Mikhail Kuzmin

Mikhail Kuzmin

A LIFE IN ART

JOHN E. MALMSTAD
NIKOLAY BOGOMOLOV

HARVARD UNIVERSITY PRESS

Cambridge, Massachusetts
London, England   1999

Frontispiece: Mikhail Kuzmin, 1909. Engraving by Nadezhda Voitinskaya.

Library of Congress Cataloging-in-Publication Data

Malmstad, John E.
    Mikhail Kuzmin : a life in art / John E. Malmstad, Nikolay
  Bogomolov.
      p.   cm.
    Includes bibliographical references and index.
    ISBN 0-674-53087-X (alk. paper)
    1. Kuzmin, M. A. (Mikhail Alekseevich), 1872–1936.
    2. Authors, Russian—20th century—Biography.
    I. Bogomolov, N. A. (Nikolaĭ Alekseevich)   II. Title.
  PG3467.K93Z76   1999
  891.71'3
  [B]—DC 21   98-44379

Contents

Illustrations

Preface

Every book has its own story; this one is more complicated than most. In 1966 I went to Russia for ten months as an exchange student to pursue research on a dissertation about the poetry of Andrey Bely. During my stay in Leningrad I had the good fortune to meet and become close to some of the most remarkable survivors of the old literary intelligentsia—people such as my adviser, Dmitry Maksimov, and critics, scholars, and translators such as Lidiya Ginzburg, Naum Berkovsky, Boris Bukhshtab, and Elga Linetskaya, to name only those of whom I became especially fond—and to an equally remarkable group of younger critics, scholars, and poets. Long conversations with these friends, often interrupted by polite, never demeaning suggestions that "you might like to take a look at . . ." gave me the finest tutorial in Russian literary history imaginable. What a tragedy for generations of Russian students in Leningrad (and Moscow, where I became friendly with many similar people) that they were not permitted contact with the great majority of them—yet another of the numerous crimes of the Soviet state that should not be forgotten or forgiven.

These Leningrad encounters invariably turned to Russian poetry, and one name kept coming up again and again—Mikhail Alekseevich Kuzmin. I had read about him in various literary histories and knew the usual anthology pieces, always a few of the "Alexandrian Songs" and a handful of early lyrics. By the time I left Russia in June 1967 I was well acquainted with the full range of his writings, and had fallen completely under his spell.

One person in particular, Gennady Shmakov, a young critic and translator, kept urging me to take up Kuzmin once I had completed my dissertation. He knew that I had turned from a study of Bely's verse to establishing its corpus in a variorum edition, and suggested I do the same for Kuzmin, none of whose original writings had been printed in his homeland since 1929. I began to do just that in the autumn of 1968, reading and re-reading a writer who exerted a fascination I had never experienced with any other Russian author except Bely (his polar opposite). Fate happily intervened when I learned from Simon Karlinsky that Vladimir Markov was already embarked on just such a project. I wrote to him, and he invited me to join him as co-editor of what would become a three-volume Russian edition of Kuzmin's collected verse, the *Sobranie stikhov* issued by the Wilhelm Fink Verlag in the mid-1970s. As Markov had already begun work on a critical preface, he suggested I do a biographical introduction. I knew little about the writer's life, but agreed. By the time the third volume appeared in print in 1977, my "introduction" had grown into a three-hundred-page monograph entitled "Mixail Kuzmin: A Chronicle of His Life and Times."

In September 1969 I made a one-month research trip to Leningrad. There Shmakov introduced me to several of Kuzmin's contemporaries, and he selflessly shared with me everything that he had found time to locate in Soviet archives. (My requesting archival access to work on such a project would have been pointless at that time.) I left Leningrad with a trove of biographical documents, both primary and secondary. Much remained to be done, and I intended to return the next summer to continue research. That was not to be. I was repeatedly denied a visa over the next decade. Shmakov and I were able to keep in contact through friends who took on the risky task of acting as couriers, bringing out a bit more material. (He himself had to give up his own work on Kuzmin when, following a purge of its editorial board, the series "Biblioteka poeta" ["The Poet's Library"] canceled his planned edition of the poet's selected verse and he lost access to the archives.) Work in Western libraries and interviews in Paris, London, and New York with acquaintances of the writer allowed me to bring the project to completion, although no one realized better than myself how many gaps remained in the life, and how much rested on conjectures and copies of materials I had never myself been able to check. Friends kept pressing me to make the biography accessible to a more general reading public, but every time I looked at the text, all I could see were the gaping holes, which neither I nor anyone else at the time could fill.

I was finally allowed to return to Russia in the autumn of 1981. By then I had gone on to other projects, though I never lost my interest in Kuzmin, and continued to write about him. In 1986, the fiftieth anniversary of his death, Jean-Claude Marcadé and I organized a symposium to mark that occasion and the centenary of the births of Nikolay Gumilev, Vladislav Khodasevich, Aleksey Kruchenykh, and Benedikt Livshits. Held in Paris under the auspices of IMSECO (Institut du monde soviétique et de l'Europe centrale et orientale), it resulted in my editing *Studies in the Life and Works of Mixail Kuzmin*, a special volume (*Sonderband* 24) of the *Wiener Slawistischer Almanach* (1989), the first book of critical essays about the writer ever published. None of the invited Soviet participants had been allowed to attend the Paris gathering, but cracks had started to appear in the barriers to the Kuzmin archive, and a few publications were coming out. One of them, fragments of his Diary from 1905–6 (based on a very defective copy of the original), only made me all too aware, however, that until that document in particular, held from all prying eyes under the proverbial seven seals, became available, there was no point in thinking of revisiting my old text. The few new materials in print would permit only tinkering.

Again, fate intervened. At the beginning of my four-month research visit to Moscow to work on a biography of Bely in the spring of 1989, an acquaintance at the Gorky Institute of World Literature introduced me to Nikolay Bogomolov, an affiliate of the institute who was teaching modern Russian literature at the School of Journalism of Moscow University and doing research and writing on a variety of shared enthusiasms, Kuzmin among them. Things were changing fast in the new climate of *glasnost'* and *perestroika*. The works of long-suppressed writers were filling the pages of Soviet magazines of every variety (the first publication, for example, of Nabokov in a chess magazine), and doors long sealed were opening up, including that which barred access to Kuzmin's Diary and other intimate papers. Bogomolov was among the first to see them, as he had been commissioned to prepare an edition of Kuzmin's verse for the "Biblioteka poeta" and was hard at work digging up everything possible in archives both in Moscow and in Leningrad. On one visit to his apartment, when he showed me a well-thumbed copy of volume three of the Munich edition, a Xerox made from a copy I had given to a mutual Leningrad friend (the only copy, I think, that was in private hands in Russia), he suggested that we together translate the text of the biography into Russian, correct its errors, and fill in the lacunae by incorporating the archival material he was gathering. I agreed (again pushing poor Bely onto a back burner), and during a four-month period from October to January 1990–91, we completed our initial work on it in Cambridge, where Bogomolov was visiting as a Senior Fellow at Harvard's Davis Center for Russian Studies. We finished it in 1992, all the time forced to continue adding to the text as a new generation of Kuzmin scholars saw previously unpublished materials into print. (Klaus Harer has surveyed the story of Kuzmin's rediscovery in the West and then in Russia in an excellent article for the Moscow literary journal *Novoe literaturnoe obozrenie*, 3 [1993].) After one after another contract to issue the book was broken as a result of the publishing crisis affecting all scholarly literature in the new Russia, it finally appeared in Moscow in the spring of 1996 as *Mikhail Kuzmin: Iskusstvo, zhizh', epokha.*

Having done all that, I felt it was right finally to turn my old text, now in quite another form, into English. I thought it would be a fairly simple task, largely a matter of translating all the new (and old) Russian material. But as I began work on it during a stay at Bellagio in the summer of 1992, I quickly realized it would be no such thing. I had written the original text with an academic audience specializing in things Russian in mind; the new text addressed them and Russian readers. I very much wanted this "third variant" to reach as wide a readership as possible. This meant that things taken for granted in the previous two texts had to be expanded or spelled out here. Then, too, the West orders matters biographical somewhat differently than Russia, even one in which restrictions have been lifted and many taboo subjects have been opened up. Bogomolov and I certainly did nothing to hide the nature of Kuzmin's sexuality in translating the original English version into Russian, but this is a subject that offends many in Russia (and here, for that matter), who are, in fact, often upset by any inquiry, biographical or critical, that seems "too personal." (Witness the uproar that any discussion of Tsvetaeva's bisexuality causes among almost all Russian specialists in her works.) There is no need for such caution here. Kuzmin's gay identity is not the main subject of this book, but it and many other personal matters and issues are treated far more fully in this account of his life than in the Russian version. In short, this book is a total recasting of the two earlier texts, not simply a revision of one and a translation of the other. To be sure, certain fundamental passages differ hardly at all among the three texts, but such instances are rare exceptions. Readers, including those who will want to consult the Russian text for its many archival citations, should consider this our final word on this subject, at least for the moment.

Many people and institutions have assisted in the research for the writing of this book. Fellowships from the International Research and Exchange Board (IREX) enabled me to make research trips to Russia, while the Villa Serbelloni, the Bellagio Study and Conference Center of the Rockefeller Foundation, provided me with a magnificent place in which to begin work on the volume in a country Kuzmin loved almost as much as his native land. Bogomolov and I are grateful to the Davis Center for Russian Studies of Harvard University, which provided him with a Senior Research Fellowship. We are both indebted to the staffs of many libraries and archives: Widener Library of Harvard University, Butler Library of Columbia University, the Helsinki University Library, Moscow's Russian State Library (the former State Lenin Library) and its Manuscript Division, Petersburg's Russian National Library (formerly the State Saltykov-Shchedrin Public Library) and its Manuscript Division, the Bibliothèque nationale, the British Library, the Russian State Archive of Literature and Art in Moscow, and the Manuscript Divisions of the Institute of Russian Literature (Pushkinskii Dom), the Gorky Institute of World Literature, the State Russian Museum, and the Anna Akhmatova Museum (Fountain House).

The following people shared their recollections of Kuzmin with me when I was at work on the "first variant": Georgy Adamovich, Yury Annenkov, George Balanchine, Naum Berkovsky, Dmitry Bouchêne, Bella Rein Bozheryanova, Sergey Ernst, Johannes von Guenther, Salome Halpern, Ivan Likhachev, Vladimir Orlov, Vsevolod Petrov, Igor Stravinsky and his wife, Vera Arturovna, Viktor Zhirmunsky, and a few others who asked never to be named, fearing that the mere association of their names with Kuzmin would label them as gay (sexual taboos die very hard).

Among the many people who gave assistance with this book, three deserve a special word of thanks for help and guidance that went far beyond the call of friendship. The enthusiasm of Simon Karlinsky for this project kept my own from flagging when obstacles seemed to threaten its completion. His masterly command of the nuances of both Russian and English prevented a few "howlers" and contributed to strengthening the text immeasurably. Robert Maguire took time from his own busy writing schedule to read the manuscript at every stage. He has always been the first (and best) reader of my prose, and once again, without his insightful comments and sage advice on matters of style, structure, and substance, this book would have been much the poorer.

The late Gennady Shmakov can truly be called the pioneer of modern Kuzmin studies. No one did more, often under the most difficult conditions, for the rediscovery of Kuzmin, and it is no exaggeration to call him the progenitor of this whole project. He managed to publish only fragments from his own work on the writer before his death in New York City in 1988, but they have lost none of their value. It is with pleasure, muted by sadness at the thought of his far too early death, that my co-author and I dedicate this book to his memory.

John E. Malmstad

Authors' Note

The transliteration system in this book follows that used by the Oxford Slavonic Papers. A few exceptions have been made for more user-friendly reading by nonspecialists. We ignore the palatalization marker in most proper names (an exception has been made for a few: so "Soloviev," not "Solovev," "Vasilievich," not "Vasilevich") and all place names throughout the text, but not in the index and in citations in the notes, where maximum precision must rule (thus Gorky in the text, but Gor'ky elsewhere). The names of many prominent Russians have found a standard English spelling that differs from a strictly transliterated form. These are used in the text and index, as is the original spelling of names of well-known people of foreign origin. When we refer to their published writings in the notes, however, we follow strict transliteration. Thus Tchaikovsky, Meyerhold, Benois, Nouvel, for example, in text and index, but Chaikovsky, Meierkhol'd, Benua, and Nuvel' in other instances. (Citations of books or articles employing one of the several other systems must, of course, render them precisely.) All Russian words, phrases, and titles adhere exactly to the transliteration system.

Dates up to February 14, 1918, are given in the Julian calendar, or Old Style, and after that in the Gregorian, or New Style. Before 1900, the Julian calendar in use in Russia was twelve days behind the Gregorian; from 1900 to 1918, it lagged by thirteen days. The calendar reform, like that of Russian orthography, took some getting used to, and Kuzmin, like many Russians, was not always careful in the immediate postrevolutionary years to keep to the new calendar, especially as concerned religious holidays. (The Orthodox Church stuck to the Old Style and still does so in Russia.)

An ellipsis in the original is indicated by "...," our own ellipses by ". . ." A complete bibliographical reference is given only when a book or article is first mentioned. Thereafter we give an abbreviated citation.

Mikhail Kuzmin

Introduction

ON NOVEMBER 30, 1916, Evgeny Znosko-Borovsky, who was prominent in Petersburg literary circles as a critic and dramatist, read a paper on the life and work of Mikhail Alekseevich Kuzmin at an evening sponsored by an arts club called the "Bronze Horseman." He expressed genuine surprise at how little was known about someone he regarded as one of contemporary Russia's most important writers.[1] That situation scarcely changed for more than seventy years. In 1977 Vladimir Markov had great fun demonstrating that everything printed about Kuzmin in literary histories, encyclopedias, and textbooks from the 1920s to that time was misleading, incomplete, or wrong.[2] Since then, reprints of Kuzmin's verse, plays, and prose made his works available to readers of Russian in the West, yet we still too often see the recycling of the same anthology pieces, and whenever any but the specialist ventures an opinion, we read the same stale clichés about "beautiful clarity," "simplicity," "escapism," and "lightness of tone" that dogged the writer's heels from the beginning of his career. Few can even get the date of his birth right.

Thankfully, the situation has changed dramatically in Russia, especially since the extraordinary revolution of 1991. After decades of suppression, the man admired by poets as diverse as Blok, Gumilev, Khlebnikov, Mandelshtam, and Tsvetaeva as one of the greatest poets of their time can now at last be read in his homeland. One of the best new literary magazines to emerge, *New Literary Review* (Novoe literaturnoe obozrenie), devoted much of its third issue (1993) to the writer, while the first issue of the always impressive *Annual* (Ezhegodnik) of the Manuscript Division of Pushkinskii Dom to be published since it was in effect closed down in 1984 was virtually dominated by publications by and about Kuzmin and two other modern Russian gay writers: the great poet Nikolay Klyuev, shot in 1937, and the once totally forgotten prose writer Leonid Dobychin, who simply disappeared in 1936 after being exposed as a homosexual and "class enemy," but who now appears poised to become one of the main heroes of twentieth-century Russian literature.[3] True, both venues rounded up the small band of the usual specialists, but clearly the ice has been broken. Readers in Russia, new to Kuzmin's writings and coming to them with eyes and ears wide open (and closed, one hopes, to the Soviet literary establishment's disinformation in its histories of Russian letters), will have no easy time trying to take the measure of the life and works of one of the most complex, even contradictory, modern Russian writers. We read through the rich variety of the works that span three decades (not all that long for a writer who lived more than sixty years) and, now that they are becoming available, the voluminous personal papers. No sooner do we think that we may have begun to pin Kuzmin down than like quicksilver, he slips away. So it goes throughout his career. He brings one style to perfection and drops it, seemingly to start from scratch. He establishes one mood in a work, only to turn it abruptly into its opposite. We read and re-read, and often are rewarded with an answer to the "secret" of one of the perfectly crafted works. Can we get to the heart of the life as well?

We turn to other sources, such as the reminiscences of contemporaries who knew him well or at least saw and heard him often, and the door slams. Take Georgy Ivanov, who was acquainted with him for more than a decade.[4] Here is how he characterized Kuzmin's life in his famous quasi-memoir *Petersburg Winters* (Peterburgskie zimy):

> Silk vests and the coats worn by coachmen, the Old Belief and Jewish blood, Italy and the Volga—all these are pieces in the kaleidoscopic mosaic that makes up the biography of Mikhail Alekseevich Kuzmin. . . . Kuzmin's life took a strange path. He began devoting himself to literature when he was about thirty. Until then he had devoted himself to music, but not for long. And before

that? Before that there was life, which began very early—passionate, intense, restless. Running away from home at age sixteen, wanderings through Russia, nights spent on his knees before icons, then atheism and being near suicide. And religion again, monasteries, thoughts of becoming a monk. Searchings, disillusionments, enthusiasms without number. Then—books, books, books, in Italian, French, Greek. Finally, the first glimmer of spiritual tranquillity in a remote Italian monastery, in conversations with a simple-hearted canon. And his first thoughts about art—about music.[5]

Here and there Ivanov's memory retained a kernel of truth, but invention runs wild in a description dictated by the laws of fiction, not reminiscence, and by Ivanov's compulsion to create a myth of his own past and of the cultural milieu that had shaped him.

Irina Odoevtseva managed to repeat most of her husband's colorful fabrications in her own no more reliable memoirs, and she added a few more, none more piquant than the sight of Kuzmin dancing the cancan in Paris with Toulouse-Lautrec's models (he never visited Paris).[6] And so it goes with a strange sameness, as if memoirists were relying on one another and were allowing the Kuzmin "legend" to color any actual recollection. (Its outlines already existed by the second decade of our century; Kuzmin at times indulged it, but, unlike some contemporaries—Akhmatova and Mayakovsky spring to mind—he did not fashion it.) As Marina Tsvetaeva remarked in her own "An Otherworldly Evening," a beautiful evocation of her one meeting with Kuzmin in 1916 interwoven with a subtle appreciation of his poetry, "Legends go round about every poet, and it is always the same envy and malice that compose them."[7] Details and the memoirists' attitude to the subject may vary, but one thread runs through them all: the "mystery" of the man and his work.

We must also carefully sift fact from legend when evaluating the evidence taken from interviews conducted by one of the authors in the late 1960s and early 1970s with people who had known Kuzmin and who eagerly shared their reminiscences. Even then all were old; by now all have died. They, no less than those who had committed their remembrances to paper, were subject to the legend and to the caprices of memory.

We have to exercise equal caution when reading Kuzmin's personal papers—the Diary and letters. The information in them must be checked against every other source at our disposal, keeping in mind the "law" about documentary evidence that Yury Tynyanov formulated: "There are ceremonial [*paradnye*] documents, and they tell lies just like people."[8] While a personal document may seem to hold wide open the front door (the other implication of Tynyanov's adjective *paradnye*) to a life, truth may be slipping out the servants' entrance. Kuzmin on occasion deliberately presented different sides of his personality to the people he encountered, giving to each of them what he thought they wanted, and he could play the sincerity game very well, to judge by the reaction of the artist Margarita Voloshina (née Sabashnikova), first wife of the poet Maksimilian Voloshin, who knew him in 1906–7: "From time to time he read his diary, without any abridgment, to his friends with an unparalleled openness and innocence." "His conduct was extremely unpretentious, without pose," she concluded, putting herself at sharp variance with numerous other memoirists who do nothing but emphasize the "poses."[9]

Close examination of all the varying accounts of his personality, however, reveals less the chameleon than the diversity of responses Kuzmin stimulated. Znosko-Borovsky noted that problem of Kuzmin's "reception" by his contemporaries, while not trying to deny the complexities and seemingly irreconcilable contradictions:

> That confusing mixture of contradictory connections and combinations which mark Kuzmin will not surprise us. Those who know the famous portrait of him painted by Somov will imagine him in the guise of the dandy and modernist. Many will also remember a photograph, in which Kuzmin appears in a peasant's heavy overcoat [*armyak*] and with a long beard. Some conceive of him as an aesthete, a partisan of form in art, almost of the doctrine "art for art's sake," while to others he is an adherent and creator of moralizing and tendentious literature [a reference to what some viewed as Kuzmin's "propagandizing" of same-sex love]. An elegant master of stylization, an affected marquis in life and in art, and at the same time a genuine Old Believer, a man who loves the simplicity of the Russian countryside.[10]

Later writers followed the dubious implication that there were two (or more) Kuzmins, while ignoring Znosko-Borovsky's attempt to determine lines of continuity in the art and life and to establish the unity of the integrated creative personality, something no less remarkable than its multiple facets.

For several decades a number of critical schools have been proclaiming the "death" of the author, if not that of the critic. (The author may be dead, the joke goes, but the publisher still knows where to send the royalty checks.) Of late that impulse has been on the wane or has been subtly modified, and we add our voices to those who believe that there is a relation, complicated and complex, to be sure, between a writer's life and art, and that one need not fall into the crude aesthetic determinism so soundly condemned by the Russian Formalists in charting that relationship. The interrelation of the private life of a writer and the work that translates one into the other and "writes" both in an act of simultaneous creation of life and text rarely offers so many fascinations as are to be found in the case of Kuzmin, not least in part because he was engaged in a project without precedent in Russian and, for that matter, the western European literature of his time: living an openly gay life, making it a central subject of his art, and writing about it with absolute candor. That honesty made him incorporate many details of his life into his works, maximally blurring the distinction between poet and poetic persona. We are well aware (as was Kuzmin) that the "literary personality," to borrow Tynyanov's term, that intersection of the actual person and the lyric persona, is far from identical with the "real" Mikhail Kuzmin. We have tried to avoid confusing or equating biographical and literary facts, while remaining attentive to both in this biography, and our account of Kuzmin's "life in art" has called for the most careful constant shuttling between text and context.

If writers, as Cocteau remarked (in *Opium*), are "quite unable to write their own lives. There are too many mysteries, too many lies, too much of a tangle," they do write them in their works, which often provide the best clues and the most penetrating answers to the questions we put to them and to the life. If we have thrown light on some of the mysteries of the life and the art, have laid to rest as many of the lies, half-truths, and clichés as possible, have unraveled some of the tangle, and in the process have helped restore Kuzmin to his rightful place in the history of Russian literature, we will have accomplished what we set out to do.

But let him speak for himself for the first time. On June 8, 1907, when he was already well known, indeed "infamous" to many for the novel *Wings* (Kryl'ya), he wrote in his Diary: "We [Kuzmin and the family of his eldest sister] were reading Pushkin's letters; he praised several contemporaries; where now are Küchelbecker, Pogodin, etc.? It is curious, who will [Vyacheslav] Ivanov, Blok, Bely be for posterity? And who would I like to be: unrecognized and great, or celebrated and abandoned, like Kukolnik, Benediktov?" He did not consider a third alternative: celebrated, abandoned, and rediscovered because great. Let him have the last word, too, in the sagacious couplets that close the second poem of the November 1907 poem cycle "The Joyful Wayfarer," and that could not be bettered as an epigraph for this book:

> And when we've grown tired, we shall sit down amidst the
>   green grass,
> having read the remaining chapters in an old book:
>
> You are the reader of your life, not its scribe,
> you do not know the end of the story.[11]

1

"The Edifying Story of My Beginnings"
1872–1897

IN 1906, while preparing to leave Petersburg to spend the summer in Vasilsursk, a small town on the Volga, Mikhail Alekseevich Kuzmin took time to make one promise to some new friends staying behind in the capital. He vowed to set down something like an autobiography before returning. On August 5 he wrote to one of them, the artist Konstantin Somov, "Thus far I have managed to write a short introduction (forty pages) to my diary: 'Histoire édifiante de mes commencements.'"[1] This "introduction," rather oddly located not at the beginning but in the middle of the second surviving notebook of Kuzmin's Diary, opens with the expected phrase, "I was born on October 6. . . ."[2] Then the mystery begins. Kuzmin first gave his year of birth as "1872." This he crossed out. He then wrote "1875," and still later, apparently, penciled in "1874." We now know that the year 1872 is correct.[3] Kuzmin thus began the "Histoire édifiante," a work intended to be read to his closest friends and one which, according to their own testimony, created an impression of total openness and sincerity, with a deliberate falsehood. He was probably motivated by nothing more than a reluctance to reveal to those friends, many already with considerable reputations in the arts, that he was about to make his own real literary debut when well over the age of thirty. Yet from the outset he gave his life an aura of enigma.

If the date of Kuzmin's birth remained a puzzle for decades, the place was never in doubt. He was born, as he often noted with pride, in the beautiful old Russian city of Yaroslavl, studded with ancient churches and monasteries and standing high above the banks of the Volga. He indulged in poetic license about even something this simple, however, when he wrote in the poem that begins "I know you not by hearsay, o cities of the upper Volga!": "I thank my stars for having *grown up* in Yaroslavl!"[4] In actuality he lived only a year and a half there before his parents moved to Saratov, on the lower Volga, and though on occasion he visited the cities of the upper Volga, he always preferred to return for visits to places around Nizhnii Novgorod and the city in which he spent his childhood.

Kuzmin was proud of his ancient lineage, and insisted throughout his life on the proper spelling of his last name—Kuzmin, not the plebeian "Kuz'min."[5] Yet here is all he has to say about his ancestors in the "Histoire édifiante":

> I was the next-to-last son in a large family. My father was sixty at the time of my birth, my mother—forty. My grandmother on my mother's side was French, by the name of Mongeaultier, and the granddaughter of Aufresne, a French actor at the time of Catherine. All the rest were Russians from the provinces of Yaroslavl and Vologda. In my childhood I remember my father as a very old man, and everyone in town took him for my grandfather, not my father. In his youth he had been very handsome, with the good looks of someone from southern climes in the West. He had been a seaman and then served as a *zemstvo* election official. He lived, they say, a stormy life, and in his old age he was a man with a capricious, spoiled, even difficult and despotic character. My mother, who was perhaps a bit frivolous by nature, loved dancing. Just before her marriage she fell in love with a former suitor who then turned her down. After that her only concern was her children. She was shy, taciturn, unsociable, and, in the end, stubborn both in her love for or in her incomprehension of something.[6]

There is relatively little to add to the description.

Kuzmin's immediate relatives were of the provincial pre-Petrine nobility, small landowners with estates near both Saratov and Yaroslavl. Many members of the family on his father's side had pursued careers in the army and navy, as the poet noted in the blank verse lines of "My Ancestors," the work he chose to open his first book of verse: "Sailors of ancient lineage, / enamored of distant horizons, / drinking wine in mysterious ports, / and embracing jolly foreign women . . . / imposing generals bedecked with medals."[7] Kuzmin's father, Aleksey Alekseevich, had been no exception. After a career as a naval officer, he served out his retirement as a provincial judicial official and provided his family with a modest but adequate income.[8] Kuzmin's mother, Nadezhda Dmitrievna, née Fedorova, was the daughter of a landowner from the province of Yaroslavl who had once served as inspector of classes in the Imperial Theater School and who had married one of its pupils and wards. His young bride was a granddaughter of the famous French tragic actor Jean Aufresne, who had known Voltaire and had acted in several of his plays.[9] He came to Petersburg in 1785 and remained there, teaching and acting, until his death in 1804.

Kuzmin's mother, who as a child had seen Gogol when he paid calls on her actress mother, instilled in her son an interest in French culture from childhood, and it became so native to him that he, like the young Pushkin, might well have been dubbed "the Frenchman" in his youth. Aleksey Remizov probably heard of this ancestry from his fellow writer, as Kuzmin liked to make mention of his "Frenchness."[10] He attributed Kuzmin's strange "un-Russian" looks to this when he wrote, after Kuzmin's death: "A woman with a little girl entered the [Paris] Metro. I looked at the mother and suddenly understood where those familiar 'Bethlehem' eyes came from—Kuzmin's mother had French relatives."[11] The poet's enormous eyes, which reminded some of a Russian icon and others of an Egyptian mummy, dominate all descriptions of his physical appearance. Memoirists rarely fail to note them. Tsvetaeva was no exception in "An Otherworldly Evening": "His eyes and nothing else. His eyes—and the rest of him. There was very little of the rest of him: almost nothing."[12] In 1921 she immortalized his eyes in the poem that begins "Two fiery sunsets! No, two mirrors!"[13]

We have no direct evidence about Kuzmin's childhood. No member of his family left any record of it. Everything comes from his own accounts, recollections lodged in the fallible, perhaps fictional, medium of memory and set down many years after the fact. We should therefore keep in mind that it is not so much a "real" childhood as the presentation to friends of what, on reflection, the writer found most significant and formative, of what he imagined his childhood to have been. That almost all of his reminiscences of his early years, be they in letters or the "Histoire édifiante," hardly fit the Edenic tradition of Russian male autobiography is their most striking feature.

We encounter one word over and over again in all Kuzmin's accounts of his childhood: "loneliness" (or "solitude," *odinochestvo*). Znosko-Borovsky reports his saying that he "was reserved and solitary" as a child,[14] while in the "Histoire édifiante" he wrote, "I grew up alone and in a family both uncongenial and rather difficult and willful and stubborn on both its sides."[15] He also emphasized that he had grown up surrounded by women in a kind of "gynaeceum" (as, incidentally, had Pushkin, Blok, and Khodasevich, good evidence to support Milan Kundera's observation that lyric poets generally come from homes run by women):

> I was alone. My brothers were in Kazan, at cadet school, my sisters away at women's college in Petersburg, and then married. I had only girls for friends, not boys, and I loved to play with dolls, to play at pretend theatricals, to read and perform light potpourris of old Italian operas, as my father was a great admirer of them, especially Rossini. Marusya Larionova, Zina Dobrokhotova, and Katya Tsarevskaya were my friends. I felt a kind of worshipful adoration for my male school companions, and finally positively fell in love with a student in the seventh class of the gymnasium, Valentin Zaitsev, who later became my teacher at school. I was also in love with my aunt, however. I was terribly possessive.[16]

A love for a world of play centering on the theater and opera and an awakening of sexual impulses are the two focal points of the account of his early life which he set down for his closest friends.

Same-sex love is the defining fact of Kuzmin's life and art. As he repeatedly notes, he realized the nature of his sexual inclinations at an early age. None of his accounts of his development articulate to what extent such awareness of gender nonconformity may have intensified his feelings of isolation and the sense of being an outsider in the environment in which he was reared, although by the time he was in the gymnasium he realized it was a characteristic that distinguished him from his classmates. Homosexuality may have been widespread—if usually private, disguised, or out of the public eye—in the Russian Empire (and evidence suggests that it was), but gay men in Russia, as elsewhere, had to face public opinion and the law. The dominant culture had marked out the boundaries of acceptable behavior in the strictest manner possible in the Legal Code, which considered male same-sex acts a criminal offense, however rarely or stringently the penalties against them seem to have been enforced.[17] Some circles, particularly in the capitals, had a tolerant attitude, but in most segments of society, certainly those in which Kuzmin was raised, same-sex love between men was considered contemptible or was treated with derision as a moral transgression condemned by Church and State and therefore a taboo, something to be kept hidden were one "afflicted" by it. Yet from his very first works, Kuzmin refused to hide the nature of his sexuality or to encode it in some way detectable only to the initiated. (Nothing so brought down his scorn as those who engaged in this strategy.) Nothing in the world of his art seems more ordinary than the gay sexuality of many of his characters and alter egos. When the second edition of *Nets* (Seti), his first verse collection of 1908, appeared after the outbreak of World War I, the rigid military censorship mutilated the poems with cuts to eliminate any suggestion that they were addressed to men or treated the love of men for men. Perversely enough, it is the clusters of dots, not the deleted words or phrases, that seem indecent, creating, as they do, an aura of pornography.[18]

None of his writings about his formative years raise the "nature-nurture" question of whether his inclination was predetermined or brought about by events that have fateful effects in shaping sexual identity. Kuzmin came to view it as simply a biographical and biological fact, one behavioral possibility on a continuum of desires, not a matter of one alternative or another or a "weakness" or medical or moral problem. His acceptance of his nature and his struggles with the gender scruples of his society provide, as we shall see, much of the drama of his youth. But his memories of childhood keep turning most insistently to art— what he first heard and read—and how first impressions formed his artistic tastes and helped shape the artist he became. Left unsaid is how they, like his sexual feelings, may have intensified a keen sense of "otherness" and differentness from his fellows. The child who will become gay conceives his sexual self in isolation. So too the artist.

A letter to Georgy Chicherin of July 18, 1893, remarkable for the manner in which it prefigures the hallmarks of Kuzmin's mature poetic style with its eye for vivid sensual details, provides a glimpse of some of those earliest impressions:

> I keep recalling Novalis's story about the blue flower, about which Heinrich von Ofterdingen dreamed and yearned. No one has ever seen it, yet the whole world is filled with its fragrance. Not all can smell it, but those who have once inhaled it will never know any peace in life. For all time they will seek it—the fantastic, the all-powerful, the mystical. Where is one to find it? Perhaps in music, perhaps—in love! And the smell of it makes me weep when there is a pale-yellow sunset, and it awakens a desire to fly far, far away with a bird. I inhaled that smell in my early childhood, and I don't know whether for the sake of joy or grief! And all my memories, like a flock of gulls, circle without end. . . . I remember when I was quite small, in the autumn at dusk, when our servant was chopping cabbage in the shed. The smell of fresh cabbage and the first chill of autumn were so invigorating. The sky was pale yellow, and my nanny was sitting on a log knitting a sock. And with an agonizing heartache I gaze at the sky where a flock of birds is flying to the south. "Nanny, tell me, where are they flying?"—I ask her tearfully. "To warm countries, my dear boy." And at night I see an azure sea and a pale yellow sky and rose-colored birds in flight. A sort of Japanese landscape without shadows—coquettish and touching! . . . I dreamed about the kinds of creatures I had made up myself. . . . When I told other children, they laughed.[19]

In this same letter, Kuzmin wrote of his affection for his younger sister Anya, who "had the spark of God in her and knew about the blue flower." It was she who first introduced him to Shakespeare and the mysterious worlds of Hoffmann. Both were to remain among his favorites, soon to be joined by *Don Quixote*, the novels of Walter Scott, and, somewhat later, Molière and the *fabliaux*.[20] Music, too, offered a powerful stimulus to his imagination and an atmosphere of magical enchantment, as when, hidden behind a heavy curtain so he would not be sent to bed, he listened to his mother perform excerpts from operas for friends on moonlit nights. His loyalty to the musical preferences of his parents, the "dear music of the 1830s," as he put it to Chicherin—Weber, Rossini, Meyerbeer, and the songs of Schubert—would, with the exception of a brief period when he became disenchanted with Rossini, waver hardly at all throughout his life.

Kuzmin's interest in the theater, in which he would be closely involved for most of his life as a dramatist and composer, also dates back to this earliest period. At first, as he wrote in the "Histoire édifiante," there were improvised plays, then his sister's gift of Shakespeare and visits to the local Saratov theater. The special enchantment of the puppet theater and opera most fired the young boy's imagination and prompted his first tries at composition, as he wrote in the same letter to Chicherin:

> And my first puppet theater! A marvel! Even now I blush all over from pleasure! And the magic lantern and the Chinese shadows, and the opera and the drama. I always composed operas and sang them in my reedy but lissome voice, and I also always wrote my own librettos. For drama I always took Shakespeare. I was, perhaps, a funny and pretentious little boy, but I was so happy, so happy and proud! And silhouettes, my eternal passion!

Typically for Kuzmin, memories of another kind provide a coda to the reminiscences of childhood:

> How bitter and empty it was when I walked home from the Bol'shoi Prospect [on Vasilievskii Island in Petersburg] after a conversation with Stolitsa [a young male acquaintance]. I was in a very religious mood at that time, and every day I begged God to grant me good looks or the power of speech so that I might persuade Stolitsa to be friendly, tenderly friendly with me. *Une amitié amoureuse.* Honestly, I really loved [him], and would then have been glad to die for just one kiss.

The memories of early childhood keep circling around the world of art, and they shade into sensual memories inseparable in nature from those aroused by works of art: an indefinable longing for an ideal, some kind of intimate friendship, and a world unlike that of his home and his "reticent and reserved" parents. The aroma of the "blue flower" may have "strengthened and refreshed" him, but its vision impelled him restlessly to search not for some lost paradise of childhood (the impulse for so many writers), but for something that art or feelings for another ("in music, perhaps—in love!") seemed to hold out tantalizingly for the seeker. The way in which indeterminacy and lack generate fascination and desire creates the dynamic that would drive Kuzmin's experiences well into his maturity.

He had begun his formal education in Saratov, where he attended classes in the same school where Chernyshevsky had once studied. He also took lessons at the local music school, where, as he remarked with the deprecating humor typical of the "Histoire édifiante," "as always in childhood and in the provinces I was considered to be making great progress."[21] In the autumn of 1884, when his father was declared redundant in the civil service, he and his parents moved, at his mother's insistence, back to the city she considered her "homeland": Petersburg. Saratov was left behind; as a place it had little impact on the writer's later art beyond some reflections of the "coloring" of the city in some of his fiction, as he once remarked to a friend.[22] Visits to relatives on the Volga would frequently take him away from the capital in future summers, and his love for provincial Russia would often surface in nostalgic reminiscences in his mature verse and in the settings of some of his stories. But now it was Petersburg, the city he would call home for the rest of his life, his "second homeland," that moved into the center of his consciousness.[23]

After a year in an apartment on Mokhovaya Street, the family settled across the Neva, on Vasilievskii Island, where Kuzmin would live with his mother until her death in 1904. At first, as he remembered later, "things were very uncomfortable in Petersburg: a small apartment in a courtyard, Father's illness, his operation, the mandatory round of visits to relatives, lack of success at school, darkness, hurdy-gurdies in the courtyards—everything inspired an inexpressible despondency in me," so much so that he "poorly recalled" the time.[24] Nevertheless, after his 1904 move back to the heart of the capital, across the Neva, he would be overcome, on revisits to his old haunts, by other memories of a later period, as he noted in his Diary on September 11, 1905:

> Here is where I walked home from school, the embankment where I strolled, making plans and thinking over new works, the Kievskoe *podvor'e* [a church with an adjacent hostel for pilgrims]— a place where I used to pray, the shops that Mama frequented, the barbershop where Pavlusha Konovalov cut my hair (at one time I was not entirely indifferent to him), the restaurant that I would

visit with Senyavin and Repinsky, and even the cabby, who either resembled Nikita or really was him, who drove me to Prince Georges's [he uses the French] place. And it's strange that you're not walking home, that you won't meet [the artist] L[idiya] M[ikhailovna] Kostrits in her white collar, that you won't catch up to Liza carrying the shopping and chattering away by the gate, that Mama, dear Mama, won't be waiting for you, and that you won't be writing your compositions in your old room, the sunny one, at the piano you used to have. While right there, at the far edge of a clearing, are the graves of Father and Mama.

No major Russian writer enjoys more of a reputation, deserved or not, for being carefree and lighthearted than does Kuzmin. Yet these lyrical reminiscences conclude with a reference to the graves of his parents. As more and more of his private writings become available, we are discovering that thoughts of death, his own in particular, were never far away. After learning of the death of the writer Fedor Sologub (whom he often called "Fir-Sprite" [*Elkich*], from a fantastical character in one of Sologub's short stories), he wrote: "Funerals suit Sologub, as they do Vyacheslav Ivanov and, perhaps, me. The incense of the deceased. Dying did not at all suit, let's say, Blok, and he is just Blok the deceased, while Sologub, like Gogol, seems to have found his true calling in being a corpse" (Diary, December 5, 1927). His was no decadent death-haunted imagination, however. From his earliest years he had faced death, as he would have to do throughout a life marked by poor health, and he had had to come to grips with it. There is probably no more stoic figure in all Russian literature, but he was not callous, as some have shallowly concluded. He had purchased his indifference and calm composure in the face of death at the price of facing his own with disdain, not despair, on more than one occasion.

His recollections of the death of his father, which occurred when he was not yet fourteen, show this well. They occupy a prominent place in the "Histoire édifiante" (significant in itself, as the event could have had no importance for the friends for whom he set down the account of his early life), and they have an immediacy and, at the same time, a distance that startles:

We had moved to a large apartment when Father died (before his death he had had a falling out with my aunt). I remember how he died. Mama, all tired out, went to bed to take a nap; a servant sat by Father's bed; I was reading *The Grainfield* [Niva, a popular magazine], where it told about how some Samoyeds swallowed a medicine not to be taken internally . . . and I laughed out loud. Nastasya said: "Mishenka, how can you?"—"Well, I'm reading something funny."—"But your papa is going to die: listen, he's wheezing. You'd better wake up the mistress."—"He's always wheezing. I'll finish what I'm reading." Father really was breathing heavily and wheezing. "Mishenka..."—"Well, what now?"—but suddenly there was a wheezing sound, louder and slower, and then one wheeze, then another—and it became quiet. Then Nastasya screamed: "Mistress, our master has died!" I sat down on the sofa. Mama, who had started to cry, hugged me. As for me, I did not cry the whole time. My aunt, who had not come once during his illness, sobbed loudly as she clutched at the coffin. The Myasoedovs would take me for days on end to distract me. Our affairs went badly, we again changed lodgings, moving to a small apartment in the same building.[25]

By the time he set down this memory, he had reached maturity. In his early childhood he had experienced the death of his youngest brother, the sight of him in his coffin, the onset of epilepsy in a servant, the madness of a brother-in-law, and his mother's attack of smallpox, which had almost taken her life.[26] He himself had attempted suicide while still a child, when his beloved sister Anya left for Petersburg, and he described it in his letter to Chicherin of July 18, 1893: "I felt dismal and wanted to die. *Bêtise!* I spent nights on the floor, I drank cold water, and finally fell ill with the most terrible diphtheria and an abscess in the throat. For two weeks, as in a nightmare, I lay between life and death on an enormous bed, covered up with a silk winter blanket embroidered in a convent. I lay there, full of strange dreams, as if on a catafalque."[27] He tried again, apparently in the autumn of 1894, and could talk about it dispassionately with friends twelve years after the event. For if life had taught him anything by then, it was to view death as but the natural final stage of life, a "full stop" no more to be feared than anything else in the lot assigned to us.

   This attitude had already formed to a certain degree when, in 1886, there occurred an event so important that Kuzmin gave it special mention in the "Histoire édifiante": "Chicherin entered our fifth class [at the Eighth Gymnasium], and soon we were fast friends and his family had an enormous influence on me."[28] This was Georgy Chicherin, who would replace Trotsky as Foreign Commissar in 1918 and become Soviet Russia's first important diplomat. He too had come to the capital from the provinces, and in him Kuzmin finally found a close male companion and confidant. He remained such for almost two decades, an admirer of Kuzmin's music (rather less so of his writings), and in many ways his mentor in the early years of their friendship.

Chicherin came from a large and close-knit family of considerable culture and social position, a "gentry family [*barskaya sem'ya*] 'as it should be,'" as Kuzmin later put it, comfortable and well off, and the young Kuzmin reveled in a way of life so dissimilar from the straitened circumstances and squabbling, distant environment of his own family.[29] The members of Chicherin's immediate family—his mother, Baroness Georgina (Zhorzhina) Egorovna, née Meyendorff, and his brother Nikolay, the two names most often encountered in Kuzmin's correspondence with Georgy—welcomed their son's new friend into their household. So did the whole Chicherin clan, gregarious and expansive, whether in Petersburg or on their estates in the province of Tambov, where summers seem to have been movable family feasts. Rather shy and withdrawn, like the young Kuzmin, Chicherin was far more self-confident and assertive in intellectual matters. He had received an excellent education at home, already knew several languages (and learned new ones easily), and had an erudition well beyond his years. He shared Kuzmin's cultural interests, and at least until the opening years of the new century, he had a forceful, often decisive influence in shaping his friend both personally and intellectually. He set about broadening Kuzmin's reading to include philosophy, chiefly Schopenhauer and Nietzsche (who impressed him little despite Chicherin's insistent preaching), and Renan and Taine. He also introduced Kuzmin to Italian culture and urged him to learn the language, just as he later encouraged him to undertake the serious study of German.

Chicherin's assured taste and self-confidence made him adopt the role of teacher, as we see in a typical letter of January 18, 1897. He tells Kuzmin about the *Chansons de Bilitis* and the "really dirty" *Aphrodite* of Pierre Louÿs; urges him to read the Gnostic *Pistis Sophia* and recommends the best edition and the most reliable article about it; praises

Hilferding's collection of the "majestic" *Byliny of the Onega Region* (Onezhskie byliny); hopes to introduce him to the Czech poet Vrchlický, whom he compares to Kalidasa; and, always generalizing, concludes that he finds a "closeness between the world of the Slavs and India in their mystical, contemplative, pessimistic propensities." In another respect, however, Chicherin felt distinctly inferior to Kuzmin. Time and again he tried his hand at writing both literature and music. Every attempt came up short. At last, aware that he lacked any creative skills, he gave up. Kuzmin, he realized very early on, possessed just those talents, and it made Chicherin regard his friend, even as he kept trying to form his taste, from a decidedly Romantic point of view as a higher being, endowed with special gifts. We see this in a letter Chicherin wrote on January 25, 1903, when virtually nothing of Kuzmin's had yet been published or performed at a public concert:

> *You also have* . . . that same kind of receptivity that Pushkin had to all that is shared by humanity. You have incarnated world after world in your art. And, as in Pushkin, this is no simple aimless wandering. This has its culmination, that most profound Pushkinian sense of the ideal that we find in your [musical compositions] "Acteon" (which can be idolized!), "The Pale Sun of an Autumn Evening," "The Mermaid Princess," "The Winter Forest," and in the summery "Noon." There are works that fade with the passing of time, and there are works that only become more splendid, more magnificent, more inimitable, more divine—such is your marvelous "Acteon!"[30]

We should not discount the possibility that Chicherin's desire to encourage his friend (in terms derived from Dostoevsky's famous 1880 panegyric of Pushkin) may have in part dictated the exaggerated praise of this evaluation, as Chicherin was well aware of Kuzmin's penchant for depression and doubts about his creative powers. This qualification, however, does nothing to diminish the intensity of Chicherin's obvious admiration for Kuzmin's musical art, in which the "pupil" had far outshone the "mentor."

Yet another circumstance made the friendship with Chicherin particularly momentous in Kuzmin's life. We now know that Chicherin, too, was gay. His family kept sending him for long stays in German clinics that specialized in treating "nervous disorders," which did nothing to "cure" him. There is no evidence to suggest that Chicherin "seduced" Kuzmin or that they were ever anything more than very close friends. Both men do mention their sexual inclination in their letters, and for Kuzmin, at least, the possibility of discussing the subject could only have deepened feelings of intimacy and shared experience. All this certainly helps explain the exceptional intensity and duration of the friendship, which lasted right up to 1904, when Chicherin went into political emigration and Kuzmin began making his entry into Petersburg modernist circles. (Even then they corresponded for several years and kept in touch through relatives.) By the time Chicherin returned to Russia after the political upheavals of 1917, the two men had drifted apart, and the discreet, even secretive Chicherin was probably glad of that.[31]

Their friendship initially sprang up because of a shared interest in literature and music. The two young men started attending concerts and operas together and studying Mozart.[32] Kuzmin, of course, had already been studying music for many years when they met, and he, Chicherin, and several of their classmates tried a hand at composing as well. The abundant references to music in Kuzmin's early correspondence reflect the formation of his tastes. He states his preferences forcefully, but refuses to generalize artistic theories from them or make "global" conclusions. "I love" or "I like" are the most common locutions Kuzmin uses when he talks about art. So it remained until the end of his life. His preferences are anchored in the particular, in the experiential reality of the senses, the concreteness of everyday experience. Some of his tastes, to be sure, would change. To judge by his verse, for example, he would recapture a lost admiration for Rossini, who is one of the few composers mentioned in it, while *Tristan und Isolde*, which he had told Chicherin he liked "least of all" of Wagner's operas, served as a subtext for individual poems and a whole verse cycle in the 1920s. (Over the years he would develop a real love-hate relationship with Wagner.) Other enthusiasms—*Die Zauberflöte, Don Giovanni, Le nozze di Figaro, Das Rheingold*—never flagged, and they surface, often in surprising contexts, in his later writings.

Kuzmin rarely let go of those works which had first revealed to him the power of art, and he invariably referred to them in the same way he had in his early letters: in the context of a comparison with literature (or vice versa), since for him music and literature go hand in hand. When he mentions Berlioz, for example, the name of Hoffmann follows, as here, in the "Histoire édifiante," when he discusses his first formal musical compositions: "After I had written some art songs . . . I turned to operas and kept writing prologues . . . and, finally, the actual text and music for *King Millo*, based on Gozzi [his *Il Corvo*]. That was the first thing I ventured in literature. After that I became captivated by the Romanticism of the Germans and the French: Hoffmann, J. P. Richter, [La Motte] Fouqué, Tieck, Weber, Berlioz, etc., completely captivated me."[33]

Kuzmin's last years at the gymnasium witnessed not only his ever more serious involvement with music and literature but also his growing psychological self-definition, which he hints at it in his letters and the "Histoire édifiante." The very nervous jumpiness of the "Histoire" is as revealing as any detailed psychological narrative. In setting down the account for his friends, Kuzmin must have realized that he was describing something that became a pattern of experience in his early life—a liaison accompanied or followed by a bout of intense religious fervor or sexual denial, a sign of deep psychological conflicts about his same-sex inclination. (He writes in the "Histoire édifiante" that in early childhood he was "indifferent to religion, like my whole family.")[34] Even before leaving for Petersburg in 1884, his older brother had introduced him to sex under the pretext of games, and had frightened him by the "sweet and dim feeling" it aroused in him. This had led to "onanism" after the move to the capital.[35] At school, surrounded by other adolescents, he found different expression for his feelings:

> I was a bad student at school, but I loved to attend, as I loved studying languages and loved my classmates. Here I had for the first time an affair [*svyaz'*], with an older student. He was tall, half-German, blond, with eyes that were almost white [readers familiar with Kuzmin's writings will recognize here the first appearance of a constant motif], because they were so bright, innocent, and depraved. He danced well, and we saw each other, besides during recesses, at dancing classes, after which I would go home with him. . . . My first bout of religiosity, directed for the most part at fasting, going to mass, and rituals, also happened at the same time. Alongside both went my fascination with classical

literature, and I started using eye and eyebrow makeup, which I soon stopped. . . . One summer I lived in Revel, and since Yusha [Chicherin] fancied himself in love with Myasoedova, I imagined myself in love with Ksenya Podgurskaya [a mistake of Kuzmin's memory or a slip of his pen—her name was Podgorskaya]. . . . My religious mood—so intense that I asked to become a priest, and they laughed at me at school, where they knew about that and also about my unhappy infatuation with Stolitsa, about my affair with Kondratiev, and then with other young men in my own class— passed; I was totally occupied with the new Frenchmen [Kuzmin means, it seems, the so-called Decadents]. I was intolerant, arrogant, rude, and impassioned.[36]

In the summer of 1890, which he spent with his mother at a resort area near Revel, Kuzmin's letters to Chicherin and other friends reflect the conduct of a young man preoccupied with his composing and with his feelings for both young men and young women. Yet on July 3 he wrote:

I am not disposed to self-deception. I know that given my looks and my behavior, *young ladies*, or, as you put it, "maidens," cannot fall in love with me, and falling in love is their main goal in life: they often take infatuation for love. . . . I say that "young ladies" fall in love; yes, the majority of people, "decent chaps," fall in love instead of loving. Someone will fall in love with some Marya Ivanovna or other, he will get his "rank," and they start to pine for each other and to "wall themselves off from the rest of the world"; the wall keeps on contracting and contracting, like a circle, and finally it turns into an engagement ring that Petr Petrovich adroitly slips on Marya Ivanovna's dainty finger. And after that *he* loves *her* as he loves pancakes, overstuffed furniture, and his Voltaire chair. I'm not capable of such love.[37]

It would be easy to dismiss the Romantic tone of this rejection of the cozy bourgeois nature of such love as a commonplace at worst or at best as the clumsy self-defense of an adolescent (Kuzmin was not yet eighteen at the time) mocked at school with casual cruelty by his fellow students and convinced that he was physically unattractive, even ugly (in some letters of the time he describes himself as a "freak" [*urod*]). More than that, we would argue, lurks beneath the surface. The positivist and Populist ideologies that still dominated the Russian intellectual elite in the late 1880s and early 1890s, the worn-out clichés of the "fathers," as Bely dubbed them in the first volume of his memoirs, were utterly alien to Kuzmin when he encountered them in school and in conversations with the Chicherin family. But the seductive perfumes of the French fin de siècle were starting to waft through the dusty attics of Russian thought, and Kuzmin, ever alert to the slightest changes in artistic taste, may have come across some of them in his reading. The "new trends," as Russians first called them, rejected codes and conventions that enforced social (and sexual) conformity. Just such a rejection of the most powerful social institution and ideal of the nineteenth century, the bourgeois family, is implicit in Kuzmin's description of Petr Petrovich and Marya Ivanovna, who play out roles which so constrict them that they cut themselves off from the world of the senses and from the experience of love itself. Unstated as yet in Kuzmin's mocking dismissal is its corollary: the call to build life according to personal ideals, usually aesthetic, drawn from art in the broadest sense, rather than to social prescriptions. As one of the heroes of his novel *Wings* (Kryl'ya) remarks: "Military service, like a monastery, like almost every carefully worked-out dogma, has an enormous attraction in the amount of ready and definite opinions it provides for every variety of phenomena and ideas. For the weak this is a great support, and life becomes unusually easy when it has been deprived of the necessity for *ethical creation*."[38] In less than a decade the same seismic upheaval in cultural and social life that was already shaking western Europe would rock Russia, and Kuzmin would play a crucial part in that revolutionary redefinition of artistic and sexual roles.

After finishing school in 1891, Kuzmin enrolled in the St. Petersburg Conservatory. (Chicherin had decided to enter the university in Petersburg and then to pursue a career in the foreign service.) He spent the summer at Karaul, the estate of Chicherin's uncle, Boris Nikolaevich, a prominent jurist and historian of the "progressive" school whom he found "rather unbearable" for his opinionated opposition to "new" ways of thinking.[39] It was not a happy time, and his friendship with Chicherin almost ruptured: "I was getting ready for the Conservatory, was rude to everyone, said things deliberately to shock, and strove to make my behavior fantastic. Everyone tried to persuade me to enter the University, but I snorted and spoke in paradoxes."[40] When he returned to the capital in August, he entered the conservatory as planned, where he studied with Rimsky-Korsakov, some of whose music he admired, as he later (1897) wrote to Chicherin: "In general I like Rimsky-Korsakov more than the other Russians. After Dargomyzhsky, Serov, Musorgsky, and Tchaikovsky he seems enchantingly elegant, although his almost miniature style in *The Snow Maiden* [Snegurochka] is tiresome."[41] He stayed for only three years, leaving after his suicide attempt in 1894. His teachers had been dissatisfied with his work, and he returned their feelings by refusing to do assignments or failing to show them what he completed.[42]

Kuzmin made excellent use of his abundant free time in these years, devoting all of it to composition, for the most part vocal. He wrote songs to texts of Musset, Eichendorff, and the then-popular Russian poet Konstantin Fofanov, but as in the summer at Revel, when he worked on an ambitious operatic treatment of the Don Juan legend, operas preoccupied him. He based the majority of them on subjects from the past, especially classical antiquity, as treated by relative contemporaries. In 1891 he was hard at work on *Elena*, using as his text Leconte de Lisle's "Hélène," from the *Poèmes antiques*. A year later his letters mention two operas "in progress," *Cleopatra* and *Esmeralda*, the latter obviously based on Hugo's *Notre-Dame de Paris*. The letters of his conservatory years abound in comments not only about Mozart, Weber, Wagner, and Berlioz, but also about the Italians. His initial conclusions could be categorical at times: "I've analyzed Verdi's *Otello* thoroughly—1/2 is commonplaces without music, 1/4 is banal, 1/4 charming. *Aida* is 6/7 banalities, 1/7 is *passable*. *Otello* not only fails to reach the level of Shakespeare, but is twice as bad even as Boito's translation. Yet all the same Verdi is head and shoulders above all the rest of those piddling Italians [*ital'yanchiki*]. I'm not speaking about Paganini and [indecipherable] Palestrina" (June 29, 1893). It was the French who for a time held the center of his attention, as he recalled in the "Histoire édifiante": "I wrote a lot of music at the time [1893–94], enamored of Massenet, Delibes, and Bizet."[43]

References to literature seem almost incidental, and are invariably provoked by a comparison with music. Of French writers, Musset, Maupassant, and Pierre Loti (titles of various of his idealized romances of adventure set in tropical or Oriental settings) appear most often.[44] But he reserved his highest praise for Victor Hugo, who figures whenever Kuzmin discusses favorite writers and composers. Most remarkable, however, is the infrequency of references to French and Russian literature (even in childhood, he had known very little of it), probably because he had taken up the study of Italian at Chicherin's urging.[45] But it was German literature, Hoffmann in particular, that still exerted its old singular appeal. On July 16, 1890, he had written to Chicherin: "I'm mad about Hoffmann. You, it seems, have no use for him. I'm mad to the point of worship, he's on a level with Berlioz, Wagner, Liszt, and Hugo!" Now he was about to embark on learning the language and reading his revered authors in the original: "In the winter I absolutely must study German so I can read Hoffmann, Goethe, Schiller, Wagner. A whole world! And what a world! Even through the mist of translations I am always enchanted and dazzled. Especially by Hoffmann and Goethe" (August 3, 1892). Only Shakespeare rivals the Germans for the number of times he is discussed.

Kuzmin's study of German made yet another discovery possible: Ibsen. His measured view of that writer is all the more remarkable in light of the unqualified superlatives his plays would provoke at the turn of the century when they finally entered the repertory of Russian theaters and the consciousness of Russian writers: "At first he seemed rather ponderous to me, but now I'm delighted. In part he reminds me of Wagner: there's something powerful, somber, high-strung, and exalted in the extreme. But all the same he is sometimes drab and ponderous" (May 21, 1893). The majority of Russians at least initially took Ibsen as a social critic—as we might expect, given the critical tradition, stretching back to Belinsky, which had disposed readers to view literature as little more than a weapon in the struggle for "progressive" goals. Of this idea Kuzmin's evaluation contains not a trace. Nor do his other letters of the time, in this respect so different from those of Chicherin. He gives the impression of being entirely untouched by the social and political passions that so engaged Chicherin and other students of the capital. On July 18, 1893, he wrote him: "For some reason or other I have always had little interest in social matters; class interests, comradeship, speeches in honor of somebody, benefit concerts—all this is utterly insignificant for me. To me personal interests have always been in the forefront."

An epistolary discussion conducted at the end of the spring and over the summer of 1893, when Chicherin was in the countryside, shows this peculiarity very clearly. On May 27 Chicherin wrote, "I am going to take up Russian history—I'd like to become a Russian historian." A few weeks later, that and other dreams had merged with what, following Berdyaev, might be called the "Russian idea": Chicherin's fascination with the "enchantments of the world of the people," a "radiant world, miraculous in its wholeness" to which he kept "returning with bowed head and with an unquenchable desire, like a repentant sinner" (June 16). His conviction of the just need for revolutionary action to improve the lot of the peasantry and, later, of the rightness of Marxist theory would ultimately bring him, as they had so many Russians before him, into the radical camp and political exile.

Kuzmin, for his part, spurned these enthusiasms with a bemused awareness of how little they had to do with reality: "I have nothing against muzhiks, even drunk ones, nothing against peasant women, even dirty ones . . . nothing against dirty-faced kids; perhaps I am even more likely to chat and laugh with them than you are. You would turn aside and wait until they had washed up and gotten sober, and would find them poetic" (June 23). For the time, questions about art and its relationship to human life claimed his attention far more. Chicherin had only to joke about himself as a "gourmet of aesthetic pleasures" in one letter to receive an irritated response from his friend: "Again you have struck up your previous song, have pulled on your epicurean mask and are off and running. Here's your 'gourmet of aesthetic pleasures' and your comparison of music with a beefsteak, etc., etc. And how dare you play Mozart and Wagner after that? You need music for your digestion, for the arousal of all manner of appetites, you need Rossini and Offenbach. And I am deeply offended if you in any way like my music" (July 14, 1893).[46]

After he received this and the long letter in which Kuzmin reminisced about his childhood, Chicherin replied:

> I am even more convinced about the closeness of our moods, even if some nuances of my own do shock you. In you an unquenchable thirst for the "blue flower" holds sway, as "artistic feelings" do in me. Is it not just a difference of words? We are searching for the same thing, but not always in one and the same place—the whole difference lies in that. You are shocked that I can search for it in base objects. You are shocked that I can speak about the most

beautiful spiritual stirrings with a cynical half-smile, but turning romance into dogma frightens me, that is, when it happens in me, not in you. (July 22)

On some fundamental level Kuzmin took Chicherin's gentle reproach to heart, especially his warning about turning pretty words and sentiments (politely called "romance" [*romantika*]) into dogma divorced from life in all its manifestations, be they "high" or "low." When he replied on August 8, he wrote: "I cannot abide allegory. There is none of that living poetic fantasy per se [in the second part of *Faust*] that Shakespeare and Hoffmann have, but just an overly contrived form that is stuck on, form alone, and therefore cold." And he let his friend "in on a secret: Ariosto fascinates me far more [than Dante]: there is a free and easy life full of adventures there."

Most striking in Kuzmin's letters from this time is his decided preference for literature that has stood the test of time (the only vaguely modernist Russian writer mentioned in the letters is that easy purveyor of world-weariness, Fofanov), and for literature and music that avoid disharmony and celebrate the beauty and harmony of life and creation. Such preferences in art and an attendant joie de vivre dominate Kuzmin's mood in the years 1890–1894, at least insofar as the surviving private papers reflect it. In a letter of July 3, 1893, he wrote: "How joyous that nature and art exist. And you feel your powers, yes, your powers, and poetry penetrates everywhere, everywhere, even trifles, even the humdrum of life!... And the world is beautiful!"

This passage anticipates the concluding stanza of the poem in *Nets* that begins "Where will I find the right style to describe a stroll," written thirteen years later. It became Kuzmin's "signature" for most readers of Russian verse:

> The spirit of trifles, charming and airy,
> Of nights of love, now caressing, now stifling,
> Of the blithe frivolity of life without a care in the world!
> Ah, [I am] remote from miracles at one's command,
> I am faithful to your flowers, merry earth![47]

The serene, untroubled view of the world underlying this poem and scores of others in every collection of Kuzmin's verse is already evident in the letter of July 1893. The famous article of 1910 "On Beautiful Clarity" ("O prekrasnoi yasnosti") at times seems almost outlined in some of the letters of the early 1890s. We are not, then, surprised to discover in them how close to Kuzmin was the philosophy of Plotinus, who argues in the *Enneads* that beauty is the indispensable attribute of existence and that love is the force enabling humanity to assimilate this beauty, enrich itself spiritually, and move to perfection (the unity with the One). Kuzmin, though at times sorely tried, would remain true to these ideas.

Kuzmin read Plotinus selectively; like most writers, he took from him (and others) only what coincided with and bolstered conclusions he had reached already. There are explicit references to Plotinus after 1895, and his name need not appear for the reader to recognize his imprint, as in this letter of June 8, 1896: "Despite all the variety, I sense beauty everywhere, the same kind that is also incarnated in perfect love.... And worlds, and all art, and perfect love, perfect life fill me in such a wide stream—not of joy or even happiness—but of a feeling that takes me beyond the boundary of happiness or unhappiness." The letters to Chicherin of this period provide abundant evidence of the amazing intensity with which Kuzmin seized on everything in his personal and intellectual surroundings, whether new works by favorite writers and composers or a whole series of personal discoveries (more in literature and philosophy now than in music), with the eclecticism indicating a voracious rather than a disorderly appetite for knowledge: Plotinus, Plato, Apuleius, the Acts of the Apostles, Augustine, Francis of Assisi, Fogazzaro (a then popular and controversial Italian novelist, poet, and playwright), De Quincey (whom he read in French), the Goncourts, Flaubert, and Leskov.

Kuzmin's personal and aesthetic views did not, however, develop in the neat linear way a biographer might wish. Rather, there was a pendular swing from confidence and assurance about the future to growing doubts and lack of faith. We notice this with particular clarity in the urgent desire, which grew in intensity from month to month, to define art itself and its role—and to define himself through it. He disliked playing the "raisonneur" about art, indulging in what certain angry German philosophers used to call "higher nonsense"; but by the mid-1890s his letters disclose more than his usual vivacity of opinion and inquisitiveness as he tried to fit conceptions about art, no matter how derivative, into a personal system. His preoccupation with the artist's role becomes more insistent in the letters to Chicherin of 1895. It manifests itself most often as an awareness of isolation and a fear of being totally absorbed in art itself: "How strange. More and more I am losing touch with life (in the narrow and literal sense) and everything for me is concentrated in but a few people, books, and all-important concepts. And this does not oppress but somehow cleanses me, and when I see people from the 'world' it seems we're speaking different languages" (September 6, 1895).

The lack of many close friends or even acquaintances and the recent death of a lover only enhanced his perception of the artist's essential loneliness. Reality, as it were, reinforced the Romantic notion, constantly encountered in his reading of Hoffmann and others, of the artist's tragic nature, as one who is specially chosen but thereby isolated from his society and fellows by that very calling and nature. He expressed this clearly in an undated letter written most probably in the second half of the 1890s: "Pure art is generated and reaches perfection in its very own closed sphere, which is separated from the whole world. That sphere has its own special demands, laws, beauty, and needs, like the world of the ill and the mad (it may be ideal and harmonious, but it is mad in its utter isolation and abstraction). The purest poet, with no embellishments or compliments for reality—it is Shelley, but you see he is a dreamy, pure, and proud king from a madhouse."

Feelings of guilt and a yearning for purification from some "sin" accompanied such musings on the artist's tragic dilemma: "How can one lift the weight of sin that cannot be washed away, how can one be purified? Purification can only come in journeyings and ordeals. It was not only Adonis but Hercules, too, who attained divinity." Ambivalent feelings about his sexual inclination could only have exacerbated this nagging sense of sin. By the early 1890s, Kuzmin had completely embarked on what he called the "other path" (inoi put'), but he was only too well aware of the gender rules encoded and enforced by his society. The emergence of homosexual identity at the end of the century reached widespread public attention with Oscar Wilde's trial and conviction in 1895. The Russian press gave wide coverage to it and wrote openly about the reasons for the scandal. The press of Right and Left pilloried English society and the English system of justice, not Wilde, and on occasion went so far as to call for the formation of defense committees. No petitions, of course, were signed in Russia as far as we know. None of this should be construed as a defense of Wilde's gay identity or any kind of special tolerance by Russian society as a whole for same-sex practices. "Highly moral" English society was either accused of sullying the name of a great writer or of "hypocrisy" for condemning a "secret vice," which, some in the Russian press insisted, represented but the tip of the degenerate iceberg that was England.[48] To be sure, the Russian modernists would fix on Wilde and his life as "exemplary" of the artist-martyr hounded to death by a philistine society which could not understand him, but that came only later.[49] It provoked stern warnings from the conservative press about the dangers of biting into the "Sodomic apple" of Wilde's art, beautiful on the outside but rotten to the core.[50]

Many of the young pass through a phase in which everything is exaggeratedly exalted or debased, and Kuzmin was no exception. The dispassionate tone of the "Histoire édifiante" provides evidence that for him the extremes were neither insincere nor unnatural: "In 1893 I encountered a man with whom I fell deeply in love, and my affair with him promised to be lasting. He was about four years older and an officer in a cavalry regiment. . . . This was one of the happiest times of my life, and I wrote a lot of music. . . . My mother did not particularly approve of my life. Strangely enough, my attempt to take poison dates from that time."[51] After confiding in Chicherin, another of his former school friends, and a cousin about his love for the cavalry officer, a man he never identified in any other way but as "Prince Georges,"[52] Kuzmin attempted suicide:

> I don't understand what led me to take that step. Perhaps it was the hope that they would save me. I think I was impelled to do it by my lack of knowledge about life, by my sense that my situation [with Prince Georges] was somehow special, by my dissatisfaction with the Conservatory, the impossibility of leading an affluent life, by romanticism, and by frivolity. . . . I bought a lot of laurel-cherry drops and drank all of them after writing a letter of farewell. Physically it was very pleasant, but the terror of death gripped me, and I woke up Mama.[53]

His mother asked only, "Misha, why have you done this?" and summoned the doctor, who rushed him to a hospital, where he was made to vomit (a "repulsive experience," he recalled). He spent the night, raving in French, on a bed in which someone had died that morning. He was released after a few days. The doctors forbade him to study, and he left the conservatory.

> My love redoubled. I confessed everything to my mother; she became affectionate and candid, and we would chat for hours on end during the night or in the evening over a game of piquet. For some reason or other we always spoke French. [A subtle way, of course, of distancing the revelation.] In the spring I traveled to Egypt with Prince Georges. We visited Constantinople, Athens, Smyrna, Alexandria, Cairo, and Memphis. It was a fairy-tale–like trip because of the enchanting nature of this first-time *collage* [he uses the French] and the unprecedented nature of the sights. On the way back he had to go to Vienna, where his aunt lived; I returned home alone. My friend died from heart disease in Vienna; I tried to find forgetfulness by studying hard.[54]

We know nothing certain about why Kuzmin decided, on what he makes sound like an impulse, to go to Egypt with "Prince Georges." The anonymity of travel, of course, offered him an opportunity to pursue his affair openly (two young men traveling together and sharing a cabin or hotel room would hardly have raised eyebrows), and travel has been the age-old prescription for illness, "nervous" or otherwise. Kuzmin's friends and mother, mindful of his suicide attempt, may have urged a sea voyage to warmer climes. Neither explanation can be discounted, even if the first seems more likely, because the chronological compression of the "Histoire édifiante" seriously misleads: the journey took place not in 1894, as one might conclude, but in the spring and summer of 1895. (This means, too, that the affair was no passing infatuation, but lasted more than two years.) Whatever the reason, and despite the journey's brevity (it lasted about two months), few events in Kuzmin's early life were more formative, if only for his art. The Egyptian past—not the distant dynasties of the Pharaohs, but Hellenistic Alexandria—would provide themes and inspiration for his music, verse, and prose for the rest of his life.

The actuality of Arab and colonial Egypt figures not at all in any of his later works. Nor does it in the one firsthand impression of the trip that we have (Kuzmin destroyed his diary for 1894–95 for reasons that remain unknown), a letter to Chicherin, written from Alexandria on May 17, 1895, with few details (that he does not mention "Prince Georges" is not surprising, as Chicherin strongly disapproved of the relationship):

> How to describe to you Constantinople, Asia Minor, Greece, Alexandria, Cairo, the pyramids, the Nile, and Memphis—I don't know. I am in a state of the most absolute mad intoxication. The only thing that really amazes me is that the sky is not blue but pale gray, and that it is not particularly hot. I have just returned from Memphis and am sitting in Alexandria at night, and from the street, through the jalousie, one can hear someone improvising infinitely doleful and languid music on a mandolin. I cannot write, there are too many impressions. [I was] in the pyramid of Menkaure, climbed up Cheops, sailed on the Nile at night: Lord, what ecstasy. I have jotted down four Egyptian tunes: a dance played at a wedding, one for a belly dance, one played when a caravan set off for Mecca, and then a men's song of some sort for the beginning of a festival in Alexandria when everyone runs about carrying torches and flowers and singing loudly and in a Bacchic manner. Honestly, I cannot write about it.[55]

The death of his lover followed not long after, and death is inextricably bound up with many of Kuzmin's evocations of life's pleasures in ancient Alexandria, that image of a kind of earthly paradise, in the free verse of the "Alexandrian Songs" ("Aleksandriiskie pesni"), written ten years later. No more is this so than in the almost programmatic second poem of the cycle "Wisdom":

> What's to be done . . .
> if my poems,
> as dear to me
> as his are to Callimachus
> or to any other great one,
> wherein I invest my love and all my tenderness,
> and airy thoughts sent by the gods,
> the solace of my mornings,
> when the sky is clear,

and the scent of jasmine drifts through the windows,
will tomorrow
be forgotten like everything else?
If I shall no longer see
your face,
hear your voice?
If the wine shall be drunk up,
fragrances evaporate,
and the most precious fabrics
will rot
centuries later?
Would I start loving less
these dear and fragile things
because they must decay?[56]

"Dear and fragile things" were the hallmark of Kuzmin's verse to generations of careless readers and critics, as though that were all that interested him in life. The poem's subtle movement gives the lie to anything so simple. It begins with encrimsoned clouds at sunset that slowly dissolve into twilight. This picture extends through the whole poem (with its interrupted journey, a constant symbolic motif in Kuzmin's work), in which the speaker likens verse, love, and, in the final reckoning, all human life to the immutable universals of nature and creation itself. "Death and Time reign on earth," to borrow from Vladimir Soloviev, and while they may deprive us of "dear and fragile things" (all the more precious for their perishability) and life itself, they inscribe each person's fate into a design as old as time itself.[57] Here is the core of Kuzmin's hard-won view of life (and of his stoic composure in the face of death), and the best of his lyrics in all periods heighten our awareness of the impermanence of the fleeting world and the permanent fact of transience and change.[58]

A deep new interest in the history of mysticism and early Christianity also explains why Kuzmin chose to visit Egypt rather than western Europe with "Prince Georges." It now shaped the denial phase that, following the pattern noted earlier, inevitably succeeded his first love affairs (and is reflected in the suicide attempt): "I thought that with the death of my friend I had to be, as it were, condemned to the absence of love. As I was already then fascinated by the Neoplatonists and the mystics of our era's first centuries, I tried to build my life on that model, strictly regulating my studies, diet, and reading; I was trying to be a kind of abstemious Pythagorean."[59] He resumed his study of music and worked on composition, harmony, and musical arrangement with Vasily Kühner, a composer, pianist, and violinist who had left Germany in 1882 to open a private music school in Petersburg. His friendship with Chicherin, who was keeping a watchful eye on him, intensified, as his friend "tried as hard as he could to support in me the notion of a Providence that was leading me to the necessity of correctness of the sentiments and to abstinence [from sex]."[60] This "honeymoon," as he called it, in his relationship with Chicherin and the denial of sensuality that he was trying to impose on himself could not last, and the familiar pendular swings of mood returned, outward indications of a psychological state so fragile that doctors ordered a trip abroad after a severe illness in the winter of 1896–97. It bears all the marks of a nervous breakdown: "I fell ill with hysteria, I started having cataleptic seizures, and underwent treatment at [the clinic of Dr.] Klimenko all winter long."[61] Kuzmin discussed the matter with Chicherin, who was living in Europe, and in the gloomy spring of 1897, unusually cold and damp even by Petersburg standards, he decided to follow his doctors' advice.

Nothing, especially not the renewed attempts to write both texts for his songs and poems in their own right, had restored any sense of balance. Letters sent just before his departure for abroad disclose Kuzmin's terrible feeling that something as yet undefined but crucial was missing, as he wrote to Chicherin on February 11: "I utterly lack a positive rite, as you call it: I love the Orthodox liturgy very much and am now rather dutiful toward it, but something does not satisfy me; an impression of the universe and of collective spirituality [*sobornost'*], the grandeur and symbolism, the personal exaltation that replaces general devoutness—all that is profound and beautiful, but something is lacking in Orthodoxy, or there is something superfluous in me."

Kuzmin's inability to give himself up utterly, without the slightest rational calculation, to some kind of faith, religious or otherwise, tormented him. He longed for the instinctive, unquestioning faith of the child and for the possibility of creating the kind of naive and powerful art he found among the common people and the ancients:

I love the Apocrypha and spiritual rimes even more [than the *byliny*]. . . . No sooner do I touch the centuries around our first one than I positively go mad; Alexandria, the Neoplatonists, the Gnostics, the emperors drive me mad and intoxicate, or rather, don't so much intoxicate as fill me with some kind of ethereal air. You don't walk, but fly, the whole world is accessible, everything is attainable, near. Let me be forgiven if I am conceited, but I feel that sooner or later I will be able to express this and will to some degree become like Valentinus and Apuleius. For this alone one can endure not one but three lives. Perhaps and not only for this. (January 13, 1897)[62]

We already have here an inkling of a resolution of the personal crisis that had brought on his breakdown, but a hint only and in the hypothetical mode. The resolution would be long in coming.

2

"I Am Searching . . . the Long, Long Path": 1897–1902

AS FOR so many Russians before him, Italy, the country Kuzmin would more than once call "blessed," became the focus of a possible alternative to his present impasse. When he started studying the Italian language in the summer of 1892, he found it "much more harsh and coarse" than French, but superficial first impressions of the language and culture softened rapidly. By 1897 he was highly proficient in both, and at last was about to see firsthand what had vividly existed only in his imagination as a "radiant paradise." The brief journey, which lasted from April to mid-June 1897, played such a major role in Kuzmin's life that it deserves our closest scrutiny.

His account of the whole trip in the "Histoire édifiante" makes clear what it meant to him:

> Rome intoxicated me. There I fell in love with a lift boy [he uses the English], Luigino, whom, with his parents' permission, I took with me to Florence so he could later accompany me to Russia in the capacity of my servant. I was very short of money, because I spent it freely. I was very jolly, and all the Neoplatonists influenced me only insofar as I regarded myself as somehow demonic. Mama in desperation turned to Chicherin [whom Kuzmin had stopped to see in Munich for some days on the way to Italy]. He unexpectedly

rushed to Florence. I was already tired of Luigino and readily allowed myself to be saved. Yusha brought me together with Canon Mori, a Jesuit, who at first took me firmly in hand and then made me move in with him, since he had decided to convert me. We sent Luigino back to Rome, Mori dictated all my letters. I was not deceiving him; I yielded of my own free will to lulling Catholicism, but formally all I said was how much I would like "to be" a Catholic, not "become" one. I ambled about visiting churches, his acquaintances, his mistress, the marquise Espinosi Marati, at her country estate. I read the lives of the Saints, especially St. Luigi Gonzaga, and was ready to become a clergyman and a monk. But Mama's letters, a sudden change of heart, the sun that I suddenly noticed one morning, the renewed attacks of hysteria—all that made me ask Mama to send a telegram demanding my return. The Canon and I parted tearfully, promising to see each other again very soon. I took with me a prayer book and letters to Catholic clergymen living in Petersburg. We corresponded often in Italian, but then the letters became rarer, and finally just stopped. I returned dissatisfied, Mama and everyone else were more alien to me [than when I had left], not knowing what to do.[1]

The trip failed to resolve his personal dilemma, even as it closed the door on one way he thought might lead out of the impasse. Yet memory transformed dissatisfaction into its opposite, as the homesickness he felt almost immediately upon returning to Petersburg gradually evolved into a cult of Italy, which finally assumed the proportions of a private myth. Nothing can exaggerate the hold Italy exercised on Kuzmin. Italy, Akhmatova liked to say, is a dream that keeps returning for the rest of your life. For Kuzmin it was a dream he kept returning to all his life in his imagination, especially at moments of greatest trial.

Nothing in his reading had prepared him for the actual encounter with Italy. Everything seemed extraordinary and larger than life, especially Rome ("in the heart of it all—Rome, *urbs!*") and Florence ("enchanting"), which exerted their magic on him no less than on previous generations of Russian travelers. Rome of the republic and early empire held little interest for him; he was far more taken with the very early Renaissance and with the Rome of the late first century A.D., the Rome of early Christianity and mystical sects, as he wrote to Chicherin on April 16:

> The ancient mosaics in many churches are magnificent in Rome, and the Christian museum attached to St. Jean de Lateran is exceptional in interest; the wondrous sarcophagi, the bas-reliefs; an altogether special world. And what a new light for me on the earliest Christianity—meek, dear, simple, almost idyllic, still in contact with classical antiquity, somewhat mystical, and not at all gloomy: Jesus is everywhere without a beard, handsome and gentle; the attendant spirits gathering grapes; the good shepherds. There is a sarcophagus with the story of Jonah that is a pure masterpiece of grace and subtlety. The catacombs were only a custom; there are underground pagan sepulchers and Jewish catacombs that differ not at all from those of the Christians; services were performed there only out of necessity, during persecutions, and not because of any penchant for gloomy surroundings. The fourth-century mosaics are something very different—here there is asceticism and mysticism—a whiff of the East.[2]

So full of impressions were the days in Rome that his thoughts again turned to composition: "I've myself been thinking about a similar 'Roman' suite: 'Colysée,' 'Via Appia,' 'The Good Shepherd,' and 'Apollo.' . . . For musical variety I would like to include, in a sort of scherzo, one of the fountains of Rome, but they're all ghastly baroque" (April 25).

He wrote the "Suite Romaine" in July, after his return to Russia, but it was his discovery of the remnants of early Christianity, so different from the somber majesty of the art and religious philosophy of Byzantium and the Orthodox East, that made an impact, as he said, "forevermore." He drew on these memories all his life. Compare the letter of April 16 with the opening of the magnificent meditation "The Catacombs," written a quarter of a century later, in 1921:

> With the innocence of infants, the shades were lost in listening to the singing of Orpheus.
> Under a willow Jonah keeps remembering the depths of the whale.

> But the Shepherd, feeling pity, lays a sheep on his shoulders,
> and gracious is the curved sunset beyond the top of the
>   cedar.[3]

Here myths of the return from the dead and promises of resurrection in three cultures—pagan, Judaic, and Christian—conclude, in a way similar to the "Alexandrian Song" discussed earlier, with a natural image that validates the timeless truth of myth: the arch of a sunset on the horizon, a glimpse of the circle's perfection in nature that will be fully realized with the sun's next rising.

It was the strange mixture of pagan and Christian in early Christianity that most intrigued Kuzmin; he later devoted several works to the subject (the play *On Alexis, Man of God* [O Aleksee cheloveke Bozh'em] and the unfinished novel *Roman Marvels* [Rimskie chudesa]). He saw it in the early Renaissance, in Pisa's Camposanto, with its collection of sarcophagi blending classical and Christian motifs, and in the adjacent Baptistery, with its pulpit by Nicola Pisano that consciously incorporates elements of classical antiquity into Christian iconography. But Rome, with its oldest churches built on the ruins of pagan temples and constructed from stones pillaged from those temples and other ancient buildings, seemed to him the very image of this curious syncretism. His fascination with it induced him to read the writings of the early Fathers of the Church, and, even more important for his conception of Italy as it is reflected in the verse of the 1920s, to take up the Gnostics with renewed attention.

His affair with Luigi Cardoni brought the stay in Rome to an end, and on April 29 he left with the young man for Florence, where he planned further to investigate Palestrina and other early Italian religious composers.[4] That interest brought him together with Canon Mori, to whom he was referred for liturgical books and instruction. Chicherin, still profoundly troubled by his own sexual feelings, had been shocked by the affair with the young Italian. His visit to Florence in the first week of May helped bring it to a decisive rupture. After Chicherin's return to Germany, Kuzmin wrote to tell him that Luigino had been sent back to Rome, and he kept him informed about his relationship with Mori, which was assuming a closer character with the passing of each day. On May 16 he wrote from Sant' Agata, a small village in the Mugello region north of Florence where friends of Mori had a villa: "For you I will say that I must read a lot, pray, and train under [Mori's] direction so as to learn a bit about the truth. I myself have written to Mama to tell her he is a monsignor, what he has done for me, what the conditions of my life are, and that my goal is tranquillity and oblivion."

The peace of the countryside, far removed from the bustle of Rome and Florence, with their memories of his love affair, gradually helped restore a measure of balance, as Mori had no doubt intended. Signs of crisis erupted at times ("Now indifference has given way to nerves; now it's caprices, now it's tears, now strivings for upper regions so intense that I must get myself under control" [May 18]), but the attentiveness of Mori and his friends helped him find a certain equanimity, enough at least to resume composing (he sketched out themes for a Requiem) and do some reading of the lives of the saints and Dante.

Kuzmin accepted Mori's invitation to take a room in the apartment he shared with his sisters in the heart of Florence, on the Borgo Santi Apostoli (no. 12), only steps away from the Uffizi and Piazza della Signoria, and he moved there on May 21. Shortly thereafter, in a letter written in Florence between June 11 and 22, Kuzmin sent Chicherin a long portrait of the man who was playing such a crucial role in his life, noting just what he could and could not give him:

> He used to be a missionary, and as a missionary he had to be excellent: he has a strong belief, is very strict, and diligently fulfills his religious duties. . . . He is a bit too *terre-à-terre*—this is a missionary for America; his is not by any means a monastic sanctity. This is an uncommonly jolly man, full of life, reveling in his fantasy. . . . You hear his sonorous Tuscan accent everywhere, now scolding, now offhand, and also the mighty peals of his laughter. On the public square he is in his element; everybody knows Canon Mori and he knows all there is to know about them. He can't help talking—this is one of the worst prattlers I have ever known. Inexhaustible anecdotes and even gossip. And then he revels in his fantasy and plans one thing after another, carrying out none of it. Not to speak of the fact that I have already turned into "one of the most famous Russian composers." . . . Today he wants to study

Spanish with me, tomorrow he promises to publish my compositions, then he intends to translate my poems, and a day later he
forgets all about his plans.

Interestingly, Kuzmin would later incorporate anecdotes from his
stay with Mori in *Wings*. All his life he rejected the well-known
Proustian argument that there is no necessary connection between the
individual-in-the-world and "le moi profond," which produces the
work. Mori, Signora Poldina, his sister, and the Marchesa Marati all
appear in the novel under their own names. Passages in the Italian
letters and in the novel coincide to a singular degree; they reveal how
heavily and directly Kuzmin drew on his experiences in Florence, Fi-
esole, and Sant' Agata (and, no doubt, Rome) when writing *Wings*. He
even went so far as to use his actual Florence address: the Italian composer Orsini lives with his aunt, the Marchesa Marati, in the same
house on the Borgo Santi Apostoli where Mori's apartment was located.
Georgy Chulkov did not know how right he was when he wrote in his
memoirs, "M. A. Kuzmin acquired a rather ambiguous notoriety at that
time when the magazine *Libra* [Vesy] printed his short novel *Wings*,
biographical in part."[5]

Many passages in the novel help recreate the special atmosphere of
Kuzmin's life in the late spring and early summer of 1897, filling the
gaps left by other documents.[6] Several details in the novel's description
of the young hero's room disclose the atmosphere of Catholicism to
which the robust Mori, equally at home in nature or the city, full of tales
both uplifting and scabrous, was introducing Kuzmin and in which the
still deeply troubled young man hoped to find solace from the tumult of
his personal and spiritual life:

On the somewhat bare walls hung engravings of saints and of
the Madonna of "Good Counsel"; there was a plain table, a shelf
with books of edifying contents, a painted wax doll of St. Luigi
Gonzaga, an *enfant de choeur* dressed in a hand-sewn costume and
standing under a glass dome on a chest of drawers, a stoup of holy
water by the door—all lent the room the character of a monk's cell,
and only the upright piano by the balcony door and the dressing
table by the window prevented the resemblance from being complete.[7]

Mori liked to call his intense young friend "St. Luigi," and Kuzmin elaborated on the affectionate nickname in the letter that describes Mori:

I am often called St. Luigi here, because people find a remarkable resemblance between me and portraits and images of St. Aloysius Gonzaga. I haven't seen a picture of him, but I read the life of this enchanting Jesuit who died in his twenty-fifth year [the saint was twenty-three when he died in 1591, a victim of his labors among the plague-stricken in Rome]. Thoroughly imbued with his life and deducing mystical trifles from the fact that he resembles me and died in his twenty-fifth year, when I am entering my twenty-fifth year as well, I disdained the rule that forbids putting questions and that prescribes giving answers and showing obedience only, and I asked whether I had the strength to imitate Him and continue His life. Mori said that he felt I did and was ready to vouch for it.

This personal acceptance of the saint, noted for his chastity, apparently brought Kuzmin to the brink of formal conversion to Catholicism, something not at all unheard of for Russians living in Italy before him, although the notion seems quite incredible given what we know of Kuzmin's later life. He did not convert, however, and remained Orthodox. In a letter to Chicherin written a year later, Kuzmin recalled his stay in Florence as a time when he lived with a "thirst for ultimate enslavement." If that craving brought moments of spiritual assuagement that approached mystical ecstasy, they could not be sustained for long. It was simply not in his nature. He was immersed in religious literature and was as drawn to the Franciscan poets and their ideal, Francis of Assisi, as he had been before.[8] He was attempting to subdue sexual feelings, which he had been persuaded, largely by Chicherin, to regard as sinful, by prayer and asceticism as he tried to sublimate desires in an *imitatio sancti*. With two of the greatest ascetics and mystics of the Western Church, Saints Francis and Aloysius Gonzaga, as his ideals, he had set himself a noble but impossible goal. He began to doubt not only himself but also those he had once viewed as the potential agents of his salvation.

Mori proved incapable of understanding the depth and nature of his moody young friend's crisis, and he took as "earthy" an attitude toward it as he did toward everything else, blaming it on Kuzmin's constitution: "Mori, incidentally, for the sake of my tranquillity, advised me to go see a doctor specializing in nervous disorders whom he knows well and who is the best one here. The latter examined me thoroughly, but when he found nothing, prescribed only daily lukewarm baths" (letter of June 11). He assured Chicherin, as he continued in the letter, that he was "very calm" and "satisfied" with his life, but only a few lines later added: "Not in vain did God save me. I would like to devote my life and talents to Him. But how can I, not yet purified, not yet [living] in truth, know how to do this myself? I must find people to whom I might give myself blindly, who might see how and in what I can do work for the Lord, who might direct me and bring me up to sanctity. And I am searching."

Mori clearly was not the man for this task, though Kuzmin retained a warm affection for him, as evidenced by the affable portrait in *Wings*. Plagued not just by doubts about the canon but by a shortage of money as well (he had already had to ask Chicherin for a large loan), he decided it was time to return to Petersburg. He arrived on the twelfth of June (June 24, New Style), with his "thirst" for a new spiritual guide lessened not at all. The attacks of "nerves"—the external symptoms, as he realized, of his failure to find the path to what he called "sanctity"—continued.

Kuzmin gradually but decisively cut all ties with Mori, but he never severed the ties with Italy. It remained a source of personal and artistic inspiration for the rest of his life. He used his actual memories of his short stay in a number of works, and he made several journeys of the imagination to Italy, in cycles of poems or in individual lyrics.[9] In the 1911 poem that begins "How I love the smell of leather," a Proustian sensation so disorients the lyrical subject that for a moment past and present, recollection of an encounter in Florence and the present perception of a young man mingle and merge. (In general in Kuzmin, it is memory and recollection that provide the sexual "charge," not anticipation, which is so common in much homosexual writing.) The speaker is forced to draw himself up with:

> We never saw each other in Florence:
> You have not been there, you were three years old then,
> but the jasmine branches swayed
> and love and anxiety were in my heart.[10]

In the late verse he would rely as much on his voluminous reading for these journeys as on his actual recollections.[11]

In an undated letter, written probably about a year after his return to Russia, Kuzmin was able to recall to Chicherin the "love and anxiety" of the trip with a certain objectivity and with a sobering awareness of the extent to which it had failed to ease the personal crisis that he had still to resolve. The letter is a testament of despair, self-accusation, and spiritual aridity:

> I have been writing with no love or pleasure, regarding my work as a burden. I am indifferent to what results and am not looking beyond tomorrow, as I do not know why I am writing. . . . At one time in the past I had purely personal and private reasons for existing; all that passed, and everything kept returning to one and the same thing. There was a time after that when I dreamt about renunciation, about incarnating in art that beauty and that love, which was filling me to overflowing, so that every instant, every breath was a hymn to love. Having renounced personal feelings, I would bring others to happiness through music, beauty, and metaphysics (as in Plotinus). . . . All that gave me wings. . . .
>
> Afterwards, as I studied it all more closely, that which was near proved to be distant, my dreams vanished. And I myself proved to be weak and frivolous. God saved me, but I was saved too easily, and that lessened the purifying power of suffering. . . . While I got better physically, my main feeling was of being dulled and stunned. There was no one to whom I could cry my heart out, before whom I could fall on my knees. Had Mori been more sly, he could have had an immense influence on me, but he didn't want to or couldn't. Enormous yearning and a thirst for ultimate enslavement, a feeling of being besotted (without even ecstasy), a total absence of thought brought me to S.J. [the Society of Jesus], so as only not to have to act and not to think. God saved me a second time. I returned healthy, alert, but utterly, utterly devastated. . . . I do not dare to think about my earlier dreams while I am not cleansed.[12]

This wrenching confession so alarmed Chicherin that he tried, as Kuzmin later recalled, "to give me a guard in place of Mori, and after my refusal to resort to Peiker, he directed me to Father Aleksey Kolokolov, a *conducteur d'âmes* fashionable in society, but this archpriest's sanc-timoniousness of the sort that was *à la mode* in society repelled me, and after the first confession I stopped going to see him."[13]

Religious searching, based on a longing for perfection and renuncia-tion of any form of openly expressed sensuality, had remained the focus of his life after the return from Italy. He was living with his mother, giving music lessons, which he detested, and trying to write. The only two of his first works in prose to have come down to us date from the late 1890s. They provide dramatic evidence of the nature of the relig-ious quest on which their author had embarked. Here are excerpts from one of them, entitled "In the Desert":

> Long did I walk through a barren desert, ever farther and farther, driven on by the curse of unwashed sins. My arms, from the bur-den of past embraces, had no strength, my eyes, exhausted from the gazes of lovers, had grown dark. . . .
>
> From out of the boundless desert, from out of the distant sky came a great radiance. It was enormous, like a sandstorm, like the pillar of Babylon. In terror I closed my eyes. It seemed that I had died already. In the oppressive mute stillness I did not hear my heart beating.
>
> When I opened my eyes, a Radiant One stood before me. His hands were concealed in the folds of his garment. Visible through his white chiton was a bloody wound, as from a lance or the tusk of a wild boar. I was unworthy to look upon his face. I only crawled up to his feet, and heavy large teardrops, like the first drops of rain, fell into the sand of the desert. I fell prostrate and wept and wept. . . .
>
> It seemed I wept for years and years on end. And I looked up at him—he was smiling, gracious. Merciful, he stretched out arms of forgiveness to me. . . . His smile and his radiance marked the whole desert. The barren steppe had turned into a paradise not of the earth, into the bright vales of the Jordan. I arose full of mighty powers—I had fallen a weeping sinner. I arose God's warrior.[14]

This fragment, redolent of Kuzmin's reading in religious literature in its deliberately archaic diction and obsessive inversions, suggests noth-ing at all of the admired prose stylist to come; but one psychologically arresting detail (not to speak of the pervasive homoeroticism, albeit of a mystical variety) hints at his still unacknowledged ambivalence about a quest grounded in asceticism: Is the "Radiant One" *(Siyayushchii)* when he first appears Christ, pierced on the cross by a lance, or Adonis, gored by a wild boar?[15]

One imagines that Kuzmin continued to work and read and make the rounds of acquaintances from sheer habit, in order to maintain minimal contact with the life and people around him. As before, the lives of great ascetics and mystical writings, especially Italian works of the fourteenth and early fifteenth centuries, most attracted him. In 1921 Kuzmin remembered one of them, Saint Catherine of Siena (and her Alexandrian predecessor), in an exquisite poem, and his reading of the Franciscan poets would influence the themes and imagery of his own verse.[16] The "tenderness" and "sweetness" he found there, like the ecstatic apprehension of reality, not excluding the most humble details of life and nature, and the immediacy provided by the pervasive "diminutive tone," left an indelible impression on his poems about love and religion in *Nets*. Similarly, the close relationship between mysticism and eroticism that characterizes the writings of the Franciscan poets ("In the Desert" contains glimmers of it) runs through that whole collection, most notably in the poems on the soul and the "holy warrior" *(svyatoi voin)* or "guide" *(vozhatyi)*, a decidedly homoerotic spiritual ideal, to be sure.

All such reading only intensified his own nagging sense of not belonging to anyone or anything, his sense that everything he did was only "for the time being" (that casually devastating word *poka*). The words "definition" and "determinacy" occur over and over again in the letters. Some higher goal, to which he could devote himself wholeheartedly, continued to elude him, but it beckoned all the more insistently. As once before, Kuzmin, "oppressed by being in the state of *un être flottant*," felt impelled to make some final definition of the role of art. He wrote to Chicherin on August 28, 1898:

> Is not its aim to awaken the slumbering creativity in every person? And the more chosen the person, the more profoundly he has apprehended [the world], must not his art be the more powerful? But who then knows *how* to awaken this? That is something totally undefined and less palpable than is absolute beauty, which, once

attained intuitively, abides forever, if only by recollection. This does not mean that I attach great significance to transient and passing thoughts, but this means that I doubt, that I am uncertain about areas where once I thought I had faith. And it is like that about everything: an enormous need for faith, a large store of faith, vague and fundamental, and the impossibility of directing it to a defined point.

In Kuzmin's definition of art's task we recognize the influence of the metaphysics of Plotinus, where the goal is to reach a state in which the soul "feels" an ineffable Presence in a joyous ecstasy of blissful plenitude. The key word is "absolute." This Kuzmin sought desperately, with that passion for finality at all costs which seems so characteristic of the Russian creative personality. It is hardly surprising that the only Russian author whose name appears frequently in Kuzmin's letters of the period is Dostoevsky.

Self-conscious and painfully turned inward, he noticed everywhere confirmation of his sense of internal division. As despair mounts in the letters, Kuzmin questions every former passion. Nothing could resist it, not even music and musical performances, which, in one undated letter, he holds up to ridicule in terms reminiscent of Tolstoy's acerbic polemic *What Is Art?* (published in 1898):

> A concert provides the maddest picture of all: people who are by no means stupid gather (if not from boredom or from the lack of anything better to do, then because they have no core) to sit for three hours and listen while 200 people play, pluck, and pipe away at a symphony, i.e., at something to the highest degree incomprehensible and absurd to the uninitiated. . . . And the symphony is the most characteristic product of pure music, where everything takes place as if on the moon, where its laws, feelings, and so forth are incomprehensible, alien, and dead for people who are not mad. And this really is the *temple* of art (sometimes of deceit and tricks), and how far it is from satisfying music's vital needs.

Not long afterwards, by contrast, he described a new composition of his and how much he looked forward to hearing it performed. In fact, in late October 1898 he made his published musical debut, when the Moscow firm of Jurgenson issued the score for piano and voice of his

Three Romances (Tri romansa), with, as fate would have it, his name misspelled on the cover because of that bedeviling palatalization marker ("Kuz'min").

His "opus one" contains "Dans ce nid furtif" (1896), a song for baritone set to a text by Sully-Prudhomme and accompanied by what must be Kuzmin's parallel translation; "Tranquillity" ("Uspokoenie," 1895), set to a slightly altered text of a Merezhkovsky poem originally entitled "Tranquil Ones" ("Uspokoennye"); and "Pale Roses" ("Blednye rozy," 1895), dedicated to a school friend of Kuzmin and Chicherin's who is often mentioned in their letters, A. I. Anichkov.[17] Kuzmin set the latter song to one of his own poems, a verbless text much like an earlier poem, "Pines and Firs," which he had sent to Chicherin before going to Italy.[18] In a letter of December 9, 1898, he reacted to his friend's reproach for laziness and indifference to the fate of his works: "I don't agree that my first publication had such paramount and decisive significance. . . . As for the matter of how [the critics] will rank me, that, honestly, is absolutely all the same to me."

The letters of the time read like a fever chart in their abrupt changes of mood, often in the space of one letter, from almost manic intensity to extreme depression. On October 13, 1898, Kuzmin informed Chicherin that he was giving up his formal studies and that

> if it were now suggested to me that I completely give up writing operas, even music itself, I would agree. Understand the full horror of the fact that it is *"all the same to me."* My soul is all trampled, like a vegetable garden by horses. And sometimes dying seems to me so beautiful, so desirable. I will not kill myself now (although I do not know what my thirst for love and religion might lead to), but I think to myself that dying would now be best. Forgive me for thinking only about myself, for being an egoist, petty, unworthy, and obstinate, but can't you see, can't you feel, that I—healthy and laughing—am dying from thirst for love, and I love no one and I am afraid to love, although I know I would be resurrected by it. . . . I don't see anything, anything at all ahead of me, and I pray that God grants me death if He denies me fullness of life.

The striking image of the third sentence, indeed the mood of the whole passage, prefigures a poem written ten years later, which reads like a gloss on his earlier impasse:

> What is my heart? An unweeded vegetable garden,
> trampled as though by a herd of wild horses.
> How shall I live a life that is rent asunder,
> when all my thoughts are about one thing?

It concludes with a truth that in 1898 still eluded him:

> And to which saints shall I appeal,
> Who could help me, who could hear?
> For it was he who was the gardener here
> who has himself trampled his own garden![19]

He craved "love and religion" (the dual concerns that provide one thematic core of his later verse), yet by rejecting one (or not fully accepting the form it took in his makeup), he denied the possibility of the other in a life that was "rent asunder." His inability to incorporate sex into life meant that he, not God, was denying "fullness of life" and intensifying his sense of a bifurcated self.[20] When he recalled the period in the "Histoire édifiante," he wrote: "I limited myself to visits to warm climes [gay argot for the bathhouses] from time to time, without enthusiasm and without making it a habit, all the more so since an irresistibly 'Russian' way suddenly revealed itself to me."[21]

The reference to an "irresistibly 'Russian' way" that revealed itself to him (the passive construction presents it almost as an act of Providence) at the turn of the century brings us to the most mysterious period in Kuzmin's life and the one that gave birth to the greatest number of legends about him. Of all the periods of his life, the years 1899–1902 are the most difficult to follow. In a 1927 autobiographical statement he wrote only that "for reasons of a purely biographical nature, I had occasion to be in the north of Russia and along the Volga, places where the schism is particularly widespread,"[22] while near the end of his life, as he reminisced about the past, he wrote that the "Russian element revealed itself to me very late and therefore with some fanaticism, to which I have little inclination. And then too it came to me in a certain roundabout way, through Greece, the East, and homosexuality."[23] In the "Histoire édifiante" he described the time with even more reserve than usual in that document:

As I went deeper into "the Russian," I became fascinated by the schism and once and for all cooled towards official Orthodoxy. I did not want to join the schism, and by not joining I could not take advantage of their religious services and the whole apparatus in the way I would have liked. At that time I met Kazakov, an antique dealer and Old Believer of my age, a bit of a swindler, eternally making plans, muddleheaded, and changeable. I started to study neumes, met Smolensky, tried to behave like a *nachetchik*, and was proud when I was taken for an Old Believer.[24]

The schism (*raskol*) to which Kuzmin refers had been precipitated in the mid-seventeenth century when Patriarch Nikon instituted a series of reforms in the Church service books and liturgy to bring them closer to Greek practices. The changes may seem minor to our eyes, but they rocked tradition-minded Muscovite society and split the Church in two. The Old Believers, as the schismatics called themselves, all refused to recognize the authority of the Moscow patriarch and the state organs. They survived the fierce persecutions that followed the onset of the schism, and over the centuries divided into many factions, primarily the "priestly" (*popovtsy*) and "priestless" (*bezpopovtsy*), the latter in turn fracturing into numerous sects. Despite constant harassment and periods of severe persecution, it has been estimated that by the end of the nineteenth century as many as 10 million such nonconformist believers were living all over the Russian Empire. They covered the whole social spectrum, although peasants, shopkeepers, and merchants, some of whom rose to be major industrial entrepreneurs, predominated.

Kuzmin's account in the "Histoire édifiante" seems reticent to the point of obscurity, as though deliberately concealing something from those friends, all Petersburg sophisticates, for whom he wrote the account, and it raises more questions than it answers. We lack any kind of documentation that would allow us to clear up the enigmas of Kuzmin's life at that time. Did he really, for example, live for long periods in the secluded hermitages of the Old Believers, which we know for a fact he did visit?[25] Did he become an Old Believer or not (and if so, of what "compact" [*soglasie*]?), or did he limit himself to what he stated in the "Histoire"? Indeed, he need not have studied the Old Belief for a long time to have been thoroughly familiar with it. As we have seen in the case of Italy, even a brief sojourn in an Old Believer milieu could have given Kuzmin, with his talent for soaking up impressions (not for nothing would he later compare the artist to a sponge), a clear conception of its special ways that reading would have deepened further. We know from his letters that he maintained contacts with adherents of the Old Belief well into the new century, and we can draw some conclusions about just what attracted him to the schism that had ruptured the Russian Church and that persists to this day.

Kuzmin thirsted for faith while to a degree fearing it as much as its opposite, "feeling." As he wrote to Chicherin on August 28, 1898:

> If now, as in our second century, there existed Eastern cults of great antiquity, I do not exclude the possibility that I would accept them. Even the Catholicism of society ladies is not a closed book to me. . . . The more passionate faith there is, the more oppressive, even dangerous it is. As concerns feeling, it is a void, consciously and voluntarily accepted, since it would be risky, given my inclinations, to set off into its abyss, lacking, as I do, sufficient perfection. . . . But I thirst for living with all my powers.

Catholicism had been tried and rejected. (The variety of "society ladies" is clearly as hypothetical a possibility in this context as "Eastern cults of great antiquity.") The Orthodox faith, into which Kuzmin, like the huge majority of Russians, had been baptized, and which was observed by many from habit (so it had been in his family), did not offer an attractive alternative. The atmosphere of extreme hostility to religion in general in the 1880s and 1890s and the atheism that was the rule among "progressive" Russian intellectuals and in student circles had touched Kuzmin but little. For him, however, as for many intellectuals of his generation, the moral status of the Church had been compromised irredeemably when it became "official," simply another arm of the state apparatus.[26] The revival of Russian religious thought, one of the most notable achievements of the Silver Age, was still several years away.

For Kuzmin, the Old Belief offered what he called the "definite material form and a palpable symbol" that he craved and an antiquity free of any taint by the modern world, from which he felt so alienated. The "marginal," "outsider" status of the Old Believers, hounded by the authorities and in some cases driven totally underground (in this resembling the early Church), may also have offered a deep psychological attraction for him. His letters to Chicherin, though chary of details about his actual activities, illuminate yet another dimension of his decision to turn to the Old Believers: his conception of contemporary Russian culture and his place in it. Chicherin, who was no longer naively infatuated with "the people" but committed to its salvation by revolutionary means, was agitated by similar questions. This makes their protracted epistolary debate a mirror of the thinking of an important part of the Russian intelligentsia at the turn of the century.[27]

A letter written by Chicherin on August 15, 1904, provides an important context as he tried to explain to his friend the differences between his own course of action and the one he ascribed to Kuzmin:

> Our time is just such a time of the bubbling and turbulent germinations of the birth of a new humanity as was the time of Christianity's first centuries or the Reformation. The revaluation of values! One of its realms is very familiar to you, it is *your* realm—the new art, hymns of praise to the earth, the new mysticism, the new, more intense human being. Another realm seems opposed to that one, seems alien to it and remote: it is the realm of the new humanity's *social* quest. And *here too* germinations are bubbling, and something is being born both in contrasts and in a kaleidoscope of tossings and turnings, extremes, and magnificent insights. By your very nature this realm is *absolutely* alien *to you. You* are not a *political animal* [he uses Aristotle's Greek term]. *It* is by its nature alien to you, and therefore must remain alien. But I want only to draw your attention to the fact that we also see in this realm the birth pangs of the new humanity. It is as if there were two parallel streams: the spiritually aristocratic new art and the democratic social movement. In both, however, is some sun of the future, as they combine in Klinger. Wagner, too, wanted whole peoples to hear his *Bühnenweihfestspiele*, that whole peoples would throng to Bayreuth *en campant* around the new holy place.

This conception of a social movement of the masses and an elite aristocracy of the spirit, consisting only of the chosen, as but two forms of one and the same historical process was hardly original to Chicherin (its roots can be traced in the Russian context to the writings of Konstantin

Leontiev). Attempts to reconcile social concerns with the new "individualism" would keep troubling Russian modernist writers and thinkers throughout the first decade of the century, Kuzmin among them, even if he felt very uneasy with the notions.

Chicherin understood the lure the Old Believers' world had for Kuzmin in the face of modern fragmentation and rootlessness, but he believed his friend, having "yielded" to it, was fooling himself if he thought that he, an *"homme moderne,"* could ever be anything more than a "naturalized citizen" in it, as he wrote in a letter of August 7, 1901. No less deceived, he wrote, had been two previous members of the intelligentsia, Nikita Gilyarov-Platonov and Nikolay Strakhov, both sons of priests and "Russian Hegelians," when they created their ideologies about Russia's special way. Both had attacked extremes of Western rationalism, and viewed nihilism, revolutionism, and materialism as symptoms of the sickness of western European society that now threatened Russia. Gilyarov-Platonov had defended the Old Belief as a natural reaction to Russia's betrayal of its own traditions (and thus to be tolerated, not persecuted), whereas Strakhov became the leading ideologist of the "return to the soil" movement, whose holistic view of the world was grounded in his insistence that nature and society form an organic whole.[28]

Kuzmin resented Chicherin's comparison of him to a "naturalized citizen" in the milieu of the Old Believers. His "roots," like those of all Russians, he argued, lay in the Russian antiquity that had been miraculously preserved among the Old Believers, a living cultural and historical force that could help him resolve his personal conflict with a modern society in which he felt homeless. He felt insulted by Chicherin's implication that it was but a cultural phenomenon of an antiquarian variety, yet another of those fads to which he had turned, like a dilettante, when something else became "unserious," and which he would likely come to see as constricting by its exclusion of modernity. He denied, too, the notion that the Old Belief was a kind of petrified culture because of its adherence to old ways of ritual and life and that it was doomed to irrelevance by the "progressive" movement of history. For Kuzmin it was a kind of living and thriving counterculture, and he now saw himself as just one part of the mass of Old Believers, with certain individual characteristics, to be sure, but still part of an undivided and indivisible whole: "I have found and I rejoice. . . . I was an *'homme moderne'* and had become one since everything that lives is *moderne*. I will not make a broken piece of glass whole, but I will wash the filth from that old glass so it will be transparent" (Autumn 1901).

Other intellectuals of his day, both in Russia and in western Europe, shared the sense of loss that underlies Kuzmin's elegiac disdain for a present age of inorganic disunity (compounded in his case by still ambivalent feelings about his sexual identity) and his hunger for authenticity and that integrity of both ancient ways and modern life that he believed he had found among the schismatics, who lived full lives in the contemporary world while keeping to age-old customs and ways. Others of his generation would also have been in sympathy with his scornful rejection of a positivism and "progressivism" that had left man bereft of faith. More revealing for Kuzmin personally, however, is his pointed attack on Chicherin's worship of the power of the human intellect to create grand schemes. Dostoevsky and Leskov (two of his favorite authors) had seen that as *the* fatal attraction for generations of Russian intellectuals, and it now, Kuzmin believed, held his friend under its spell:

> You say "impossible" about what exists, and you say it is fictitious, like a sign reading "buffalo" on an elephant's cage. What can one say to that? Is it not the sacrifice of tangible reality to a fictitious and harmonious theory? In theory it cannot exist, which means it does not exist, so anything that contradicts the theory is a deception and fiction? But the very harmoniousness of the theory and the syllogisms forces one to suspect that it is at variance with reality, where everything is clear and muddled, simple and contradictory, and scarcely susceptible to systematization. (Autumn 1901)

He rejected any kind of system, philosophical or otherwise, as a distortion of the complexity and infinite variety of life, and he made clear his outspoken preference for life over any system, for the particular over the general ("I couldn't care less for the general"). This preference lies at the core of his later refusal to allow anyone, even his closest friends, to command his allegiance to any literary grouping or school. Even the central tenet of his one venture at forming a group of like-minded writers around himself, the very short-lived "Emotionalism," a product of the polarized literary climate of the mid-1920s, has its roots in opinions expressed at the turn of the century: the predilection for experience itself over all else as the source of art. Related to this belief is his confidence that beauty and truth are *one* with the world, not opposed to it. His hostility to those who would intellectualize the spiritual, and his insistence on the need for simplicity and a personal faith, something he repeats again and again, help explain why the Religious-Philosophical Society and its attempts to bring together the intelligentsia and members of the official Church or the related activities of Merezhkovsky and his circle never attracted Kuzmin, despite his concern with religion. They all positively repelled him.[29] Most significant is Kuzmin's movement in his letters from an emphasis on and defense of the traditions of a universal, unchanging church ("I have *never* imagined faith and the church as anything but strictly ordered intrinsically and extrinsically, common to all times and peoples, but itself unchanging and unchangeable" [Autumn 1901]) to an extremely personal conclusion about his own art. It was still imperfect, he felt, and still unequal to the beauties of the world and his experiences in it: "What I write is so pathetic in comparison with the way I apprehend it and the way it all thrills me! And it is altogether superfluous" (Autumn 1901).

In an undated latter from this time, which he called a "big-sounding and grandiloquent epistle," a joking reference to the opening of Prince Kurbsky's second letter to Ivan IV,[30] Kuzmin confessed that several times in the 1890s he had thought of entering a monastery, and then expressed what he felt the Old Belief could now offer him:

> And the mysterious ineffable treasures that one receives from devotions and prayers said during the night, and, then, inevitably from the same book, before the same icon, when using the same *lestovka* (for in just such a way do I, by my connection with a certain church and a certain way of life, feel myself a link full of meaning, not alone, impotent). . . . Here are the mysterious sources of life itself, deep and tenacious shoots, and they are accessible to all, and they live in all who have substance. . . . Hard and fast faith, an unchanging rite, harmoniousness of the way of life, and in its midst a living earthly cause—there is the obligatory ideal of life and happiness.[31]

When there is a "way of life, faith, life (with the mysteries of birth, love, and death), nature, and a cause," he went on, "what else can one want?

All else is but words, art's madness, journalism, charlatanism, political and other adventurism." He was convinced that "happiness exists, it can be touched and felt, it is of life and living—it is the way of life and the life of the Old Believers." Here at last was the "bond and communality" with life for which he had been searching for so long, and he "accepted it all and in full."

He then addressed his present situation:

> All that I do, I do *"for the time being,"* and I do it in part so I won't become groggy from doing nothing, and in part for Mama. . . . On the outside, everything is as it was. An. France and D'Annunzio are still on the shelf, in the mornings I work on an opera. . . . This hypocrisy and duplicity are not easy for me, but I will take on this burden. There can be no talk at all about the seriousness of such pursuits. I stand on the border of a promised land, like someone standing in the church's vestibule and not yet allowed in, but I belong to it already and I have the happiness of community and of a bond, since I know that that church is no myth, that it is open to me, and that I have only to step over the threshold to enter it. . . . If I remain steadfast, I will go either to the hermitages along the seashore [of the White Sea] in the province of Olonets or to Belaya Krinitsa, but if fainthearted (for I must foresee everything) to a good Orthodox monastery.[32]

Kuzmin never entered a monastery, but he may indeed have left the capital for long periods to wander among the Old Believer communities on the Volga or in the Russian far north, where they had gone to escape persecution. We simply cannot say. All he wrote in the "Histoire édifiante" about the years 1900–1903 was: "My sister was then living in Nizhnii [Novgorod], and in the summers she lived in areas around it, where I would come for visits. So one year we lived in Chernoe, one year in Yurkino, and two years in Vasilsursk."[33] He added only that he particularly enjoyed the company of a group of people who seemed like types out of the novels of Melnikov-Pechersky, a native of Nizhnii Novgorod and a chronicler of the ways of the Old Believers in the backwoods areas beyond the Volga, implying that they too were adherents of the Old Belief. He maintained similar contacts with Old Believers, such as Kazakov, who were living in Petersburg, and steeped himself in the customs and traditions of the schismatics, collecting icons, old books, and manuscripts.

We get a glimpse of what his life was like from *Wings*, when one of its heroes, the mysterious Shtrup, adds Russia's age-old ways to his interests:

> Dealers with manuscripts, icons, ancient fabrics, and metalwork (obviously forged) began making visits to him, some chatty and wearing Western-style clothes, others "pious and Godly" [*ot Bozhestva*] and wearing long half-caftans, but rascals one and all; he began to take an interest in ancient Church music, to read Smolensky, Razumovsky, and Metallov, to go to Nikolaevskaya [Square] from time to time to hear the singing [in the Cathedral there], and, finally, to study the neumes himself under the tutelage of a pock-marked chorister. "I was totally ignorant of this secluded corner of the world spirit," Shtrup kept repeating.[34]

Kuzmin did not abandon the idea of a total transformation of his way of life by giving up his culture (as late as 1903 he was still discussing with Chicherin the idea of becoming an Old Believer *nachetchik*), but for now, well aware of clothing's ability to proclaim opinions, he transformed himself externally and served the "Russian idea" as "Russian dress": he grew a long beard and wore a *poddevka* (a kind of long coat favored by merchants and coachmen), heavy peasant boots, and a peaked cap that fooled some into thinking he was an adherent of the Old Belief. He showed up for the first time at the "Tower" of Vyacheslav Ivanov, the meeting place of the Petersburg cultural elite, in just such an outfit at the beginning of 1906 and with exaggeratedly "Russian" turns of phrase and manners, which astonished other guests for the contrast it presented to the easy sophistication of his talk about every aspect of ancient and modern European cultural matters.

The fruits of this involvement with the Old Believers are obvious in every period of his creative life, and this profound "Russianness" cannot be overlooked for an understanding of his view of the world, as a few contemporaries such as Remizov, who grew up in an Old Believer section of Moscow, and Aleksandr Blok noted: "Kuzmin's art has roots, perhaps the deepest, most forked and twisted, that have burrowed their way into the remote darkness of the Russian past. The name of Kuzmin is always for me connected with the awakening of the Russian Schism. . . . With what is not his art connected in the Russian literature of the eighteenth and nineteenth centuries, which gropes its way along the long dark trunk of sectarian expectations? One of the branches of that living trunk is the art of Kuzmin."[35]

The best way, however, to appreciate the special appeal the Old Believer milieu and culture had to his imagination is to allow Kuzmin to speak for himself in lines from the wonderful poem of 1922 that begins "'And this is a hoodlum's song,' she said." Here he fixed once and for all memories of a way of life fated to be brutally exterminated in everything but memory in less than a decade, and he reveled in the magic names and places of Old Russia. Even in translation, the place names lose none of their evocative, almost incantatory power:

> I wanted
> in a second wave [of memory]
> to enumerate the saints
> and local holy places,
> the kind that are depicted
> on ancient images
> in two, three, and four tiers.
>> Hands in prayer,
>> eyes raised heavenward—
>> the sounds of Kitezh
>> in the wintry sunset.[36]
> Pechora, the Kremlin, forests, and Solovki,
> and Konevets Korelskii, dark-blue Sarov,[37]
> thrushes, vixens, youths, princes,
> and the uniquely Russian family of holy fools,
> and the traditional village cycle of worship.
>> And when this
>> tide ebbs,
>> another will surge
>> inexhaustibly: forbidden,
>> without processions of the cross,
>> without bells,
>> without patriarchs...[38]
> Smoke from log cabins, tundras without roads,

> The police will never get to Vyg.
> Those gone underground, Khlysts, and fugitives,
> and graves while alive on distant river islands.[39]
> The most holy and disowned host
> of the free and Divine Spirit![40]

This catalogue, Kuzmin's favorite device for reminding readers of the joyous multiplicity of the world, creates a sacral unity of Russian faiths, which he would have rejected in the beginning of the century—that of the official Church and that of the Old Believers. The "saints" of the official Church and the "local holy places" of the schismatics and sectarians are not opposed in the opening of the fragment but interwoven in one "wave" of memory. "Pechora" functions similarly: what might at first glance seem a slightly skewed rendering of the Pskovo-Pechersky Monastery, a greatly revered Orthodox pilgrimage site in the small town of Pechory, probably alludes to the river Pechora that flows into the White Sea. The city of Pustozersk stands on its banks, and it was there that the archpriest Avvakum, the most celebrated seventeenth-century schismatic, and several of his followers met their martyrdom by being burned at the stake in 1682.

Direct reflections in Kuzmin's later poetry and prose of his involvement with the Old Belief are numerous. Summing up its impact on the works he actually wrote during this "Russian period" presents some difficulties, as we have very few by which to judge. The Old Believers prohibited secular art, and Kuzmin may have destroyed many of the works that he "sinfully" kept working on despite his continuing doubts about their worth and validity. Yet in a letter to Chicherin in which he discussed the prohibition, he also singled out something else about the "Russia of old": "the beauty that enters life" in a variety of forms, "as it did in antiquity and in the Renaissance, and among our common people (not hidden away at concerts and in museums)." Several of his letters begin to document an important shift of perspective as he attempted to examine his experience of the special milieu of the Old Belivers in a new light: to see it not as he once had—as something totally excluding the temptations of modern life, art above all—but as providing *models* of how art and life can interact for the *homme moderne* who feels he must, despite all misgivings, create.

On July 11, 1902, away from Petersburg in Vasilsursk, where he was living with his sister, and where he has Vanya, the young hero of *Wings*,

spend the summer with the Old Believer family in the second part of
the novel, he wrote of his life with great zest:

> I am living surrounded by apple orchards on a high bank above the
> confluence of the Sura and the Volga; beyond the Sura are groves,
> fields, and meadows studded with villages, but I'm sitting here with
> my back to this view that resembles and suits the center of black-
> earth Russia . . . [to where] a dark pine forest towers on the hori-
> zon and stretches to the northeast halfway to Siberia. You can't tear
> your gaze away from it, and this expanse of rivers and forests just
> makes the heart ache. Before that I was in various places and in
> Kazan. . . . But I am not writing anything, and I don't yet know
> what I might write. People are sitting at work in a large, bright
> room surrounded by windows, and singing:
>
> > Dear Vanya, you dashing fellow,
> > I hear that you are going far away from me.
> > With whom will I live through the winter?
> > With whom would you have me stroll during the fair
> >   summer?
> > Stroll all alone, my dear, during the fair summer—
> > I'm off for distant cities.
>
> And curly-headed Vanya . . . goes off to some Kungur or other,
> while she . . . strolls all alone on the banks, gazing at the forests,
> beyond which her Vanya has disappeared.[41]

Here, he was starting to realize, was a milieu in which life and art
were not opposed but organically linked, growing into and out of each
other, the one validating the other. The experience gave him renewed
confidence in his own ability to do something similar, and he was soon
at work on the song cycles "Spiritual Rimes" ("Dukhovnye stikhi"), the
"Times of Life" ("Vremena zhizni"; "The Seasons" ["Vremena goda"]
was an alternate title), and one, now lost, entitled "Cities" ("Goroda").
These vocal cycles, very different from his earlier works on "antique"
themes (what he called his "Babylons and Cleopatras"), at least as much
as we can tell from what has been preserved, represent Kuzmin's attempts to create in his own music and texts analogues to the kind of art
that he saw and heard every day among the folk and the Old Believers
(in their case icons, religious frescoes, book illumination, sacred writ-

ings and music, folk pictures [*lubki*], folktales, legends, and utensils for daily use). This is an art that is inscribed in life, not separate from it, or, as he put it to Chicherin, an "aestheticized way of life," an art that does not so much "reflect" as create life itself. Kuzmin's experience to a degree parallels that of Vasily Kandinsky, who, while still a law student, visited the Vologda region in 1889 on an ethnographic expedition. In his "Reminiscences" (1913) Kandinsky describes the "living art" he saw there in "magical houses":

> The table, the benches, the great stove (indispensable in Russian farmhouses), the cupboards, and every other object were covered with brightly colored, elaborate ornaments. Folk pictures on the walls: a symbolic representation of a hero, a battle, a painted folk song. The "red" corner (red is the same as beautiful in old Russian) thickly, completely covered with painted and printed pictures of the saints. . . . When I finally entered the room, I felt surrounded on all sides by painting, into which I had thus penetrated. . . . It was probably through these impressions, rather than in any other way, that my further wishes and aims as regards my own art formed themselves within me.[42]

We feel Kandinsky's intense admiration for a milieu in which art is part of life and in which, as he put it, one "'strolls' within the picture." It inspired his own commitment to become an artist and try to achieve the same result, much as it did Kuzmin slightly more than a decade later.

The compositions Kuzmin was at work on reflect his new affirmation of the possible wholeness of contemporary life, whether "the Russian" or "the Western Russia," both of which were but organic parts of a historical process unfolding in Russia itself and in anyone living there, himself included. The "Spiritual Rimes," on the one hand, so faithfully capture the form and spirit of the authentic Old Russian folk poem that they seem transcriptions of some lost original.[43] Yet on the other hand, the partially preserved song cycle "Times of Life" well shows his growing new conviction. One of its parts, "Petya, get up, the rooks have come back!," a joyous evocation of the wonder of spring's overnight arrival in a Russian village as seen through the eyes of a country boy, gets just right the folk idiom of the songs he heard sung all around him.[44] The "Prologue" to the whole cycle, however, draws on altogether different literary and cultural associations (and provides the first example of a conceit Kuzmin would employ in many later works, drawing an analogue between a natural phenomenon or cycle, be it the seasons or something man-made, such as the calendar, and human life):

> The world consists of four things:
> of air, fire, water, earth...
> and a human being, as if a small world,
> consists also of four elements:
> of blood, phlegm, red and black bile.
> Blood is air, red bile—fire,
> black bile—earth, water—that is phlegm.
> And every age, just like a season,
> governs its own element. . . .
> Thus in a human being, as if in a small world,
> one may see the rotation of the universe.[45]

Here notions going back to antiquity exclude any suggestion of the Russian mode. In the context of the cycle as we know it, the whimsical combination of both modes (unnoticeable if we take the poems as separate units, a perennial problem with reading Kuzmin, who wrote most of his verse to be read in cyclical contexts) makes the point that Blok and other contemporaries noted with amazement: everything, be it Russian or Western, of the most remote antiquity or the most modern, seems absolutely "organic" and "natural" in Kuzmin's artistic universe.

Kuzmin disliked Chicherin's talk of the age's drive for "synthesis" and rejected it for himself. He instead sought and finally found a balance for the different elements in the world and himself, each living harmoniously with the others. No matter how much Kuzmin tried to prove the possibility of his transformation into a "true Russian," at times into an almost ethnographic specimen, no matter how much he dismissed every "temptation," his memory retained everything, and he remained as "natural" an heir of Russia's most remote past as of classical antiquity, the Italian Renaissance, and contemporary Western culture (in fact, this quality in itself makes him seem uniquely Russian).

Kuzmin came to moderate the fanaticism of his rejection of his own age and his devotion to the Old Belief, but at the time he held to it fervently, if unsteadily. A passage in a letter to Chicherin of October 3, 1901, offers the best clue to an understanding of what was going on in his life at this moment. It well formulates the wisdom Kuzmin had achieved by the time he approached his thirtieth year, following one after another crisis of faith and identity: "And nothing is repeated, and the returning worlds and their contents reappear with a new light, with another life, but with a beauty unlike their former one. And so it is a long, long path, and ever onwards, to yet another ecstasy without end and without tranquillity."

Here, in highly concentrated form, is the central theme and image of all Kuzmin's art: the journey, the "long, long path." As he accepted the Greek mystics' metaphor of the soul's journey to perfection, he rejected the Plotinian (and Gnostic) insistence on the wretchedness of that soul in a sinful world. So, too, he found the love of Saint Francis for all aspects of God's creation very close to his own temper, but he repudiated Franciscan asceticism. In *Wings*, Vanya's closest friend in the Old Believer family, Sasha, remarks (in a statement very similar to some in Kuzmin's letters), as he and Vanya gaze out over the Volga:

> A person must be like a river or a mirror—he should accept whatever will be reflected in him. Then, as in the Volga, the sun and storm clouds and forests and high banks and towns with churches will all be in him—you have to be open and just to everything, and then you will unite everything within you. But if just one thing gets its hook in a person, it will devour him, and most of all the obsession with gain or, even more, with the divine.[46]

He echoes, surely, Kuzmin's acceptance and affirmation of the variety and concreteness of life in all its richness and complexity and contradictions, and his ultimate acceptance of his own sexuality as well, for as another of the Old Believers remarks in the novel, "It's hard, Vanya, to go against what's God-given in you—and sinful too, perhaps."[47] He would then remember and appreciate fully Mori's advice to enjoy and revel in life, but so too his own deprecation of what he called "flitting about." A goal in life is essential: life must be a personal and perpetual quest for the ideal. Kuzmin would somewhat refine these views (and certainly his notion of what constituted an "ideal") and would find further support for them in other reading, but they remained virtually unchanging throughout his whole life and the basis of a personal vision adequate to both life and creation. At the opening of the new century the "long, long path" of his future life in art still lay ahead, but he had marked out the way.

✧ 3 ✧

"Will a New Russia Arise?"
1903–1905

DURING the first years of the new century, before Kuzmin began work on the novel and poems that would bring him fame and a degree of sensational repute in Russian culture, the subtle, tempting narcotic of "Russianness" and the "ever-present past" of the Old Believers still exerted its pull on his imagination. The longing for perfection had not lessened in intensity; nor had his moral uncertainties, the moments of mystical exaltation, and those of black despair that on occasion prompted the old talk of entering a monastery or the possibility of suicide, only to be followed by sober awareness: "What do I know? Nothing. I want only to know the truth, not to indulge in fantasies, not to be sly, not to speak without thinking" (November 23, 1901). When he summed up the period in the "Histoire édifiante," he concluded: "I see now that it was as if there were two extreme points between which fluctuated a clock's pendulum. . . . On the one hand, I wanted nothing except churchliness, the old way, the way of the people, and I rejected all art and our present, while on the other, I was delirious about D'Annunzio, the new art, and sensuality."[1]

We see the attraction of both in the letters he sent to Chicherin in 1901–1903. In one, of June 28, 1901, he reveled in the life around him. Its descriptive mix of animate and inanimate used to convey a jumble of impressions would become characteristic of his poetry and prose:

I am writing to you from a place one can reach only on the most disgusting and miserable little steamboats, which are packed with peasants carrying piles of boxes for the berries they travel to our Yurkino to obtain; . . . where you take a ferry surrounded by piles of boxes, foul language, and shouting, and constantly run aground on sandbars; where our balcony looks out on a daily berry bazaar full of shouting, clamor, and the smell of dried cod; . . . where people sit behind window frames draped in muslin to keep out the flies and mosquitoes, because of which, nonetheless, I have acquired the looks of someone with smallpox; . . . where the new church of the synodal variety, which the people don't attend, has a greedy priest who's too fond of the bottle; where there are marvelous and varied views with hills and thickets; where there are so many orchards that in the spring you can smell their aroma over the whole Volga; where the people are handsome and independent, of good build and inhospitable; where they eat, drink, go for walks, go boating, and sleep—in a word, I'm in the village of Yurkino.

He added that he was reading Anatole France and had finished orchestrating the song of Hyacinthus and Apollo from his "opera di camera" *Hyacinthus and Apollo* (Giatsint i Apollon), a work with an explicitly homoerotic subtext.

A year later, however, on May 11, 1902, when he examined his life and all the "old junk" that he had to "drag after him" as he tried to "begin a new, renewed life," old doubts assailed him. Was, he wondered, "something new" really possible "after yesterday's Hellenism and today's *Domostroi?*"[2] And what if his Old Believer friends, those "real people, who do me the joyous honor of regarding me almost as one of their own, and who often do not even suspect that I engage in musical pursuits (except for my study of their neumes)," were to learn that the "pagan and sinner" was still up to his old habits? There seemed only one exclusionary way out:

These compositions (up to the last two, three years) have to be hidden or burned, as suitors burn their love letters to demimondaines. No matter where I will go, I will come to grief. Whether I am sitting at Kazakov's, living at my sister's in the summer, traveling along the Volga or through forests with people I've met over the summer, or studying neumes at home, I feel life and poetry and soak them in, and I see the foolishness of music; . . . I see clearly, so much that it hurts, all the artificiality and literariness of daydreamings about music and the pointlessness of combining the uncombinable.

The gulf between his apprehension of life and his ability to capture it in his music seemed as unbridgeable as before.

So it went as he groped his way toward his own personal solution for the meeting of Russian and Western cultures in himself and his art. As he grappled with the question of how his art could somehow bridge the chasm that Chicherin kept arguing would separate the two cultures forever, Kuzmin came to realize that his place was in the milieu in which he had been born and raised. There he would stay, and talk of fleeing to a monastery or becoming an Old Believer *nachetchik* became more and more rare. He never regretted his attraction to the "Russia of old," and he maintained his contacts with it (and his Russian dress) for several more years. He tried to remain loyal to the virtues he saw in it, but he knew, too, that he could never fully become a part of it. He never said as much in any of his letters, but a remark by the Old Believer Sasha Sorokin to Vanya in *Wings* has the ring of Kuzmin's own final awareness: "You, being an outsider, can, perhaps, understand and see our life, faith, and rites better than we can ourselves, you may be able to understand our people, but they will not understand you, no, or only one part of you, not the main one. . . . You would always be a stranger, an outsider. And there's nothing to be done about it! . . . The difference is sure to become apparent in some particular, and wishing it to be otherwise won't change a thing."[3]

He was not a stranger in another milieu. Kuzmin first mentions the name Verkhovsky in a 1902 letter to Chicherin that notes people for whom he was playing his compositions. Yury Verkhovsky, to whom Aleksey Remizov would give the nickname "Slon Slonovich" ("Elephant, Son of the Elephant") in his bizarre "Great and Free Monkey Chamber," was an aspiring poet and amateur musician when Kuzmin was introduced to him, apparently by Chicherin. He shared Kuzmin's interests in classical antiquity and the Renaissance, and moved in those circles of the Petersburg intelligentsia that were active in the arts and that were already playing a defining role in the development of Russian culture at the beginning of the century. In his cultivated family Kuzmin found a sympathetic and encouraging audience for his work.[4]

In December 1904 the Verkhovsky family sponsored the publication of a new miscellany under the name *The Green Collection of Verse and Prose* (Zelenyi sbornik stikhov i prozy). There Kuzmin appeared in print as a writer for the first time with a cycle of "Thirteen Sonnets" and a "dramatic long poem in eleven scenes" (one of his opera librettos) written in September–November 1903 and entitled "The History of the Knight d'Alessio" ("Istoriya rytsarya d'Alessio"). In his letters to Chicherin of 1901–2, Kuzmin wrote over and over again that creative work was a sin, to whose temptation all manner of external circumstances, but never any powerful inner creative drive, kept impelling him. He writes of the "Thirteen Sonnets" (which he always calls "Il Canzoniere"), by contrast, as though they had arisen of their own accord in 1903. He discusses them with Chicherin without the slightest tinge of guilt for having given way to "sinfulness," even though in style and spirit they are far removed from the notions about art and its goal that he had once insisted he must cultivate. We need not look hard for an explanation of this startling change: an infatuation with a young man provided the stimulus for the writing of the sonnets.

After his Italian adventure with "Luigino," Kuzmin had tried to avoid any kind of physical relationship that might impinge on the spiritual condition he was so determined to maintain. If one occurred, he resolutely repented, usually to Chicherin, and vowed to "sin" no more. There is not a trace of that sense of repentance, however, in Kuzmin's account of the summer of 1903 in the "Histoire édifiante": "The second summer I fell desperately in love with a certain boy, Alesha Bekhli, whose family was also staying at the same dacha of Varya's acquaintances in Vasil [Vasilsursk]. When we parted, I to Petersburg, he to Moscow, we carried on a correspondence, which was discovered by his father. He raised an awful row, got my sister involved in it, and so brought an end to this adventure. . . . I had once again to resort to art."[5]

Kuzmin first mentioned beginning work on the sonnet cycle in an undated letter (clearly from July 1903) sent to Chicherin from Vasilsursk:

A strange incident. When the four of us—my sister [Varvara], my nephew Serezha [Auslender], Serezha's friend Alesha Bekhli, and

I—were traveling through a forest on the way to a convent, I suddenly wanted, in the midst of these entirely incongruous surroundings, to depict a series of scenes from the Italian Renaissance, passionately so. There could be several sections (*Canzoniere*, the Alchemist, Venice, and so on), and I have even begun the words for the *Canzoniere* (3 sonnets) and the introduction.

This sudden appeal of the Renaissance (and, no less, of the young man) so surprised Kuzmin that he felt he had to explain himself in the same letter: "I look at this attraction without dread, hoping only that it will last long enough for me to finish what I have planned."

By August 20 Kuzmin had finished the texts of all thirteen sonnets and music for eight, writing to Chicherin from Nizhnii Novgorod that "I am very pleased with them, although the music is not always better than the words." For obvious reasons Kuzmin could not openly dedicate the sonnets to young Bekhli when they were published a year after the "awful row" that brought the relationship to an end (only the initials "A. B." appear in the dedication), but they are the first of his works for which we can precisely name the person who inspired them.[6] Only readers aware of the young man hidden behind the initials would, perhaps, have taken note of the "youth with a secret in his eyes" ("otrok s tainoyu v glazakh") who figures in the introductory sonnet, but they might have spotted hints throughout the cycle that the poems are addressed to a man, not a woman, even if Kuzmin is careful to use the personal pronoun "you," genderless as a fig leaf, not "he," and present-tense verb forms that mask the gender of the object of feeling. (Past-tense verb forms in Russian are marked both in number and in gender.) Still, the terms that, as it were, stand in for the beloved "other" are invariably masculine in gender: a "desired messenger" ("zhelannyi vestnik"), a "desired friend" ("zhelannyi drug"), or "your gaze" ("tvoi vzor"). None of the critics, at least, noticed.

Kuzmin, as always, lacked confidence about the worth of what he had written, but the Verkhovsky family praised the poems and encouraged him to publish the texts separately. They arranged for their appearance in *The Green Collection*, which they personally financed. Only works by their son and family friends appeared in the volume, and the entirely fictitious "publishing house" that issued it bore the name of their estate near Smolensk, "Shchelkanovo." One also detects the hand of their son

Yury in the neutral title "Thirteen Sonnets," despite the fact that only "Il Canzoniere" stands at the head of the full manuscript score; using the title of Petrarch's greatest poetic achievement must have seemed virtual blasphemy to that fervent young admirer of the Renaissance.

Critics of *The Green Collection* wrote with sympathy about young Verkhovsky's poems, and some found Vyacheslav Menzhinsky's wretchedly written short novel "Demidov's Love Affair" ("Roman Demidova") worthy of note for its curious reflection of the ideological climate. (An acquaintance and a kind of "sponsor" of Kuzmin at the time, Menzhinsky became a prominent Chekist in the immediate postrevolutionary period.)[7] They hardly took note of Kuzmin. Nikolay Korobka, who had regularly savaged the budding Symbolist movement in the Petersburg press in the late 1890s, found little to praise, but did not dismiss him out of hand.[8] Blok gave both works a real drubbing. He dismissed the sonnets in one sentence as "much more rough and naive, but at the same time too facile," and concluded, "The same author's narrative poem (in dramatic form) consists of eleven scenes, but it could as easily contain fifty, since the knight d'Alessio (a hodgepodge of Faust, Don Juan, and Hamlet) has still not by a long way despaired of all countries and all women on the face of the earth."[9]

Valery Bryusov, writing in the pages of the new but already influential Symbolist-oriented magazine *Libra*, was the only critic to pay close attention to the sonnets. He took their author to task for a series of formal blunders, and declared: "Almost all the sonnets are marred by inept, unsuccessful conclusions. In all of them unnecessary stanzas and utterly empty lines, in terms of imagery, have been stuck in to glue them together, but successful, beautiful lines are occasionally encountered in the first quatrains."[10] Kuzmin, like many of his contemporaries, respected Bryusov as a master of verse technique long after he had stopped admiring his poetry; he never republished the sonnets.[11] He certainly read Bryusov's review and paid close attention. Not a single critic would ever again be able to reproach Kuzmin for technical lapses in his verse. Quite the contrary: he attained a mastery of verse technique—complex strophic forms, new and daring rhyme possibilities, sound orchestration, *vers libre*, acrostics so subtle we hardly notice them—that makes his verse among the most formally perfect in all Russian literature.

Some parts of "The History of the Knight d'Alessio," which the critics unfairly snubbed (and whose genealogy they pretty much got wrong: it is a quest narrative with an explicitly homoerotic conclusion), call to mind in an eerily prescient way the plots of some of the "Orientalist" ballets with which Diaghilev's Ballets Russes would conquer Paris in a few years, and they make one wonder how closely some of the men associated with that enterprise might have read and later remembered Kuzmin's work. For he was now on occasion seeing just those people while he was writing it in the autumn of 1903. The circle "Evenings of Contemporary Music" ("Vechera sovremennoi muzyki"; "Les Soirées de musique contemporaine" was used as much as the Russian), founded in the autumn of 1901, was a kind of godchild of the renowned "World of Art" ("Mir iskusstva"), most famous in the West for the Ballets Russes, its most glorious offspring and the perfect exemplar of its ideals. As chance would have it, Verkhovsky's older sister was married to the composer and music critic Vyacheslav Karatygin, one of the most active participants in the "Evenings." Through the Verkhovsky family Kuzmin became close to several of the circle's leading figures.[12] Although Kuzmin had no formal connection with the World of Art group, his affinity with its guiding spirit made his contacts with it, developed through his growing participation in the "Evenings," one of the key events in his biography.

The World of Art had developed from an essentially dilettantish association of young students. Bored with their studies and disaffected with the state of Russian art, they gathered at the Petersburg apartment of Dmitry Filosofov in the early 1890s. Guided (some of them would have said driven) by the missionary zeal of the indomitable Sergey Diaghilev, they became a force that changed the whole course of Russian culture. A loose grouping of individuals with highly individual outlooks, they subscribed to no one philosophy of art, but used their magazine, *World of Art* (Mir iskusstva), started in 1899 under the editorship of Diaghilev, to further and embody their one shared aim: the liberation and revival of Russian culture. Artists, most famously Alexandre Benois, Léon Bakst (the pseudonym of Lev Rozenberg), and Konstantin Somov, constituted the majority of the group's original nucleus. The visual and plastic arts predominated on the pages of its elegantly printed journal, full of high-quality reproductions and designs prepared especially for each issue. This in itself represented a revolution in the history of Russian publishing, which until then knew only the prim stolidity of the so-called "thick journals." The exquisitely designed magazine, like the slim books issued by the modernist presses, suggested a new image of art and literature by its very appearance.

Alfred Nurok and Walter Nouvel, members of the original World of Art nucleus, were devoted to music, and they chafed under the movement's orientation toward the visual arts and under Diaghilev's authoritarian direction. The "Evenings" were the result of their mild disaffection, and they were careful to keep Diaghilev, who immediately wanted to sign on, at a healthy distance. The magazine and the exhibits organized by the movement aimed to revitalize Russian art and culture by drawing it into vigorous contact not only with the contemporary West but also with aspects of Russia's own artistic heritage that had been neglected or denigrated at home. (Whole issues of the magazine were devoted to Russian religious and folk art, which must have helped smooth Kuzmin's path to the group.) The "Evenings" tried for no less at their public concerts. Their seasons, always hampered by meager financial resources, were relatively modest affairs by comparison with Diaghilev's grandiose undertakings, and rarely went beyond recitals of chamber music and songs. Still, their activities, which lasted until 1912, introduced audiences in Petersburg to the music of Debussy, Ravel, d'Indy, Franck, Fauré, Dukas, Reger, Richard Strauss, Schoenberg, Stravinsky, Prokofiev, Myaskovsky, and many others. Debussy, Ravel, Reger, Strauss, and Schoenberg even traveled to Russia to perform their works at the concerts.

Kuzmin felt that he owed an artistic and intellectual debt to the two groups, and he acknowledged it all his life, proudly describing himself to one friend in the 1930s as *"un homme de Mir Iskousstva,"* and in 1923 remarking to a young interviewer, "If I had not met Diaghilev, Stravinsky, Somov, Sapunov, Sudeikin, and others at the right time, I, of course, would not be now what I am now."[13] One cannot speak of any direct influence, for by the time Kuzmin encountered both groups, his own ideas on art had by and large been formed. They attracted him because they shared his outlook on art and life, and with the encouragement of some members of both groups, Kuzmin began to move, very tentatively at first, in Petersburg modernist circles.

One word best sums up the atmosphere in which Kuzmin now found himself: aestheticism. The term has taken on so many negative connotations in our century that readers may regard it as a term of abuse. We should remind ourselves that it has not always been so, especially at the turn of the century. The cult of beauty, the devotion to good taste, and the impulse to spiritualize life by turning it into a quest for beauty, to, as it were, turn life itself into a work of art, have attracted some of the greatest artists in modern Western culture, and aestheticism, carefully defined, represents a major strand in Russian modernism. (The "high Symbolist" obsession with art as the "creation of life" is one such extreme instance.) When we now think of aestheticism in Russia and Europe, we tend to think of its fin-de-siècle variety: Pater, Wilde, Beardsley, and the French Decadents, those aesthetes who so powerfully challenged the dominant myths and constrictions, both artistic and sexual, of the Victorian age and who redefined the meaning of art and masculinity. That variety of aestheticism attracted Kuzmin (and many in the World of Art), and he would shortly play a similar role in Russia, but he also stood apart from it in more interesting ways.

Until August 1906 he hardly looked like someone belonging to the Petersburg artistic elite. The Russian-style dress he still affected marked him as "other" in the thoroughly Westernized capital, particularly in the milieu of the "Evenings" and the World of Art, where it must have seemed positively exotic.[14] His literary debut in December 1904 had attracted the attention, albeit negative, of two of the leading figures of the Symbolist movement, Aleksandr Blok in Petersburg and Valery Bryusov in Moscow. The movement's formative phase was over, and it had now started decisively to shape the modernist literary climate in Russia's two cultural capitals and beyond. We might expect Kuzmin, once he had broken out of his isolation from, even boycott of, the contemporary cultural scene, to have tried to make some contacts with it. He did not, and until the spring of 1906 he went his own very different way.[15]

He was spending most of his time alone, working on his compositions, or in the Old Believer atmosphere of Kazakov's antique shop, or in travels with him or with his sister Varvara's husband, Prokopy Moshkov, around the provinces near Petersburg. (His sister and her family had moved back to the capital in the summer of 1904.) The people he met at the Verkhovsky apartment and his acquaintances in the Evenings of Contemporary Music represented his only contacts with artistic circles. All others he avoided. How much so we can see in a Diary entry for January 17, 1906, when he learned he was to attend for the first time one of the "Wednesdays" at Vyacheslav Ivanov's "Tower": "At home a blow awaited me, a letter from Nouvel saying he'll pick me up tomorrow to go to Ivanov's. My existence has been poisoned: such are the fruits of ill-considered consents." He may have been living for the most part in physical isolation from the capital's artistic world, but he had a profound inner connection with it: in 1904–5 he was at work on the compositions that would make and define his literary reputation as Petersburg's leading "aesthete," the "northern Wilde," when he made his first real appearance in that world, the works that can truly be said to mark the beginning of his literary career—the novel *Wings* and the cycle of "Alexandrian Songs."[16] An explanation for this strange incongruity must be sought in a close look at Kuzmin's deepest roots, which go back to the art and ideas of an earlier age, to which the term "aestheticism" can be applied only with great caution.

The German "Sturm und Drang" movement was a lifelong passion for Kuzmin, and we find many parallels between his views on art and literature and those of its leading figures.[17] Kuzmin had long admired Goethe, and the aestheticism of Goethe's early and middle period struck a particularly sympathetic chord.[18] In the early years of the twentieth century, particularly in 1904–5, two other German writers, relatively little known then, certainly in Russia, moved to the center of his attention: the philosopher and theologian Johann Georg Hamann and the writer and art critic Johann Jakob Wilhelm Heinse.

The quixotic figure of Hamann, "der Magus des Nordens," as he was called by his contemporaries and by Kuzmin himself in an essay of 1922, certainly stands out in Kuzmin's reading list of the time.[19] A friend of Goethe and Herder, and an acquaintance of many other important German writers and thinkers of the eighteenth century, Hamann was largely forgotten or dismissed as a crazy eccentric in the nineteenth. Yet he exerted, as we now know, a profound influence on Kierkegaard, who revered him, and the Expressionists would "rediscover" and reinterpret him in the twentieth century. (He thus provides a crucial link between Kuzmin and German Expressionism, which Kuzmin promoted early in the 1920s.) Even in a culture whose philosophers rarely count grace or clarity of style among their virtues, Hamann occupies a special place. Some have called him the most obscure of German philosophers, and one critic goes so far as to maintain that "no other work in the German language is as hard to understand as any one of Hamann's writings."[20]

Kuzmin probably discovered him through his reading of Goethe and other "Stürmer und Dränger," for despite Hamann's contempt for that movement, its members regarded him as a major influence and alluded to him often. How deeply or "correctly" Kuzmin understood his writings is beside the point. Like other creative minds, he took from Hamann only what he found congenial to his own outlook and what gave it further support. Hamann, like Plotinus, was a thinker who would particularly appeal to a creative artist; he expressed his ideas in images, metaphors, and numerous other poetic devices, and his work abounds in wordplay (he could never resist a pun), all part of the reason for his legendary obscurity. Hamann's affirmation of the sensuous life and his defense of experience as the means to truth drew the special attention of Kuzmin no less than it had the writers of the "Sturm und Drang." Truth in Hamann's teaching is tied to the sensual and the physical. (Pure truth, by being abstracted from the sensual and material, must be inaccessible under the conditions of existence.) This not only helps explain Kuzmin's attraction, but also helps account for Hamann's withering attack on Kant, something of no less importance for Kuzmin, whose aesthetic views, like those of Goethe, are pre- if not anti-Kantian in orientation.

Hamann rejected the Kantian (and Platonic) idea of transcendence, and this, too, was of equal importance to Kuzmin, who shared that belief. To him beauty and truth were *inherent* in God's creation, not opposed to it or located in some inaccessible higher sphere. For this reason alone (if not for several others), Kuzmin stands fundamentally apart from the ideological core of Russian Symbolism, despite some seeming affinities with it in his own mystical impulses and his close personal ties with several of its leading figures, who tried to draw him into their activities and who opened the pages of their publications to him. For Hamann, a deeply Christian thinker, God is clothed always in the world he created, just as Christ is clothed always in the flesh. One of his favorite quotations was the Hippocratic aphorism "All is divine, but all is also human." Kuzmin could easily have repeated it, and many of the poems of *Nets* and all the poems of the opening section of *The Guide* affirm it.

Creation itself, for Hamann, is an example of God's "condescension" and "humility." Hamann compares such humility to the concern, the single-mindedness, the tenderness, and the sensitivity (what Kuzminian notions!) that we observe between friends, and particularly between lovers. (Sexual imagery is as common in Hamann as in Kuzmin when they write of the divine, and both frequently conflate moral and erotic impulses.) Pride separates us from God.[21] The greatest sin to Hamann lies in pride and in the human being's passion for total autonomy and self-dependence. He taught that the revelation of God comes in concealed forms, as the lowly and the foolish, the "rags of life," and he even used the expression "little domestic details," which Kuzmin's famous line about the "dear trifles" of life seems deliberately to echo.[22]

Salvation, Hamann maintained, takes place not as flight from the flesh but in it. He ridiculed asceticism, remarking memorably, "Need your loins as you need the limbs of your body!"[23] That stance must have been agreeable to Kuzmin, whose own attempts at salvation through denial of the flesh had failed so dismally. In *Wings* he dismisses the attempt, as Mori had once advised. Kuzmin would also have found encouragement in another of Hamann's central concepts, the belief that we must not regard any natural drive as evil or anti-Christian. There is no area of life from which we must flee as innately evil, nor one to which we can turn as a haven incorruptibly good. Kuzmin addresses the issue directly in his novel: "It is not true what the old women say about the body being a sin, about flowers and beauty being a sin, about washing the body being a sin. Has not the Lord created all this—the water and the trees and the body? The sin lies in resisting the Lord's will. For example, when someone is marked out for something and longs for it with all his might, and it isn't permitted, now there's sin for you!"[24] Furthermore, in Kuzmin only the *attitude* toward something natural, not the act itself, can make it a vice or sin. Mori makes the point for the author in *Wings* when he explains to Vanya that the love of Hadrian for Antinous had nothing in common with the depravities of Tiberius on Capri: "What is important in every action is the attitude toward it, the aim, and also the reasons that have brought it into being. Actions themselves are but the mechanical movements of our body, and they are incapable of offending anyone, much less the Lord God."[25] Kuzmin's reading of Hamann, who insisted on sex itself as a fundamental aspect of man's nature and a crucial expression of the divine, can only have helped him to accept his own sexual nature, not reject it as sinful.

Believing as he did in the primacy of the natural and concrete, of intuitive insight and an imaginative grasp of reality over the artificial and abstract, Hamann rejected any fixed system of ideas, which caused some to accuse him of "frivolity," a word never far from the lips of Kuzmin's detractors as well. Critics also charged Hamann, as they would Kuzmin, with passivity because of his total acceptance of the world. They missed what is probably the essential point in his writings, something that does not merely allow room for change but makes it essential: that every person of his own free will must strive in this life for salvation and perfection.

Hamann's attitude toward classical antiquity, Greece in particular, and early Christianity also drew Kuzmin to his writings. Hamann saw no breach between the traditions of Hellenic culture and the advent of Christianity, but rather what he called a "coincidence of opposites." Christianity had absorbed and further developed and transformed the best in Hellenic religion, not rejected it. Hamann found support for his belief both in Gnosticism, with its insistence that God lies within us and that the search for personal salvation begins with internal experience, and in the sects of the early Church. Kuzmin, of course, shared this fascination with the varieties of belief from which Christianity was forged, as well as this notion of the continuity, not discontinuity, of the two traditions. After the revolutions of 1917, when anxious voices in Russia were raising questions about another kind of rupture of tradition, he gave expression to his own syncretic vision in works such as the verse cantata "St. George" ("Sv. Georgy," in the collection *Otherworldly Evenings* [Nezdeshnie vechera]), where he merges the myth of Perseus and Andromeda with the apocryphal Life of Russia's patron saint. Hamann's concern to reconcile Greece and the Rome of Christianity represents but another facet of his Germany's intellectual and cultural involvement with antiquity. Another aspect of that story could not have escaped Kuzmin's attention. Italy often mediated the German fascination with Greece, for it was in the great art collections of eighteenth-century Rome, begun in the Renaissance, that Winckelmann and Goethe made their personal commitment to the ethos of ancient Greece. When the young hero of *Wings* makes his own journey of self-discovery to Italy, he visits those same collections in the company of the man who has invited him to make the trip: his teacher Daniil Ivanovich, one of the book's ideological heroes, who is himself of mixed Greek and Russian blood.

Wilhelm Heinse, an art critic of major stature who gave best form to his utopian vision of life and art in the novel *Ardinghello und die glückseli-*

gen Inseln (1787), occupies a special place in the history of the German dialogue with Greece. Although he set the novel's utopian conclusion in the Greek archipelago, the action primarily unfolds in Italy. Heinse proclaimed a philosophy of life based entirely on sensuous enjoyment, and his novel is a "passionate call to throw away all convention and let all passions fulfil themselves, no matter how destructively or how great the scandal to the respectable."[26] The extravagant plot of the book, whose hero is a painter and dreamer, concerns the founding of a new society devoted to the cult of beauty and pleasure. Kuzmin, having once and for all rejected asceticism, was strongly pulled toward his sensual vision of life, which Heinse expounded in prose of clarity and precision. Heinse's belief in the "emancipation of the flesh" and his sexualization of the myth of Greece (absolute sexual freedom is a fundamental tenet of his utopia) particularly attracted him. All this, as well as Heinse's assertion that the nude human form represents the highest beauty, is reflected very directly in *Wings*. A group of gay men (clearly implied, if not stated) have gathered in the Petersburg apartment of the novel's major ideological hero, Shtrup, a place "haunted by echoes of Rameau and Debussy," where, in its book-lined rooms, "they read Marlowe and Swinburne." One of them says:

> We are Hellenes: the intolerant monotheism of the Hebrews is alien to us, their rejection of the representational arts, as well as their attachment to the flesh, to progeny, to seed. . . . Love has no other goal apart from itself. Nature, too, is devoid of any trace of the idea of finality. The laws of nature are of another order altogether than the so-called laws of God and the laws of man. The law of nature does not rule that a given tree must bear fruit, but that in certain conditions it will bear fruit, while in others it will not and will even perish itself as truly and simply as it would have born fruit. . . . When they say to you, "It is against nature," just look at the blind fool who has said it and pass by, not acting like those sparrows who fly up in all directions because of a scarecrow in a vegetable garden. People walk about like the blind, like the dead, when they might create a most ardent life. . . . Those who link the conception of beauty with the beauty of a woman in the eyes of a man show only vulgar lust and are the very farthest of all from the true idea of beauty. We are Hellenes, lovers of the beauti-

ful, the bacchants of a life to come. Like the visions of Tannhäuser in the grotto of Venus, like the clairvoyance of Klinger and Thoma, there exists an ancestral homeland, flooded with sunlight and freedom, where dwell handsome and bold people, and thither, across seas, through fog and darkness, we sail, argonauts![27]

Reading this hymn to the senses we can believe that Shtrup's library must contain Heinse's novel and that the unidentified speaker has just put it down, so closely does this resemble Heinse's vision of the "blessed isles." It is as ringing an affirmation of what one critic has called Heinse's "aesthetic immoralism" as we will ever encounter in Kuzmin, except that the female, not the male, nude was for Heinse the highest form of beauty.[28]

The nature of *Wings*, a gay *roman à thèse*, sometimes led Kuzmin to commit to paper statements more categorical than his views as a whole. Although strongly attracted to extreme aestheticism in the years 1904–1908, he never surrendered to it completely. Heinse's "aesthetic immoralism," his belief in an absolute beauty beyond distinctions of morality and utility, had, like his hedonism, a very real appeal for Kuzmin in these years, but not his cult of "grand nature" or his concept of the survival of the fittest, the aestheticism of the "strong man."[29] The primary attraction of Heinse remained his cult of sexual freedom and his sexual approach to art, his definition of the beautiful as that which we know and *love*. To these elements of beauty and love Kuzmin added something that Heinse, who was defiantly anti-Christian, had left out of his writings: the soul and its movement to perfection, which has both Plotinian and Gnostic roots. Kuzmin had no irreligious habit of mind. His is a Christianity of kindness, love, and tolerant generosity to others, which are just the characteristics he always gave to his favorite heroes, and just those he emphasized in his reading of the Franciscan poets.

It is difficult to speak of any pure aestheticism of the fin-de-siècle type in Kuzmin in this period. A far more accurate term is "aesthetic paganism," where pagan implies not an anti-Christian but a pre-Christian, "this-worldly" view of life.[30] In opposing Christian dualism, "this-worldliness" *(Diesseitigkeit)* implies a belief in divine forces inherent in nature and man, preaches the enjoyment of life, not asceticism, and vindicates the physical as well as the spiritual side of life, often with a special stress on the sexual element. It plays down concepts of sin and guilt-ridden conscience while stressing Epicurean joy and a Stoic dignity. In extreme form it could lead to Heinse's position, but with a proper mixture of idealism it could lead equally to the views of the middle-period Goethe, which Kuzmin's "aesthetic paganism" closely resembles. Like Goethe, Kuzmin was neither amoral nor cynical, and he rejected, as did Goethe, Schiller's limitation of man's choice in life to the harsh alternative of sensual pleasure *(Sinnenglück)* or spiritual peace *(Seelenfrieden)*. He recognized the tension between the two, as we have seen in the letters to Chicherin, but he now rejected his earlier exclusionary fanaticism and insisted on the possibility of their resolution. The young hero of *Wings* tries to do just that. The novel charts his successful attempt to find personal freedom and liberation in a fusion of ethical and aesthetic elements, to steer a course between hedonism (condemned by the example of mindless pleasure-seekers throughout the novel) and asceticism (rejected explicitly in the Old Believer section of the novel and condemned by the fictional Mori). The goal and ideal is a free life expressed in a balanced and serene affirmation of sensuous natural existence. We must but open ourselves to life; as Shtrup says in *Wings*, "People realized that every form of beauty and every form of love are from the gods, and they became free and bold, and they grew wings."[31]

Not every work of Kuzmin's early period, of course, expresses this ideal vision. The prose, though interesting for its subject matter and stylistic and narrative experimentation, often falls short of the mark in achievement. In the verse, by contrast—in the finest poems of *Nets*, for example—he gives perfect expression to his ideal. To be sure, there are instances of aestheticism in the purest form; others are "frivolous" and lack "seriousness," while displaying unfailing good taste, charm, and a dose of ironic contemplation that at times recalls the world of Somov (or Watteau) at his best. Many of the critical dismissals or slightings of Kuzmin's work, on the grounds of "refinement," "sensitivity," "delicacy," and so on, betray an unconscious homophobia: a "man's" art should not have these "feminine" qualities, and if it does, the work is "limited." A number of these works refuse depth, but this refusal springs not only from Kuzmin's aesthetics or from his facility in composing seemingly ephemeral lyrics, but also from his loyalty to the immediacy of life. His attention to the inexhaustible particulars of which the world is composed can be seen today as one hallmark of the period in general. Never before, except in the age of Pushkin, and never since did life's minutiae so freely and unashamedly enter the highest art. This should hardly surprise us: Russian culture, after decades of heavy seriousness and humorlessness, needed a breathing spell, as did Kuzmin himself after a long period of loneliness and doubt. Here, at the beginning of his career in literature, he seems to want to try his hand at everything, to live life and experience it to its fullest. But in the best works he never loses sight of the ideal that would focus more and more of his attention after the excesses of the early period had passed into memory.

Hamann, Heinse, Goethe, the "Sturm und Drang," the reading of Plotinus and Saint Francis: all these became fundamental parts of a personal synthesis that resulted in a strong belief in the possibility of spiritual rebirth through love and beauty. Kuzmin had once seen art and religion in conflict and had rejected the one in the name of the other. Now, once he realized that the one could *serve* the other in the quest for an ideal of beauty and life, he could abandon his old fanatical opposition of the two and devote himself to art without guilt. How he achieved this balance and came to his new conviction we really cannot say, for his Diary is for the most part silent about his inner experiences. One thing, however, is clear: he had accepted his own personality. Many of his convictions would change, others would be tested again and again, and his searching would continue, but his gaze remained fixed on what is best formulated by Daniil Ivanovich in *Wings* after he and Vanya have seen in Rome the statue called "The Running Boy" ("The Youth of Subiaco"), through which the blood still seems to course: "The body itself, matter will perish, and works of art—Phidias, Mozart, Shakespeare, let us assume—will perish, but the idea, the model of beauty contained in them cannot perish, and this, perhaps, is the only thing of true value in the changing and transient motley of life. And no matter how crude the realizations of these ideas, they are divine and pure."[32] To that vision Kuzmin remained true to the end of his life.

As these views were taking shape and finding their form in the works he was writing in 1904–5, only a tiny circle of intimates knew of them before he entered the Petersburg artistic world in 1906 and, finally, at the beginning of 1907, the consciousness of a relatively wider reading public. One man in particular did much to ease that transition and to open the doors that made it possible: Walter Nouvel. The man who became Diaghilev's devoted "attaché" (his official position in the Russian bureaucracy demanded little of his time) had pronounced intellectual and artistic interests, was widely read in all the arts, and had an aptitude for music that raised him above the level of gifted amateur. His opinions carried great weight among the members of the World of Art. One of them, the artist Anna Ostroumova-Lebedeva, remembered him in her memoirs as an uncommonly active and cheerful young man of exceptional intelligence, who always made her think of sparkling and fizzing champagne, whereas another recalled him as an "aesthete from head to toe."[33] "Valechka," as all his friends called him, was exactly the right man at the right time in Kuzmin's life. In the spring of 1904 Chicherin had gone to Europe, where he stayed in political emigration until January 1918. With his departure Kuzmin lost his closest friend and confidant in Petersburg. Not long after, he found a new one in Nouvel, and their friendship lasted throughout the decade.[34]

Like Kuzmin, Nouvel was a great partisan of Mozart and the French and Italian music written before him. Kuzmin did not share the World of Art enthusiasm for Tchaikovsky—"the Russian Massenet," he sniffed.[35] But he shared something far more fundamental with his new friend: Nouvel, only a year older than Kuzmin, was gay and openly so, without the slightest tinge of guilt or awkwardness, and he was accustomed to moving in a milieu that endorsed such candor in sexual matters. Kuzmin's new awareness of the openness and assertiveness of articulate groups of gay men such as Nouvel and his friends Somov and Diaghilev could only have acted as reinforcement for his own "coming out" and emboldened him to give literary voice to an emerging homosexual identity. Their attitude and behavior differed markedly from that of Chicherin, who could never come to terms with his sexuality. As Kuzmin jotted in his Diary after returning from a walk with Nouvel: "It seemed that I was strolling with Yusha Chicherin. That is the best I could imagine in the sense of a friend, only without his moralizing" (May 29, 1906). With Nouvel and his friends he at last found the comradeship of differentness he had once hoped to find among the Old Believers, and, far more important, one that both valued his art and recognized his sexual orientation.

Nouvel's friends—Somov, Bakst, Benois, somewhat later Vyacheslav Ivanov—soon became Kuzmin's as well. Nouvel introduced him to the inner circle of the World of Art and encouraged his musical and poetic interests.[36] Kuzmin had fewer ties with Nouvel's best friend, Diaghilev. We know that Diaghilev had high regard for Kuzmin's works and considered him one of Russia's finest contemporary writers, but he never tried to bring Kuzmin into any of his activities. The two men saw a great deal of each other only in the autumn and winter of 1907, so much so that on October 31 Kuzmin noted in the Diary: "Gossip is making the rounds about me and Diaghilev. *Quel farce.*" He had, in fact, considered following up on some of Diaghilev's advances, but thought better of a "fling" with him, and only dedicated his story "Anna Meyer's Decision" ("Reshenie Anny Meier"), finished in December, to him out of a feeling of friendship and of admiration for all that Diaghilev had done for Russian culture.

At the time Kuzmin met Nouvel and his circle, some of the most cherished ideals of the World of Art were reaching fruition. Their magazine had ceased publication in 1904, but Diaghilev was striving to give their interests new, even more striking form. These interests embraced all areas of the world of art—literature, the visual arts, music, ballet, theater, each but a facet of one crystal—and they regarded them as changing subtly but decisively in a period of transition. Kuzmin shared this perception, and he deemed an earlier period, for which he had a singular love and understanding, to be similar:

> On the threshold of the nineteenth century, on the eve of a total change of life, of a way of life, feelings, and social relationships, all of Europe was swept by a feverish, loving, and convulsive aspiration to engrave and fix this fleeting life, the trifles of a way of life doomed to disappear, the charm and the bagatelles of a peaceful existence, of domestic comedies, of "bourgeois" idylls, of feelings and thoughts that were already almost obsolete. It was as if people tried to stop the wheel of time. . . . From everywhere sounds a kind of swan song of a vanishing society. This phenomenon was, of course, unconscious, as unconscious as was this haste and this avidity for the real and silly joys and sorrows of humdrum life.[37]

Many of the artists of the World of Art, Somov in particular, were equally drawn to this period, but the "retrospectivist" spirit of their works should not obscure the fact that they, like Kuzmin, were no less concerned with the present and future state of art. They were all convinced of the necessity of summing up the past and taking stock of its achievements (and failures) in order to move art into what they believed would be a glorious future. Stravinsky said it best when he wrote: "A *renewal* is fruitful only when it goes hand in hand with tradition. Living dialectic wills that renewal and tradition shall develop and abet each other in a simultaneous process."[38] Kuzmin would second that view in many of his essays, and would demonstrate its truth in a subtle interplay of invention and convention in his own best works.

Diaghilev's organization in March–September 1905 of an unprecedented exhibition of Russian and Ukrainian seventeenth- and eighteenth-century portraiture in the refurbished Tauride Palace in Petersburg gave this belief concrete embodiment. He gathered four thousand paintings and sculptures from museums and private collections all over the empire and western Europe, catalogued and documented them, and arrayed before an astonished public a panorama of the art of an age that seemed gone forever in rooms designed by his artist friends and full of period porcelain and furniture, itself a startling innovation in exhibition practice. More than 45,000 people visited before it closed, Kuzmin among them.

The disturbances that had begun on January 9, 1905 ("Bloody Sunday"), and that culminated in the "October Days," a full-scale revolution, shook the palace walls and the great manor houses from which Diaghilev had borrowed portraits for the exhibition, and provoked an apocalyptic climate of oppressive foreboding and gloom.[39] We do not know how Kuzmin reacted to the events that signaled the revolution to come, as the Diary that has come down to us begins on August 22, 1905.[40] He had never before shown the remotest interest in political matters, and for the time being he remained preoccupied by private affairs.

On November 21, 1904, his mother had died. Apart from the emotional shock, this entailed a break of another kind, as he had been living in her apartment on Vasilievskii Island (Eighth Line, no. 28) and had no source of income other than what little money his music lessons brought in or he received from the sale, now and then, of an icon or rare book from his large collection. Chicherin had immediately come to the aid of his stricken friend, and at least until the end of 1909 he sent Kuzmin one hundred rubles a month, a decent sum, but never enough, given Kuzmin's spendthrift habits. He also had high hopes of receiving a large sum from the division and sale of his grandfather's Vologda estate, but by the time it was settled two years later, court fees and a lawsuit had devoured almost all of his portion. For the rest of his life, the threat of penury made money an obsessive concern.

The "Histoire édifiante" describes his life until the summer of 1905:

I was often at the Kazakovs, went to visit them in Pskov, traveled with them to the province of Olonets and to Povenets, and returned via Finland. Finally I moved in with them, taking my icons with me, when we rented an apartment together. . . . In the spring [of 1905] I met Grisha Muraviev, with whom I soon began an affair, thinking to settle down in time with him in Pskov. In the summer I stopped in at Zaraisk, where he was living, and we spent six days together with the curtains drawn to keep out the heat, making love and plans, and strolling in the evenings in the quiet fields beyond the city. Then I lived at Shchelkanovo with the Verkhovskys. There, simply from boredom, I started paying more attention than I should have to the youngest brother, which provoked the jealousy of his wife, the indignation of others, and almost a falling out. Everybody then made up, but he left for Kiev.[41]

Little can be added to his own account. In 1904 he had completed another cycle of "Sonnets" addressed to Aleksey Bekhli,[42] the *Comedy from Alexandrian Life* (Komediya iz aleksandriiskoi zhizni), which in May–August he turned into the opera *Eulogius and Ada* (Evlogy i Ada),[43] and a vocal suite entitled "Charicles from Miletus" ("Kharikl iz Mileta"), which he subsequently dedicated to Nouvel.[44] In 1905 he was hard at work on *Wings* and the "Alexandrian Songs."

In the autumn of 1905 he decided to leave the Kazakovs and live with the family of his eldest sister, Varvara, in their apartment on Suvorovskii Prospect (no. 34): "The poetry of large families, of large apartments, of more or less open life wafted over me. . . . *Vita nuova*" (Diary, August 29). Her letters to her brother make clear that she can in no way be said to have belonged to any intellectual circles, although Kuzmin did on occasion encounter some of the minor players in the revolutionary movement at her apartment, when friends of her first husband, Abram

Auslender, came to call. He had belonged to the violent People's Will organization, and had been arrested in 1883. He was exiled to the Siberian Province of Tobolsk and died shortly after his wife gave birth to a son, Sergey, in 1888 or possibly 1886. Mother and child had then lived for a time with Kuzmin and his mother in Petersburg.[45]

Even before moving in with them, Kuzmin had become particularly friendly with his nephew, Sergey Auslender, who was still at the gymnasium when Kuzmin joined the family. Their closeness, which set some nasty tongues wagging in the Petersburg artistic circles both frequented when Auslender himself began to write, lasted for several years.[46] Kuzmin wrote poems for Auslender's stories, introduced him to his friends, and shared his artistic plans with him. Auslender himself took to the limit in his own prose one of the lines of Kuzmin's: stylization. As early as 1906, when both men were just starting to publish, people were already confusing the two: "They sent Serezha an answer from *The Golden Fleece* [Zolotoe runo] that they could not accept his story, but that his 'The Story about Eleusippus' [by Kuzmin] was accepted; that they are getting us mixed up is fatal" (Diary, October 5). The confusion continued for years in the public and critical mind, though Kuzmin for the most part gradually dropped the manner that his nephew had made his own trademark.

By the time Kuzmin moved in with his sister, no one could pretend to ignore the rapidly deteriorating political situation. Yet, judging by the Diary, one would hardly guess at the extent of the disruptions in the capital and throughout the empire. Through August and September, Kuzmin was in one of his rare moods of self-confidence—full of plans for future compositions, at work on more of the "Alexandrian Songs," reading Shakespeare, studying the Italian Renaissance with renewed passion ("Ave Italia bella!" he wrote), and fixing up his room in the new apartment. On September 10 he noted that despite his "flippancy and thirst for pleasures," he had a "kind of altogether un-Russian, very bourgeois need for order." By October, when revolution was in the air, he could not fail to notice the disintegration of order all around him. Not surprisingly, the ideology of his "schismatic-Russian" phase would shape his response to the revolutionary upheaval.

At times during the autumn crisis, Kuzmin's mood had not been all that different from Flaubert's in the France of 1852, when he wrote to Louise Colet: "Don't bother with anything but yourself. Let's let the

Empire go its way, let's close our door and climb to the highest part of our ivory tower, on the last step, the closest to the sky. It's cold up there sometimes, isn't it? But so what! One sees the stars shining clearly and one no longer hears the turkeys."[47] No tower could now offer refuge from the gabble of revolutionary turkeys, as young Auslender, thrilled at the opportunity to reenact the role of his radical father, ran from one rally to another and reported back to his uncle about all the excitement. At first Kuzmin found the news so "romantic" that "it almost attracts even me," but by the thirteenth of October his patience snapped:

> Today we stocked up on provisions as though for a month-long siege. Serezha is delighted by the justness and the lawfulness of the strikes, but to me any kind of force and outrage (I cannot find any other word for it), whether it be from the police or the strikers, is disgusting. Anyone may express his just protest by refusing to do something, but using force to disrupt the carrying out of the most vital functions of cultural life is barbarism and a crime, and the government, pleading its impotence to put a stop to it, will have to answer fully for not having punished it. Blood! Was less spilled in [the war with] Japan for the fiction of wealth and influence, for a political adventure? Calm is needed. . . . In the evening I was at the "contemporaries" [his frequent name for his friends in the "Evenings of Contemporary Music"], and when I went there and then returned along Nevsky I saw that the coffeehouses and stores were all open, the crowds had their usual appearance, but tomorrow, of course, I will learn from the newspapers that everything had been boarded up, that gangs of hooligans were on the loose, etc.

"Incidentally," he added, "I have always had and now have even more a tender spot in my heart for them [the hooligans]."

The very word "hooligans" had only recently entered the Russian language, but their attacks on social authority and their challenges to conventions of public propriety were provoking tremendous anxiety in society.[48] Kuzmin's sympathy for the bravado and insolent defiance of these rowdy lower-class males, violent expressions of the anger and social discontent seething beneath the surface of urban Russian life, reveals that he had not yet completely overcome his own sense of alienation from the dominant culture around him. Throughout his life he was intrigued by and identified with outsiders, but in this case his bizarre conception of the socially marginal "hooligans," urban riffraff, not representatives of "the people," was as wide of reality as some of his political viewpoints.

Some of his friends in the "Evenings" and the World of Art were firmly on the side of the revolutionaries. Others supported the autocracy out of snobbery, because of its emphasis on ritual and order, and as a symbol of the blessings of civilization, which now seemed threatened by revolutionary chaos. Those attitudes held some appeal to Kuzmin, but as serious social disturbances multiplied and the old order found itself under siege, the oppressor became the oppressed in his mind. At a time when all levels of society were nearly united in their opposition to the tsarist regime, he identified the autocracy with Russia itself and the revolutionaries not with the common people but with the bourgeoisie and the liberal intelligentsia that he despised. While claiming to speak for the masses and in their name, they were, he believed, utterly alien to them and their way of life. On October 18, when he, like other Russians, learned of the contents of the manifesto that revolutionary events had forced Nicholas II to issue the day before, he at last gave vent to his feelings about the political crisis, filtering everything, as usual, through his own very private perspective:

At City Hall revolutionaries with a red banner were speaking. . . . A group of sympathizers kept applauding the speakers in advance as they explained that the whole manifesto was a fraud. . . . The speeches of the speakers, the ladies strolling around staring, the vulgarity and common popularity of liberalism put me in a state where I now think with yearning and a kind of thirst, contrary to nature, about B[oris] Nikolsky and the "Russian Assembly" precisely at a time when they, no less vulgar perhaps (but less popular), are drowned out by all this triumphant prattling.[49] Even the "contemporaries" are talking about politics. Where are those aesthetes, or even blockheads, even officers of the Guards, who stupidly burn the candle at both ends, who would not talk about political meetings and universal suffrage? O, Somov, preoccupied with your ladies of the 1830s, *nachetchiks* who are finding the events of our times in Revelation, can even you be talking about it?[50] Where are they, those blessed ones who have taken a vow of silence? When Cossacks (or hussars?) galloped by at full speed on their white horses, a young worker said, *"Oprichniks,"* and how could he better have praised what is beautiful and strong?[51] Their time is over, but I hate those who kick people who are down, and a building, abandoned by everyone, becomes dear to me, and the spot at which all the purer-than-pure and the ascetics, the charlatans and dirty-faced swine, the prattlers and impudent know-it-alls are spitting— it becomes sacred for me because of that. A hatred for the popular, for "what's for everybody," for this terribly vulgar prattling is consuming me.

Kuzmin, it is true, came from an old gentry family, though one that by the opening of the century could be considered only middle class in financial terms. He might certainly have included himself among the have-nots of Russian society, as he was penniless at the time, constantly having to borrow money from friends or barter with Kazakov. Yet, fascinatingly enough, he viewed the upheaval as not so much a class but a cultural conflict between two groups: the Europeanized intelligentsia and bourgeoisie on the one hand and, on the other, the Russian masses and those few Russians, such as the Chicherin family or the Old Believers around Kazakov, who, to his mind, had retained traditional values.

At a time of unprecedented public unrest, his "Russianness," his conservative and Old Believer distaste for the secularized and modernizing tendencies that were so rapidly and chaotically transforming Russian society, asserted itself with a vengeance. He was convinced that liberal and radical opinion, which he, like many others, identified with the Jews, was making this revolution, not the traditionalist mass of common people who were standing silently apart from the events in the capital. They alone—the peasant masses—had the right to overturn the system, because they alone were Russia. (Thus he could support what he called the "really proper revolt of Finland" for autonomy [Diary, October 22], because he saw it as a genuinely popular revolution.) The Right, not the Left, spoke for them. This was as naively dangerous a conclusion as his attitude toward hooligan mobs, but it served as the main "ideological" underpinning of his own support for the autocracy. Blind to the worst abuses of the regime under which he lived, he saw only the vices of those he believed were removed from the real life of the people and ignorant of their ways. He recognized only the individual and his own temperament, and judged events by that standard.

He found confirmation for his view of the revolution of 1905 in literature, particularly in Dostoevsky's *Devils* (Besy) and in the anti-ni-hilist novels of Leskov, *No Way Out* (Nekuda) in particular. He loved only Pushkin as much as he did Leskov, and no writer to him had better known, and written with greater penetration about, the Russian people than had Leskov. He read through Leskov's works again and again at various periods in his life for guidance and support in literary and personal matters. Now the writer kept coming to his mind, bringing thoughts of his own earlier life among the common people: "I was at the Chicherins' in the evening; whenever I'm there I always think of Leskov, his starry-eyed, slightly eccentric, splendid Russians and society ladies, and his members of the higher clergy, and sectarians, something dear, warm, and Petersburgian" (Diary, October 3). He wondered, "Where is the peace of former years?" as he sat in a "disgusting, thrice disgusting, politically bustling and politically unbeautiful rainy" Petersburg (October 20). The only haven he found was at home: "All by myself. At first I played through all of *Mlada* and remembered the blissful times of the [Mighty] handful, of what was Russian, forever Russian, the epigones of the Slavophiles, the coziness and luminosity that one sees in Leskov and now does not see anywhere. Let's admit we now need swords, prophets, leaders" (November 21).

At times some of his reactions to the "October days" shock by their appalling callousness: "This morning, at the barbershop, as I read the news about armed clashes everywhere, about pogroms, about Feodosiya, where people who had been set on fire were thrown from the roof into the crowd and were severely beaten, I came out of my depression; in war you have to take things as they come" (October 21). "As regards politics, I am in a rage," he wrote two days later. That rage may help explain, if not excuse, his deplorable myopia about the real nature of the events going on and the people involved in them, which brought him at times not only to illusory hopes for the future, but to quite fantastic utopian dreams, in which the weak and vacillating Nicholas II would assert the medieval system of personal rule from the throne, or would "shut himself up somewhere in Yaroslavl and turn loose a Pugachev rebellion along the Volga, having temporarily given up power with all the bells in Moscow chiming, to perish in a beautiful and striking manner" (October 29).[52]

The absurd political naïveté of Kuzmin's romantic conservatism (not very different from that of the tsar himself insofar as he was fervently convinced of the loyalty of "the people") is equally clear from an entry of November 3: "O Lord, will Grisha [his lover, Grigory Muraviev] come, will everything be arranged as I now dream, will Russia blush brightly, blaming neither the one side nor the other for being at fault in openly wanting disorder, will a new Russia arise, tempered by its passage through fire and blood? Or will everything drown in hidden, not open repressions, in childish, deceitful demands of one side or the other, in salon dissent and parliamentary prattle?" It was fear of this last that led him to commit an act he was later to regret.

On November 1 he wrote in the Diary, "I am becoming more and more convinced in my extremism—it has no relationship to the Right or, God knows, any other party; . . . and I am somehow embarrassed that I am not yet in the Black Hundreds" (rowdy, drunken gangs of the disaffected who sided with the monarchy). A visit to Kazakov's shop on November 11 convinced him that he was "not alone . . . the Old Believers are uniting, rising. . . . Black Hundred is not a nickname, but a historical name," and that evening he found further encouragement when he read Leskov's story ridiculing the revolutionary movement, "An Enigmatic Man" ("Zagadochnyi chelovek"). Throughout November his obsession grew with a mysterious "Union of Russians" that he had heard about at Kazakov's. It culminated at the end of the month when he enrolled in the "Union of the Russian People," the archconservative and viciously anti-Semitic organization, established in October, which the court and police camarilla tried to use to halt the spread of revolution through the promotion of monarchist rallies and, later, of pogroms that it portrayed as "spontaneous" and justified reactions of the loyal masses against Jewish and revolutionary "troublemakers."

Until 1905 Kuzmin had been an apolitical man with some of the uglier prejudices of his age and class, not least a pronounced social anti-Semitism, which was not at all uncommon in every Russian milieu at the time. As we learn from the Diary, however, he knew nothing at all about the Union of the Russian People and its fierce anti-Semitism. He believed it represented and was made up of the common people, with whom he was determined to re-cement his old ties. (He was toying with the idea of abandoning Petersburg for a life surrounded by the Russia of old in Pskov.) He got his first real inkling of what it was and of what it consisted when he went to the offices of the Union to sign up on November 29:

There was a mob; workers were bringing membership dues and lists of people who wanted to join by the score, boys from shops, officers, ladies, the most typical bureaucratic types, peasants. . . . Members were chatting back and forth: the hoariest anecdotes about Jewish solidarity [and "knavery"]. . . . A gentleman with a Ukrainian-style mustache was ardently rejecting the word "political rally" [*miting*] as non-Russian in front of two really disgusting university students. The ladies were twittering, a Guardsman, rolling his *r*'s in the French manner, was asking for some "proclamations," having in mind the newspaper *Russian Banner* [Russkoe znamya]. And the questions—"Are you Orthodox?" "Are you a patriot?"—sounded somehow strange. The common people were sitting along the walls bug-eyed, sweating and blushing assiduously when the sweetie-pie types [*dushanchiki*] darted up to make flattering remarks. I bought the newspaper *Word* [Slovo], but, o, mercy, how terribly boring it is! . . . Khrustalev has turned out to be Nosar;[53] of course the [revolutionary] movement isn't the work of two yids, but why are Lassalle and Marx and Bebel all Jews? And the Russian emancipation activists, and Nosar, and Goldstein, and Gapon, and Gershuni. They are comparing socialism to Christianity (also a Jewish utopia); isn't it just as inapplicable without changes that would make it unrecognizable to the point of abolishing it in political life? All the more so for Russia.[54]

Interestingly enough, he would himself develop the comparison between Christianity (in its earliest forms) and socialism twenty years later in a penetrating article entitled "Wood Shavings" ("Struzhki"), but in Soviet Russia he could not risk asserting, as he does in the Diary, that socialism was hardly applicable to Russia in light of its state of development. A republic in the ideal would be fine, he concluded in the Diary, but it would be absurdly unsuitable in Russia. As it would satisfy no one, it would inevitably be transformed unrecognizably, a surprisingly shrewd observation given the naïveté of most of his other political notions and evidence that his opposition to the revolution was no simple matter of Black Hundred obscurantism.

Although some strikes continued, overt resistance in the capital, at least, was coming to an end. News of the armed uprising in Moscow in December made Kuzmin wonder what he had to do in order to be something more than just a registered member of the Union of the Russian People, but he did nothing. Instead he went off on a five-day trip through the province of Novgorod with his brother-in-law. By the end of the month he was preoccupied again by his plans to move to Pskov with Muraviev and by professional matters. His old raging against "progressivism, liberalism, intellectualism and for the physical appearance of, the life, and the faces of its bearers" (November 15) and his hatred for the "traitors and scoundrels" who were trying "to destroy Russia" disappear from the Diary, as he lapsed into apathy: "Empty days; . . . I am writing verselets and little songs; have no money; Kazakov is gone; . . . I did not go to an assembly of the 'Union of the Russian People' [he never, in fact, attended any of its functions]; . . . melancholy, what is to be? Tomorrow is the eve of the New Year" (December 28, 29, 30). The Revolution of 1905 sputtered to an inconclusive end. The monarchy had survived, but the absolutist state, despite the stubborn opposition of the tsar and his wife, was gradually forced to give up its claims and pretenses to control the life of the body and mind.

As far as may be judged by his personal papers, Kuzmin never later tried either to defend or to justify his joining the Union of the Russian People. He probably forgot all about it, as references to it simply disappear from the Diary.[55] The Union was, of course, totally at odds with the "Russian fantasy" in whose imaginary world he was again living, and his anti-Semitism had nothing in common with the violent variety propagated and practiced by the Union. He would himself in later years become a target of its propaganda pamphlets and of one of its leaders, the notorious Vladimir Purishkevich. His fiercely antirevolutionary zeal and his hope for the appearance of some savior of Russia, arising from the common people like a new Minin, passed as the revolutionary onslaught itself subsided.[56] By the beginning of 1906 he could sit at the apartment of Vyacheslav Ivanov, where revolutionary politics were debated seriously and openly, and calmly hear opinions that only months before would have called down his anathema. Still, the incident, like his anti-Semitism, which he never entirely overcame, is the most justly censurable in his whole biography.[57] It calls to mind Chesterton's remark that if ordinary people hold "battered forms of truth," intellectuals hold "perfected forms of error."

4

Buoyant Days: 1905–1906

THE POLITICAL ATMOSPHERE of Petersburg in the autumn of 1905, where the "spirit of social concerns is insinuating itself everywhere like a bad odor" (November 10), had plunged Kuzmin into another of those moods of self-searching and doubt that he thought he had overcome once and for all. A self-portrait of October 25 reveals his powerful insecurity, and develops into an attempt to analyze his own divided personality:

> I have to be candid and truthful, if only before myself, as regards the chaos that is reigning in my soul. But if I have three faces, there are even more men within me, and all of them are howling, and at times one of them shouts down the other, and how will I harmonize them—do I know myself? Now, my three faces are so dissimilar, so hostile one to another, that only the subtlest eye would not be attracted by this difference, which outrages all those who love one or the other of them. They are: the one with a long beard, resembling in some way da Vinci, very pampered and seemingly kind, of a certain suspicious holiness, seemingly simple, but complicated. The second, with the pointed goatee—a bit foppish— of a French correspondent, more coarsely subtle, indifferent and bored. . . . The third, the most terrifying of all, without a beard or a mustache, not old and not young, the face of a fifty-year-old

youth and old man, of Casanova, half-charlatan, half-abbé, with a crafty and childlike fresh mouth, a face dry and suspicious.[1]

His awareness that he was a creature of contradictions who would like "completely simple people or the most refined flower of culture" (November 2) only intensified the old anxiety that he might never belong to one milieu or the other. Over the next few months, through the help of his new friends, he would have to regain his former confidence that "day is my leader, morning and fiery sunsets" (September 7, 1905).[2]

In the days immediately preceding the outbreak of actual revolution, Kuzmin gave some of those friends a foretaste of the prose and poems on which he had been working all year, the "Alexandrian Songs" and *Wings*. On September 1 he noted the reaction to the novel from some listeners at the Karatygins': "There was no talk at all about the subject matter from an ethical standpoint" (Diary). A month later, on October 6, he played a "new series" of "Alexandrian Songs" for a group of the "contemporaries," and promised to read from the novel the next Monday at Alfred Nurok's. He described that reading to Somov, Nouvel, Karatygin, and others in the Diary: "I didn't even expect such success and all the talk . . . [saying] that in translation into French all this will have a great success since what they have in this line is so inferior, sentimental, and indecent that it has nothing at all in common with my 'chaste' novel" (October 10). *Wings* made such a strong impression on its first listeners that, still in manuscript, it became a literary event among the capital's cultural elite: "Somov is so delighted by my novel that he grabs people on the street and says that he has never read anything like it, and now a whole group of people (L[eonid] Andreev, incidentally) wants a second hearing" (October 13).[3]

No work of Kuzmin's has been more written about than *Wings*, and none provoked more of a sensation when it finally appeared in 1906, taking up the entire November issue of *Libra*, in itself an unprecedented event in the magazine's history. It brought Kuzmin instant notoriety, and the "Scorpio" ("Skorpion") publishing house, which put out *Libra*, took advantage by quickly issuing it in book form. When the first edition instantly sold out, it was reissued just as promptly, again something unheard of for a concern that published and promoted the leading modernist writers in print runs of five hundred to a thousand elegantly designed copies. *Wings* sparked a noisy debate in the literary world and beyond.[4] To some it marked a new and necessary frankness in literature; to others it provided proof of the moral decadence of the whole modernist movement in the connection some perceived between its sexual (or homosexual) and aesthetic transgressions (the "un-Russian" disregard of psychological analysis, for example). Certainly no reader had ever before encountered anything in Russian or western European literature like this frank defense of same-sex love. The book could not, in fact, have been published in any form in Russia before the 1905 Revolution. In its aftermath, the preliminary censorship of books and periodicals had been virtually abolished. Ironically, Kuzmin, who had taken so hostile a stance against the forces of revolution, benefited from them more directly than many other writers.

For the public at large, *Wings* was a pornographic novel whose author had depicted a hitherto taboo topic and given a kind of "physiological sketch," shocking for its candor. The word "homosexuality" never appears in the book, perhaps because Russian lacked any "morally neutral" word for same-sex love, and Kuzmin carefully avoided any depiction of sex, gay or otherwise, leaving his readers to use their imaginations. Nevertheless, the newspaper attacks, the critical articles, and the many parodies that followed the publication all fixed on the same-sex aspect alone, creating for Kuzmin by the summer of 1907 a literary reputation and image that he could never shake, no matter how much he wrote on other subjects.

Kuzmin should have known that most readers would focus on the sheer fact of his writing about same-sex love rather than on how he presented it. Even in his most intimate circle some viewed *Wings* only as a quasi-naturalistic depiction of one milieu, a dimension that Kuzmin, of course, never denied. (The reaction of his gay friends also discloses an awareness of self-difference and a kind of group identification.) Little wonder, then, that even critics such as Andrey Bely, who had shown in his writing on Chekhov or Ibsen that he could see beyond their discussions of controversial contemporary issues to some "symbolist" core, saw only "vulgar aestheticism" and the taboo dimension, which he pronounced "nauseating" *(toshno)* to read.[5] Only Blok hinted that there might be something else, when he wrote in his 1907 essay "On the Drama" ("O drame"): "Contemporary criticism has the tendency to regard Kuzmin as an *advocate*, to consider him the carrier of some kind of dangerous ideas. Thus, I have had occasion to hear the opinion that *Wings* corresponds to Chernyshevsky's *What Is to Be Done?* for our time. I think this opinion, not without wit, although highly tendentious, cannot stand up to the slightest criticism."[6]

Read from the perspective of our time, the furor around the homosexual aspect of the novel seems more surprising than anything in it, but we should remember how much courage it must have taken to publish anything like *Wings* in the moral climate that then prevailed in the Western world. Wilde hinted in *The Picture of Dorian Gray* (1890) that his hero's suppression of his true nature caused his inner corruption, but he never made this explicit; Gide dared not name the attraction of his hero in *L'Immoraliste* (1902); Forster wrote *Maurice* for the desk drawer; Proust felt impelled to engage in all manner of subterfuge. And so it went. Gide's apologia of pederasty, *Corydon*, written in 1911, did not go on general sale until 1924 in France, a country without legal penalties against homosexuality. By writing about same-sex love and presenting it in a nonjudgmental fashion, Kuzmin had challenged that climate of secrecy and put the limits of society's boundaries to the test, although we can find no signs that he was aware of doing so. In this he validated Gide's comment in *Corydon*, "It is remarkable that each renaissance or period of great activity in whatever country it occurs is always accompanied by a great outbreak of homosexuality."[7] Not surprisingly, both the popular press and many in the modernist camp fulminated, for if it was one thing to lead a discreet gay life, it was quite another to make it the subject of one's art.

The young hero of *Wings*, Vanya Smurov, literally and symbolically an orphan, learns through his growing capacity for experience to accept all aspects of life and to value his sexual orientation. At the novel's conclusion, set in Italy, he agrees to live with an older man, Larion Shtrup, and, a stranger no more, "opens the window onto a street flooded with bright sunlight."[8] (The Russian language has no equivalent for the expression "coming out," but the novel's last sentence provides a symbolic counterpart of that action in the hero's throwing open of the window, a kind of final barrier between him and life.) Like Shtrup, he escapes the constraints of his society's sexual anxiety, but— and this is most remarkable in the cultural context—he and his creator also escape those of fin-de-siècle decadence, which showed, albeit in masked form, the homosexual as a pariah who paid for his creativity by his marginality. *Wings* is a kind of breviary of fin-de-siècle aestheticism, worthy in this regard of comparison with Huysmans's *À rebours*. Shtrup, though no artist in fact, is an artist in his aestheticization of sexuality and the ideals of same-sex love, and in his conception of art as a means of regeneration through the recovery of true emotional life and deliverance from constricting social and moral conventions. He does feel and think differently from the mass of people around him, and does refuse to acknowledge current sexual codes. In this he cuts himself off from his country (his nationality throughout the novel is unclear—is he English, half English?) and any fixed place. This "nomad of beauty," to borrow the title of one of Vyacheslav Ivanov's programmatic lyrics, is in constant movement throughout the book, as he seeks and aspires to recover a golden age of beauty and sexual openness.[9]

What we see here is the familiar fin-de-siècle vision of the gay man as artist and *l'étranger*, but Kuzmin's novel stands apart from it in one striking way that makes it a true predecessor of later gay fiction. Shtrup is an individualist and sexual nonconformist, but he refuses to regard himself as marginal in any way. He seeks no outlaw status (he moves as freely and openly in Petersburg society as in that of Rome or Florence) or martyrdom. Surely it is significant that Antinous figures in the novel as the ideal of gay love, not Saint Sebastian, that martyr–patron saint of fin-de-siècle literature and visual art, erotically charged but a victim nonetheless. He nowhere appears in Kuzmin; nor do the guilt, fear, and self-hatred so obvious in Wilde's novel or in *L'Immoraliste*. Shtrup, as the young hero will learn to do, accepts his life as natural for him and easy, and thus outraged some critics. He is exceptional only in that he answers the call of an unusual, but untragic, destiny.

The very title of the novel should have alerted a literate reader to its most significant dimension. Here was not so much a "same-sex physiological sketch" as a kind of philosophical treatise, an analogue to the Platonic dialogues, from one of which, the *Phaedrus*, Kuzmin chose the title to suggest the novel's real themes: the quest for freedom and beauty, the soul's journey to perfection through love, and Hellenism's vision of male love as the agent of personal and cultural transformation.[10] Chicherin was the first, it seems, to remark that aspect of the work, when he wrote to Kuzmin on December 31, 1906, that there was "too much disquisitioning in *Wings* . . . (as though it is a treatise in the form of a dialogue, as was done in the times of the Encyclopedists), and always about one and the same thing, panmoutonism [*panmutonizm*], so to speak, or panheart-of-the-matterism [*panzarytosobakizm*]."[11]

Chicherin noted, too, a real flaw in the novel: weak characterizations and a lack of firm plotting. He also discerned its genre instability in a comment on the frequent discrepancy between dialogue and setting. The characters, except for Vanya, who most often listens or asks questions, do talk at great length in a variety of well-captured settings (a Petersburg middle-class family and Shtrup's gay circle, Old Believer communities on the Volga, expatriate and native bohemian milieus in Rome and Florence), while a hint of scandal, involving the suicide of a young woman who loved Shtrup, follows on the heels of his mysterious appearances and disappearances throughout the book. The novel stubbornly resists any neat categorization into philosophical dialogue, naturalist sketch, or adventure story. Kuzmin had never tried to write one or the other, but he lacked the skill at this stage to make all the elements, whether of dialogue or setting, advance what might be called the "homoromantic" (as opposed to homoerotic) theme, the same-sex messianism in a work in which the discourse on love *is* the plot. There is indeed far too much "disquisitioning," and much of the novel is all conversation and little action, with the result that the plot throughout the work often gets murky, as Kuzmin seems simply to forget about it altogether. This uneasy succession of sketches and dialogues was bound to confuse critics, even those few who tried to read it seriously, and made them focus on one element only, obscuring the intimate link between morality and aesthetics in the novel.

Whether he resented the remarks of Chicherin or not, Kuzmin did take them to heart. He rejected the overly ambitious scale of *Wings* and deliberately "simplified," as he turned to short prose forms in which he cultivated one or another of its several manners, but not all of them at once. Many of the resulting works are real gains in terms of artistry, but few are as interesting intellectually and as significant culturally as the "failure" of *Wings*, whose very uniqueness makes us judge it by standards other than that of workmanlike proficiency. Only after 1916 would Kuzmin write very different works of comparable complexity, this time with success.

The "Alexandrian Songs," published in part in the July issue of *Libra* in 1906, four months before *Wings*, met with a much happier reception than the novel from the critics and reading public alike. The "Songs," too, have their legends and mysteries. Commentators have traditionally viewed them as imitations of the widely popular "Chansons de Bilitis" of Pierre Louÿs, even though Kuzmin called those stylizations "hollow beads."[12] To be sure, one of Kuzmin's own "Songs," beginning "There were four of them that month" ("Ikh bylo chetvero v etot mesyats"), carries the subtitle "In imitation of P. Louÿs," but that was no more than a tribute to the fashion of the times.

All the "Songs" actually represent what their title states: song texts meant to be performed to piano accompaniment. The relationship of the texts to music has never been explored.[13] That they are song texts might in part explain the ease and fluidity of their free verse, a form with which Russian poets have never felt entirely comfortable and in which many fine ones have tripped up badly. Kuzmin's "Songs" set a standard that very few have ever matched. The number of unanswered questions about them makes a report read by the young poet Nina Volkenau at the literary section of the State Academy of Artistic Sciences (GAKhN) in Moscow on December 4, 1925, all the more valuable, because she had had long discussions with Kuzmin in December 1924, and her comments reflect his own thoughts on his roots and evolution. The following excerpt touches on the "Songs" and on Kuzmin's interest in the Hellenistic culture of Alexandria.

The "Alexandrian Songs" can hardly "be taken for a translation of some Greek poet of the second century B.C.," as Valery Bryusov stated.[14] The elegance, wit, and brilliance of the epigrams of Callimachus, the enchanting and gentle frivolity and gaiety of Asclepiades, the light and virtuoso tone shared by Alexandrian epigrammatic poetry are at times close to Kuzmin, but they are just what is alien to the "Alexandrian Songs," to their complex world of passion, wisdom, and the secret of that feeling of doom, merry and obedient. The "Alexandrian Songs" are also alien to the rather outwardly amorous elegy and to the direct, simple feeling of the idylls of Theocritus. In their mythological reminiscences, all the Alexandrian poets of the second century mentioned above are pure Hellenes and alien to Kuzmin's syncretism. And it goes without saying that the poem on Antinous permits us rather to place Kuzmin's Alexandria in the age of the Greek renaissance of the second and third centuries A.D. Kuzmin himself, when asked what he regarded as the source of the "Alexandrian Songs," directed the speaker to translations of ancient Egyptian texts that were published in the 1870s under the aegis of the English Society of Biblical

Archaeology and that came out for many years as a series under the name "Records of the Past."[15] In the author's opinion, this material gave him the tissue of everyday life; general historical information supplemented it. Kuzmin said that he had never read the Alexandrian epigrammatists and elegists.[16]

Only a classicist could test the truth of many of these statements (one is obviously incorrect: all the Alexandrian poets named lived in the third, not the second, century B.C.), but they do point us to a major source yet to be investigated and overturn some common misconceptions about the "Songs."

So does another even more surprising influence, which Kuzmin neglected to mention to Volkenau. On December 27, 1934, in a passage in his Diary entitled "Sources," he wrote: "The things that stimulate and jolt us to the discovery of whole worlds are often completely insignificant. Thus, antiquity, which has played such a central role in my consciousness and creative works, was revealed to me through the novels of Ebers, and the genuine treasures of Aeschylus or Theocritus had a much weaker impact on me. Namely, his *Emperor* and *Seraphis*. One can trace their influence not only on the 'Alexandrian Songs,' but right up to the most recent years." Forgotten or dismissed as *Professorenromanen* today, the two novels share a setting in Roman-dominated Alexandria of the imperial period, and the first treats one of Kuzmin's favorite subjects: Hadrian, Antinous, and early Christianity.

The key word in Volkenau's evaluation is "syncretism." We have already remarked Kuzmin's fascination with syncretic periods of ancient history, when different cultures met and mingled: the Hellenistic period in the eastern Mediterranean and late imperial Rome, when Christianity, paganism, and a host of other doctrines challenged one another and East and West fused. The combination and harmonization of two such seemingly disparate tendencies as the spirit of antiquity and that of his own time, a sense of the past pervading the present and allowing for a rich deployment of ironic perspectives, are characteristic not only of this work (and others) of Kuzmin, but also of a line in modernism in general that used antiquity for its own purposes.[17] Indeed, Kuzmin encountered an instance of it in the letters of Chicherin, who found analogues in ancient myths for his own belief in the inevitability of a social revolution that would shatter modern consciousness. In a letter of May

16, 1906, Chicherin praised the "Alexandrian Songs" for the greatest artistry. He called them "Kuzmin *le plus pur*, unalloyed. Your very first inspirations are reborn in them and combine with your most recent complexity, concision, rejection of the superfluous and excessively material, with a framework and scheme of the *lignes déterminantes* only." More important, Chicherin believed, was the fact that here at last his friend had produced something "adequately ancient," by which he meant an antiquity adequate to contemporary times and problems. Kuzmin had given "a slice of reality as a whole" in all its "morbidity, elegance, pantheism, and primordial intensity." He had finally realized that "palingenesis," as Chicherin put it, could not take place if art stood aside from life, but only when the "aesthetic mystical factor," which Chicherin had always seen in Kuzmin, joined life and thus began its regeneration.[18]

We do not know what Kuzmin thought of that reading of his work. He had created a world quite unlike anything in his previous poetry. He had united an almost Doric severity of thematic structure with a Hellenistic delicacy of detail and decoration, and had fused the spiritual and the profane, imbuing the whole with a feeling of bliss so lofty that death by one's own hand is no less desirable than continuing to exist amid all that we hold dear. We may as easily, like Antinous, become gods as remain mortals in the lowliest of guises, like the seller of charcoal and the old woman rocking a cradle in his hut in the poem that begins "What a downpour!" ("Chto za dozhd'!"). The certainty of proportion and the fully reasoned significance of the details create a vision of harmony and beauty so complete that questions of allegory or symbolic projections of problems agitating contemporary times fade before the reader's awareness of an ideal that existed "then and now" and may once again be fully realized.

It was as the author of the "Alexandrian Songs" that Kuzmin made his first entrance into the cultural world of Petersburg after several were played at the November 28, 1905, concert of the "Evenings of Contemporary Music." He had been performing them in private for members of the group throughout the year, and on November 5 they formally invited him to become a member. He did not attend the concert on the twenty-eighth, but his sister and other family members did: "They say that Goltison's singing was nothing special, but that he was called out for a bow after my works, there were a lot of people." The newspaper *Our Life* (Nasha zhizn') published a highly critical review of the concert on November 30:

> I was given such a drubbing in *Our Life* that it could not have been worse. "The Society of Contemporary Music made a big mistake when it allowed the performance at the evening of works by M. Kuzmin, who revealed a total lack of talent as a poet and as a composer; it was terrible, and insulting for the listeners, who, it seemed, were at times offered the works of a complete degenerate," something along those lines. It does not, of course, disturb me very much, nor, I think, the "contemporaries." (Diary)[19]

In the summer of 1905, Vyacheslav Ivanov and his wife, Lidiya Zinovieva-Annibal, had settled into a large, oddly shaped apartment on the top floor of a building overlooking the gardens of the Tauride Palace.[20] Their "Wednesdays" started in September, and the "Tower," as the apartment was dubbed, soon became the leading modernist salon of the city. Kuzmin, once again bedeviled by doubts about the future and upset by the unraveling of his relationship with Muraviev, made his first reluctant visit to the "Tower" on January 18, 1906. The usual "Who's Who" of Petersburg's intellectual and artistic elite was there. Leonid Gabrilovich, a physicist teaching at the university, read a paper on "religion and mysticism" that Kuzmin found "extremely long and dull." He did not make a very favorable impression on his hostess (whom he described as "Hera in a red chiton"), perhaps for having made some antirevolutionary remark, because not long after she included him among those she called "Black Hundred poetasters."[21]

Kuzmin did attract the favorable attention of another of the guests: among the forty or so people crowded into the apartment that night, drinking "red wine poured out of enormous bottles," was the "severe Bryusov," who had decided to recruit the authors of *The Green Collection* for his *Libra*. They were introduced, and Kuzmin was asked to stop by the Karatygin apartment two days later to discuss the matter. On January 20 he wrote in the Diary: "After dinner I went to the Karatygins'. . . . [Bryusov] is very decent and not without *charmes*, only I don't know how sincere he is. . . . [He] declared that . . . the 'Alexandrian

Songs' would be in *Libra* no earlier than April, most likely, and that should I decide to write something, I should send it in, and that *Libra* would be sent to me regularly. I don't know how true that is or not, because his main aim was to recruit Yurasha [Verkhovsky]." Kuzmin was quite mistaken about the latter, because not long after the meeting Bryusov told Sergey Polyakov, who financed both *Libra* and the "Scorpio" publishing house, "I have found the whole membership of *The Green Collection*, of whom *Verkhovsky* and *Kuzmin* may be useful as workers in various respects."[22]

On March 3, 1906, he sent Bryusov a group of poems from the "Alexandrian Songs." Kuzmin's virtually unclouded collaboration with the most important of the literary magazines of Russian Symbolism, *Libra*, then at the height of its influence, began with the publication of the eleven selected by Bryusov in the July issue, followed by *Wings* in the November number.[23] Kuzmin's name never left the list of regular contributors, and even after the magazine ceased publication in 1909, he remained closely tied to the "Scorpio" publishing house. In the years that followed, Bryusov, who had acted as Kuzmin's first significant literary sponsor, promoted his works, defended him from criticism, and reviewed his books favorably, if at times rather shallowly.[24] Kuzmin remained grateful all his life for Bryusov's help in launching his career.[25]

After his first exposure to the "Wednesdays," Kuzmin, who had still not entirely given up the idea of settling in Pskov, went about his usual routine. He worked on his music and a play, and saw the Chicherin and Verkhovsky families, the "Contemporaries" and friends in the World of Art from time to time, and, most often, Kazakov and his Old Believer merchant colleagues. The "Russian way" had lost none of its old appeal: "How alien and boring to me is the life that is now opening up as possible and that everyone else thinks is desirable and necessary for me. . . . How foolish must 'Torches' ['Fakely,' a miscellany edited by Ivanov] and the like seem to some *nachetchik* or other. And the *Ustav* [a book of religious service regulations] is more poetic and right than a thousand Maeterlincks and Balmonts. I've got 18 kopecks to my name" (January 22, 1906). Kuzmin's financial state made any move to Pskov out of the question, and, as in the past, the prospect of a bleak future turned his thoughts to suicide. His growing friendship with Nouvel and Somov, whom he particularly liked, gradually drew him out of his black mood and away from the world of Kazakov.[26] Thanks to their propagandizing, especially that of Nouvel, who was doing everything in his power to find a publisher for *Wings* and his other works, Kuzmin was acquiring a name for himself. As winter passed into spring, he began to feel at home in those Petersburg circles and with a way of life he had so recently censored as "alien and boring."

Vyacheslav Ivanov and his wife, Petersburg's new arbiters of excellence, overcame their initial irritation with Kuzmin and began issuing invitations he could not refuse to their "Wednesdays."[27] In the middle of April 1906 they asked him, through Nouvel, to take part in a much more intimate gathering that Ivanov was planning. Ivanov dubbed his new circle the "Hafiz-Schenken" or the "Tavern of Hafiz" (Kabachok Gafiza) in honor of the fourteenth-century Persian Sufi poet whose poetry of wine and love salutes a Beloved who may be read symbolically or mystically as the Ideal, thus intimating that the flesh and the spirit are equally valid paths to the divine.[28] Ivanov, like Kuzmin, had probably come to admire Hafiz's affirmation of life's pleasures and stoic acceptance of the burdens of daily existence from encountering him in Goethe's "West-östliche Divan," whose ninth section is entitled "Saki Nameh: *Schenkenbuch*" (emphasis added). The participants at the "Evenings of Hafiz" were the Ivanovs, Somov, Nouvel, and Kuzmin (all three virtually inseparable at the time), Bakst, the poet Sergey Gorodetsky, Kuzmin's nephew Sergey Auslender, and, only at the first few gatherings, Nikolay Berdyaev and his wife. Each participant received a nickname, chosen for the most part from the history and mythology of classical antiquity or Middle Eastern culture. Kuzmin was known both as Antinous (at the time he usually sealed his letters with wax imprinted with a profile of Antinous) or Charicles (taken from his own "Charicles from Miletus").[29]

Kuzmin and Ivanov, as the "chroniclers" and "bards," wrote "hymns" and sometimes recorded the "minutes" of the meetings in "Petrobaghdad" in verse, while the artists were responsible for designing the stylized "Eastern" clothing the members (all of whom used the intimate "thou" form in addressing one another) put on before entering a room decorated in a similarly stylized Oriental fashion—hung with brilliantly colored swatches of cloth, huge pillows scattered over Persian carpets— for a light supper, accompanied by large quantities of wine and conversation and musical entertainments supervised by Nouvel and Kuzmin that went on into the morning hours. Mindful of the boy cupbearers who serve Hafiz in his verse, they at first planned to invite handsome young men to pour the wine and serve as further "decoration" for the eye, but they abandoned the idea, much to Kuzmin's disappointment.

Here is Kuzmin's description of the first evening on May 2:

> I had not expected to experience such a sense of an enterprise, which was felt in the silence when Ivanov said "Incipit Hafiz." And the clothes, and the flowers, and sitting on the floor, and the half-circular window in the depths of the room, and the candles be-low—everything disposed us to a certain freedom of speech, ges-tures, feelings. Like clothes and an unaccustomed name, "thou" changes relationships. . . . And the conversation and everything seemed special, and special for the best. I was extremely touched when L[idiya] Dm[itrievna] called me Antinous. I enjoyed myself very much.

Several others followed throughout May and June.

The easy hedonism, frivolity, and total avoidance of any talk of social issues that were the "call of the evenings" created an atmosphere of "pure art" which not only poked fun at the high seriousness of the discussions of philosophy and politics at the "Wednesdays," but deliber-ately inverted their manner and substance as well. The costumes and code names suggest another and deeper dimension to this "play": the use of naming and clothing to "fashion" identity and personae that could destabilize the identity assumed in the larger society of the "Wednesdays," in effect a variant of the central Symbolist notion of the "creation of life." The gatherings turned topsy-turvy the hierarchical binary oppositions in the value system of an intellectual society that for decades had looked with suspicion on art (except as social criticism), the aesthetic, individualism, and gaiety. They, as did the art of several of the participants, "privileged" the private sphere in all its manifestations.

The "Hafiz-Schenken" was no homosexual club, but the "compan-ions of Hafiz" were dominated by people who were gay (Kuzmin, Nou-vel, and Somov) or sexually ambiguous (Ivanov and his wife, Goro-detsky, and Bakst at the time). "Art," Ivanov wrote, "is a sphere that is saturated with the sense of sex."[30] The talk about both sometimes led to highjinks that deliberately confused gender boundaries, as when on May 22 all the members (Zinovieva-Annibal was the only woman present) were blindfolded one after another and then kissed. ("There were kisses of different kinds: dry and gentle, moist and biting, and *furtifs*" [Diary].) At the next gathering, a week later, things went somewhat further, as Kuzmin described in the Diary: "Only I don't remember why he [Gorodetsky] embraced me and I stroked him and kissed his fingers, while he kissed me on the hand and on the lips, gently and fleetingly, as I like it most of all, and he kept pressing me closely and would not let me go and praised the caress he received from my eyebrows. There was something light and divine, sad and winged, and a new face of Hafiz."[31]

On June 13 an event Ivanov had long been anticipating took place: Kuzmin read part of his Diary to the "Hafizites." He was accustomed to praise from Nouvel and Somov, who had already heard parts of it, but he can only have been astonished by Ivanov's reaction to what he called this *"lecture édifiante"*:

> The reading was captivating. The Diary is a work of art. . . . He is gentle and in his own way chaste. At times slightly demonic (passively, that is, in the sense of hysterical possession). . . . In his own way a pioneer of a coming age, when, with the increase in homosexuality [*gomoseksual'nost'*], the aesthetics of our time and its ethics of the sexes, understood as "men for women" and "women for men," with its vulgar *appas* of women and its aesthetic nihilism of male brutality, will no longer disfigure and impair humanity. This is the aesthetics of savages and a biological ethics. . . . Homosexuality is inseparably connected with humanism.[32]

Ivanov added only that he found bisexuality preferable to exclusively same-sex love, which he feared was threatened by sterility.

After that reading the two men were on the closest of terms. Ivanov's "preachiness" sometimes irritated Kuzmin, and they did not always agree on artistic matters, as we see from a Diary entry of June 6, 1906, describing a "huge quarrel" about Oscar Wilde: "V[yacheslav] I[vanovich] places that snob, that hypocrite, that bad writer and faint-hearted man, who besmirched that for which he was put on trial, next to Christ—that's really terrible." They would later fall out for personal reasons, but each always valued the other's art, opinions, and erudition, and each found in the other a confidant for artistic and personal questions.

Kuzmin's talents blossomed in this atmosphere in which his works and his personality were admired, not censured ("I have never before had such a band of friends" [Diary, June 18]), and we sense a new confidence in his private papers and projects of the time. Over the next months he finished the music and words for the *Chimes of Love* (Kuranty lyubvi), which he variously called a narrative poem *(poema)* and a play.[33] He began and finished (on October 7) his first large-scale venture in "stylization," the short novel *The Adventures of Aimé Leboeuf* (Priklyucheniya Eme Lebefa), a beautifully crafted entertainment. Its eighteenth-century hero, Kuzmin's usual naif away from home for the first time, does not so much embark on a quest, as does Vanya in *Wings*, as undergo a series of picaresque escapades, among them the advances of predatory women and one explicitly gay encounter. He dedicated the fast-paced narrative of action to "dear Somov" when "Scorpio" published it in 1907 in the artist's design.[34]

He had been working since April on his first play (as opposed to the many opera librettos), *The Dangerous Precaution* (Opasnaya predostorozhnost'), a "comedy with singing in one act," for which Nouvel wrote music that Kuzmin found "scandalous, sometimes to the point of impudence." He now completed it, as well as a "mime ballet" with his own music, *The Choice of a Bride* (Vybor nevesty), which became a favorite of the capital's choreographers.[35] When these rococo divertissements, which consciously evoke the traditions of another age of deliberately "theatrical" artifice, were published with the "pastoral for a masquerade," *Two Shepherds and a Nymph in a Hut* (Dva pastukha i nimfa v khizhine), a lighthearted tale of male friendship almost destroyed by a woman, in the *Three Plays* (Tri p'esy, 1907), the authorities confiscated the elegant pocket-sized volume.

Kuzmin's is not an art of indignation and it does not accuse society, but these playful works bear the seed of radical change in attitudes toward sexuality, and provoked the very strict theater censorship.[36] The gender bending at the heart of the intrigue of erotic concealment and disclosure in *The Dangerous Precaution* must have been as disturbing as the equivocal sexuality of one of its heroes, the young man Floridal. The young prince René has been courting him, having taken him for a girl in disguise. When he learns the truth (after Floridal sings a song that asks "Are women's embraces as passionate as mine?"), René nevertheless "kisses him slowly" and orders a merry jig, with which the curtain falls. No less provocative for its destabilizing of gender identity is the song of the courtier Gaetano that dismisses the differences between men and women as "only trifles, only trifles," a remark that renders same-sex love nontransgressive by reducing it to a slight difference. Kuzmin may have been a fatalist, but he was no determinist, and he delighted in subverting the age's socially imposed gender antitheses.

More important for Kuzmin's personal life and for his development as a poet was the cycle "The Love of This Summer" ("Lyubov' etogo leta"), his first major verse work written with no connection whatever to music. The "love of this summer"—how typical of Kuzmin is the phrase "*this* summer," the very emblem of his poetry's orientation to the immediacy of experience rather than to "that" world of the Symbolists—was a short but intense and often stormy affair with a young man named Pavel Maslov, who sounds, to judge by the Diary, like something of a gay hustler. Nouvel pronounced him an "obvious professional" after Kuzmin read him the June 11 Diary description of their encounter in the Tavricheskii Garden and the assignation that followed, and some of Kuzmin's other friends were also unimpressed, which bothered Kuzmin not at all: "Bakst finds Pavlik *inférieur à nous mais gentil*, but you don't, after all, talk about Merezhkovsky and Nietzsche during *rendezvous* and merry escapades. He is jolly, kind, and well built, and that's that" (Diary, June 19). Kuzmin openly dedicated to him the cycle, which records the affair that developed against the background of the "evenings of Hafiz" and then Kuzmin's long absence from Petersburg.

Kuzmin had left the capital, after spending several weeks living at Nouvel's apartment, on July 13. Full of doubts about the course of the affair with Maslov, as he confessed to Somov, he spent the second half of July and August with his sister and her family in Vasilsursk. He hoped there to economize on money, which, as usual, was in short supply, and which he owed to several people. As before, his financial straits prompted thoughts of suicide. He wrote the twelve poems of the cycle while the affair was being played out during June–September, and promised it to Bryusov for *Libra*, where it was published in 1907 in the third number.

Kuzmin chose the cycle to open his first book of verse, *Nets*, which

"Scorpio" published two years later in April 1908. The cycle itself begins with one of his most famous lyrics: "Where will I find the right style to describe a stroll, / Chablis on ice, toasted white bread, / and the luscious agate of ripe cherries?"[37] Nothing better characterizes Kuzmin's poetry than its privileging of detail, but the objects are never random. There is, as he knew, a great difference between clutter and art, and the choice of details demonstrates his sharp alertness to the everyday and the contemporary: chilled Chablis, we know from memoirs of the period, was the drink of choice in Petersburg bohemian circles, in which semiprecious stones were also the new rage, while "toasted white bread" ("podzharennaya bulka") not only captures a then-current culinary mode among Anglophiles, but places the cycle firmly in Petersburg as well. *Bulka*, as anyone who has spent any time in St. Petersburg knows, simply means "white bread" (a kind of baguette, not "bun," its common meaning and the usual mistranslation) in the local argot, to distinguish it from the more common and plebeian black bread *(khleb)*. Typically, too, the details capture the poet's immediate experience: on June 27 he wrote in the Diary, "On Thursday it would be fine to go to Sestroretsk together, bathe in the sea [something described in the final two lines of the same first stanza], eat cherries, dine," while on the next day we find, "We [Kuzmin, Nouvel, and Maslov] drank Chablis and ate dessert."

It is hard now to recapture the effect these lines had on readers of the time who followed verse and who were accustomed to the hieratic vocabulary and imagery of Symbolism. (The lines acted like a bombshell on the young Mayakovsky, who found them "revolutionary.") They may now appear to be no more than those "trifles, charming and airy" that the poet salutes in the poem's conclusion, while the cycle as a whole, with its strong narrative element, strikes us at first glance as nothing more than a "love story in verse," with all the expected elements: an infatuation, the fleeting nature of which both parties sense from the outset; the torments of separation, which only intensify the poet's love; and his expectation of their new encounter as a Volga steamboat bears him back to his beloved. Commentators rarely go beyond the cycle, even its first poem, before summing up Kuzmin as a refined and carefree hedonist reveling in the ephemeral pleasures of life, a kind of literary equivalent of the *style moderne* in the sharp and sinuous clarity of his imagery.

The poem's brilliant second stanza hardly appears to contradict such a reading:

> Your tender gaze, sly and alluring,
> like the dear nonsense of a tinkling comedy
> or Marivaux's capricious pen.
> Your Pierrot-like nose and the intoxicating cut of your lips
> drive my mind dizzy, as does *The Marriage of Figaro.*[38]

The cultural references create the aura of charm and merriment the young man evokes in the speaker just as they in a sense distance us from any clear physical picture of him. Familiarity with the Diary reveals how closely the verse portrait corresponds to the "real" Maslov: "Pavlik's thin face . . . now recalled the Italian primitives, then Harlequin, tender and sly, the eighteenth century" (June 24, 1906); "Somov . . . found that his [Maslov's] *forte* is his nose, very Pierrot" (July 3). The accent on *Figaro*, which concludes a dizzying series of sound repetitions in the Russian, also points the reader to a hidden dimension in the poem and the cycle as a whole, in which melancholy, anxiety, and doubts about the other have as much place as gaiety and frivolity. The cycle is really the first of Kuzmin's major works fully to demonstrate the hallmark of his verse and prose at their best, in which the disparate moods of "lightness" and "gravity" find a rare balance.

The reference to *Figaro* points directly, of course, to the Mozart opera. Many references to the opera dot the Diary throughout June. But the context as a whole will also recall, for any Russian reader at least, Salieri's remark to Mozart in scene two of Pushkin's *Mozart and Salieri:* "Beaumarchais used to say to me, 'Listen, brother Salieri, when black thoughts come to you, uncork a bottle of champagne or re-read *The Marriage of Figaro.*'" Pushkin, of course, knew that his reference to Beaumarchais would also trigger an association with the opera, thus creating a subtle and unsettling contrast with the dark mood of his "little tragedy." Kuzmin's lines work in a similar way, if in a different direction, causing a disjuncture that strikes to the deepest level of the cycle. They call to mind the duplicity and betrayal at the core of the Pushkin play and suggest their presence in what is to come in the cycle beneath the surface gaiety of the Marivaux, commedia dell'arte, and Mozart opera allusions. If sensitive to that, the cycle's important theme

of the inconstancy and falseness of passion insinuates itself and tinges
everything with disquieting irony: "Our masks smiled, / our gazes did
not meet, / and our lips were mute."[39] There, with the lovers singing arias from Gounod's opera of betrayal (and salvation), *Faust*, is the
culmination of a "night full of caresses" in the cycle's fourth poem. The
lyrical protagonist tries to convince himself otherwise in the sixth
poem:

> Why does the risen moon turn pink,
> the wind blow, full of warmly sensual languor,
> the boat not sense the serpentine rippling of the waves,
> while my spirit keeps fasting in preparation for you?[40]

The "spirit's fasting" seems answered when the mail brings a letter from
his friend that renews his obsession ("I cannot escape from captivity"
["Ya ne mogu uiti iz plenu"], in the tenth poem). The cycle ends, however, only with the poet's "sweet hope" for a love to come that will be
stronger after separation. The banks of the Volga flash by "playfully, as
though motifs of Mozart" ("Berega begut igrivo, / Budto Motsarta mo-
tivy") in the final poem, bringing us full circle with the cycle's opening.
But the poet sleeps "anxiously," fearful of losing his "radiant thoughts,"
while hearing "calm down, my friend," and a hypothetical promise of a
new meeting and renewed love in the even, thudding sound of the
paddle wheel. (Compare the Diary for August 17, 1906: "Every turn of
the paddle wheel brings me closer to . . . Pavlik, and, perhaps, to my
death.") In that ambiguity, not the "blithe frivolity of life without a care
in the world," we see the real theme of the cycle as a whole, as it is of the
Mozart opera, if we are mindful of the story of the count and countess
and of her great third-act aria "Dove sono," as well as the final-act *tutti*
of reconciliation and hope.

When we look at *Nets* as a book (excluding the prefatory poem "My
Ancestors" and the final cycle of "Alexandrian Songs"), we see that its
lyrical plot has three distinct phases: the first part, with the cycles "The
Love of This Summer" and "An Interrupted Story" ("Prervannaya
povest'"), deals with love that is possibly deceptive and certainly lacking
in any spiritual dimension, thus ending in emotional unease or outright
betrayal by the other. The second part, made up of "Skyrockets"
("Rakety"), "The Deceiver Deceived," and "The Joyful Wayfarer"
("Radostnyi putnik"), treats the rebirth of hope for a new and comfort-

ing future that the poet senses but cannot will into being. The cycles of the third part, "The Wise Encounter" ("Mudraya vstrecha") and "The Guide," lexically marked by a specifically scriptural vocabulary, and "Streams" (or "Rillets" ["Strui"]) introduce Love, the animating and uplifting force of Kuzmin's life and art, the love to come, and the guide who leads us to it, a man and at the same time a heavenly warrior in shining armor. This figure, who appears throughout Kuzmin's art, is obviously associated with the poet's namesake, the Archangel Michael, the leader of the heavenly hosts, and with iconic images of the patron saint of Russia (and Kuzmin's native city of Yaroslavl), Saint George, as well as with the Roman belief that every human being is guarded and guided through life by an ever-present personal tutelary spirit, whose dictates the individual, with little volition of his own, must follow. The book as a whole represents Kuzmin's variant of the Platonic tradition of the aspiration for Eros, a Dantesque trilogy of the incarnation of true love in carnal passion that approaches and partakes of a mystical and divine Ideal.[41]

Kuzmin himself might well have disputed such an "overreading" of his book. In May 1907 he told Bryusov that while Vyacheslav Ivanov regarded his play about Eudoxia as an "attempt at reconstruction of the mystery of a 'pan-national ritual action' [*deistvo*]," he saw it as nothing but a "touching, frivolous, and mannered story about a saint seen through [the prism of] the eighteenth century."[42] We are mindful, however, that Blok, one of Kuzmin's best early readers, called that play "the most perfect creation in the sphere of *lyrical drama* in Russia," and found it "imbued with a kind of captivating sadness and infused with the most subtle poisons of that irony which is so characteristic of Kuzmin's art."[43] Then, too, the polemical context of Kuzmin's remark must be kept in mind. He was trying hard to steer an independent course through the shoals of the controversy that had erupted about "Mystical Anarchism" and that had set his two friends Bryusov and Ivanov at loggerheads.[44] He did not want to be drawn into either side in the conflict, and certainly did not want Bryusov to think that he had allied himself with Ivanov, who planned to publish the play in a miscellany issued by "Oraea" ("Ory"), his private publishing venture. He wanted to maintain his friendship with both, as well as the possibility of continuing his collaboration with *Libra* and its various rivals in the world of modernist periodicals.

Kuzmin's deliberately disparaging remark about his own play cannot really be taken seriously. *The Comedy on Eudoxia of Heliopolis, or the Converted Courtesan* (Komediya o Evdokii iz Geliopolya, ili obrashchennaya kurtizanka) and the two other "religious comedies" written at the same time—*On Alexis, Man of God, or the Son Lost and Found* and *The Comedy on Martinian* (Komediya o Martiniane)—are, despite their doses of amiable skepticism, polar opposites to the capriccios included in the *Three Plays*.[45] In these variations on apocryphal accounts of saints' lives, the holy naïveté of their title characters, who find grace by not resisting the wisdom concealed in the mysterious working out of divine will, embodies Kuzmin's deepest and most hard-won belief about life, and the words that close *On Alexis* could serve as the epigraph for *Nets* or any other of Kuzmin's books: "No matter how much we may strive, God's Will invisibly directs the fates of men. Our swift lot catches us up."

Kuzmin returned to the capital near the end of August 1906. As Remizov recalled, his name "suddenly blazed" on the horizon of the Petersburg literary world that autumn.[46] Most of those who left memoirs of the period first encountered him then, as did the minor Symbolist poet Vladimir Pyast, who met him at the writer Fedor Sologub's "Sundays."[47] At one of them, on November 12, 1906, Kuzmin performed the song that begins

> If it's sunny tomorrow,
> we'll take a trip to Fiesole;
> if it's rainy tomorrow—
> then we'll hire a carriage.

and ends

> If you fall in love with me,
> I'll believe you with delight;
> if you don't want to—
> We'll find somebody else.[48]

Pyast admired the verse form of the "little song" (or "ditty," *pesen'ka*, Kuzmin's own title), which, he writes, he was to hear everywhere in the years that followed: "We noticed a tiny subtle touch—the feminine ending in the third line of every even stanza. That feature revealed the most expert master of versification." He also remembered that the song's title was the "solution of all difficulties" (it has none). It was just that quality which had such an obvious appeal for Kuzmin's listeners after the revolutionary upheaval of the year before. The song became the virtual anthem of Petersburg bohemian circles, nowhere more so than among the new group of people Kuzmin met in the autumn of 1906.

In 1906 the celebrated actress Vera Komissarzhevskaya had invited the young Moscow actor and director Vsevolod Meyerhold to join her theater in Petersburg. Founded in 1904 to further the cause of the "new drama" and to provide a showcase for her own talents, Komissarzhevskaya's company, which her stepbrother, Fedor, directed with her, had increasingly fallen under the spell of Symbolism, and the theater's repertory began to drift toward Russian and Western modernist plays with antirealistic tendencies. The invitation to Meyerhold climaxed the shift in direction. As if to symbolize this decisive break with its past, the theater moved to a new building on Ofitserskaya Street (no. 39) in the autumn of 1906. Meyerhold brought with him not only new ideas about the theater, but also a large number of Moscow friends, both actors and artists such as Nikolay Sapunov, Sergey Sudeikin, and Nikolay Feofilaktov. The theater soon became a magnet for the capital's cultural elite.

Before the opening of the new season in November, regular gatherings took place on Saturdays in the theater's studios in the Latvian Club. Meyerhold, concerned about the crippling influence of traditional acting practices on the members of the company and fearful of how they would respond to the nonrealist plays and productions he was planning, decided to expose them to the "new art" by inviting its representatives in Petersburg to attend the gatherings. Kuzmin and his friends were naturally among those Meyerhold welcomed. The new Moscow visitors made a strong impression on Kuzmin.[49] "They were so unlike the representatives of the World of Art whom I knew in Petersburg," he later recalled, "that I could not help thinking that now a new kind of people had arrived."[50]

Upon his return to Petersburg, Kuzmin had found himself as "captivated" by Maslov as before, but the young man began pressing him for money, oblivious to Kuzmin's replies that he had none. Kuzmin was coming to the sad realization that they had nothing whatsoever in common except sexual attraction ("Ah, if only the magical gardens of the arts were even slightly accessible to Pavlik!" [Diary, September 12]). By

September 20 he concluded: "It seems to me that the cycle of the 'love of this summer' has closed," adding, two days later, "His [Maslov's] summer has passed." Maslov, for his part, refused to pick up on Kuzmin's hints that their relationship had come to an end, and Kuzmin, in the grip of his usual amorous indecisiveness, did not push it. They would see each other on and off for many more months, with their encounters sometimes ending in some form of sexual relation, what Kuzmin called a *"fatalité."*

As he was bringing the relationship with Maslov to an end, and as he concluded a very brief *"camaraderie d'amour"* with Somov (with whom he remained on the best of terms), Sergey Sudeikin moved to the center of his attention: "Somehow fate keeps bringing me together with artists" (Diary, October 29). The affair with Sudeikin was not to last long: Kuzmin met him on October 14 at one of the theater's Saturdays, and by the end of December they parted when the artist left for Moscow to marry the actress Olga Glebova. Sudeikin, who was twenty-four at the time, tried to draw back from intimacy and to keep the relationship a matter of friendship alone, but his own passion got the upper hand, as the Diary makes clear.[51]

The poem cycle "An Interrupted Story" and the story "The Little Cardboard House" ("Kartonnyi domik"), the two works of Kuzmin's that recount the course of the affair, are not just closely related to each other but transparently autobiographical. On December 3 he wrote in the Diary: "I have the idea of writing a cycle, analogous to 'The Love of This Summer,' to Sudeikin. How happy I am, how happy I am, how happy I am!" Although the story is truly "interrupted" because the printers managed to drop its last four chapters when they were assembling the page proofs for the miscellany *White Nights* (Belye nochi), readers easily recognized the close ties between the two works when they were published together in the miscellany in 1907.[52] Kuzmin was well aware that he had provided an unusual dual perspective on one event; when he sent the poem cycle to the miscellany's editor, Georgy Chulkov, on May 8, 1907, he wrote, "I am sending you, as I promised, 'An Interrupted Story,' but . . . it may be awkward to have two accounts of one and the same event, each of which, as it were, throws light on the other."[53] Reviewers, of course, paid no heed to that. Many were shocked at the openness with which Kuzmin described a same-sex affair in both the verse and the prose narratives.[54]

Kuzmin used the same names for the principals in both these *romans à clef*, and his friends certainly had no difficulty recognizing the real-life prototypes and themselves in the characters, who are virtually copied from nature and whose pseudonyms are easily deciphered. The composer Mikhail Aleksandrovich Demyanov, for example, is obviously Kuzmin himself (Kuzmin/Demyanov points to the popular blacksmith brother saints, Kozma and Demyan, the Cosmas and Damian of the Greek Church, the traditional patrons of Russian peasant marriages), whereas Nikolay Pavlovich Temirov is a composite of Nikolay Nikolaevich Sapunov (both last names are derived from Turkish) and Nikolay Petrovich Feofilaktov. Only the name of the artist, Pavel Ivanovich Myatlev, with whom Demyanov is in love, can really be said properly to camouflage someone—Sudeikin in this case.[55] There is no question either about the extent to which Kuzmin transposed the affair into the fiction. In many cases, passages in the story are astonishingly similar to the Diary, and Kuzmin made hardly any changes at all when he incorporated Sudeikin's letter ending their relationship into the story.[56] The affair, like the story that transcribed it, ended calmly enough, with a decisive break, but without scenes or moralizing from any of the participants, including Olga Glebova, who knew what had transpired between Kuzmin and her husband-to-be and who, like her husband, remained on the closest of terms with Kuzmin right up to the time of her emigration in 1924.[57]

Was the relationship, however, over so painlessly, or had Kuzmin donned a mask of seeming indifference? A memoirist who knew Kuzmin well at this time in his life wrote: "He succumbed to a passion for his friends as to some higher power, and he suffered unspeakably with every breaking off of a personal relationship."[58] We certainly see evidence of that tendency in the days before Kuzmin learned of the impending marriage. Sudeikin, who had returned to Petersburg in the middle of December, treated Kuzmin's affections with callous indifference, not even bothering to tell him of his return from Moscow and not once troubling to contact him, to Kuzmin's misery: "As [Maeterlinck's] Béatrice cries out: 'Angels of heaven, what have you done with me?' so I could say: 'Sergey Yurievich, what have you done with me?'" (Diary, December 18, 1906). For months afterwards, Kuzmin referred to Sudeikin's "betrayal" *(izmena)*, a word he never used in either the poem cycle or the story, whose hero says only that he is not "now" suffering.

Bitterness and "unspeakable suffering," of course, are absolutely anti-
thetical to the "major note" of Kuzmin's art, and we are reminded again
that the deepest roots of that art are in no way necessarily equivalent
with life, no matter how closely he at times drew on it for his fictions.
Parts of the Diary itself may be as deceptive as the fictions: in both
Kuzmin created structures for interpreting experience and distancing
himself from its suffering. He used "The Little Cardboard House" in
just such a way. The day after Sudeikin wrote to end the affair, Kuzmin
read the Diary's account to Somov: "His tough, disenchanting, and
nasty words sounded like comfort to me, although he cast Sudeikin in
the light of someone who had played a double game, vain, heartless,
desiring only a victory over me and nothing more. He advised me to
write a story about it, something like *Il fuoco*. Isn't life more interesting
than any novel whatsoever?" (December 27). D'Annunzio's novel *Il
Fuoco*, published in 1900, had caused a furor because of its transparent
allusions to the author's affair with the celebrated actress Eleonora
Duse. Kuzmin, however, settled no scores in his story. He simply set
down what had happened in life, and in his art, at least, put it behind
him.

Kuzmin used none of the pseudonyms of "The Little Cardboard
House" in "An Interrupted Story," but he hardly needed to, as many
other details link the two narratives and intimately connect them with
Kuzmin's biography. The poem "The Whole Day" ("Tselyi den'")
mentions Auslender ("Serezha") and his mother, Kuzmin's sister, with
whom he was still living, while "A Happy Day" ("Schastlivyi den'")
brings Sapunov in by name and even contains a "self-citation" so bla-
tant that the work proclaims its autobiographical nature, when the lyrical persona refers to his "Chablis on ice." Only Kuzmin's friends, however, would have recognized the real-life incident behind the poem "At
the Party":

> You and I and a fat lady,
> having softly closed the doors,
> withdrew from the general din.
>
> I played you my *Chimes* [*of Love*],
> the doors constantly creaked,
> fashion plates and dandies kept coming in.

I understood the hints in your eyes,
and together we went through the doors,
and everyone else at once became remote.

The fat lady remained at the piano,
the dandies crowded in a herd at the doors,
the skinny fashion plate laughed loudly.

We climbed up the dark staircase,
opened the familiar doors,
your smile became even more languid.

Our eyes became veiled with love,
and now we locked other doors...
If only such nights would occur more often![59]

Here is the Diary of November 22, 1906:

The first presentation of [Maeterlinck's] *Soeur Béatrice*. A sensational success. . . . I saw dear Sudeikin. The little actresses tried to drag us off somewhere after the performance, but we drove to the Ivanovs'. The drive was marvelous. We caught up and passed Somov and Nouvel and Leman's cousin. There was already a large crowd at the Ivanovs'. We did not go into the room where, it turned out later, they were discussing the Komissarzhevskaya theater. Sudeikin and I, who had been together the whole time, and Serafima Pavlovna [the obese wife of Remizov] withdrew into a neighboring room and occupied ourselves with music; an audience of sorts crawled in, Vilkina was talking with Nouvel and Somov [the "skinny fashion plate" and the "dandies" of the poem] so loudly, although there were two empty rooms next to ours, that we were forced to stop the music. S[ergey] Yu[rievich Sudeikin] said that he could stop by my place, which induced me to leave early, incognito, although I thought people would look for me. At home I read my Diary and poems; then we became affectionate, then we put out the candles, the bed was already made; there was again a long journey with ineffable joy, bitterness, hurt, and delight. Then we ate cutlets and drank water with jam. We heard how Serezha came home. S. Yu. left at five in the morning. I love him madly.

Kuzmin left only enough details in the poem to make a narrative, but we easily recognize the close coincidence between life and art in the poem. (In this poem there are no gender-specific endings for the verbs because of the use of the formal "you" [*vy*], but the lover is referred to throughout the cycle as "he.") He, of course, carefully shapes the experience in the poem, with its subtle repetition of "doors" (*dveri*) in every second line's rhyme position in the Russian, an erotic detail whose mutual "opening" and "locking" is the opposite of the common fin-de-siècle image of forced penetration through locked doors, as in the archetypical *The Strange Case of Dr. Jekyll and Mr. Hyde* or *The Picture of Dorian Gray*, where locked doors hide the central characters' most fearful secrets.

The reference in both works to the *Chimes of Love* would also have "marked" the texts in Petersburg cultural circles and, after their publication a few years later, for any reader. Demyanov, who seals his letters with an image of Antinous, is asked to play them at a gathering of an unnamed theater company. We have no need of the Diary to recognize the theater as Komissarzhevskaya's when we compare Kuzmin's description of it in the poem "In the Theater"—"How I love the slightly damp walls / of the white auditorium [of the theater]"—with that given by a contemporary: the auditorium was "entirely white, with columns, devoid of any manner of decoration at all."[60]

Komissarzhevskaya's theater opened on November 10, 1906, with a production of *Hedda Gabler*, with costumes by Vasily Milioti and sets by Sapunov. Kuzmin, no longer an admirer of Ibsen, found the play itself "old, unnecessary, false, and boring" (Diary) and criticized the acting, but he admired Meyerhold's direction and the "excellent" sets and costumes, and was furious at Somov and Nouvel's "Russian provincial, snobbish" criticism of the production, suspecting that they were jealous of the Moscow artists and resented his closeness with Sudeikin. The artistic "left" on the whole hailed the production as a revelation, while the majority of critics reviled it as a travesty. This set the pattern for the critical reaction to the plays that followed in the winter of 1906–7. The season's major success (or scandal) was reserved, however, for the first performance of Blok's play *The Puppet Booth* (Balaganchik), one of the most famous productions in the history of the Russian theater.

Blok had read his "lyrical drama" *The King in the Square* (Korol' na ploshchadi) on October 14, 1906, at the theater's first Saturday get-together, the night Kuzmin first met Sudeikin.[61] Meyerhold wanted to produce the play, which Kuzmin found "boring and abstract" (Diary), but was blocked by the theater censor, who wanted no depictions of revolution, no matter how "symbolic," on the stage. He turned instead to *The Puppet Booth*, and asked Sapunov to design the production and Kuzmin to write incidental music, which he agreed to do, as he professed to admire it.[62] The play, paired with Maeterlinck's *Miracle de Saint Antoine* (the censor demanded that its title be changed to "The Miracle of Anthony the Pilgrim"), opened on December 30, 1906, to the expected uproar, which began, Chulkov remembered, from the moment the sounds of Kuzmin's "piquant, heady, disturbing, and sweet music" died down.[63] The partisans of the enigmatic play, which used commedia dell'arte characters in a modern setting in the ironic game of reality and identity so beloved of the Symbolists, and whose puppet hero prefigures the tragedy of *Petrushka*, called the participants on stage for bows to an ovation, while an equally demonstrative group tried to shout them down with whistles and catcalls. One reviewer dubbed both play and the premiere "Bedlamchik."[64] Blok, for his part, was delighted by the whole production, and in the introduction to his *Lyrical Dramas* called Kuzmin's music "ideal." He stipulated use of Kuzmin's music in all future performances.

With the collaboration on *The Puppet Booth*, Kuzmin began his active career in the theater and his friendship with Blok. The negative review of *The Green Collection* was forgotten as Kuzmin fell under the spell of Blok, whom he pronounced a "splendid [*slavnyi*] fellow," and Blok, in his turn, took an immediate liking to Kuzmin, whom he saw often during the readings and rehearsals that preceded the December opening. Blok's appreciation for Kuzmin's talent grew apace, as we have seen, and in the years to come he forcefully defended his friend against charges of "immorality." Blok valued Kuzmin's innate sense of theater, and invited him to a reading of his play *The Song of Fate* (Pesnya Sud'by) on April 30, 1908, and two months later he persuaded Fedor Komissarzhevsky to commission music from Kuzmin for a production of Grillparzer's *Die Ahnfrau* in his translation.[65]

Kuzmin continued the habit of drawing directly on his biography in his works. He oscillates between the most obvious references, easily recognizable to his immediate circle of friends and beyond, as in the story and poem cycle we have been examining, to the most obscurely private, decipherable only if we have his private papers, and often simply enigmatic. (The Diary, our primary source of information and so revealing in the early years, offers small help as it gradually grew into little more than a record of people, places, and events.) The "aesthetic potentiality," as Lidiya Ginzburg would put it, of his own life and experience presented the models that the fiction and verse of others, where openly gay thematics remained taboo, could not. As he realized them (and broke the taboo) in his own works, he became less and less direct, as he was able, with the years, to make incidents from his life "disappear" into a personal myth. No matter how subtle the practice, Kuzmin continued so often to compound matters of fact and matters of fiction that he encouraged invasions of his private life for those in search of a more rounded understanding of the public one and for those who wonder about the methods and extent of the intricate encoding of the life in the art, a process of self-awareness in which the author, in the interdependency, indeed the indissoluble interconnectedness, of creative subject and the figures he creates, reflects and realizes himself in his characters.

The description in "The Little Cardboard House" of couples "conversing politely and amorously," and of people "in some gentle and quiet way having a good time," captures perfectly the social atmosphere of the parties, outings, and intimate dinners that accompanied the first Meyerhold season of 1906–7, when art invaded daily life, aestheticizing its everyday course. Long after it was over, those who had been involved remembered it as a special time of "lightness" and grace, when they opened themselves to a total enjoyment of life as never before, and when, as one wrote, "There was nothing real about it—no lacerating emotion, no melancholy, no fear, just a lighthearted whirling of masks on white snow under a dark starry sky."[66]

The costume parties and the elegant dress codes for the presentation of self at these gatherings, with their theatricalization of life, had a singular appeal for Kuzmin, who had just entered the "dandy phase" that so many memoirs describe, the legendary possessor of 365 vests, the "Prince of Aesthetes." He had only just bidden farewell to his "Russian phase," by the end of which no one would have taken him for an Old Believer or seminarian. Remizov describes him shortly before he abandoned the Russian dress and shaved off his beard on September 9:

> At that time Kuzmin had a beard—black as black can be!—and went about in a maroon velvet *poddevka*, while at home at his sister's . . . he appeared in a brocaded golden-colored shirt worn

outside his trousers. His eyes looking aslant, just like a horse!—Somov caught it very well in his portrait!—and besides, there was a touch of eye makeup, so that he looked either like the Pharaoh Tutankhamen himself or like someone who has escaped from a bonfire in the hermitages beyond the Volga, and he used a lot of rose-smelling scent—so he reeked like a [scented] icon on a holiday.[67]

On October 1, 1906, Kuzmin characterized his new look in a letter to Somov: "Gorodetsky found that I have a terrifying appearance, and he kept making the sign of the cross with his left hand. Vyacheslav Ivanovich [Ivanov] found that I look better, *plus troublant, inquiétant,* and more piquant, but he loves to make compliments. In my opinion, my face is unpleasant, perhaps a bit repellent, but stranger and more interesting, hardly younger."

Kuzmin, always keenly aware of costume as a means of proclaiming difference and indifference to reigning tastes and moral proscriptions, skillfully fashioned this new public persona to live up to his reputation, but also to affirm an independence and inner freedom from petty bourgeois restrictions, symbolized for him and many others in modernist circles by the colorless uniformity of contemporary dress, whose prosaic conventions they consciously violated. Andrey Bely, no dandy himself, wrote, "Our [men's] clothes are the least aesthetic of all the clothes I know of. And our fashions are hideously ugly,"[68] echoing, without the final *pointe*, Lord Henry Wotton's remark that "the costume of the nineteenth century is detestable. It is so sombre, so depressing. Sin is the only real colour-element left in modern life."[69]

Kuzmin refused to live artlessly in the world, and for a short while he pushed his protest against ugliness to the limits with his colorful vests, makeup, and even special beauty marks designed by Somov after those worn in the eighteenth century: "They glued a heart near my eye, a half-moon and star on my cheek, and a small phallus behind my ear, but when we went outside I took them off my cheek as it's too *voyantes*" (Diary, June 21, 1906). That phase passed, but the legend of a "Frenchman from Martinique of the eighteenth century in Petersburg of the twentieth century," as Tsvetaeva affectionately put it, lived on.[70] Somov's 1909 portrait of his friend wearing a pale blue suit and bright red necktie, locks of hair carefully curled over the receding hairline, captured the look, as did Aleksandr Golovin's 1910 portrait of Kuzmin in

one of the famous vests and a turquoise-colored suit, the very image of
the fashion rebel.[71] Not long after Golovin finished the work, Kuzmin
dropped some of the outré eccentricities, and he did so no less consciously than he had assumed them. By then dandyism itself had become a fashion. When Barbey d'Aurevilly's *Du Dandysme et de G. Brum-
mell* appeared in Russian translation in 1912, Kuzmin wrote in the
preface: "In this sphere, as in any other, of course, individual and collective creativity differ one from another. But cannot that which today is
the opinion and paradox of a d'Aurevilly or Wilde tomorrow be a clause
in the general rules and regulations of fashion! And although they may
understand dandyism as the rebellion of individual taste against the
leveling and tyranny of fashion, does not this very protest serve as a
certain fashion?"[72]

Kuzmin used readings from his Diary no less skillfully than his appearance and fictions and music to create a series of public images. On
June 30 he wrote with exasperation after reading from the Diary to the
Ivanov circle, who had found it becoming "monotonous," that "*reading
it* [the Diary] *is a real evil. Can it be I am supposed to live in such a way
as to make the Diary interesting? What nonsense!*" That autumn, however, he continued his readings from it in the close-knit Ivanov circle
and elsewhere, and on November 13 he commented, "Somov said that
all that's left is for me to read my Diary in public auditoriums next
season." That, of course, he never did, but Somov had intuited something crucial about Kuzmin's readings: for all the appearance of sincerity, they were a form of performance art. He read from the Diary very
selectively, picking and choosing and grouping sections to suit the person or persons whom he seemed to be initiating into the secrets of his
private life. At no point did Kuzmin ever say what the chief meaning of
the Diary was for him, although in a sense it allowed him to become a
spectator of his life and that of others and thus allow distance from
both.

When friends complained about the Diary's "monotonousness," he
mused about "inventing" episodes that would amuse them, but instantly
rejected the very notion, continuing to the end of his life to make it
a record that preserved some trace of the events of his private life.
Kuzmin, unlike Wilde, did not feel compelled to lead a double life, and
he did not found a life or an art on the tension between a pose and the
"real" self nor ever conceal his sexual identity in either. (The result is

that the strategies of encoding the discourse of gay experience in other societies are largely irrelevant for the study of Kuzmin.) While he was acutely aware of the various aspects of his self, which he strove to balance, we see no evidence of the Wildean view of the sense of self as a fictional construct. Nevertheless, his readings from the Diary by their selectivity helped foster an air of mystery about him, of "various Kuzmins," as people to whom it was read described or remembered their different impressions of what they had heard. He could play that impression against the public personas it also crafted—a game of identity acting in counterpoint to the seemingly autobiographical fictions, as both they and the Diary implicated life and art: "I asked K[onstantin] A[ndreevich Somov]: 'Can it be possible that our life will not survive for posterity?'—'If these terrible diaries are preserved [Somov, like Nouvel, had started to keep one and read from it], it will survive, of course; in the next age we will be regarded as Marquis de Sade.' Today I understood the importance of our art and our life" (Diary, September 15, 1906).

The publication of *Wings* in November set another facet of that persona before the larger reading public, as did the appearance in the final double issue of *The Golden Fleece* for 1906 of "The Story about Eleusippus" ("Povest' ob Elevsippe," written in February), another of Kuzmin's works to set a young man wandering, this time in ancient Greece, in search of a true path in life. *The Golden Fleece*, which, like *Libra*, now listed Kuzmin among its regular contributors, had announced in its tenth issue a competition for works of literature and the visual arts on the theme of the Devil. Kuzmin responded with the brief epistolary tale "From the Letters of the Maiden Clara Valmont to Rosalie Tütelmeyer" ("Iz pisem devitsy Klary Val'mon k Rozalii Tyutel'maier"). There were sixty-two entries; and the jury, which included Blok, Bryusov, Ivanov, and the magazine's Maecenas, Nikolay Ryabushinsky, divided the first prize in prose between Kuzmin's exercise in deviltry and Remizov's "Little Devil" ("Chertik"), giving Kuzmin one hundred badly needed rubles. Both stories were published in its January 1907 issue with drawings by some of the leading Russian artists of the day.

It is a wonder that Kuzmin found time to write anything at all, given the round of activities at the "Tower," the Komissarzhevskaya theater, and his work for it. As the season whirled on, Kuzmin's songs and

Somov's paintings of an idyllic utopia of *fêtes galantes* and flirtatious rendezvous best caught its mood of seductive charm and subtle harmony. When the season ended in the spring of 1907, Kuzmin, inspired by Somov's paintings and those of Sapunov and Sudeikin, wrote the poem cycle "Skyrockets," where scintillating fireworks and rainbows, real and artificial, highlight harlequinades that mythologize the special time when the "wounds of the heart" were "only deceptions," as he wrote in the poem "Masquerade." It had been "his" winter, Blok's wife told him on May 2, 1907, a time when his elegant artistry and the unsettling ambiguity of the games of life and death in his works had "poisoned" everyone. Re-reading the Diary several years later, Kuzmin could only marvel at "what brilliance there was in 1906–1907: it seems unbelievable now" (August 2, 1909). He never forgot those months of poeticized carnival, which he captured in an acute appreciation of Somov's art as late as 1921.[73] For, as he wrote in "Masquerade,"

> Though the beauties of rainbows are but for a moment,
> dear, fragile world of enigmas,
> for me your [illumination] arc glows![74]

❧ 5 ❧

"Burning with a Double Love"
1907–1909

AS EARLY as January 1907, the bloom of Kuzmin's association with the Komissarzhevskaya theater had begun to fade: "Ever since the sense of enthusiasm in the theater died out and intrigues started up, it interests me considerably less" (Diary, January 8). He saw some of the people often, especially Sapunov, who was working on a portrait of him that month, attended performances, and dropped by backstage, but he had less and less to do with the troupe over the course of the spring.

The theater group had never displaced Ivanov's "Tower" as the dynamic hub of the capital's modernist intellectual life. The style of the "Wednesdays," where erudition and culture did not exclude high spirits and novelty, perfectly suited Kuzmin in 1906–7. During a lecture or debate, with the listeners seated in ranks around the speaker's table, Ivanov's wife or one of her more bohemian friends might be perched on the same table, while high-spirited members of the audience pelted the speaker with apples or oranges when they felt he was becoming boring. If too wearied by the discussions, they would abandon the others altogether to disport themselves in the neighboring orange study of the hostess, who had covered its floor with mattresses upholstered with bright-colored fabrics and strewn with pillows, to sing, read verse, and drink wine.[1] Kuzmin could most often be found there, and he usually arrived late, often after "escapades" in the Tavricheskii Garden, as he and Somov and Nouvel called sexual encounters in what was the capital's leading "cruising" territory.

Kuzmin was now a fixture at the "Wednesdays" and his musical performances part of the regular entertainment. Ivanov had to discontinue the evenings for a short while in the winter when Zinovieva-Annibal fell ill, but Kuzmin and a few others continued to stop by almost every day. None of that changed in the spring of 1907, when the "Wednesdays" resumed, if on an irregular basis. The bond between Ivanov and Kuzmin, who were brought together by their shared interest in classical antiquity, early Christianity, and the varieties of religious experience, grew because of Ivanov's desire to create a spiritual and sexual collective. This had led to his and his wife's experimentation with "triadic unions" involving Gorodetsky and then Margarita Sabashnikova, the wife of his poet friend Maksimilian Voloshin.[2] Ivanov wondered what Kuzmin's same-sex orientation might contribute to this "collectivity," and he soon made Kuzmin his most intimate confidant about sexual matters, often to Kuzmin's puzzlement, even mild irritation, suspicious as he was of extreme "mystification of the flesh," no matter how great the appeal to him of the Platonic ideal of Eros.

Kuzmin and Ivanov had high regard for each other as poets. In 1924, twelve years after the two men had had a serious falling-out, Ivanov, casting a disenchanted eye over the contemporary Russian literary scene, would remark to a friend: "Everything is insignificant, I'm dissatisfied with everything. You tell me, who is there in poetry? Only Kuzmin. Kuzmin I love."[3] He never changed his estimation of his old friend: Olga Deschartes, Ivanov's secretary and closest confidante during the last two and a half decades of his life, wrote that he "fervently loved" Kuzmin "for his impeccable artistic taste and genuine poetic gift."[4] Kuzmin sometimes joked with friends about the excessive "learning" of Ivanov's verse, but he appreciated its depth and exceptional craftsmanship, and its mastery of the most complex poetic forms.[5] He found much that was alien in Ivanov's view of the world and of art—so much, in fact, that it would be erroneous to speak of Kuzmin as in any way his "pupil." Rather, Ivanov guided Kuzmin's poetic development into new, more serious directions, as Chicherin had once done, by bringing to the fore elements that other friends were unable to encourage.

Then, too, friends such as Nouvel, irritated by what they saw as the drift of Kuzmin's prose toward stylization after *Wings*, were urging him to deal exclusively with contemporary themes. They failed to see that at their best, Kuzmin's dialogues with the past, as exercises in style and language, show a deep affinity with the aesthetic position of the World of Art in their attempt to recover the sense of style lost in the great mass of Russian fiction in the final decades of the nineteenth century. Nouvel also missed the fact that several of them refract highly contemporary issues of sexual morality, poetics, and cultural continuity through the prism of history. A contemporary setting, in fact, presented greater dangers of producing "entertaining, light, slightly scandalous reading, *amusement*" (Diary, September 15, 1906), which was all Nouvel really wanted from Kuzmin's verse and prose. Kuzmin's explorations of the interface of past and present, history and modernity, which Ivanov encouraged and cultivated, better served the artistic expression of the very disparate elements of his background.

Kuzmin would never turn his back on composing, but by the beginning of 1907, bolstered by the praise of Ivanov, Bryusov, and others, he decided that his real future lay in literature, noting on January 7 that "it makes me mad when people think of me first and foremost as a musician" (Diary). With the notoriety of *Wings* and the success of the "Alexandrian Songs," a literary career seemed a possibility. The few modernist magazines began vying for his works, but with that came problems: he now found himself in the middle of the quarrels that were splintering the modernist literary scene into rival camps. The previous autumn, even before the "Russian Beardsley," as Nikolay Feofilaktov was called, had met Kuzmin,[6] he had "implored" him in a letter not to accept the invitation of *The Watershed* (Pereval), a new Moscow magazine, to become a contributor.[7] Kuzmin, who had been led on to no purpose by several Petersburg publishing houses with promises to issue his works, realized how heavily dependent he was on the good will of *Libra* and "Scorpio," with which Feofilaktov was closely allied. (Feofilaktov had undoubtedly written his letter on Bryusov's instructions.) He had thus felt obliged to comply with the request in the autumn of 1906, although he kept looking for other sources of income from publishing.

By the summer of 1907, matters had become a good deal more complicated, and we see something new both in the Diary and in the writer's correspondence: Kuzmin the professional man of letters, closely following the literary scene and watching for comments about his works in the press, motivated not by vanity but by concern about his precarious financial state. Although *Wings* had been something of a best-seller, he had received all of 450 rubles for all the printings.[8] He could ill afford to be pulled into the polemics raging between *Libra* and

The Golden Fleece, and rivals such as *The Watershed* and "Oraea," and hoped somehow to stand above the fray and play his own game.

On June 1, 1907, he received a letter from Likiardopulo, the secretary of *Libra*, asking him to join other contributors to the journal in boycotting *The Golden Fleece* should it publish anything critical about its Moscow rival,[9] and the next day he noted with some bitterness in the Diary: "Again quarrels in Moscow with *The Fleece*; since they're getting ready to leave it, they invite me to join in. Well, then, having deprived me of *The Watershed*, they now want to deprive me of *The Fleece* as well."[10] On July 14 he wrote, "I would like it if everybody either made peace or clearly parted company and then divided themselves up among the magazines, like the artists, who almost do not have the right to participate in different exhibits" (Diary). Not long after, out of loyalty to Bryusov, he did sign, with some reluctance, a collective letter announcing the signatories' intention to boycott *The Golden Fleece*, even though he had closer friends, such as Ivanov, in the rival camp, and detested the Merezhkovskys, who, with Bely, were Bryusov's main allies.[11]

He now felt free to accept the old invitation from *The Watershed*, whose editor, Sergey Sokolov, warned him, "Strategy and my awareness that the circle of our readers far from coincides with the circle of, let's say, *Libra*, force me, alas, to wish for 'minimal eroticism.'"[12] Kuzmin responded with the play *On Alexis, Man of God*, published in September in the eleventh issue, and with an "innocent" cycle of poems entitled "At the Factory" ("Na fabrike"). The latter reflects a long stay with his sister Varvara and her family at Porakhina, a village not far from Okulovka, a station on the Nikolaevskii railroad line between Petersburg and Moscow, where his brother-in-law worked as the manager of a factory. When his whole family joined him there in May 1907, Kuzmin, pressed for money, and, with their departure from the capital, homeless, had no choice but to leave Petersburg with them.

The isolation of life in the provinces made Kuzmin entirely dependent on friends for news about cultural matters and the progress of his own affairs, about which he continued to fret. On August 2 Nouvel, in Moscow on business, filled him in on what was transpiring there:

It goes without saying that all the Muscovites are raining down abuse on the Petersburgers. You are about the only happy exception. . . . Bryusov scolds Vyacheslav Ivanov now and then. But the one who can't talk about him without foaming at the mouth, that's Ellis. . . . Bryusov is very nice, correct, academic. He sings your praises very much. Incidentally, even Bely "finds repose" when he reads you.[13] Bely is also very nice, but to carry on a long conversation with him is exhausting. You're afraid all the time that what if he up and jumps out the window. And so everyone loves you, and you are to everyone's taste, with the exception of Gippius, Leonid Andreev, Burenin, Botsyanovsky, and others like them.[14]

Heartened by that "consoling news" (Diary, August 4) and full of plans, Kuzmin returned at the end of the month to Petersburg. There he accepted the invitation of Elizaveta Zvantseva, an old friend of his and Somov's, to take a room in her apartment, which housed her studio and art school and which was located in the same building where the Ivanovs lived, on the floor immediately beneath the "Tower," and connected with it by a rear staircase.

Kuzmin managed to reestablish ties with *The Golden Fleece* quickly. Early in September, Nikolay Ryabushinsky met with him and invited him back into the fold, commissioning some poems and a portrait of him by Somov. Kuzmin succeeded in doing this without alienating Bryusov, who realized that, unlike the other boycotters, Kuzmin had no ideological axes to grind with either side in their polemics. The "Egyptian" story "The Shade of Phyllis" ("Ten' Fillidy") appeared in a triple issue of *The Golden Fleece* (no. 7–9, 1907), and "Aunt Sonya's Sofa" ("Kushetka teti Soni") in the tenth issue of *Libra*.[15] In the latter story, which Bryusov published at Kuzmin's insistence, the sofa itself narrates a gay love story in Kuzmin's witty and extremely well told variation on a threadbare conceit of erotic literature that he had probably encountered in the eighteenth-century French novel *Le Sopha* by Crébillon *fils*.

Kuzmin had no such success with another old acquaintance, Vera Komissarzhevskaya. The idea of writing a series of "mystery plays" had arisen in his mind in February, and on the twenty-second, he got his well-thumbed copy of the *The Reading Menaea* (Chet'i Minei) out of an old trunk. Kuzmin used Dimitry Rostovsky's edition of that huge collection of saints' lives and songs in honor of the saints as the primary source for the three "religious comedies" he wrote in 1907. As we see from his correspondence of the summer, he had been encouraged to hope that one of them, *The Comedy on Eudoxia of Heliopolis*, might be produced in the autumn at her theater.[16] Meyerhold pledged to "make the case for *Eudoxia*," as he was "simply enraptured by the play."[17] The actress, however, rejected it for her company at the end of July, dismissing it as "a picture without any ideas and needed by no one inside an elegant picture frame."[18]

Kuzmin learned of Komissarzhevskaya's decision only after he returned to Petersburg. The difference of opinion about the play was only one more sign of the growing tension between Meyerhold and his friends on one side and Komissarzhevskaya and her brother on the other. By the middle of October, the trouble was out in the open, and after the failure of Meyerhold's second production of the new season, Maeterlinck's *Pelléas et Mélisande*, he was fired. Many of his friends cut all ties with the theater immediately, among them most of the artists; the majority of the actors he had brought into the company left when their contracts expired. Kuzmin, who by then so little bothered himself with the theater's affairs that he did not even mention the scandal in the Diary, did fulfill contractual obligations for incidental music for one production, and then drifted away from the enterprise.[19] The bitter atmosphere of charges and countercharges for a time poisoned memories of the carefree season of 1906–7, for which Kuzmin had unwittingly written the epitaph when, at Bryusov's request, he did his first theater review for *Libra* (no. 5, 1907), a summary of the theater's achievements.

The gloom intensified when news reached Petersburg of the death, on October 17, of Zinovieva-Annibal. She and Kuzmin had been part of the same intimate circle, but he had never been as close to her as to her husband. Expressions of irritation, even dismay, about her "malicious" behavior punctuate the Diary, and he clearly had to work hard to disguise his growing antipathy toward her. She had further complicated matters when she asked him to write incidental music for her verse comedy *The Melodious Ass* (Pevuchii osel).[20] He did not want to offend Ivanov, yet he disliked the play, as he did her other works. He also regarded the way she used motifs from *A Midsummer Night's Dream* in the play to poke fun at the life of the "Tower" in the summer and autumn of 1906 as tasteless and another instance of her tactless maneuverings to alienate him and other friends from her husband. Even so, the Diary entry is shocking for its total absence of his usual generosity of spirit: "Diotima has died: it is hard to get used to the idea that a person, who was still alive not long ago, is no more. But it means Vyach[eslav] Iv[anovich] will arrive soon."

When Ivanov and his stepdaughter, Vera Shvarsalon, Zinovieva-Annibal's child by her first marriage, returned to Petersburg at the end of the month, Kuzmin's relations with the grieving poet and his family became even closer. The "Wednesdays" were suspended for a time, but Kuzmin stopped by the apartment almost every day, and was soon drawn even further into the family circle, with important consequences for his life and art. On November 1 he noted in the Diary: "I dropped in at Vyach[eslav] Iv[anovich's], that old bag Mintslova has installed herself there. Vyach. is dolorous, melancholy, but not crushed, in my opinion. We chatted. My thoughts [directed] toward the future." Those thoughts, although Kuzmin did not yet realize it, would soon be connected with the "old bag."

Anna Mintslova, a great pudding of a woman with an eerie resemblance to Madame Blavatsky, appeared in the Ivanov apartment at the end of 1906 or beginning of 1907 as mysteriously as she would disappear from it in 1910.[21] "She would burst in," Bely remembered, "floundering about in a black sack . . . her enormous heavy head would force its way among us; her yellow locks stood on end above it . . . like serpents . . . and the small, weak-sighted, and watery sky-blue little eyes would narrow; but tear them open—they were like two wheels: not eyes; and when they would darken, it seemed that they were bottomless."[22] Presenting herself as a psychic adept and an emissary of various European esoteric movements, theosophy and Rudolf Steiner's teachings among them, she established herself as someone to whom Ivanov and his wife entrusted their most private secrets, for, as Berdyaev recalled, "Mintslova was an intelligent woman, gifted in her own way, and she possessed great art in the approach to human souls."[23] Zinovieva-Annibal had fallen totally under her spell. After the death of his wife, Ivanov did so no less, mesmerized by her talk of being an intermediary between this world and the next and by her promise that with her help he could commune, even be reunited with, his wife in this world.

Like most of his contemporaries, Kuzmin had an interest in mystical and occult literature as a part of European intellectual and cultural history, and imagery from his reading of it found its way into some of his poetry and prose. As far as we can judge by his personal papers, he took a highly skeptical attitude to the comprehensive cosmologies of occult or esoteric doctrine of any kind, and he had a keen nose for mummery. Yet he, too, felt the force of Mintslova's hypnotic personality in the months after the death of Zinovieva-Annibal, when his status in the Ivanov household brought him into almost daily contact with her. He had first met her on November 19, 1906, at the apartment of Voloshin and his wife, both of whom had the deepest interest in theosophy and later in anthroposophy. He saw her there again on November 29, and reported in the Diary, "Mintslova said that I had been someone very close to Cesare Borgia, then the Chevalier des Grieux, and then in some Russian sect or other, a fanatical and depraved one." He kept running into her throughout late 1907. By then he was involved with a young cadet, Viktor Naumov.

On February 21, 1907, the young poet Modest Gofman had introduced Kuzmin to Naumov, an old acquaintance from Cadet School. At first he took little notice, although he was pleased to discover Naumov well read and with a fine appreciation for music. On April 8, when Naumov dropped by for a visit, Kuzmin "insistently and clearly questioned him," and learned that "everything that I say in *Wings* etc. has agitated him all his life. . . . *Il est des notres*, is not afraid, is not shocked, is looking for advice" (Diary). The next day Kuzmin learned that Somov "thinks that Naumov is in love with me, no more, no less, but that, of course, is not true." A week later he heard, much to his irritation, that Chulkov and other acquaintances were spreading gossip about him and the handsome cadet. The next day, however, he confessed to himself, "It seems to me that I am thinking about Naumov," and he was happy that "dear Naumov" was now writing to him. A game of confidences and coquetry soon ensued: "I must make him consider himself my muse" (Diary, April 28). It continued throughout May, and, to judge by the letters the young cadet wrote, he entered into its spirit with no less gusto than Kuzmin.

When Kuzmin left the capital for Porakhina, he was still unsure about his own feelings and totally at sea about Naumov's real attitude toward him. Despite the encouraging tone of the letters he received from him over the summer, enough so that he dedicated to him the cycle "Skyrockets," written in July, he found the situation in Petersburg, when he returned in August, as murky as before. The poem cycles "The Deceiver Deceived," written in October, and "The Joyous Way-

farer," in November, plot with the same certain self-referentiality we
find in "An Interrupted Story" the course of the wild emotional roller-
coaster that the young man had set in motion in September when he
told Kuzmin that though he did not love him, he did not *not* love him or
reject the possibility of love. Professions of love from the young cadet
followed, only to be denied, and then repeated.

On October 6 Kuzmin finally "thanked Heaven," which had sent him
"such happiness. . . . Such an *ange gardien*" (Diary). But by the end of
that month, during which he wrote the young man fourteen times (and
received five replies), he was convinced that Naumov had been toying
with him and with the affections of other close friends, with whom he
shamelessly flirted.[24] On October 31, when Kuzmin visited him at the
hospital, where he was recovering from a riding injury, they "talked for
about an hour and a half about the necessity of making a choice, sensi-
bly and drily." When Kuzmin got up to leave, Naumov told him that he
would tell him "when the choice has been made." Kuzmin "thanked
him drily and left unhappy," wondering just what he could expect from
this "youth *sans équilibre*" (Diary). Two weeks later Naumov told him
that he had "chosen" him, but nothing happened. Despite all Kuzmin's
strategies and entreaties, Naumov betrayed not the slightest sign that
he would ever allow the relationship to pass from friendship to any kind
of physical intimacy.

Caught in a state of mind between desire and fulfillment, hoping and
having, Kuzmin appealed to Vyacheslav Ivanov for advice. At his urging, Kuzmin, practical, playful, and deeply religious (and superstitious),
decided to turn to this last aspect of his personality to achieve his ends.[25]
Practicality and playfulness had accomplished nothing; perhaps mysticism and the occult would do the trick. Ivanov himself, convinced that
his wife's death held mystical significance, had been listening to advice
not only from Mintslova's "voices" but also from Boris Leman, who was
involved in every manner of occultism. Kuzmin, surrounded by this
atmosphere of mystical exaltation, submitted to their guidance as well.
His Diary entry of December 23 is typical of entries at the end of 1907
and the beginning of 1908, in which he charts his passage from initial
skepticism to credulous belief that they could indeed help:

Leman came, said astonishing things derived from numerology,
which weren't clear to me. In about fourteen days the business

with V. A. will become clearer, in a month everything will be firmly in place, in April–May there will be enormous light and happiness, an awakening like a bright morning. He very much reassured me. . . . An April morning will come no matter what I do. I will live to be 53, and could reach 62–67, were it not for the present involvement. No threat of insanity. . . . I still cannot go out alone without [my] *anges gardiens.*

Six days later, "during the day," Kuzmin "saw an angel in a golden-brown cloak and in golden armor, with the face of Viktor or, perhaps, Prince Georges. He was standing by the window. . . . This most distinct vision lasted about eight seconds."

On December 30 a clock which had not worked for over four months started to run, and the next day, finding it still working, Kuzmin pronounced it a "miracle" and an omen for the beginning of the new year. On New Year's Day he "took some scores, poems, and so on to the castle [*zamok*]." This was the famous Engineers' Castle, a palace built by Paul I after the Archangel Michael commanded him in a dream to erect a church on the site of Paul's birthplace in Petersburg; the church and surrounding royal residence were converted to a military engineering academy two decades after Paul's assassination in the building. Naumov was in an infirmary there, and Kuzmin must have been struck by the connection of the place with his patron saint. "He was very affectionate and Christian," Kuzmin continued. "What light ahead! . . . An angel is watching over me." He now spent all his time in idealized chastity, seeing Naumov at the hospital almost every day with a feeling of a "divine worship service." On January 10 Ivanov and his family presented him with a "candlestick for two candles, with shields, crosses, and lances," and four days after that "Vyacheslav gave me formulas 'Rose Cr.' [presumably Rosicrucian]."

On January 18 Kuzmin experienced another vision: "Suddenly [at Ivanov's] a presence was so clear to me that I could not move, was shattered, I clearly saw Vik[tor] Andr[eevich], anxious, with something in his hands. . . . All the time 'he' was with us. I walked as if I had wings." He concluded, on January 21, that he had a "mystical connection with Viktor," and seven days later, at Ivanov's urging, he "began meditations, having accepted all the formulas. What a beginning!" In the middle of February, Mintslova "led me to her room, and after ordering me to renounce everything around me, to fix myself on the one thing, to attempt to ascend, to withdraw, she herself, in a great paroxysm, embraced me. Coldness and trembling. Through a thick shroud I saw Viktor without a sack over his head, his hands on a blanket, ruddy-cheeked, as though sleeping. When I returned [to my rooms], I saw a sword, my sword, and pieces of shrouds for a long time" (February 16).

All this might best seem material for a history of the mystical obsessions of the age and of the hermetic preoccupations of early European modernism if it did not have the most intimate bearing on the verse Kuzmin was writing at the time. Images of spring, wings, golden armor, the erotically charged sword or lance, the cloak, radiance, the angel with the face of Naumov or Prince Georges or Kuzmin himself mirrored in a window are all the attributes of the "holy warrior" Guide, Kuzmin's protector and male muse, with which he associates Naumov, whom we encounter in the three cycles, dating from December 1907 to February 1908, that make up the third part of *Nets*.[26]

None of these cycles has the transparently autobiographical quality of the narratives of the first part of the volume. To be sure, they too are narratives, but they are records of a mystic quest, of dedication and ascent to a mystical ideal of Love beyond the imperatives of desire. In them Kuzmin transforms present experience to an extent never before seen in his mature poetry, yet he does not lose sight of the *realia* in his quest for the *realiora*. Their elusive presence, no matter how heightened and transmuted by the sacral context, gives these poems a feeling quite unlike the verse of Ivanov and other religiously inclined Symbolists such as Bely and Blok.

After December 18 Kuzmin took to calling every meeting with Naumov in the "castle" "vespers," thus bringing the military and ecclesiastical realms together, just as both merge in the Guide in shining armor in the cycles. (In the final stanza of the fifth poem of "The Wise Encounter" he writes simply, "I loyally go to vespers / again and again / so as to be more inaccessible to filth.")[27] On January 19, 1908, he discovered that at the same time that he had so strongly experienced Naumov's presence at Ivanov's the day before, Naumov had "had a dream . . . he was told, 'You do not need an anchor!' (Now I understand that he had an anchor in his hands)," and the second stanza of the seventh poem of "Streams" begins, "You do not need an anchor" ("Yakorya tebe ne nado"). In that cycle's fourth poem we find "You are hearing the sounds of a sonata" ("Ty slyshish' zvuki sonaty"). That detail, which is striking in a poem otherwise governed by the expected religious dominant of an icon lamp, prayer, armor, and radiant eyes, and which is just the kind of detail that is so characteristic of all of Kuzmin's verse, can also be traced to Kuzmin's experience at the Ivanov apartment on February 8: "When An[na] Rud[olfovna] was playing *The Kreutzer Sonata*, I knew clearly that Naumov was hearing this music, and it seemed so to her too." Obviously, we do not need the Diary to take the meaning or import of any of these poems, but such evidence of the "autobiographical imperative" at work in poems that we never suspected had anything to do with Kuzmin's immediate experience beyond an erotic idealization of Naumov offers the biographer satisfaction.

The Diary also offers us help of another kind in reading these cycles. Several of the poems allude to so many Western mystical traditions for their iconography that biographical background provides a useful extratextual control, nowhere more so than for the symbolic cluster of rose and heart imagery employed with such a sure hand in the final cycle, "Streams." In reading it, one is tempted to turn to Ivanov's "Rosarium" cycle in *Cor Ardens*, even though it was written in 1910, to explicate the opening stanzas of the second poem of Kuzmin's cycle:

> Bleed, o heart, bleed!
> Blossom, o rose, blossom!
>   The heart, drunk on the rose, is aquiver.
>
> It is love that burns me up, it is love;
> do not call me, o dear boy, do not call me:
>   from beyond the rose the threatening sword glistens.[28]

No reader is likely to miss the homoeroticism of the final line, and the direction of meaning becomes almost obvious when, apart from the "wound of love" conceit (borrowed most probably from the verse and mystical writings of the Italian Renaissance), we turn to the Diary. Here is an entry of February 7, 1908: "During the day I clearly saw two transparent roses, and it seemed blood flowed onto the floor out of my heart," followed on the next day by "My chest hurts from where it was bleeding." Several days before, while waiting to see Naumov at the infirmary where he was hospitalized with typhus, Kuzmin had performed the Rosicrucian formulas Ivanov had given him a few weeks earlier and which he had begun on January 28. When he was admitted to Naumov's room, he saw him "lying there, burning in a fever, like a mysterious rose" (February 4).

Here are the third and fourth stanzas of the same poem:

> Protect, o heart, protect.
> Do no harm, sharp sword, do no harm:
>   Sink onto sky-blue moisture.
>
> I will deflect misfortune with love,
> I will come, o dear boy, I will come,
>   and I will lie together with you under the sword.[29]

These stanzas similarly draw on and reshape the poet's immediate experience: "I am alarmed, I saw him in a dream, in a glade. . . . I cry out: 'I will come immediately'" (February 5); "A sword, shining brightly, sank into sky-blue water" (February 11). We are thankful to have been able to name what was likely the major source of the imagery—Rosicrucian literature, probably Masonic writings as well—and to better understand the circular process at work, as the mystical reading and meditations gave rise to the visions, which in turn found their way back into another text, the poetry itself.

Kuzmin's "holy warrior" cycles are full of the hieratic imagery of religious rites, and, not surprisingly, Kuzmin dedicated one of them, "The Wise Encounter," to Ivanov.[30] He "particularly liked" these poems and certainly understood the mystical impulse that had given them birth better than any other of Kuzmin's friends, even if all three cycles were inspired by Naumov, whose first name, Viktor, Kuzmin encoded in the Latin dedication of "The Guide": "Victori Duci."[31] Love, death, and confidence in spiritual resurrection through a new perfected love provide the dynamics both of the cycles and of Kuzmin's and Ivanov's experiences in the winter of 1907–8. The two men shared these experiences so closely that at times both felt they were becoming parts of one personality, wracked by an erotic and mystical upheaval and devoted to the spiritualization of earthly love.

After the completion of "Streams" late in February, which left

Kuzmin with a feeling of "utter emptiness," and after Naumov's release from the hospital, when the cadet "denied everything that had been before the illness" (Diary, March 21, 1908), the two saw less and less of each other. Finally, on March 29, on the eve of Naumov's departure from Petersburg with his unit, Kuzmin was "in the castle, bade farewell, he gave me his blessing." Kuzmin had never reached what had once been a physical goal, and, to the bafflement of Nouvel and Diaghilev, had ultimately not pursued it at all. Art itself had provided the catharsis and a spiritual consummation, that "burning with a double love," as he wrote in the final poem of "The Guide," in which physical and spiritual are inseparable, mutually dependent, and simultaneous. He seemed to realize that as he came to terms with the end of something that had consumed him for four months. "How long it has been since I've been in church; at times these meditations etc. seem to me somehow gray and dirty, very sinful and unmerry" (Diary, April 6, 1908). This was as close as he ever came to being sucked into the treacherous currents of the "secret doctrines" that destroyed or deformed the lives of so many at the time. Like Mintslova and her neurotic smothering protectiveness, they were cast aside, despite Ivanov's continuing absorption in his own mystic concerns and his attempts to keep his friends involved in them.

Shortly before Kuzmin began work on the mystical cycles that mark such an important new direction in his art, he set down one of his most definitive statements about his preferences in art. He had established the core of his interests by 1907 and never abandoned them. He would write hundreds of articles and reviews in the years to come, but nowhere did he lay out his views so candidly and categorically as in two letters that he sent to Vladimir Ruslov in November and December 1907. They come close to being the artistic credo Kuzmin never wrote as such.

On September 1 Kuzmin noted that Diaghilev "talked about a gymnasium student in Moscow named [Vladimir] Ruslov, a proselytizer and *casse-tête*, who considers himself Dorian Gray, who always has about thirty comrades at the ready *par amour*, who himself tracked down Diaghilev, etc." Exactly two months later he received a letter from the young Muscovite. Other letters followed, each of them carefully noted in the Diary, which reveals the special significance Kuzmin attached to them. He took the young man seriously enough to copy out and send him the dropped chapters of "The Little Cardboard House," and even contemplated a trip to Moscow especially to make his acquaintance, fascinated as he was by the aura of legend that surrounded him and by the idea that a new kind of "gay society" of unprecedented sexual openness might be formed with Ruslov and his young friends as the Moscow nucleus.[32] The trip did not transpire because of pressing obligations in Petersburg.[33] Neither did the new "society" or the meeting with Ruslov (Kuzmin would meet him only in September 1909), but on November 15 and December 8–9 he responded to Ruslov's questions about what he liked in art with two long letters. Put in the highly personal tone typical of Kuzmin ("I like . . . I don't like"), as though the writer has no pretense either to objectivity or to authority, the letters do bear witness to a curious mind that knew few boundaries and to a teasing sense of humor that delights in deliberately mixing "high and low":

I don't like Beethoven, Wagner, and especially Schumann, I don't like Schiller, Heine, Ibsen, and the majority of the new Germans (excepting Hofmannsthal, Stefan George, and their school), I don't like Byron. I don't like the 1860s and the Itinerants. I almost don't like animals, I don't like the smell of lilies of the valley and heliotrope, I don't like the color dark or sky blue, I don't like fields of growing grain or conifers, I don't like chess, I don't like raw vegetables. . . .

In art I like things that are either indelibly alive, even if a bit coarse, or that are aristocratically aloof [*uedinennye*]. I don't like moralizing bad taste, things that are drawn out and purely lyrical. I lean toward the French and the Italians. I like both sobriety and the unconcealed piling up of opulence. And so on the one hand I like the Italian *novelliere*, French comedies of the seventeenth and eighteenth centuries, the theater of Shakespeare's contemporaries, Pushkin, and Leskov, and on the other hand several of the German Romantic prose writers (Hoffmann, J. P. Richter, Platen), Musset, Mérimée, Gautier, Stendhal, d'Annunzio, Wilde, and Swinburne. I like Rabelais, *Don Quixote, The Thousand and One Nights*, and Perrault's fairy tales, but I don't like *byliny* and narrative poems. I like Flaubert, Anatole France, and Henri de Régnier. I like Bryusov, Blok in parts, and some of Sologub's prose. I like old French and Italian music; Mozart, Bizet, Delibes, and the newest French (Debussy, Ravel, Ladmirault, Chausson); I used to like Berlioz; I like vocal and ballet music more, I like intimate music more, but not quartets. I like cakewalks, the maxixe, and so on. I like the sounds of a military band playing outdoors.

I like ballets (traditional ones), comedies, and comic operas (in the broad sense; operettas—only old ones). I like Swift, Congreve's comedies, and so on, I adore Apuleius, Petronius, and Lucian, I like Voltaire.

In painting I like old miniatures, Botticelli, Beardsley, painting of the eighteenth century, I used to like Klinger and Thoma (but not Böcklin and Stuck), I like Somov and some of Benois, some of Feofilaktov. I like old folk prints and portraits. I rarely like landscapes.

I like cats and peacocks.

I like pearls, garnets, opals, and such semiprecious stones as "bull's-eye," "moonstone," "cat's-eye." I love silver and unalloyed bronze and amber. I like roses, mimosa, narcissuses, and stock, I don't like lilies of the valley, violets, and forget-me-nots. I don't like vegetation without flowers. I like to sleep in the nude under fur.[34]

To comment in detail on this extraordinary mix or to trace the ties of Kuzmin's writings with each person named would tip the balance of biography in the direction of the source criticism we leave for others. Notwithstanding, we must highlight several salient features, while keeping in mind that the "style" of his correspondence with Ruslov left its imprint on the listings. In all the letters Kuzmin worked hard to craft an immaculate incarnation of the dandy, an aesthete from head to toe, so much so that he presented his relationship with Naumov as a love intrigue like any other, "this game," as he called it. He never gives the slightest hint of the misery that Naumov's platonic attitude was causing, let alone, in his two letters of January 1908, of the mystical exaltation recorded in the Diary (he mentions only living a life of hermit-like seclusion and his "very relative sanctity"). This is yet another instance of his donning a mask to conceal the deepest feelings, knowing how inappropriate these would be for the "gay plot" that the young Ruslov was trying, à la Dorian Gray, to live in Moscow.

The formulaic statement "In art I like things that are either indelibly alive, even if a bit coarse, or that are aristocratically aloof" succinctly defines his aesthetic position. It helps explain the seemingly incompatible range of interests, which so puzzled the many contemporaries who left memoirs, on the part of a writer who could listen to (and later review and translate) the greatest operas and the most ephemeral operettas with equal enthusiasm. Johannes von Guenther's description of the "wonderful surprise" of Kuzmin's library reflects the diversity—Hoffmann in the original; *The Thousand and One Nights* in French translation; an edition of Leskov in many volumes; the novels of Melnikov-Pechersky; Dante in Italian; the Slavonic Bible; scores by Beethoven, Mozart, Borodin, Musorgsky, Rimsky-Korsakov, Viennese waltzes of Lanner, and Russian spiritual songs—and he clearly based it on actual memories.[35] Georgy Ivanov, by contrast, obviously selected titles to create a picture of polar opposites in Kuzmin's tastes and thus a "mystery" of his own calculation, not Kuzmin's: "a motley selection. Saints' Lives and Casanova's *Memoirs*, Rilke and Rabelais, Leskov and Wilde. On his desk an open volume of Aristophanes in the original."[36]

No less impressive than the scope of Kuzmin's allegiances is his predilection for writers hardly known in Russia in his day and for lesser-known works by major authors. We see instances in the letters to Ruslov, and especially in a publication plan (almost all to be translations) he drew up for the "Petropolis" publishing house at the beginning of the 1920s. In the rough draft we find the expected stars of magnitude, but also Heinse *(Ardinghello)*, Klinger, Giambattista Casti, Jean-Paul Richter, T. G. Hippel (his four-volume *Lebensläufe nach aufsteigender Linie*), German popular chapbooks of the seventeenth century, Karl Immermann, the Apocrypha, *Ephesian Stories (Abrocomes and Atheia)*, the novel *Historia Apollonii Regis Tyrii*, *Die Nachtwachen* by the pseudonymous Bonaventura, Jean de Gourmont, and a collection of tales from the *Prolog*, *Paterikons*, and the *Leimonarion*. Alongside works like these, we encounter relatively obscure works by Tieck, Defoe, Smollett, Henri de Régnier, and Leskov, all of them testimony to Kuzmin's habit of approaching his "centuries of choice" parabolically, probing their peripheries carefully as he moved to examine central figures.[37]

Others in Petersburg shared Kuzmin's interest in areas of cultural history ignored by previous Russian generations. In the autumn of 1907 the director Nikolay Evreinov and the theater historian Baron Nikolay Drizen announced plans to open the "Theater of Old" ("Starinnyi

Theater"), dedicated to the education of the public in the history of the development of Western theater from medieval times.[38] They invited Kuzmin to join in, and he responded in October by translating a twelfth-century mystery play on Adam and Eve. His association with the enterprise did not last long (nor did the theater—only two months, from December 1907 to January 1908), but it testifies again to his increasingly active involvement in the capital's theatrical life, as does his participation in discussions at the "Tower" about how to realize Ivanov's dream of a "theater of myth."[39]

The circle of Kuzmin's literary acquaintances also kept growing. He had first met Andrey Bely at the apartment of Evgeny Anichkov on September 2, 1906, and the next day they saw each other again, at Sologub's, when Bely read some poems that Kuzmin found *"macabre,"* adding, "Bely as a person I didn't like at all, uncommonly so." Nor did he care for Bely's early prose "Symphonies," one of which (the Third) he believed exhibited the "coarsest lack of taste" (January 11, 1907). In 1907 Bely, with a paranoid eye fixed on the Petersburgers, had anathematized all those he believed to be ruining Russian letters: the "liberals, bourgeois, aesthetes, Kadets, whores and lechers, idlers, men and women alike, mediocrities, losers, ignoramuses, cynics and Maecenases, vampires, the self-loving and self-indulgent, orgiasts and pederasts, sadists and the like."[40] The violent polemics of 1907 had ended by the time of his visit to Petersburg in January 1908, and Bely expressed his admiration for Kuzmin and his work. Even then, Kuzmin still found Bely "alien in some way" (Diary, January 25, 1980).[41] At Bely's request, Kuzmin sent him most of the score for "The Wise Encounter," and a respectful relationship continued for several years, as poem cycles like that one persuaded Bely that Kuzmin was no "enemy" of Symbolism. They could never become close friends, however, separated as they were by a chasm of differences in temperament and art.[42]

With the completion of the three cycles dominated by the archangel-like Guide, the poems that would make up Kuzmin's first book of verse were ready. After close work with Bryusov concerning its contents and the ordering of the cycles, *Nets* went on sale in April 1908.[43] A few predictable complaints about "pornography" greeted the volume because of "The Love of This Summer" and "An Interrupted Story," but the majority of critics found much to praise, while hardly probing very deeply. Typical was the reaction of the poet Sergey Soloviev, nephew of the philosopher and one of Bely's closest friends and literary allies: "His world is a small enclosed world of day-to-day cares, warm feelings, light, slightly mocking thoughts. We would seem not to have encountered in poetry such intimacy, such simplicity, such a poetization of everyday interactions since the times of Catullus and Martial."[44] Bryusov did not manage much better. When he received the manuscript he saluted Kuzmin with: "As a whole this book has made a most happy impression on me. If you will permit me to express my opinion briefly and simply, I will say 'a beautiful book.'" But four years later he wrote, "His poetry resembles a brilliant butterfly fluttering about in a splendid bed of flowers on a sunny day."[45]

Only Blok, who alone amidst a chorus of abuse had called *Wings* "wondrous," saw a great deal more in *Nets*.[46] In reviewing the collection in the article "Letters on Poetry," he alone among Kuzmin's contemporaries formulated an adequate, and at times penetrating, critical response, even if it does rather too coyly talk around the gay dimension:

> It is as if there are two writers in Kuzmin: one is young, with a heart open and sad because it bears the sins of the world in itself, like the heart of a person of "ancient piety"; the other is not old, but only experienced, is sort of covered with dust, mocks himself without repentance, but with some kind of ulterior motive, and is slightly embittered. . . . By donning a mask, Kuzmin has condemned himself to being misunderstood by the majority, and there is no reason to be surprised that the most sincere and noble people shy away from his lonely and malicious but very likely innocent pranks. . . . If Kuzmin will shake off the tatters of capricious lightness, he can become a national bard.[47]

Kuzmin was not troubled that the public at large, the "bol'shaya publika," as he put it, did not see his "true face," remarking to Ivanov after reading Blok's review, "The person who wants to, who is able to—does see it, and isn't that enough?"

He certainly never sought a bardic role, national or otherwise, even if what might be called the gay community gave it to him, as we see from Ruslov's letters. Many critics, mainly Kuzmin's fellow writers, took his work seriously. The majority of those writing in the popular press, by contrast, assigned him the status of "pornographer" at worst and "gay spokesman" at best, and in the years to come they scanned every new work for the slightest hint of homoeroticism, which they could turn up even when it was absent. "Homosexuality" was "in the air," as Zinovieva-Annibal had once remarked to him, and Kuzmin more than anyone else had helped to bring the subject into the open and give it a kind of "modernist cachet."[48] In an age rife with sexual experimentation, some felt they were not really up-to-date unless they had tried it. Often the results were comic, as Kuzmin described in the Diary on August 23, 1907, after a visit to "Vienna," a popular haunt of Petersburg's writers and, like the ones mentioned here, of near-writers and literary journalists desperately trying to seem "bohemian":

> I went to "Vienna" to have a bite to eat, where I immediately fell into the arms of Pilsky, [Anatoly] Kamensky, Manych, and some kind of Armenian. Lazarevsky and Muizhel were at another table. . . . Manych claims that after reading a lot of me, he and the artist Troyanovksy wanted to give it a try; so long as they were embracing, etc., everything was all right, but when they started shoving it in and moving it, it all fell out, and they couldn't manage anything. His naïveté almost charmed me.

Kuzmin never shunned the kind of popularity *Wings* and *Nets* brought him, although he realized its transient significance. Constantly pressed by the sorry state of his monetary affairs, he too often in the years that immediately followed failed to offer much resistance to the dynamic that the public reputation had created, letting it drive the agenda of his writing with at times damaging effects for his art. He looked back over his career as a poet in 1931 and gave it a blunt appraisal, with which it is hard to disagree:

> I've been rereading my poems. Frankly speaking, I came across many slack and slipshod poems from the period 1908–1916. Now it is a different matter. Self-delusion perhaps. In my opinion, using the five-point grading system to evaluate all the collections, it comes out *Nets* (nonetheless a five), *Autumnal Lakes*—3, *Clay Doves* [Glinyanye golubki]—2, *Echo* [Ekho]—2, *Otherworldly Evenings*—4, *The Guide*—4, *Parables* [Paraboly]—4, *The New Hull* [Novyi Gul']—3, *The Trout* [*Breaking through the Ice; Forel' razbivaet led*]—5. (Diary, October 10)

After the indisputable achievement of *Nets*, one of only a handful of great "first books" in the history of Russian verse, Kuzmin began to repeat himself and to write too fast. Far too much of the poetry collected in *Autumnal Lakes* (1912) and *Clay Doves* (1914) represents just the kind of "lightness" Blok had urged him to abandon, "automatic writing" typical not of the poet at his original best but of the numerous epigones who sprang up in imitation. We can find, to be sure, a few of his finest poems in each of these books and even in *Echo* (1921), a small collection of some occasional poems from 1915–1919 that he excluded from *The Guide* and *Otherworldly Evenings*. Those two volumes preserve the best of an art which in 1916 developed, at first unsteadily, but then inexorably, in a rising curve until reaching the "five" of his final book. The same strictures apply to the prose he wrote in 1910–1915.

With the end of the relationship with Naumov, Kuzmin entered into one of those phases of aimless drift, dejection, and passive lethargy that typically followed the cooling of some obsessive passion ("I am doing nothing. Am like an unweeded garden" [Diary, April 1, 1908]). He stayed away from the bathhouses and other old haunts, but he was miserable, for, as he confessed over and over to the Diary, life without loving seemed a nullity. He was also under severe financial pressure, as usual, and had to resort to loans from family and friends because of partial creative paralysis: "How much time one wastes without love. D'Annunzio is an excellent school for the imagination, but love is the one and only, the one and only" (Diary, July 16, 1908).

In the past Kuzmin had had affairs and sexual encounters with some of the typical male pinups of the period (guardsmen, bathhouse attendants, coachmen, tradesmen), but he never fetishized or rated virility according to occupation or social class. Nor did he keep any of his lovers, no matter of what background, hidden away from his own intellectual and cultural milieu. His attraction to younger men always contained a strong aesthetic and artistic as well as physical component. In 1905 he had observed, rather wistfully, in the Diary: "I often think that to have a friend whom I could love physically and who would be receptive to all the paths in art, an aesthete, a comrade in tastes, reveries, delights, a bit of a disciple and admirer, with whom to travel together through Italy, laughing like children, bathing in beauty, with whom to attend concerts, go for drives, and to love his face, eyes, body, voice, to have him—that would be bliss" (August 27). A few months later he recognized that only with "Prince Georges" had there been a "total coincidence of interests and level of culture and tastes" (October 3). Since then, only Sudeikin had for a brief time promised similar fulfillment.

By the summer of 1908, it seemed that Sergey Poznyakov, a student at the university and an amateur writer, might be another such person. A remarkably handsome young man, Poznyakov had been trying to insinuate himself into the Kuzmin-Somov-Nouvel circle since the autumn of 1907, without any success. On December 7, 1907, he came with Auslender to Kuzmin's rooms and lingered on "with the firm intention of taking the matter to a conclusion, in which he succeeded. There's chance for you. But I would not say that it wasn't agreeable" (Diary). Not long after, Kuzmin surrendered to the mystical obsession with Naumov. He saw Poznyakov now and then, and the young man kept writing him, but he kept him at a distance. After Naumov's departure from Petersburg at the end of March 1908, however, Kuzmin began to see Poznyakov almost every day despite wondering "just what kind of lad is he really."

Voloshin met him on April 26, and he recorded Poznyakov's pithy self-characterization in his diary: "I am eighteen, that is my only merit. I am a member of the Russian gentry."[49] Two days later Kuzmin observed, "I am becoming more and more closely attached to S[ergey] S[ergeevich], am jealous, make demands, beg. . . . We are making visits *comme des jeunes mariés*," and by the end of the month "dear Serezha is almost living at my place, has been spending the night. Complete happiness. But if we were to live, work, read, drink, eat together: what ecstasy that would be!" (April 29–May 3). Realization of that, however, had to be postponed, because, with the end of the school term, Poznyakov departed with his family to spend the summer in Volhynia, leaving Kuzmin to mope in the capital. Ivanov did not help matters. Although he called Poznyakov "an enchanting, jolly lad" (May 22), he tried to persuade his friend "to live *maritalement* with Naumov" (May 28), from whom Kuzmin was still from time to time receiving letters. Throughout June, Ivanov kept urging Kuzmin to pray to the Archangel Michael for the resolve to "give up Poznyakov [and] take up with Viktor."

Before Poznyakov's departure, Kuzmin, eager to promote the young man, whom many began viewing as his protégé, had brought him into his own wide circle of friends. A young Baltic German writer and translator, Johannes von Guenther, had joined that circle at about the same time. He met Kuzmin late in April 1908 at the "Tower," where his interest in Russian modernist literature and his involvement with German had naturally brought him to present his credentials to the Germanophile Ivanov several years before. Now, charmed by the air of "quasi una fantasia" that Kuzmin created when he performed *The Chimes of Love* and music of Mozart, Chopin, and Beethoven for Ivanov and his guests, he asked if he might be allowed to translate them and the "Alexandrian Songs" into German.[50] Kuzmin agreed, and repaid the favor by offering to render into Russian, with Ivanov's help, one of his plays, *Die reizende Schlange, oder das wunderbare Spiel der Liebe*, practice that would later serve Kuzmin in good stead for his many translations from the German.[51]

Guenther was soon living at the "Tower," where the family, which had a pet name for every friend, called him "Gyugyus." Kuzmin himself had also taken up residence there. When Elizaveta Zvantseva closed down her studio, he had to find new quarters, and Ivanov, aware of the desperate state of his friend's finances, offered him his late wife's room. He moved in on May 12, and, although supposed to leave for his sister's at Okulovka, he kept postponing his departure at Ivanov's and especially Guenther's insistence. The latter's account of the late spring and early summer of 1908, when he was particularly close to Kuzmin, offers the kind of detail that readers may relish but that no memory can provide.

Typical is his claim to have "introduced" Petersburg poets to the *ghazals* of Count August von Platen, which the German poet had himself taken from Hafiz.[52] In the summer of 1906, at the time of the Hafiz-Schenken, Ivanov had planned to translate Platen's works in that form, while Kuzmin had mentioned Platen to Ruslov in his 1907 list of favorite authors, which is not surprising considering the lightly veiled homoeroticism of the German's verse. Kuzmin had also known and had an abiding interest in Arabic and Persian literature long before he met Guenther. He read and reread Mardrus's translation of *Le Livre des mille nuits et une nuit*, and he mentioned it in a note to the cycle of thirty *ghazals* that he wrote in May–June 1908, perhaps, indeed, at Guenther's urging.[53] Called "A Wreath of Springtimes" ("Venok vesen") in *Autumnal Lakes*, the cycle, Kuzmin later told Nina Volkenau, was his tribute to the "splendor and passion" of Persian and Arabic literatures.[54]

Guenther's omissions and distortions of emphasis present greater and

more interesting problems. When asked early in the 1970s for information about "The Rider" ("Vsadnik"), a narrative poem in twenty-eight
Spenserian stanzas that Kuzmin wrote in July 1908 and dedicated to
Guenther, he responded that Kuzmin had transposed into verse the
story of Guenther's love affair with a Riga actress, and had done so
"with a light touch of irony and out of the devotion of friendship."[55]
The text of the medievally tinged poem, one of the most explicitly
homoerotic of Kuzmin's early works, offers no support at all for the
statement. In its twenty opening stanzas, a rather androgynously handsome knight, one of Kuzmin's typical wanderer figures, rides through a
forest resembling Klingsor's garden, where a series of temptresses ac-
cost him and try to stop him on his search for love, each insisting that
she represents the end of his quest. None of these Kundrys succeeds, as
he rejects one after another. He finally reaches a mysterious castle, in
which he finds a naked youth bound to a pedestal, and realizes, in
stanzas that are suffused with radiance, that he has reached his goal. He
swears that he is unsullied by other forms of love, and frees the youth,
called Eros, with his sword, whereupon he is led by him to an inner
chamber, and the poem concludes in a bold series of metaphors for
male same-sex lovemaking.[56] There is not a trace of irony in the allegory; and by writing only of the "devotion of friendship," Guenther
tried to camouflage the nature of his relationship with Kuzmin in May–
June 1908, when his "charlatanry with mysticism and his visions" and
his "playing the coquette" had irritated Kuzmin, who was not at all
interested in him. "The Rider" looks like Kuzmin's warning to the
German to beware the guile of women and to take Eros itself seriously
or be made a fool.[57]

Over the summer of 1908, which Kuzmin spent at Okulovka, he
wrote "The Rider" (an "Ariosto-Byronic mongrel," albeit "not without
charm," he remarked shortly before finishing it on July 21) and two
stories. In "Florus and the Bandit" ("Flor i razboinik"), a bizarre tale of
sexual obsession, a wealthy Roman so identifies himself with a man he
has glimpsed on the street that he dies, a mysterious bruise around his
neck, at the same moment the man, a criminal, is hanged. "The Double
Confidant" ("Dvoinoi napersnik") is about a confused relationship between two men who try to hide their attraction for each other by convincing themselves that they are in love with the same woman. Kuzmin
rightly worried that the story's transparent mockery of Mintslova's

mummery, his use of details from the recent affair with Naumov, and the obvious modeling of other characters on visitors to the "Tower" would offend his host, but Ivanov forgave him for the indiscretions.[58]

Work on *The Exploits of Alexander the Great* (Podvigi velikogo Aleksandra), which he had sketched out in the spring, also resumed over the summer. In the novel, which is based on the rich tradition of legends, both classical and medieval, about the historical figure, he slipped effortlessly into the narrative stance and manner of a pious and naive medieval chronicler, mixing the ordinary and the miraculous in the tale of a man driven inexorably by fate. Curiously enough, he is so true to the medieval manner that he makes nothing of the relationship between Alexander and Hephaestion, characterizing them only as tender friends, and the hero's major failing is never to know love. He published it, one of his most accomplished early long prose works, in the first issue of *Libra* for 1909 with a dedication to Bryusov.

Throughout July and August 1908 Kuzmin lived in a state of tense anxiety about what the autumn would bring in both financial and amorous terms. The two issues were inextricably linked in his mind. He had notoriety, but had yet to translate it into success in the literary world at large, something he knew to be essential if he were ever to solve his financial problems. Without money he had no way of making plans for his living arrangements with, he hoped, Poznyakov, and the constant references to "money, money" in the Diary reflect that persistent concern. On the day of his arrival at Okulovka, he had received the first of what would initially be a stream of letters and telegrams from Poznyakov declaring, "I love you, desire you, kiss you" (July 1). The young man was never far from his thoughts, but then, on July 13, Naumov sent a surprising invitation, which Kuzmin noted in the Diary: "Viktor is going to Petersburg soon and calls me to join him, but where can I go without money? And then what will I say to him given Serezha's [Poznyakov's] presence? Like Lear, I said that I love the one who himself loves me the most, but by what is that measured?" The "mad desire to see, touch, possess Sergey or Viktor" that "took possession" of him held him in its grip in the weeks that followed, always coupled with the thought, "How will I disentangle this whole story?"

In August, Poznyakov moved once and for all to the center of Kuzmin's indecisive attention. So penniless that he could often not afford to buy stamps to reply to Poznyakov's letters or send telegrams,

Kuzmin despaired of ever being able to settle again in Petersburg. He took comfort only in the exquisite landscape of an early autumn, reflected in the opening poems of the "Autumnal Lakes" cycle, which he began at the time. Late in August, however, his publishers finally paid him some long-overdue royalties. Most of the sum went to pay debts to his brother-in-law, but on September 10, after receiving a telegram from Poznyakov with the news that he would arrive in Petersburg the next day, Kuzmin returned to the capital.

He took a room in the Severnaya Hotel (the Grand Hôtel du Nord) opposite the Nikolaevskii railroad station in the heart of the city. Ivanov had invited him to return to the "Tower," but he had reacted to his telegram of August 31—"The Tower is open to you alone"—as to a "slash of a whip across my face," interpreting it as a not so subtle hint that he, but never Poznyakov, would be welcome to live there: "Can it be that I will again stay with those nasty hypocrites? Of course not, of course not!" (The breach was healed in October.) On the eleventh, after going from one railway station to another in the vain hope of encountering the returning Poznyakov, Kuzmin learned from a letter forwarded by his sister that his lover would be arriving two days later. After steeling his nerves, he made the visit to Naumov that he had been dreading ever since coming back. They parted on good terms, and would see each other from time to time. On July 31, 1909, Kuzmin wrote in the Diary: "I perhaps loved Naumov most of all. That is what is most clear."[59]

The year before, however, it was Poznyakov, who arrived on the fourteenth, with whom Kuzmin was prepared to fall in love, and whom he made his new muse and the addressee of a series of poems. Poznyakov accompanied Kuzmin just about everywhere, but it was an uneasy relationship from its new inception. "How much I love him," Kuzmin wrote on September 20, "although, all the same, it seems he does not love me, and is probably unfaithful, but it's nothing." External circumstances caused many of the doubts and much of the dissatisfaction. He was still badly off, and again reduced to asking friends for money, which now had to cover both his and Poznyakov's expenses on outings and at restaurants. By the twenty-fourth, there was nothing to do but return to his sister's in the country, with Poznyakov promising to join him there.

On October 7 he set to work on a project conceived late in August, a new novel that had the title *Gentle Joseph* (Nezhnyi Iosif) from the start and that was finished only as it was being serialized in the first ten issues of *The Golden Fleece* in 1909. It is the first of a kind of trilogy of novels, made up also of *Dreamers* (Mechtateli) and *The Quiet Guard* (Tikhii strazh). All are set in contemporary times and are linked by their similarity of plot, by their predominantly conversational structure, and by the air of mystery that surrounds the journeys of the heroes. At the center of each stands a rather blank Parsifal-like young hero whom a series of morally unworthy characters try to tempt from a higher path. In this case it is a predatory widow who pursues and marries Joseph for his money. Thanks to the efforts of a "Guide figure," here an officer, Andrey Fonvizin, the hero, always quite passive, remains on his journey to spiritual regeneration through love. In the novel's final pages, set shortly after Easter in Petersburg, where Joseph has moved after breaking with his wife, he is back on his path. Saved by his guide, by the company of an Old Believer family who deal in religious objects and who are obviously modeled on Kuzmin's old friends the Kazakov family, and by his conversations with a saintly peasant woman, Marina, he is about to set off for Rome. Kuzmin dedicated the novel to Poznyakov.

He found time, too, for music and the theater. He composed a "March of the Monkeys" for a play that Remizov had based on an apocryphal tale and entitled *On Judas, Prince of Iscariot* (O Iude, printse Iskariotskom). Komissarzhevskaya accepted it for production and asked Kuzmin for music, but neglected to pay him his fee when the piece had to be dropped for "reasons beyond the control of the theater management," an allusion to the strict theater censorship that forbade the depiction of biblical personages on the stage.[60] On October 3 Kuzmin also finished the first draft of an operetta, *The Maidens' Amusement* (Zabava dev), whose action is set in Istanbul. Several theaters expressed interest and even made vague promises, which buoyed his spirits with the thought of regular royalties, but he had to wait almost three years to find a theater to produce it.

Broken promises of another kind created far greater anxiety. Poznyakov either wrote nothing or suddenly dispatched telegrams announcing his imminent arrival, only to fail to show up without any explanation or excuse. This behavior deepened Kuzmin's concern about the depth of the younger man's feelings and suspicions about his conduct, especially his flirtations with "that vile condom," as Kuzmin now started calling Nouvel. A visit to Petersburg between October 19 and

26 cleared up nothing. The opening lines of the poem "Glossa" (a small fish, *Platessa luscus*), written perhaps not long after the brief but costly visit to Petersburg, offer the best commentary on it and the whole autumn of anxious frustration: "Without you I languish in boredom, / in your presence I languish, jealous; / all the same, I would prefer kisses / to the languor of separation."[61]

In November, Poznyakov and Kuzmin spent ten "sweetly happy days" together at Okulovka, taking sleigh rides, playing with the children, reading Leskov, and writing side by side in Kuzmin's rooms overlooking the snowy landscape. Emboldened by a new mood of confidence about the future, Kuzmin, who only two years before had himself needed literary sponsorship, recommended several of his lover's works to Bryusov on November 12. Five days later he accompanied Poznyakov back to the capital, and the next day all his old anxieties resurfaced: "Well, back in Petersburg again, without money, without hopes, without friendship" (Diary). Bryusov's positive response about the young man's "Dialogues" ("Dialogi") and some of his own works brought him out of his self-pity.[62] He also reestablished some old ties in the theater. Blocked by the conservatism of the majority of the theaters in both capitals, Meyerhold had invited some friends from the days of his work with Komissarzhevskaya's troupe to found a new type of intimate theater called "The Cove" ("Lukomor'e") for the main hall of the Theater Club.[63] After only a week of performances, the venture collapsed in December, primarily, Auslender explained in his theater column in *The Golden Fleece* (no. 1, 1909), because of lack of repertory. Kuzmin and the others did not forget that lesson when, a few years later, the same impulse to create a theater-cabaret led to the establishment of two longer-lived enterprises, in both of which he played an important role with many of the same people, most notably Meyerhold.

By the time two of Poznyakov's "Dialogues" appeared in the February 1909 issue of *Libra*, the "blue flower" of the relationship, in which Kuzmin had invested so much of his hope for a "creative friendship" of love and art, had begun to wilt. Poznyakov managed to fritter away the money Kuzmin had begged for him, while breaking a promise to move in with him by the twentieth of January 1909. Then came the greatest blow: the young man announced that he did not love him. Dejected, Kuzmin nevertheless declared: "Perhaps [he] will marry—I will accept everything. . . . But some other man, perhaps a woman, is caressing this face, this body—how can I endure it? . . . But I love him more and more and will never give up until he discards me like a rag, like a squeezed-out lemon" (January 23, 1909).

Because of the sexual tolerance of the circles he frequented and the virtual lack of prosecution for male same-sex conduct, Kuzmin had never had to consider a marriage of convenience to mask his sexual preference or to protect himself from the public odium surrounding his literary name, a sham that would have condemned him and a wife to wretchedness of the kind that drove Tchaikovsky and his wife in name only to the edge of madness. Nor had he ever pretended now and then to a bisexuality he did not command. In a period of profound cultural insecurity marked by a battle between and with the sexes, as women in Russia asserted their rights no less vigorously than their counterparts in western Europe and America, and the "women's question" moved from the margins of Russian society to its center, Kuzmin kept out of the fray. He was certainly no male feminist, and he was happy with women in traditional domestic roles. He enjoyed their company, and had many close women friends all his adult life, several of them among his greatest admirers. To judge from the Diary, he had a special rapport with many women, an easygoing relationship that most men, whatever their sexual preference, might have envied, and he was a man to whom women liked to tell confidences and toward whom they often took a protective, sisterly attitude. He certainly did not perceive women as a threat in society or the arts, and he championed the careers of Akhmatova and several other women writers.

In his works Kuzmin presents women with sympathy and insight when they are motherly or stand at the margins of his heroes' lives. They also often play the important role of agents for the gay protagonists' wrestling with questions of identity. Let them, however, get in the way of male bonding or endanger a male relationship (an obsessive plot motif in his works), and the portraits crackle with misogyny. (On April 24, 1907, during a visit to old family friends, he noted that one of them, to whom he had once been attracted, had "gone to seed" [*opustilsya*]) after his recent marriage, adding tartly, "*comme les femmes dégradent toujours.*") The women who pursue the two heroes of *Wings* are unattractive, if not downright repulsive, like Nata in part one, or typical fin-de-siècle temptresses, like Veronica Cibo with her "depraved mermaiden eyes in a pale face" in the Italian section of the novel. The most appealing, Ida Golberg, kills herself when she learns of Shtrup's sexual nature and realizes the hopelessness of her love for him. So it goes in

Kuzmin's fictions, where masculinity always bears a positive affective charge, femininity a negative one. Male companionship is idealized, while his young heroes' relationships with women are entanglements at best or literally destructive passions at worst that separate the males from some higher ideal and "transcendence." (Each opera mentioned in *Wings*—*Carmen, Samson et Dalila, Parsifal, Tannhäuser, Tristan und Isolde*—presents a different model of passion, each destructive in its own way, even if the last does offer transcendence through love-death, a theme to which Kuzmin would return in the 1920s.)

Kuzmin's art and private papers show no ambivalence or defensiveness about same-sex love. He had no personal anxieties about manliness and virility, no longing to be the male mother or the authoritarian father, and none of that rationalization of same-sex desire as aesthetic experience so common in the fin de siècle. (This does not, however, exclude the fact that an erotic ideal in his verse is an aesthetic and spiritual one at the same time.) He explores the nature of human relationships and art, not that of masculinity, in his writings. He was always drawn not to "aunties" *(tetki)* or "fairies" *(tapetki*, from the French *tapette)*, as he derisively referred to effeminate men, but to virile men of his own milieu or, if that were impossible, to a "simple bathhouse attendant or a soldier" (Diary, July 18, 1910). Often these men turned out to be bisexual, and more than one left him for a woman, as had happened with Sudeikin. Now the increasingly querulous, even viciously unstable Poznyakov seemed to be repeating the pattern (or at least so he, a consummate tease, liked to pretend in order to pain and manipulate his older lover).

After paying his debts in January 1909, Kuzmin was broke again. Depressed by the seeming hopelessness of his affairs, he at times thought again of a monastery or suicide as the only way out of a predicament that seemed insolvable. Nervous and on edge because of the behavior of his on-again, off-again lover, who refused to make any kind of commitment, Kuzmin left for Okulovka on February 15 and spent the rest of the winter, the entire spring, and the early summer in its environs. He finished the poem cycle "The Feasts of the Most Holy Mother of God" ("Prazdniki Presvyatoi Bogoroditsy") in February. For the most part he worked in fits and starts on *Gentle Joseph* and on the short picaresque novel *The Journey of Sir John Fairfax* (Puteshestvie sera Dzhona Firfaksa), published in the February issue of *Apollo* (Apollon) in 1910 with illustrations by Sudeikin. He set the adventure tale in the late seventeenth century, and his usual hero-naïf is in this case an orphan with a lack of will and a propensity to encounter and give in to the worst, or at least the most colorful and treacherous, temptations the world has to offer.[64] This is a splendid entertainment whose narrative moves along briskly in a series of episodes that are blithely (and very deliberately) innocent of questions of verisimilitude or psychological analysis, its spare prose calling to mind a comment Kuzmin would make about "poets' prose" a few years later: "When poets write prose (Pushkin, Lermontov, Gautier, Bryusov), it turns out to have a special precision and, if you like, a dryness that particularly captivates us and that one will not encounter in prose writers who do not write verse (Gogol, Dostoevsky, Remizov)."[65] If he "relaxed" with *Fairfax*, he encountered little but frustration with his work on the narrative poem "The New Rolla" ("Novyi Rolla"), his attempt to continue Musset's 1833 Byronesque *Rolla*, which he had begun the year before.

In February the distance from Petersburg had at first only intensified his feelings for Poznyakov ("How jealousy is calmed by expansive space all around, and how love increases" [February 17, 1909]). He waited anxiously for his letters and any sign of remembrance, but while winter slowly turned into spring, they came with less and less regularity. As at similar bleak moments in the past, his thoughts kept turning to the idea of a "Russian refuge," of retiring to a monastery or to one of the Old Russian cities he so often saluted in his verse. That notion passed, as did his listlessness, as he found resolve for work and existence in reading Leskov. By the beginning of April, he had lost touch with Poznyakov (and patience with his clumsy lies): "No matter what Sergey Sergeevich answers, I don't think I'll go to the city. And just what kind of love is this anyway when it demands so much time for an explanation of it post factum!" He began to acknowledge to himself the mistake he had made: he had loved a pouting narcissist of small talent who milked his admirers for what they could do for him, and who was incapable of returning love or even affection. On May 7 he received news of Poznyakov from Auslender with indifference: "S[ergey] S[ergeevich] is 'wan and heavy,' well, so the hell with it! He will be the ruin of himself."[66] He had once planned to return to Petersburg after Easter, but with the end of the relationship with Poznyakov and with no solution to his financial problems in sight, he lingered on and on at his sister's, caught up in the bustling activities of his relatives and their many friends in the neighborhood. He worked on his novels, wrote a few poems, read Pushkin,

Ostrovsky, and Leskov, practiced the piano, gave music and French lessons to some of the neighbors, studied English with a visiting Englishman, and enjoyed the outings, card parties, and amateur theatricals of the Porakhina community.

He returned abruptly to the capital at the beginning of July, after quarreling with his sister and brother-in-law, who demanded that he leave. (They were furious that one of their neighbors, with whom their daughter was in love, was becoming too close to him.)[67] He again took up residence in the Severnaya Hotel. He was glad for the renewed company of friends such as Somov and the Ivanovs, even if the poet, himself comfortably well-off because of the estate of his wealthy late wife, did upbraid him for the mismanagement of his literary affairs and the failure to curb expenses, which still kept him desperately in debt. His prospects, indeed, looked as miserable as before. He had no money and no place but a hotel to live, and he feared that soon he would have nowhere to publish on any kind of regular basis, as both *Libra* and *The Golden Fleece* were on their last legs. Then, as unexpectedly as everything had fallen apart the year before, a series of providential events, the kind of thing in which he always placed so much faith, presented solutions for all his problems. On July 14 he noted that "as I was accompanying Gumilev [home from the Ivanovs'], I met S[ergey] Makovsky, who invited me to contribute to *Apollo*." The next day "Scorpio" sent a check, and on the seventeenth the Ivanovs, who had decided to "try to save him from the hotel," again offered him sanctuary in the "Tower": "Thank God, *vita nuova?* How many times it has begun. . . . Quiet, calm. To work. *Il n'y a que l'art*, as Bakst says after the collapse of his affairs of the heart."

He did not know it at the time, but the combination of Gumilev, Makovsky, *Apollo*, and Ivanov would prove an explosive one in the near future. For now, however, his *vita nuova* seemed on course, and he thanked the Ivanovs in a gracious poem that he addressed to Vera Shvarsalon:

> The homeless wanderer has found shelter
> after a nomadic life;
> no longer a wanderer or an exile,
> I am not myself from happiness.[68]

✥ 6 ✥

Disciple to Master: 1909–1910

DESPITE the promiscuity of his sexual life, Kuzmin craved the sense of permanence and place that a family, even if not of his own making, could offer. The move to Ivanov's apartment in 1909 brought the domestic stability he cherished, and his life resumed its old patterns, to his and Ivanov's satisfaction. The latter wrote:

> The abbé is pleasant. One needs Philostratus—he has that. With him one can talk about poetry, philology, music, Catholicism, the Old Believers, icons, Romanticism, the eighteenth, the seventeenth, etc., centuries, about antiquity—with the exception of any ideology and even generalizations that are too abstract. Therefore there is elegant culture without forced witticisms and skepticism, a cult of clear form, and the wisdom of pure phenomenology, and the aesthetics of pragmatism. Humanists of this kind still exist only among the Catholic clergy. In the evening he continued [his playing of] Mozart's *Don Giovanni*. . . . The abbé is reading his Diary for November 1907. (August 1, 1909)[1]

Soon Kuzmin's two small rooms, which had their own entrance from a back staircase, became a nucleus within the larger center of the Ivanov apartment, in and out of which went a stream of people at all times of the day and night.[2]

The atmosphere of the "Tower" had an immediate effect on Kuzmin's prose. He had been working on *Gentle Joseph* since January to meet deadlines as *The Golden Fleece* serialized it. In the novel's fourth and final part, the saintly Marina comes every day to read a saint's life from the *Prolog* to Joseph, and Ivanov believed that the novel's conclusion had taken this turn because of Kuzmin's return to his apartment:

> Kuzmin brought the concluding chapters of Joseph that he had finished writing today. As I read the scenes with Marina, I could not refrain from tears. . . . Kuzmin not only has beautifully fulfilled what I advised him to do about the final chapters . . . but has surpassed all my expectations. . . . He does not reason, but all the same, thinks, and the constant harmony of his consciousness is conditioned by the clear and profound solutions he has reached in the realm of spiritual problems. No doubt about it, the novel is something significant despite expectations. I am happy for Kuzmin. Friends find him radiant and joyful. He is happy, it seems, that he is living here, and his soul is serene. (August 6)[3]

Ivanov reiterated his high opinion of the novel in the critical article on Kuzmin's prose that he published several months later in the April 1910 issue (no. 7) of the new magazine *Apollo*.[4] That enterprise was now taking up much of his and Kuzmin's time.

Kuzmin had met Nikolay Gumilev, Aleksey Tolstoy, and Osip Mandelshtam, young writers who were starting to make a name for themselves, very early in 1909. He and Gumilev had particularly hit it off. The younger poet had invited him to take part in his new literary magazine *Island* (Ostrov, an "island of poets" [*ostrov poetov*]), where Kuzmin's "Feasts of the Most Holy Mother of God" appeared in May, in the first issue.[5] He also arranged for Kuzmin to publish, as he did himself, in "Glagolin's cheap rag" (*afishka*), as Kuzmin dubbed it, that is, in the *Magazine of the Theater of the Literary-Artistic Society* (Zhurnal Teatra literaturno-khudozhestvenogo obshchestva). Kuzmin was glad for the exposure, but the meager choices only demonstrated how badly he and others in the modernist camp needed more outlets for their works, especially now, faced as they were with the imminent demise of *Libra* and *The Golden Fleece*.

Sergey Makovsky, an energetic and enterprising young art critic and sometime poet, had conceived the idea for a new literary and artistic magazine in late November 1908. He at first thought to name it "Acropolis" (Akropol'), but decided instead on the name of the god of beauty and measure, Apollo, a "classicizing" gesture that shows the initial aims of the magazine.[6] Following his meeting with the no less ambitious Gumilev in January 1909, the two of them went about the job of gathering supporters for the venture.[7] That spring, Gumilev and his friends had asked some of the capital's "masters" of verse such as Ivanov, Voloshin, and Innokenty Annensky, Gumilev's former teacher and poetic mentor, to give a series of formal lectures at the "Tower" on the history of poetry and verse technique. (Kuzmin, in the countryside, first learned of this "Academy" on May 7, when Auslender mentioned it in a letter.) They used the large crowds of young writers attracted to the lectures, which were most often read by Ivanov, to form the nucleus of contributors for the magazine.

After his return to Petersburg, Gumilev and Makovsky drew Kuzmin into the inner circle that was planning *Apollo*. While grateful for Ivanov's "quiet refuge," Kuzmin soon became dispirited, "without money, without real projects, without love" (Diary, August 25), though he was enlivened by their attention even as he kept a wary eye on their mentors. He took a very guarded view of Ivanov's religio-theurgic conception of art, and he had reservations about Annensky the man and poet, as is revealed in an entry in the Diary, made after Gumilev introduced them at Tsarskoe Selo: "Annensky is rather strangely prim, with poetic emphasis, too unsystematic for a skeptic and wit, without *clarté* and definiteness. His verse now resembles Sluchevsky, now Zhemchuzhnikov" (August 9, 1909).

Annensky, for his part, obviously found much in Kuzmin's verse that was not to his liking, to judge by the less than flattering pages he devoted to him in the "They" portion of his quirky article "On Contemporary Lyricism," which dominated the critical section of the first three issues of *Apollo* in 1909:

The volume of his verse [*Nets*] is a book of great culture, even erudition, it seems, but also of considerable oddities. . . . In M[ikhail] Kuzmin's lyricism, amazing in its musical sensitivity, there is at times something almost terrifyingly intimate and tender, and all the more terrible because it is impossible not to believe him when he weeps. Our soul, *urban*, partly petrified, museum-like, has changed everything and has distorted a great deal.[8]

Vyacheslav Ivanov received a similarly ambiguous mixture of praise and censure in the same article, as Annensky advised him to work on his syntax and provide commentaries to his poems, whose "pedantry" made them inaccessible to a modern reader.[9] Still, uneasily or not, they all shared, with Balmont, Bryusov, Gumilev, and Voloshin, the poetry pages of the first issue of *Apollo*, which came out on October 24 with a critical preamble, much of it based on Annensky's and Ivanov's suggestions, proclaiming its "purely aesthetic" goals and its commitment to the Apollonian ideals of a "strict search for beauty" and poetic mastery.

When Guenther returned to Petersburg in October, he often found what Evgeny Znosko-Borovsky, the magazine's secretary, called the "young editorial board" of *Apollo*—Gumilev, Makovsky, Auslender, Aleksey Tolstoy, and Kuzmin—noisily gathered in Kuzmin's rooms at the "Tower" or, surrounded by other chattering young people, at its offices.[10] Kuzmin was of course much older than most of the others, and Znosko-Borovsky's words remind us just how tangentially Kuzmin seemed attached to the Symbolist camp in the eyes of some, especially the young, who would soon challenge its hegemony and the authority of the older generation. At the request of the young poets, the "poetic academy" had moved from the "Tower" to the editorial offices of *Apollo* in a two-story dark red private residence with a balcony facing the Moika Canal, not far from the house in which Pushkin had spent his last years, a bit of symbolism not lost on those associated with the magazine. It was formalized as the "Society of Devotees of the Artistic Word" ("Obshchestvo revnitelei khudozhestvennogo slova"), with a broad program of poetry evenings and lectures by a variety of speakers, and an executive committee (*sovet*) consisting of Kuzmin, Annensky, Blok, Gumilev, Ivanov, and Makovsky (a careful balance of the "young" and "old"), which presided over its activities.[11] Kuzmin was not thrilled by the idea of so official an organization, but, flattered at being chosen, he agreed to take part.

Such recognition did not translate into automatic publication in the pages of the new magazine. Kuzmin had been working on the narrative poem "The New Rolla" since 1908, and Ivanov was now reading it critically, suggesting revisions and twists and turns for its complex plot.

Kuzmin offered what he had written so far to *Apollo*, but it met with a cool response from Makovsky, who agreed to publish only a few fragments in the third issue. Though disheartened, Kuzmin kept laboring away, rather fruitlessly for the most part, before abandoning the task in 1910 and publishing it as an "unfinished novel in fragments" in *Clay Doves*.

He had hardly any more luck with the "Boring Conversation" ("Skuchnyi razgovor"), a programmatic statement of the goals of *Apollo* that he put together in September, at Makovsky's request, for "The Bees and Wasps of Apollo" section of the first issue. He used ideas, mostly those of Makovsky, Annensky, and Ivanov, which had been debated at an editorial meeting on September 12, and he thought up identities (the philosopher, the poet, the young composer, the skeptical lady, and so on) to mask the real people behind the participants in the imaginary dialogue.[12] On the twenty-first he read what he had written to Ivanov, who "became enraged, said that this is a caricature, etc." Kuzmin found the incident "extremely unpleasant," and two days later told Makovsky that he would no longer make any contributions to "The Bees" column. He dropped any plans he may have had to play an active part himself in working out the magazine's program.

After the shock of these experiences, Kuzmin might have thrown up his hands in exasperation and have had nothing more to do with the venture. He understood, however, that his own aesthetic position had much in common with several of the magazine's stated aims, especially its World of Art–like insistence on craftsmanship, good taste, and "defense of the cultural heritage," as the editors wrote in the first issue. The air of aestheticism and the high spirits that reigned among its young staff also attracted him, and we find entry after entry in the Diary throughout late 1909 and 1910 noting visits to the editorial offices and long conversations with Znosko-Borovsky and the other contributors, Gumilev in particular. On October 7 Makovsky asked him to be the reader for prose submissions and later persuaded him to edit the "Notes about Russian Fiction" section, for which he wrote regular reviews, some of the best criticism of contemporary Russian fiction published at the time. He also contributed often to the "Letters on Russian Poetry" section, which was supervised by Gumilev, and published poems and articles on occasion throughout the first three years of the magazine's existence. His career as a critic really began with the association with

Apollo, and the opportunity to exercise on a regular basis his critical sensibility and intelligence would serve him well after 1917, when he had to do reviewing on an almost daily basis.

Gumilev had been a frequent visitor to the "Tower" since 1909, presenting himself as Ivanov's humble pupil, while all the time organizing ventures, such as *Apollo*, that would allow him to take on the role of *maître* and mentor. His energy and spirit of adventure appealed to Kuzmin, who was certainly flattered by Gumilev's high opinion of his verse ("Among contemporary Russian poets, M. A. Kuzmin occupies one of the first places"), and by his repeated assurances that his poems and songs best expressed the spirit the new magazine wished to cultivate.[13] Gumilev, for his part, counted on Kuzmin as a useful ally in his attempts to seize the high ground of Russian letters. In the autumn of 1909 they were constantly in each other's company, Kuzmin a welcome guest of Gumilev's in Tsarskoe Selo, Gumilev often staying the night in Kuzmin's rooms when he missed the last train home. Throughout 1909–10 they exchanged chatty letters and dedicated prose and poems to each other.[14]

In November 1909 the friendship got Kuzmin into the middle of one of the oddest incidents in the history of Russian modernism. Early that month Makovsky had informed Annensky that he had decided, under pressure from Voloshin, to postpone publication of a large selection of his poems, already in proofs, in the second issue of *Apollo*, and replace them with twelve poems by an entirely unknown poet named Cherubina de Gabriak. (Some, like Akhmatova, blamed Annensky's death on November 30 from a heart attack on this gratuitous slight.)[15] They appeared accompanied by Voloshin's laudatory article about the young writer, "The Horoscope of Cherubina de Gabriak." What few knew was that no such person existed and that Makovsky had been the victim of a practical joke that soon took an ugly turn.

The real young woman behind the exotic pseudonym that Voloshin had dreamed up was Elizaveta Dmitrieva, a lame schoolteacher studying as an auditor at the university. After Makovsky had rejected some of the poems she sent him in September for the new magazine, Voloshin had urged her to send some others under the false identity. Her sad story has been told from several points of view (usually Voloshin's), which present Kuzmin's role as peripheral.[16] In fact, as the Diary relates, Kuzmin was in the thick of it, for he was the one to reveal to the astonished and mortified Makovsky ("Papa Mako," as he was known to the *Apollo* insiders) the identity of the mysterious woman from whom he had been receiving poems and letters. Makovsky not only had been completely taken in, but had become infatuated with the woman whom he had never seen but only spoken to from time to time over the telephone. He confessed all this to Voloshin, little suspecting that it was Voloshin himself who was writing all the letters and directing the course of the prank. (Dmitrieva herself was writing the accomplished poems.) That both Gumilev and Guenther were admirers of the real Dmitrieva further complicated the matter.

On November 11 Guenther "betrayed" to Kuzmin, no special admirer of her verse, "that de Gabriak is none other than Dmitrieva and still other unmaskings" (Diary). Three days later Kuzmin noted, "Gossip about Cherubina; I am now positive that it is El[izaveta] Iv[anovna]." On the sixteenth, the day before he told Makovsky what was going on, he wrote: "I dragged myself to *Apollo*. Makovsky conferred about the course of events. The thought that I have to reveal Cherubina to him torments me. The Count [Aleksey Tolstoy] corroborated everything about Cherubina. . . . How amazing that Dmitrieva–Cherubina keeps being pictured in an unattractive light. Really, a dirty business. The mistress of Gummi and of yet someone else [Voloshin himself, it was believed], and now of Guenther . . . what a respectable crowd" (Diary).

What had begun as a mischievous "mystification" took on an air of scandal when the men involved, each with a large and easily bruised ego, reacted to the revelation as though they had been cuckolded. A series of "explanations" followed, during one of which Gumilev made remarks to Dmitrieva that she found offensive. She reported them to Voloshin, who, on November 19, slapped Gumilev in front of most of the people associated with *Apollo*, who had gathered at Aleksandr Golovin's large studio high above the stage of the Mariinskii Theater to pose for a group portrait.[17] "When I returned," Kuzmin reports (he had slipped off to listen to Chaliapin singing *Faust* on the stage below), "and walked over to say hello to Maks, who was approaching, Gummi took me aside, saying that Vol[oshin] had just slapped him in the face, and he wants me to be his second. It turns out that it's all true. Maks had come up from behind and with his huge fist almost broke the nose of N[iko-lay] S[tepanovich], who had to be restrained. Everyone was astonished, especially Annensky" (Diary).

Three days later the two writers met with dueling pistols on a swampy field of honor outside the city, not far from Chernaya Rechka, the site of Pushkin's fatal encounter. The seconds—Kuzmin and Znosko-Borovsky for Gumilev, Tolstoy and the artist Aleksandr Shervashidze for Voloshin—had done everything they could to prevent bloodshed by arranging for the combatants to shoot at fifteen paces (other accounts say twenty-five). Gumilev had at first insisted on five and a duel to the death, and had been persuaded only with difficulty to change his mind. Kuzmin hardly cut a heroic figure: as the duel began, his nerves and legs gave way, and he plopped down in the snow, using a medical bag to cover his eyes. Gumilev's first shot missed, and Voloshin's pistol misfired twice. Gumilev did not take his second shot against the unarmed Voloshin; he would have continued, but the seconds brought the affair to an end, much to the dissatisfaction of Gumilev, and the two parted without shaking hands. Dmitrieva, on the verge of a nervous breakdown and with her reputation in tatters because of the wide and gleeful coverage of the scandal in the tabloid press, would write little for five years. Makovsky published one poem under her real name in the September 1910 (no. 10) issue of *Apollo*, along with thirteen poems of "de Gabriak." With that she disappeared from the mainstream of Russian literature, the real victim of the whole sorry affair.

As the rift in the circle connected with *Apollo* gradually mended following the duel, the old buoyancy, what Auslender called a "swirl of gaiety" (December 11), resumed. The Diary is full of testimony to Kuzmin's state of constant emotional excitement throughout the end of 1909, when he had a brief affair with the young artist Veniamin Belkin, who would illustrate "The New Rolla" for *Apollo*, and the beginning of 1910, as the business of the magazine occupied all his time. It took an obvious toll on his poetry: he had written a brief cycle entitled "The Three" ("Troe") in July–August 1909, but aside from the rare occasional poem and work on "The New Rolla," Kuzmin did not write another cycle of any kind until the summer of 1910, when, inspired by a new love affair, he set down "Autumnal May" ("Osennii mai").

Prose better suited his mood and the frenetic pace of the first half of 1910. He finished *The Journey of Sir John Fairfax* and several stories: "The Story of Xanthos, the Cook of King Alexander, and His Wife, Kalla" ("Rasskaz o Ksanfe, povare tsarya Aleksandra, i zhene ego Kalle"), a charming anecdote that could have been included in the novel about the exploits of the Macedonian conqueror; "A Hunter's Repast" ("Okhotnichii zavtrak") in March; "The Dangerous Guard" ("Opasnyi strazh") in the autumn (in both it and the previous story a man uses the pursuit of a woman to mask his real involvement with a man); and "Unexpected Provisions" ("Nechayannyi proviant"), a little Leskovian frame tale. In the best of them, "Lofty Art" ("Vysokoe iskusstvo"), written in August and dedicated to Gumilev, Kuzmin continued the habit of peppering his works with personal references: he gives his first name and patronymic to the narrator, has him accompany "his nephew, S. Auslender," to the railway station when the latter leaves for Florence, and recalls his own life there, "when I spent many months at the place of a jolly and strict canon who is still alive and well."[18] He composed quite a bit of music as well, and began work on his first important translation, Boccaccio's *Elegia di Madonna Fiammetta*, which he tried hard to find time to work on throughout the summer and autumn of 1910.[19]

Kuzmin's closeness with Gumilev and Makovsky following the de Gabriak scandal resulted in his first contribution to the "Letters on Russian Poetry" (in the December 1909 issue of *Apollo*) and the invitation to take over the "Notes on Russian Prose" column. The January 1910 issue of the magazine contained Kuzmin's reviews of a mixed bag of now forgotten writers and an article, "On Beautiful Clarity," which remains one of the best known and least understood parts of his literary legacy. In the years that immediately followed its publication, Gumilev and his young allies distanced themselves from the Symbolist masters, notably in papers read at the "Society of Devotees of the Artistic Word" on February 18, 1912, more than two years after the publication of Kuzmin's article. Appearing as it did, however, at the beginning of the year traditionally viewed as the "crisis of Symbolism" in Russia and shortly before a whole series of articles in which the leading Symbolists took stock of their past and future, "On Beautiful Clarity" has been taken by some to be the opening salvo in an attack on Symbolism itself, and has been viewed as a kind of "pre-manifesto" of the rival Acmeist movement, which Gumilev and Gorodetsky announced only in 1913 in the first number of *Apollo*.[20] This neatly linear cast of mind merely muddles a complex issue that requires careful reappraisal.

A remark in Ivanov's diary for August 7, 1909, further complicates matters: "I've thought up for Renouveau [Nouvel] the scheme for a union, which I christened 'clarists' (on the model of 'purists') from *'clarté.'*"[21] The term "clarism" figures prominently in Kuzmin's article, and the "ism" helps give it a programmatic air. Should we conclude, then, that the article was indeed a manifesto of some half-mythical union about which we know nothing more, and that Kuzmin had picked up on a suggestion of Ivanov's and organized some kind of opposition to Symbolism? Kuzmin enjoyed pranks, but after the recent fiasco around the Cherubina de Gabriak mystification he would have been unlikely to launch one of his own. In any event, we can find no mention of "clarists" or "clarism" in Kuzmin's writings either before or after the publication of the article and not a hint of anything in the Diary, although the word *clarté* does appear there from time to time as a mark of praise. Ivanov often used the word "clarity" to describe Kuzmin's art, but we can trace the exact formulation "beautiful clarity" not to him but to Heine, who used the phrase "schöne Klarheit" in the seventh letter of his 1837 *Über die französische Bühne.* Kuzmin certainly knew it, and when he finds the "cradle" of his *beau idéal* for prose style in "Latin lands" ("Romance countries were the cradle of the novella and novel, for there the *Apollonian* view of art was more developed than anywhere else, . . . exact and harmonious"),[22] he echoes Heine: "The French language, and also French declamation, are, like the people itself, reserved for the day and the present; the twilight realm of memory and premonition is closed to it: it thrives in the light of the sun, from which derives its *beautiful clarity* and warmth; foreign and inhospitable to it is the night, with pale moonlight, mystical stars, sweet dreams, and ghastly apparitions."[23] If Ivanov recognized the context from which Kuzmin had drawn the phrase "beautiful clarity," he would hardly have been pleased, for Heine was implicitly reproaching just the variety of German Romanticism that Ivanov so admired: he was translating Novalis's *Hymnen an die Nacht* at the very time Kuzmin's article appeared.

The Diary notes that on December 11, 1909, "Vyach[eslav] is expressing a desire to hear the article, which doesn't particularly suit me. But [when I read it to him] it did not turn out badly at all." Publication of the article did irritate the increasingly dogmatic and authoritarian Ivanov. As far as firsthand evidence permits us to judge, however, that was primarily because he suspected that Makovsky and others among "the young" were trying to appropriate Kuzmin for themselves and to use the article as a tool to exclude him and others from the magazine. Unfortunately, the letter of Znosko-Borovsky to Makovsky, in which the magazine's secretary outlined Ivanov's grievances, has apparently not been preserved, but Makovsky's reply to Ivanov has been.[24] His letter of February 2, 1910, gives a good picture of the rift developing between the literary generations and the way in which its editor personally viewed the article.

Makovsky challenged Ivanov's "most serious accusation," namely, that *Apollo* had "scorned the gains of modernism (speaking in general) of recent years" by turning "for the most part not to the masters, but to the young," by asserting that "all I ever did was invite the masters. . . . I began by recruiting you, Annensky, Bryusov, Balmont, Benois, and, finally, Volynsky." He could not be blamed if "internecine disagreements between them began from the first issue." Only Annensky, moreover, had really given himself "heart and soul to the cause of *Apollo*," and with his death and the failure of the others to take an active part in the magazine's affairs, to whom could he turn "for constant work, without which no magazine can exist?" "To whom," he continued, "if not to the *young* writers, whom I love and whom you yourself value so highly? In particular, was it not you who called Kuzmin a 'master'? . . . Kuzmin has truly proved to be a selfless worker in the magazine." Makovsky then turned to the key point of contention:

> But is Kuzmin the spokesman of *Apollo*'s "credo"? I think that he himself would hardly make such a claim. The word "clarism" that he launched accurately characterizes his personal evolution and coincides with one of those eternal ideals of art (clarity, simplicity), which, of course, the magazine cannot reject as it bears the name of the "god of measure and order," and which you too, of course, do not reject. But does that mean that "clarism" exhausts the task of literature, of good literature? For my part, in any case, it would be naive to resort to such unnecessary rigorism. For art always has many faces, and only he loves art who knows how to value the variety of enchantments within it. . . . The name *Apollo* covers everything that is genuinely artistic precisely because it cannot be defined with the exactness of a mathematical formula. . . . I protest against any doctrinaire attitude, especially a collective one. . . .
>
> Yes, the magazine must belong to no party, while remaining

deeply principled, not indulging either the coarse tastes of the public or the egos of individual contributors. . . . That is why I was so deeply pained by the reproaches you directed at *Apollo*, in which I hear some kind of incomprehensible ultimatum: either— or... Either "clarism" or "me." But it is utterly impossible to imagine a greater "clarist of thought" than you. "Clarism" is not a slogan that excludes an "open forum," but simply an old truth, often forgotten in our day, that one must strive for perfection of thought and word.[25]

As we see, the editor of *Apollo* gave no kind of special significance to "On Beautiful Clarity," and one day later he wrote to Znosko-Borovsky: "I was much amused by the incident with Vyach[eslav] Ivanov, in particular when it became clear that, in the end, his attacks on *Apollo* are simply his vexation at the fact that we are somehow making do without him too easily. . . . Is the magazine really worse because it has no 'ideology'? Who needs this Russian pontificating . . . ? Symbolism, neorealism, clarism, etc.—the public and we writers are, truly, sick and tired of all those . . . bugbears."[26] Nothing in the private papers of Kuzmin (or anyone else) suggests that he took a different view. Diversity of opinion about all the arts rather than any one "party line" marked the magazine from its inception, as is clear from the lively, often contentious debates that accompanied the working out of its program for the first issue and then continued on its pages. Kuzmin's article contributed to that climate of debate about art's aims.[27]

Above all else, we should remember that "On Beautiful Clarity" appeared in the same issue of *Apollo* in which Kuzmin began to review fiction, and that the article's subtitle, too often overlooked, is "Notes on Prose" ("Zametki o proze"). At a time of obsessive theorizing by writers, Kuzmin had always avoided making pronouncements about art, but he may well have thought it only proper now to put his cards on the table in a critical *profession de foi*, just what Ivanov had encouraged him to do in September 1909.[28] Far from being an attempt to avoid controversy, the subtitle accurately conveys what he discusses in the article, most of whose generalizations about prose style rest on his own practices in that medium, and not in verse, to which they have little relevance. His remarks about "style" call to mind Thomas Hardy's observation that "the whole secret of a living style . . . lies in not having too much style—being, in fact, a little careless, or rather seeming to be," as neat a characterization of Kuzmin's prose style as one could imagine. Mindful of Russian culture's increasing devotion to pastiche and appropriation, Kuzmin draws a careful distinction between what he calls a "sense of style" (*stil'nost'*, the writer's choice of a style appropriate to a given topic) and "stylization" (*stilizatsiya*, the writer's cloaking of his subject in the "exact literary form of a given era"), a clear warning to critics of his own prose and to those writers, such as Auslender and Remizov (whom he names), who at times lost sight of the difference.[29] Couching his words as friendly advice to prose writers (and to himself, as he remarks in the final sentence), Kuzmin employs an easygoing and delicately ironic manner that masks, but cannot conceal, enormous sophistication and broad reading as he goes about inventing his alternative culture in prose. He rounds up his usual suspects, unexpected only to those unfamiliar with his own art, from Western (Apuleius, the Italian and Spanish *novelliere*, Prévost, Lesage, Hoffmann, Poe, Flaubert, France, Henri de Régnier) and Russian (Pushkin, Leskov, Pechersky, Bryusov) literature who exemplify his "Apollonian" ideal of obedience to the "*laws* of clear harmony and architectonics." The call to be "logical in conception, in the work's structure, in syntax," regardless of the matter or manner, hardly offers anything so grand as an aesthetic theory, something about which the skeptical Kuzmin was deeply suspicious.[30] He never republished "On Beautiful Clarity" and excluded it from his one volume of collected critical essays, a sign, surely, that, unlike the critics who used its title as a catchall phrase to describe his writing, he did not regard it as an all-embracing aesthetic credo, much less a manifesto.

We by no means want to belittle the significance or the impact of the article. Regardless of Kuzmin's intention, an article that discussed art in such a deliberately modest way and without any of the metaphysics that Bely and Ivanov were advancing at the same time in their closely reasoned but often abstruse theories of Symbolism was bound to attract the attention of Kuzmin's fellow writers, especially the young. So must the comparisons of the writer to an architect (these may have influenced Mandelshtam's 1913 essay "The Morning of Acmeism" ["Utro akmeizma"]), and remarks such as "Besides immediate talent, knowledge of one's material and of form and a correspondence between it and the content are essential," or the very terms "clarity," "logic," "crystalline form," and "balance" *(stroinost')*—all of which are reminiscent of Pushkin's aesthetics. The very introduction of a new "ism" at a time when another—Symbolism—seemed to reign supreme had to strike many as a deliberate provocation. In fact, it may well have provoked the peevish Ivanov.[31]

Ivanov was concerned by the attention Kuzmin's article was receiving in literary circles and by the way some in *Apollo*, in his view, were using it. He laid out a ringing defense of Symbolism in a lecture he delivered in Moscow on March 17 at the "Society of Free Aesthetics" and then in Petersburg on the twenty-sixth at the offices of the magazine. Bryusov, who in January 1910 had urged Ivanov to speak out on his ideas about art, had attended Ivanov's Moscow reading, and he had not at all liked what he heard: "His fundamental idea—art must serve religion. I sharply protested."[32] A few days later, in a letter of March 23 to Petr Pertsov, his old friend from the heady days of the "new art's" first notoriety, Bryusov seized on Kuzmin's term: "The 'clarists' are defending *clarity*, clarity of thought, style, images . . . ; in essence they are defending 'poetry, whose aim is poetry'. . . . The mystics . . . in essence want poetry to serve their Christianity, for it to become *ancilla theologiae*. . . . I, as you suspect, am with the 'clarists' heart and soul."[33]

The Symbolist camp had ruptured in the theoretical dispute about the very nature of Symbolism that followed the publication in *Apollo* of Ivanov's "Testaments of Symbolism" ("Zavety simvolizma"), which was a reworking of his two lectures, with Ivanov, Blok, and Bely lined up against Bryusov's position that art serves art, not other aims, be they religious or theurgic.[34] Here the younger generation clearly sided with Bryusov, as did Kuzmin. On August 27, 1910, after the publication in *Apollo* of Bryusov's rejoinder to Ivanov and Blok, Kuzmin wrote Bryusov a letter that cleverly managed both to make his opinion clear and to distance himself from the fray by denigrating his own importance: "By a caprice of fate I have acquired the false appearance of someone who means something and who slightly signifies something in *Apollo*, and how difficult it was, there were so many reprimands, 'tongue-lashings' from all sides (mainly, of course, from Vyach[eslav] Ivanov). . . . When you sent us your article, you cannot imagine what good spirits, almost rejoicing, there was in the 'young' editorial board."[35]

After 1910 Kuzmin never again used the term "clarism," and he certainly never made the slightest attempt to set up any kind of group, much less a "school," under its banner. He returned only once to something resembling the ideas outlined in "On Beautiful Clarity" when, in a 1911 article about Gluck's opera *Orfeo ed Euridice*, he argued his own view of art from an appeal to the composer's words about "beautiful simplicity" *(prekrasnaya prostota)*.[36] By immediately adding, however, that Wagner might have said the same thing about his art, Kuzmin rather muddied the waters about just what he meant by "simplicity" or "clarity." And he ended the 1911 article with a sharply worded protest against the habit of evaluating creative artists in terms of schools and manifestos, which, he maintained, have nothing to do with artistic achievement.

With all this in mind, "On Beautiful Clarity," like the article about Gluck's opera, can best be seen as a declaration of artistic independence, a warning that the author was not about to allow himself to be made a partisan of any one side in the mounting polemics about the direction literature was to take in Russia. For Kuzmin this was a matter of principle. He stood apart from literary schools all his life, not because he was flippant and not because he found wrangling about definitions of artistic tenets boring, but because he opposed any attempt to "systematize" art and believed above all else in the independence of the artist, who must work out the principles of his own art by and for himself. Herein lie both the legacy of his lifelong devotion to Hamann and a deep personal conviction. Given Kuzmin's clearly expressed views on the poetic grouping that would variously call itself "Adamism" or "Acmeism," any suggestion that "On Beautiful Clarity" was a kind of pre-Acmeist treatise, written some two years before Acmeism was even a gleam in the eye of Gumilev or anyone else, must be challenged just as vigorously.

Gumilev, who had begun his poetic career as a self-proclaimed disciple of Bryusov and had then missed no opportunity to express his devotion to Vyacheslav Ivanov before becoming more and more critical of his view of art in 1910–11, finally asserted his independence once and for all with the founding of the "Poets' Guild" ("Tsekh poetov") in October 1911. Many of the older writers in Petersburg found its meetings highly offensive, for Gumilev imperiously presided as the new *maître*, maintaining a strict hierarchical discipline. Kuzmin simply regarded the whole enterprise and Gumilev's role in particular as preposterous, and he was amused by the very idea that one was somehow to perfect one's mastery as a poet in such a climate. Blok had taken one look and never reappeared; Kuzmin did attend a few meetings and, always in need of a place for his works, published some poems in the guild's magazine, *Hyperborean* (Giperborei), but he took no role in its activities. The poet and critic Vasily Gippius, a regular participant in the guild, recalled one of Kuzmin's visits: "Once, after Kuzmin—a rare guest at the guild—had read his poems, it suddenly turned out that no one had the urge to talk; the lyric power of the poems was so convincing that the previous cerebral analyses seemed insipid, and to talk about Kuzmin's poems would be like diluting wine with water."[37] It was at meetings of the guild that Gumilev and Gorodetsky, the "syndics" of the Acmeism to come, worked out its ideology over the summer and autumn of 1912.

One could certainly make the case that Kuzmin's early verse has something in common with the principles that Gumilev, Akhmatova, Mandelshtam, and, to some degree, Gorodetsky were practicing in their verse in those years. If, however, that is all it means to be an "Acmeist," then Vladimir Narbut and Mikhail Zenkevich, whom the other four always named as part of the movement, would have to be excluded from it because of their quite different poetic stance. Yet the poetics of writers such as Boris Sadovskoy, Vladislav Khodasevich, Georgy Ivanov, and others would give them a place in it, although that would mean ignoring the fact that the first two were outspokenly hostile to Acmeism (Sadovskoy even tried to start a specifically anti-Acmeist magazine, *Galathea* [Galateya]), while none of the six "official" Acmeists ever included the third in their group, despite his very close contacts with the guild and all its activities. From the outset, Gumilev drew a sharp distinction between those who took part in the guild and Acmeists proper. In March 1913, in a letter to Bryusov, he wrote, "It is imperative that everyone writing about acmeism knows that the 'Poets' Guild' stands completely apart from acmeism (there are twenty-six members in the first, there are only six poet-acmeists)."[38] As Akhmatova never tired of saying, only six people represented Acmeism as historical phenomenon, and, in an echo of the famous remark about the Third Rome, a seventh there was never to be.[39] As the six went about working out certain general positions on art, they paid equal attention to formulating special principles of conduct to oppose to Symbolism's "creation of life" *(zhiznetvorchestvo)*, that variation of Romantic idealism that sought to merge art and life in a supreme religious act that might reach the Absolute. Not a single one of the six ever invited Kuzmin to participate in either activity, and Akhmatova categorically rejected the suggestion that Kuzmin had had anything whatever to do with Acmeism.[40]

Kuzmin always disputed the notion, no less vehemently, that he had had something to do with the origins of the movement or had been a part of it, and his many statements about the matter leave no room for doubt. He made no mention of it in any autobiographical utterance, and in one he put the matter bluntly to rest by saying, "I quickly parted with the *Apollo* group, just as I did with the Poets' Guild."[41] Indeed, by late 1912, when Gumilev became the literary editor of *Apollo* and tried without success to make it the organ of the views that would be called Acmeism, Kuzmin was no longer writing his columns for it. A year after Acmeism had launched its "official" existence, Kuzmin definitively stated his position in the article "The Meditations and Perplexities of Petr Otshelnik [Peter the Hermit]":

> Everything that is complete and perfect is already intolerance, ossification, an end. But then how do Symbolists, Acmeists, and Futurists exist? To the eye of the impartial observer, they do not exist. Individual poets, who have joined with one or another school, do exist, but there are no schools. Since the time our Symbolists began talking about the symbolism of Dante or Goethe, Symbolism as a school ceased to exist, because it is obvious to everyone that it is now a matter of poetry in general, which often has a symbolic property. A school is always a summing up, a deduction from the works of a generation that saw things in the same way, but it is never a postulate for creation, which is why I dare to assure the Futurists and especially the Acmeists that concern for theoretical and programmatic proclamations can perform a service for anything you like, but not for art, not for creation. . . . And in the abundance of schools one can see only the ferment of critical thought (but not creation), if not personal ambitions.[42]

The remarks bear all the signs of Kuzmin's deeply held views, and he would repeat them more than once in the 1920s as well, always setting himself apart from Acmeism or any other school, and always in the same terms: rules and theories, like guilds and manifestos, have no place in art and creation. He would repeat, too, the comment about "personal ambitions," a transparent allusion to Gumilev, in the 1921 article "Dreamers," where he asserted that Acmeism was a literary school "fabricated by one person (in this case by Nikolay Gumilev)."[43]

Although Kuzmin had nothing to do with the organization of the Acmeist movement and wanted no part of it, the question of Kuzmin and Acmeism requires convincing resolution. In all his statements Kuzmin carefully disassociates himself first and foremost from *formal* alliance with the group and especially from those characteristics (primarily represented by Gumilev) that he found distasteful: its attempts to teach poets how to write and its excessive concern, from his point of view, with problems of form at the expense of poetry itself. But it is impossible to imagine that the poet who had daringly written of "Chablis on ice, toasted white bread" at the high point of Symbolism's triumph in Russian letters did not have an influence on the young poets who were distancing themselves from the Symbolist view of the world. The example of much (by no means all) of Kuzmin's early verse, especially those poems which took their subject matter from the provocative immediacy of experience and the reality of contemporary life in its most public, familiar, widely shared aspect, profoundly affected this younger generation as they looked for new "masters" and predecessors. Akhmatova, after all, called him her "wondrous teacher" in inscribing one of her books to him.[44] Kuzmin's view of the world is by no means identical with that of the Acmeists—nor did its three major poets share a single view—but it is closer to theirs than to that of Symbolists such as Sologub, Gippius, Blok, Bely, and Ivanov.[45]

We perhaps see the closeness most clearly in a short letter Kuzmin sent to the editorial board of *Apollo* in the spring of 1912 in the aftermath of the mutilated publication of his review of the first book of Vyacheslav Ivanov's *Cor Ardens* in the first issue of the new Symbolist magazine *Works and Days* (Trudy i dni), whose editors had cut the ending of the review because the "views and opinion expressed there did not coincide with the opinion of the editorial board."[46] He protested against such high-handed treatment, and used the letter as a platform for stating his major disagreements with the ideas of those Symbolists—most notably Bely, Ivanov, and Blok—who had started the magazine as a forum for their views. Kuzmin's first point contained his primary objection:

Religious or moral demands of any kind, no matter how right they may be, cannot be applied to the theory of art, which does not need the constrictions of religion and philosophy for its origin. While fully recognizing the necessity of a religious principle for the poet as a creative personality, it is impossible not to see that meditations about it go right past art. . . . All the same, theoreticians of art are not John Chrysostoms, although the latter, perhaps, were more important for poets.[47]

Kuzmin may have taken no part in formulating the positions of Acmeism, but Gumilev certainly read this letter with eyes wide open, and it sounds in this point like a draft for parts of Gumilev's manifesto "Acmeism and the Legacy of Symbolism" ("Nasledie simvolizma i ak-meizm"), published eight months later in *Apollo*, even if Kuzmin's views have their source in quite different premises.

Oddly enough, one of the most revealing testimonies to Kuzmin's skeptical attitude about Acmeism is the great interest he showed in the poetic experiments of the Russian Futurists, to whom one might have thought the apostle of "beautiful clarity" and "simplicity" would have been irredeemably hostile. It began from the time that the young Viktor Khlebnikov (not yet either Velimir or a Futurist) appeared at Ivanov's "Tower" at the end of 1908. Throughout 1909 he attended Ivanov's lectures on verse and showed up on occasion at the "Wednesdays." Ivanov and Kuzmin took an immediate liking to him, and gave the shy and modest young student encouragement. On September 12, 1909, Kuzmin wrote in the Diary, "They are saying that I am acting as his patron, but there is something striking and unusual in his poems," and on September 20 he called Khlebnikov's poems "mad and full of genius" (*genial'no-sumasshedshie*).[48] Not long after that, Khlebnikov broke his slender ties with the *Apollo* circle and strengthened his contacts with those poets in Petersburg and Moscow who would take the name Futurists. He and Kuzmin saw each other very rarely, but remained on excellent terms, and in 1917 Khlebnikov included him in his utopian society "Chairmen of the Earth."[49] Kuzmin, who often criticized the Futurists' relentless penchant for composing manifestos, wrote in 1921 that "Khlebnikov and Vyacheslav Ivanov are wonderful poets *in spite of* Symbolism and Futurism and not because they belong to these schools."[50]

Another guest at the "Tower" when "On Beautiful Clarity" appeared in print was Andrey Bely, who came to Petersburg at the end of January 1910. He and Ivanov spent long hours working on a program for the new Symbolist "collective" called "Musagetes" ("Musaget," a clear challenge to *Apollo* by the very title) and its related "Orpheus" and "Logos" publishing ventures, and they struggled without success to find some resolution for the triangular "Brotherhood" that Mintslova was now trying to create. This "period of excruciating misunderstandings" with Ivanov and Mintslova took its toll on Bely's nerves, already worn thin by a demanding meditative regimen imposed by Mintslova, and Kuzmin's charm and attentiveness did much to keep him to some degree on an even keel.[51] Bely loved the impromptu concerts organized late in the evening or early morning when Kuzmin sat at the piano, responding to the requests of Ivanov and the most intimate regulars of the "Tower," and sang, often until four in the morning, his own songs in his "wheezy, cracked voice, but it came out marvelously."[52] When the various inhabitants of the "Tower" reassembled around one in the afternoon, Bely invariably found Kuzmin, "cozy, black-haired, knitted brows, totally at home, baldish," sitting in a Russian shirt at the table in the dining room and working on a manuscript, activity he would cheerfully interrupt to make tea from the boiling samovar and have a chat and a smoke.[53]

At the summons of Mintslova, Bely left for Moscow with Ivanov early in March, but he and Kuzmin remained on cordial terms. In the summer, in a review of the prose published on the pages of *Libra*, Kuzmin singled out Bely's "symbolic-realist" novel *The Silver Dove* (Serebryanyi golub') for special mention, and wrote that despite flaws in plotting and characterization and some stylistic excesses, its "vision blinds" and this "finest work" of Bely had opened up new paths for the Russian novel.[54] Bely late that summer wrote Kuzmin that he still remembered "with pleasure" the days they had spent together, and invited him to contribute to a miscellany that "Musagetes" was planning. Kuzmin responded with the newly written "Autumnal May," which appeared in the *Anthology "Musagetes"* the next year.

Before leaving for Moscow, Bely had memorialized his days in Petersburg with a verse "improvisation," two lines of which—"The carpet is no longer a carpet, but a meadow—/ Flowers bloom, vales glitter"—indicate that he may have witnessed some of the rehearsals at the "Tower" for what was to be one of the most celebrated amateur experimental theatricals in the history of the Russian stage.[55] The lines sound like a description of one scene of that production, in which a flowered green rug thrown on the floor by the actors represented the meadow in which they stood. In the autumn of 1909, Vera Shvarsalon had suggested to Meyerhold that he direct a production of Calderón's *Devoción de la Cruz* (*Poklonenie Krestu* in Balmont's translation) at the Ivanov apartment. Kuzmin had taken an active role in all the planning, which had gone on since early November of 1909.[56] It opened at the "Tower Theater" on April 19, 1910.

True to the habits of the "Tower," the performance began at 11:15 in the evening. The guests, admitted by special invitation, found a small, low stage in the largest room of the apartment. Behind it hung a black and dark green backdrop, resembling a large carpet, decorated with bright red and yellow flowers. Sudeikin had designed the vividly colored sets and costumes, or rather had improvised them from the variety of fabric scraps that Zinovieva-Annibal had collected over the years. Only lamps and candles illuminated the action, which took place virtually in the midst of the audience, which was seated and standing on all sides. Meyerhold, fascinated by all forms of popular entertainment and determined to integrate sound, color, and movement, made every aspect of the production stress deliberate theatricality, what he called the "theater of conventions" (*uslovnyi teatr*), even artificiality, in order, as one reviewer noted, to evoke the naïveté of the sixteenth- and seventeenth-century Spanish theater.[57] The use not of professional performers but of members of the Ivanov family and of their and his friends as the cast underscored this intention, although by all accounts they played their parts with great skill. (Kuzmin performed two roles, Curcio, an old man, in one scene, and a young man in another; there was no music.)[58] Meyerhold wanted to break down the artificial barriers between audience and players that the very design of contemporary theaters created, and the whole production conformed to his evolving concept of the theater as "fairground booth" (*balagan*).[59] Painted throws of various kinds suggested the scenery; the actors themselves carried the few props on and off the stage, often right through the audience; and two boys costumed as blackamoors (they were actually the sons of the building's awe-inspiring doorman) operated the curtain, one of several innovations employed in the production which Meyerhold later incorporated into his celebrated staging of Molière's *Dom Juan* at the Aleksandrinskii in November 1910.

Aleksandr Golovin, an older associate of the World of Art and one of

the greatest scenic designers of the age, did the costumes and sets for
that production, as he did for most of those that Meyerhold directed at
the Imperial Theaters, where he had received an appointment in 1908.
In 1909 Meyerhold had introduced Kuzmin to the courtly Golovin, a
man with the manners of a grandee and the cultivation of a savant.
Not long afterwards, the editors of *Apollo* had commissioned him to
do a group portrait of their closest collaborators. Annensky, Ivanov,
Voloshin, and Kuzmin assembled on November 13 at Golovin's studio
in the Mariinskii to work out the picture's formal arrangement. The
backstage atmosphere, which brought back a flood of memories of
the Komissarzhevskaya 1906–7 season, once again captivated Kuzmin:
"Golovin was downstairs and himself escorted me past the dressing
rooms. The wings of a theater intoxicate me. His studio is marvelous,
the designs for *Orfeo*, the portrait of [Count Vladimir] Kankrin . . .
Golovin himself with his gray hair and young face, affectionate and
courteous—everything was enchanting" (Diary).[60] After Voloshin
slapped Gumilev on the nineteenth during what was to have been the
first sitting for the group picture, the painter abandoned all thought of
continuing the project. But, as he wrote in his memoirs, he had been
struck by Kuzmin's appearance, and was determined to do a portrait of
him.[61] He asked Kuzmin the very night of the nineteenth, and began
work on the portrait on December 18, 1909 (not in October, as Golovin
erroneously writes in his memoirs), not finishing it until the spring of
1910, after some twenty sittings. The portrait, depicting Kuzmin standing in one of his famous vests, partially turned to the viewer, in one of
the Mariinskii's large scenery workshops, is by far the finest of many
pictures of the author. It fixes forever what Golovin observed in a verbal
portrait: "Kuzmin has a peculiar non-Russian appearance. At the time
that I painted his portrait, he had a mustache and goatee . . . later his
appearance changed, he started shaving his mustache and goatee, and as
a result his outer apppearance became perhaps even more distinctive
and expressive."[62]

Golovin already admired Kuzmin's verse when they met, and he
never wavered in his opinion that Kuzmin was the "most outstanding
poet of the *Apollo* circle," an "incomparable . . . absolutely out of the
ordinary, and striking poet."[63] The painter shared the poet's interest in
the culture of the eighteenth century and, of course, in the theater,
and during the long sittings for the portrait, when Kuzmin impressed
Golovin with his cleverness and the breadth and availability of his cul-

ture, mutual sympathy grew into a friendship that lasted until the artist's death in 1930. Because of his influential position, Golovin, prodded no doubt by Meyerhold, saw to it that his friend received several well-paid commissions from the Imperial Theaters in Petersburg.

Kuzmin first collaborated with the Aleksandrinskii when he wrote music for Meyerhold's production of Ernst Hardt's five-act drama on the Tristan theme, *Tantris der Narr*, which opened on March 9, 1910, in a translation edited by Kuzmin and Ivanov. Golovin's high opinion of Kuzmin's talents as a translator led him to arrange for several commissions to translate opera librettos as well. Kuzmin finished the first, Massenet's recently written *Don Quichotte*, for Moscow's Bol'shoi Theater in August 1910. (The premiere, with Chaliapin in the title role, took place on November 12.) Kuzmin then embarked on Richard Strauss's *Elektra*, which he speedily completed, although it had to wait until February 18, 1913, for its first performance at the Mariinskii, in a production by Meyerhold and Golovin.[64]

Kuzmin's employment by the Imperial Theaters marked the onset of a period in which projects for the stage took more and more of his time. He seriously began his long career as a drama critic with a review in the "Petersburg Theaters" column in the "Chronicle" section of *Apollo* in January 1910. There he gave a highly favorable notice to Yury Belyaev's "dear and captivating" play *Putanitsa or the Year 1840* (Putanitsa ili sorokovoi god), in which Olga Glebova-Sudeikina returned to the stage in the title role after a two-year absence.[65] (It is one of her several guises in the "1913: Petersburg Tale" section of Akhmatova's *Poem without a Hero* [Poema bez Geroya], in which Kuzmin also figures prominently; Akhmatova alludes to Sudeikin's portrait of his wife costumed for the role.) Sudeikin and his wife were again living in Petersburg, and after Kuzmin's return to the capital in 1909 they became constant companions and made him the confidant of the course of their turbulent relationship.

At the "Tower Theater" Meyerhold had been able to try out some of his ideas for a "truly theatrical theater," but he wanted a wider public than that one-night occasion had offered, and he needed a more permanent testing place for ideas still too daring for the Imperial Theaters.[66] He also believed that "short forms" would best allow him to put a variety of his experiments into practice. He particularly valued Kuzmin's talents for just that type of theatrical diversion, which rejected the tendentious approach that both men believed had marked the nineteenth-century Russian theater and had brought it into such decline. In the 1911 article "Russian Dramatists," he included Kuzmin among those "founders of the New Theater" (others were Ivanov, Blok, Sologub, Remizov, Bely, Zinovieva-Annibal, Znosko-Borovsky, and, looking decidedly odd in this company, Vladimir Soloviev), who were "trying above all else to revive one or another peculiarity of one of the theaters of truly theatrical ages," as opposed to the "antitheatrical" works of the "realists" and "decadents." He saluted Kuzmin for "writing plays in the spirit of medieval drama and also reconstructing the French comic theater" on Russian soil, for only by returning to the origins of western European drama could the Russian theater overcome its crisis.[67] Kuzmin reflected just that spirit in the two playlets on which he set to work late in the summer for the new venture that Meyerhold was planning and in which he took the closest part.

In September 1910 Auslender added a "P.S." to his regular "Petersburg Theaters" column in *Apollo* informing his readers of the imminent opening of a new theater, the "Interlude" ("Intermediya"), in the former headquarters of the Folktale Theater (Skazka), on Galernaya Street. He explained that its repertory would consist of "old and new farces, comedies, pantomimes, operettas, vaudevilles, short dramas, and individual numbers."[68] Although it was run in name by an "Association [*tovarishchestvo*] of Actors, Artists, Writers, and Musicians," only three people in fact composed its artistic board and gave the "House of Interludes" ("Dom intermedii"), as it was officially named, motivation and direction: Meyerhold, Sapunov, who had returned to Petersburg and was in charge of all artistic matters, and Kuzmin, responsible for literary and musical arrangements.[69] Vladimir Telyakovsky, director of the Imperial Theaters, had advised Meyerhold to adopt a pseudonym to avoid any appearance of conflict of interest with his duties at the state theaters. At Kuzmin's suggestion he chose Doctor Dapertutto, the magician and eerie genius of Hoffmann's "Geschichte vom verlornen Spiegelbilde" from the *Fantasiestücke in Callots Manier*. It became the alter ego he used throughout this phase of his career.

The "House of Interludes" opened formally on October 12, 1910, the most "brilliant and lively evening" one reviewer could remember.[70] The audience took its places not in the usual serried rows of seats, but at small tables that created an informal atmosphere of "graceful, easy merriment." Meyerhold had removed all the footlights, thus destroying that artificial division between stage and viewers, and he used a wide staircase to integrate the tiny stage with the audience, one of his favorite devices. Kuzmin wrote text and music for a short "prologue" entitled "The Reformed Eccentric" ("Ispravlennyi chudak"; the work has not survived). It was intended to induce a mood of "Hoffmannesque fantasy" and "mocking grotesquery" in the audience as "dolls metamorphosed into live actors" (an allusion to Hoffmann's Doctor Coppelius) and people who were ostensibly members of the audience stepped onto the stage to take part in the pantomime that followed, with a "wooden Schnitzler and Dohnányi," the pantomime's author and composer, on stage with them.[71] Meyerhold's "transcription" (actually a very free adaptation) of Arthur Schnitzler's harlequinade pantomime *Der Schleier der Pierrette* (called *Columbine's Scarf* [Sharf Kolombiny]), the brilliant centerpiece of the program, was followed by Kuzmin's "elegant pastoral" *The Dutch Girl Liza* (Gollandka Liza), a one-act play "with music and dancing" loosely based on the thirteenth-century French *Jeu de Robin et de Marion*. The troupe performed it in a setting designed by Sapunov, who, with Anatoly Arapov, did the sets and costumes for the whole evening.[72] A "playlet-grotesque" called *Black and White* (Blek end uait) by Petr Potemkin and the actor Konstantin Gibshman, described as a "Negro tragedy," although it appears to have been the Russians' idea of a minstrel show and was played for laughs as though written in English, concluded the program. The theater repeated the program twenty-five times before closing to work on a new evening of entertainments.

The second program, once again prepared by Meyerhold, opened on December 3, 1910. It included Ivan Krylov's 1793 comic operetta *The Rabid Family* (Beshenaya sem'ya), with Kuzmin's music, and Znosko-Borovsky's comedy *The Converted Prince or Amor omnia vincit* (Obrashchennyi prints), for which Kuzmin wrote music and the lyrics for several songs and Sudeikin did the costumes and sets. A series of concert numbers performed by Gibshman, Nikolay Petrov (better known to Petersburg friends and audiences as "Kolya Peter"), and Bela Kazaroza, a popular variety hall singer, brought the evening to an end.[73] She sang Kuzmin's "songs for children" ("pesenki dlya detei") with "enormous success," among them "If it will be sunny tomorrow" and the no less renowned "The Child and the Rose":

> Child, don't reach for a rose in the spring,
> you can pick all the roses you want in the summer,

> violets are gathered in the early spring,
> remember that there are no violets in the summer.[74]

For Kuzmin's contemporaries, the "subtle poison" of these songs captured all the *carpe diem* lightheartedness of the time, even when it had vanished irrevocably and seemed a distant fantasy.

The second program of the "House of Interludes" enjoyed less success than the first, but it was repeated many times throughout the spring of 1911. The theater closed for the summer, but preparations began for a new season in the autumn. The troupe visited Moscow in October, where it presented an evening of numbers from its first two programs, among them *The Reformed Eccentric* and the "songs for children." Critics received it well, but there was little public success. On the fourth of the month Kuzmin, who had stayed in Petersburg, noted in the Diary, "The 'Interlude,' it seems, has bombed (*shlepnulas'*) in Moscow." The theater had stretched its meager financial resources to the breaking point, and it could not reopen when it returned to Petersburg.[75]

Kuzmin had by no means been ignoring other genres. "Scorpio" issued two volumes of his collected prose, the *First Book of Stories* and the *Second* in 1910, but they included only works written between 1906 and 1909. Far more significant was his return to poetry after a lull precipitated by the end of his relationship with Sergey Poznyakov and the brief affair with Veniamin Belkin. What he called a "parched spell" in his amorous life had followed, but he more than made up for that drought in the two years after the summer of 1910, as the array of dedications in *Autumnal Lakes* demonstrates. One name, however, does stand out there and in a listing of his works that he compiled in 1923, where, under the 1910 heading "Poetry," we find only "Poems to Knyazev." Kuzmin wrote other poems that year, but the starkness of the entry indicates how unique a place Knyazev occupied in both his personal and his creative life at the time. There would be only one other such listing in all the years to come.

We now know what little there is to know about the biography of Vsevolod Knyazev thanks to the work of commentators on the mysteries and mystifications of Akhmatova's *Poem without a Hero*, in which he appears as the "cornet of the dragoons with his verse / and a meaningless death in his breast."[76] Guenther writes only that he was a "handsome, slender young man with warm brown eyes and severely parted brown hair, from a good St. Petersburg family," a description that accords with surviving photographs.[77] Kuzmin was close to thirty-eight when he met the nineteen-year-old Knyazev for the first time on Sunday May 2, 1910, at Pavlovsk, where he was in the company of the infamous "friend of poets," the actress and poetaster Pallada (or Palladiya) Starynkevich, but Gross or Berg or Deryuzhinskaya or Peddi-Kabetskaya (and several others) by her various marriages. (She published her poems, meretricious imitations of Kuzmin and Akhmatova, under the name Bogdanova-Belskaya.)[78]

Georgy Ivanov immortalized her in the poem beginning "A January day. On the shore of the Neva / a wind sweeps by, wafting destruction" as among those women who "shone in the year 1913": "Where is Olechka Sudeikina, alas! / Akhmatova, Pallada, Salomeya?"[79] Akhmatova, incredulous that Lidiya Chukovskaya had never heard of the notorious libertine, was decidedly less lyrical in her succinctly catty characterization: "She was renowned. Ankle bracelets, Homeric fornications *(blud)*. Once in my presence she said to a woman friend: 'I had a fabulous apartment on Mokhovaya. Do you remember who I was living with then?'"[80] Knyazev, like many others, fell under the spell of this femme fatale, who disgusted Kuzmin (certainly no prude in such matters, to say the least) by the flagrancy of her domestic and sexual *moeurs*, which he depicted in a very thinly disguised fashion in the misogynous portrait of "Polina," who does no man any good, in his 1914 novel *Travelers by Sea and Land* (Plavayushchie-puteshestvuyushchie).

Kuzmin had found himself immediately attracted to Knyazev's signal good looks, and by the middle of May he was seeing the young hussar almost every day, very often in the company of the twenty-five-year-old Pallada, whose reputation was no secret to him. The Diary for this whole period creates a vivid picture of the hysterical atmosphere, filled with jealous scenes and recriminations, in which Knyazev played out his affair with her. Kuzmin's growing involvement with the young man put him in the middle of their erotic skirmishes, and on occasion Kuzmin witnessed scenes that made him wonder if he had wandered into a parody of the worst "scandals" in Dostoevsky's novels.[81] He was puzzled by Knyazev's coquettish behavior—he kept asking Kuzmin to dress him in his clothes, sent flowers, vowed he wanted to be Kuzmin's "one and only friend," said he was not afraid of an affair, while professing his love for Pallada in her and Kuzmin's presence—and on May 27 Kuzmin warned himself that he must not give himself up to this "aimless love" or else he would "perish." Nonetheless, infatuation slowly evolved into something like what he had experienced earlier when he thought he had at last found the "companion in life and art" he kept seeking, even if from the outset he kept fearing that his relationship with this "slightly revised edition of Viktor Andreevich," that is, Naumov, might turn out the same way that had.

Kuzmin had never before, however, found himself embroiled in such a bizarre ménage as this one. On May 24 he wrote in the Diary: "Vsevolod says that Pallada is jealous of him and me and so on. . . . Pallada told Valechka [Nouvel] a lot, even more than a lot, that she's in love with me, that if he will make me available to her, she will fix him up with Knyazev, etc. In general, an incredible mess *(kasha)*." At the beginning of June, Knyazev swore to Kuzmin that he had broken with Pallada once and for all. Kuzmin wondered if he could believe him, but soon after the young man began his involvement with Kuzmin. It would prove hardly any less complicated and stormy than his affair with Pallada had been, and was colored by what Kuzmin called the "Palladism" of Knyazev's behavior, his synonymn for sluttishness, unreliability, and gratuitous cruelty.

In the past, Kuzmin's love affairs had rarely seen out more than a year, often just a few months. The relationship with Knyazev lasted for two and a half years, until September 1912. Its longevity may have been attributable to the fact that the young man was a poet, if of no unusual talent. Kuzmin immediately introduced him to the circle around *Apollo*, where on occasion he read his poems, but he could never persuade his friends there or, with one exception, anywhere else to publish his verse.[82] The affair was also very much on and off, complicated both by Knyazev's character (Kuzmin was once again involved with a man of ambiguous sexuality) and by the long absences from Petersburg that his military service made necessary.

On June 9 Knyazev, "extremely tender and desirable," left Petersburg to spend the summer at his family's home in the Baltic, and Kuzmin found solace for his absence (and surcease for the lingering doubts about Knyazev's real feelings for him) in verse. Between June and August he wrote the eleven poems of the first of the "Knyazev cycles," "Autumnal May," which he dedicated to him when it was published in *Autumnal Lakes*. In its first poem, the poet acknowledged that this new love ("May," like "April," invariant metaphors for love in his verse, in the "autumn" of the poet's life) had broken the logjam of his long poetic silence:

> With what should I begin? Poems, like a herd of frisky goats,
> are rushing in an impatient throng
> to my soul, silent for so long. . . .
> You appeared . . .
> Now I know, proud and happy,
> with what I should begin.[83]

Two letters came in June, but then, as with Maslov, Naumov, and Poznyakov, nothing. Kuzmin fretted in the capital, but finally, on July 12, he received a "letter from Vsevolod, he is coming on August 9. He writes that he is pained by my jealousy at his smiles for others; ah, how well I know arguments like that!" (Diary). Knyazev then disappears from the Diary for almost a month; he also does so in a "real" sense from the verse written at the same time. As Kuzmin remarked in the Diary on July 26: "I am becoming lyrical, because I cannot embrace the unembraceable."

"All first names are pale, and all names are old, / but love is new every time," Kuzmin wrote in the cycle's sixth poem, adding, "the words grow old, but not the heart."[84] As in the poetry addressed to earlier lovers, Kuzmin "embraces the unembraceable" by foreseeing an ideal resolution of his doubts—"'May will ensue for us in August too!'"—and by creating in "Autumnal May" an ideal spiritual and physical "other," in which the "real" object of the love virtually disappears behind a depersonalized mask.[85] In this Kuzmin follows a Neoplatonist tradition widespread in the Italian Renaissance and celebrated in a quatrain by Michelangelo, whom he translated:

> Love, your beauty is not a mortal thing:
> there is no face among us that can equal
> the image in the heart, which you kindle and sustain
> with another fire and stir with other wings.[86]

We can know the person who inspired the verse, he can even be named directly, but he appears only as certain attributes which, specific though they may sometimes be (Knyazev's "green hussar jacket" in one poem, for example), move the reader from a "real" to an "ideal" level.[87]

During the first months with Knyazev, Kuzmin often found his thoughts returning to another young officer: Naumov. Consciously or unconsciously, that left its mark on the poetry of "Autumnal May." Two figures long absent from his verse, but closely associated with the poems to Naumov (they do not figure at all in those addressed to Poznyakov), now reappear: Eros, in the sixth poem of the cycle ("As before, winged Eros hovers / and threatens with his sharp arrow," a major motif in future poems to Knyazev), and the Guide or Holy Warrior, with whom he associates the idealized figure of Knyazev.[88] In the cycle's second (and third) poem we reencounter the exalted eroticism of the "mystic cycles" of the third section of *Nets:*

> Thrice you came, sword-bearing messenger,
> into the dark crypt of oppressing passions,
> and you were luring me into another land.
> How can I now avoid your call?
> I burn, my bridegroom, the yellow frankincense,
> as I sense the nearness of shining white wings.[89]

During the years of his involvement with Knyazev, Kuzmin worked on a prose study of the heavenly figures, archangels, and warrior saints who guide human beings on the path to perfection. Announcements for a "Book about Holy Warriors" ("Kniga o svyatykh voinakh") repeatedly appeared in the press, but it was never published, and not a trace of it remains in his archive.[90]

In the cycle's seventh poem, Love, "our mother," assures her "foolish child" that she "tightly binds hearts together in the hour of parting," and when Knyazev returned to Petersburg in early August, her promise seemed fulfilled.[91] They spent five days together before Knyazev left for Tver and Moscow on the sixteenth. During their time together Kuzmin sometimes found him "capricious and jealous," and wondered why he "does not appreciate me." Uncertainty colors the final lines of the concluding poem of "Autumnal May," which he completed when he returned to the capital at the end of the month after attending Auslender's wedding at Okulovka: "But what if volatile Fortune suddenly makes our autumnal May October?"[92] Letters from Knyazev did little to set his

mind at ease (they "touch and bother me" [Diary, September 15]), but
by the middle of the month Kuzmin was so preoccupied by the affairs of
the "House of Interludes" that he thought of little else. When, on
September 27, he learned that Knyazev had returned for a month, he
"was more surprised than gladdened. He will take up a lot of time."

On September 29 Knyazev "showed up, resplendent," and presented
Kuzmin with a "charming" poem that he had written for him entitled
"M. A. K—nu," that is, "To M. A. K[uzmi]n." It was written in September 1910 and is one of only two poems bearing a dedication to Kuzmin
in Knyazev's posthumous book of verse, which in its diary-like quality
very much resembles Kuzmin's collections. The other's eyes, the
speaker assures himself, will tell him "in an instant" whether the two
"had fallen out of love or were still in love." We do not know what
Kuzmin's eyes told Knyazev on that or later occasions, for a month-
long gap succeeds an entry for September 30 in the Diary. But the "lost
paradise" was not to be so quickly "found again," as the lyrical persona
of Knyazev's poem had confidently predicted in the poem's conclusion.[93]

On September 20 the "House of Interludes" had hired a "sweet
young actor" (*milyi akterik*) named Nikolay Kuznetsov, and by the
twenty-fourth, three days before Knyazev's return, Kuzmin was "courting" him. The relationship with Knyazev still remained ill defined in his
mind and had yet to involve any physical intimacy. We do not know
what transpired after September 29, but on October 28 he wrote in the
Diary:

> My God, a whole month has again been left out of this poor
> notebook, which is precious to me. And yet how much has taken
> place during it: the whole brilliance and the whole tragedy of our
> theater, my love for Kuznetsov, Knyazev's arrival [and departure],
> my works, hopes, disenchantment, having money and having
> none. Muscovites, quarrels, friendships. I am now losing everyone
> and everything with Nik[olay] Dmitr[ievich]. But today I am so
> happy, so tranquil, although I have no reason at all to be so.

The affairs of the "House of Interludes" made Kuzmin and Kuznetsov inseparable in the weeks that followed, and on November 13 they
made a trip to Moscow to try to arrange a visiting engagement for the

theater. The next day Kuzmin wrote, "What happiness to live in one room with Kuznetsov, to dine, drink tea, go to sleep, get up together." He was delighted by the impression the dashing young actor made on his friends: at the restaurant Prague with Somov and the actor Yury Rakitin "Ryabushinksy was telling everyone that I had arrived accompanied by a young man of rare beauty, completely sprinkled with diamonds, and now Nosova [a wealthy Moscow patron of the arts] wants to arrange an evening not only for me, but for N[ikolay] Dm[itrievich] as well" (Diary, November 18). The next day he noted, "I love him more and more strongly all the time," but added, "still, he is a man not altogether reliable, especially in relation to me."

Back in Petersburg he did not doubt his own feelings, and he dedicated *The Dutch Girl Liza*, in which Kuznetsov had played the role of Luka, to him as a sign of his affection. Yet, as so often in the past, he wondered if he was really loved in return. By the thirteenth of December he was beginning to fear that Kuznetsov had fallen in love with another actor in the troupe named Andrey Golubev, but he did not give up hope, writing the next day, by way of comparison with Poznyakov, who had unexpectedly stopped by, "Dear Nikolay Dmitrievich, one may be washed clean in him, as in pure water, and draw out fresh, ever fresh strength." Kuzmin would have been better advised, as 1911 would show, to heed his misgivings about Kuznetsov's reliablilty and to wonder if he had really so easily eradicated Knyazev, absent from Petersburg for over two months, from his heart.

7

"Where Is Life's Enchantment?"
1911–1912

IN THE MIDDLE of February 1911, Kuzmin found himself right in the thick of one of the ugliest theatrical-political scandals of the season. On February 25 Vladimir Purishkevich, an odious Duma deputy and quasi-official ideologue of anti-Semitism, interrupted a debate in the Duma on the budget estimates of the Ministry of the Interior with a long tirade on the state of the Russian theater.[1] Employing quite fantastic statistics, he tried to prove that the Jews had taken over. He attacked Vera Komissarzhevskaya, who had died in February 1910 of smallpox while on a tour in the provinces, and ridiculed the many articles that had mourned her death as an irreparable loss.[2] He accused the theater of actively contributing to, if not actually causing, revolution, warned that it posed even more dangers for public order than did the cinema, and identified it as the source of the "decline in morals," especially among university students. Naturally, Kuzmin was condemned as a "pervert" (*The Chimes of Love* was specifically named), but he found himself in good company: Blok, Meyerhold, Bely, and Sologub were among those included in the attack. As discussion from Right and Left followed in the press, Meyerhold and his collaborators feared that because of Purishkevich's close connections at the court, they might face dismissal from the staff of the Imperial Theaters or risk losing commissions. Kuzmin, busy juggling his personal affairs, did not note the matter in the Diary, even though he could have been adversely affected by it. Fortunately the tempest died down, and on March 23 Meyerhold's production of Yury Belyaev's play on the life of Baron Münchhausen, *The Red Tavern* (Krasnyi kabachok), opened on schedule and to acclaim at the Aleksandrinskii, with sets and costumes by Aleksandr Golovin and music by Kuzmin.

Throughout early 1911, Kuzmin had been waiting with impatience for the first performance of his full-length operetta *The Maidens' Amusement* (Zabava dev). Not long after the opening of *The Red Tavern*, rehearsals got under way for it at Aleksey Suvorin's Malyi Theater. This was Kuzmin's first opportunity to work with one of Petersburg's large non-state theaters, in this case one well known for the conservatism of its repertory and rather middlebrow audience. He must initially have conceived of it as a play with music, a "singspiel," as he described it to Nouvel, since he approached Komissarzhevskaya about producing it in the summer of 1909. He worked sporadically on it in the years that followed; then, on March 14, 1911, Boris Glagolin, "who wants to stage my operetta in May, called. Very profitable terms. It is probably Sudeikin's idea. . . . If this works out, it will be excellent" (Diary). A great deal of curiosity surrounded the production, as this was the first time the theater was to mount a work by one of the capital's most important "modernist" writers, as the press kept calling Kuzmin. He was understandably agitated about the theater's realization of his work (and about the censor's clumsy meddling with the text), but the opening night on May 1, 1911, was a "success, unexpected and complete. . . . I feel as if I am in a dream" (Diary). Reviewers greeted the operetta with coolness, but the enthusiastic public reaction kept it running for twenty-four performances, and it was revived for the autumn season on August 16.[3]

The plot is a kind of Oriental fairy tale involving a young Venetian merchant who is in love with the sultan's favorite wife (a role played by Lyubov Delmas, the Carmen of Blok's 1914 cycle of that name). He gains access to the harem in Istanbul to woo and win her by disguising himself as a magical bird (the "maidens' amusement"). The setting allowed Sudeikin to give full rein to his coloristic fantasy and exotic stylization (and Kuzmin to make some sly allusions to the gay "penchant" of some of the Turks), and the lavish spectacle contributed a large part to the public success of the production.[4] Some suggested that Kuzmin was pushing his musical talents to impossible limits in such a large-scale form, but one song, beginning "Let us fly far beyond the sea," the duet between the young Venetian Uccellino and the sultan's wife which closes the second act and the operetta, became the musical "hit" *(gvozd')* of the season.[5]

The operetta and other forms of what we now call "popular culture"—the puppet theater, the circus, vaudeville, motion pictures—always attracted Kuzmin for their exaggerated theatricality and deliberate flouting of conventions.[6] He called the operetta the "Daughter of Public Squares, Companion of Revolutions" in a 1918 essay, and considered it an underrated genre.[7] He resented the fact that French works, which he admired, still dominated the Russian stage, largely because critics so scorned native products that Russian musicians and writers feared soiling their hands with the genre. The patronizing tone of Znosko-Borovsky's reaction to both *The Maidens' Amusement* and Kuzmin's second operetta, on which he had worked over the summer of 1911, *Woman's Faithfulness, or the Return of Odysseus* (Zhenskaya vernost', ili vozvrashchenie Odisseya), seems to offer confirmation of his belief. Znosko-Borovsky dismissed both works and accused his friend of betraying his real talents and of playing up to the "mob."[8]

The second production, again directed by Glagolin, but this time with sets and costumes by Sapunov, opened at the Malyi on September 8 and was a total critical failure. On September 13 Kuzmin noted "its unbelievable savaging in the newspapers, the complete silence of my friends, the departure of Nik[olay] Dm[itrievich Kuznetsov], financial troubles" (Diary). His witty use of deliberate anachronisms—contemporary idioms, literary and cultural references, and snatches of French in a work set in ancient Greece, a practice he certainly had learned from Offenbach's *La Belle Hélène*, which he mentions in the text—had contributed to the work's lack of success with a puzzled public and irritated many critics, who dismissed the operetta as a "bag of tricks." He had toyed with the device in *The Maidens' Amusement*, but took it much farther here, and he went right on experimenting with it. All that his friends could remember from *Odysseus* was a couplet from one song, whose surreal silliness, a harbinger of the more inspired nonsense to come in some of Kuzmin's works in the 1920s, can perhaps be captured

by a loose translation: "Poor, oh poor Telemachus, / he fears hippo-
potamus!"[9]

Both Knyazev, who had returned to Petersburg at the end of January,
and Kuznetsov had often accompanied Kuzmin to the spring rehearsals
of *The Maidens' Amusement*, and the triangle raised no eyebrows. Their
high spirits kept him in a good mood even when their antics at first
made him wonder just what the relationship of the two young men
might become. After realizing at the beginning of the year that Kuznetsov was to be a friend but never a lover, Kuzmin had reassessed his
feelings for both men. His attraction to the young actor hardly diminished at first, but Kuzmin found himself becoming more and more
attached to Knyazev, who was now willing to have some kind of affec-
tional and even, for the first time, sexual contact with him. Two verse
cycles written between February and May 1911 testify to Kuzmin's
wavering affections: "Winter Sun" ("Zimnee solntse," February–May),
a celebration of the warmth of his feelings for Kuznetsov, to whom it
is dedicated, and "Vernal Return" ("Vesennii vozvrat," March–May),
dedicated to Knyazev and celebrating the love and passion he had
brought back to Kuzmin's life. His feelings for Kuznetsov, to whom he
dedicated both operettas, did not so much dwindle as evolve into a
lasting friendship. When he saw Kuznetsov for the first time since the
actor's abrupt departure from Petersburg in September (unexplained,
given the lack of Diary entries for the time), Kuzmin wrote: "I love him
sincerely, like a nephew or a son" (December 6, 1911).

Throughout February 1911, Kuzmin pronounced Knyazev "very
sweet" whenever they saw each other, especially on the occasion when,
"laughing and joking," they went to the fashionable establishment of
Boissonnas et Eggler on Nevsky to have their picture taken at the end
of the month. On February 26 Kuzmin inscribed a copy of *Wings* to the
one "I now love far more than before. That is the truth."[10] A week later
the young officer, who was now attached to the Sixteenth Irkutsk Hussar Regiment, which had its headquarters in Pskov, left for duty. In the
past, when distance separated him from a lover, Kuzmin had experienced torments of anxiety. He certainly missed Knyazev, but he was
confident enough of his promises of love to mention the March 9 Feast
of the Forty Martyrs of Sebaste, traditionally associated in Russia with
the onset of spring (Kuzmin's invariant metaphor for love), in the sec-

ond poem of "Vernal Return," which he wrote on the day of Knyazev's departure:

> Perhaps I am foolhardy
> in not fearing unexpected traps,
> but although your departure is difficult,
> I do not fear distant Pskov.
>
> Happiness blunts my doubts
> with a certain and sure piece of news:
> "The Forty Martyrs" will come—
> and you will return home.[11]

A prayer to those martyrs, crowned by angels sent from Heaven at the moment of their death, is offered during the Orthodox wedding service when crowns are held over the heads of bride and groom, and in the days that immediately followed Knyazev's return from Pskov on March 25, the two men made the round of their friends like newlyweds. Znosko-Borovsky told Kuzmin that he had rarely seen such "gushing and sincere joy" in Knyazev as now, while Gumilev reported that he and his wife and Mandelshtam had been "captivated" by "sweet Vsevolod" when he and the proud Kuzmin visited them at Tsarskoe Selo on April 2.

The diary-like quality of Knyazev's poems reflects the twists and turns of his relationship with Kuzmin with such clarity that his father, when preparing them for publication, had to take pains to conceal how many were addressed to Kuzmin by changing the gender of pronouns and verb endings in some and by removing all but two dedications. Anyone familiar with Kuzmin's verse will, however, easily recognize his presence in many others, for Knyazev's texts often work variations on themes of Kuzmin's own poems. When Knyazev writes in one poem of kissing the "black and white piano keys" only just touched by fingers that had been playing some "forgotten old waltzes," the identity of the addressee could not be clearer.[12] It is no less so in the poem that Knyazev wrote at about this time in 1911 which begins, "It seems to me that my gentle, / my sweet, longed-for, mysterious friend will soon come to me."[13] Its decidedly homoerotic imagery of Eros, a "tightly

strung bow," and a "sharp arrow" (all taken from Kuzmin's poems addressed to Knyazev), and the identification of that friend with Antinous
might have prompted the devoted father to remove the poem had he
recognized the references.

Kuzmin could still be as direct, but he more often refracted experience far more obliquely than he had done before in his verse. The third
poem of "Vernal Return" offers a ready example of how his always
referential aesthetic now worked:

> How joyous is spring in April,
> how enchanting it is for us!
> In the beginning of next week
> let's go to have our picture taken at Boissonnas.
>
> Obedient to the rituals of love,
> not thinking of anything,
> hand in hand, shoulder to shoulder.
> we'll affectionately get side by side,
>
> Were not tears of doubt just a dream?
> (Dreams can be deceitful!)
> And, after all, are the charming whims of spring
> really strange to us in April?[14]

By 1911 Georgy Ivanov had come to know Kuzmin (when they first
met, Kuzmin referred to him as an "insufferable little snot," but he got
used to him), though not well enough to support his assertion that the
poem is nothing more than an "accidental" trifle prompted by Kuzmin's
discovery of the unusual rhyme *vesná* (spring) / *Buasoná* (Boissonnas).[15]
There is nothing accidental about the poem, written on April 5, 1911,
and it is connected with events of the day before: "Knyazev arrived and
suddenly started expounding various theories about virginity, knavery,
etc. He was fascinated precisely by the possibility of deceiving someone,
so to speak, in male-to-male love. So his alteration [into a homosexual]
is worth very little. A scene ensued. I don't know if he understood or
not, but all the rumors about him revived in my memory. We somehow
or other made up. We had our picture taken in a merry mood" (Diary).
The "real" psychological state underlying the third stanza does become
clearer with the extratextual evidence of the Diary entry, but in the

world of the poem Kuzmin has erased the existential imperative of the world "out there" that gave rise to the text itself. The aesthetic act integrates "self" and "other" in the photograph that would be taken, and the wrenching conflicts of love, the bitter reflections about Knyazev's conduct, and the doubts about his affections become nothing but the "deceits," not of the lover but of dreams, "charming whims" in April, Kuzmin's frequent metaphor for spring and love.[16]

Near the end of May, Kuzmin received a letter "in the Palladian style, hysterical, and shady," from Knyazev's sister, who was married to Pallada's brother Leon, asking for a loan of five hundred rubles. Another arrived the next day, even more insistent in tone. He, of course, had nothing like that sum, and he was irked by her assumption that just because he was her brother's "lover" (*lyubovnik*, the first time he so refers to Knyazev in the Diary) he would extend it. The Diary betrays no sign of any irritation with Knyazev for her action, and in the days before Knyazev left for posting to summer camp near Moscow, Kuzmin wondered only about his own "excess," the "mad desire for ever new bodies" that kept driving him to the baths, so much so that on May 31 he asked himself, "Can it be possible that I am a heartless libertine?" He also sought in vain to explain to himself the reasons for his "swinishness towards Vsevolod" (June 10), whose beauty had so recently acted like a narcotic on him. What that "swinishness" had been he did not say, but with that reference Knyazev disappears from the Diary without comment. On June 24 Kuzmin himself left for Okulovka, where he spent the rest of the summer working on *Odysseus*, "reveling" in reading Gozzi, and translating some poems of Aubrey Beardsley for a book of drawings Mikhail Likiardopulo was putting together.[17] He went to Petersburg on August 1, but only to deliver and play what he had written to Glagolin (and have sex at the baths) before returning to the country the next day to finish the operetta.

He was back in the capital for the "flop" of *Odysseus* in September, where for a week or so he fell under the spell of the good-looking tenor Vladimir Sabinin, who had sung the part of Telemachus. In the absence of Kuznetsov, who had seemed to serve as some kind of check on the worst of his impulses, Kuzmin passed the remainder of the year in a state of totally aimless drifting: "Again ennui, idleness, lack of money, lassitude. . . . What would I like? A return to a very simple solitary life, *Apollo*, 'Contemporary Music,' what? I would like for Nik[olay]

Dm[itrievich] to be here, not especially to have to think about money, to write, answer all the letters. But I am bored to tears, to death. How can people live and where is life's enchantment?" (Diary, September 16). Kuzmin was again seeing Nouvel almost every day, and he and his dissolute entourage of hustlers, pretty boys, and actors and dancers from the city's gay demimonde brought out the worst in his own restless eroticism. He upbraided himself for the mindlessness of his behavior even as he drew up a plan with Nouvel and Diaghilev, who was back in Petersburg rounding up talent for his European enterprise, to visit, one by one, the bathhouses of the city, about the only systematic thing he managed to accomplish that early autumn. They did not carry it out, although they succeeded in patronizing a goodly number of the twenty-five on the list, something that only further increased Kuzmin's poverty without at all lessening the frequency of his refrain, "I am bored to death."

His mood improved when he met a twenty-year-old student at the School of Jurisprudence, Sergey Ionin, a "captivating lad with whom I fell in love at once" (Diary, October 17). He was the brother of Yury Rakitin, a friend of Kuzmin's since his recent arrival in the city to work as an actor and director at the Aleksandrinskii Theater, which had ac-quired a decidedly homosexual notoriety because of its leading man, Yury Yuriev, the most popular actor in Petersburg. Yuriev made no secret of his same-sex inclination and kept, Kuzmin observed in the Diary, a veritable male harem at his apartment.[18] The encounter with the student did not do much to change Kuzmin's habits, but his "great fondness" for young Ionin reawakened an impulse for poetry, dormant since the late spring, and three days later he was at work on the nine poems that make up the cycle "The Thaw" ("Ottepel'"), which he completed in November. He had not been at all sure about the nature of Ionin's sexuality from the outset: "He scarcely, I think, understands what's what" (October 27). His puzzlement had no effect on the quality of the poems, and it did make him exercise discretion by heeding Ionin's request, on March 8, 1912, not to publish the work with a dedication to him. When it came out in *Autumnal Lakes*, the dedication read only "To S. L. I."[19]

He still heard from Naumov now and then, and when the latter wrote to say that he was coming to Petersburg and suggested a meeting, Kuzmin was curious enough to agree. Their encounter on October 28 put a full stop to whatever fantasies might have lingered in his mind: "Naumov arrived. *Une tante classique*, in my opinion—pinkie rings, a bracelet, has put on weight. Shaved off his mustache yesterday or today. We had a rather strained chat" (Diary). The next day, at the apartment of Pallada, Kuzmin met a "very noisy, flighty officer, Miller, who is thought to resemble Vsevolod [Knyazev]." Kuzmin lost touch with the officer, whose first name, like that of young Ionin, was Sergey, for several weeks until, on November 16, he ran into him again at Pallada's. Two days later they were lovers: "He spent the night with me. He was mine, and that was great happiness and joy. How delightful, fine, and splendid. I must remember this date" (Diary).

No one reading the "Lighthouse of Love" ("Mayak lyubvi") cycle that Kuzmin addressed to Miller would suspect that their affair in December 1911 and January 1912, during which he wrote its twelve poems, was anything but an idyll. But in life it was a nightmare, no less tawdry and sordid than the worst days of his relationship with Poznyakov three years before, a destructive cycle of recriminations and passionate reconciliations punctuated by Miller's flirting (usually with Nouvel, although he was not choosy) and the occasional "scandalous incident," such as the drunken brawl at Pallada's on November 21 that left everyone but Kuzmin black and blue from the exchange of fisticuffs and slaps. Kuzmin was "terrified by the consequences" of his "passion" but unable to end it: "I love him so much that I am ready to go anywhere at all with him" (December 7), he wrote, a major motif of "The Lighthouse of Love."

From the start, money shadowed the relationship, as Miller, like Poznyakov, expected to be kept amused, always at Kuzmin's expense. Some time earlier, Golovin had arranged a lucrative commission from the Imperial Theaters for Kuzmin to write incidental music for a new production of Lermontov's play *Masquerade*, which Meyerhold was to direct at the Aleksandrinskii, but it never panned out.[20] Friends in Petersburg, disgusted by his profligacy with Miller, refused to help with any more "loans," and so, on December 11, he decamped for Moscow, with Miller in tow, to try to plead for more money from "Scorpio" for his collections of stories and advances from other publishers for work that he had already done: an introduction for a Russian edition of Barbey d'Aurevilly's *Du Dandysme et de G. Brummel* and translations of the verse portions of Rémy de Gourmont's *Livre des masques*.[21]

The first few days seemed like a "lost paradise" when Kuzmin re-called them later. They made the rounds of his Moscow friends, visited exhibitions, lunched with Gordon Craig in the company of theater acquaintances, some of whom promised to try to set up commissions, and cadged money from everyone possible. Kuzmin did not doubt his own love, but by the middle of the month he feared that "all this will end in calamity" (December 15). Trapped in the old game of "he loves me—he loves me not," and faced with having to find money on a day-by-day basis, he finally fled Moscow alone on the twenty-eighth, wondering why he was "not happy with this salvation." An unexpected surprise awaited him in Petersburg. Kuzmin had sometimes thought about Knyazev that autumn and had daydreamed about Rakitin's ar-ranging a rapprochement, even though he had heard that "Vsevolod continues to be furious with me" (Diary, October 24). On December 30 he ran into him at the offices of *Apollo*: "Very handsome in a new uniform. We exchanged kisses. He thinks that everything transpired because of his sister." Kuzmin might have lingered, but he rushed back to Moscow to Knyazev's surrogate (and that, he realized later, was all Miller had been), who had been sending telegrams and letters promis-ing "I am yours forever." They spent what turned into a miserable New Year's Eve at the mansion of the Nosovs, fabulously wealthy patrons of the arts, and quarreled again as soon as they returned to the hotel.

On January 6, 1912, they were back in Petersburg with nothing in the relationship changed. By now Kuzmin's friends, who were appalled by his emotional and economic serfdom to the officer, were urging him to send Miller packing. Kuzmin, reduced to pawning his wardrobe piece by piece, believed that he still loved Miller and let him continue sharing his rooms at the "Tower." He realized, however, that there was nothing he could do to "rescue the pathetic lad" from himself and that he had to save himself from a life of idle dissipation and creative impo-tence by fleeing Petersburg if necessary. He kept postponing anything like such "cruelty" to Miller, until, on February 1, 1912, the officer himself unwittingly forced his hand with one of his typical brush-offs. Kuzmin responded with the same casual rejection and left for the Gu-milevs' at Tsarskoe Selo: "How quiet and peaceful in Selo. The Gu-milevs have electricity, a bulldog. The 'Guild' assembled. I slept in the library. Sad, easy, and sweet. Very strange" (Diary).

Gumilev and Anna Akhmatova had married in April 1910, and at the beginning of June, after a month-long honeymoon abroad, they settled in Tsarskoe Selo at the house of his parents. Kuzmin pronounced her "affected" *(manerna)* when they met on June 10, but three days later, after a pleasant evening at the "Tower," where she read her verse, he decided, "She's all right—she'll manage and will be quite nice" (Diary). He had seen much more of his old friend than he did of Akhmatova after Gumilev returned from his second trip to Abyssinia at the end of March 1911, but he enjoyed the company of both. He tarried with the Gumilevs for several more days "thinking only of Miller," who had been thrown out of the "Tower" and was now begging Kuzmin to live with him in Finland, where his regiment was to be stationed. On the seventh Kuzmin gave in to his entreaties to return to Petersburg, only to learn three days later that "Serezha has gonorrhea. He was at some whore's on the thirtieth. How disgusting, how disgusting, how disgusting, and then he came to me, lay down in my bed. Phooey!" Kuzmin lived "like a nomad" for a few days, now at the Gumilevs', now with Miller, until accepting Kuznetsov's offer of a hiding place on the fourteenth. Miller, fearful that Kuzmin was going to leave, had hidden his manuscripts, but he found them, packed up his few things, and left once and for all. He missed Miller, but he resisted the officer's attempts to see him, knowing his own weakness: "If I glimpse him, I cannot restrain myself from staying. He does not know his power over me." Ten days later, when they bumped into each other on Nevsky, they shared a bottle of wine, but no more: "Now I fear nothing. It turns out that he belonged to Valechka [Nouvel] at the same time. Valka's just a scoundrel, but the other's a slut" (Diary, February 23). By mid-March the relationship had limped to a conclusion.

With the end of the affair and the completion of the cycle it had called into being, Kuzmin had enough poems to gather for the second collection he had long been promising to "Scorpio." It appeared under the title *Autumnal Lakes* early that autumn, but not before Miller, whom Kuzmin kept running into at the beginning of August, caused a fuss. He had once told Kuzmin he would "revenge" himself were the writer ever to leave him, and he now "threatened unpleasantries and misfortune," as Kuzmin wrote to his publisher in August, over "The Lighthouse of Love." Kuzmin removed the dedication and the cycle's final poem, in which Miller's name was mentioned, but some copies of the book did come out with the dedication intact. Miller blustered, but did nothing except dog Kuzmin's path for many more months. Fellow poets such as Bryusov and Khodasevich gave the volume enthusiastic reviews, while Gumilev wrote no fewer than three separate pieces on it.[22] The first of them he concluded with a carefully worded compliment to Kuzmin for having expressed the views of a gay community that was now taking its rightful place in society: "Kuzmin occupies one of the first positions among contemporary poets. . . . Furthermore, as the spokesman for the views and emotions of a whole circle of people who are united by a common culture and who have quite justly risen to the crest of life's wave, he is a poet with organic roots."[23]

The volume troubled one critic, the novice poet Mikhail Lopatto, who knew Kuzmin rather well, as their correspondence testifies, before he emigrated from Russia in 1920. He read it with care when preparing an article for the prestigious *New Encyclopedic Dictionary*, and remarked an unsettling "duality" *(dvoistvennost')* in the collection as a whole: "In his *Autumnal Lakes* one senses a certain lack of confidence in himself and searchings for something that is alive which will agitate his heart. . . . Kuzmin tries to find that living quality in a love that is rather base and egotistical."[24] His last comment is puzzling, because nothing else in the article suggests that he found anything immoral or offensive about the undisguised same-sex orientation of Kuzmin's love poetry in the volume. Had he, unlike any other critic, noticed, but been too discreet to point out, that the collection opens with a crude provocative gesture: the first three lines of the opening poem form an acrostic for a common Russian obscenity (*khui*—"cock")? *Nets* had naturally culminated with the mystical cycles of its third section, as it unfolded the story of the path to ideal love and developed the Neoplatonic idea that the love of beauty can draw the lover upward to a sense of the divine origin of all love. *Autumnal Lakes* simply ends with its two religious cycles—the "Spiritual Rimes," written between 1901 and 1903 and preceded by a dedicatory poem of 1912 to Knyazev in the Guide vein, and "The Feasts of the Most Holy Mother of God." Nothing evolves in a collection that zigs and zags from one tone to another in a dangerous balancing act between the profane and the sacred. The instability suggests nothing so much as the onset of a crisis in Kuzmin's life, of which the affair with Miller in 1912, Kuzmin's *annus horribilis*, was the first symptom.

Kuzmin had moved back to Tsarskoe Selo on February 21 at Gumilev's insistence, where he continued work on *Dreamers* (Mechtateli), the new novel he had started shortly before. (The novel's Masonic subplot reflects his recent discussions on the subject with Ivanov.)[25] He enjoyed reading from it to Akhmatova, but worried that he was crowding his hosts, and after a few days he was back in the city, first with Kuznetsov and, finally, at the Ivanovs', working with little inspiration on the novel while translating the *Bibliotheca* of Apollodorus of Athens.[26] Bely and his young wife, Asya Turgeneva, had spent over a month at the "Tower" after their arrival on January 21, 1912, and Kuzmin heard Bely read "excellent fragments" from *Petersburg*. On one occasion he also overheard several heated arguments between Bely, Ivanov, and Gumilev about Symbolism. On February 18 the long-simmering differences between the generations came out in the open during a discussion of two talks on Symbolism given by Ivanov and Bely: "There was an uproar in the Academy. Who should be elected? The Symbolists or the 'Guild'? The second, I think. I will ask Zhenya [Znosko-Borovsky]." He elected to stay out of the fight, and on March 1 pretty much dismissed the business: "To the 'Guild.' Gorod[etsky] and Gummi expounded their not particularly coherent theories" (Diary). Two weeks later, however, when "Gummi expounded intelligent nonsense" during a meeting at the offices of *Apollo*, "Zhenya and I rebelled" (March 17).

Kuzmin made clear his own views on the issues dividing the "old men," as he called them, and the "young" when Emily Metner, a rather unprincipled polemicist and a fanatical advocate of a Symbolism oriented exclusively toward German idealist philosophy, cut the final paragraph of Kuzmin's review of volume one of Ivanov's verse collection *Cor Ardens* when it appeared that month in the first issue of *Works and Days*. Neither Bely nor Ivanov, who had conceived the venture as a forum for the discussion and defense of Symbolism, had anything to do with the action. Ivanov himself wrote Metner to protest on March 29 and again on May 3 in a letter that reinforces a point already made, namely, that Ivanov took no exception to Kuzmin's holding views on art that differed from his own: "I totally disagree with the amputation. . . . An author's signature does mean something. . . . An artist and critic such as Kuzmin has the right to his own opinion. . . . Just what kind of *criticism* is possible without freedom for personal evaluation?"[27] Kuzmin's thoughtful review, in fact, contained the only serious contemporary consideration of the bedeviled matter of Ivanov's "difficulty." But that was obscured for many readers by its often perfervid rhetoric. Blok, for one, called the dithyrambic tone of the final sentence "loathsome."[28] By that time the two old friends hardly ever saw each other, and when they did, Kuzmin was appalled by Blok's "degeneration" and heavy drinking.

Kuzmin did not confine his own protest of Metner's high-handedness to a private letter: he read his "reproach" *(otpoved')* at the offices of *Apollo* on April 2, and published it as a letter to the editor in the May issue. Nor did he limit himself to the matter of journalistic etiquette. He used his measured response, as we have seen, as a platform to state his major disagreements with those who would apply "religious or moral demands . . . to the theory of art" and to dispute the magazine's attempt to equate its exclusive view of Symbolism with poetry itself:

> No matter how unpleasant it may be to *Works and Days*, the fact remains that the school of Symbolists appeared in the 1880s in France and had as its first representatives here V[alery] Bryusov, Balmont, Gippius, and Sologub. To make the genealogy read Dante, Goethe, Tyutchev, Blok, and Bely is not always convenient, and the conclusions following from that premise are not always convincing. But if a new movement of several writers, fully formed masters and theoreticians, so differs from what it is customary to call Symbolism, then it would be better to give it another name—I do not know what to call it: "theurgism" perhaps—so that there would not be any confusion in possible discussions.[29]

He also took strong exception to the magazine's "aggressive polemic" and to its tactlessness in publishing in the same issue as his review an article by Bely, under one of his numerous pseudonyms, "Cunctator," that contained a polemical aside aimed at Kuzmin in its reference to a "police station of clarity." The letter ended with an expression of "respect and enthusiasm for the works" of Bely, Blok, and Ivanov, but no one could doubt that its author resented having been made to appear partisan, that he had put a distance between himself and Symbolism, and that he would continue to resist any attempts to categorize him.

Ivanov had not known that Kuzmin was writing the letter until it appeared in print, and he could not have failed to notice that it challenged some of the views on art he had himself expressed in the programmatic "Thoughts about Symbolism" ("Mysli o simvolizme"), which had been published in the same issue of *Works and Days* as the review. All he remarked to Metner about the letter, however, was that "*formally* he is correct in everything," for by then he was well aware of his friend's positions.[30] A year before, Ivanov had called Kuzmin his "ally on Helicon" in the first poem of the cycle that he dedicated to Kuzmin and entitled, alluding to their shared life in the "Tower," "Being Neighbors" ("Sosedstvo"). But he had continued with "My brother in Delphic Apollo, / but in the other one, on the Moika, all but my enemy!"[31] He immediately softened the pointed reference to the location of the editorial offices of *Apollo* by adding that it was not their fate "to try to out-argue each other" and "to be at odds." Events in May 1912 would prove him to have been a poor prophet in this, even if it was a personal drama, not literary differences, that provoked the rupture that brought life in the "Tower" to an end for everyone.

Kuzmin had always adored the vivacious company of Ivanov's daughter Lidiya, who was ever ready to join him at the piano for improvisations that parodied other composers (usually Scriabin), and whose sprightly good cheer and teasing could bring him out of the blackest mood. The often moody behavior of her stepsister, Vera Shvarsalon, sometimes perplexed him, as well it might have: unbeknownst to him or anyone in her family, she had been in love with him since the end of 1907.[32] He had learned of this on November 20, 1908, when he and Ivanov made up the differences that had clouded their relationship over the summer. He assumed that her feelings had passed by then, as did Vera, who had felt betrayed when she recognized herself in the young woman in the story "The Double Confidant" with whom the two heroes become infatuated; but she forgave him. When he moved back into the "Tower" in August 1909, Kuzmin sensed her affection, but interpreted it as that of a sister for a prodigal returned to the fold. Vera, however, her lips pressed in a wistful smile, her head, like a "bowed ear of ripe grain," always slightly inclined, as though from the weight of her heavy bright-gold braids,[33] had never been out of love with him, as she confided only to her diary.

She had seen too many of the young men Kuzmin had introduced to the "Tower" to have any questions about his sexual preference, but for a time she indulged her delusion that were he only to fall in love with a "*real* woman," that would "make him a real human being" capable of returning her love.[34] She soon realized the folly of that fantasy, but the intensity of her feelings for Kuzmin diminished not at all. Kuzmin and Ivanov suspected nothing. On October 15, 1911, as Kuzmin and Vera sat quietly waiting for Ivanov to return home from a night out on the town, she "made a declaration of love to me. There is a surprise for you and a not altogether pleasant one" (Diary). He would have been even more astonished had he known that in 1910, when Vera had joined her stepfather, twenty-four years her senior, in Italy, where he had gone to collect materials for his ongoing investigation of the Dionysian cults, the Eternal City had played the same decisive role in their life as it had in that of Ivanov and her mother, and they had "joined their fates." Ivanov associated her with Persephone, daughter of Demeter and an ancient symbol of rebirth, and he believed that in this "Childlike copy of the daughter-goddess / who stepped across the forbidden threshold," his love for her mother, the all-consuming passion of his life, lived again in a union urged by her voice from beyond the grave.[35] A threshold of another kind had been violated in the eyes of the Russian Church, which regarded such an alliance as tantamount to incest, and after the couple returned to Russia in November 1910, they kept the relationship secret even from members of their family.

On January 19, 1912, Ivanov finally spoke with Kuzmin "about Vera, for a long time and candidly" (Diary). He was also talking with a few other intimates, as it was becoming impossible to hide what was going on. Kuzmin sensed an "air of devastation at the 'Tower'" on February 1. He had been able to distance himself from it for a while when he lived with other friends, but not for long: "Dear little Lidiya's birthday. Now there would be a bride for you. During the day, when everyone had gone out, Vera told me that she was pregnant by Vyacheslav, that she loved me and without that love could not live with him, that this had been going on for a long time, and she proposed a fictitious marriage to me. I was dumbfounded. And besides, the ghost of L[idiya] Dm[itrievna] is dragged into all this" (Diary, April 16).[36] The long-simmering tension in the household finally erupted on May 6: "Ivanov railed at me at dinner, said I had gone stale, am acting common, am an idiot, etc.—in front of everyone. . . . It is evidently all over with Vyach[eslav]. Oh, to move away from them as soon as possible." Penury made such a move impossible, but Ivanov solved the problem for Kuzmin by departing himself: "Everyone is busy with the departure. . . . Vyach[eslav] spoke with me candidly, about the same thing again" (Diary, May 18). The next day, Ivanov and Vera, accompanied only by Lidiya, left for France, where Vera gave birth to a son on July 12. They were married a year later in Livorno in the same Greek Orthodox church and by the same priest who had performed the ceremony for Ivanov and Zinovieva-Annibal in 1899. They did not return to Russia until that autumn, settling in Moscow.

Mariya Zamyatnina, the "guardian angel" of the "Tower," whose special favorite Kuzmin had long been, and Ivanov's stepsons had stayed in Petersburg to close up the old apartment. Aware that Kuzmin had nowhere else to go, they did not ask him to leave immediately. He knew, though, that he had to if only for his peace of mind, but, as so often in the past, he was paralyzed by lack of will and money. "What am I to do, what am I to do?" closes virtually every Diary entry in the weeks that followed, as he considered and rejected as unsuitable one after another offer to stay with friends, his only way out. Nikolay Sapunov, one of his closest friends and collaborators, migrated back and forth between Moscow and Petersburg, where he always kept a studio, but it and his way of life were too disorderly even by the bohemian standards of Kuzmin's own reckless behavior: "It is impossible to move in with Sapunov: it will be endless drunkenness, pennilessness, and chaos" (Diary, May 22, 1912).

Kuzmin had been spending long hours in Sapunov's studio on Vasilievskii Island for over a year while the artist worked on his portrait. Sapunov had first taken care to design a colorful Italian Renaissance coat and turban for him in January 1911, and before beginning the picture in March, he had tried out one pose after another until he settled on a very young-looking Kuzmin standing, one arm extended and looking to the side with dreamy eyes, as though about to declaim something. The portrait was still unfinished in May 1912 because of Sapunov's dilatory ways and because small black spots had appeared on the surface, since the artist had apparently failed to prime the canvas properly.[37] The deeply superstitious Kuzmin and Sapunov might have taken that as a sinister warning to stop work on it, but they persevered with the posing and painting.

After the closing of the "House of Interludes" in 1911, those associated with it had considered various schemes to get a similar theater group started again. In late spring 1912, Boris Pronin, a director and the founder of the recently opened cabaret the "Stray Dog" ("Bro-dyachaya sobaka"), and a few others revived the old "Association of Actors, Artists, Writers, and Musicians" and invited Meyerhold to head it. They rented a small theater in the Casino Hotel at Terijoki, a popu-lar seaside resort northwest of Petersburg, and in May moved there to prepare their first program.[38] Kuzmin and Sapunov had both been in-cluded in the "association," and Sapunov had designed the flag, a smil-ing commedia dell'arte figure on a lilac background, which waved over the theater. Kuzmin missed the opening on June 9, but he accepted Sapunov's invitation to take part in organizing a special carnival pro-gram for June 29, the feast day of Saints Peter and Paul.

On the fourteenth, accompanied by some artist friends, they went to discuss the details with Meyerhold:

> We went to the "Dog," where Pronin and Tsybulskaya already were. We stopped the cab to pick up Nazarbek. Waited for Yak-ovleva and Bebutova at the station. Departed. Damp and gloomy at Terijoki. . . . We decided to go boating. Found a boat with diffi-culty. The sea was like milk. It wasn't bad, but when I changed places with the princess [Bebutova], she fell down, pulling me along, and all of us fell into the water. As I was sinking I thought: "Can this be death?" We came to the surface groaning. We did not start shouting at once. Sapunov said: "Why, I don't know how to swim," grabbed hold of Yakovleva, pulled her off, and the boat capsized again. And this is when Sapunov went under. The boat turned over and over about six times. Shouting, despair at Sapunov's death, the screams of the princess and Yakovleva—aw-ful, awful. The sea was empty. Finally, Yakovleva caught sight of a boat. Another two minutes and we all would have perished. We had held on for 20–25 minutes. A sailor pulled us out like piglets. In the boat now sobbing about Sapunov. All the time I thought: "O God, tomorrow my dear Knyazev arrives and I won't be alive!!" . . . How awful, awful. I kept imagining Sapunov playing some kind of exhausted leapfrog. (Diary, June 14)

Aleksandr Mgebrov, an actor with the troupe who later recalled that he had never seen faces "so pathetic and hideously tormented" as those of the saved, gave Kuzmin forty drops of valerian, a massive dose of the popular tranquilizer, and put him to bed.[39] The next morning Nikolay Kulbin, a doctor and artist-patron of the nascent avant-garde, detected "neurosis of the heart" and ordered his patient to "introduce some 'clarity' into his life." Back at the "Tower" that evening, his friends "offered sympathy and rejoiced" that he was alive, "but all of this is awful. My heart is hardly beating." Sapunov's body was not found until two weeks later, when the tides threw it up on the headland of Kronshtadt. At the Requiem Mass celebrated on June 23 in St. Isaac's Cathedral, "there were few people," Blok wrote to his mother, "and it was very touching. Kuzmin prayed and made the sign of the cross very nicely."[40]

The death of his friend, who was not yet thirty-two, shook Kuzmin profoundly. At the end of 1913, when asked to respond to a questionnaire "On the Terrifying and Mystical," he wrote only, "How I almost drowned with Sapunov at Terijoki."[41] One thing in particular haunted him, and he addressed it in the reminiscences he wrote in 1913 for the memorial volume that he helped plan and edit: "It was repeatedly predicted to [Sapunov] that he would drown, and he believed it to such a degree that he was even careful not to cross the Neva by ferry. Therefore, one must really marvel at that fatal momentary mental lapse that induced him voluntarily, on his own initiative, having forgotten all his fears, to set out on that boat ride that so sadly and irreparably vindicated the predictions of fortune-tellers."[42] He alluded to it as well in the 1914 lyric "To Sapunov," who had "sailed to where fate had borne" him, knowing, "without telling fortunes" ("ne gadaya"), what fate had been marked out for him. The poem concludes with one of those instances of *realia* that we so often encounter in Kuzmin:

> You said: "I don't know how to swim,"
> and off you swam, poor swimmer,
> to where glory had already plaited
> a laurel wreath for you.[43]

We see another in the first two lines of a quatrain that he wrote after Sapunov had appeared to him, "aged and grown a bit swollen" (Diary), in a terrible nightmare in August 1926. In his memoirs of Sapunov, Kuzmin had noted the Moscow artists' "manner of clattering their heels as they walk," and in the quatrain, part of the "Second Introduction" to the cycle "The Trout Breaking through the Ice," a "Drowned artist / who makes a tapping noise with his heel" appears among the "unbidden guests" who have dropped by for tea. In the same quatrain's final two lines, he is "followed by a hussar lad,"[44] just as at the moment of Sapunov's death, Kuzmin had also thought of Vsevolod Knyazev, with whom he was destined to end his long relationship in the same dreadful year 1912.

After running into Kuzmin at the offices of *Apollo* at the end of 1911, Knyazev, who was in Petersburg on holiday leave, had seen him twice after Kuzmin's return from Moscow at the beginning of 1912: "Vsevolod has cooked up some kind of incredible imbroglio with Sonechka Tolstaya [the artist wife of Aleksey] and asks me to help. Thanks a lot" (Diary, January 7, 1912). By the time he came back to the capital for the Easter holiday in March, his involvement with her was over, as was Kuzmin's "mutual enslavement" to Miller. Knyazev made an Easter call to the "Tower" on March 25, and by the thirtieth, after seeing each other every day, Kuzmin wrote, "I love him very much, and he's devilishly handsome" (Diary). On April 3, the day the young hussar had to leave to rejoin his regiment in Riga, Kuzmin summed up their week-long interlude with "The sweet, sweet, sweet boy. Mine."

Confidence waned during his long absence, but the news, on June 2, that Knyazev would be arriving in a few weeks made Kuzmin give up any thoughts he had had of leaving Petersburg to move in once again with his sister and brother-in-law at Okulovka. Despite the intense rekindling of their passion upon Knyazev's return on June 24, when they spent the day in bed together "as if in paradise," Kuzmin wondered: "But is he happy? Why do I think not? I can give him too little" (Diary, July 9). What he could offer was poetry. Knyazev had recited his own poems "like a hussar-like Pushkin" during his March visit and had asked Kuzmin for some of his. Inspired by that request, Kuzmin responded with enough to make up several cycles in his third book of verse, *Clay Doves*.

During his infatuation with young Ionin and the affair with Miller, Kuzmin had at least remained faithful to his old feelings for Knyazev in his verse: the Guide figure, so prominent both in the poems to Naumov and in those to Knyazev of 1910, appears in neither of the cycles addressed to them. His attributes often do so in the poems that he was now writing, whose tone explores the full gamut from the sacred to the profane. Among the latter is the erotic masterpiece that begins "Nine delightful birthmarks," in which the poet explores the geography of his lover's body:

> Nine delightful birthmarks
> I count with my kisses,
> and as I count them, I read
> a mystery, sweeter than heavenly mysteries.
> On your cheeks, on your dear neck,
> on your chest, where your heart is beating...
> That which is darker than musk
> will not be erased by kisses.
> Thus, along the heavenly staircase,
> as I tell the beads of caresses,
> I shall reach the gates of paradise
> of your miraculous beauty.
> Now, that eighth birthmark
> is dearer to me than everything in the world,
> sweeter than the shade in sultry summer
> and dearer than the breeze of May.
> And when I reach the ninth one—
> I no longer bother counting...
> I simply melt, I melt, I melt,
> enveloped in a tender flame.[45]

In the very different poem beginning "I quietly walk away from you," one of the most simple and perfect love lyrics in Russian verse, the poet resolves *realia* (the apartment of Knyazev's parents had a balcony from which he sometimes watched Kuzmin walking home, while the "Tower" overlooked the Tavricheskii Garden) and any perplexity about Knyazev on a mythic level of the lover's perfection:

> I quietly walk away from you,
> and you remained on the balcony.
> The trumpets in the Tavricheskii Garden play
> "How glorious is our Lord in Zion."
> I see a pale star
> on the radiant warm horizon,

and I will not find better words
when I walk away from you
than "glorious is our Lord in Zion."[46]

The speaker says nothing about the relationship between himself and
the man who remains on the balcony (the ending of the past-tense verb
in line two is masculine), a spatial dimension that intimates his elevated
and ideal status. Yet we know everything because of the poetic context
of a lyric without a single trope or poeticism, unless it be the "warm
horizon," as fresh and unexpected an epithet as is the "extra" eighth line
that subtly shifts the rhythmic pattern to prepare for the personaliza-
tion of the refrain in the final line. Any Russian knew what followed
"How glorious is our Lord in Zion" in the sacred anthem that was
reserved for Church ceremonies in which the military took part, and
was thus particularly appropriate for Knyazev: "The tongue cannot
express."[47] The poet validates the truth of that statement by refusing
any direct expression of his own feelings, leaving everything to the
indirectness so characteristic of much of Kuzmin's best early verse, in
which the very sparseness of the diction paradoxically invests certain of
his favorite words (the "quietly" and "radiant" of this poem) with great
force.

A "green hussar jacket" performs synecdochic duty for Knyazev in
many of the poems, often accompanied by imagery as old as Anacreon,
with Eros and his bow and stinging arrows. Another, "Do not burn, but
guard well / the hands I covered with kisses," engages in open dialogue
with its two-line epigraph, taken from one of Knyazev's poems, and
goes so far as to incorporate in quotation marks the opening line of that
poem as its own final verse.[48] Knyazev's poem that begins "Captivated
by the melodious charm," in fact, so successfully mimics its models that
it might be confused with one of Kuzmin's minor efforts of the time.[49]
The referentiality of both poets was deliberate. They had been ex-
changing poems since the spring, and Kuzmin had hit on the idea of
doing a book of verse with Knyazev. They first considered "The Jab of
the Arrow" ("Ukol strely," from Knyazev's "Captivated") for its title
before deciding on something from one of Kuzmin's poems: "An Example for Those in Love" ("Primer vlyublennym").[50]

On June 3, 1912, Kuzmin wrote to Aleksandr Kozhebatkin, who
owned "Alcyone," a small Moscow publishing house, to propose the

idea of a "scandalous book" with "25 or so of my poems and about 15 by Vsevolod Knyazev."[51] Most of the writers who had dealings with Kozhebatkin excoriated him for the slowness with which he realized their projects, but Kuzmin could blame only himself for the fact that the little book never appeared in print. He had doomed it when he suggested that Sergey Sudeikin could do the cover. Sudeikin's wife, Olga ("Olenka"), had played small parts in both of Kuzmin's operettas in 1911, and she and her husband were on such good terms with him that by the summer of 1912 they were suggesting that he share an apartment with them. The artist wanted to do a double portrait of Kuzmin and Knyazev for their book of verse, and on July 11 they stopped by the Sudeikins', who took them and some other friends off on an outing to Peterhof to see the famous fountains. During the train ride, Knyazev, "according to his rule," kept vanishing, to Kuzmin's obvious displeasure, and once there,

> Vsevolod and Olenka abandoned us, and we couldn't find them. We all pouted. . . . In the railway coach [on the way home] I invited Vsev[olod] to have supper; he refused, but as soon as the Sudeikins invited him, he accepted. I was offended and was about to have it out with him, but he interrupted me and ran on ahead. . . . I thought that everything was over. Vsevolod chases after any skirt. Everything has fallen apart, our love, and the book, everything. . . . He is suffering from Palladism. (Diary)

Knyazev seemed sullen the next day, but posed with him for the picture while the artist's wife read their poems aloud. The portrait itself was "turning out splendidly: mysterious and enchanting" (July 14), yet Knyazev, affectionate one minute, then out of sorts and withdrawn the next, kept on "Palladising" (*palladiruet*). Something indefinable gnawed at Kuzmin, but on the twentieth, at Knyazev's parents', "Vsevolod was . . . incredibly bold. . . . But it was all done as a challenge to his parents. He got out his copy of Wilde [*The Picture of Dorian Gray*], embraced me, read his poems. . . . I love him like a son, like a friend, like a lover, like unbelievable beauty" (Diary). The next day Kuzmin sent Kozhebatkin their poems, among which was one beginning "Dearer than a son, closer than a brother" and ending "My devoted, my desired friend."[52] Two weeks later, "ever impartial," as he assured his friends, he was recommending his lover's poems to Bryusov, now the literary editor of Russia's most prestigious "thick journal," *Russian Thought* (Russkaya mysl'). The "severe" Bryusov took one of Kuzmin's ("We should set out o'er the whole wide world" ["Pustit'sya by po belu svetu"]), which he published without its "V. K." dedication, but none of Knyazev's.

By then Kuzmin was living at the Sudeikins' new apartment at Rynochnaya, no. 16, only steps from the Summer Garden and the Fontanka Canal. Knyazev was in Riga, where he had returned on August 1. Znosko-Borovsky had refused to take *Dreamers* for *Apollo*, but Kuzmin sold it to the popular magazine *The Grainfield*, which issued the novel in seven installments at the end of the year. This was his debut in the mass-circulation press. He ran through the money in a matter of days and had to borrow from friends to make the trip to Riga that he had promised Knyazev. When he arrived in that city on August 31, Knyazev was waiting at the station, but Kuzmin noted that he seemed a "bit cold and wants to act, as before, or like Miller, that is, to drive me away often, thinking up excuses and business matters" (Diary).[53] On September 2 Kuzmin thought "everything is fine. Vs[evolod] was very passionate and nice. To sleep together at night—that is a kind of journey through a varied and wondrous country of love. Enchanting." The next morning, however, they "quarreled a bit. He is on the verge of giving up our poetry, everything. He said that in 1911 I had gone to the baths immediately after he had given himself to me, that that is not love, but something disgusting, like what goes on in Maupassant's 'Vie.' . . . All the same, he called me to bed."

On the fifth it was as though they were "in love again for the first time," when Guenther arrived to invite them to visit him in Mitau. Kuzmin, who believed that Knyazev was basing his thoughts about their relationship on the Diary, which he kept asking Kuzmin to read to him, hid it. When he returned to a Petersburg blanketed by an early snow on the twentieth, he summarized the period of September 6–18 in the Diary: "Throughout that time a peaceful amorous life, one could not imagine better. We wrote, read, translated. We were in Mitau, in the hotel where Karamzin, Casanova, and Cagliostro had stayed. . . . My God, I thank you for everything!"[54] Knyazev had begged him to postpone his departure, but had at least gotten a week's leave to come to Petersburg. He arrived on the thirtieth: "Today is a day to remember. Vsevolod arrived and I have parted with him forever. It was awful, like a nightmare, all the more so because the Sologubs, Kolya [the young director Nikolay Petrov], and [Georgy] Ivanov were at our place. Again I have to begin life all over, and each time I lack the strength I once had. He is stubborn, cruel, and insensitive, says different things at different times" (Diary). The next day Sudeikin tried to cheer him up, but Olga studiously avoided him.

The next seven days in the Diary are blank, and we learn nothing from it about why Knyazev abruptly ended the affair. Kuzmin had complained before about his lover's "secretiveness" and believed that he "loved a lie" in his relationships (Diary, July 29). He had also suspected for a long time that something was going on between Knyazev and his hostess, who had turned the heads of many men and women in Petersburg artistic circles. Knyazev had constantly been at the Sudeikin apartment in July, and Kuzmin had not liked it: "The sight of a woman's skirt positively hypnotizes him. No matter how nice the woman, whenever one gets mixed up with men, there is always something a bit disgusting about it" (July 27). He did not know, however, that at least since July, Knyazev had been writing poems not only to him but to Olga as well.[55] Kuzmin hinted at his suspicions in the three-part cycle "Beaded Purses," which he wrote in September.[56] In its first poem, a French rondeau set on a Russian country estate during the Napoleonic Wars, a young girl sits daydreaming of her officer lover, who is away on those campaigns, while "Alone, at leisure, I am stringing beads: / crimson, green, yellow— / your colors."[57] The colors were those of Knyazev (his father used them for the border of his son's posthumous volume), and Sudeikin had depicted his wife as just such a girl, offering a rose to a captured wounded French officer quartered on her estate, in a recent drawing that he had shown Kuzmin and Knyazev.[58]

The striking physical image of Sudeikina—tall, full breasts, broad white shoulders that she liked to keep as bare as possible, transparent blue eyes, and a cascade of pale blond hair—haunts memoirs of prewar Petersburg, just as it does the works of her husband, who included her portrait in one after another of his elegantly stylized pictures. Yet she impressed observers as strangely delicate, almost as doll-like as the porcelain figurines she designed and the puppets she made out of scraps of cotton wool and pieces of her old dresses, a remote and fragile shell into which others could pour their fantasies. The commedia dell'arte, with its conventions and disguises hinting at fluid sexual identity, obsessed the creative artists of the time, who realized its illusions both in their works and in the theatricalized roles they played in their personal lives.[59] Sudeikina seemed created for the role of Columbine, with which she was so often associated and which she now assumed in Knyazev's new verse: the first poem directly addressed to her in his collected verse is immediately followed by one that begins, "You are sweet, gentle Columbine" and that ends with the poet's pained awareness that he is "only Pierrot, Pierrot."[60] Akhmatova would later borrow the imagery for the "1913: Petersburg Tale" section of *Poem without a Hero*, while Kuzmin, who is portrayed there as a murderous Harlequin, wrote in 1912 of the young man who had failed to return his love as a "blind Pierrot" acting out his life wearing "melancholy and pale grease-paint."[61]

Kuzmin, only days from his fortieth birthday, tried to pick up the pieces of his life. He heard not a word from Knyazev, whose mother, at her son's request, sent back on that October 6 birthday the books Kuzmin had inscribed to him. He could still hardly believe that everything was over, and surrendered to the lure of self-deception in several poems that he later included in the cycle entitled "The Stop" ("Ostanovka"), as if this were but a halt on the journey of love, not its end. The accent falls on jealousy and anxiety in these poems, one of which, "I know that you love [a female] another," contains what must be the most embarrassing line that he ever wrote: "My sweet one [male], I beg you, imagine / for an instant that I am she."[62]

The parasitical Miller had now attached himself to the Sudeikins, at whose apartment he was practically living, sponging off their hospitality (and engaging in petty thievery) and begging from or threatening Kuzmin. The dispirited writer found little forgetfulness in work ("How disgusting I am to myself" [Diary, November 24]), but write he must if he was to pay off his debts and his share of the communal expenses. The Sudeikins, who had wide ties in the theater, arranged for some commissions for incidental music, and the artist and Kuzmin "cooked up Venice" (*zadumali Venetsiyu* [Diary, September 20]). This was the idea for the play that he worked on throughout the autumn and titled *Venetian Madcaps* (Venetsianskie bezumtsy).[63] He wrote a couple of what he called "fairy tales," but he devoted what energies he had for prose to the short novel *The Dead Woman in the House* (Pokoinitsa v dome), which he had been promising Bryusov for *Russian Thought* since August. It finally appeared there in 1913, while Vyacheslav Ivanov and his immediate family were still abroad, but they would easily have recognized its variation on their own story in the tale of a vibrant young woman who is transformed into the passive victim of the desires of others through shady mysticism.[64]

That kind of indiscretion got him into an unsavory scrape in October 1912. Ivanov's abrupt departure from Petersburg in May had set tongues wagging among his many friends and acquaintances, almost none of whom knew anything about the real reasons for it, but who suspected plenty. Rumors had soon spread beyond that circle to the literary world of the capital at large, so much so that in the autumn, the poet and parodist Nikolay Venttsel, writing under the pseudonym "Benedikt," published a "Morality Play of the Twentieth Century," *Playacting about Mr. Ivanov* (Litsedeistvo o gospodine Ivanove), which the popular cabaret theater the "Crooked Mirror" snapped up for performance.[65] The playlet ridiculed the conventions of the Symbolist theater as it travestied the Ivanov family drama as a matter of incest between a daughter and her father, a "mediocre gentleman" with classical pretensions named Ivanov, a "satyr" who chafes under the "yoke" of a conventional marriage and hungers for "Dionysian" passions and "love in the *style moderne*," but who meets his downfall when the Legal Code appears on stage to bring down the curtain on his "vile ventures."

Kuzmin knew about the gossipy mores of the circles in which he moved, but he had stupidly not kept his mouth shut about something that discretion, not to speak of his long friendship with the Ivanov family, should have made him conceal. One word about the Ivanovs' suggestion of a fictitious marriage and the reasons for it, apparently to the Sudeikins, had been enough to start more and more people tittle-tatt!ing. An old enemy of Kuzmin's, Aleksandra Chebotarevskaya, the aptly nicknamed "Cassandra," blamed him alone as the "evil source" responsible for spreading what she first dismissed as groundless slander when she wrote a melodramatic letter about it to Ivanov in early October. She professed horror about what would happen should Vera's two brothers hear of the story, but did nothing to try to keep it from reaching them. In mid-October the elder of them, Sergey Shvarsalon, challenged Kuzmin to a duel, which he was able to get out of only after agreeing to a "humiliating" formal protocol. The Diary for October 2–18 says only: "Shvarsalon sent Skaldin and Zalemanov with a challenge, Sudeikin wrangled with them and sent them away. He says that everyone is against me, but I went out, called at the Sologubs', where all of Ivanov's friends were very nice to me. I am exceedingly bored. Don't know for what reason. I should get away from here!"

Kuzmin thought the matter over and done with. On December 5, however, during the second intermission of the premiere of Jacinto Benavente's *Intereses creados* (*Iznanka zhizni*; The Seamy Side of Life, in its Russian translation) at the Reineke Russian Drama Theater, the twenty-five-year-old Shvarsalon slapped Kuzmin in front of a crowd of friends backstage, breaking his pince-nez and bloodying his nose.[66] A few advised a lawsuit, but cooler heads brought about peace between all parties, even if they could not keep the incident out of the newspapers. Ivanov refused to allow Skaldin, who was preparing the collection *Tender Mystery* (Nezhnaya taina) for print in the poet's absence, to remove the poems he had addressed to Kuzmin from its section "To My Friends," but Vera expunged that "old woman, not a man at all," from her heart forever. The laconic Diary records events, not feelings: "A big gap again [from November 27 to December 7]. *The Seamy Side of Life*, friendship with Reineke's theater, that cretin Shvarsalon's insult to me, friendship with Nagrodskaya" (December 8, 1912). Kuzmin never saw any of the principals again.

Benavente's play, for which Kuzmin wrote the incidental music and Sudeikin designed the flashy sets and costumes, mixes characters from the traditional Spanish theater and the commedia dell'arte for its satire on the world of business. Reineke's company, from which Kuzmin hoped to receive further commissions, only to see it close after one season, held dress rehearsals for Aleksandr Tairov's production of the play not in its theater but in the "Stray Dog," some of whose rooms were decorated with motifs from the *commedia*. Since late 1909 Boris Pronin, the cabaret's "Hund-Director," and a group of like-minded friends had been discussing starting something like Moscow's famous "Bat" ("Letuchaya mysh'") cabaret.[67] They took two years to settle plans and search out a location for the "Society of Intimate Theater," as the venture was formally called. When Pronin found an abandoned cellar with an entrance from the courtyard, not the street, in the old Dashkov mansion on the corner (no. 4–5) of Italyanskaya Street and Mikhailovskaya Square in the heart of Petersburg, he invited friends such as Sapunov, Sudeikin, Kulbin, and Belkin to decorate the walls and ceilings of the small arched rooms and design all its appointments. He opened its doors on the eve of the New Year 1912 to an elite group of artists, musicians, and writers, who regarded it as their intimate private club. There they could socialize with their friends at all hours of the night and realize, at what were at first twice-weekly programs, the projects that were unsuitable for other venues. It lost a good deal of its serious purpose with the passage of time, turning into a popular bohemian haunt that attracted what the regulars called the "pharmacists" (*farmatsevty*, analogous to the dismissive shrug of the French, *les pompiers*), those from the public at large who were willing to pay a hefty entrance fee for the right to gawk at the behavior, not nearly so bad as they were hoping for, of the famous guests. (Someone, Pronin knew, had to pay the bills.) But it never entirely lost the loyalty of those original patrons from the worlds of art who filled the low-ceilinged cabaret during the first two years of its existence for playlets, sketches, readings, lectures, and concerts both planned and improvised, and it soon entered into Petersburg legend.[68]

Kuzmin was a member of the "Society" that had founded the cabaret, but, oddly enough, since he is so much a part of its legend, he repeatedly declined Pronin's invitations to visit, and did not descend the fourteen steps that led to the din of its still exclusive rooms until April 28, 1912: "Gyugyus and Astafieva stopped by in the evening, dragged me to the 'Dog.' The premises there are nice, but the public is nothing special." For the Sudeikins, by contrast, the cabaret served as a virtual extension of their apartment, and once they and Kuzmin began living under one roof, it also became part of his nightly ritual in the autumn. (It did not hurt that Pronin, delighted to see him now as one of the most notorious regulars, always picked up the tab.)

It was against this background of Pronin's "theater of masks and Columbines," its walls decorated by Sudeikin with fantastic birds and "flowers of evil," that the modern drama of a self-styled Pierrot and his Columbine was played to an end. On December 10 Guenther had "stopped by, talked a lot about Vsevolod, who has been confessing in his letters to him and about everything. How bitter!" (Diary). The next day Sudeikin, who had had an open marriage for several years, also spoke about the matter with Kuzmin, and when the infatuated officer arrived in Petersburg on holiday leave, Kuzmin and Sudeikin both saw with their own eyes what they had only discussed. Knyazev had never stopped writing poems to Sudeikina, and she had made at least one trip to Riga. Now she "keeps disappearing with Knyazev and does not even bother to hide it from me" (Diary, December 20). One day later "Olenka asked S[ergey] Yu[rievich] to pass on that Knyazev wants to make things up, but without the main condition. That circumstance and Vsevolod's tactlessness really upset me." Her empty-headed insensitivity only made matters worse: "O[lga] A[fanasievna] keeps saying the same things about Knyazev. S. Yu. is a bundle of nerves, cannot do anything, wants to get away from all these psychologies, and again makes me swear an oath not to write about him and his wife in the diary. I took a nap and had nightmares" (December 24).

On the twenty-sixth Kuzmin

> went to the 'Dog,' quaking at the very idea of seeing Vsevolod there. The Auslenders, Grebenshchikov, Tairov, and Jacques [Yakov Izrailevich, a young dilettante composer interested in the theater] were protecting me. Knyazev behaved like a whore. He all but tried to get a table in the very same room. Incidentally, that was just what Olenka wanted to do, but he has not yet lost all shame to such a degree. . . . I seem to have lost the feeling I once had for Knyazev, and it has been replaced by another one, a not very pleasant one. And then I do not at all want to be a pimp for their happiness.

Three days later, nothing could get him to the "Cabaret artistique," but he found no refuge at home. Sudeikina decided not to go out and spent the evening embroidering the little pictures that she fancied as art: "I find it very hard with her now. As soon as anyone shows up, she starts to make her move, almost up to and including Miller."

Kuzmin had to be dragged to the "Stray Dog" on New Year's Eve to hear the performance of the jocular "Hymn" that he had written to mark its first anniversary. It closed the evening's "Cinematograph" program of the highlights of that first year, and guests received a copy of it designed by Sudeikin. Kuzmin celebrated many of the cabaret's habitués, the "refined artists" and "singers, ballerinas, and artistes of all types" by name, but only Pallada felt the sting of his wit. She had enraged him with her "disgusting gossip" that summer about Knyazev, his sister, and her brother Leon ("It is all utter nonsense. . . . Why is it that wherever Pallada is there is a kind of noxious intoxication and lacerating hysteria?" [Diary, July 8]), and she paid for it now in the final verse of the "Hymn":

> A!..
> And Pallada is not forgotten
> in this titled circle,
> just like an ancient dryad
> who gambols in the meadow,
> love alone is her delight,
> and where necessary and where not
> she will never ever answer (3 times) "I cannot."[69]

In the first verse Kuzmin had written that one "rested one's woes" when "descending into the depths of the cellar," but he found no more merriment that night than he had throughout the end of the year. The Diary, which makes no reference to the "Hymn" or to the "Order of the Stray Dog" that he received, notes only: "Vsevolod came straight from O[lga] A[fanasievna]. Miller was not admitted. I drank such a mixture of things that I got a headache. Belkin had drawn a homosexual hanging for me. It wasn't all that bad. Here's the New Year."

"Everything Will Be as It Is Destined"
1913–1916

"I FEEL very good," Kuzmin wrote, to his surprise, on January 1, 1913, after sleeping until the early evening, "although I am wasting money" (Diary). That good mood persisted over the next few days as actor friends rehearsed his 1912 "puppet play" *(vertep kukol'nyi)* entitled *The Nativity of Christ* (Rozhdestvo Khristovo), a charming faux-naïf variation on a Ukrainian folk form, which received its sole performance at the "Stray Dog" on Twelfth Night, January 6, with decor by Sudeikin.[1] The Diary gives no hint of the head of steam that was building in the artist's apartment. On January 7, however, the pressure cooker exploded: "There was an enormous scene today. Our life is unbearable because of women: we cannot hire a manservant because of the Veras [the incompetent maid and cook who had been irritating him for months], I cannot take a lover because of O[lga] A[fanasievna]." They "made up" that evening, but the situation was impossible. Not long after, he moved out before the next inevitable explosion, which might have brought to an end his friendship with Sudeikina, and thus with her husband.

Sudeikina broke off her affair with Knyazev at about the same time. (The Diary offers no help in pinpointing dates: entries abruptly stop after January 12 and resume only on March 3.) The officer had written of "love's passing" and the nearness of death in the anemic clichés of his last poem of 1912.[2] There is nothing of that, however, in the next two poems, "January 1, 1913" and "I was in a land where roses bloom eternally" (dated "Riga, January 17, 1913"), in which the poet, the "happiest of men," celebrates his lover in that often tasteless mingling of sexual and religious imagery so common to the age: "I kissed the 'gates of Damascus' [an allusion to Bryusov's notorious 1903 poem likening the sex act to the road to Damascus], / Gates with a shield entwined in fur."[3] They are his last poems. On March 29, 1913, he put a Browning to his chest and pulled the trigger. He died in a Riga hospital on April 5 and was buried several days later in Petersburg's Smolenskoe Cemetery.[4]

Some said that he took his life when a woman he had seduced in Riga demanded that he marry her and complained about his refusal to his commanding officer, others that he had proposed to the daughter of a "good family" and had been rejected because of the gossip about his relationship with Kuzmin and Sudeikina.[5] In both versions he committed suicide out of a sense of besmirched honor. At the funeral in Petersburg, Knyazev's mother, looking Sudeikina directly in the eye, said, "God will punish those who made him suffer!"[6] The family certainly did not blame Kuzmin. Knyazev's mother wrote him about the death of her son and asked him to come to the funeral. He was a welcome guest at their apartment for several years after, and when he ran into the mother on September 28, 1922, at the Scholars' House, he wrote: "Knyazeva hailed me. Anya has taken the veil, Kirill is under arrest. Had Vsev[olod] not quarreled with me, he would not have shot himself—that is her opinion" (Diary).

We shall never know what drove Knyazev to his action, but at least one person put the onus on Kuzmin. Anna Akhmatova castigated him in her strenuously allusive *Poem without a Hero* as a satanic Cagliostro "Who does not weep with me over the dead, / who does not know what conscience means / and why it exists."[7] This verse indictment accords with a passage in the "sixth fragment" of her own "Prose about the *Poem*," which she wrote in the autumn of 1961: "I do not particularly want to talk about this, but for those who know the whole story of the year 1913, it is not a secret. I will only say that [Kuzmin] was probably born under a lucky star. He was one of those for whom all is permitted. Right now I will not enumerate what he was permitted, but were I to do so, a contemporary reader's hair would stand on end."[8]

Other of Akhmatova's comments on Kuzmin were no less accusatory.

On September 5, 1940, Lidiya Chukovskaya recorded Akhmatova's reaction to his last collection of poems, *The Trout Breaking through the Ice*: "The obscenity makes a very depressing impression . . . I would have liked dots in many places. . . . Kuzmin was always homosexual in his poetry, but here he exceeds all bounds. Before, one could not do this: Vyacheslav Ivanov might wince. But in the twenties, there was no longer anyone to be wary of... Perhaps Villon might have pulled it off, but as for Mikhail Alekseevich—no. It is utterly repulsive."[9] Not long after, Akhmatova began work on her own *Poem without a Hero*, which polemicizes with the first cycle of Kuzmin's collection, where he made a personal myth of the triumph of love between two men that is threatened by the destructive passion of one of them for a woman.

Aside from the fact that Akhmatova must have meant Verlaine, not Villon, who never wrote about same-sex love, and the preposterous assumption that Vyacheslav Ivanov (for whom she had developed a pathological hatred) would have disapproved of the book's gay dimension, there is something very sad about her remarks. Kuzmin "exceeded" no more "bounds" in the collection than in any other of his writings, including *Nets*, which Akhmatova professed to admire.[10] There is nothing at all explicit in the book or any of his others, and nothing remotely "obscene," unless for Akhmatova it was the fact that Kuzmin addresses, as usual, same-sex love. That had not shocked her, it would seem, when he lived under her roof in 1912, nor in the years 1921 to 1923, when she shared an apartment with Sudeikina (sparking rumors of a lesbian relationship), where Kuzmin, usually accompanied by his lover, was a constant and welcome visitor.

By the middle of the 1920s, friends of Akhmatova were noticing more than a bit of hostility in some of the remarks she made about Kuzmin. Her attitude may have stemmed in part from her quite mistaken belief that he had come to dislike her. That he was also a close friend of Anna Radlova, whom she detested, and had championed her poetry made matters worse. Then, too, Kuzmin's apartment had become a mecca for young writers, indeed for all who were engaged in anything innovative in the arts in Leningrad, while she lived in growing enforced isolation, officially condemned and banned from publishing her verse from 1925 to 1940. (Attacks on Kuzmin were no less vile after 1925, but he at least managed to get one book into print and played a certain role in the city's cultural life.) All that may help explain the

sourness and the tone of prudish moralizing in her statements about
him throughout the thirties and after, when most of her contemporaries
felt the lash of her tongue, although none to the extent of the puritanical vindictiveness of her portrait of Kuzmin.

Then, too, more than a bit of the anxiety of influence is evident here.
In 1912, at the time he was living at the Gumilevs' in Tsarskoe Selo,
Akhmatova had asked Kuzmin to write a preface for her first book of
verse, *Evening* (Vecher). He responded with a perceptive, even enthusiastic appreciation of it, and with an elegant poem, beginning "Like a
passing dove she flew down to us."[11] But then as now, no literary good
deed went unpunished. And what better way to distance herself from
the "wondrous teacher" to whose poetics her own verse owed so much
than to demonize him as the villain of the *Poem?*[12]

Akhmatova's fiercely protective attitude about the memory of Nikolay Gumilev also played a part in her change of heart toward Kuzmin.
She had been delighted when she learned that Kuzmin had taken the
time in 1925 to search through the Diary for references to Gumilev at
the request of the twenty-three-year-old Pavel Luknitsky, who was assembling everything he could for a biography. "She said that it was
evident at once that Kuzmin was indeed a real man of letters and that
she would thank him very much when they met," wrote Luknitsky.
"Kuzmin really had acted nobly when he gave me what he could. One
had to take into account his dislike for Nikolay Stepanovich... A[nna]
A[ndreevna] had complimented him highly—that too was noble: one
had to take into account her dislike for Kuzmin."[13] But that was all that
could temper her enmity. She thought she knew what black cat had
crossed the path of her husband's close relationship with Kuzmin, and
she spoke about it with Lidiya Chukovskaya on August 8, 1940:
"Kuzmin was a very bad man, malevolent, spiteful. Kolya wrote a review of *Autumnal Lakes* in which he called Kuzmin's verse 'boudoir
poetry.' Before publishing it, he showed it to Kuzmin, who asked him to
change the word 'boudoir' to 'salon.' All his life he never forgave Kolya
for that review."[14]

Gumilev had indeed begun his review with: "The poetry of M[ikhail]
Kuzmin is primarily 'salon' poetry, which is not to say that it is not real
poetry or beautiful. On the contrary, the 'salon quality' gives it something additional which makes it unlike any other poetry."[15] The tone of
the rest of the review and of the two others that he wrote later was

positive, at times laudatory, but even if "boudoir" had been qualified to "salon," the slightly patronizing opening sentence had done its damage. One can understand Kuzmin's offended feelings if not excuse his response. He had published a cautious but favorable review of Gumilev's fourth book of verse, *Foreign Skies* (Chuzhoe nebo), some months before in *Apollo*. There he had, quite correctly, called it transitional and a step forward for Gumilev, but pretty much left unsaid what he thought of the poetry.[16] Now he took the unprecedented step of reviewing the book again in *The Grainfield*. He again insisted on its transitional nature, but paid Gumilev back for the word "salon" by calling it "empty" ("that is all that one can say about it").[17] Kuzmin was full of compliments for Gumilev's mastery of form and predicted that his "striving for greater simplicity and liberation from romantic aestheticism" would yield a significant book. But that did nothing to assuage Gumilev, irritated as he already was by Kuzmin's refusal to pledge allegiance to the recently proclaimed Acmeism. The Diary makes no mention of any of these reviews and records many meetings between the two touchy poets without any hint of bad feelings between them,[18] but a strain had entered the relationship, and they never recovered the closeness of the years 1910–1912.

Kuzmin's relationship with Knyazev, which the latter's "Palladism," not Kuzmin's actions, had brought to an end, had been over for more than six months when Knyazev committed suicide. Was Kuzmin, however, as utterly indifferent to his fate as Akhmatova later accused him of being? The mask of composure that he wore for the Sudeikins and others might have made them think so. The memoirs of the little-known writer Fedor Ivanov provide an example of the way he donned it:

> Kuzmin once read me his diary. It is odd. Somehow there were no people in it at all. And if something is said, then it is somehow in passing, indifferently. About a man he had once loved:
> "Today they buried X."
> Literally four words. And then, as though nothing had occurred, about how T. K. has written a novel, and it is not as bad as one might have expected.[19]

Close study of the Diary reveals that Kuzmin had not simply read from it selectively to Ivanov, as he had done with others in the past, but had in this instance done so to create, for reasons known only to him, an image of callous indifference. The portion touching on Knyazev's funeral, which Ivanov clearly has in mind, actually reads, "Today is the funeral of unhappy Knyazev, his mother wrote to me" (April 8, 1913), and nothing else, while the comment about the novel of "T[atiana] K[rasnopolskaya]" occurs not only under another date but under another year: "Ryurik [Ivnev], Tatiana, and Semenov showed up. Tatiana read. It was not as bad as one might have expected" (April 28, 1914). Akhmatova had very probably heard of Kuzmin's "heartlessness" from Sudeikina (who herself may have heard a similar reading) or from Ivanov himself, who writes about Akhmatova in his memoirs. What might she have thought about him had Kuzmin crafted for them and others a different self-image? What if he had followed the sentence about Knyazev's funeral with this, an entry of June 23, 1910, about the death of an acquaintance who had shot himself two days before: "Figaro [one of his barbers] told me how Bekman died. I remember him very well. And now those lips, those eyes, hands, feet, the smell of his body are no more. If someone loved him, then it is simply unendurable. I could not work at all."

Kuzmin kept his own feelings about Knyazev's death to himself.[20] He certainly harbored no bitterness toward Sudeikina, whom he asked to accept the "modest gift of an old friend" in the poem of July 11, 1918, that he addressed to her. Its opening lines refer to the "merry and sad fate" that "had been linking us for a long time," an obvious allusion to her role in his affairs with Sudeikin and then Knyazev.[21] He made direct reference to her conduct only once, on May 16, 1921, when he gave vent to what he had felt after Sudeikina's December 1912 revelations in recalling the "petty and loathsome demonism that kept prompting Olenka to give herself to Knyazev right on my own sofas" (Diary).

He reserved his deepest thoughts and feelings for his verse. There are poets who, like Tsvetaeva, direct magnificent poetic invective at those love objects who scorn or reject them. Kuzmin never wrote a single poem of reproach. He did rearrange the poems of "An Example for Those in Love" into new cycles when he published some of them in *Clay Doves*, and, perhaps to spare the family, dedicated none of them to Knyazev. (Only one poem in the collection bears a dedication to him, a discreet "V. K.")[22] The sheer physicality of Kuzmin's passion for Knyazev had almost totally crowded out the Holy Warrior–Guide figure in most of the poems addressed to him. He is very much present in one of them, the sonnet that begins "Aspiring always for an elusive love," which originally formed a perfect acrostic for "Vsevolod Knyazev." When Kuzmin published the poem in *Clay Doves*, he destroyed the acrostic by changing the first word of its eleventh line from "I" (*ya*) to "and" (*i*), as though distancing Knyazev from his spiritual ideal of love and the Guide who presides over a life moving toward it.[23]

Knyazev was not, however, to be so easily erased from his art. On May 11, 1913, a month after his death, Kuzmin wrote of the "modest, ineffable miracle" of a love he "would never forget" in the poem that begins "Earth, you gave me a flower,"[24] and he dedicated to his memory an exquisite elegy that had been prompted by his death:

> At times a strange silence
> comes upon us,
> but within it lies hidden the crowning,
> the calm hour of happiness.
> Our angel, pensive above
> the ladder's rungs, looks down to
> where a golden haze hangs
> suspended amid autumnal trees.
> Again our steed, spurred on,
> will neigh in greeting,
> and will carry us forward at a good clip
> over an untrodden road.
> But do not be troubled by the halts along the way,
> my gentle, gentle friend,
> and do not disrupt our orbit
> with awkward explanations.
> Everything will be as it is destined,
> a guide leads us.
> For those hours lost here
> we shall partake of the honey of heaven.[25]

Its subtle amalgamation of beauty and sadness, loss and consolation, makes it one of Kuzmin's most personal and powerful meditations on death and his seraphic acceptance of it as an inevitable but never final moment in individual lives that move in a larger scheme toward perfection. It is hard to imagine more fitting tributes to the death of his former lover than these poems. The family knew to whom they were dedicated, but the world at large did not. Some feelings were too personal: when Kuzmin published the poems a year later, he removed the dedication, which is found only in the autograph.[26]

When he put together the collection *Clay Doves*, largely made up of his poetry of 1912–13 (the major exception being "The New Rolla"), he forsook chronology by opening it with a poem of 1913 dedicated to Evdokiya Nagrodskaya, the one that gives the volume its title,[27] and immediately followed it with a cycle, "On the Journey" ("V doroge," dated February–August 1913), which he dedicated to Yury Yurkun, thus acknowledging to the world the centrality these two people had assumed in his life. The Diary, which resumes on March 3, 1913, as abruptly as it had stopped on January 12, says simply, "I just cannot get my writing going; the closest possible friendship with Nagrodskaya, my love for Yurkun, my departure from the Sudeikins—that is all that has happened."

We know almost nothing about the early life of Yury Yurkun except that he was Lithuanian and Catholic by birth and, having been born on September 17, 1895, was not yet eighteen years old when Kuzmin met him in Kiev in February 1913.[28] What he was doing there is a mystery. Some say Kuzmin saw him in a theater, where he was acting under the slightly preposterous pseudonym "Mongandri," others that he was working as a clerk in a store that sold books and musical scores, where Kuzmin encountered him. Even his name poses a puzzle. He was apparently born Iosif Yurkunas, which he "Russianized" to Osip Yurkun. He first appears in the Diary as Yurkun, and then only as Yurochka, the affectionate diminutive of Yury. Kuzmin himself seems to have given him the name that he used for the rest of his life: it is another form of George in Russian, and that name had had a special meaning for Kuzmin ever since his love affair with "Prince Georges" twenty years before. Kuzmin had known the bitter disappointment that every intimate acquaintance yielded over and over in his life, yet he never lost faith in the inextinguishable force that guided him: "Love—my constant faith."[29] What better way to signal his confidence than by giving to the young man with whom he fell in love at first sight the name of that Holy Warrior saint who watched over his life? Yurkun returned to Petersburg with Kuzmin, and, though hardly inseparable, they were friends, lovers, and companions for the rest of Kuzmin's life, the "Petersburg Verlaine and Rimbaud" of so many memoirs.[30]

Yurkun for a time shared a room in Petersburg with a young acquaintance of Kuzmin's, and he immediately started paying court to and may have had an affair with Nadezhda Zborovskaya-Auslender, the actress wife of Kuzmin's nephew. Once again Kuzmin was involved with what we would now call a bisexual many years his junior, and the consequences were just what he might have expected. Yurkun kept company with what sounds from the Diary to have been the most bohemian young crowd that frequented the "Stray Dog," to which Kuzmin was "dragged" far too often considering the state of his pocketbook. Kuzmin introduced him to friends, including Sudeikin, whose portrait of him captured the seductive smile but not the color of his thinly browed, heavy-lidded gray eyes, a constant motif from then on in Kuzmin's verse.[31]

"No, life's windmill has not ground out / love's boldness in my blood,— / I want to break into a boyish song / of love at the top of my voice!"[32] Those lines begin the first poem that Kuzmin addressed to his new muse in February, and throughout 1913 poem after poem celebrated both the "unexpected guest" who had brought him "youth and light" and his love for him, which combined the "tenderness of a brother, the loyalty of a friend, and the passion of a lover."[33] But he knew also that this was, as he wrote in one poem, "not the love of a young man, / but of a child and of a man / (perhaps an old one),"[34] and its course was anything but smooth during their years together.

Kuzmin's anxiety about his lover's feelings for him shadowed the relationship for a very long time, especially at the beginning, when he was often worried, even exasperated by Yurkun's behavior: "I love him very much, but his obstinacy and hooliganism will destroy him, no doubt about it" (Diary, May 27, 1913). On June 19 he experienced a "surge of boundless tenderness for Yurochka, whom everyone is persecuting because of the fact that I love him too much" (Diary). Some well-intentioned friends, believing that he had fallen into the clutches of a younger version of Miller, tried to separate him from his new lover. They could never succeed, for "Without you my life is empty. / I will be with you to the grave," as Kuzmin wrote in the poem that fixed in verse forever the "tear-stained violets" of his lover's eyes on the dreadful day, June 21, when they "thought everything was over" and almost parted because of the scheming of Yakov Izrailevich.[35]

Kuzmin had to support Yurkun to keep him in Petersburg, and to do that he had to put his own disordered life in order and get his writing going. He thought that he had found the financial and psychological support to do both in his friendship with Evdokiya Nagrodskaya and her wealthy husband, Vladimir, an engineer and high official in the Ministry of Transportation. Nagrodskaya had been an actress, but she was the daughter of Avdotya Panaeva, a prose writer more renowned as the hostess of one of Petersburg's most famous mid–nineteenth-century literary salons, and she had literary talents and ambitions herself.

Most critics sneered at the popular success of women writers like Anastasiya Verbitskaya, dismissing their fiction as sensationalist trash (what the Russians call *bul'varnaya literatura*, literally, "boulevard literature"). Most were merciless toward Nagrodskaya's first novel, *The Wrath of Dionysus* (Gnev Dionisa), a melodramatic tale of a love triangle between two men and a "liberated" woman painter, which became hugely successful when it was published in 1910.[36] She probably expected the worst from the arbiter of excellence for prose in *Apollo*, but Kuzmin pronounced her novel a good read in his review and noted the "tact" and "boldness" with which it touched on "dangerous and contemporary questions."[37] (There is a gay subplot.)

Kuzmin met the neither fashionable nor quite respectable writer on December 8, 1912, at the "Stray Dog," remarking that, like Zinaida Vengerova, another "fag hag," to use the slang of a later age, she was "comforting" (Diary). By spring 1913 he was taking an early afternoon dinner with her almost every day, and on the third of July, unable because of his chronically desperate financial straits to set up a living arrangement with Yurkun, he accepted her invitation to move from the hotel where he had been living since leaving the Sudeikins' to her spacious apartment on the Moika (no. 91), at the Sinii Most (Blue Bridge).

Many of Kuzmin's friends, remembering his long stay at Ivanov's illustrious "Tower," were shocked that he had now become a "member of the family" at what one, Ryurik Ivnev, called Nagrodskaya's "questionable salon." Ivnev, a novice poet of Futurist leanings who met Kuzmin there in 1913, wondered how the "poet-aesthete" could "live in the same apartment with the author of vulgarly popular novels," and noted "how ill assorted were the people in this salon, which could be called literary only with the greatest stretch of the imagination, for aside from Kuzmin, there was not a single genuine writer."[38] Georgy Ivanov, another visitor, sniffed at the atmosphere which surrounded

Kuzmin in the apartment, its walls covered with signed pictures and autographs of those who had paid a call, where "in [Kuzmin's] absence and in his presence, they call him a genius," and where the hostess tried to "instill this in her new author: 'You are subtle. You are sensitive. These decadents have been forcing you to ruin your talent. Forget what they instilled in you... Be yourself.'"[39] She may never have called him the Russian Balzac, as Ivanov asserted, but in one letter she did style him a Goethe in prose, and her flattery at times tried Kuzmin's patience: "Yurochka was with me [at Nagrodskaya's], but I got sick of all the conversations solely about my and his genius" (Diary, December 21, 1913).

He was well aware of the difference between this milieu and that of the past. A year after he had moved into her apartment, he observed: "As I was writing, I thought of the 'Interludes,' *Apollo*, Somov, Nouvel. All the same, there was brilliance then, interest, society, culture, and recognition, but now some backwoods or other" (July 17, 1914), adding a few days later, "It is as if I am in captivity. I am sinking lower and lower to an unbelievable degree" (July 29). When one of his friends later asked him why he had stayed so long, he replied with a joke: "But she fed me very juicy cutlets!"[40] Irritating as she soon became after he moved in, she and her husband did for a time provide the semblance of a family atmosphere to someone who found "no real peace in solitude" (April 1, 1914). But by August 1914, when their relationship had become irretrievably frosty, he asked himself, "Why do I lack the strength to leave?" He was unsparing in his answer: "The fear of losing comfort? Yes. There you have it, enslavement to a placid life, and a lack of courage. . . . And I depend on her money" (August 16).

He later recalled the "difficulty and gloom of my life at the Nagrodskys'" (Diary, March 21, 1922), and the Diary, despite a long gap from July 5 to December 3, 1913, provides ample evidence of her "lack of tact and intelligence" and her touchiness: "We argued about Debussy [whose music she detested], and Evd[okiya] Ap[ollonovna] became terribly offended. I never know how to act with her, and to conduct myself as Sazonov [an actor] does, to flatter and every minute worry about what side to show, is very difficult" (March 1, 1914). She wanted, he came to realize, a "lapdog," and any sign of an independent opinion provoked jealous scenes, "doubly unpleasant" to him because they resembled, he thought, quarrels between lovers, not friends. What finally drove him from the apartment, however, was her jealousy of his feelings for Yurkun and her clumsy attempts to break up the relationship. On October 13 he rented two rooms on Spasskaya Street (no. 10), "in the same building, it seems, where Naumov lived and where Knyazev was born" (Diary). Five days later he moved. Nagrodskaya kept up her "filthy intrigues" for many months, but once she gave them up, he made his peace with her, and in 1916 dedicated the novel *The Quiet Guard* to her.

By the time they parted ways in 1914, Kuzmin was convinced that Nagrodskaya, in order to make him totally dependent on her, was trying to sabotage the relationships with publishers that he had established with her help. That she failed to do. In June 1913 she had introduced him to her publisher, Matvey Semenov, whose prosperous Petersburg firm put out an array of prose, poetry, and nonfiction. He was unreliable at the best of times and liked to dole out royalties piecemeal, which often enraged Kuzmin, but the contract Kuzmin signed with him in 1914 for an edition of his collected works promised to provide some kind of reasonably steady income, even if his finances were precarious in the first months on his own.[41]

Before embarking on that venture, Kuzmin had had to launch Yurkun's career. He had taken charge of his education from the moment they arrived in Petersburg, reading Plato, contemporary poets, Leskov, and Pushkin with him. He also from the start encouraged him in his writing, and recommended him to his own publishers. Lyubov Gurevich, who had replaced Bryusov as literary editor of *Russian Thought*, and her prose referees repeatedly turned down his submissions,[42] but Kuzmin's persistence with Vladimir Bondi, editor of the mass magazine *Little Fire* (Ogonek), finally paid off when Bondi published his protégé's "Lithuanian legend" "For He Knew What He Did" ("Ibo On znal, chto delal") in the second issue for 1914.

Kuzmin had similar luck with some other magazine editors who owed him a favor, but at first the young man's stories more often met with rejections, and the humiliating dependency on his mentor at times put a severe strain on their relationship. He desperately needed, Kuzmin believed, some affirmation of his talent, and he did everything in his power to get it for him. He managed, despite Nagrodskaya's intrigues, to persuade Semenov to issue Yurkun's first novel, the autobiographical *Swedish Gloves* (Shvedskie perchatki). Kuzmin saw the novel's "distant relatives" in Lesage, Sterne, and Dickens (critics saw Anatole France and Kuzmin himself), but he insisted on its uniqueness in the preface that he wrote for it in February 1914 and in the lecture about contemporary Russian prose that he delivered on April 13, 1914, at the "Stray Dog." There, in effect, he "presented" the novel and its author to the public by using excerpts from it to illustrate his talk.[43] It came out in June with the dedication "To the person who is dearest of all to me and a friend," a few weeks after Semenov had issued *Clay Doves* as volume three of the collected works, to the praise of friends such as Gumilev: "I met Babenchikov [a young art critic]. He says that Gumilev thinks *Clay Doves* is the best of my books" (Diary, July 8).[44] Kuzmin had spent weeks going over Yurkun's novel, "correcting" it in January and February, yet he had to note in the preface that it had "its own language, at times apparently incorrect, with Polonisms and a not very rich vocabulary." (Yurkun's first language seems to have been Polish, not Russian, which was not odd for someone growing up in Lithuania at that time.) The critics took Yurkun to task for just that in their reviews. One wrote that Kuzmin would have done the author a greater service by translating the novel into Russian instead of writing a preface. The acerbic Vladislav Khodasevich judged the novel's language "definitely illiterate," while noting that Yurkun "undoubtedly" had a "genuine literary gift."[45]

Somov found the diary-like novel an "interesting document . . . sincere and tender," but he doubted that a writer would emerge "from this Yurkun" and predicted it would be his only book.[46] He was wrong about that. Yurkun worked hard on his language and improved a great deal (if not quite enough) of his craft under the careful guidance of Kuzmin, who, like a proud parent, took pleasure in every one of his modest successes and who suffered from his lover's bad reviews and rejections by publishers far more than he ever did for those he received himself. Yurkun started a new novel, *Bad Company* (Durnaya kompaniya), in April 1914, which he dedicated to Sudeikin. In it the influence of his reading with Kuzmin of Hoffmann is obvious. *Russian Thought* turned it down for publication, but that was one of his few failures in 1915, when he managed to publish a number of stories.

At the very end of 1915, "Cove" ("Lukomor'e"), another of Kuzmin's publishers, issued a volume of Yurkun's *Stories Written on Kirochnaya Street in House Number 48* (Rasskazy, napisannye na Kirochnoi ul., v dome pod No. 48), its title taken from the address of the building, near the Tavricheskii Garden and not far from where Knyazev had lived, where he had rooms (apartment 16). The first story is dedicated to Kuzmin, and each of the others also bears a dedication. In the aggregate these provide a virtual compendium of his and Kuzmin's acquaintances of the period: Ryurik Ivnev; E. M. Miklashevskaya, probably the sister of the theater specialist Konstantin Miklashevsky; Boris Mosolov, a young actor and director; Yakov Gishpling, the frequent "Yasha" of the Diary, a young gay friend; Tatiana Shenfeld, who wrote under the pen name Krasnopolskaya (for a time in the autumn of 1914, when she intrigued against him and Yurkun, Kuzmin found "her stupidity is matched only by her insolence" [Diary, October 8]); Georgy Ivanov; Leonid Kannegiser, a young gay poet who, Kuzmin believed, had a harmless crush on Yurkun; Yury Slezkin, a prose writer from Vilnius who headed the Petersburg arts club the "Bronze Horseman," in which Yurkun and Kuzmin took part;[47] Nagrodskaya; the artist Boris Grigoriev; Glebova-Sudeikina; Georgy Adamovich, another novice poet who was gay; and the artist Aleksandr Bozheryanov, whom Kuzmin had known since 1909 and who did the cover for the book, as well as for *Swedish Gloves* and all the volumes of the Semenov collected edition.

In 1912 Kuzmin had pondered the "strange" prophetic power that poets sometimes possess: "Future misfortune / is now brought down, / is now staved off / by incoherent hints."[48] His own fiction had provided an unhappy instance of this power: one of the plot lines of *Dreamers* involves a young officer who betrays the affection of his male friend for the seductions of a woman and commits suicide. Less than a year later Knyazev had taken his own life. Kuzmin returned to the theme in the novel that he was working on while he helped ready Yurkun's first novel for print. He finished *Travelers by Sea and Land*, its title taken from the Orthodox prayer of intercession, on March 21, 1914, and dedicated the roman à clef to his young companion when Semenov published it in February 1915.

Glebova-Sudeikina easily recognized herself in the femme fatale Elena Tsarevskaya, who stands at the center of several tangled liaisons. Although married, she does everything she can to attract the attentions of two men, a young poet named Lavrik Pekarsky (clearly modeled on Yurkun), and a young officer, Dmitry Lavrentiev. Unlike Knyazev, the obvious source for Lavrentiev, both escape her clutches. Acquaintances had no trouble spotting real-life prototypes for some of the other characters (the merciless portrait of Pallada as "Polina") and for the setting where much of the action takes place, a cellar cabaret called the "Owl" ("Sova"), which Kuzmin portrays as a place of mindless frivolity and amorous intrigues, ephemeral but potentially destructive. Suicide threatens several of the characters, among them a young officer named Viktor Frolov, who manages to conquer the impulse only through the help of an older Englishman named Stock, who is given some of Kuzmin's most cherished views of love and life as a journey. The actress Zoya Lilienfeld, whom Kuzmin modeled on the dancer Ida Rubinstein and Akhmatova, does take her life when her lover rejects her, but the others avoid that fate. Some, including the Sudeikins, were "a bit hurt" by the novel (Diary, March 14, 1915), while others, such as Akhmatova, were deeply offended by what they saw as a lampoon of Petersburg artistic circles. (She later made several polemical allusions to the novel in her *Poem without a Hero*.) But as in so many of his works, Kuzmin had only made "life" follow the paradigm of his gay fictional world. Once the major male characters leave the city and the cabaret behind, they "bond" at the country estate of Lavrentiev, named "Lakes" (a transparent allusion to the title of Kuzmin's second verse collection and its gay "examples to those in love"). They are close to but far enough away from the neighboring estate with a no less symbolic name, "Backwaters," where the women, who no longer pose a threat to male friendship, have gathered.

Throughout his stay at Nagrodskaya's, Kuzmin had complained that "her constant grudges and chatter" (Diary, January 7, 1914) took up all his time, forcing him to rise early in the morning if he were to get any writing done at all before she "descended" on his rooms for hours. Once he was out of her apartment, prose poured from his pen. Verse was by no means forgotten, but prose paid far better, and in the years from 1913 to 1916 he wrote more of it than at any other time in his life, much of it calling to mind Degas's rebuke to Whistler: "Mr. Whistler, you behave as though you had no talent at all." Nagrodskaya had never encouraged an atmosphere of self-criticism and careful craft: during the same years she published four novels and three volumes of stories, each of them immediately reprinted. Now, with no one to help support him (and as careless with money as ever), he followed her example: whatever he wrote, he published, enough to make up five volumes of the collected works.[49]

He did not, however, delude himself about its worth. On September 30, 1915, after reading some harsh criticism of his new fiction, he had to conclude that "all the same, all the failures began after the move to the Nagrodskys'. That was a *faux pas* that is hardly reparable" (Diary). Three days later he was even more brutal: "I am losing everything little by little. I am trash." He was too hard on himself. In the best of the works, his experience as a gay man is everywhere apparent in his appreciation of the liberating power of honesty and his humanizing treatment of marginal characters. But in too many, no matter how skillfully told, we have little but anecdotes, diversity, but with little complexity or depth, stories nicely crafted for the space limits and tastes of the popular magazines and newspapers for which he was now doing almost all of his writing. At the end of 1920, after re-reading some of this work, he had to admit that the novels in particular were simply "boring," one of the most damning words in his vocabulary.

In his April 1914 lecture at the "Stray Dog," he had remarked that the mass-circulation press, which catered to the demands of Russia's growing readership for entertainment, sensation, and easily digestible information on current events, the arts, medicine, and science, now welcomed Russia's leading writers, almost all of whom took advantage of the high royalties. He called this development the "triumph of modernism," and added, "After *Libra* closed, there was no stronghold of modernism, and all writers went not to the people [an allusion to the slogan of the nineteenth-century Populist movement] but to the public, taking part in magazines large and small." Since Znosko-Borovsky had turned down *Dreamers* in the summer of 1912, Kuzmin had contributed little to *Apollo* except for the occasional poem; in any event, it was evolving into an art journal.[50] He did continue his association with serious magazines such as *Russian Thought, The Contemporary* (Sovremennik), the distinguished new *Northern Annals* (Severnye zapiski, a Petersburg literary journal put out by a wealthy Jewish couple, Sophia Chatskina and her husband, Yakov Saker),[51] and with the liberal-conservative daily *Stock Market Gazette*, where most of Russia's finest writers appeared regularly, and where in 1915–1917 Kuzmin reviewed the productions mounted by the permanent French company of the Mikhailovskii Theater. But readers could most often encounter his prose, poems, and critical writings in the pages of *The Grainfield*, *Little Fire*, *Satyricon* (Satirikon), *New Word* (Novoe slovo), *Russia's Sun* (Solntse Rossii), *Argus*, and even the lowbrow *Cove* (Lukomor'e), a literary-satirical magazine that many writers avoided because of its association with the right-wing Suvorin family. ("To what have I come? I am going into Suvorin's magazine" [Diary, March 28, 1914].) To their credit, the magazines did publish some of Kuzmin's best verse, hardly "light reading," but the poems seem lost in the swamp of trash surrounding them, and they came into their own only when gathered in the collection *The Guide*.

The "writer's existence," Kuzmin remarked, is "wretched, carefree, and sacred" (Diary, July 1, 1914). Wretched financially he was at least determined to be no longer, as he now turned also to translations (Alcaeus, Rimbaud, Cazotte, Schiller) and especially the theater to help augment his income. The "Stray Dog" had meant to offer regular theater evenings, but without a well-thought-out program, it soon "perished from chaotic and monotonous improvisations," as Kuzmin wrote in 1916.[52] It was that aimlessness which kept him away. While his name is indelibly associated with the legend of the cabaret, he very rarely visited it after he moved out of the Sudeikin apartment, just as he distanced himself from it symbolically in *Travelers by Sea and Land*, in which fire destroys the "Owl."[53] Guenther and Izrailevich had tried to start a Pushkin theater with Kuzmin as its literary adviser in 1913. They planned to stage Russian classics and works by Kuzmin, Gumilev, Auslender, and other friends, but they could find no financial backing. Other dreams for a new theater also came to nothing. With no alternative, Kuzmin turned to Moscow's "Bat" and the "theaters of miniatures" in Petersburg such as the Liteinyi Intimate Theater, the Troitskii Theater, the Intimate Theater of B. S. Nevolin, the Queen of Spades, and the Pavillon de Paris (a cinema with "live" interludes). They specialized in evenings of light entertainment, programs of readings, vaudevilles, stagings of stories and poems, ballet-pantomimes, "living pictures," and the "living dolls" for which Baliev's "Bat" was particularly famous.[54] Kuzmin had an obvious flair for the kind of repertory they demanded, and his own experience as a performer meant that he worked well with them and could produce a text, usually with his own music, on short notice.

Few of the playlets, vaudevilles, and ballets that he wrote in the years 1914–1917, works with titles such as *Alice, Who Was Afraid of Mice*

(Alisa, kotoraya boyalas' myshei, 1913), *The King's Kitchen Boys* (Korolevskie povaryata, 1914), *The Fairy, the Bassoon, and the Stagehand* (Feya, fagot i mashinist, 1915), *The Windiest Place in England* (Samoe vetrenoe mesto v Anglii, 1917), left a lasting impression. They were ephemeral in every sense of the word (we cannot even be certain when and where most of them were performed), but now that their texts have been disinterred from the archives and published, we can see how well crafted and stageworthy they were, works of wit and invention by a consummate theater professional.[55]

No strictures apply to *Venetian Madcaps* (1912).[56] In the summer of 1913, Somov had asked Kuzmin to write a play that he wanted to design for a private production at the house of Evfimiya Nosova, an heiress of the millionaire merchant Ryabushinsky family. Kuzmin, who had met her at the end of 1911, responded to the lucrative commission with *The Würtemberg Twins* (Vyurtembergskie bliznetsy, text lost), but Somov rejected it as unsuitable. She persisted, however, and Kuzmin sent the two-act *Venetian Madcaps*. It received its first and only performance at the Nosov mansion on February 23, 1914, with sets and costumes by Sudeikin (Nosova had quarreled with Somov), Kuzmin's music, and choreography by Mikhail Mordkin, the *premier danseur* of the Bol'shoi Theater. Kuzmin heard from Dobuzhinsky on March 4 that it had been "acted very badly" (Diary) by its largely amateur cast drawn from some of Moscow's wealthiest families, but his spirits picked up on the twelfth, when he heard that it was "being praised in Moscow." A year later, an elegant limited edition of the play (555 numbered copies) appeared for sale with color plates of Sudeikin's costume designs, as memorable an example of the printer's art in Russia as the performance had been in the annals of its amateur theatricals.

Set in the "Venice of Goldoni, Gozzi, and Longhi," the play, a melo-dramatic tale of love and jealousy, fate and retribution (once again in Kuzmin a seductress disrupts a male friendship, with murderous re-sults), would not be much more than a graceful conceit were it not for one factor: the improbable stone mirage of Venice itself. Kuzmin im-bued the text with the spirit of the city, that "perpetual fluidity" to which its cult of masks and masquerades pays literal-minded tribute. The songs, dances, and pantomimes skillfully integrate the intrigues of several love triangles, and the powers of dissimulation blur any line between "reality" and the stage more thoroughly (and modernly) than the Venetian master Gozzi could have imagined, as Venetian aristocrats and members of a traveling commedia dell'arte troupe assume a series of disguises and roles in this drama of fantasy and extravagance. "Of course," Kuzmin once remarked, "Venice and St. Petersburg are no further apart than Pavlovsk and Tsarskoe Selo,"[57] and the play is his finest tribute to the city he loved above all others in Europe and to his beloved Gozzi. The "luxury of the staging" had been "taken to its limits," one memoirist recalled,[58] and in a matter of months, anything like the "exquisite spectacle" the select guests had seen would be unthinkable, indeed, even immoral to many.

"War has been declared on Serbia" (July 13, 1914); "War. So many will be killed. Life is the only irretrievable thing" (July 18); "So many young people will die. My God" (July 20). Stark Diary entries like those in July and the months that followed evince none of the patriotic fervor, the almost holiday spirit ("everyone but me is rejoicing," he remarked), with which Russians, like people in all the belligerent countries, greeted the outbreak of war. War fever gripped writers, artists, and intellectuals no less than the purveyors of mass culture.[59] The subtle philosopher Vladimir Ern, German and Scandanavian by origin and a close friend of the Germanophile Vyacheslav Ivanov (who gave vent to one strident anti-German diatribe after another), set the tone as he thundered, like a modern Savonarola, his famous "From Kant to Krupp" from a Moscow stage and predicted, before catastrophic setbacks to Russian arms put an end to fantasies, that "The Time is Slavophilizing" ("Vremya slavyanofil'stvuet").[60]

No Germanophobe himself, Kuzmin was not immune to the mood that prevailed in the first year of the conflict, as intellectuals of every stripe rushed to denounce the enemy. His few statements on Germany do, however, show a nuance missing from the militant posture taken by most commentators, especially after the "rape" of Belgium and the shelling of the cathedral at Rheims, when everything "Teutonic" was labeled barbaric and inhuman. It was the "ugly Germans" Kaiser Wilhelm and Richard Wagner, about whom his old reservations now resurfaced, who became the favorite targets of his scorn. In answer to a questionnaire entitled "Everyone on the Germans," published in the autumn of 1914, he wrote:

At the present moment, when one says "German" one is saying "Prussian." [The Russian word for "Prussian" can also mean "cockroach"; German slang for the insect was "Russen"!] One must not forget Luther, Goethe, and Mozart, but one thinks about the Emperor Wilhelm, Wagner, and war. . . . We see what a culture built on a neurotic striving for external greatness and "major art" comes to and at what cost. It is clear that the disgusting and savage manifestations of German "might," Berlin's Ziegeralle, Wilhelm, Wagner, and all of Germany's art of the past fifty years are one and the same. God grant that this evil mirage, this hypnotic spell will disappear, and that Germany will once again cultivate those genuine cultural values that have not, perhaps, been totally trampled to death there by this farcical megalomania.[61]

He sounded a similar note in a poem written at the same time: "Will Germany reconsider and decide / to abandon this ruinous itinerary / to which a ridiculous mania and / a Wagnerian buffoon in a helmet are leading?!"[62]

There was a widespread aversion to Wagner that stemmed from the belief in his alleged imperialist ideology. But Kuzmin's suspicions about his "pernicious talent" lay elsewhere: "A truly grandiose and lofty conception of the world . . . almost always leads to the tender-heartedness of St. Francis ('Water, my little sister'), to the comic operas of Mozart, and to the serene satires of Anatole France. Underdeveloped or badly understood ones to the clanging of spurs, Romanticism, and Wagner."[63] He never tired of iterating that "the more an age and art strive toward *grand art*, the more lifeless they become,"[64] and the art of Wagner offered the best example of his axiom, as he exploded in conversation with Georgy Adamovich:

Wagner? You're talking about him again?. . . Listen, I'll explain something to you. Works of genius? Yes. Grandiose? Yes. New? Yes. Yes, yes, unusual. Long before you, Rimsky-Korsakov used to drone on and on to me about this newness of genius. But it is inhuman. And I suffocate from boredom. There is something, somewhere in *Tristan*... That English horn of the shepherd... Yes, unforgettable. But as a whole inhuman. Like some never-ending military review on the Kaiserplatz.[65]

Only later, in the 1920s, would he regain respect for several of the composer's operas, and he would evoke the "unforgettable" shepherd's horn solo in the 1921 poem "Tristan's Elegy."[66]

Poems, stories, and feuilletons on the war by writers young and old flooded the Russian press, so much so that only two months into the war, Kuzmin wrote with some exasperation: "They brought me a copy of *Russian Thought*. That cheered me up somehow, that there is still literature apart from all the journalese war drivel" (Diary, September 30, 1914).[67] He could hardly avoid the theme of the war himself, as the periodicals he relied on for income wanted nothing else in 1914. The handful of poems he wrote in the immediate aftermath of the declaration of war and the more numerous stories from 1914 and 1915 are hardly distinguished, but they do differ sharply from the glorifications of war and the caricatures of national stereotypes that the philosophical and literary armchair warriors were writing on demand. Some of the poems, with their religious imagery and evocations of warrior saints, suggest a holy war against the infidel Hun and Turk, and indulge the age-old Russian dream of reclaiming Constantinople for Orthodoxy, but the majority invoke divine protection for the common Russian soldiers and convey a sense of their ordeal and that of their families without any false heroics. They avoid the rhetorical invective and the "high diction" that dominated the early "heroic" stage of the war, and mercifully lack the homoeroticism so common in much of English war poetry, with its celebration of male friendship and beautiful youths laid low by death.

Eight of his stories appeared in a separate volume of *War Stories* (Voennye rasskazy, 1915), while another six made up the "Troubled Life" ("Smutnoe zhit'e") section of the 1916 collection *Interlude in the Ravine* (Antrakt v ovrage). Almost all are sentimental tales set on the homefront, in the far north of Russia, and in Belgium, and deal with the plight of refugees, families facing separation, or personal dramas exacerbated by the call to military service. If set at the front, they treat a simple regimental chaplain or soldiers stoically going about painful duties, not performing feats of bravery. Kuzmin was, of course, too old to face any form of service, but not Yurkun and other young friends. At the beginning of September 1915, it looked as though Yurkun would be called up, and he and Kuzmin spent three agonizing weeks of uncertainty before he received a medical exemption. Long before conscription threatened him, however, we see in the Diary an awareness, unusual as early as 1914, about the senseless slaughter in the trenches. The military censorship did its best to hide the real truth from those at home, but a sensitive eye could imagine it: "Then we went to the cinema [*v kinemo*]. Film of a battle. How people are dying. This is irreparable, for everyone is loved by someone" (Diary, December 23, 1914). As so often in Kuzmin's life, a personal moral compass set him a truer course than that provided by accepted opinion. He never refused a request to participate in charity benefits for aid to the wounded and refugees, but after 1915 he declined to write about "this loathsome war which is poisoning everything" (Diary, August 31, 1915). If he could not address its pain with truth, he preferred to keep silent, even if it meant that his income suffered. Similarly, he rejected orders for the kind of patriotic spectacles that theaters were now commissioning. In one of the war stories, "The Cue" ("Replika," 1915), he even quietly satirized the mock-heroics of those stage potboilers by having a character, an actor of modest talents in a provincial theater, transcend the maudlin sentimentality and false bravado required by his script by replacing his lines with the actual words uttered by his brother, who was murdered when trying to save the honor of his daughter from German officers.

Ever since meeting Yurkun, he had become an avid moviegoer. Unlike some writers (Khodasevich comes to mind) who feared the new medium as a threat to literature and high culture in general, Kuzmin, always drawn to forms of popular culture, enjoyed it for what it was, and he dismissed as ridiculous its supposed dire effects on society.[68] He also felt that it posed a stimulating challenge to age-old and rather threadbare theatrical habits (especially the "psychologizing" of so many contemporary Russian plays) and offered fascinating means of transcending traditional narrative linearity through its ability to move viewers seamlessly from one time and space to another. He waited until the 1920s, after exposure to the brilliance of German Expressionist cinema and the movies of D. W. Griffith, to experiment with nonlinear narration in his plays, but in 1914 he explored the possibilities of "silent acting," that is, pantomime. In the brief theoretical article "On Pantomime, Cinematograph, and Conversational Plays,"[69] he called on playwrights to write pieces for the stage combining words (the fewer the better) and gesture in a way that would make them "coincide" in "exact" harmony. He put his idea into practice in *Whit-Monday in Toledo* (Dukhov den' v Toledo), a "pantomime in three scenes," which Aleksandr Tairov commissioned in December 1914 for his newly opened Chamber (Kamernyi) Theater in Moscow.

Tairov, one of the most innovative directors of the golden age of the

Russian theater, tried to steer a course between the naturalism of Stan-islavsky's "method" and the "conscious theatricality" of Meyerhold. He had been impressed by Kuzmin's innate sense of the theater when they collaborated on the staging of Benavente's *Intereses creados* in 1912, and Kuzmin's ideas about the untapped potential of pantomime intrigued him. Kuzmin gave him music, brief stage directions, and rudimentary dialogue (reminiscent of silent film titles) for the outlines of a plot of jealousy and death set in Spain, in which "live" actors invert the tale performed by marionettes during a second-act commedia dell'arte pup-pet show. He left it up to Tairov and the cast to find the appropriate gestural panache. Kuzmin was not to know if what he had called for in his article could be achieved, for Tairov ignored his instructions and produced the play, which opened on March 23, 1915, with sets and costumes by Pavel Kuznetsov, as pure mime. The audience enjoyed the color and atmosphere of the spectacle, but the critics did not, pro-nouncing it a fiasco. Kuzmin was undeterred, and his next major work for the theater would employ his cinematic conceptions about the stage even more radically.

In some of the belligerent countries, the coming of war had at first brought a feeling of liberation from constraints and conventions. Not so in Russia, where the imposition of a strict military censorship and public austerity measures brought back memories of the worst days before the reforms of 1905. The "Stray Dog" was among the victims of the official puritanical spirit: on March 3, 1915, only a few days after the publication of *Travelers by Sea and Land*, the authorities closed the popular cabaret, ostensibly for violations of the stringent new liquor regulations. Even before that happened, Pronin had been making plans to open a new cabaret theater dubbed the "Comedians' Rest" ("Prival komediantov"), where he and like-minded friends could experiment in a way that had long been impossible at the "Stray Dog." He wanted Meyerhold as the centerpiece of the enterprise, and he hoped that Kuzmin, who was a member of the advisory group for the director's "Studio," would also play an active role.[70]

Pronin located another cellar suitable for his purposes in the historic Adamini House at the intersection of the Moika and the Field of Mars in central Petersburg and completely refurbished it with the help of the artists Boris Grigoriev and Aleksandr Yakovlev and the architect Ivan Fomin, who designed colorful tiled stoves and elaborate fireplaces. But it was Sudeikin, the guiding "decorative spirit" at the "Stray Dog," who took charge. He named the cellar's largest room, where theatrical performances were to be given, the "Hall of Carlo Gozzi and Ernst Theodor Amadeus Hoffmann," and studded its walls and ceiling with mirrors that entrapped the viewers in a maze of shifting reflections. It featured a portrait of Gozzi and figures from his *Fiabe*. Meyerhold had given the name *A Love for Three Oranges* (Lyubov' k trem apel'sinam) to his new theater magazine in homage to Gozzi's first theatrical triumph, the 1761 *L'amore delle tre melarance*. In recognition of that, Sudeikin designed a special costume for him, an eighteenth-century-style rose satin camisole with silver buttons, a blue cloak, a three-cornered plumed hat, and a Venetian carnival mask with a large beak. Wearing it as his alter ego, Doctor Dapertutto, he was to greet visitors to the hall, as if Gozzi or one of his characters had stepped from the walls.

When the cabaret finally opened on April 18, 1916, Kuzmin welcomed the first-nighters with:

In this place, all are children and all are beautiful. Here reigns fantasy, here wafts the spirit of Count Gozzi and the divine Hoffmann. . . . The poets who are prepared to share their inspirations with us may, perhaps, belong to different schools. They may even be their leaders, but here they are only poets, children, and dreamers. When you cross the threshold of the "Comedians' Rest," leave behind all divisions, all burdens. . . . Give yourselves up to sweet and beneficial fantasy! . . . Give us your hand! Lady Fantasy will usher you into her kingdom. And you will be simple as children.[71]

Meyerhold's new staging of the Schnitzler pantomime first given as *Colombine's Scarf* at the "House of Interludes" in 1910 followed, this time with sets and costumes by Sudeikin. Kuzmin expressed reservations about the work's "unpleasant naturalism" and loathed Dohnányi's "unusually flat and repulsive music." In an article about the cabaret published two days later, he attributed the play's success with the public in 1910 and now to the brilliance of Meyerhold's "incomparable staging."[72]

Meyerhold resigned as director several months after the opening, and the cabaret never became the "theater of underground classics," with a repertory of plays by Cervantes, Tieck, Claudel, Maeterlinck,

Strindberg, Miklashevsky, Kuzmin, and others, that he and Pronin had envisaged. It did, however, feature far more regular productions and planned programs throughout its existence than had its "improvisational" predecessor. Kuzmin's old friends Nikolay Evreinov and Nikolay Petrov immediately replaced Meyerhold. They were determined to work out a "metatheatrical" cabaret style and repertory, something that kept Kuzmin interested in the enterprise as long as they were in charge. When Pronin's wife, Vera Lishnevskaya, became the guiding spirit in the spring of 1917, his participation waned, even though he remained much more of a "regular" than he had ever been at the "Stray Dog."

On October 29, 1916, the cabaret marked the ten-year "jubilee" of Kuzmin's literary career with a special program of his works for the theater.[73] The evening opened with the first performance of *The Comedy on Martinian* (retitled *The Legend of Silvian* and with its text slightly revised to avoid the censorship problems that had blocked its production in 1908), directed by Petrov with sets by Natan Altman, a young artist of avant-garde leanings. Evreinov, who remembered the whole evening as an enchanting dream that made the terrible news from the front seem a distant nightmare, directed *Two Shepherds and a Nymph in a Hut*, which followed, with sets by Sudeikin. That old favorite, *The Choice of a Bride*, staged by the choreographer Boris Romanov in a "style of exaggerated parody (grotesque)," concluded the first part of the program. Speeches in the poet's honor, among them a verse tribute from Balmont, brought the evening to a close when Petrov directed an improvised choir in a salutatory hymn which ended with a verse where the adverb "jauntily" *(likho)* cleverly rhymed with the first two syllables of the guest of honor's first name *(Mikha-)*: "Be jauntily celebrated, / celebrated, Mikha- / il Alekseevich Kuzmin!"[74] The audience kept calling him onto the cabaret's tiny stage to wave after wave of "enthusiastic applause," but he preferred to sit quietly with Karsavina in an alcove, where he accepted his friends' tributes.

Kuzmin and his friends had reason to celebrate. He had lost his special voice for the first time in his poetic life in the 1914 war poetry, and manner had veered dangerously close to mannerism in far too many of the poems collected in *Clay Doves*. He had become expert at a certain way of writing, but as it had grown easy, he had become as suspicious of it as of the rhetoric of facile patriotism. In 1915 and 1916 he found his voice again as he worked toward a new style in poem cycles whose titles—"Russian Paradise" ("Russkii rai") and "The Fruit Ripens" ("Plod zreet")—point both to their matter and to their new maturity. The "fiery-icy, frosty-hot Russian paradise," that "longed for, ineradicable dream of my soul for a long, long time," had lost none of its hold on Kuzmin's imagination.[75] Inspired by it, he gave voice to his passionate attachment to Russia's age-old ways and beliefs, his love of its "gentle" landscape, and his fear for its future in deeply personal meditations on history and culture, love, and the powerlessness of death in the face of human renewal through love and nature.

A few of the poems do not escape the easy clichés of a kind of *style russe*, but just as we fear he may slip into them, as in the opening of the second stanza of the great 1916 poem that begins "Lord, I see that I am unworthy," with its "plowed-up field," "roadside brook in the shade of birches," and "the smell of rye," different referents and memories color a specifically Russian landscape in his mind:

> I am bothered by a rebellious sigh
> (from such sighs, oh Lord, save me!),
> when I hear the gentle call
> now of Mozart, now of Debussy.
> I still want to forget about grief,
> and my gaze blazes up with hope
> when I feel a wind from the sea
> and dream of you, o Bosporus![76]

Here, as in other poems from this period that are addressed to Debussy, to Mozart, to the paintings of Gauguin, to ancient Greece and Rome, as well as to Russia's past and present, Kuzmin reestablishes his identity and destiny as a writer in the creative intersection of Russia and Europe, and reaffirms the World of Art conviction, so characteristic of the best of his own works at all times, that "the Russian" finds "true expression by turning with open arms to occidental culture."[77]

Moscow's Kremlin precincts, the city's bustling market square, Okhotnyi Ryad (Hunters' Row), and "Spain and Mozart—*Figaro!*" entwine in another work of the time, the curious long poem in Spenserian stanzas entitled "Someone Else's Poem" ("Chuzhaya poema"). In it, the poet places people and events in what seems an arbitrary web of cultural associations that defy time and space, a method he was to use more and more in the future. Its dedication to "V. A. Sh." and "S. Yu. S." in the 1921 collection *Echo* had long been a puzzle until the first of its dedicatees, Vera Arturovna de Bosset, the wife of Igor Stravinsky, explained it to one of the authors in May 1970 and told him the story behind the poem. In the early autumn of 1915, Sudeikin, recently separated from his wife, had gone to Moscow at the invitation of Aleksandr Tairov to design a production of Beaumarchais's *Mariage de Figaro* for the Chamber Theater. Vera Arturovna, who was married at the time to a ne'er-do-well Balt named Robert Shilling, had long shown a talent for the arts, and she was determined to realize her old love for the theater. Intrigued by reports of Tairov's radical innovations, she let it be known that she was interested in joining his troupe. When he paid a call—probably, she admitted, because he hoped to take advantage of the rumors about her money—she told him honestly that she had little experience and almost none of the latter. Charmed by her determination and by what Thomas Mann would later call her "specifically Russian beauty" (actually, she had not a drop of Russian blood, as her father was French and her mother Swedish—so much for national stereotypes),[78] he invited her anyway. She began to attend rehearsals, where Sudeikin fell in love with her and insisted that Tairov find a place for her in the production. As she had attended some ballet classes in Moscow, the director devised a Spanish dance, for which Sudeikin designed a costume sprinkled with tiny stars.

When the artist returned to Petersburg in March 1916, the twenty-seven-year-old Vera accompanied him and settled with him in his old apartment above the "Comedians' Rest." There she met and captivated Kuzmin no less than she had many others. He was particularly taken by the story of the couple's courtship, and on Easter 1916 he surprised them with the poem, dedicated to "V[era] A[rturovna] Sh[illing] and S[ergey] Yu[rievich] S[udeikin]," which that tale had called into being. (It is related from the point of view of Sudeikin, thus "someone else's" love story.) He captured her dance and Sudeikin's costume ("for you I poured out the magic of starry realms, / for your fiery and swift dances"), their favorite places of rendezvous (the Kremlin, with its Assumption and Annunciation Cathedrals, and the oldest sections of Moscow), and the production of the play, which used Mozart's music. Even the multiple references to *Don Giovanni* reflect their courtship: Sudeikin's reluctance to call her Susanna, the name of Beaumarchais's saucy heroine, because he felt it inappropriate to her languid dark beauty. "I am Figaro, but you... you are Donna Anna. / No, there is no Don Juan [Sudeikin refused to allow her to call him that], and Susanna will never come!"[79]

We experience an invigorating sense of risk in many of the poems Kuzmin wrote between 1915 and early 1917. Their complexity of syntax and the at times deliberate coarseness of verbal texture, as in this fragment from the "ode" entitled "The Hostile Sea," so unlike the sharpened transparency of other of his new poems, made critics talk of a new "Futurist" Kuzmin:

> A specter of shapeless freedom,
> swampily false, like white-eyed people,
> you divide nations as
> you mumble about a miracle that never was.
> And now,
> like a racetrack horse,
> you will rush like an explosion of waters,
> will be enraged, will snort, fling
> wet fire
> at the white sky, as you are crushed and
> crush, drilling with a whirling funnel,
> your own insides![80]

The poems' frequent use of "high" and "low" diction and of what one critic, characterizing Futurist poetics, called the "combination of weirdly unrelated ideas,"[81] as well as the dedications to those closely associated with Futurism and "left art"—people such as Yury Annenkov, Konstantin Bolshakov, Lili Brik, and Mayakovsky—point in the same direction and testify to the poet's working out of a new style.

Kuzmin had called the program of the Italian Futurists "ill defined ... heterogeneous, haphazard, and inconsistent" in an informative 1910 notice about the group, one of the first to appear in the Russian press.[82] He thought no more highly of the ones dreamed up by the Russians. He had laughed off the Hylaen Futurists' summary dismissal of him in their provocatory 1912 manifesto "A Slap in the Face of Public Taste," perhaps because he savored the notoriety of being cast aside with the likes of Pushkin, Dostoevsky, Tolstoy, Bunin, Balmont, Bryusov, Blok,

Sologub, Remizov, Andreev, and Gorky. Not so poor Khlebnikov, who had been mortified that his colleagues David Burlyuk, Aleksey Kruchenykh, and Mayakovsky had included the name of his "gentle teacher" in the manifesto against his wishes. Kuzmin later assured him that he had been able to take a joke.

Sometimes he thought they went too far with their provocations, as when Ilya Zdanevich, creator, with the painter Mikhail Larionov, of the aesthetics of "everythingism" *(vsechestvo)* and later famous as the "beyonsense writer" *(zaumnik)* "Ilyazd," proclaimed a shoe more beautiful than the Venus de Milo in an April 17, 1914, lecture at the "Stray Dog": "An outrageous incident. . . . We've become utterly bankrupt" (Diary). Four days earlier, however, in his own report on contemporary Russian prose (which included a good deal on verse as well), he had remarked, after making his usual attack on the idea of literary schools, "One can expect new forces only from the side of the Futurists and the wild men [*dikie*]."[83] Their flamboyant behavior and highjinks appealed to the bohemian in him, and, unlike most, he refused for the most part to be "shocked." But it was their "liberation of the word," their Slavic "primitivism," and their "intoxication with the Russian language" that most fascinated him and that was now exerting a powerful influence on some of his new verse.[84]

Late in 1914 he found himself invited to share the pages with them in a miscellany entitled *Archer* (Strelets) that an ambitious fledgling writer named Aleksandr Belenson was trying to put together to unite avant-gardists and more established writers, most of them, like Blok and Sologub, associated with Symbolism. Kuzmin found Belenson "tedious" *(nudnyi)*, but agreed despite his irritation that the latter, contrary to repeated promises, did not ask Yurkun. The editor presented the collection to a curious public on February 25, 1915, at a special evening at the "Stray Dog." Mayakovsky had grumbled about appearing between the same covers with a bunch of, to his mind, has-been decadents, but he gave a fragment from his "Cloud in Trousers" ("Oblako v shtanakh") for the first issue and participated, as did Kuzmin, in the February presentation.

Two weeks earlier, on February 11, Mayakovsky had caused a furor when he read the poem "You there!" ("Vam!") at the cabaret, unusually crowded that night with respectable "pharmacists." Its invective had caused just the outrage Mayakovsky had hoped to provoke by his im-

promptu "shock treatment" aimed at "stirring up the bourgeois bas-
tards a bit!"[85] (Kuzmin, who was present, contributed his part to the
rumpus.) Four months later, Mayakovsky dropped by uninvited at the
Sudeikins' apartment: "He became a bit tiresome," Kuzmin thought
(Diary, June 25, 1915), but the moody, often intractable Mayakovsky
certainly fell under Kuzmin's spell that night, for he left a little verse
improvisation in Sudeikin's album before he left: "It is pleasant of a
Mars evening / to drink the rum of Kuzmin's talk."[86] Not long after, he
took up residence in the Petrograd apartment of the critic Osip Brik
and his wife, Lili, his erotic and emotional obsession. He showed up at
Kuzmin's apartment on August 6 ("He's a hooligan, but somehow childlike" [Diary]), and soon, to the amazement of many of his friends and
the shock of most of Kuzmin's, the older poet and Yurkun were regular
guests of the Brik ménage and remained so right up until the time the
three of them returned to Moscow in March 1919.

No one had expected Kuzmin and the poet-provocateur to hit it off
so splendidly or for Kuzmin to lend such an attentive (but never uncritical) ear to his verse and that of his Futurist comrade Velimir
Khlebnikov. We can hear them both in the prophetic authority of "The
Hostile Sea," which Kuzmin wrote in April 1917 and dedicated to
Mayakovsky. But if its freely rhymed accentual verse recalls him, the
blend of images from ancient Greek legends, *The Iliad*, *Agamemnon*, and
Xenophon's *Anabasis* that Kuzmin, writing at a time of revolution and
the fall of empires, used to create a sense of death and catastrophe rife
with ominous premonition does not. It seems, rather, a polemical swipe
at the tradition-bashing pose of its Futurist dedicatee, even while the
ode's manner and crunching consonants often recall Futurism.[87]

Mayakovsky's self-promotion and bragging could try his patience,
but Kuzmin genuinely admired his enormous talent, and found touching the insecurities that no amount of boasting could hide. In the 1922
article "Parnassian Thickets," a provocative survey of contemporary
Russian literature, Kuzmin wrote:

> The name of Mayakovsky does not now scare anyone, I think,
> since he has grown from the champion of Futurism, an official
> revolutionary, and a voluntary scarecrow into Mayakovsky the
> poet. . . . His rich inventiveness in the area of rhetorical images, his
> oratorical temperament, his feeling for rhythm (but not that feel-

ing for the word that Khlebnikov has), his durable breath control, and his inner sentimentality—there for the present are the distinctive features of this outstanding poet. But it seems to me that the first circle of his art is near an end. . . . All the same, Mayakovsky's most perfect work of art so far is "Man" ["Chelovek"].[88]

Kuzmin would later hear and admire some of Mayakovsky's new poems from *About That* (Pro eto), but he knew that the closing of the "first circle" of his friend's art had been the beginning of the end. In a passage that he cut from "Fish Scales in the Net" to spare Mayakovsky's feelings, he noted with regret the poet's lapse into what he regarded as empty posturing: "All the same, there are Hugo and Verhaeren and Nekrasov in Mayakovsky. The images are audacious, but this is very external."[89]

Kuzmin had closed a circle of his own in the prose of the war stories and his other slight fiction of the time, but striking out in as new a direction in his prose as he had taken in his verse took a bit longer. In September 1914 he had begun work on the novel that Semenov published in 1916 as the seventh volume of the collected works, *The Quiet Guard*, a celebration of the power of self-effacing love written in his usual manner, but with an unusually dense complex of plots and subplots, replete with allusions to the fictional world of Dostoevsky.[90] The effort on it and the writing of several tales and novellas of adventure and the supernatural set in eighteenth-century Italy all paid off, however, when he turned his hand to a new novel in 1916.

He had had the idea of writing what he called a "New Plutarch" as early as June 28, 1907 (Diary), and after immersing himself in February and March 1908 in the writings of the mystic Mme. Guyon, the seventeenth-century French advocate of Quietism who was much on his mind during the "mystical affair" with Naumov, he thought for a time that she might be an appropriate candidate for its first volume. Her name appears in the ambitious plan he drew up in August 1915 for what he conceived of as a series of semi-fictionalized lives of historical figures under that title. Though laid out in two parallel columns, the list does not suggest that Kuzmin intended to write it, like Plutarch's forty-eight lives of Greeks and Romans, in paired couples for comparison and contrast. The names do give an exemplary picture of his tastes and intellectual interests: "Alexander of Macedonia, Cagliostro, Shake-

speare, Descartes, Virgil, Swedenborg, Mozart, Hoffmann, Chodowiecki, Gluck, Suvorov, Friedrich [Frederick the Great], [Emperor]
Paul [I], Somov, Debussy, A. France, Sudeikin, Musorgsky, Borovik-
ovsky, V[an] Gogh" (the left-hand column); "Apuleius, Balzac, Verlaine, Pushkin, Goethe, Mme. Guyon, J[akov] Boehme, Klinger,
M[ichel] Angelo, Botticelli, M[arco] Polo, Leskov, Palestrina, Callot,
Klinger [sic!], Weber, Dante, Cavalcanti, Rachel" (the right-hand column).[91] In the introduction he wrote for *The Wondrous Life of Giuseppe
Balsamo, Count Cagliostro* (Chudesnaya zhizn' Iosifa Bal'zamo, grafa Kaliostro, 1916), he spoke of "about fifty biographies" that he planned for
the series, but the life of the audacious Italian adventurer and charlatan
was the first and only volume that he completed.[92] He would never
again write a prose work of comparable length.

Kuzmin, no believer in the "objectivity" of history, raised the issue of
the "truth" of history and the "truth" of the imagination in the introduction by alluding to the "chief literary difficulty" faced by Mr. Boffin,
the "Golden Dustman" of Dickens's "fine, but little-known novel" *Our
Mutual Friend:* "What to believe . . . ; for some time he was divided in
his mind between half, all, or none; at length, when he decided, as a
moderate man, to compound with half, the question still remained,
which half? And that stumbling block he never got over."[93] He had
no intention, he continued, of "frivolously asserting that Michelangelo
lived in the twentieth century," nor would he "settle Plato among the
Zulus," but readers of the "New Plutarch" were warned to expect novels, not "biographical compilations" or "historical studies." "With the
exception of the most basic biographical outlines," he reserved for himself "complete freedom in the details, colors, and sometimes even the
course of the events depicted."[94] He gave full rein to his "fantasies" in
the "wondrous life," yet managed to compel credible, often humorous
life through the mesh of omniscience and fact required by the biographical novel in this, his most perfectly achieved long fiction.[95]

In the novel, as in the new verse he was writing, Kuzmin demonstrated what now interested him most in the lives of the legendary
figures he planned to address and in his own and that of Russia itself:
"the diverse paths of the Spirit, which all lead to one goal, but sometimes, before reaching it, allow the wanderer to turn into side roads,
where he will undoubtedly lose his way. What is important to me is the
place that my chosen heroes occupy in the general evolution, the gen-

eral building of God's world, while the motley external change of scenes and events is needed only as an entertaining shell, which imagination, the younger sister of clairvoyance, can always replace."[96]

Some, like Georgy Ivanov, resented the poet's need to change and began murmuring about a decline in his talents, while others, like Adamovich, were simply dismayed that their mentor had "broken his delicate and pure voice" in works like "The Hostile Sea."[97] Kuzmin ignored the complaints about his interest in "left art" and a supposedly new seriousness unsuited to his "modest" talents as he savored the admiration of young poets such as Sergey Esenin and Marina Tsvetaeva, whom he had met at a literary soirée in Petersburg in January 1916. Although they never saw each other again, Tsvetaeva would not forget the encounter or his verse: in 1923 she wrote to Boris Pasternak that "from neither Akhmatova, nor Mandelshtam, nor Bely, nor Kuzmin do I expect anything but themselves," her highest praise, and in 1936 she recaptured their 1916 meeting in the memoir "An Otherworldly Evening."[98]

That year too, Yurkun and his mother, who had come to Petersburg in 1915, moved into Kuzmin's rooms in Spasskaya Street, no. 10. Sometime after 1917, they moved to no. 17, and shared the apartment for the rest of their lives. Their life together was never the ideal that Kuzmin so often expressed in his writings, and his lover's sulks and mysterious disappearances at times maddened him (while keeping him in thrall), but its relative constancy provided an atmosphere in which both creativity and happiness were possible. As they settled into a life of domestic dependency that takes affection for granted and accepts as inevitable a certain level of boredom and discontent, Kuzmin looked ahead. When the leap year 1916 drew to a close, he invoked the New Year to come in a poem. He "thanked God" that 1916, still a time of war, "had made itself scarce," but he asked with impatience whether Russia would continue to weep or would offer prayers of rejoicing for the coming of peace in the new year. "The meaning of the Tarot is unknown to us," he knew, yet neither he nor anyone else could have imagined what the year "with the shapely number seventeen" would actually bring.[99]

Kuzmin, probably late 1880s. *Authors' collection.*

Kuzmin, 1893. The inscription reads: "To dear Yurochka Yurkun. M. Kuzmin.
1913. How I looked 20 years ago and how I do not ever plan to look again."
Courtesy of the Anna Akhmatova Museum (Fountain House), St. Petersburg.

Kuzmin in Russian costume, ca. 1900.
Authors' collection.

Kuzmin, ca. 1910.
Authors' collection.

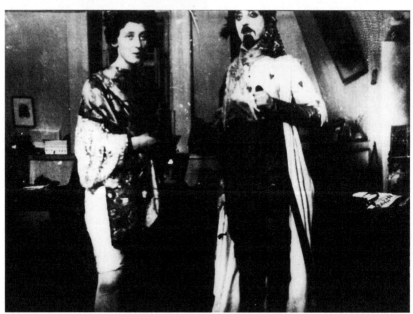

Vera Shvarsalon and Kuzmin in costume for the "Tower Theater"
performance of Calderón's *Devoción de la Cruz*, April 19, 1910.
Authors' collection.

Yury Yurkun and Kuzmin, 1913 or 1914.
Courtesy of the Anna Akhmatova Museum (Fountain House), St. Petersburg.

Twentieth anniversary of Kuzmin's literary debut, October 11, 1925,
Leningrad. Kuzmin is seated in the center. Anna Akhmatova stands immediately
behind him, Anna Radlova sits to his immediate right, while the bearded man
seated to his extreme left is Nikolay Klyuev.

Courtesy of the Anna Akhmatova Museum (Fountain House), St. Petersburg.

"Visiting Mikhail Kuzmin. 'White Night,'" 1932 drawing by
Vladimir Milashevsky.
Private collection, St. Petersburg.

Yury Yurkun, Kuzmin, and Aleksey Stepanov. Summer Garden, Leningrad,
August 18, 1934. When Kuzmin received a copy of the picture from Stepanov
on September 15, he wrote with amazement, "In certain pictures even
we could look like men about town" (Diary).
Courtesy of the Anna Akhmatova Museum (Fountain House), St. Petersburg.

Yury Yurkun and Kuzmin, 1936. One of the last pictures taken of the writer.
Courtesy of the Anna Akhmatova Museum (Fountain House), St. Petersburg.

✣ 9 ✣

"The End of Everything"
1917–1920

LA DIVINA COMMEDIA

With clanging, creaking, and squeaking, an iron curtain is low-
ering over Russian History. "The performance is over." The
audience got up. "Time to put on your fur coats and go home."
We looked around. But the fur coats and homes were missing.

—Vasily Rozanov, *The Apocalypse of Our Times* (1918)

"RUSSIA HAS to win this war," Kuzmin had remarked to a friend in
October 1914, after hearing bleak news from the front. "Or else it will
be the end of everything. And the end of us." With a tone of finality he
cut off the objection his puzzled friend was about to make: "Yes, the
end... And the main thing is that the war must not last for a long time.
You know how sometimes when you begin writing a poem and you feel
that it's going to be two stanzas and no more? That's just the way it is
with this war. Otherwise, God only knows what will happen."[1] The
perception of social events through the immediacy of his own very
different personal experience is characteristic of the poet, and for one
who professed utter indifference to such events and to politics, he demonstrated amazing prescience.

As the war dragged on inconclusively, as the economy turned into a
shambles, and as the government lurched from one crisis to another,
the air of the capital was thick with a sense of malaise and ominous
foreboding. Still, the outbreak of revolution probably caught Kuzmin
by surprise, as it did all Russians. He must have been no less astonished
by the collapse of the Romanov dynasty in a matter of six days between
February 23 and 28, 1917. We say "probably" because we lack a crucial
piece of evidence. Book seven of the Diary, covering the period Octo-

ber 29, 1915—October 12, 1917, has either been lost or destroyed, or it still lies somewhere in the archives of the secret police. The testimony of several other sources indicates that Kuzmin was as weary of the senseless killing at the front as were most Russians, and that he welcomed a revolution that he hoped would bring an end to the war. (His constant anxiety about the draft status of Yurkun should also never be ignored in assessing his reponse to the events of 1917.) The heroic spirit, the holiday atmosphere, and the air of euphoria he saw everywhere, especially on the "simple faces" of the peasant soldiers crowding the streets, thoroughly seduced him.

He had excoriated the revolutionary disturbances of 1905 as the work of troublemakers alien to the mass of the Russian people. Now, he chronicled with amazement the events that had brought down the government in a poem written only days later ("It is as though a hundred years have passed, and it was only a week! / What do you mean, a week ... twenty-four hours!"), and he wrote with hope of a Russian revolution, "youthful, chaste, righteous," which was marching forward "like an angel in a worker's blouse."[2] By late April he was sounding notes of positively socialist fervor in a poem hailing the first legal May Day demonstration in Russia. It concluded with his most heartfelt wish: "Dispersing the bloody shadow [of war], / a red May Day will trumpet / that all the peoples of the world are brothers!"[3]

Sentiments like those astonished many old friends, but not a circle of new ones, radical young members of the avant-garde whom he had met through his closeness with the left-leaning Mayakovsky and the Briks. He usually encountered them at the apartment-studio of the artist Lev Bruni at the Academy of Arts, which he had often visited in 1916. Friends from the World of Art looked with horror on the variety of "isms" that had revolutionized Russian painting after 1905, but Kuzmin found much to admire and praise, just as he had in the painters' Futurist allies. The adherents of "left art," accustomed to nothing but abuse and scorn from most members of Kuzmin's generation, valued his opinions and welcomed his company. Now, as the generations prepared to do battle over who would work out policies toward the arts in the new government, they looked to Kuzmin as an ally and found one.

On March 12 more than 1,400 people gathered in the Mikhailovskii Theater for a meeting that was without precedent in the history of Russian culture. The public forum on the future of the arts in Russia soon turned into a noisy attack on the call that Benois and his allies in the World of Art had issued for the creation of a ministry of culture, which they, of course, hoped to control. Kuzmin did not speak, but the audience elected him, along with Blok, Mayakovsky, and Nikolay Punin, a brilliant young theoretician of the avant-garde, to the presidium of the "Union of Practitioners of the Arts" (Soyuz deyatelei iskusstv), which was established that evening. This was all the more remarkable considering that widely popular writers such as Gorky, Kuprin, and Leonid Andreev had also stood for the seats.[4] Somov, still the impeccable dandy, had been shocked by Kuzmin's ratty appearance when he saw him at the end of 1916, and he could hardly conceal his contempt when noting Kuzmin's election the next day in his diary.[5] He was no more pleased by the active role his friend was playing throughout the spring and summer in a group that called itself "Freedom for Art" (Svoboda iskusstvu). There Kuzmin joined Mayakovsky, Meyerhold, Punin, Chagall, Malevich, Annenkov, Bruni, Vera Ermolaeva, and other radicals in opposing any attempt by conservative factions to dominate the art scene.

Of course, Kuzmin still made room for personal matters. In April 1917 a young bisexual poet named Yury Degen, who had a crush both on him and on his verse, founded a literary circle to which he gave the name "The Sailors of Marseilles" (Marsel'skie matrosy), and he invited Kuzmin to be its "captain." (Rumor made him Kuzmin's lover, but there is no evidence for that whatsoever or for the notion that the circle was some kind of gay literary salon.) Taking its name from a poem by Evgeny Baratynsky entitled "The Steamship" ("Piroskaf"), the group united young writers who admired Kuzmin. Yurkun, of course, and Ryurik Ivnev were members, while several others, including Georgy Ivanov, Adamovich, Anna Radlova, Mikhail Struve, and Degen himself had been members of the Second Guild of Poets, at whose informal gatherings Kuzmin had served as the favorite chairman. The rest, poets including Lazar Berman, Vsevolod Kurdyumov, and Boris Evgeniev, all of whose verse showed the strong imprint of Kuzmin's, would leave little more than a trace in Russian letters. Kuzmin himself wrote the words and music for the jaunty anthem that begins "Marseilles is a fine little city" ("Slavnyi gorodok Marsel'") that opened the circle's never very serious sessions, during which the members read and argued about one another's poems before adjourning to the "Comedians' Rest" for serious carousing. Degen planned to publish the anthem and one of his own, as well as an illustrated edition of "The Hostile Sea," a series of works by his fellow "sailors," a miscellany, and the collected works of E. T. A. Hoffmann in his own translation. All that came of those ambitious plans were two slim volumes of poems by Moisey Bamdas (financed by his parents), for one of which Kuzmin wrote a brief preface.[6] When Degen left for the Caucasus in September, the little circle disbanded.[7]

Kuzmin had had to learn to accommodate himself to the chronic indigence that for many went with the literary life, but he was always looking for some way out of his hand-to-mouth existence. On January 28, 1917, he had signed a contract for a "selected verse" (izbornik) with the prestigious Moscow publishing firm of Mikhail Sabashnikov. He received a generous advance and sent off the manuscript in April. Only in October did he learn that the editors had found his personal selection "a bit one-sided in the sense that poems of a special nature, ones such as 'Nine Birthmarks' and the like, predominate in the volume."[8] To put it less delicately, the book was too openly gay for their taste. They hoped that Kuzmin would "slightly change the selection of poems in the interests of completeness and balance of material, especially keeping in mind that the edition is intended for a broad, ill-prepared circle of readers, in part even 'for family reading,' as they used to say in times of old." Kuzmin understood that unless changes were made, the volume would not be printed, and he complied with the request. The publisher kept listing it in his advertising right up to 1921, but it never appeared.

Two commissions took up much of his time in 1917: work on a translation of the *Metamorphoses*, or *The Golden Ass*, of Apuleius, whose artful, self-conscious literariness he admired, and a version of Casanova's memoirs.[9] As so often in the past, promises came to nothing. (The Apuleius, on which he resumed work in the twenties, was published in 1929; it remains the standard Russian translation.) He tried to keep up his spirits as soaring prices devoured whatever he managed to earn, but by the summer his financial situation, chancy at the best of times in the past, approached destitution, and the threat of outright penury would haunt him for most of the rest of his life.[10]

Because uncertain publishing schedules caused by the unstable economic climate made magazines and newspapers reluctant to accept prose, Kuzmin's old standby for income, he turned to poems. While that may account for their large number in 1917, it cannot explain their high quality. In one of them, written in June, his desperate straits found expression with all the immediacy of a diary entry:

> I am not tortured by grief, my soul,
> but I weep, my flighty pilgrim.
> We are selling everything, we are in debt to everyone,
> soon we won't have anything left.
>
> Of course, there is God, and the heavens,
> and the imagination, which is not idle,
> but when you live almost without bread,
> you become like a ridiculous captive.
>
> The Muse will jump up, will tell of love
> (she's a bit stupid, after all, the little fool),
> but you will look at how our sweet Yurochka
> ties up the last bundle with a rope,—
>
> and you will stop. Momentary
> solace, petty suffering,
> but, my God, who needs that
> I go round and round like a squirrel on a treadmill?[11]

Neither this nor the splendid verse of the cantata "St. George" ("Sv. Georgy"), written at the same time, could find a publisher, wary as many were of what critics were starting to call the "new Kuzmin."[12] The sale of books from his library went on, and he now had to part with drawings and paintings given as gifts by Somov, Sapunov, Sudeikin, Kandinsky, Larionov, Goncharova, and others. Soon he would be reduced to selling his manuscripts to collectors.

Kuzmin had little more luck with the theater. The first production of *On Alexis, Man of God*, previously unperformable because of Church censorship, at Fedor Komissarzhevsky's Moscow studio-theater on March 18 brought a pittance in royalties. Several other playlets found no takers at all in a city where little law and less order kept many theaters dark because of the citizenry's prudent reluctance to venture out at night. The far more ambitious *Mary's Tuesday* (Vtornik Meri), a verse play "in three parts for puppets alive or wooden," fared no better, but at least found a publisher, though not until several years later. In it he explored cinematic techniques, especially a montage-like, associative linking of the many briskly changing brief scenes that fade in and out on the story of Mary and her two rival lovers, a plot that is mirrored by the classic commedia dell'arte triangle that is played on the stage in the work's final part.

Thankfully, caution meant nothing to the denizens of the "Comedians' Rest," where puppet shows, which can point up the artificiality and conventions of the theater, had on occasion been staged, to Kuzmin's fascination. He probably intended his own play for performance there, but he had to settle for a far more modest program of musical numbers, songs, and dances put together by his young friend Arthur Lourié, a composer of "left-art" persuasion and the new companion of Glebova-Sudeikina. She performed in the little "conversation" *Two Dances* (Dva tantsa) that Kuzmin specially wrote for the program. The music for Blok's *Puppet Show* opened the evening of August 2, 1917, and Kuzmin himself played and sang his ever-popular songs. He had to do so at the cabaret almost every night until the middle of September, when a flood closed down performances at the cellar for several months.[13]

By late autumn, Russia's "resurrection" still remained a distant dream, and life had become unpredictable for the average citizen. As the country drifted rudderless, rival organs of authority vied for power, while the Bolsheviks and their Military-Revolutionary Committee plotted to seize it. Kuzmin found the mounting atmosphere of crisis curiously invigorating, as he wrote on October 24: "Dangerous and alarming. All the same, I like days like these." The uncertainty finally broke that evening, when the Bolsheviks struck, seizing all objectives of strategic importance in Petersburg with little resistance. On the next day, life in the capital had an outward appearance of normality. Few of its citizens had any inkling of the armed insurrection of the night before, and those who knew of Lenin's early morning declaration announcing the deposition of the Provisional Government did not take it seriously. Kuzmin's Diary reflects the dawning awareness of what had occurred: "News reports: the bank is occupied, the pre-parliament dissolved, Kerensky has fled. Lenin is the premier, Trotsky the foreign minister. Already announcements to the people from the Bolsheviks. Gunfire. . . . S[ophia] I[saakovna Chatskina] suddenly asked me why am I a Bolshevik and said that it's unpleasant to have Bolsheviks in the house. How stupid. . . . Quiet, warm, shooting in the distance, as though artillery. If only there will be peace!" (October 25).

On the night of October 25–26, Bolshevik forces seized the Winter Palace, the thinly defended seat of the Provisional Government, and arrested its ministers. "Miracles are happening. Everything is occupied by the Bolsheviks. I doubt they will last, but bless them. The majority of people, of course, are goddamned panic mongers, beasts, and scum. They are afraid of peace, are all atremble about their [property?—illegible] and are ready to defend it to the last drop of someone else's blood. . . . Warm and merry on the streets. A fine *esprit*" (Diary, October 26).[14]

On the twenty-seventh, his doubts about the future of the new government deepened:

Everything really is in their hands, but everyone has turned their backs on them and they are terribly alone. They won't be able to hold on to power. Panic in the city. The loathsome bourgeoisie and the intellectuals will take credit for everything and they won't even be hanged. Kerensky, Kornilov, Kaledin, all but Savinkov are approaching [Petersburg]. But who is supporting them, it would be interesting to know. Someone was here. Ah, yes, Lenechka [Kannegiser]. He gave a fine account about the Winter Palace. Almost a Bolshevik. . . . Once again the hopes of the simple, nice young soldiers and workers won't be fulfilled.

Despite stiff resistance in Moscow from those loyal to the Provisional Government, the Bolsheviks set about solidifying their hold on power in the face of massive boycotts by the civil service and opposition from rival parties. It would take three years of civil war and terror to accomplish their goal.

In the two months that followed, references to the political situation in the Diary are rare and anecdotal: the closing of newspapers; "political conversations at the Briks'"; surprise at a friend's having become a commissar; grumbling about having to do his turn at night watch behind the barricaded doors of his apartment building; the "insufferable saboteurs" who cut off the electricity without warning, making writing impossible; shooting on the streets; even rumors about negotiations with England for Chicherin's return from abroad ("If he comes home, will he drop by to see me?" he wondered on December 1). Only on December 4, the day the Bolsheviks and their Left Socialist-Revolutionary allies broke up the Second Congress of Peasants' Deputies and demonstrators filled the streets, do we find an entry of some length (and with the same note of almost aesthetic pleasure that we see in some of the earlier ones, so different from the exalted mysticism with which writers such as Blok, Bely, Esenin, and Klyuev reacted to "October"): "Soldiers are marching to music, the little boys are rejoicing. Peasant women are cursing. Now they walk about freely, with grace, merrily and with dignity, they feel themselves their own masters. For this alone, blessed is the *coup*." It is the last unequivocally positive response to the events of 1917 that we find in the Diary.

Far more mundane matters crowded out all else from its pages as day-to-day survival preoccupied him: fending off the landlady, who threatened to evict him for nonpayment of rent; begging for "loans" from friends, such as Tamara ("Tyapa") Persits, his new standard of feminine elegance; the old worry about the "caprices" of Yurkun, whom he still loved "without measure." As the year drew to a close, he looked at the future with sober awareness and not a trace of self-pity: "Could not stop remembering Mama, my sister, the Chicherins. Everyone has died, aged. All well-being has just been swept away. Peaceful life—farewell! And I too am getting old and am becoming superfluous. Dear Yur[ochka], Mamasha [Yurkun's mother]. Soon I'll have to think of death" (December 24).

As he struggled daily to make ends meet, Kuzmin wondered how he was ever going to keep on finding the resources to keep himself and his little family fed and sheltered. He had had the courage to disregard the tastes of his admirers and fly in the face of their desire to have him go on repeating himself, even as he realized that that meant losing a large part of his former readers. Now, however, he wondered if he was to have an audience at all: "Ivnev, Esenin, Klyuev, Blok, Remizov, Chernyavsky, Lyandau have merged with Ivanov-Razumnik and Lunacharsky in *The Banner of Labor* [Znamya truda, a Left Socialist-Revolutionary newspaper]. Do I feel envious? I am not a gangster and am not a proletarian. I am not among those or the others—and none of them want me" (January 6, 1918). Preoccupied by that concern, he mentioned the Bolsheviks' illegal disbanding of the Constituent Assembly the day before almost as an afterthought ("Stopped by the Kannegisers'. Had lunch. The Assembly has been dispersed, it seems"), little realizing that with its closing, any hope for a genuinely democratic government in Russia had come to an end.

While uncertain of the future and his place in it, Kuzmin kept writing. His work on the biography of Cagliostro had broadened his already wide reading in mystical and occult literature. Now a time of disorientation and ruptured connections rekindled his old interest in Gnosticism, which had arisen in the ancient world in a period of political and religious crisis. As the October coup was being carried out, he had begun work on a cycle of eight "Gnostic poems" he entitled "Sophia." He finished it in 1918, and would return to the subject many times over the next five years. He was writing a very different cycle at the same time, the erotic poems he later published under the title *Pictures under Wraps* (Zanaveshennye kartinki). Typically for Kuzmin, at a time of cataclysmic social change, he asserted the importance of the most intimate sphere of life. Some of the "pictures" recall the elegant artifice of the worlds of Boucher and Fragonard, while others evoke the coarse vigor of the neoprimitivist canvases of Russian provincial life that his old friend Mikhail Larionov had painted in the decade before 1914. The very stylistic variety of the poems captures, as it salutes, the heterogeneity of erotic experience, be it hetero- or homosexual.

That he could set down poems many dismissed as pornography, while composing a series of hymns to the Pleroma, the Gnostics' world of plenitude and divine perfection, would seem to offer proof perfect to those who charge Kuzmin with cynicism and amorality. But only those addled by prudery can confuse the witty erotica of *Pictures under Wraps* with pornography, and any critic would make a fundamental error in seeing an opposition between the two cycles. In the opening poem of "Sophia," the Divine Wisdom, the "crucified bride," addresses Her "bridegroom" in that mixture of elevated mysticim and eroticism that we find in many Gnostic and Neoplatonic texts:

> On a throne of seven pillars
> I, like a ruby, blazed,
> and with unwilling desire,
> I desired You, Christ!
> I said: "It is lawless

to solder the soul with law,
of or without my will,
I will transgress the ban of love!"[15]

During and after the writing of both cycles, Kuzmin made entries like
these in his notebooks: "Love unites. God is the source of Love, while
the creative act is a work of His love. The first law is love. The appearance of that law is truth. Truth and love are Divine Wisdom"; "The act
of exertion of Divine love—the Passion of Christ. Is it not sexual? The
channel of love is the cross. The phallus. Only in the life of the flesh is
there the union of creativity with oneness"; "The Annunciation (conception) used to be celebrated in antiquity on the same day as the
Passion or the Resurrection. Does this not confirm my thoughts about
the erotic significance of the Passion?"[16]

Keeping these in mind, we can better understand an otherwise puzzling remark in the Diary on April 6, 1929, in which the poet glimpsed
the coherence of a life that might seem to others merely an accumula-
tion of incidents:

> Why in my diary do I never touch on the two or three most
> important points of my present life? As I see now, they always
> existed, I even see their development in sudden leaps. Much from
> the past has become understandable. I am totally self-aware, and
> even Yur[ochka] begins to guess. Egunov is right, it is religion.
> Madness, perhaps. But no. There is an immense chastity and oth-
> erworldly logic here. I do not write about it because, although I
> have a clear realization of it, it does not need formulation. I myself
> will never forget this, of course, since this is what I live by, but it
> will also be revealed to others not in the form of discourse, but
> from the impact of all my works on them. I do not even know why
> I am writing this now. The point is that without these two things,
> the diary becomes, as it were, a dry and heartless enumeration of
> petty facts which are enlivened (for me) only by their essence.

The other of the "two things" is, of course, Eros. To miss or ignore the
centrality of both religion and love in Kuzmin's view of the world can
lead only to incomprehension of works as diverse as *Wings*, the Gnostic
and erotic cycles of 1917–18, "The Birth of Eros" ("Rozhdenie Erosa,"

1920), and the great lyrics gathered in *Parables*. The last collection closes with the long poem "The Ladder" ("Lesenka"), in which Kuzmin's view of life as the soul's journey of ascent to a reunification with the Ideal, with Love and with an Art impelled by Love urging it toward perfection, finds its culminating expression. "Love moves us to art," he wrote in 1922,[17] and "One's own will is like a ray of God's Will. The aim is to realize in full the work of the artistic Creator."[18] In statements like those and in the poems of 1917–18 we find the core of the credo that he would develop and explore in his poetry and prose of the next decade: the primacy of the creative act, be it sexual or artistic, with the varieties of erotic experience only aspects, each with equal rights, of one impulse.

He could find no one interested in publishing "Sophia" (printing the erotic cycle was out of the question at a time of censorious prudishness), but an artists' artel called "Today" (Segodnya) did issue a tiny pamphlet, *To the Two* (Dvum), containing two occasional poems, one addressed to the Pronins' new baby daughter and the other to Lili Brik, who was recovering from a long illness. He also persuaded Nikolay Mikhailov, owner of the Petersburg firm "Prometheus," to put out a small printing of the collection he called *The Guide*, a selection of his finest poems of the years 1913–1917. "They want to buy four books of verse *at once*. That would be wonderful! Our wretched affairs would really improve," he had written on February 16. "Prometheus" did list four other volumes of his verse in a brief catalogue included in *The Guide*, but only one of them, the "Alexandrian Songs," ever appeared, and not until 1921. Plans for a luxurious edition of *The Exploits of Alexander the Great* with special illustrations by Pavel Kuznetsov fizzled out with nothing more than a prospectus, dated Moscow, 1918, to show for the effort.[19]

The adoption of the policies that came to be called War Communism did nothing to stabilize the publishing world. That massive and brutal attempt not only to mobilize all resources to win the civil war but to forge utopia *now*, was, of course, unrealizable, but it did manage in less than three years to devastate a battered but not crippled economy, and exposed all but the party elite to extreme privation and famine. "Hysterical decrees" was Kuzmin's verdict on Lenin's "Socialist Fatherland in Danger!" of February 21–22, 1918, which authorized summary executions of opponents and forced labor. But not until March 10 did he make his first overtly critical comment about the Bolshevik state: "Really, the comrades who have finally got power are acting like Attila, and only agile operators like Ryurik [Ivnev] and Annenkov or Lourié and Altman can make a go of it." That night, Lenin moved the government and capital to Moscow. The secret departure by heavily guarded special train, "like thieves in the night," disgusted Kuzmin, and six days later he noted: "Odessa has been captured. Now, when the Germans have successes, one says 'Thank God.'"

As one outrage followed another—forced conscription, the declaration of war on the "peasant bourgeoisie" and armed requisition of grain in the villages, the reintroduction of capital punishment, the imposition of total press censorship—Kuzmin's disgust and disaffection hardened into outright rejection of a regime that seemed the very embodiment of evil. After learning of the murder of Nicholas II and his family in Ekaterinburg on the night of July 16–17, he could not shake the "loathsome impression: the graves of cholera victims, the high cost of living, indolence, mobilizations, and this despicable murder. All of this merges into such a smell that you have to plug your nostrils. Brainless loutish scum, no other word for them. And there will never be any kind of universal social revolution. Our example will serve to all others as a kind of emetic" (Diary, July 20). As the heroine of one of his stories remarks, "I think the most hardened counterrevolutionaries are those who at first sympathized with the revolution."[20]

He was unsparing about his own earlier naïveté, and he longed for the overthrow of the "rotten Bolsheviks" (Diary, August 2). He had no choice, however, but to do everything in his power to "make a go of it." He joined a group of other writers in organizing a bookshop where they could sell books, prints, and engravings from their collections and those of others without a middleman. Both he and Yurkun walked all over the city examining and buying up books for the store, and they took their turn sorting and pricing them, manning the counters on Morskaya, no. 14, or serving tea to the shoppers, many of them drawn to the "Writers' Bookshop" by the chance to see the city's leading writers and artists acting as tradesmen. Before long, as the crisis in publishing worsened, the shop, like its counterpart in Moscow, was issuing "editions" (usually only one or two copies) of a poem cycle, playlet, or story that the authors themselves wrote out by hand for sale to collectors. ("Sophia" first saw the light of day in that format in 1920.) An inveterate bibliophile himself, Kuzmin delighted in the "enchanting" atmosphere of the store and the chance to examine rare volumes. Neither that trade, which took up a great deal of the time he should have been spending writing, nor the measly royalties from his publishers, nor the occasional performance at the "Comedians' Rest" or one of the other nightclubs still open could keep hunger from the door for long. "I have no impression at all that it is Easter," he had written on March 30. "Poor Veronika Karlovna [Yurkun's Catholic mother]: 2 eggs, sour cream, some mutton, a tiny piece of white bread—there is our whole Easter." Not long afterward, he would remember this as a feast.

His plight stemmed in no small way from his insistence on keeping his distance from the cultural agencies that the regime was setting up to run the arts. He had nothing but contempt for the "shameful collaboration" of those who rushed to "serve," but he knew that many, while no less hostile than he was to the new order, had to accept jobs given that the alternatives were starvation or emigration. Fortunately, he saw nothing compromising in accepting the invitation of the Theatrical Department (known by the acronym TEO) of the People's Commissariat of Enlightenment (or Education, NARKOMPROS) to write for the Children's Theater it set up in the late spring. It opened on June 15 with an adaptation of Hans Christian Andersen's tale "The Shepherdess and the Chimney Sweep," for which he wrote a prologue in the voice of the narrator. Pleased by the success of the performance, Meyerhold, the deputy head of TEO, and Andrey Golubev, head of its Petrograd section, asked Kuzmin to write a full-length play. Meyerhold felt that the anti-naturalism of his old friend's earlier plays and his insistence on a "theater for grown-up children" made him an ideal collaborator for the new venture.

On August 13 Blok, who headed the Repertory Committee of TEO, professed guarded admiration for the three-act *A Happy Day, or Two Brothers* (Schastlivyi den', ili Dva brata), for which Kuzmin also wrote the music, but he found the "Chinese drama" totally unsuitable for children of any age.[21] (Blok was untroubled by the fact that Russia's most openly gay writer had been asked to write a play for children; it was the plot, in which a thief commits a murder that goes unpunished, that gave him pause.) To Kuzmin's dismay, Meyerhold sided with Blok: "I spent the whole day at the department. Blok and Meyerhold have stirred up a whole campaign against me. . . . Yur[ochka] stopped by for me and really lit into me. Maybe they are right and I have written myself out and no longer have any talent. But I do not think so" (Diary, August 23, 1918). He was "afraid of quarrels with Blok," but still tried to make a case for the play, all to no avail (and no fee). He cheered up a bit knowing that the new publishing house of Tamara Persits, "The Wandering Enthusiast" (Stranstvuyushchii entuziast), was finally getting off the ground and that Mstislav Dobuzhinsky was working on illustrations for the first book edition of the Cagliostro novel that it would issue in March 1919. Then, at the end of the month, he and Yurkun suddenly found themselves right in the middle of that "arena of history," as Bolshevik propagandists liked to describe the misery all around, a phrase that so often brought down his scorn.

Before 1917 he had often enjoyed the lively company of Leonid Kannegiser, a talented budding poet, and the hospitality of his wealthy and cultivated Jewish family, at one of whose literary soirées he had met Tsvetaeva in January 1916. As with so many other friends, he saw less of them now, as the brilliance of Petersburg cultural life dimmed to candlepower, like the electricity which was off more than on. The twenty-two-year-old "Lenechka" had a well-known penchant for handsome young officers, several of whom after October 1917 were active, as he was, in anti-Bolshevik underground organizations. When in August the Cheka (the Bolsheviks' dread security police) arrested and executed one with whom Kannegiser was particularly close, Vladimir Pereltsveig, he carefully plotted a desperate revenge. Early on the day of August 30, he shot and killed Moisey Uritsky, chief of the Petrograd Cheka, as he was arriving at his office. Kannegiser almost made good his escape, but was captured by Red Guards. That same evening Fanny Kaplan shot and seriously wounded Lenin in Moscow. Suspecting a terrorist conspiracy, the Cheka held Kannegiser at their headquarters on Gorokhovaya, no. 2, the most feared address in all Petrograd, where he was questioned, often under torture, for several weeks. He named no names, and was finally executed in October. His remains were destroyed without a trace.[22]

On the morning of Saturday, August 31, Kuzmin was awakened by a loud noise:

A search. They started with Yur[ochka's] room. Veronika Karlovna was very agitated. I had tea. I was late getting to the bookshop. Suddenly someone says: "Yur. has been taken." I'm off on the run. An investigator is sitting there, Red Guards. "Yur., what's going on?" "I don't know." He is being arrested, they say, but not for long, a misunderstanding. They seized his novel and some notes.... I will never as long as I live forget his smiling, perplexed, dear kindred face, his uncombed hair. I will never forget that.... I raced to Lyandau's. It transpires that Lenya Kannegiser has killed Uritsky. He avenged the execution of Pereltsveig. All his relations are under arrest.... Everything is as in a dream. Lord, Lord, dear Yur. Where else did I run? To Altman: cold and official. It's all nonsense, he says. Some nonsense, the mangy Jew! They would not accept my package [at the prison]. Not on the lists. I looked at them. No. But how many acquaintances.... Gorky has refused to try to help and thinks that I am under arrest myself. It is terribly bitter, but what is *he* going through!

Altman, who had ties among the Bolsheviks, had been worse than insensitive in dismissing the matter as "nonsense," as the secret police arrested everyone mentioned in Kannegiser's address book. On the fourth, the party organ *Petrograd Truth* (Petrogradskaya pravda) announced the "discovery" (read: total fabrication, a grim prefiguring of the Stalinist fictions of the 1930s) of a "grandiose conspiracy of party organizations [Right and Left Socialist-Revolutionaries] and foreign agents of Anglo-French capitalism."[23] That day an order that hostages be taken was announced, and on September 5 the Bolsheviks officially launched the Red Terror, in which their opponents, both real and imagined, were rounded up and executed without investigation or trial, as were thousands of randomly chosen hostages.

In the days that followed, Kuzmin was on the verge of collapse. He tried to console Yurkun's mother, and had to keep up Yurkun's spirits with letters, visits to the prison ("the scenes there are heartbreaking"), and food packages. Yurkun's letters did nothing to ease his mind; nor did the lists of those executed, which he scanned every day in the newpapers, terrified that he might encounter his lover's name there. Some friends, such as Tamara Persits, did all they could to help, while others shocked him by their "odious" concern only for themselves, fearful as they were that their addresses might have been among Yurkun's seized papers, and by their reluctance to have anything to do with anyone close to him. (It was, in fact, a miracle that Kuzmin himself was not taken, as Gorky had assumed.)

Kuzmin never forgot the horror of those days, when he returned

home, exhausted by his efforts on Yurkun's behalf, as to a "grave," and
when people spoke in whispers about the sinking of two barges loaded
with former officers and the shooting of every tenth hostage held at
the Deryabinskie Barracks on the shore of the Gulf of Finland, where
Yurkun, members of Kannegiser's family, and other friends were im-
prisoned. He waited for news of Yurkun's fate in an atmosphere of
general intimidation, and his dread is reflected in the cycle "Captivity"
("Plen"), which he wrote a year later. The very existence of its counterrevolutionary poems caused alarm among his friends. It was not until
1925, however, that his despair of those weeks found expression in
purest lyrical form in the cycle "The Northern Fan" ("Severnyi veer"),
which he dedicated to Yurkun. Its poems are among the most enigmati-
cally personal that Kuzmin ever wrote, but one is startlingly direct if we
know the events of 1918. Needless to say, he did not bother (or dare) to
submit the poem to the censor, and when the cycle appeared in *The
Trout Breaking through the Ice* (1929), eight rows of dots follow "No. 5."

> They sank the barges at Kronshtadt,
> every tenth [person] was executed—
> Yurochka, my Yurochka,
> God grant that you were the eighth.
>
> Barracks on the shore of a backwater,
> once I would have shouted "People!"
> Now I pray in the cellar
> while I think of the white miracle.[24]

The "white miracle," of course, was the White Army, which he kept
hoping would triumph in the civil war.

On September 18 he had the first bit of good news in almost three
weeks: Gorky, he learned, had sent to Grigory Zinoviev, dictator-vice-
roy of Petrograd, a list of names, Yurkun's included, of those he argued
were innocent of any conspiracy, and a few acquaintances of Kannegiser's had been set free. Lourié, who was now a "commissar" in the
music section of TEO, had also persuaded Lunacharsky, the Commissar of Enlightenment, to send an appeal. Lourié and Gorky kept up
the pressure on Zinoviev, but nothing happened. Yurkun's letters, with
complaints that he was forgotten and reproaches about Kuzmin's failure

to gain his freedom, at times reduced the latter to despair. And he had been "completely dismayed" (October 20) by Yurkun's diary. He had taken the "despicable" step of reading it, thinking it might explain why others were being freed but not Yurkun. All he learned was how bored his lover often felt with him and how he believed that "only possessing a woman of a well-known type could return him to life." Kuzmin spent the next week in a daze: "The thought that I am nothing to him is killing me" (October 24). He managed to reassure himself about Yurkun's feelings, but almost three months after the arrest, matters still seemed hopeless: "Yurochka, return, return, love me! I just do not know what to do. . . . Come back, my dear one, my joy" (November 22). Then, the next day, "suddenly, Yur. calls from the bookshop. My God, my God! I run into the kitchen, out on the steps, watch for him. There he comes with his red blanket. What joy, what joy. One story after another. He did not get on too badly in general and was not hungry. . . . Yur. put me to bed with him 'for all night,' the poor boy."

Just as unexpectedly, several ways of easing his desperate financial impasse had presented themselves in the months that preceded the joyful homecoming. On September 14 "Gorky [called and] invited me to stop by. A very interesting matter regarding translations and editing." Two days later, unshaven and dirty, he followed up on the invitation and had a long conversation with Aleksandr Tikhonov. The experienced editor of several of Gorky's former publishing ventures, Tikhonov had now been entrusted with the direction of an ambitious new project. On September 4 Gorky and Lunacharsky had signed an agreement to establish "World Literature" (Vsemirnaya literatura) as an autonomous department of NARKOMPROS to publish in Russian a series of classics of European and American literature of the eighteenth to twentieth centuries, and another devoted to the literatures of the Middle Ages, the Slavs, and the Orient. Gorky and Tikhonov drew up the plan, advised by a team of writers, critics, and scholars who were to do the translations and provide the introductions and annotations.[25]

Like so many of Gorky's projects, this endeavor was quixotic from its inception. Plagued by paper shortages, by presses idled from lack of spare parts, and, later, by opposition from the increasingly monopolistic State Publishing House (Gosizdat), "World Literature" succeeded in putting out only fifty-nine titles during its first three years. Given the rapidly collapsing economy, that was an amazing figure, and around two hundred managed to appear before Gozisdat forcibly absorbed it in December 1924. Its service to the history of Russian culture, however, cannot be overestimated. Once the finances were in order, employees, hired regardless of their political sympathies, received small but fairly steady payment as they worked on their assignments. Even more important, as government functionaries, they were entitled to ration cards and emergency packages in the years 1919–20, when that was almost the only access to food available to those inept at speculation or with nothing left to sell on the black market. Several hundred members of the literary intelligentsia owed their lives and those of their families to "World Literature" and to Roza Vasilievna, who ran a little shop in its foyer. No one knew her last name (it was Rura) or where she got her provisions, but most royalties went for immediate purchases from her (usually at black market prices), and her grudging credit helped save many a writer, Kuzmin among them, from probable starvation.

Kuzmin, suspicious as always of "teaching" writers, kept his distance from the Literary Studio set up to train the inexperienced, but he took an active part in the other activities of "Vsemirka," as the enterprise was affectionately called.[26] The long discussions drawing up plans for the French section, headed by Gumilev and Andrey Levinson, tried his patience ("They have fobbed off Musset on me, a bit of Balzac [the *Contes drolatiques*], and France. No advance" [October 19]). But he liked and trusted Tikhonov, who made him feel that he still had something to contribute to Russian letters, and he seized on the assignment of Anatole France, his favorite contemporary author, with alacrity. He drew up a plan for the nine-volume edition of France's selected works, which he was to supervise, and finished introductions for two of its volumes before the year 1918 was out.[27]

Because of his preoccupation with Yurkun, Kuzmin made no reference at all in the Diary to another venture beyond saying, "We [he and Izrailevich] talked about the newspaper" (October 8), "turned down the editorship . . . was asked to stay on the editorial board" (October 12), and "Meetings, plans, work" (October 21). He did not even remark the appearance of the first issue of the newspaper *The Life of Art* (Zhizn' iskusstva) on October 29, 1918, with two of his long articles, nor the thirteen pieces that he wrote for it in the next three weeks, as he used work to try to numb his anxiety and misery. The newspaper's editorial board consisted of Viktor Shklovsky, Boris Asafiev (a composer who wrote under the pseudonym Igor Glebov), Gerasim Romm, and Kuzmin. There was never an absolute division of labor, but Shklovsky concentrated on literature, Asafiev on music, and Kuzmin on the theater in the broadest sense. The reviews and articles, the programs for all theaters and concerts, lists of daily cultural activities, bibliographies of new books and publishing projects, even addresses and telephone numbers of major cultural figures and organizations, make it indispensable for a history of the day-to-day "life of the arts" in Petersburg, and it was no less crucial as a source of income for its staff and contributors.

Kuzmin took a dim view of Formalism: "One should start a campaign against being formalistic. Or is it harmless and will collapse on its own? Perhaps laziness and inertia are holding me back. Literary quarrels, of course, are ridiculous, but essential in this little life."[28] He thought Shklovsky "awfully abusive" *(rugatel')* in his writings, but he was "nice and very talented" (Diary, April 29, 1921), and he appreciated that his invitations to young Formalist colleagues such as Tomashevsky, Eikhenbaum, Jakobson, and Zhirmunsky made the newspaper a hotbed of provocative critical debate, while the other editors kept the writing on music and the pictorial arts no less pointed and principled at a time of ferment and contention in all the arts. Kuzmin could be outspoken in the more than one hundred articles and reviews he wrote for the newspaper over the next five years, but all of them offered judiciously informative comment and elucidation. They are testimony to his immense knowledge and range of interests, his analytical power and quirky taste, and he at times used them to set down statements of principle and to outline his attitudes on art and life. (In 1923 he included a selection of the most consequential in the book he called *Conventions*).

The theater took up most of his energies. Indeed, a complete collection of his reviews would provide a panorama of the life of the Petersburg stage (drama, opera, operetta, even the circus) in the years 1919–1923. As a playwright himself, he was especially concerned by the problem of repertory. He knew that Russian literature had produced only a handful of first-rate dramatists and that their works could never sustain a varied repertory. Inevitably, foreign works, a few native classics, and a large number of third-rate (or worse) local products dominated the Russian stage. What the country needed, he argued, was what he called "good second-rate plays," of the kind at which the French were such masters, and he proposed the establishment of a "theater of new plays" where authors, directors, and actors could all collaborate to develop and produce them.[29]

He did not confine his concern for the future of the Russian theater to his reviewing. Most of the "theaters of miniatures" were now gone, but "Bobish" Romanov staged *The Choice of a Bride* in November before an audience of several thousand enthusiastic children at Tsarskoe Selo.[30] The "Comedians' Rest" finally opened a new season on November 2 with a program that included Kuzmin's "Prologue" and Konstantin Tverskoy's much-delayed staging of Kuzmin's vaudeville *Dancing Master of Harrow Street* (Tantsmeister s Khërestrita), which played until the end of the month. Despite Blok's reservations about the suitability of *A Happy Day, or Two Brothers* for children, the actor Aleksandr Bryantsev had liked the script. He gave the play its first performance on January 1, 1919, at the "Workshop" of Pavel Gaideburov and Nadezhda Skarskaya's popular Itinerant Mass Theater (Peredvizhnoi obshchedostupnyi teatr). It ran for months, and is considered the first production in the history of Soviet theater for children.[31] A few of Kuzmin's old works continued to be performed from time to time, but after 1918 he spent far less time as a playwright than as a playgoer, composer of incidental music for the plays of others, and adviser to theaters such as the new "Theater-Studio" that opened early in 1919 after months of discussions about its repertory.[32] Kuzmin's *Nativity of Christ* played at its puppet theater section in April, but two months later the enterprise broke up.

His collaboration with the Bol'shoi Drama Theater proved far longer-lived. The most prestigious of the projects of the Petersburg TEO, it was organized in the autumn of 1918 by Gorky and his second wife, the actress Mariya Andreeva, whose pretentiousness and imperious ways irritated Kuzmin and others. Blok served as the chairman of the board of directors and supervised the repertory. The theater attracted some of the city's finest actors, Yuriev and Monakhov among them, and intended to produce only the best plays of European and Russian literature. A theater of "heroic tragedies and lofty comedies," as Kuzmin wrote in his review of its first production, Schiller's *Don Carlos*, which opened on February 15, 1919, it performs to this day in the former Suvorin Theater on the Fontanka.[33] Kuzmin was placed in charge of musical arrangements, a job he shared with Boris Asafiev and the composer Yury Shaporin from 1919 to 1924. He dismissed Sem Benelli's drama *Il Mantellaccio* (1911) as "utterly banal nonsense," but he wrote music for its production in September 1919, his first work for the new theater.[34] The play had no place, he wrote, in a repertory dominated by the works of Shakespeare and Schiller, about whose early plays he wrote an essay for the first issue of the little illustrated magazine that the theater put out about its activities and sold in the foyer.[35]

By the end of 1918 he could still see no end in sight to the "vile" Bolshevik regime, and life seemed not so much a dream as a phantasmal realm (simply a nightmare at times), with Petersburg a "city of the dead"—"Letheburg," as his friend the "absurdist" poet Daniil Kharms would later dub it. On November 12, as he walked, ill-clad, aching with hunger, and "almost in tears," through the late evening streets, he saw only "ghosts of some kind, abandoned and frightened. But all of them are specters—Lunacharsky and the Red Guards. There is no place for this in nature, and everyone senses that. What a terrible dream" (Diary). On February 20, 1919, he, Blok, and several others read their verse "rather somberly" at a poets' evening at the "Comedians' Rest," and he could not shake the impression of "something spectral and dead" when he wrote an account of the evening on March 5.[36]

News of the violence and savagery on both sides in the civil war revolted him. His greatest indignation, however, was stirred by the steady erosion of hard-won freedoms and especially the daily diminutions of private life and its small pleasures, always for him a mark and measure of a civilized society. Those he could "not forget or forgive," as he wrote in the Diary on the last day of 1918. Some, like Gippius and Bely, excoriated the Bolsheviks for their betrayal of abstractions like "the revolution" and Russia's "messianic destiny" to transform mankind itself. In the four poems of the 1919 cycle "Captivity," Kuzmin lashed out at a contemptible tyranny that scorned life itself. The evocation of the varied wonders of life and art that opens the freely rhymed verse of the first poem, "The Angel Announcing Good Tidings," is suddenly shattered:

> Bang!
> They smacked us in the face with a dirty rag.
> They took away bread, light, warmth, meat,
> milk, soap, paper, books,
> clothes, boots, blanket, butter,
> kerosene, candles, salt, sugar,

tobacco, matches, cereals.
Everything,
and said:
"Live and be free!"
    Bang!
They locked us in a cage, in barracks,
in an almshouse, in a madhouse,
sowing sadness and hatred...
Is not your ideal being realized, Arakcheev?
"Live and be free!"
    Bang! . . .
Trampled underfoot
not even by boots,
not by bast shoes,
but by shoes stolen from someone else's feet,
we live free,
shiver by an unheated stove
(Imagination).
We walk through the dark to similarly shivering friends.
There are so few of them—
eat garbage, greedily glancing at somebody else's
    piece out of the corner of the eye.
The mind is dulled, . . .
Despicable gunshots,
gray hatred,
the hard underground life
of unborn worms.
Can it really be
that we are manure,
as that heap of manure says. . .
that has buried us under it.
    No.
Crushed, frightened,
dismayed, perhaps despicable,—
but we are people,
and therefore this is only a dream
(oh God, a two-year dream).
The angel announcing good tidings

has not flown away from me forever.
I wait for him as
I think about a miracle.[37]

The poet can imagine when "the dream will pass," when he will again "not know what to do: / to write, / to stroll, / love, / make purchases, / drink, / simply look around, / breathe, / and live, live!" and when another pleasure long gone will also return:

> Then freely, without any burden,
> we will sweetly tie a knot,
> and freely (do you understand: freely) will go
> to hot—privately owned,
> by a free person
> who earns two thousand a year
> (by then that will be an enormous sum)—
> bathhouses.
> I am ending the poem
> with that rather repellent word,
> I have been subjected to so many attacks
> because of this word. . . .
> But then that was long ago,
> I have changed since then.
> Any impartial reader can assure himself of that.
> And besides, there is the English *motto* (in French),
> which one can see
> on any cigarette case, garter, and bar of soap:
> "Honi soit qui mal y pense."[38]

Kuzmin found refuge (and humor, never far away in what he wrote even at the hardest of times) only in the imagination, however, and through it he returned to his "second homeland" (Diary, June 4, 1919) in the eight "Poems about Italy" that he began in 1919 and completed in May–June 1920. There is nothing "escapist" about them. Informed by his reading rather than by specific reminiscences of his 1897 journey, the poems celebrate the history, myths, art, and literature of "golden" Italy, his "second mother." By remembering, he affirmed his faith in everything that was faced with extinction at home, and it is tempting to

see his hope for the fate of Petersburg in the one he prophesied for
Ravenna in the poem of that title. There he writes confidently of the
day when the "drowsy" city, the glories of her Byzantine past seemingly
long gone, will awaken from slumber and her saints will "sternly step
out of the icons."[39]

Life was now a grind of journalism, editing, and translation, and a
daily struggle to find food as the daily ration dropped to four ounces of
adulterated bread. Kuzmin convinced himself that with the coming of
spring, the regime, "so hateful to everyone," would fall, but things only
got worse. He castigated himself for lethargy ("I want to sleep all the
time," he writes over and over) and an inability to work, not realizing
that the permanent state of undernourishment was draining his energy
and undermining his health. (He frequently complained of swelling in
his feet and chest pains, the first signs of the heart disease that would
kill him.) Yurkun's military status also caused enormous anxiety. In
March 1919 he was called up for service and pronounced fit, but he was
only assigned to occasional guard duty in the city. More and more
people of his status, however, were being called to the front as the army
of General Yudenich threatened Petersburg ("Everyone is in joyous
expectation" [Diary, May 26]). Yurkun's turn came in the autumn. He
deserted, but with thousands of other men following the same course,
the police, faced with a soaring crime wave, could not be bothered to
hunt him down. After hiding out with friends for a time, he returned to
the apartment and went on with his old ways, but the thought that he
might be found and executed on the spot haunted Kuzmin.

A Writers' House (Dom literatorov) had been set up in December
1918 to help writers obtain basic necessities, and it later opened a communal dining room in its building on the corner of Basseinaya and
Ertelev Lane, no. 11–17. It could hardly begin to cope with the crisis
facing all the members of the intelligentsia in the cities in 1919. At the
end of that year, the House of Arts (Dom Iskusstv), offering members rooms, heated work areas, a canteen, ration cards, and firewood,
opened in the former mansion of Stepan Eliseev on the corner of the
Moika and Nevsky Prospect, and in January 1920 the Scholars' House
(Dom uchenykh) opened its doors in the palace that had once belonged
to the uncle of Nicholas II.[40] "We plodded to the House" or "I dragged
myself to the House" are regular Diary entries, as is the "cold porridge"
they usually got for lunch. Like several other writers, Kuzmin had

managed to receive a so-called academic ration in addition to those from the Writers' House and the House of Arts, and several times a week he waited in long lines at the Scholars' House for rations, often with the cooks and maids of the few academicians who were more comfortably settled.[41] (For his part, he quite enjoyed their company: they knew all the rumors and were full of tidbits of information on where food could be found.)

Faced with abysmal conditions, many writers, artists, and musicians abandoned their apartments for the dormitories of the House of Arts or fled Petersburg altogether. (It is estimated that Petersburg lost approximately two-thirds of its population during the civil war years.) Kuzmin stayed on, and it was in the winter of 1919–20 that Nina Kannegiser, a cousin of Leonid, first saw him. Many close friends of their family had dropped them after the events of 1918, but not Kuzmin. During his long imprisonment in the autumn of 1918, Yurkun had become friendly with Isay Mandelshtam, Nina's stepfather and a relative of the Kannegisers'. Kuzmin met him at the apartment of Leonid's family and invited him, as a practiced translator, to take part in the Anatole France edition. Kuzmin was soon a visitor at Mandelshtam's apartment, which had a large stove, rather than steam heat, which had long ceased to function in almost all but government buildings. Nina later recalled:

Kuzmin and Yurkun would come simply to warm up, most often in the early evening, sometimes before my stepfather's return from work. Once Yurkun said to my mother: "I have brought Mikhail Alekseevich a bit earlier today. I'm afraid that he might freeze to death." One had to understand that literally. . . . The sub-zero temperatures that year were harsh, and because of hunger, the fierce cold in their rooms, and constantly being in the same insufficiently warm and dilapidated clothing (wool coats and felt hats), they would arrive numb from the cold. . . . Mikhail Alekseevich, taking tiny little steps (he had a very characteristic gait), would go into the dining room, lean against the tiled stove, and gradually thaw out: he would turn slightly pink, cough, have a cigarette. Mama, carrying our only candle, would disappear into the kitchen (soup made out of cereal and an additional course—the hateful rutabagas), having instructed my sister (a year older) and me [she was nine at the time]: "Sit with Mikhail Alekseevich, only don't pester him." He was very courteous to us, used the polite form of "you," and we would staidly chat about ways to cure frostbitten fingers and about the exceptional talent of our cat. . . .

He was extremely thin—his clothes hung on him. A puffy face (from edema?). . . . His face and hands were a yellowish blue gray from the cold and dirt—a smoky fire supplied the light and heat in their apartment at the time, and water had to be carried out of the cellars.[42]

If asked, he would "readily" read his new poems: "He spoke quietly, slightly lisping and swallowing the last syllable. The result was a very distinctive kind of gibberish, which intensified when he read his poems, for then he somehow stammered too."[43]

Public readings had always been popular, but by the winter of 1919–20, they were virtually the only means most writers had to communicate.[44] Kuzmin, to be sure, had better luck than many with his books, but aside from his reviews, he published only three poems and one story, and all in the same magazine, *Moscow* (Moskva), from 1918 to early 1921. Cultural life was reviving, but not publishing, and Russia was becoming an oral, pre-Gutenberg culture. On December 29, 1919, Kuzmin opened the series of poetry evenings that the House of Arts sponsored with a reading of "Sophia" and poems from the Italian cycle,[45] and he read, often to "noisy applause," at the "living almanacs" that the Writers' House held throughout 1920.

If the listeners' enthusiastic response picked up his spirits, it was never for long, as a ghostly quotidian reality reasserted itself: "My mood—lie down and die" (Diary, March 6, 1920). Four days earlier he had seen Blok, Bely, and Sologub at the offices of "World Literature." "Ghosts of some kind," was his impression. He realized that he and his household were eating a bit better, but it was the "creeping sense of insurmountable hopelessness" that made everything seem bleakly unreal: "It seems to me all the time that this is not life, these are not people, not rehearsals, not streets, but some kind of boring, Satanic play of ghosts, ghosts, ghosts. Yusha Chicherin [now Commissar of Foreign Affairs], previously a source of genuine good spirits, is also wandering about like a ghost somewhere or other" (March 17, 1920). A week later he wondered "can it be that the only thing left is to go headfirst into a hole in the ice?"

He spent April in a state of "total apathy," unable to work and consumed with guilt that he was a burden to Yurkun and his mother. At the end of the month an "appetite for life" suddenly returned and with it a desire to write, perhaps because his thoughts had again turned to Italy. He resumed work on his "Poems about Italy," and on May 22 finished the "Venetian Tale," "From the Notebooks of Tiburtius Penzel," which came out in the first miscellany published by the House of Arts in 1921.[46] Set in late eighteenth-century Venice, it is full of pictorial reminiscences of Venetian painting from Carpaccio to Longhi and Guardi, and is a witty escape into the world of Gozzi, Goldoni, and Mozartian artifice, with an embedded tale of twin brothers who love each other so much that the death of one inevitably leads to that of the other. He also wrote another story, "The Hand on the Plow" ("Ruka na pluge"; the unpublished text is lost), and two articles on the opera for the series he called "Conventions," translated France's novel *Le Lys rouge*, and reviewed a production of Schiller's *Verschwörung des Fiesko in Genua*— quite a month for someone who upbraided himself for "laziness."

On May 24 the Writers' House gave him a "personal evening." Viktor Zhirmunsky opened it with a lecture on Kuzmin's works. The author then gave the first reading of *Mary's Tuesday*, some poems, and an excerpt from a new novel, *Roman Marvels*.[47] In the Diary he did not even mention that he had participated in the event, only that the concert section which followed "had come off all right," and that during the intermission he and Yurkun had had a glass of milk. "I was satisfied," he concluded, but now, when something as simple as a glass of milk was remarkable, it took little to achieve that: "I do not consider myself the hub of the universe, but the life around us is such that it severs various earthly inclinations. At first sexual ones, because everything was directed toward food. And now food too. At first I thought it was impotence, but no. It has simply been made the tenth most important thing. Of course, the Bolsheviks are not responsible, but still they are accursed and condemned. But a regime of slavery has its effect. Cruel, but perhaps beneficial" (May 27).

He was dismayed by how many friends were setting themselves up with a "Soviet situation": "Mrs. Khovin [the wife of Viktor Khovin, a critic, publisher, and book dealer] told me that Brik has joined the Cheka. No surprise in that. Lili Yurievna is in charge of an institution" (June 7). Kuzmin would have none of that, but he did have work to do, and he kept up the pace of May throughout the summer, even giving a few more lectures on poetry to students at the Writers' House, something he hated but had been cajoled into doing. And at times he could for a moment forget the "Soviet nightmare": "There are still five splendid things: (1) the consciousness that God, angels, the Last Judgment, and the saints exist; (2) to read and play charming things, although there is the apprehension: hasn't the time for this come and gone?; (3) to look at the sky, the clouds, the sun, the moon, and the stars (where the Bolsheviks cannot befoul things as they have done with the earth); (4) to see Yur. and know that he loves me (with my heart rent, since he is in rags, is hungry); (5) to drink real tea, despite it all" (July 6, Diary).

In February, Mariya Andreeva, a party member, and Evgeny Kuznetsov, another Bolshevik and a young theater critic whom Kuzmin found very handsome, had replaced him and Shklovsky on the editorial board of *The Life of Art*. (The masthead listing changed on February 13.) For a while it looked as though he had been forced out completely, but in mid-March, Kuznetsov and Romm invited him back. His articles and reviews now appeared less regularly, though that meant there was more time for other work, which perforce had had to give way to journalism, and he wrote over a half-dozen poems during the summer.

At the end of May the "proletarian" *Red Newspaper* (Krasnaya gazeta) savaged the works he had read at his evening on the twenty-fourth as "nonsensical muddle" that had nothing to do with the times.[48] Deeply offended and alarmed that he could be "abused" in such terms in the Bolshevik press, he replied in *The Life of Art* with the article "The Fleet-Footed Men of History." He dismissed the "art of a single day," produced by a "swarm" that "glorifies the deeds and days of the victors," as having nothing to do with art. If to some such work seemed "revolutionary," then it was only in the "narrowly party, mechanical meaning of that word," for "Art always was, is, will be, and must be ahead of history and life. In this lies its innately revolutionary character and its meaning. There is no 'reflection of life.' . . . It is clairvoyant, rebellious, always about the future. . . . It is a prophet, not a parrot."[49] He gave another kind of answer to his critics in his new fiction. No matter that it is set in the distant past, it is "all about the present, my friend," to borrow the opening line of the poem that he wrote on July 9.

He had begun the novel *Roman Marvels* the year before, and started the second chapter late in September. Reflecting his fascination with

Gnosticism and the esoteric tendencies of early Christianity, the first chapter deals with Simon Magus and Helen, whose story he had related in the 1904 *Comedy from Alexandrian Life*. But he moved these half-historical, half-legendary figures from the first century to the Rome of the Emperor Hadrian or Marcus Aurelius, a time of persecution for Jews and Christians, and he placed them in the center of an early Christian-Gnostic sect.[50] The change of time, of course, allowed him to return in the second chapter to a favorite hero, Antinous (in this, too, the novel looks back to another work of 1904, "Charicles of Miletus"). Far more important, it provided a setting in which he could work out his growing belief that the catastrophic change taking place around him was only part of some more general process. "With ever-growing alarm and doubt, you ask yourself the question: could these be new forms of life, the devil take them!" he wrote on July 17. The times seemed to him reminiscent of another revolutionary age, when a dynamic early Christianity spread throughout the ancient world. Driven, he believed, by an unrealizable utopian vision that it was determined to realize in life, early Christianity, which was still more a collection of sects than an organized church, had been faced by a powerful alternative—the esoteric world of Gnosticism that required humankind to transcend physical being itself. "Our time is the crucible of the future," he wrote. "Positivism and naturalism went bankrupt, throwing us back not to the third quarter of the eighteenth century, when they were beginning, but to a far more primitive age. . . . Every beginning, wishing to be self-sufficient, reaches a dead end, and leaves behind everything of value. . . . It looks like it is *the second century*, perhaps some others as well. Khlebnikov would have made calculations about which."[51]

It is hard to say how he meant to develop these ideas in the novel: only the first two chapters were published in 1922 in the last issue of the miscellany *Archer*. He wrote at least two more chapters in 1924–25, but by then there could be no thought of printing the novel, and the manuscript has apparently been lost.[52] We can say just as little about the second volume of his "New Plutarch," a life of Virgil that he began in 1919 and dedicated to Golovin, who was to illustrate the text. Again, only two chapters appeared in print, under the title "The Golden Heavens."[53] A three-page list of sources in Latin, German, and French in one of his notebooks, and the work's subtitle—"The Life of Publius Vergilius Maro, the Sorcerer of Mantua"—suggest that the biography of the Roman poet was to be shaped by the popular apocrypha and medieval legends that made him out to be a great magician. Kuzmin could thus have explored one of his most cherished beliefs: the possibility of the miraculous as such in our world, where it exists side by side with the everyday and gives those who are open to it the chance to enter another realm. (In this respect Cagliostro, every bit as much as Virgil, is the creative artist as sorcerer and enchanter.)

After May 1920 the name of Yakov Blokh, whom Kuzmin had met during the days of Meyerhold's "Studio" before the war, begins to appear almost every day in the Diary, crowding out that of Zinovy Grzhebin, who had once been Kuzmin's major contact in the postrevolutionary publishing world.[54] Blokh had started "Petropolis" in 1918 as a book cooperative, but it was not until 1920 that he could get its publishing plans off the ground. He bought the rights for *Mary's Tuesday* and a volume of verse (the future collection *Otherworldly Evenings*, 1921) on May 31. For the next five years his firm would put out works by many of Russia's finest writers and a series of those both old and new by Kuzmin, first in Petersburg and then in Berlin, where its main office moved in 1922.[55] Kuzmin became a member of its small literary board, and, as the publisher remembered, "very quickly became attached to my wife and me. He would come to see us every evening, and we would sit down to play 'kings' [a card game] with enthusiasm—a way of passing the time that, it would seem, corresponds very little to the image of Kuzmin as an erotic poet."[56] One commision from Blokh that June, a translation of Henri de Régnier's "Sept estampes amoureuses" from the 1911 verse collection *Le Miroir des Heures*, ensured that the "erotic" reputation would stick for a bit longer. It came out at the end of 1920 as *Seven Amorous Portraits* (Sem' lyubovnykh portretov) in an exquisite printing of 327 copies, with illustrations by Dmitry Mitrokhin, an artist Kuzmin admired.

The little Régnier volume went almost unnoticed, but not another, *Pictures under Wraps*, which "Petropolis" printed in large format and, considering the times, on remarkably fine paper. There was not a trace of the publisher's name in any of the 307 numbered copies, and the place of publication was given as "Amsterdam," in honor, perhaps, of the timeworn eighteenth-century tradition of printing erotica in Paris but listing Brussels or Amsterdam as the place of origin to avoid legal prosecution.[57] Kuzmin never intended the book for public sale. Costing ten thousand rubles, and with delicately salacious drawings by Vladimir Milashevsky, it was published with an "author's copyright" *(na pravakh rukopisi)* only, and was meant for exclusive purchase by wealthy bibliophiles and fanciers of erotica directly from the author or Yurkun. But it did not take long for news of the book to spread at home and abroad.[58] The story of how the poems reached print makes quite a tale.

A year earlier, in June 1919, Kuzmin had offered a special handwritten copy of the cycle, then called "The Forbidden Garden" ("Zapretnyi sad"), to Lev Melin, a well-known collector and bookseller with whom he had been dealing for several years. Melin always drove a hard bargain; he had "given very little" for the manuscript on June 7, and the deal seems to have fallen through. At least two other such manuscript copies exist, and Kuzmin even asked Gorky to try to sell another abroad.[59] In the late summer of 1920, he decided to risk printing them with "Petropolis." On the ninth of November he received Milashevsky's illustrations, but the next day he learned that while the censorship had passed *Seven Amorous Portraits*, it had forbidden *Pictures under Wraps* and verse collections by Akhmatova and Sologub which "Petropolis" also wanted to print.[60] Apparently it was only then that Kuzmin and "Petropolis" concocted the strategy of anonymous publication. The book was set in print by November 18; a month later he received his first three copies, and sold one immediately. A week later he noted only, "Panic with *Pictures*." One wonders just exactly what the "panic" was about, but obviously news of the book, which was meant to be secret, was spreading, and with it the possibility of unpleasant consequences. For the moment nothing happened, but as late as 1924, unscrupulous critics were trying to use the "pornographic" *Pictures under Wraps* to drive him off the literary scene.

A far happier occasion had taken place three months before. Late in the spring Kuzmin had joined the Petrograd branch of the new All-Russian Writers' Union with some reluctance (its name smacked too much of hateful Soviet organizations), and Blok had had to dispatch the young poet Vsevolod Rozhdestvensky to persuade him to become a member of the city's section of the All-Russian Poets' Union in June. But once he accepted, he took his responsibilities as a member of its selection committee seriously, as his meticulous evaluations of the submissions of those seeking admission to the Union reveal.[61] On September 29, 1920, its grateful members, joined by hundreds of others, assembled in a packed, stuffy hall at the House of Arts to honor one of their own on the fifteenth anniversary of his literary debut. Blok, as chairman of the Poets' Union, opened the evening. He set his warm praise for Kuzmin in the larger context of the need to preserve culture itself:

> We are all . . . concerned about how to preserve you. To lose a poet is very easy, but to acquire a poet is very difficult; and there are very few poets like you in the world today. In your person, we want to preserve not civilization, which, in essence, has not yet existed in Russia (and when will it?), but something of the Russian culture that was, is, and will be. . . . And with all our heart we wish that eventually a milieu should come into being in which the artist will be able to be capricious and whimsical, as he needs to be, where he will be able to remain himself without being a bureaucrat, a member of a board, or a scholar.[62]

Congratulations followed from Gumilev, Shklovsky, Remizov, and others, after which came a musical program of Kuzmin's songs put together by Karatygin. Glebova-Sudeikina then recited his "Beaded Purses," and Kuzmin ended the evening by reading "From the Notebooks of Tiburtius Penzel" and the "Italian poems." On display, too, was a special exhibit of books, manuscripts, music, and portraits.[63] For a writer who, after the savaging in *Red Newspaper*, was still haunted by the fear that he had no real recognition (thus, how was he to make a living?), the evening and the flattering critical appraisals that followed in the press can only have been gratifying.[64]

With the onset of another severe winter, the old lassitude and sense of ill-defined malaise reasserted themselves. He found it hard to drag himself out of bed into the unheated rooms of what was now a communal apartment that he shared with several other families, but he had to keep working. He still drew the line at anything smacking of collaboration with the Bolsheviks, whose downfall he kept hoping for. In October, Aleksandr Belenson, the publisher of *Archer*, was, to the surprise of all, asked to edit the literary section of the magazine *The Red Militiaman* (Krasnyi militsioner). He persuaded Blok, Remizov, Annenkov, Mandelshtam, and other of Kuzmin's acquaintances to contribute, and he "pestered" Kuzmin to take part. (On October 27 Kuzmin heard that "Akhmatova has not been able to resist. Her business"; it turned out to be only a rumor.) Despite the high royalties Belenson offered, he refused point blank, and on April 2, 1921, when Belenson brought him an issue, he dismissed it as a "lousy rag."

The theater, at least, was uncompromised. He had been translating for it (the libretto of Mozart's *Entführung aus dem Serail*) and writing incidental music all year long—in March, for a program of plays by Molière that included *Sganarelle* and *Le Malade imaginaire* at the Petrograd Drama Theater; in August for a production of Rudolf Rittner's four-act "Spielmannsdrama" of 1906, *Narrenglanz*, which opened at the same theater in October; and, in December, for its production of Lope de Vega's *Perro del hortelano*, for which he also composed an "interlude" that was performed between acts three and four. The panoply of culture represented by such a repertory, which also included *Othello, King Lear,* and *The Merchant of Venice* at the Bol'shoi Drama Theater and the Mozart, Cimarosa's *Matrimonio segreto*, and Massenet's *Werther* at the Theater of Comic Opera (he reviewed all six productions), can hardly be imagined in any foreign capital at the time. No less incredible is the fact that all his exertions could barely keep food on the table.

On November 4, *On Alexis, Man of God*, set as a "dramatic oratorio" by the composer Anatoly Kankarovich, a self-proclaimed "disciple," opened at the "Workshop" of Gaideburov's Itinerant Mass Theater. Kuzmin admired the music, "although there is something of me, Musorgsky, and Massenet," but he thought that it had "flopped spectacularly. But I'm in a fighting mood" (Diary). He rounded out a year that had unexpectedly been his most "Italian" with music for Lev Nikulin's pantomime *The Italian Comedians* (Ital'yanskie komedianty), which Nikolay Petrov directed at the Free Comedy Theater in December, and with a commission from the Bol'shoi Drama Theater for incidental music for a new production of Goldoni's *Servitore di due padroni*.[65] But how very far away was Italy from the reality of that December, when snow piled up on uncleared streets and sidewalks, and Petersburgers, again shivering in barely heated apartments in buildings that took on the appearance of icebergs, wondered if things would be as bad as the last grim winter. (They were to be worse: being able to remove one's overcoat indoors became worthy of note in the Diary.)

On returning from a reading with Gumilev in Moscow to Petersburg on November 4, Kuzmin had been struck by the "emptiness" of the former capital: "It is as though we have arrrived in Kazan." "I am suddenly in the dumps," he wrote a month later. "Not the thought, but the premonition of the thought that suddenly this is forever, until the end of our lives, horrified me. But God, of course, will not allow it." With hands so swollen that he could not wash them from the pain, he was tormented by nightmares that his fingers would fall off. Unusually rosy sunsets could at times make the "frosty weather" seem "charming," but not for long: "We are living as if in exile" (December 22).

In the story "The Cave" ("Peshchera"), Zamyatin imagined the city inhabited by cave dwellers, with mammoths roaming its deserted streets, and Dobuzhinsky captured the bleak beauty of what many believed to be a dying city in a series of engravings ("Petersburg in [the winter of] 1921"). Kuzmin so emblematized the fate of the city and a generation in a poem that he wrote on December 8, 1920, that its text quickly spread far beyond the immediate circle of friends to whom he dared read it:

> December spreads frosts in the rosy sky,
> the unheated house grows gloomier.
> And we, like Menshikov at Berezov,
> read the Bible and wait.
>
> And wait for what? Do we know ourselves?
> For whose rescuing hand?
> Our swollen fingers have already cracked
> and our shoes have fallen to pieces.
>
> No one talks of Wrangel,
> the senseless days pass on and on.
> Only lights shimmer sweetly
> on the Archangel forged in gold.
>
> Send us firm endurance,
> and a meek spirit, and easy sleep,
> and the sacred reading of dear books,
> and the unchanging horizon!

But if an angel bends in sorrow,
sobbing: "This is forever!"—
then let the star that guides me
fall, like a lawless woman.

No, only in exile, we are only in exile . . .[66]

"This is no beyonsense [*zaum'*]. An exact copy from nature," one friend commented.[67] By the end of the month, an unexpected trial was to put the endurance that had gotten the poet through forty-eight years to the severest test.

✌ 10 ✌

"Will I Have Time to Show the Magic in Me?" 1921–1923

KUZMIN HAD KNOWN from the beginning of their relationship that Yurkun was not indifferent to women. The young man, while not objecting to the sexual practice, resisted any identification of himself as gay: "He kept lashing out at homosexuality [*gomoseksualizm*] and me. . . . When we got home he immediately spent some time [*pobyl*, the Diary's code word for having sex together], but as though he had thrown a bone to a dog" (Diary, April 4, 1915). That "rebellion," as Kuzmin dubbed it, passed, but not his flirtations, and Kuzmin had been pained to learn from Yurkun's diary that at times he resorted to prostitutes. Convinced of his companion's genuine affection and concern, however, he was willing to endure the occasional infidelity, as he still loved him "without measure." He blamed Yurkun's sulks, "caprices," and frequent depressions not on their relationship, but on the young man's failure to find any kind of recognition as a writer, something that particularly pained Kuzmin, given his belief in Yurkun's exceptional talents and the special vision of his "pure, childlike soul."[1]

But in late December 1920, when Yurkun took up with Olga Gildebrandt, a striking young actress who used the stage name of her actor father, Arbenin, as her own, Kuzmin realized that a "courtship" that he at first had dismissed with an ironic shrug was no infatuation.[2] On January 4, 1921, he noted: "Today, as usual, I had a terrible day. Yur., as I thought, is involved with Arbenina, and, it seems, seriously. At any rate, things are falling apart. . . . And then the gossip, everybody know-ing, feeling sorry for me. That, of course, is all nonsense. If only he does not distance himself in soul and spirit. And also I just can't overcome a slight physical squeamishness." When Yurkun brought the timid young woman to the apartment for the first time the next day, Kuzmin tried to put the best face on it. He addressed them both in the gracious poem that begins "Someone else's love suddenly blossomed under a New Year's star," but two days later he wrote: "Something bad has entered my life. . . . Desertion, dismay (Diary).[3]

The young couple announced their relationship to the Petersburg artistic elite at a masquerade ball on January 11, when they appeared dressed as a shepherd and shepherdess in costumes borrowed from the Mariinskii Theater. Kuzmin stayed home in the blackest depression: "I am sinking into non-being. I am sick to death of everything. Everything is a dream. Only memory, daydreams, and sleep save me. . . . I, like a corpse, can do nothing." Yurkun and Arbenina never married, but from then on they considered themselves husband and wife. Kuzmin did not like the situation any more than did Yurkun's mother, who could hardly hide her distaste for Arbenina, but he could not think of life without Yurkun and was resigned to accepting him on his terms. And then, too, the sexual relationship between the two men continued at the time and for years after.

To judge by her memoirs, Arbenina knew nothing of that fact, but from the start she had to accept that Yurkun was not going to leave Kuzmin or his apartment.[4] She tried not to complicate matters: "O[lga] N[ikolaevna] came. She is very sweet, treats me affectionately and re-spectfully" (Diary, January 20, 1921). Kuzmin responded in kind, dedi-cating to her his long poem "The Birth of Eros," written the year before. Still, during the first few months, his patience was sorely tried at times: "The same petty and vile demonism that impelled Olenka [Gle-bova-Sudeikina] to give herself to Knyazev on my very own sofas is also guiding this other Olga. I nearly caught them *en flagrant délit.* Yur. then told me, laughing, that she had forced him to undress and to have a look, but to do this at my place is either unclean or unnecessary demon-ism and mockery" (May 16, 1921). He had little respect for her intelli-gence: "She's a little fool, and her female, all too female side expresses itself in her utterly empty ambition and Gumilev-like attitude of sam-pling poetry" (November 1, 1921). He never really changed that opinion, but he gradually reconciled himself to her presence in their life, and grew genuinely fond of her and sympathetic to her awkward position in the ménage à trois.

Kuzmin, as usual, castigated himself for his "disgraceful" idleness, but he could hardly rouse himself from lethargy at the beginning of 1921. He wrote almost nothing at a time when everything seemed "stale" and the terrible cold and "microscopic" rations ("not enough for a mouse") numbed him. Battered no less than Petersburg itself by neglect and deprivation, he desperately needed something to celebrate. The city's intellectuals found a rather unlikely pretext to do just that in the eighty-fourth anniversary of the death of the writer who had saluted the city's "stern, harmonious aspect" and laid the foundations for the literary myth that attached to it. The "Pushkin Days," a series of exhibitions, concerts, readings, and memorial meetings planned by a presidium made up of scholars, critics, and writers, Kuzmin among them, opened on February 11 with a gala evening at the Writers' House attended by "all literary Petersburg."[5]

Kuzmin had been "very nervous about the Pushkin evening. But everything was festive and warm. A mass of acquaintances. It was extremely pleasant. They liked the poem it seems" (Diary). One observer found most of the proceedings a "tasteless caricature," which would have made Pushkin "say for the second time 'God, how sad is our Russia.' Koni was trite, Blok boring. Only Kuzmin's poem to Pushkin was charming."[6] Most of those present would certainly have disagreed with the observer's assessment of Blok's speech, "On the Calling of the Poet," in which he warned of the danger posed to the poet's "secret freedom" by the "stifling" atmosphere that the new regime was creating. The public received it with long applause, and Blok repeated his triumph two days later, when he and Kuzmin, who read his poem again, were joined by Vladislav Khodasevich, who pronounced his passionate jeremiad on the threatened eclipse of Pushkin (and Russian culture itself), "The Shaken Tripod."

Kuzmin's contempt for the Bolshevik regime and his hope for its fall had not lessened, as the repeated phrase "counterrevolutionary conversations" in the Diary testifies. At a time when Yurkun's relationship with Arbenina was uppermost in his mind, he still carefully noted reports of peasant uprisings in the countryside, massive industrial unrest, soldiers' mutinies, and even the rumor that Nicholas II was alive and in Germany. On February 22 he concluded that "we are again on the threshold of major events of some kind." Entries such as "state of siege, can be out on the street only to eleven" and "proclamations plastered all over" fix the first rumblings of the disorder that erupted in total revolt on March 2, when Trotsky's "pride of the Revolution," the sailors of the naval base at Kronshtadt, mutineed and called on all Russia to sweep out the Bolsheviks.

"Can it really be a historic day?" Kuzmin wondered on March 3 and during the initial days of stalemate, when, with the imposition of total press censorship, rumors ran rampant and "nothing is really known for sure" (March 5). We see firsthand in the Diary how Kuzmin lived through the anxious time that followed:

How many years have we been asleep!? [March 7]. Gunfire in the distance. Thank God, it means that they haven't surrendered [March 8]. I am very agitated about Kronshtadt. . . . If only they don't dream up some kind of socialism there [March 9]. A wonderful day. . . . Things are fine at Kronshtadt. . . . I have dreams about the Whites all the time [March 11]. Fog and cold, the shooting has stopped. This silence is horrible [March 15]. It seems that Kronshtadt really has fallen. . . . No shooting, the city is as though it died out. . . . Everyone is gloomy [March 18]. Yes, for this time, everything is over. No one even wants to talk about it. Well, we'll have to wait. But what an ignoble people. No, it will only be saved by the absence, even in stupid dreams, of any sort of "soviets" for a long time [March 19]. Everything is over. The Soviet yoke again [March 20].

Only on March 28, when he met an acquaintance who had been on Kronshtadt throughout the events, did Kuzmin learn that it was "not at all the way they wrote and the way we thought. This was the outburst of the people's indignation from the lower classes."

Strangely enough, the revolt energized him for a while. During the height of the uprising, he wrote an appreciation of Somov that has never been bettered, and on the twenty-second a review of Anna Radlova's new book of verse, *Ships* (Korabli). He had met her and her husband, Sergey, an innovative stage director, in the summer of 1914. He invited her to participate in "The Sailors of Marseilles," and he gave her first verse collection, *Honeycombs* (Soty), a favorable review in 1918.[7] After that, he and Yurkun encountered the couple on occasion at the apartments of friends such as Tamara Persits. Within a year of the review of *Ships*, they were close friends and collaborators.

In the review Kuzmin declared that Radlova had taken "her lawful place in the family of major contemporary lyric poets like Akhmatova, Blok, Vyacheslav Ivanov, Mandelshtam, and Sologub."[8] The high praise irritated the rival "Anna," but the following passage gave offense in another quarter:

> Her appearance on the scene differs sharply from the herd-like burgeoning of schools with studios and a party line, where strength is measured in numbers and by devotion to the *maître* and the school's discipline. *Ships* is not the result of formal training and is not a collection of exercises. . . . One remembers the definition of some naive person or other: "Poetry is the best words in the best order." One may utter any stupidity one likes, but all poetry and the poetry of Anna Radlova . . . protest against that.

The closing shaft was directed, of course, not at Coleridge but at Gumilev, who liked to repeat the remark to his pupils, and he did not miss the reference: "Gumm and Odoevtseva have obviously read what I wrote about Radlova, and it found its target, judging by their manner [when we met at the House of Arts]. I will acquire enemies. But to fear enemies is not to live" (March 28).[9] Kuzmin softened the remark about the "naive person" when he republished the review two years later, but it had put a strain on his relationship with Gumilev and all those associated with his Guild. In the future some of them would use Radlova and Kuzmin's high opinion of her verse to settle scores.

After the frisson of the review and some sharp remarks about a new production of Goldoni's *Servitore di due padroni* at the Bol'shoi Drama Theater, Kuzmin fell into another slump.[10] He blamed it on his "stupid weakness": "If I am to have an appetite and love for my writing, I have to have a comfortable life. . . . Works written in haste, catch-as-catch-can, on revolting scraps of paper, when half-starving, wearing rags— how can they be interesting?" (April 10). Goods had started to enter the shops with the introduction of the New Economic Policy (NEP) in March, but, with his only income deriving from tiny salaries from TEO and "Petropolis" and money from the sale now and then of a copy of *Pictures under Wraps*, he could afford to buy little. To make matters worse, he lost some of his ration permits. What he called "hungry meals" *(golodnyi obed)* continued, and if he noted some "delicacy"—real tea, a piece of candy—on his table or that of equally poor friends, he usually added, with no hint of condemnation, "stolen, of course." His shabby appearance and that of his friends reminded him of the retreating Napoleonic army in 1812, and the state of his shoes, their soles flapping as he walked, became an obsession when foot power was the only reliable means of transportation: "The rusty nails in my shoes bothered me [on the way to Somov's]; because of them I have deep rust-colored holes in my feet" (May 10).

He cheered up a bit on April 18, when he learned that his young friend Ignaty Bernshtein, who put out a few books under the imprint "Kartonnyi domik," named in honor of Kuzmin's early story, had received permission to issue a small volume of his poems under the title *Echo*. (It appeared in an edition of one thousand copies in September with an elegant cover design by Golovin.) He did not snap out of his ill-defined malaise, however, until the end of the month, when suddenly, to his own surprise, he began to write verse again. He upbraided himself for taking the time he should have been devoting to reviews and translations—"I wrote poems again. That's downright shameful" (April 29)—but he could not stop, even though a rainy May sometimes brought on his old depression. Over the next several months he wrote "a lot of poems," as the entry for 1921 reads in a list of his works, enough to make up half of the 1922 collection *Parables*.

In a world of violent change dominated by a sense of inconclusive endings and uncertain beginnings, Kuzmin's art moved toward myth, the mystical, and the universally significant. He became one of the great poets of culture and memory in these new poems, and we are reminded of his attachment to Petersburg, that fluctuant city of canals on the Neva and its tributaries, the epitome of the mutability of political fortunes and the permanence of cultural and spiritual values, no matter how threatened they were at the time. Often memory of past experience impelled him, nowhere more so than in the cycle "A Journey through Italy," written at the end of April and in May. The seven poems form an imaginary trip with a beloved friend (it is dedicated to Yurkun) through a kind of Elysian Fields in which the lovers wander, "awakened

in April" and released from the "prison" of Soviet reality. The Petersburg literati heard it and other new works on May 21, when the House
of Arts organized an evening for him: "Few tickets sold. Gum was
reading stupidities of some kind in an adjacent room. [The reading]
turned out not too badly. I was given some lilies of the valley at the
beginning and that perked me up."

One of the first tangible effects of NEP was renewed vigor in the
publishing world. "Petropolis" was finally able to issue *Mary's Tuesday*
on June 4 and *Otherworldly Evenings* ten days later. Reviews of both
were good, and Kuzmin had been invited to join two new groups, the
"Free Community of Poets" in May and the "Ring of Poets in Honor of
K. M. Fofanov" in July, both of them ephemeral.[11] Yet the matter of his
reputation, not to speak of his vexation at the refusal even of many
friends to give his new works the attention they deserved, still troubled
him: "I hope that I'll manage to survive, but I don't know what I will
become and what the attitude toward me will be. My situation, after all,
is still very problematic. Some still recognize me, but others stubbornly
do not want to" (June 4).

As in the spring, the "slightest effort" was again difficult, but write he
did: more poems, *Roman Marvels* and the life of Virgil, to which he
returned, reviews and an appeal for help for the famine-stricken Volga,
and a translation of two farces by Henry Fielding for "Petropolis."[12] At
the end of June, inspired, he thought, by his reading of a book about
Mozart, he was "thinking, like a fool, about music" (June 29). He was
still reading the Mozart and "thinking of 'The Grove' (isn't this an
obsolete aesthetic undertaking?)" the next day, and on July 1 he began
writing his most ambitious and innovative large-scale work of the year,
a kind of singspiel with poems (to be sung) and a prose narrative, cinematic in its use of short scenes that dissolve in and out of one another.
Each of its three parts pays tribute to a favorite author—Shakespeare,
Hoffmann, and Apuleius—in a very private associative montage of
characters and themes from their works that set out his own view of art
and love. As he labored on the "chamber work," he was assailed by that
old conflict between the need to follow an inner creative drive and the
self-doubt that eroded his ability to do so: "Just what remains of me?
Laziness, ineptitude, apathy, insensibility, petty caprices, of course,
some sort of uninspired (perhaps obsolete) plans and idiotic daydreams.
I am not altogether sure that I still have faith" (July 5). The text was
completed, however, by the twenty-fourth, when he read it at the apart-

ment of Glebova-Sudeikina to Akhmatova, Lourié, Milashevsky, and a few other friends, who liked it. (Most of the critics would find it incomprehensible.) In January 1922 "The Burning Bush" ("Neopalimaya kupina"), a small private firm, published *The Grove* (Lesok), a "lyric long poem for music with explanatory prose," in an edition of five hundred copies with illustrations (and a silhouette of the author as the frontispiece) by his old friend Aleksandr Bozheryanov, which Kuzmin did not at all like.[13]

To some, the NEP years look like a period of relative intellectual freedom given what was to follow, but that view must be severely qualified. Some private publishing houses and new periodicals did appear, but press censorship was further tightened, the paper supply was a government monopoly, and room for dissent was very narrow. Witness the continuing fierce persecution of all forms of religion and the mass deportation of more than one hundred of the country's academic and philosophical elite in September 1922, an action without precedent in Russian history.[14] Zamyatin and Blok had expressed alarm at the encroachments on intellectual freedom at the beginning of the year. Now, at the onset of NEP, the "apolitical" Kuzmin made a bold statement of protest (he assumed it would not be published) on the pages of *The Life of Art*. In a long article entitled "Cabbage on Apple Trees," he stated his long-held belief in the absolute freedom of art:

> Almost from the creation of the world, the most varied standards
> . . . have been applied to art: ethical, utilitarian, political, aesthetic,
> philosophical, and so on. All this, of course, misses the point. . . .
> Only an immoral and unfree society can fear the influence of
> art. . . . Art is metaphysical, moral, and free, but it is impossible to
> deduce either a philosophical system or a moral code or a party
> program from it. . . . Art is timeless and by its very nature revolu-
> tionary. . . . And every society which asserts that it is free and moral
> must have full trust in true art.[15]

There were no immediate consequences, but Kuzmin's "un-Soviet" opinions and his explicit rejection of censorship and "social commands" would not be forgotten.

"Away, away! . . . For we have seen hell with our own eyes and do not fear Gehenna," the lyrical hero of "The Journey through Italy" exclaims at the sight of the ghost of Virgil in one of its poems.[16] Events in

August only deepened Kuzmin's conviction about the nature of the monstrous society in which he was living. "Gumilev really has been arrested," he learned on August 5. Ever since the review of Radlova's *Ships*, Kuzmin and Gumilev had met only if they ran into each other at one of the Houses or at the offices of "Petropolis." Kuzmin's alienation from his old friend did not lessen his anxiety about his fate now, but another event for a time overshadowed that for him and others.

Kuzmin had been moved by Blok's remarks about him at the 1920 celebration of his jubilee, and the two poets had chatted warmly at the Pushkin festivities, but after February they seem not to have seen each other again, as Blok, seriously ill, rarely left his apartment and withdrew into himself.[17] Kuzmin was thus unprepared for the news of August 7: "Blok is dead. Olenka cried, but Yur. started to *raisonner* and be malicious. This was somehow indecorous. . . . And I too will have to die. My God, just what have I accomplished? Everything seems lightweight to me." Arbenina persuaded him to go to the Requiem Mass in Blok's apartment the next day:

> It's good that we went. Everyone was there. Weeping. The words "poet" and "tenderness," of course, are inseparable from him. Many were mourning their own past, a whole period of artistic life, and their own, perhaps, imminent deaths. The women in tears. Disheveled Delmas stood next to Blok's severe widow, and Bely, and Olga Afanasievna, and Akhmatova, and Annenkov right up front. . . . Bruni, Kankarovich, Ershov, Lourié—everyone. The Radlovs, Tyapa. Astonished, dismayed, tear-stained faces. The sun, the small room, the old houses, the meadow on the bank of the canal, the incense, and the words of the mass. We barely managed to get home.

On August 10 all that remained of literary Petersburg followed the coffin through the dusty streets from the apartment to the Smolenskoe Cemetery on Vasilievskii Island: "The open coffin was carried by hand. Priests, wreaths, a crowd. Everyone was there. One could more easily list those who were absent. . . . How Blok had changed. How terribly, and what an air of decay. They overcooked him and roasted him in the sun. . . . A lot of people with nothing better to do kept asking just who is this Blok person" (Diary). "The most loved, the first of contemporary poets. He was and remains so. . . . A poet with a capital letter," Kuzmin called Blok in the brief tribute that he wrote three days later.[18]

In the days that followed, "gloomy rumors" about arrests and executions and news about "decrees, one more outlandish than the other" (August 15), swept through a city sweltering in an unusual August heat wave. Only on September 1 did the authorities announce the execution of Gumilev and sixty others for their alleged involvement in the "Tagantsev conspiracy": "Yes, the news about Gumilev is true, a terrible list, there are people I know. . . . Horrible." The next day it was "still the same. Everyone is depressed by the executions. . . . I am despondent too." On the sixth he heard the "most fantastic rumors that those who were executed were not killed but sent to Arkhangelsk (?)," adding "God grant it may be so." But five days later, when a friend who had been arrested and released told him "terrible" stories about Gumilev's last days in prison, he knew that he and the others were dead, their bodies cast into a mass grave whose location has never been identified.

In the middle of September some friends gave him two rabbits, and Kuzmin took comfort in watching the "dear little animals" hop about and hide under the tables in the kitchen of his apartment. The twenty-fifth brought sadness of another kind: "A rabbit died this morning. . . . Yur. wept. It was very sad. An unenlightened little beasty, what could you ask of him, and yet he suffered so much. The live one licked him, as if he understood nothing. It seems they were both boys. Like on Mt. Athos." Typically for Kuzmin, this domestic "trifle" figures in the September poem that begins with the ironic "We are not living too badly: slush and sand." He reflected on the events of August in its second stanza:

> I am not sick, not drowned,
> not crazy, not murdered!
> Our rabbity hermitage knows
> no howls.[19]

The hermeticism of private associations in the stanza was becoming typical of Kuzmin's new verse, and a Diary entry for August 26 fixes the stanza's terrible referents:

Nothing but melancholy news. Veiner has been stricken by paralysis. And Nastya Sologub has thrown herself from the Tuchkov

Bridge in a fit of frenzy. The poor old man! How will he live? And everyone is indifferent. . . . The unenlightened rabbit, obtuse Gummi, the poet Blok [he was rumored not to have been in sound mind in the days before he died, so "crazy" in the poem], unbearable Nastya—find rest, find rest. Will my heart and my tired bones also find rest? Will I have time to show the magic that is still accumulating in me? And is this needed after all?

Only the "invisible" presence of a third force, God or Love, blesses the stoic poet and his lover in the poem's final stanza: "Whom he has once welcomed will not die an orphan."[20]

Hundreds of thousands of Russians from all ways of life had sought refuge abroad after 1917, among them a number of Kuzmin's good friends. The events of August 1921 hastened the flight: "Tyapa is leaving on Tuesday. The Blokhs are packing. In general, people are crawling away in all directions as in the eighteenth century" (September 9). "One can live in poverty for a while, but it is impossible on a regular basis," he wrote on October 15, adding, "And the Bolsheviks are more and more (if only because of their durability) becoming the norm." Yet he gave no thought to leaving, even if during a performance of Musorgsky's *Boris Godunov* "[Grigory] Otrepiev's questions about how to get to the border [to flee Russia] agitated me" (November 24).

It had been a long time since his prose fiction had appeared in print, and in December he was happy to see the little miscellany *Hours* (Chasy) that he and Milashevsky had put together to publish works by their friends. Two chapters from Kuzmin's "Melted Footsteps in the Snow" ("Talyi sled") had pride of place.[21] He was also glad to hear from Blokh on December 18 that *Gentle Joseph* and the "Alexandrian Songs" had come out in German translation. He was convinced that if he were to have any kind of reputation abroad (and some foreign royalties) it would be in Germany, through the efforts of translator friends such as Guenther and Reinhold von Walter. "Better, of course, better" than last year, he felt on New Year's Eve, but he wondered if this were just the effect of the Rhine wine that the Blokh family, with whom he now spent nearly every evening, had obtained as a special treat for him.

At the beginning of 1922 Kuzmin was often in a state of "total prostration," feeling like "Adam expelled from paradise, or like the Jews who had not yet reached the Promised Land" (January 15). He was seeing a lot of a group of actors from Rostov-on-Don who opened a

Theater Workshop (Teatral'naya Masterskaya) in Petersburg in January. They talked of producing his *Eudoxia* with music by Lourié, asked him to write music for Euripides' *Cyclops*, and ordered some translations, but, of course, fulfilled none of their promises.[22] It was not until the spring that another new enterprise, the Theater of Young Spectators (Teatr yunykh zritelei), which had opened the previous autumn, lived up to a commission. Kuzmin's three-act play *The Nightingale* (Solovei), adapted at its request from the Andersen story, opened with his music on April 17 in a production directed by Aleksandr Bryantsev. It remained in the repertory until 1924, a welcome source of royalties, tiny though they were.

Since January 1921, a group of young poets who took the name the "Resounding Shell" ("Zvuchashchaya rakovina") had been gathering to read their verse after Gumilev concluded his Wednesday poetry lectures at the House of Arts. They kept on meeting after his execution, now on Mondays, but as before at Nevsky, no. 72, in the large apartment of the leading portrait photographer of the age, Moisey Nappelbaum, two of whose daughters, Ida and Frederika, were among the group's most energetic members.[23] Kuzmin resisted their invitations until January 9, 1922, when first impressions were anything but favorable: "Gloomy and cheerless, and I would not say very respectful. They read some poor stuff. Yur. read 'Petrushka' [a chapter from his new novel]. It was like an explosion in their sleepy torpor. I don't know whether the lads understood what nonentities they are or not" (Diary).

He sent Yurkun from time to time to keep an eye on what was going on, but kept away himself. Then on March 16 he read Sergey Bobrov's review of *Echo*.[24] Famous for his poison pen, the critic and sometime poet outdid himself on this occasion. "Incredibly abusive," wrote Kuzmin. "Another person in my position would shoot himself. And could this all be true perhaps? Am I an ignorant hack with no talent . . . ? With all this, how can I work? And layer after layer of the people who value me is falling away. Without the least pride I think: would anyone else at all be treated in this manner?" He could not get the review out of his mind for days, and on March 27, perhaps to see how he would be greeted, he went to another Monday gathering, where he "stayed for a long time." After that, Yurkun visited rather often with Arbenina, but Kuzmin, who never liked the "exhibitionism" of the verse readings, stopped by rarely.

He was rather hard on some of the members and their former mentor in the article that he wrote in March, "Parnassian Thickets," but he always found an appreciative audience for his verse at the Nappelbaum apartment.[25] And there he met a young poet whose culture and modesty charmed him. His as yet immature but unmistakable gifts impressed Kuzmin so much that he singled him out for special mention in the article: "A real poet is growing in K[onstantin] Vaginov."[26] Kuzmin never changed that opinion. He regarded Vaginov as the most important poet of his generation and his poetry and prose as the hope of a Russian literature being swamped by a sea of mediocrity. From then on, Vaginov became one of the most welcome and frequent of Kuzmin's visitors.

"Like a fool, I wrote a poem instead of working on the translation [of France's *Petit Pierre*]" (Diary, April 20, 1922). As it had a year before, the arrival of spring witnessed a lyrical outpouring of poems, many of which made ever more daring "raids on the inarticulate," as Eliot put it in "East Coker." Despite his often bad mood and worries about his health, the creative spell stretched into the early summer. When Blokh and his family left for Berlin on September 23, the publisher took the all but completed manuscript of *Parables* with him, and "Petropolis" printed it there in December. The large number of misprints, even dropped titles and lines, upset Kuzmin, but even worse, he waited in vain to see the book put on sale in Russia, unaware that the government, in an attempt to bankrupt émigré publishers, was tightening the screws on the importation of virtually everything printed abroad in Russian.[27] He tried to arrange for a second revised edition with "Academia" at home and with "Petropolis" abroad, but nothing came of it.

Kuzmin always regarded the book, which contains some of the most "difficult" poems in modern Russian poetry, as one of his finest achievements. He was disappointed by the reaction of some friends who found it "too respectable and abstract" (Diary, October 14, 1923) and by the virtual absence of reviews, even in the emigration, where the book was distributed and where so many friends now lived. He addressed two of them, Tamara Persits and Tamara Karsavina, in the wonderfully supple free verse of the poignant "An Errand," which he wrote on May 10:

> Wanderer, if you will be in Berlin,
> among the Germans, dear to my heart,
> where Hoffmann, Mozart, and Chodowiecki were

(and Goethe, Goethe, of course)—
convey my greetings to the houses and passersby,
and to the old, prim lindens,
and to the surrounding flat plains.
Everything there is probably different now—
I would not recognize it, were I to go,
but I know that in Charlottenburg,
on such and such a Strasse,
fair-haired Tamara is living
with her mama, sister, and brother. . . .
Tell her that we are alive and well,
we remember her often,
have not died, but have even become more hardy,
we will soon be counted among the saints,
that we haven't drunk, haven't eaten, haven't worn shoes,
have been nourished on spiritual words,
that we are poor (but that's no news:
what possessions do sparrows have?),
have engaged in remarkable commerce:
we sell everything and purchase nothing,
we gaze at the spring sky
and then think about faraway friends.
Whether our hearts are weary,
whether our hands have grown weak,
let that be judged by new books,
which will come out some day. . . .
But if you travel farther
and meet another Tamara—
tremble, tremble, wanderer, . . .
as you watch the movements of a vatic Firebird,
as you gaze at the dark, flying sun.[28]

"Everyone is talking about leaving," he wrote over and over in the spring and summer. On May 19, after hearing from Annenkov about the life of several friends in Berlin, he had wondered if he, too, might be able to make a go of it there, only to dismiss the idea as "not worth thinking about." He never said why he refused to join the exodus, but we find a likely answer in the diary jottings of the heroine of his story

"Underground Springs," which he wrote in April. Many of them quite literally reflect his own thoughts of the time: "Aleksey Mikhailovich [the name and patronymic of Remizov] is very homesick in Berlin. I should think so. Such a Russian. . . . The language, a few customs, the climate, and the landscape—that is one's home."[29]

On the evening of July 3 he went to see a workshop performance of his *Comedy on Martinian* given by the Sky-Blue Circle (Goluboi krug). Once again his confidence was shaken: "They recited it horribly. . . . But then how horrible my own verse seemed. I wasn't the only one, incidentally, who felt uncomfortable. [The artist and stage designer Vladimir] Dmitriev said: 'What horrible verse you used to write.' In ten years the verse that I am writing now will also seem just as monstrous to them. . . . Perhaps Bobrov is right." A week later, however, he was in a fighting mood when he read Marietta Shaginyan's nasty review of Radlova's third book of verse, *The Winged Guest* (Krylatyi gost'), which had just appeared.[30] Kuzmin, always fiercely loyal to his friends, responded in *The Life of Art* on July 18 in "The Winged Guest, a Herbarium, and Examinations," and he used the article not only to defend Radlova's verse, but also to attack the so-called Formal method and set out his own view of art.[31] Shaginyan replied there two weeks later, as did Georgy Adamovich, who had been annoyed by Kuzmin's reference to the "quadrilles and polkas of the Gumilev school" and the comment that Gumilev was the "most antimusical poet in principle." When he had the temerity to attack Radlova's verse to Kuzmin's face, Kuzmin said simply, "You, Zhorzhik, are a fool."[32] They never spoke again.

In August a new wave of arrests swept up a large number of friends as the Bolsheviks prepared for the "exile of the philosophers," and Kuzmin in all seriousness awaited being taken himself. That did not happen, but in September, Trotsky, still second only to Lenin in the Soviet hierarchy, made a pronouncement on literature. The Diary notes: "Now Trotsky too is abusing us. Perhaps we are candidates for exile" (September 21). Speaking of the recently published third number of *Archer*, Trotsky had written: "How many collections of verse have come out this year, many of them bearing famous names. There are short lines on small pages, and each line is not bad, and they are connected into a poem where there is no little art and there is even an echo of some past feeling. And everything taken together is completely and utterly superfluous to today's post-October person, like a glass bead to a soldier on a march." He concluded his dismissal of this "literature of discarded thoughts and feelings" written by impotent "internal émigrés" with: "What hopelessness, what dying! It would be better if they cursed and went into a frenzy. That, after all, resembles life."[33]

Even before Trotsky's attack, Kuzmin had felt embattled as never before in the ever more polarized world of Soviet letters, with Serapion Brothers, "Islanders," Proletarian poets, Fellow-Travelers, and dozens of other "schools" and groupings all vying for position. He had warned of the dangers of government interference in the arts in "Cabbage on Apple Trees," but he was even more concerned with what he saw as the "formalistic bias" among the young and in so much writing about the arts. He dismissed the Formal method in that article with "as is said in *King Lear*, 'nothing will come of nothing,'" and in article after article he let pass no opportunity to belittle a "simpleminded," "mechanistic," and "dehumanizing" approach devoid of any spiritual or transcendent element, one that, to his mind, emphasized "devices" and "techniques" at the expense of the creative imagination. How much easier it was to "point your finger at the fourth paeon than to demonstrate the action of the creative spirit that alone makes art alive and ever new," as he had chided Shaginyan.[34] Late in August he decided that it was time to rally those friends who shared his views and take a public stand while it was still possible.

Kuzmin, Yurkun, Radlova and her husband, Sergey, Vaginov, the gay poet and novelist Boris Paparigopulo, and the artist Vladimir Dmitriev began to meet regularly with a few others at Kuzmin's apartment or that of the Radlovs, prompting talk in literary circles of the "Kuzmin or Radlov hermitage [*skit*]," as he remarked on October 28. He was particularly close to the "talented and charming" Dmitriev, with whom he thought he might have an affair, but despite rumors to that effect, the relationship remained "Platonic," as he put it at the end of 1922. (The friendship was close enough to stir strong emotions in Yurkun: on February 15, 1923, he physically assaulted Kuzmin, slamming him against a wall and choking him in the presence of Dmitriev and Arbenina.) The group decided to put out a small miscellany, and assigned organizational matters to Orest Tizengauzen, whose wife, Olga Ziv, had been one of the auditors of Kuzmin's lectures at the Writers' House. Kuzmin busied himself with attending to last-minute editorial matters and reading proofs for the first issue of the miscellany, to which he gave the

Gnostic title *Abraxas* (Abraksas).[35] The sixty-four-page collection came out early in October in a printing of five hundred copies, with contributions by all of Kuzmin's associates in the venture and a poem by Akhmatova, who had taken no part in its planning and had nothing further to do with it.

Kuzmin thought that Boris Pasternak might make a fine ally. Pasternak had written to Yurkun on June 14, 1922, saying that he was sending him a copy of the miscellany in which his story "Lyuver's Childhood" ("Detstvo Lyuvers") had appeared and a copy of *My Sister, Life* (Sestra moya—zhizn') for Kuzmin.[36] The collection had created a sensation that summer, and Kuzmin noted it in "Parnassian Thickets." He devoted most of the August article "Those Who Are Speaking" to an appreciation of "Lyuver's Childhood," calling it an "event in art" superior to Pasternak's early poems, in which Kuzmin found too great a "debt to the latest formal fashions."[37] (Pasternak himself would reach the same conclusion two decades later.)

In late summer, when Pasternak stopped in Petersburg on his way abroad, he "suddenly appeared. He's nice. . . . Conversed like friends who have not seen each other for a long time. . . . He spoke very interestingly about his meeting with Trotsky, who summoned him and Mayakovsky for a fatherly reprimand" (Diary, August 13).[38] On the sixteenth, the day before he and his wife left for Berlin, the poet came to Kuzmin's apartment, where he had a long "heartfelt and friendly" conversation with Yurkun. Kuzmin listened on the sidelines, grateful that Yurkun had at last found someone else who genuinely admired his writings.[39] Pasternak met none of the other "Abraxasists," but he left the poem "Pushkin" for publication in the first issue of the miscellany.[40] In 1924 he dedicated his story "Aerial Ways" ("Vozdushnye puti") to Kuzmin, who had been among the first to single out his great gifts as a prose writer, and in 1926 he wrote a long inscription on a copy of his selected verse, assuring Kuzmin of his "devotion."[41]

Kuzmin and Radlova, disgusted by Tizengauzen's disorganization and constant intriguing within the group, removed him from editorial responsibilities and took over *Abraxas* themselves in November. The second issue came out at the end of that month with most of the same contributors as in the first, joined by the poet and stage director Adrian Piotrovsky. The little band of friends, united only by their opposition to regnant ideologies, can hardly be called a "school" with the rules and dictates that Kuzmin hated. They did not even get around to publishing a statement of principles until the third (and last) issue of the miscellany, which came out in February 1923 and opened with Kuzmin's "Declaration of Emotionalism" ("Deklaratsiya emotsionalizma"), which was co-signed by Radlova, her husband, and Yurkun, the four people who formally composed what Kuzmin had dubbed the "Emotionalists."[42]

On February 5, 1922, at an evening at the Blokhs' apartment, Kuzmin had seen the manuscript of "[Vladimir] Veidle's article against the formalists. Grist to our mill. Even the expression 'emotional art' is used." He included it in the collection *Tomorrow* (Zavtra), which he, Zamyatin, and Mikhail Lozinsky put together for "Petropolis" and which appeared in Berlin in February 1923.[43] Kuzmin himself declared that "art is emotional and vatic" in "The Winged Guest, a Herbarium, and Examinations," while in the "Letter to Peking," a survey of recent Russian literature that he wrote in November 1922 and published in the second issue of *Abraxas*, he asserted that the "formalist wave" was on the wane and that art was "returning to its emotional, symbolic, and metaphysical sources."[44] In December he went further in "Emotionality and Artistic Means," a review of an exhibition of contemporary painting, where he wrote that art must convey the "emotional, personal, unique, unrepeatable perception" of reality, realized in form "brought about by emotional necessity," not by fruitless searchs for "discoveries and novelties."[45] The "Declaration," written in December, and the essay "Emotionality as the Fundamental Element of Art," which Kuzmin wrote in January 1923, only elaborated these notions.[46]

All the statements addressed Kuzmin's old insistence that all true art, no matter in what time or space it is set, is "contemporary and revolutionary" by its very nature. As he had once scoffed, those who chase after "galloping contemporaneity" will only find themselves left breathless in its wake.[47] The statements were genuinely oppositional in this regard, rejecting as they did not only the party's call for the "timely," but also two of the most common stances of the day: either a nostalgic wallowing in the past or an anxious groveling before a no less fictive future, both of which to Kuzmin's mind devalued the present for "meaningless and harmful utopias." "There exists no past and no future independent of our most sacred present, perceived emotionally with all the power of the spirit, a present toward which art is directed" (point nine of the "Declaration"). That affirmation of the experiential reality of human life and an assertion of the primacy of the tangible particular over lifeless "*general* types, canons, and laws" inform his own practice as a writer and all his writings about art.[48]

Kuzmin used both statements for the report with which he opened the program on April 15, 1923, at the Institute of the History of Arts, when the Emotionalists gave their first public reading: "There weren't many people and they were all strangers, but they gave us a very good reception, and in general, it went all right" (Diary). Kuzmin, Radlova, Vaginov, and Piotrovsky followed with a recitation of verse, and then Yurkun, Paparigopulo, and Vaginov read from their prose. The anonymous reviewer for *Latest News* (Poslednie novosti), who gave a detailed account of the evening, noted that Kuzmin had stressed the group's affinity with Expressionism, and he saw its impact in some of their works.[49] A month earlier, in fact, they had published in *The Life of Art* a "Greeting to the Artists of Young Germany from the Group of Emotionalists," in which they sent their "brotherly greeting to the German Expressionists and in their person to all new Germany."[50] Kuzmin, the first signatory and its author, hailed the Expressionists as "fighters against the mechanization of life" and compared them to that "wave of genius, the 'Sturm und Drang,'" which had once swept "gloriously" through Germany.

German culture had appealed to him since his youth, and his special perception of German mores only intensified a long-standing allure: "The pronounced homosexuality [there] has an attraction," he had written in the Diary on April 25, 1915, after seeing a German movie.[51] Expressionism had always fascinated him, and by 1922 it had become a passion: "Yur. brought home a lot of good books by the Expressionists and German pictures. Germanophilia and a love for America [its movies] keep on developing in our hermitage" (December 2).[52] He devoted a long paragraph to it in "Emotionality as the Fundamental Element of Art," where he wrote that Expressionism, like Emotionalism, "opposes itself not only to Futurism, Cubism, and Impressionism, but to all of a nineteenth-century culture that is based on positivism, the material, a canon, and mechanization . . . the automation, atomization, and dehumanization of life, which has led to war and the horrors of capitalism."[53]

On September 3, 1922, Nikolay Monakhov had invited Kuzmin to take the position of repertory supervisor at the Bol'shoi Drama Theater, which had been vacant since Blok's death the year before. Kuzmin fretted that his standing there was a bit "false and insecure," but it allowed him at once to realize his interest in the Germans. He asked Konstantin Khokhlov to stage Georg Kaiser's *Gas*, and Kuzmin noted with satisfaction that "everyone is talking" about it after the opening on November 5. Radlov also admired Expressionist drama, and his *Murder of Archie Brighton* (Ubiistvo Archi Breitona) had taken up much of the second issue of *Abraxas*. The abrupt shifts of its ten short acts and its detective-story tale of the tragic fate of a "common man" obviously owed a large debt to the German movement. Piotrovsky read from his own play *The Fall of Elena Lei* (Padenie Eleny Lei) at the April 1923 evening of the Emotionalists, and when Radlov staged it that year at the Theater of New Drama (Teatr novoi dramy), critics noted the clear inspiration of *Gas*. Finally, the Emotionalists united for an acclaimed production of Ernst Toller's Expressionist classic *Hinkemann*, called *Eugen the Unhappy* (Eugen Neschastnyi), at the State Academic Malyi Theater (the former Mikhailovskii) on December 15, 1923. Radlov directed Piotrovsky's translation, which was performed with Kuzmin's music and with sets and costumes by Dmitriev.[54] Only the young Georgy Balanchivadze (not yet George Balanchine), who did the choreography for the dances, had had nothing to do with the group.

Kuzmin knew that the Expressionist plays were not, as he wrote in an article on Toller, entirely "first-rate."[55] He took pride nevertheless in having helped "renovate" the too classical repertory of the Bol'shoi Drama Theater by introducing contemporary plays like *Gas*.[56] It was in Expressionist films, one in particular, that he first saw what he believed marked out a future for all the arts in the fusion of the real and the fantastic, memory and imagination, something he had himself been doing in his most recent verse. On February 12, 1923, Robert Wiene's *Kabinett des Dr. Caligari* (1919) was given a special showing for the Petersburg artistic elite. Kuzmin, who had to hock some books for admission money, sat upstairs with Yurkun, and from that vantage point "everything was distorted. But such 'El Greco' suits this movie a lot. The sleepwalker has a ravishing face. But in general, such faces, plot, and movements pierce and frighten one to the marrow" (Diary).

The film made an even greater impact when he saw it a second time on March 2 at another "closed" showing, and he did not miss its homoerotic element:

An excellent movie. And no success at all. . . . All the characters are terrifyingly close to me. And the relationship between Caligari and Cesare. A loathsome villain, a decomposing corpse, and the purest magic. Respect, peace of mind, work—to throw it all away and live like a bum in a cold carnival booth with a monster and a guest from heaven. When Cesare is shown to Jane, it is so obscene that it is as if the very worst is being done to her, worse than rape. And Francis—once he has entered Caligari's circle, good-bye to any other life. The insane asylum, like [Raphael's] *School of Athens*, like Paradise. . . . All of it is the most deeply and disgustingly humane. And everything drags one in, like a Hoffmann story. I have rarely had such a *choc*.

At a theater two days later, he noticed that "some kind of automaton was sitting upstairs. . . . I cannot get Caligari out of my mind." The extraordinarily expressive face of Conrad Veidt, who played the sleepwalker Cesare, particularly haunted his imagination, and he captured it and the film's exaggerated perspective and zigzag contours in the poem "Germany," which he wrote on February 25.[57] *Caligari* and other Expressionist films would leave their mark on most of what he wrote in the next five years.

He wrote articles about *Caligari*, Radlov, the new German and American cinema (he had no use for Soviet movies), *Anthony and Cleopatra*, *Giselle* (he had become a balletomane again), and others, but Gaik Adonts, the editor of *The Life of Art*, which had become a weekly magazine with its first issue for 1923, rejected them all. He would now accept only pieces on the operetta. Kuzmin suspected, rightly as it turned out, "intrigues" aimed at discrediting his reputation as a critic. He tried to get to the bottom of them, but except for an April theater review and an essay marking the one-hundredth anniversary of the birth of the playwright Ostrovsky, it was the operetta or nothing at all. He was able to slip some remarks about Expressionism into the operetta reviews, but after August 1923 he gave up on the periodical which had for so long been an important source of income.[58]

Abraxas had not been an alternative for a long time. The third issue, which was only half as large as previous ones because of censorship problems, had been the last: "*Abraxas* was banned for its literary incomprehensibility and extremeness. We are making efforts on its behalf.

Probably in vain. . . . In general, I am working, although the unexpected prohibitions have a depressing effect."[59] To his relief, essays commissioned for books marking the twenty-fifth anniversaries of the great tenor Leonid Sobinov and of Evgeniya Lopukhova, a member of the Lopukhov dance dynasty who was now making a career as an operetta actress, did make it into print at the end of 1923.

Several small private theaters and cabarets had sprung up in the wake of NEP, but none showed any particular interest in Kuzmin until November 1922, when Grigory Yudovsky asked him to become the artistic adviser for his new "literary cafe," "The Little Berry" (Yagodka), on Nevsky Prospect. Kuzmin admired its "charming" and "cosy" rooms with low ceilings and walls decorated by Boris Kustodiev in his *style russe* manner. His musical setting of the "Petrushka" story and his "cantata" saluting Kustodiev were performed there in January 1923, but as he had feared, the "quarrelsome" proprietor proved too difficult to work for. Collaboration with Nikolay Petrov's small new theater "Balaganchik," for which he wrote a few sketches, proved just as short-lived. Recitals of verse and literary evenings still went on, but it was proving harder and harder to find venues after the abrupt closing of the Writers' House and the House of Arts by the authorities at the end of 1922.

Opportunities in Petersburg's state theaters were also becoming fewer and fewer. Kuzmin began the music for Radlov's new production of Plautus' *Menaechmi* (*Bliznetsy*; The Twins, in Radlov's translation) in May and finished it a few weeks before the opening on September 29, 1923, at the Bol'shoi Drama Theater with sets and costumes by one of the director's favorite new collaborators, Valentina Khodasevich. After that, his work there slowly came to an end because of the indifference of its management and his own dissatisfaction with it. Kuzmin did see signs of life at the Academic Drama Theater (the former Aleksandrinskii) after years of stagnation, and he welcomed its invitation to collaborate.[60] His experience with the Theater of Young Spectators was altogether more disheartening. Bryantsev asked him to adapt Perrault's tale of Puss-in-Boots, "Le Maître Chat ou le Chat botté," for its puppet theater and invited Dmitry Mitrokhin to design it. Kuzmin submitted the text and music in August, and the theater assured him that rehearsals were under way, despite some questions about the play's suitability for children. Then, on September 7, he learned that the play had "infuriated everyone, like pornography." A month later he was told that the theater still wanted to produce it, and he agreed to revise the text. Mitrokhin kept stopping by to show him the designs, but in December the management simply dropped the play with no explanation. He never received another commission for a new play from any theater.

Kuzmin had spent most of his adult life in the company of artists, and he still saw old friends from the World of Art, such as Somov and Dobuzhinsky, usually at the ballet.[61] He had honed his skills as an art critic in the recent past with articles on Annenkov, Georgy Narbut, and Mitrokhin,[62] and he was glad of it in the summer of 1923, when the young art historian and critic Erikh Gollerbakh asked him for articles for a new art journal, *Argonauts* (Argonavty), which he was starting with Mitrokhin and Evgeny Lancéray. The magazine closed after the first issue, before it could publish Kuzmin's articles about Serov's portraits and about Ryabushkin. That August he had finished a stimulating appreciation of the World of Art painter Nicholas Roerich, who was most famous for his collaboration with Stravinsky on the libretto for *The Rite of Spring* and for his set and costume designs for its first performance in May 1913. The essay traced the impact of Russian religious and pre-Petrine culture on Roerich and a whole generation of Russian creative artists. It was printed as a small brochure in Moscow at the end of the year and remains the best brief introduction to the painter's work.[63]

At the beginning of July, Kuzmin had felt "inspiration" for his own creative work "accumulating in waves": "It is criminal and insane—to be burying myself in never-ending translating and editing work at my age"(July 8), and he worried that nothing might come after the long silence that all the "hackwork" kept imposing on him. But translating and editing he had to do: Lehár's *Blaue Mazur*, *Die gelbe Jacke*, and *Eva*, and Henri de Régnier for "Academia," a new firm that had started life as an outlet for scholarly literature in 1921 but was now taking over the role "World Literature" had played. Kuzmin had once read Régnier "with enthusiasm": "How I rest from naive and barbarian views (Russian) on the divine craft of the prose writer" (Diary, March 5, 1914). But by the 1920s he had "cooled very much. . . . The initial idea and details are engaging, the development and psychology slack and ordinary."[64] Kuzmin could not, however, afford to turn down Aleksandr Smirnov's invitation to join the editorial team that was preparing a nineteen-volume edition of Régnier's collected works.[65]

None of the work brought in enough money, and by the end of August, with debts mounting (he had to work by candlelight until the end of the year because the electricity had been disconnected, as had the telephone) and the "crash of all my undertakings" (August 20), he began to slide into deep depression. He gave the gloomiest possible assessment of his life in art on October 9, 1923:

> If I were to recall all my business affairs, undertakings, public appearances, and what is called a "career," it would show total failure, a total inability to uphold my dignity. And then the accidental misfortunes. Lately they have been becoming more frequent. Perhaps it is my own fault, I won't deny it. *The Life of Art*, *Red Newspaper*, the Bol'shoi Drama Theater, the Theater of Young Spectators, translations of operettas. "World Literature," all those "Houses." Where can I regard myself as belonging? "Academia," "Petropolis," etc. Not to speak of my music. The books about which people once talked, yes and sometimes abused—"Alexandrian Songs," *Wings, Nets, Chimes [of Love]*—they are all my first ones. What did people write about me in 1920–1921? My hair stands on end. The World of Art, *Apollo*, the House of Interludes, the [Comedians'] Rest—was I ever really in any of them? Everywhere *intrus*. So too in my acquaintances. And private undertakings? *Hours, Abraxas, Petersburg Evenings?* It is pathetic. It is all a kind of fiction.

Four days later he re-read Hoffmann's *Kater Murr:* "There's a novel for you." "I too could write, had I the time," he added, but he wrote nothing for himself until January 1924. To make matters worse, both he and Yurkun, as if testing fate, "had unexpectedly become real gamblers" (Diary, September 11, 1923). Night after night they visited the city's many casinos, wasting the little money he was receiving from abroad for the "Petropolis" Russian reprints of earlier works and for German translations.[66] (Kuzmin finally broke the habit at the end of November.) He found his thoughts turning again and again to death, as they had so often throughout 1923.

Always superstitious, Kuzmin had consulted several fortune-tellers in 1922. One had seen "talent and loneliness, more and more complete. Some kind of sad, lofty, and unintelligible genius. . . . But I would like something a bit more simple and merry" (October 3, 1922). Several times, when he caught sight of himself in a mirror, he thought that he was literally "shrinking," and Cesare's prediction of the death of Allen in *Caligari* had so struck him that he wondered: was 1923 to be "the year of my death? . . . And if I die, whom will this frighten, bring to reason, or grieve?" (February 18, 1923). The realization that he was the "last of the Kuzmins" gave special poignancy to his premonitions about the future. On November 21, 1922, he had received a letter "out of the blue" from his nephew Auslender, from whom he had heard nothing for many years: "He's turned up in Moscow, is publishing a magazine with Slezkin and Kozhebatkin. Sad news: both my sisters have died, and my brother shot himself. He was already an old man. I alone have been left to die."

"In general, the time to leave has come imperceptibly, and I have done nothing at all," he wrote on July 25, 1923, even as he pressed on with a mass of commissions. The visit of a young Moscow critic and scholar, Boris Gornung, did little to improve his bleak mood: "The Muscovite came by. They do not approve of my new course. They consider *Abraxas* to be experiments. Poetics, but not poetry. This is perhaps symptomatic, but obtuse. Gumilev's leaven is obviously active even in Moscow and rather strongly so" (August 13). Nevertheless, Gornung asked him for some poems for the manuscript journal *Hermes* (Germes) which he and some friends had been putting out in an "edition" of twelve copies since July 1922. Kuzmin, with virtually no place for what little verse he found time to write, gave him two or three poems, among them the very "experimental" (and brilliant) meditation on the Shroud of Turin, his metaphor for the preservation of spiritual values.[67]

The black border around the title of *Conventions* upset Kuzmin when he saw it for the first time on July 17, and on August 20, when he looked through the book *In Memory of Blok* (Pamyati Bloka), he thought: "Well, and I too will soon die. Isn't the black-bordered frame a sign that the end is nigh? Poor Yur., poor Yur., poor Yur." Two months later he had to conclude: "If one is to look not only the future but tomorrow right in the eye, one would have to shudder. Either hang oneself or take heart and drastically, to the point of madness, of heroism, change one's life" (October 26). Heartened by a new friendship with a young man, he would do just that, but not until 1924. As day followed day, "monotonous in their diversity," the year that had begun with the effervescent promise of Emotionalism dragged to a dreary end. Kuzmin and Yurkun, who was no longer even trying to make any money, were once again reduced to pawning or selling their furniture and other personal goods.

❧ 11 ❧

"Like a Ragged Squirrel on a Treadmill"
1924–1926

ON NEW YEAR'S DAY 1924, Kuzmin placed a small piece of incense on the glowing coals of his samovar. "Faika jumped up, barked, growled, ran toward the window, but stopped before she got there, snarled. . . . She had glimpsed a spirit, whom I had either summoned or expelled with the incense." Three weeks later, on the evening of January 21, Lenin, a paralyzed ruin for more than ten months after a series of strokes, died in Moscow. Kuzmin learned of it in the newspapers two days later:

> Lenin is dead. Perhaps this is pregnant with changes. I don't know how much this will be reflected in our day-to-day life. They're shouting, "A full detailed description of the death of Comrade Lenin," but why bother to describe the death of a man who was without the power of speech, out of his mind, and without faith. He died like a dog. At most before his death he could have uttered "beat the yids" [an allusion to the slogan of the Union of the Russian People: "Beat the yids, save Russia!"], or could have asked for a priest. But without the power of speech he could not even utter such historical phrases. (Diary)

Kuzmin's reaction to accounts of the funeral was no less ironic than his response to the earlier news, but has a touch of mystical horror: "After the funeral, the weather became calm and kinder: all the demons calmed down. What a complete pack of lies and charlatanism were all the speeches. Not even 'mass madness,' but just a mass swindle assuming such dimensions that it can be taken for madness. . . . Pulling the whole world through drunken vomit—there you have the world structure of Communism" (January 28). Later that same day he "got the idea of writing 'The Death of Nero,'" but he would not begin serious work on the play of that title until the end of 1928.

In his operettas and later, in *Roman Marvels* and "The Ladder," Kuzmin had deliberately used linguistic anachronisms and the temporal disjunctions that they produced to suggest rather than state directly his views on the contemporary scene and the historical processes at work in it. In "A Letter to Peking," he had seen the hallmarks of the best works of contemporary Russian literature in the "mixture of styles, the abrupt shift of planes [*sdvig planov*], and the total exertion of spiritual and mental forces to bring together the most distant eras."[1] He saw it in Anna Radlova's linkage of the ecstatic rites *(radenie)* of the "Flagellants" ("Khlysty"), the fall of Rome, and the Russian Revolution in some of her verse because of their supposed Dionysian and "cataclysmic" similarities. In the late 1920s, emboldened by the further example of D. W. Griffith's *Intolerance*, which he admired, Gustav Meyrink's "excellent" novels, and Vaginov's story "The Star of Bethlehem" ("Zvezda Vifleema"), in which the action shunts with cinematic speed from Rome to Russia and from one century to another, Kuzmin would go further than he had ever done before in shifting perspectives of time and space in *The Death of Nero*, arguably his dramatic masterpiece.[2]

The play's three acts and twenty-eight short scenes, most of which are set in Italy at the time of Nero and in 1919, mingle and contrast the life of the "artist" Roman emperor and that of a young Russian writer, Pavel Lukin, who has just finished a play about him. No equal sign can be placed between Nero and Lenin, but Kuzmin's reactions of 1924 to Lenin's death obviously inform the portrait of the earlier despot, as do his thoughts about the fate of crazed tyrants who promise their people every blessing but plunge them into bloody chaos, only to be turned into cult heroes after their death.[3] Nero dies a suicide, but some followers gather at his grave in the play's final scene and hope for his return. By contrast, Pavel is rescued from an insane asylum by a simple Italian girl after being confined there for setting fire to a hotel in a fit of "revolutionary" delusion. He regains his senses and his "angelic" double, his younger brother. His wife, Marie, who commits suicide, comes as close to offering Kuzmin's "moral" about revolutionary utopianism as anyone in the play: "It is impossible to benefit humanity without seeing individual human beings. And he did not see them. . . . For him we are phantoms, numbers, grains of sand. Oh, how I hate that word humanity."

In an odd irony, the January 29 issue of *The Life of Art* that was devoted to the death of Lenin contained a defamatory attack on Kuzmin that was meant to put an end to his participation in the Soviet literary process: "Volynsky is opening a campaign against me. . . . Who will stand up for me? No one, I think. I really am extremely isolated. . . . Always politics" (January 29). In the article "Amsterdam Pornography," which he signed with the initials "S. E.," that is, "Staryi Entuziast" ("Old Enthusiast"), a disguise that fooled no one, Akim Volynsky, an early champion of modernism and now Petersburg's leading ballet critic, dredged up the issue of *Pictures under Wraps.* He used it to dismiss Kuzmin as a "jolly vaudevillian versifier" without a single "monumental" work to his name. He then concluded with what really had motivated his article: Kuzmin's never, to him, very distinguished "critical muse" had now "degenerated" into nothing but hack reviews of the local operetta scene.[4] There was no place for a talentless pornographer like Kuzmin in the Soviet press.

"I never thought that he was such a shortsighted idiot," Kuzmin remarked after reading the article the next day (Diary). He did not trouble to settle the score with a public protest on the pages of *The Life of Art*, believing, as he did, that its editor had put Volynsky up to the derisive attack. As he wrote the latter on February 2: "I think that my writings lie so far outside the range of your interests that it is simply unimportant *to you just what opinion you have about me*. . . . But I think that you wrote from the dictation of others and for their interests. Be more careful with your advisers." *Pictures under Wraps*, Kuzmin wrote, was "just a pretext, and not a very good one. A book that was published five years ago with author's copyright, that was never officially put on sale, cannot be, from either a legal or an ethical point of view, the object of discussion in print." He also defended himself from Volynsky's charge that he reviewed nothing but operettas, pointing out that he had written on a variety of subjects in *The Life of Art*, "where I wrote right from the time of its founding up to the moment when G. G. Adonts clearly gave me to understand that my collaboration, in the form I felt possible, was undesirable."[5] Volynsky sent him a "triumphantly stupid" conciliatory letter on February 13, but his article had done its work: collaboration with *The Life of Art*, already in effect over for months, was no longer possible, and the newspaper lost little time in becoming his most savage critic.

When *The Life of Art* had rejected Kuzmin's fine article "Film Art in Germany" in the summer of 1923, he had been able to place it and a couple of other pieces in the evening edition of *Red Newspaper*.[6] Evgeny Kuznetsov, who had left *The Life of Art* because of differences with Adonts, edited its cultural pages. In April 1924, after the magazine *Theater* had closed its pages to Kuzmin at the end of February following a radical change in its management, *Red Newspaper* became his new "periodical home" and the sole outlet for his reviews. Ironically enough, it allowed him to do little but operetta reviews.

"Academia" was still paying him for work on the edition of Régnier, whose *Passé vivant* he was translating, but faced by mounting debts and taxes and, once again, by the loss of his piano, Kuzmin had to take on hackwork such as translating the "nonsense" of Leon Jessel's operetta *Das Detektivmädel* (1921) for the Musical Comedy Theater. He had written only eight or nine serious poems in 1923 and nothing "for himself" for months. His long poetic silence suddenly broke in February, as he told his Berlin publisher, Yakov Blokh, in a letter of March 17, 1924: "You probably think that I am no longer among the living. I am alive, breathing, have begun to write (recently), and have in general taken heart. By some sort of miracle (by the way, I know what kind), an appetite for life has revived in me and has filled me with dreams that are, in essence, rather vain ones, about fame and notoriety."[7] Kuzmin's hope that Blokh would arrange for widespread translations of his works into German and other languages would prove unrealizable. Blokh himself would find it possible to publish only reprints of Kuzmin's earlier works and none of the writings that the "miracle" had brought into being. Yet renewed creative energy inspirited Kuzmin for several months.

The name of the miracle was Lev Rakov, a handsome nineteen-year-old student when Kuzmin met him on October 9, 1923, remarking after he visited the next day that "something about him reminds me of Knyazev." Kuzmin, never good at concealing his attraction to someone, soon suspected that Yurkun was jealous, and by the end of the month, Kuzmin felt "sorry for him. It was very awkward that I was expecting

Rakov . . . [who] is very nice. But a typical young person, so far not very talented, but kind, affectionate, and graceful. Similar to Knyazev, Miller, and many others. His remarks, opinions, jokes, tastes, comparisons are almost feminine. But obliging and well-mannered. Is making up to me a bit" (October 28). By the time he left for Moscow in December to see his father, Rakov had become an almost daily visitor and often accompanied Kuzmin and Yurkun on their rounds of the city's gambling houses.

Kuzmin was "really delighted" when the youth suddenly reappeared on January 22, 1924, "as sweet as before." If Yurkun had "won the right" to have his relationship with Arbenina, Kuzmin decided that he also had carte blanche to form a new attachment himself, although he reproached himself for such "sophistry." He felt an abiding love for Yurkun, who was "life itself" to him, but his feelings for Rakov grew stronger, so much so that by March 12 he felt himself being split in two between the two men: "I am head over heels in love [with Rakov] and happy, and unhappy, and I just cannot really believe that this is serious." It was, however, and he fretted that he had lost Yurkun for good, only to have him become even more attentive and possessive. That, in turn, upset Rakov: "He is already jealous. . . . He calls the resumption of my [erotic] attitudes toward Yury Ivanovich an 'atavism'" (March 15).

Despite his repeated declarations that he could "not live without Kuzmin," "Levushka" never let matters go beyond hugs and kisses. Had Rakov allowed his feelings to express themselves, Kuzmin believed, the young man might have "appropriated" him from Yurkun. Instead he grew so moody and withdrawn that by the end of March, Kuzmin wondered why he should pursue a "gloomy and tedious egoist" when he had "sweet, tender Yurkun, my very own." Still, he felt depressed by yet another failure in a year marred by one disappointment after another. For a few days he even daydreamed about moving to Europe, where he might make the career he knew was impossible in Soviet Russia. Then, just when the affair seemed over, Rakov, now a fixture in the circle of Kuzmin's friends and flattered that everyone was aware of Kuzmin's feelings for him, again became "kindness itself" early in April. Kuzmin, however, realized that the relationship would never be consummated: "Lev Lvovich is a dazzling, charming fiction" (April 14).

By Easter, Kuzmin had come to understand that he had only been "erotically in love" with Rakov, "captivated" by his youth and "touching soul," but that he was bound to Yurkun by "art, love, life, in general by the links of one heart to another." He never entirely got over his feelings for Rakov, who came often to Kuzmin's apartment throughout the 1920s and 1930s.[8] Once again, however, Kuzmin's "dreams, plans, everything were connected with Yurochka," his "one and only sweet friend" (April 30). Their life together was now domestic and rarely sexual, but their intimacy and mutual love grew all the more deep and gratifying. Their tiffs, sometimes stormy, continued, and both remained prone to depressions, but the unshakable faith of each in the other's talent acted as comforter and conciliator.[9]

Whenever Kuzmin felt anything intensely, it came out in verse. When he fell under the spell of Rakov, he experienced a surge of "renewed strength and desires," to which he hoped he could muster the "time and energy" to give expression (February 13). The feelings poured into a "cycle of twelve amorous poems," which he began on February 17 and called "The New Hull." For several years Kuzmin had sometimes noticed a resemblance between someone he loved or had loved and various screen actors. On February 1, 1923, in one such instance, he remarked that the German Paul Hartmann was "fatally reminiscent of Pavlik Maslov." In the case of Rakov it was Paul Richter, who had played the young American millionaire Edgar Hull, who falls victim to the murderous intrigues of the sinister criminal mastermind and hypnotist of Fritz Lang's *Dr. Mabuse, der Spieler* (1922). The film made the "strongest impression" on Kuzmin when he saw it for the first time on January 23, 1923, and at least twice after that.[10]

The cycle, which contains allusions to motifs from Kuzmin's earlier verse, *Tristan und Isolde*, Jean Gilbert's operetta *Dorine und der Zufall*, *Caligari*, and alchemical treatises, makes only one explicit reference to the movie, in the "Introduction":

> The young American Hull
> was killed by Doctor Mabuse:
> he so resembles... Is this not why
> the muse began speaking about him?
> After all, I have completely forgotten
> how he looked on the screen![11]

Kuzmin actually wrote the "Introduction" after he had finished most of the other poems of the cycle, and Yurkun intuited something important about them all in an outburst of jealousy on March 21, when he claimed several of the poems for himself and told Kuzmin that he found his "love poetry so general that it could apply to anyone at all." Rakov had indeed served only as the external creative stimulus for the poems, and it was not so much his slight resemblance to Paul Richter as a "psychological" affinity—Kuzmin's recognition of his love for a charming young man—that had made him the "New Hull," love's "double," in a cycle that asserts the creativity and integrity of the individual spirit and the power of love. Lang's movie is but one element in a web of allusions, one facet of that "unprecedented crystal" (*nevidannyi kristal,* itself an allusion to the "magic crystal" of the penultimate stanza in Pushkin's *Eugene Onegin*), which refracts the hero in a labyrinth of doubling mirrors: "There he [Richter as Hull] sits (or is it you sitting?) in the loge."[12] The displacements and affinities in the textual palimpsest that results prefigured the verse Kuzmin would write later that year and in the future.

When "Academia" published *The New Hull* with the dedication "L. R." at the end of May in an edition of one thousand copies, those friends of Kuzmin who had disliked the "Khlebnikovism" of some of his recent verse were relieved by the greater intimacy and transparency of its style, though somewhat baffled by the complex play of associations. The latter quality troubled them even more in the other work that sprang from Kuzmin's infatuation with Rakov, *Hull's Strolls* (Progulki Gulya), which he told Rakov about on February 13 and finished on March 31. On March 17, in a letter to Vladimir Ruslov, Kuzmin called it a "large (rather) work, half-lyric, half-drama," while in a letter of the same date to Yakov Blokh, he described it as an "odd work, half-scenario, half-lyric, half-story, with music."[13]

In prose dialogue with verse and dance interludes, for which Kuzmin wrote the music, the action moves Hull and the other characters back and forth in time and throughout the world in fifteen brief scenes.[14] In a 1929 scenario of the work that is also a commentary on it, Kuzmin wrote, "The external form is a series of scenes and lyrical fragments that are not united by conditions of time and space, but are tied together only by the associations of the situations and words."[15] The associative principle operates purely on the basis of sound in the opening scenes. In the first, Psyche sits on the steps of Petersburg's Gostinyi Dvor feeding pigeons (*golubi* in Russian), from which she suddenly flies up into an "unusually azure sky" ("azure" or "sky blue" is *goluboi*). In the second scene, two women are searching for some "dove-colored" *(golubinoe)* material in a shop and mention Hull's name (Gul') as pigeons flutter outside the windows. The third section, a verse "intermezzo" built on the sound *guli* (the plural of *gulya*, colloquial Russian for "pigeon") and with references to Aphrodite, makes the transition to Hull's first appearance in the section that follows. Later scenes lead one into another through a spatial (a bridge) or thematic (a star) association, to single out only a few of the many linkages.

Most of the friends in Petersburg to whom Kuzmin read it did not know what to make of the work, although they might have recognized that in it Kuzmin had developed and extended the cinematic technique of "montage" that he had used in *Mary's Tuesday* and *The Grove* and that he admired in American and German Expressionist movies. (The sixth scene, set in New York City, is described as having "all the attributes of contemporary Americanism in the prism of Expressionism.") He did so to explore one of his age-old themes: the journey, a "person's search [the 'strolls'] for an organizing element in life, in which all manifestations of life and all actions would find their corresponding place and perspective," as he wrote in the 1929 scenario. It is an analogue to one of Kuzmin's obsessive concerns in the 1920s: the imagination, guided and prompted by memory—both personal, historical, and cultural—draws parallels between seemingly random phenomena and thus provides a model for art and life. The hero, like the reader, must "recognize" these parallels and move from the purely personal level to universal principles (here the power of self-sacrificing love) or be doomed to wander in a meaningless maze of *realia*. (Recognition of one's "double" in several works of the twenties, like the earlier recognition of self as "other" in a mirror, is a variant of the theme.) Kuzmin could interest no Soviet publisher in it, but he hoped that Blokh might publish what he called his "associative long poem in dramatic form," along with the score of the twelve musical numbers and with illustrations by some of the leading German graphic artists of the day.[16] Anything so complex, however, lay far beyond the increasingly limited means of his Berlin friend.

A small audience in Moscow first heard many of these new works. On March 1 Vladimir Ruslov, whom Kuzmin had not seen for fourteen years, wrote to thank him for the greetings that a mutual friend had relayed and to send an invitation from a gay group in the capital:

A small, very intimate circle made up in the main of young poets has been formed among us here in Moscow under the name "Antinous." Its aim is the revelation of male beauty in print, in the theater, and in other forms of art. In the course of 1923, we had two evenings of performances, the music of "our" composers, the reading of "our" poems, the singing of "our" songs, and also "our" male ballet. A dramatization of your "Antinous" from the "Alexandrian Songs" was given at the second evening. . . . One of this circle's next tasks is the publication of a miscellany with poems dedicated to the celebration of male beauty and love by all poets . . . in whose number there must be . . . yours. . . . We have now conceived the idea of organizing our next evening of performances . . . and devoting it to you with your personal participation.[17]

Ruslov hoped that Kuzmin would give a reading of about two hours from his unpublished poetry and prose, "most desirably works with 'our' hue," and then participate in the musical section of the evening, which would be devoted exclusively to his compositions. He offered a generous fee, and assured Kuzmin that the evening would be "intimate" and "with a strictly restricted and even more strictly censored sale of tickets."

Kuzmin responded on March 17 with thanks to the little society of like-minded men for remembering him as the "grandmother of the Russian Revolution," a witty allusion to the honorific given to Ekaterina Breshko-Breshkovskaya, one of the most prominent pre-1917 figures in the cause of political (not sexual) reform. He demurred when it came to the request for a two-hour reading, which he felt would tire him and the listeners. The program he was planning, he promised, would contain poems "where the theme has a clear ideological basis" and a story (never to be written) "from contemporary German life" set in "male nacht-locals," accompanied by his own music.

As might have been expected, a series of problems arose. None were as serious as those that made the circle's members abandon the plan for a miscellany of homoerotic verse, but it takes no reading between the lines to understand the reasons why they had trouble finding premises for the occasion. "It was hard to book immediately," Ruslov reported, "because of the certain specific nature of this evening: we had to select something both comfortable and intimate, and safe as regards the administration of the premises." The authorities, distrustful of any dissent and freethinking, kept a sharp eye on all gatherings. "Closed evenings," particularly of such a "specific nature," made them very wary.

Ruslov thought everything was set for April 14, but he again encountered a delay because a new male ballet set to the *Chimes of Love* was not ready and, as he wrote the next day,

> because of the foul atmosphere in general now reigning in Moscow both among Muscovites in general (the reason—lack of money and arrests) and among "our" people, who, as you yourself probably know, are easier to frighten than the gazelles of the desert, and therefore all of them, frightened by the mood here, are prostrate, and at the very thought of "our" evening immediately go into hysterics, and there is no way to make them buy tickets.

Ruslov's friends had good reason to be timid. In the months of contentious struggle for supreme power that followed Lenin's death, the Bolsheviks clamped down with renewed severity. Kuzmin noted purges at the university that spring and arrests that cast a pall over his circle of friends. The new Soviet Criminal Code of 1922 contained no statute against sodomy, but gay behavior could be prosecuted as a form of disorderly conduct and for endangering public morals. Throughout 1924 Petersburg (now Leningrad) newspapers were full of articles about raids on "dens of iniquity" *(pritony razvrata)*, among them alleged gay brothels employing sailors from the Red Navy base at Kronshtadt.

Ruslov swore that the evening would take place on May 12, but Kuzmin doubted it until, on May 1, Auslender showed up in Petersburg "as though from the other world" to fetch his uncle to Moscow. The two of them arrived there on the morning of May 10, Kuzmin's first visit to the capital since November 1920. Members of the "Green Lamp" circle, who numbered several old Petersburg friends, celebrated the event that evening with a banquet in Kuzmin's honor at Auslender's small house in the heart of the city, where he was staying. Kuzmin considered the city "the provinces" despite its metropolitan scale, but he enjoyed strolling through its old quarters ("The churches are still intact and the bells ring as before" [Diary]) and seeing old acquaintances.[18]

The evening sponsored by "Antinous" was held on the twelfth at the "Bluebird" ("Sinyaya ptitsa"), a cabaret located in the premises of a former Masonic lodge. Kuzmin was "scandalized" when he arrived to find that nothing at all of the promised program of singing, readings, and dances had been organized. As he sat in the green room waiting to go on stage, he "made friends with an icon specialist from Yaroslavl. There is a room there of famous people from Yaroslavl and my picture hangs in it. Invited me to visit. Aunties and *jeunes hommes* assembled. Very homespun, but warm and courteous. Two young men in the first row and some little old man gave me particular support. It was pleasant to read" from *Parables, The Grove, The New Hull,* and *Hull's Strolls.* He also performed music from *The Grove,* some of his songs, and the "shimmy" he had written for *Hinkemann.* "Even the agents from the GPU [the new name of the secret police] applauded." On the fourteenth he was back in Petersburg, as he never stopped calling it, with a much lower fee than had been promised, but with "aesthetic memories." The next night he and Yurkun made love for the first time in months.

Kuzmin immediately fell into apathy when once again he had to face his dismal finances, and he experienced a renewed sense of isolation. He had joined the All-Russian Union of Writers in March, but had been "blackballed" from membership on the boards of the Poets' Union and the Union of Dramatic Writers. He soon learned that the authorities would definitely not permit another issue of *Abraxas* which he had been planning. Even the publication of *The New Hull* failed to cheer him up: the printers had ruined Mitrokhin's cover design by reversing the colors. He did receive a commission from the Malyi Opera Theater to translate Mozart's *Die Zauberflöte* in June, and, encouraged by talks with Isay Lezhnev, the editor of the magazine *Russia* (Rossiya), he resumed work on *Roman Marvels,* whose third chapter he finished in August. Still, plagued by headaches, a terrible pain in his leg, and a feeling of utter uselessness, he remained in a sour mood for months.

Over the summer he continued work on the Régnier, edited several other translations, and in August started a translation of Henri Barbusse's antiwar novel *Le Feu* (1916), which he finished in November. He was again doing reviews for the evening edition of *Red Newspaper,* but only Lezhnev's magazine offered an outlet for articles on literary subjects. In August, Kuzmin wrote "Wood Shavings," where he made his last public statement about the similarity between the rise of Christianity and Communism and gave his final defense of "Emotionalism." A year before, on August 27, 1923, he had written: "We will have to wait several centuries until socialism, like Christianity, assumes an acceptable and comprehensible form. Of course, we are the society of paganism's fall" (Diary). Now he could not be nearly so outspoken, he knew, in print, but he opened with the categorical assertion that "the analogy between the birth of Christianity and the development of socialism is not subject to doubt" before turning to his main point.[19] Christianity, he argued, had initially undergone a period of exclusionary fanaticism. If we replace "Christianity" in what followed with "communism" (which he, of course, dared not mention), Kuzmin's comment on his own time becomes clear:

> Even more, Christianity destroys every individual distinction—class (there is neither the slave *nor the free*), national (there is neither Hellene nor Hebrew), sexual (there is neither man nor woman)—all are only Christians, slaves of God, a registered unit, an anonymous member of a collective. As a teaching and as a milieu, Christianity could not give birth to art. Early Christian art is a primitivized compilation of pagan art. Hatred for art and culture. . . . Every hint of the diversity and variety of the external and spiritual world, the national, the personal must be hateful to primordial Christianity—the gloomiest, most misanthropic asceticism, the rejection of the "devil's" world, the race to death, abstraction, and non-existence, where, of course, every unsolvable problem can easily be solved.[20]

Only when it "laid down its arms" and built on the culture that it had tried to destroy did Christianity "turn into a creative and fruitful phenomenon." This was how Kuzmin summed up his Aesopic warning that Bolshevism must tolerate pluralism and open itself to the culture that it was attacking, or else remain a stagnant and stultifying dogma.

He then turned to literature. He used irony to belittle the obsessive theorizing of the day and the increasingly militant calls of some for the party to take a "line" in cultural matters: "During the street rallies in 1917, some soldier, trying to prove the necessity of continuing the war, said: 'If we don't fight with the German, what will we do with him?' But why something had to be done with the German, no one knew. Much of the concern about art, about its nature and role, reminds me of that soldier. In general, art flourishes more when people talk less about its role." He then reaffirmed his belief in the creative autonomy and individuality of art and the artist: "The intensity of a collective feeling is sometimes stronger than an individual one, but its quality is always incomparably lower." The writer is not a "gramophone" repeating slogans and ready-made emotions, "dead likenesses that insult the living," he asserted as he passed to a defense of the "emotional" and Expressionism, which was already coming under attack from proletarian ideologues as "petit-bourgeois." Both opposed the "rationalistic dead end," "stasis," and formalistic "stupor" of so much contemporary culture, the deadening legacy of positivism that they both defiantly challenged.[21] When *Russia* published "Wood Shavings" in its fifth issue for 1925, Kuzmin thought that his article "made a vile impression" in the pro-Bolshevik company of the other articles, with their "servility and intellectual posturing": "How seriously they analyze this experiment called Communism" (Diary, June 4, 1925). The authorities were not appeased. They shut down the magazine and deported Lezhnev for his unorthodox Marxist views.

Matters had not been so grim in 1924, when Kuzmin wrote the article and, in October, a long obituary of Anatole France, who was another target of recent criticism because of his outspoken hostility to the Bolshevik regime.[22] "Petropolis" had published a Russian-language reprint of *The Quiet Guard* in Berlin in September. But Kuzmin did not know that it would be the last of its editions of his works when he wrote to Blokh on October 15, 1924, to inquire about progress on plans for German translations of his prose and Russian editions of his new works. He reported that for his part he was "translating, doing editing work, am writing reviews and similar boring occupations." That pretty much summed up what his life would be for the next few years. "Lyrically I feel splendid," he added, thinking of the visits of Rakov, with whom he was experiencing a renewed infatuation, and the poems that kept coming unbidden. (Not until 1927 would he compose as many poems in one year as the twenty-six he wrote in 1924.) "We are living quietly," he concluded, "But I am very busy, and there is never enough money and there is too little time for real work. I run round and round in circles like a ragged squirrel on a treadmill."[23]

News from abroad about the success of friends such as Karsavina and Somov in Paris could cheer him up. But reports of the undimmed brilliance of Diaghilev's Ballets Russes, as it took what he dubbed an "avant-garde direction" in *Le Train bleu* ("in swimming suits," he exclaimed) and a sexually provocative course in *Les Biches* (the influence of Cocteau, he decided), only made him feel that he was living in a backwater, as one fine young dancer after another left for the West and the Mariinskii mounted little but old chestnuts.[24] He was pleased to hear that on occasion he was praised in the Paris émigré press and that it continued to "savage" the Bolshevik regime. Nevertheless, "all these repressions," as he wrote Ruslov after his return from Moscow, and the darkening political climate were, he knew, the present and future reality. As if acknowledging that external opposition was pointless, he finally switched at about this time to the new orthography introduced by the Bolsheviks, and he even started writing "God" without a capital letter in manuscripts intended for Soviet printers.

As one country after another recognized the Soviet state, Kuzmin wavered not at all in his absolute rejection of its legitimacy. In November he gave vent to his contempt in a searing denunciation that is all the more powerful for its quiet tone. It opens with one of those definitions by negation common in riddles:

> It was not a governor's wife sitting with an officer,
> it was not an empress listening to an orderly,
> on an intricately curved gilded chair
> it was the Mother of God sitting sewing.
> And before her stood Michael the Archangel.[25]

In a manner reminiscent of those early Italian Renaissance paintings that Kuzmin loved, a scene of biblical grandeur is domesticated by its homely setting (here decidedly Russian) and a glimpse of human and natural perspective through an open window: the Archangel's horse "tapping its hoof" by the paling to which it is tied "while linen was bleaching in the sun on a hillock." The poem affirms the power of time and nature to effect historical redemption once present evil is anathematized:

> Our Lady said to the Archangel:
> "I honestly, Mikhailushka, don't know
> what to think. . . .
> It is impossible to live without faith and hope,

and without a tsar sent by God.
I am a woman. I pity even a villain.
But these I do not regard as people at all.
Indeed, even they themselves have repudiated themselves
and have renounced their immortal soul.
I will commit them to you. Act justly."
She fell silent, not interrupting her sewing,
but tears did not glisten on her eyelids. . . .
"Well, Godspeed!" said the Mother of God,
then she quietly looked through the small window
and spoke: "Another week will pass
and the linen shall be whiter than snow."[26]

That the Archangel is the patron saint and "Guide" of Kuzmin makes the poem even more pointedly personal.

The poem, of course, circulated only among friends, but Kuzmin did nothing to hide from others the "horror that gripped" him as he faced the "unreal and counterfeit" life around him (Diary, December 17). He was as candid about that as he was about questions concerning his art when Nina Volkenau, a poet friend of Boris Gornung whom he had met in Moscow, came to interview him on December 25 and 27 in preparation for a lecture she was to read in the capital. On the twenty-eighth he wrote in the Diary: "The woman from Moscow has left. I have the impression that she will talk everywhere—my suppression, scope, art, poverty, and terrible counterrevolutionary attitude."

Nothing he turned to could rouse Kuzmin from the "alarming apathy" that held him in its firm grip for the first eight months of 1925 despite a renewed surge of love for Rakov. Aside from some irksome reviews and music for Radlov's production of Zamyatin's play *The Society of Honorable Bell Ringers* (Obshchestvo pochetnykh zvonarei), all he could do was "putter away" at the fourth chapter of *Roman Marvels*, as he wrote Blokh on January 29. "If there were a stimulus from without," he added, "I would, of course, write faster, but there is the impression that one is wasting time on a totally hopeless undertaking."[27] Occasional letters from Blokh bucked up his "often wavering and weakening spirit" with their "illusion" that someone was still paying attention to his work, but at the beginning of March, Lezhnev held out little chance that *Roman Marvels* would ever be published in *Russia*, and he gave Kuzmin no encouragement to continue it.[28]

Kuzmin hoped that spring would bring a sense of renewal, but nothing could provide the seismic shock *(potryasenie)* that he required to rouse him from creative lethargy. By the end of March, his "affairs were in such a mess" that he worried not so much about how to keep up his "meager way of life" as how to "avoid a colossal scandal with my monetary and social obligations," as he told Blokh on March 21.[29] Any "external affirmation" of the simple fact of his existence helped, he added, as "at times I am ready to dry up inside." He feared he was "falling into imbecility" in May as he finished translating *Le Bon plaisir*, wrote an introduction for it, and began his next assignment for the Régnier project, *L'Amphisbène: Roman moderne* (1912), while also starting to translate the libretto of Jean Gilbert's operetta *Zwei um Eine* (1924).[30]

Despite deep misgivings, the Poets' Union persuaded him to take part in what it announced as an "evening of the Emotionalists" on May 29. Only he and Yurkun read, and the result, he concluded, could not have been more dismal: "No one understood anything. . . . Clearly a totally senseless evening" (Diary). A few days later, however, friends told him that after he had left, the audience had heatedly discussed the readings: "Better than one could have thought. Yurochka has something in common with Khlebnikov. I am comprehensible, but in the future" (June 3). Small comfort, as he now quarreled with Kuznetsov about his assignments for *Red Newspaper* and resumed writing for it only in February 1926. "Everyone is busy with something. It is as though I do not exist. Wiped clean from the slate," he noted on June 25. That month he read Franz Werfel's 1924 novel *Verdi*, dealing with the artist's crisis when his creative powers failed. For weeks he could not get it out of his mind. Over the summer, when he listed his daily income in kopecks and his diet consisted of little but bread, macaroni, and tea, he could muster the energy to work—when he had ink and paper—on nothing but translations.

On June 26 Faika, the lively Newfoundland that Yurkun had purchased in 1923 and that had become so much a part of the family that the Diary rarely fails to record her whimsical behavior, was struck and killed by a car:

> Not crushed, but killed without a drop of blood. She still managed, whirling around, to run, then collapsed. Didn't yelp, didn't bark, didn't whine. When Veronika Karlovna, all in tears, told me about

it, I was seized by terror. Yurochka was asleep. What is this? The first weak blow with continuations to come or is she the scapegoat? Perhaps the misfortune roaming around us will limit itself to this, but perhaps it snatched what was most easily available and will persecute us more. . . . Poor Yurochka is not even allowed to have a dog.

Two years before, Kuzmin had had an eerie experience when he was walking home "by daylight, but already after ten," thinking of his "depressing" situation and fate:

An automobile with unusually bright headlights, now flashing on, now off, was standing on Nadezhdinskaya Street. At times the silhouette of the driver was visible. This yellow light without rays during daylight, as though in the beyond—hopeless and unusually agreeable. Yurochka and, for some reason, Faika had gone to sleep in the dark room—little ones, little ones, as though through the wrong end of binoculars. (July 14, 1923)

Both incidents merge in the penultimate poem of the seven-part cycle "The Northern Fan," which Kuzmin began writing on September 16, the day before Yurkun's thirtieth birthday:

> On the street in daylight the headlights
> are on. The light without rays
> seemed an otherworldly dawn.
> As though now, as in antiquity,
> Orpheus has lost his way
> between winter and summer.
> Nadezhdinskaya has become a meadow
> with anemones from beyond the grave in hand,
> and you, little one, are walking with Faika,
> legs weaving in and out, in the distance, in the distance.
> The dog is barking in the twilight hall
> to say that you should not be expected.[31]

Myth—Orpheus and Adonis, from whose drops of blood sprang anemones, both figures symbolic of Yurkun as writer and lover—and actual memories of parting and death become one in a scene that is caught in the ominous light of the sinister headlights that destroys any line between "this" and "that" world.

Kuzmin dedicated the cycle to Yurkun, and its poems, each as it were a segment of the ivory fan with ostrich feathers that Kuzmin owned, abound in allusions to Kuzmin's life with him.[32] All testify to his abiding love for the man with whom he had now been living for twelve years: "Wrote poems. I love Yurochka very much" (September 24, 1925).

"Twelve is a vatic number, / but thirty is a Rubicon" ("Dvenadtsat'—veshchee chislo, / A tridtsat'—Rubikon"), he had written in the opening of the seventh poem as yet another anniversary approached. On October 5 Vaginov brought him a letter from Ida Nappelbaum inviting him to pick a Sunday evening when she and her sister Frederika and those who had a "lively interest in literary life," his in particular, could mark the twentieth anniversary of his literary debut and hear his new works, which "we do not know at all, which is really a pity."[33] Kuzmin, all too aware of the passage of time ("I am turning into a ruin, and not even a particularly imposing one" [September 10, 1925]), gave his reluctant assent, and on October 11 set off with friends for the Nappelbaums' large studio: "Akhmatova, Klyuev, Radlova, Lozinsky, the Arapovs [Anatoly Arapov was working on his portrait at the time], Fedin, and so on. Homey and cordial. What a lot of trouble: 65 people. And wine. They read the usual. I read some poems. [The gypsy singer] Nina Shishkina sang. Took our picture. I between the two Annas. . . . Better than I thought it would be." In one of the two photographs taken, Kuzmin indeed sits between Radlova and Akhmatova, who looks uncomfortably distant, perhaps from being in such close proximity to the woman she called "the toad."[34]

Seated to Kuzmin's left in both photos is the thickly bearded "peasant poet" Nikolay Klyuev, who was openly gay and the lover of Esenin when Kuzmin met him on September 25, 1915. Kuzmin might have been expected to be drawn to him, but he dismissed him as a poseur and "unsuccessful Rasputin." Kuzmin's opinion had not changed eight years later, when a mutual acquaintance relayed greetings from him: "He has written Khlysty songs, was arrested twice, and is now working for Gosizdat. If he were not a charlatan, it would be touching" (September 15, 1923).[35] He relented only in 1927, when he saw Klyuev at the apartment of Benedikt Livshits: "All the same, he is an intimate and cosy man" (February 3).

Kuzmin preferred the company of another of the guests at his evening, Olga Cheremshanova, a poet with interests similar to Klyuev's in Russian folk traditions, the Khlysty, and other sectarian groups.[36] In February 1925 he had written a preface to her only published book of verse, *The Crypt* (Sklep). It praised her "richly gifted nature, impulsive and temperamental," and the unusually "supple," "emotional" rhythms of her poetry, which were best appreciated, he thought, when she declaimed them.[37] The critics did not agree when it appeared in July: "They are tearing Cheremshanova's book to pieces today, and me too at the same time" (July 31, 1925).[38] Neither Kuzmin's belief in her talent nor his affection for her wavered, and in October, when he finished the poem cycle "The Fingers of the Days" ("Pal'tsy dnei"), he dedicated it to her.[39] Each of its poems bears the name of one of the seven days of the week, five of which Kuzmin associates with planetary bodies or Roman gods, while "Saturday" evokes the sabbath activities of his Jewish neighbors in the communal apartment, and "Sunday" playfully salutes Seurat's *Dimanche d'été à la Grand-Jatte* and the verse of Jules Laforgue.

A few of the people who had been at the Nappelbaum studio joined others two weeks later on October 26 for the only semiofficial celebration of Kuzmin's twentieth "jubilee," an evening organized by friends at the Leningrad Society of Bibliophiles. Sergey Mukhin used the rare personal editions and manuscripts that Kuzmin had once had to sell him to mount a small exhibit. The speakers included Aleksey Tolstoy, Pavel Medvedev, Vsevolod Rozhdestvensky, and Vyacheslav Karatygin. Kuzmin recited a few poems before the second part of the program began, which was devoted to a reading of his poems and performances of some of his songs. He had been afraid that they were "planning something boring" (October 16), and he felt "bored and somehow indifferent" as he listened to the official greetings and speeches. Still, he was "touched and comforted" by the presence of many old friends, and he was pleased that the Society had printed a tiny booklet with the program to mark the occasion.[40] A dinner in his honor that followed at the apartment of one of the Society's board members soon, much to his distaste, turned into "complete drunken chaos." ("I think that many have come to the end of their rope," he noted.) When he tried to persuade Yurkun to pull himself together, Yurkun struck him, breaking Kuzmin's pince-nez and knocking out a tooth. Kuzmin left him passed out on the floor.

A blow of another kind awaited him the next day when he opened *The Life of Art* and found a scurrilous attack on him, Akhmatova, and Sologub by Viktor Pertsov under the title "Along the Literary Watersheds." In it Pertsov first raised the old issue of *Pictures under Wraps*, which he called testimony to the "complete spiritual bankruptcy" of its author. He then dismissed *The New Hull* as suitable only for "those who appreciate the poetry of old" because "one feels the calm cheerfulness of personal life" in its poems. After quoting Kuzmin's remarks about positivism and art in "Wood Shavings," Pertsov sneered: "This is just what some philistine could have said in the magazine *Apollo* in 1907 [it began in 1909], but with far greater pungency. Kuzmin thinks the same way in 1925. . . . There is no hope for Kuzmin." He concluded with crude sarcasm when he noted with surprise that "after the October Revolution, M. Kuzmin stayed in Russia, continued to walk the streets, continued to eat, drink, and in general carry out all the vital functions characteristic of a human being." Nothing, however, could "galvanize a writer like Kuzmin for contemporary times."[41] If the earlier attack by Volynsky in *The Life of Art* had been intended to drive Kuzmin off its pages, Pertsov, who was already beginning to make his odious career as an "official" spokesman, meant to drive him out of "our" society and literature into silence.

Little surprised Kuzmin anymore, and, to the amazement of friends, he reacted with equanimity: "This is as yet nothing at all. Of course I am not a proletarian writer, and there is no hope for me. If contemporary times means communism, I am not contemporary" (October 27). Yet Pertsov's attack, the incident with Yurkun, and his awareness of the chasm that separated his conception of what a "proper" life should be from the "counterfeit" reality around him depressed him anew, just when he had begun to think that "things for some reason do not seem so terrible" (October 21). In the experimental prose piece "Five Conversations and an Incident," which he began a few weeks later, on November 10, and which he called "rather unpleasant" when he finished it on the thirteenth, the hero finds everything in his former homeland alien and baffling after many years abroad. "Either you have all gone insane or I am a madman," he exclaims before leaving Russia forever, having concluded with respect to its "experiment": "A dead end. Not even horror. Vulgarization of all spirituality and a complete lack of talent, the affirmation of that lack of talent and of spiritual boorishness. No one believes. Our fate is to be vomited out by life and nature."[42]

As 1925 drew to a dreary end, Kuzmin, often in ill health, worked on his translation commissions, edited a volume of Jack London's stories, and wrote a brochure about Conrad Veidt, which he never finished. He found little pleasure, now that his piano had been taken away for non-payment of the rental fee, except in reading Dickens and Hoffmann and in an occasional evening at the apartment of Aleksandr Krolenko, the director of "Academia." There he and other guests huddled "like spirits" around their host's exotic new purchase, a radio. They listened to fuzzy BBC broadcasts of news, classical music, the third act of *Die Meistersinger von Nürnberg* from Covent Garden, a jazz band, and finally the chimes of Big Ben—all of it "like something from the other world," "soothing and magical" (October 27). On December 30 Yurkun brought home a "copy of [*Berliner*] *Tageblatt*. This intoxicates me, as does any bit of news about real life. Diaghilev, Stravinsky, Gilbert, Lehár, movies, clothing, fashions—but as for us? us? Taxes, debts, [eviction from] the apartment."

Somehow, as always, he managed to keep disaster at bay. In January 1926 he started work on another Régnier volume, *La Pécheresse: Histoire d'amour*, which was later reassigned to Mikhail Lozinsky, and Evgeny Gerken, a gay poet and dramatist best known after 1917 for translations and adaptations of operetta librettos, asked him to write a preface for his new book of verse. Kuzmin found warm words for the modest talents of his old friend, and he used the preface to defend his own view of poetry: "His themes—friendship, love, a feeling for nature—are always contemporary." A book of lyric poetry like Gerken's might have been out of place in 1918–19, he continued, but not in 1926, when it was vital to "make out, through all the ardent summons to battle and freedom, the voice of simple human feelings, which are by no means subject to abolition, but on the contrary affirm joyous and robust life."[43]

He wrote three brief articles for a booklet issued by the Bol'shoi Drama Theater to mark the thirtieth anniversary of Monakhov, its leading actor, and, most important for his finances, he resumed writing reviews for *Red Newspaper* in February.[44] Over the next five months he wrote twenty-five pieces on the theater, concerts, operettas, operas such as Prokofiev's *Love for Three Oranges*, and ballets including Stravinsky's *Pulcinella*, both of which seemed to him like "breaths of fresh air from Europe." No periodical was interested in his verse, but poems still came, such as the enigmatic "Isolde's Deer" ("Olen' Izol'dy") in February and, in April, the blank-verse "The Migrants" ("Pereselentsy"), one of his greatest poems. Ostensibly a kind of variation on the American chapters of *Martin Chuzzlewit*, "The Migrants" is a prophetic meditation on the poet's own time, pitiless in its contempt for the Soviets and heartbreaking in its capture of the seemingly endless human suffering that their utopian folly had brought about:

> An alien sun furiously sets
> on its perch beyond an alien swamp,
> and it will autocratically rise tomorrow,
> not punishing, not well disposed. . . .
> Oh, my God, my God, my God, my God, my God!
> Why should we wake up if tomorrow
> we shall see the same hummocks in the bogs and the road
> where stands a stick with the sign "Victory Prospect," . . .
> And the children will grow up as swineherds:
> will forget how to read, write, pray,
> will dig about in the miserly earth,
> and keep saying that time is money, . . .
> will breed children and dully die,
> almost unconscious of the boring glory
> of the deceptive word "pioneers"!...
> Better sleep, Molly, until noon.
> Perhaps you will dream of the banks of the Thames
> and the house entwined with hops where you grew up...[45]

There could, of course, be no thought of publishing the poem, which survived in the memories of the friends to whom he read it. One, Vsevolod Petrov, thought after hearing it that its author himself was just such an "unwilling migrant into an alien age."[46]

No more publishable in Soviet Russia was the curious "A Stove in a Bathhouse" ("Pechka v bane"), which Kuzmin wrote on March 17, 1926. When he read it to Yurkun that evening, the latter "got terribly offended that I am sneaking into his territory and am anticipating his plans." The work is certainly unlike any of Kuzmin's other prose works. "Five Conversations and an Incident" was deliberately fragmentary in its jettisoning of narrative line and characterization, but "A Stove in a Bathhouse" presents fourteen anecdotes connected only by their mordant humor, each section one of the scenes on the tiles covering the stove of the title. Kuzmin sent it to Blokh on July 9, 1927, hoping that he could publish the "little example" of his "new prose" in Germany (he could not), but he recognized the problem that it presented: "It is terribly difficult to translate in my opinion, and almost inevitably demands illustrations."[47]

Some of the sections, such as the five-sentence-long "The Trip" ("Puteshestvie"), are indeed untranslatable because of their witty play on French and Russian slang. In others, such as "The Greeks" ("Greki"), the inappropriateness of the vocabulary and diction to the subject recalls Zoshchenko, whom he liked, as it mocks the debasement of language and the pretentions to education of the new Soviet "intelligentsia" with elusive sarcasm (and a trace of homoeroticism): "The Greek baths. Well, of course, marble, gold, frankincense, and myrrh. First-rate luxury, but they haven't got a roof. No one undresses, since they arrive walking naked down the avenue. Rub themselves with oil and sprinkle on sand. Why, one wonders? So that in case someone starts grabbing things, it will be both delayed and not delayed. This is the highest wisdom. And as far as soap and water go, they don't use any." Kuzmin spares no one, not even himself, as in the self-parodic "The Riders" ("Vsadniki"):

> Two military men are riding on horseback. Officers, probably just commissioned, I suppose. The horses are glossy, and they themselves are neatly dressed. Their boots shine for all their worth. They ride and keep glancing at each other. Have a look and turn away. They arrive at some place or other, just a place, nothing special. Well, they know better. They stop. One says: "Well all right Petya, dismount." And the other one covers his eyes with his hand and blushes, blushes like a cherry.

"The Fish" ("Ryba") parodies storytelling itself: "Water. And the crescent moon turned on full blast. Bushes, trees, but no people. Must have all gone to bed. It's quiet. A fish finally poked its head out, had a look at the moon, sees that it's not a worm, and went down. Not interesting."[48]

"A Stove in a Bathhouse" was anything but uninteresting to those to whom the author read it. Kuzmin, always alert and generous to the new and the young, particularly cherished companionship and signs of attention now, when he felt that he was being forgotten and driven into isolation. He welcomed the many writers who came to the apartment to read their works and also found in them a sympathetic audience for his own. Some were old friends, such as "Ben" Livshits, Neldikhen, Radlova, Ivnev, and Vaginov, but there were many new faces. In the spring of 1924, some young poets who still called themselves Futurists had often dropped by, and one of them, Aleksandr Vvedensky, whom Kuzmin dubbed a "mystic-futurist" when he met him on March 16, 1924, was soon visiting on such a regular every-other-day schedule that the Diary notes his failures to do so. He was handsome and radiated confidence, and Kuzmin pronounced him a "splendid chap and very talented" (September 10, 1924), an opinion that never changed.[49] Vvedensky, for his part, was among the relatively small band of Kuzmin's admirers who understood and encouraged the flair and freedom of the older poet's ever more daring verse, and he dedicated a number of works (now lost) to him.

On December 5, 1925, Vvedensky introduced Kuzmin to the pleasantly eccentric Daniil Kharms, one of his "beyonsense" poet friends in what they called the "Left Flank" (Levyi flang): "He looks like an Estonian or even an Estonian woman, has stature and not bad poems. Everybody read" (Diary). In 1927 they took the name "Oberiu," an acronym from "Ob"edinenie real'nogo iskusstva" (the "Association of Real Art"), and they brought their fellow members, Nikolay Zabolotsky, Igor Bakhterev, and Nikolay Oleinikov, to meet Kuzmin.[50] He followed their activities with lively interest, never letting their outlandish antics get in the way of his appreciation of their writings. Vvedensky and Kharms both heard "A Stove in a Bathhouse," and it had an undeniable impact on their own miniaturist experiments of the 1930s, as did Kuzmin's late verse on their own and that of their "Oberiuty" friends.[51]

On June 7, 1926, an editor at *Red Newspaper* had telephoned to tell Kuzmin that the new issue of *The Life of Art* contained an article savaging the whole theater section of the newspaper. Kuzmin, however, was the real target of the abusive personal attack that Mikhail Padvo published under the title "A Few Words to Reviewers and about Reviewers; about Leisure Park at the same time and a Premiere at the Musical Comedy." "There exists in Russia the poet 'by God's grace' M. Kuzmin," Padvo began. "But so respected a title and profession (a poet!) do not satisfy this venerable figure. Besides his publications as a poet, we also see Kuzmin in the role of a music critic, theater reviewer, and so on. How pleasant—a universal man."[52]

Six days before, the evening edition of *Red Newspaper* had published Kuzmin's opening night review of Robert Stolz's operetta *Ein Riviera-traum (Das Fräulein aus 1001 Nacht)* at the Musical Comedy Theater's summer home in Leisure Park. It, and several other previous reviews, served only as a pretext, however, for Padvo's denunciation of Kuzmin as an apologist for "bourgeois" phenomena such as Leisure Park and the fox-trot (already part of Bolshevik demonology) and "degenerate" Negro art (in this, as in so much else, Bolshevik ideology prefigured the Nazis):

> There is not only a restaurant there, there is even, they say, the fox-trot—what wide scope for a poet! And please stop, *I beg of you,* disinterestedly advertising and recommending our bourgeoisie's Leisure Park to the workers on the pages of the Soviet press. Stop it! You're off-key, poet! . . . Yes, about the opening night. It was indeed dressy. But a bourgeois dressiness. And what taste! Why they have the audience dancing, a "jazz band," children on the stage—it just reeks of some third-rate Western European dive. And the "new trend in art,"—is it Negro? They have borrowed nightclub twitching of the legs, and erotic poses and gestures from the Negro operetta. Here's freshness for you! What pungency! Now this is life! A marvel!

Such "bourgeois nonsense" was not to be tolerated, nor those sympathetic to it, Padvo concluded in a tone that prefigured the Stalinist polemical style to come: "Reviews like those of Kuzmin are completely unacceptable and harmful in the Soviet press—this is addressed to reviewers, so they'd better watch out. . . . What I have written about Kuzmin pertains, unfortunately, to many others as well. To things that must be eradicated."[53]

Evgeny Kuznetsov, afraid that the piece was the opening salvo in a campaign to shut down the newspaper, started rounding up supporters to sign a letter of protest. On the eighth he persuaded Kuzmin to write to Chicherin, with whom Kuzmin had been out of touch for almost two decades, in the hope that the Commissar of Foreign Affairs might add his name to the list. Kuzmin nervously awaited a response as he helped gather names. By June 14, when *Red Newspaper* published the letter of protest under the title "In Defense of the Dignity of Soviet Criticism," Kuzmin decided that Chicherin must not be in Moscow or was not going to reply.[54] Then, on the fifteenth: "Suddenly a letter brought by special messenger. From Yusha. It excited me very much. There are touching passages, but indifference to aesthetics, of course" (Diary). In the brief first part of the letter, typed on June 9 and sounding as though dictated to an aide, Chicherin addressed Kuzmin by his first name and patronymic and with the formal form of "you," something he had never done in their earlier correspondence. He begged off intervening in the polemic with: "I, unfortunately, am too overworked to follow contemporary literature no matter to what trend it belongs. I am in absolutely no position to make pronouncements on questions of contemporary literature and literary politics." In the longer handwritten postscript, however, we hear the old voice of Kuzmin's correspondent of the 1890s as he mused about "What does it mean to be cultured?" and asked, "Who represented being cultured . . . Pilate or Jesus, Cyril of Alexandria or Hypatia, Gregory of Tours or the German lummoxes of yore with loud voices, smelling of sweat and garlic, whom he described, Almaviva or Figaro? That created by the life of the past or the pulse of new life?" He concluded on a tone of reminiscence: "Aleksandra Alekseevna used to say about someone: 'Il est très vulgaire.' Should we resurrect Aleksandra Alekseevna? Le mort saisit le vif or on the contrary? In my free hours—or rather, minutes—or rather, seconds—I relax at the piano with your 'Seasons' and so on."[55]

Chicherin did write a rather vague letter, and Kuzmin was told that *The Life of Art* was receiving dozens of letters protesting the smear campaign that its editor refused to acknowledge, although he did publish a defense of Padvo signed by a group of Soviet hatchetmen on June 18. By the end of the month Kuzmin thought that the "incident was settled." On July 2 *Red Newspaper* telephoned to request a review of that night's performance by the Musical Comedy Theater at Leisure Park, and the next day his review of Radlov's production of Leo Ascher's operetta *Sonja* (1925) appeared in its pages.[56] As he worked on a translation of Lehár's new operetta *Paganini* (1925) and read Charles de Coster's "totally undistinguished novel" on the Till Eulenspiegel legend, which he had been commissioned to turn into a film scenario, Kuzmin waited for calls from Kuznetsov ("he is shaking like a rabbit"), who only two months before had promised him a permanent place on the newspaper's staff in the autumn with a monthly salary of two hundred rubles.

At last, on August 30, Kuznetsov made an "urgent" call asking

Kuzmin to review that evening's performance of S. V. Bershadsky's opera *Stenka Razin*, which Kuzmin dismissed as "unimaginably vile and brazen" (Diary). The next day *Evening Red Newspaper* "printed the article without cuts, signed *M*. That, of course, is swinishness and weakness on my part" (Diary). Four days later Kuznetsov assured him that everything was now "splendid," but in the weeks that followed, he was as "silent as the grave about work" (Diary, November 21). He did not even invite Kuzmin to contribute to the literary supplement to the newspaper that he had started in October ("No mention of me, of course, as though I'm dead" [October 9]). Kuzmin would write an appreciation of the artist Valentina Khodasevich for a booklet on her in the series "Contemporary Theater Artists" in April 1927, and in May 1928 three of his opera reviews, signed "M. A.," suddenly reappeared on the pages of *Red Newspaper*, only to disappear once again despite Kuznetsov's promises. In 1933, in a futile attempt to reenter Soviet literary life, he wrote a piece on the poetry of Eduard Bagritsky for the *Literary Newspaper* (Literaturnaya gazeta).[57] The paper's editors called it a "document of the reformation *(perestroika)* of M. Kuzmin," but cautiously distanced themselves from Kuzmin's opinions in a footnote. Kuzmin's almost twenty-year-long career as a critic had really come to an end seven years before, in 1926.

❧ 12 ❧

Dissenting to the End
1927–1936

They will come no more,
The old men with beautiful manners.
—Ezra Pound, "Moeurs contemporaines, VII"

IN NOVEMBER 1926 Chicherin, accompanied, as usual, by a handsome young aide, arrived in Leningrad to visit his family, and sent word that he wanted to see his old friend. Kuzmin visited him on the twenty-sixth in his luxurious suite at the Hôtel de l'Europe. "Mieux veut tard que jamais," he began, and he continued in French, using the familiar form of *you*, "since, in his words, he feels as if he is abroad being with me." They reminisced, and chatted about "art, polemics, friendship, wit, diplomacy," and Kuzmin's "fame in Germany." Chicherin's "optimism" and questions about why his friend now published and wrote little made Kuzmin realize that he did not have the slightest idea about the life of an ordinary Soviet citizen and his literary situation. By the time of their meeting, Kuzmin, deprived of the income from *Red Newspaper*, desperately needed help. But he refused to ask Chicherin to come to his aid: "Everyone is astonished that I did not ask him for anything, but I think that this way is better" (Diary, November 27). Two days later he "for some reason remembered Dante's 'How steep are staircases for supplicants.'"

Translations were now all that could put an "economical meal" on his table, and in August 1926 he had quickly accepted Aleksandr Smirnov's invitation to join him and Mikhail Lozinsky in preparing an edition of Mérimée's collected works for "Academia." He translated almost a third of the novels and stories included in the seven volumes it issued between 1927 and 1929. In the years that followed, "Academia," sometimes in collaboration with the State Publishing House, commissioned him to make translations for its editions of Heine, Molière, and Goethe, and in 1929 it published his translation of *The Golden Ass*, to which he had returned in 1927.[1] Payments came with such maddening irregularity that Kuzmin, often threatened with eviction or loss of electricity, was forced to take on work such as Romain Rolland's lives of Beethoven and Michelangelo for other publishers.[2] (He thought Rolland, like Gorky, a "typical vulgarian.") He found some respite from the awesome workload, which severely taxed his health, in trying his hand at the *Iliad* at the prompting of Samuil Marshak. We do not know how much he actually did, but the one fragment that Kuzmin published, Hector's farewell to Andromache, makes clear that if he had ever completed it, his supple hexameters would have stood a good chance of disputing the place Nikolay Gnedich's 1829 version still holds in the canon.[3]

Some of the translations took a real critical drubbing when Kuzmin and his friends at "Academia," partisans of "exact translation," were accused of "sabotaging" clarity and meaning in a misguided commitment to "literalism" at the expense of "creative translation." Korney Chukovsky led the attack in a savage review of new translations of Shakespeare, among them the *King Lear* done by Kuzmin, which had been published in a 1934 volume of the selected plays.[4] Kuzmin had devoted more time to Shakespeare than to any other writer in the 1930s, translating eight of the other plays. Chukovsky's review delayed their inclusion in the "Academia" edition of the collected works until after Kuzmin's death.[5] The translation of Byron's *Don Juan*, on which he labored for more than five years, met an even harsher fate. When he submitted it in March 1935, the publisher's internal reviewer, Dmitry Mirsky, while calling him "one of the most outstanding masters of Russian style," recommended that it be returned for total revision. Kuzmin had to agree, but was already too sick to start the reworking. It has never been published.[6]

Kuzmin once remarked to a friend that he "really knew only three subjects. One period in music, the eighteenth century up to Mozart inclusively, the painting of the Italian quattrocento, and the teachings of the Gnostics."[7] Smirnov, the general editor of Shakespeare's collected works, he added, knew the Elizabethan period better. He yielded to no one, however, in his love for the writer in whom as a child he had first discovered the "enchantment and mystery" of art and of whom he once said: "Shakespeare has everything" (Diary, September 29, 1905). The sonnets, for obvious reasons, particularly attracted him. He wrote music for several in 1903 and 1904, and as early as 1917 began translating them. By May 1933 he had completed one-third and by the time of his death, more than one hundred, including all those touching on the mysterious "W. H."[8] A friend, while sorting out Kuzmin's papers after his death, came upon the manuscript and remembered that he had "translated very precisely. Many sonnets had been translated splendidly, but often, when he wanted to get as much of the original as possible into the translation, he wrote indecipherable verse which it was simply impossible to understand."[9] The outbreak of war with Germany put a stop to Smirnov's plan to publish them in his revision.[10] The translation has disappeared without a trace.

Translations for Leningrad and Moscow music theaters also provided a major source of income. In June 1926 Radlov asked Kuzmin to translate the libretto of Alban Berg's *Wozzeck*. He had shown Kuzmin the piano score in May, and on June 7 Kuzmin published a brief laudatory article about it under the title "A New Word in Opera."[11] After the opera barely squeaked past a nervous censorship, Radlov, Kuzmin, Boris Asafiev, and Vladimir Dranishnikov, the chief conductor at the Academic Theater of Opera and Ballet (the former Mariinskii), met regularly to discuss and plan its production there. Berg himself, who knew and admired Kuzmin's prose in German translation, came to Leningrad for the performance.[12] Kuzmin found him "touching and nice" when he chatted with him at the Radlovs' on June 12, 1927, after the general rehearsal. The next night, after the premiere, he called the opera a "wondrous work, not particularly close to me, but profoundly impressive" (Diary).

When Radlov was appointed director of the theater in 1928, he made possible a steady series of libretto translations for his friend. Their variety suggests the richness of Leningrad musical life before the dead hand of Stalinist conformism clamped down: *Der Rosenkavalier, Carmen, Fidelio, Guillaume Tell, Don Giovanni, Benvenuto Cellini, Il Trovatore, Don Carlos, Falstaff, Les Huguenots,* and Cherubini's *Wasserträger.* Old acquaintances at the Musical Comedy Theater did not forget him either, and Kuzmin's "virtuosic" translation-adaptation of the text of Strauss's *Zigeunerbaron* in 1932 was a major critical success.[13] Kuzmin groaned under the workload, but gratefully accepted other translations from another friend, the conductor Nikolay Malko, music director of the Leningrad Philharmonic.[14] The commissions stopped when Malko stayed abroad while on tour in 1929, but his successor, Aleksandr Gauk, who had been impressed by Kuzmin's skill and reliability, ordered translations of the texts in Berlioz's *Grande Symphonie funèbre et triomphale* and his *Damnation de Faust*. On February 17, 1936, only weeks before Kuzmin's death, he led a performance of the composer's "dramatic symphony" *Roméo et Juliette*, whose texts Kuzmin had translated four years earlier.

Kuzmin had not yet given up hope of seeing his own works performed. Anatoly Kankarovich, the guiding light of the Sky-Blue Circle, had, with Kuzmin's encouragement, written music for the entire text of *Hull's Strolls*. In the summer of 1927 Kuzmin tried but failed to interest Meyerhold in mounting the quirky piece at his Moscow theater.[15] Finally, on March 31, 1929, a cast drawn largely from members of the Circle itself presented it under the title "Non-Sense" ("Che-pu-kha," certainly the result of the censor's meddling) at the Leningrad Capella. Critics found the music an interesting experiment, but Kuzmin's text was "ideologically alien" to Soviet reality.[16] His texts might have resounded one more time from a Soviet stage when, in 1933, Meyerhold asked him to write some songs for a 1934 production of *La Dame aux camélias*.[17] Kuzmin was touched that the director still remembered him ("this is now very, very important for me") and did as requested, but the songs were not used.

Poetry was never forgotten while the translation orders piled up. In June 1926 Kuzmin wrote the cycle "A Panorama with Panels" ("Panorama s vynoskami"). Among the picture panels displayed in this imaginary panorama, a counterpart in verse to the sideshow attraction that Kuzmin had once enjoyed during the Russian Mardi Gras, is the poem "Dark Streets Beget Dark Feelings," his meditation on the mysterious death of the young dancer Lidiya Ivanova.[18] Like many other balletomanes, he considered her the hope of Russian classical dance, and two days after her death on June 16, 1924, in what was reported as a boating accident, Kuzmin published an appreciation in *Red Newspaper*.[19] Not long after, her father came to the apartment to thank him, and soon became a regular if not always welcome guest. Obsessed by the unexplained circumstances of the death and convinced that he was being trailed by the secret police, Ivanov relayed rumor after rumor, each more fantastic than the next, about what he believed to have been her murder either at the instigation of a rival ballerina or at the hands of the secret police. Kuzmin made no reference to them in other poems he dedicated to her memory and in the article he wrote in 1925 at her father's request, but both versions pass through the very dark glass of the 1926 poem.[20] "In general, there is no more monastic and unerotic art, in my opinion, than classical ballet," he remarked in the Diary on November 12, 1926. Yet this "child of ballet," as he called Ivanova, had been ensnared and destroyed by just those "passions, jealousy, envy, and vengeance," that he believed were utterly alien to the realm of classical ballet, "rather abstract and, as it were, out of time."[21] Her death, a grotesque violation of a perfect art form, haunted him for many years.

Not long after finishing that cycle, Kuzmin read Freud's book *Die Traumdeutung* (Diary, July 13, 1926). The next day, after interpreting one of his own dreams in Freudian terms, he called him a "dirty Jew and speculator, of course, but he touches on interesting things." A few weeks later he had a "terrible dream" (August 4). He did not analyze it, but transcribed it in such great detail that it must have held special meaning for him. It reads like some of his best late prose:

A new room, large, but very secluded, nothing can be heard either from without or from within. . . . A knock at the door. . . . Almost no one comes to see us. A visitor. A stranger. I vaguely remember something. The usual: "You won't recognize me, we met at such and such a place." Something about him I don't like, he inspires fear and revulsion. Another knock. "It is probably Sapunov," he says. How awful. It really is Sapunov. Yurochka is already here by some miracle. The very same Nikolay Nikolaevich, only he has aged and gotten a bit swollen. In extreme terror I make the sign of the cross over him. . . . His face positively contorted from rage. "How courteously you greet old friends, Miquel." "What's next, will all kinds of corpses come calling!" . . . Yurochka intervenes. "What are you saying, Michael [he uses the English; Yurkun always addressed Kuzmin this way], the body of Nik. Nik. wasn't found, he could be among the living." "So why are you afraid of the sign of the cross?" "Ah, it's time to get rid of that sanctimoniousness. Gives me little pleasure." I calm down, overcoming my revulsion, I kiss the cold Sapunov, introduce him to Yurochka. We sit down like guests on the low sofa. We sink back on it. . . . A new visitor. An undoubted corpse. Some kind of likable musician. They are all badly shaven, their clothes are baggy, dirty, but it is obvious that even such a primitively decent appearance has cost them incredible effort. All of them deep down inside are evil and vindictive. . . . Questions about friends. "Yes, we have heard from such and such" (recently dead). How they talk there, whisper, bear malice, wait, beckon. "Where we are, they value you very much." As though they are speaking about another country. Memory from beyond the grave while still alive. They get ready to leave. "What a pleasant evening it's been. It's nice to remember old times. Now there remain only six or seven places where one can meet." My God, they are going to be coming to see me! I go to show them out. On the stairway someone says: "So they've taken to visiting you too. This is that kind of apartment, no one lives here." Did they have anything to drink or eat, I don't remember. They certainly smoked.

Is this not a depiction of our life or a sign?

Seven months later, on March 3, 1927, he received a copy of Gustav Meyrink's novel *Das grüne Gesicht*, which he pronounced "magnificent, not worse than his *Golem*." In July he saw in a shop window another of Meyrink's novels with the intriguing title *Der Engel vom westlichen Fenster*. He did not have enough money to buy it, but Ivanova's father surprised him by making a present of it on July 13. Six days later Kuzmin "began to write poems, although I wanted to write prose." On the twenty-sixth he finished "The Trout Breaking through the Ice," which he dedicated to Radlova, who thought she recognized herself in the woman "like a canvas of Bryullov" who listens to *Tristan und Isolde* in the cycle's "First Thrust." Rarely had he written with such speed, but the novels and the remembered nightmare, both of which figure prominently in the narrative cycle, provided a powerful stimulus.

None but the naive would believe that a work in which an "Angel of transformations" reunites two men after the fatal passion of one of them for a woman almost destroys their life together has "no biographical basis," as Kuzmin wrote to the suspicious Arbenina.[22] Kuzmin's best poetry had always needed the catalyst of personal relationships, in particular the excitement of those that were intense and fraught with a mixture of love and jealousy. In "The Trout" he reexperienced the archetypical pattern of past love affairs (he refers to both Yurkun and Knyazev) and gave them a mythic resolution in Love's triumph on New Year's Eve. Vsevolod Rozhdestvensky, to whom Kuzmin read the "enchanting" cycle in September 1927, immediately saw the "autobiographical" dimension, but recognized that in it Kuzmin's "whole life passes through a lyrically sharpened memory."[23] The autobiography is shaped and transformed by a dense array of cultural sources—literary (Meyrink, Pushkin, Blok, Shakespeare's sonnets, Coleridge, Tennyson, Yeats, to name but a few), musical (*Tristan und Isolde, Der fliegende Holländer*), and cinematic (*Caligari, Nosferatu*)—that is so complex that nothing better describes "The Trout" than the lyrical persona's own statement about the work's inception in the "Conclusion": "Waves of memories rushed in, fragments of novels I have read, the deceased got mixed up with the living."[24] Kuzmin's achievement was rarely if ever to be matched by other poets in the years that followed.

That September he wrote the ten poems of the odd cycle "For August" ("Dlya avgusta"): "I read 'August.' It is terrible naturalism, and I somehow have gotten stuck in it, and no one particularly likes it" (Diary, September 18). He got unstuck in the masterly narrative cycle "Lazarus" ("Lazar'"), which he began in January 1928 and dedicated to Kornily Pokrovsky, an old friend who was now Radlova's husband, when he finished it in August. Inspired, perhaps, by the story line in Browning's "The Ring and the Book," it makes constant allegorical allusions to the Gospel narrative of Lazarus, Mary, and Martha in its suggestion that new life is possible only when the full horror of the times has been experienced. Kuzmin chose the cycle to close the new collection of verse he was putting together, a book in which death and rebirth, as in "The Trout," are a dominant leitmotif.

On February 23, 1929, the "Writers' Publishing House in Leningrad" (Izdatel'stvo pisatelei v Leningrade) issued two thousand copies of *The Trout Breaking through the Ice.* A month later Kuzmin noted that "the book is gradually selling. They think there won't be any reviews. They won't allow praise and they will not wish abuse" (Diary). The book could not have appeared at a less propitious time. It was the year of the "great break with the past" and Stalin's call for a sharpening of class struggle as he forcibly shifted the economy from NEP to industrialization and violent rural collectivization. Valery Druzin, not yet the anti-Semitic hatchetman of Soviet criticism that he would become, combined his review with one of Livshits's collection *Crotonian Noon* (Krotonskii polden'). Hypnotized by the term "beautiful clarity," Druzin tore lines from their contexts to find "clarity," "concreteness," and "pleasant jocosity," making Kuzmin's book sound like nothing so much as a new *Nets*. He spotted a "few principles of revolutionary poetry" in "Lazarus," but not enough to save the collection from dismissal as irrelevant to the "most serious questions of our time" and a "curious monument of a culture that has died out."[25] There were no other reviews, only the ridicule of Boris Olkhovy, a high party member charged by the Central Committee with overseeing the "ideological purification" of Soviet intellectual life. He strained for "wit"—"In general one could say the same thing about this collection that Goethe's *Faust* says about the incantations of the witch: 'What nonsense is she saying there? / Really, my head wants to burst. / It seems as if a whole chorus / of a hundred thousand fools is muttering'"—before passing on to caricatures of Bely, Mandelshtam, and other "fellow travelers."[26] Emigrés such as Adamovich did no better; he called the book a "human document," "melancholy, feeble, very tired. Not without charm, of course."[27]

Translations left Kuzmin little time for his own work, but he never abandoned verse as some poets did in those years for the surrogate of their verse translations. There is a poem addressed to Arbenina in 1930, and friends spoke of a long narrative poem and two cycles of poems, "Tristan" and "The Simple World" ("Prostoi mir"), that he wrote in the early 1930s, enough to make up a book he planned to call "The Lesson of the Brook" ("Urok ruch'ya").[28] A remark in the Diary gives a hint of what "Tristan" must have been like: "Only in 'love in death' is there completeness—*pleroma*. From where did *der alte W[agner]* know this? Did he read the Gnostics? No one has written about this."[29] But only one of its poems seems to have escaped the destruction of the poet's archive, and then only because a friend had made a copy, which was about the only way anyone could know his new work.[30] As the poet Dmitry Usov wrote to Gollerbakh from Moscow in 1932, asking him to send any of Kuzmin's latest works for copying, Kuzmin, "like Voloshin, is becoming 'not a book, but a notebook' in his own lifetime."[31]

Friends and young people of an "uneducated and ignorant generation," as one of them put it, kept coming to Kuzmin's apartment to hear him read or just to take tea and chat in an atmosphere of an "astonishingly high level of culture."[32] Something other than Kuzmin's fabled erudition made others want to meet him. When Magnus Hirschfeld, the pioneering German sexologist and "apologist and pillar of homosexuality," as Kuzmin called him, visited Leningrad in June 1926, he "was dying to make the acquaintance" of Kuzmin (Diary). Kuzmin and Klyuev met him at a "deadly dull" gathering on the eighth, and found the "professor pompous and naive. . . . Looks at everything scientifically. . . . Optimistic imagination." The left-leaning Hirschfeld had been campaigning for years for repeal of Paragraph 175, the German sodomy law, but if he saw the Soviet Union as an emancipationist ideal, he would have been naive indeed. The regime saw homosexuality not as a crime but as a perversion, a form of mental illness to be cured. Throughout the 1920s, the People's Commissariat of Public Health waged "sexual enlightenment" campaigns that were designed to eradicate it, along with masturbation, premarital sex, and other forms of "unnatural" behavior. By 1926, had Kuzmin not simply dismissed it with a joke, he might have realized the ominous implications of things to come when he read a "wretched little [Soviet] booklet" about Conrad Veidt: "He is made out to be the representative of decadence: mysticism in art, Spengler in the [social] sciences, homosexuality in life, reaction in politics" (April 20, 1926).

The secret police had been keeping an eye on Kuzmin and his friends ever since Yurkun's 1918 arrest, and after Hirschfeld's visit they stepped up their surveillance. People he suspected of being police informers started to drop by the apartment uninvited and clumsily ask about his political views, and on November 26, 1927, a "frightened" Rakov "whispered in my ear that he had been summoned to the GPU and questioned about me. Who comes to see me, was I the one who had inculcated monarchism in him, what kind of conversations took place on the tenth anniversary [of the Bolshevik coup], what besides homosexuality ties him with me. . . . He thinks he will be thrown out of the university and exiled. I don't know. I felt as if in a dream. . . . He said that they have a fat notebook of materials on me" (Diary). That "cruel and melancholy contact with reality," as he put it the next day, might have made a more cautious man become a social hermit, but Kuzmin, as if testing fate, changed his way of life not at all.

He had not given a public reading since 1925. In 1928, unsure of how he would be received, he accepted, with misgivings, an invitation from students to read his new verse. The director at the students' institute had been no less reluctant to permit the reading, fearing that it might attract a large crowd of "undesirables," that is, members of Leningrad's gay population, but he consented when he was assured that there would be no advertising and that only students with tickets would be admitted. On March 10, 1928, one of the students, Vladimir Orlov, came to fetch Kuzmin by cab.[33] He remembered how shocked he was to see the poet, still on occasion caricatured in the press as an "aesthete," dressed in a threadbare summer coat. In the Diary Kuzmin remarked that the evening was "very crowded" and that "it was all right thanks to my friends. Read with verve, as I felt they were getting it." It was anything but "all right," however, for the organizers, who were almost expelled for the "scandal." As they watched with alarm, the ticket system broke down because of the crush at the doors, and more and more of just those "undesirables" who the director had been assured would not be admitted kept crowding in, lining the walls and sitting on the floor. During the ovation that followed the end of the reading, they pushed to the front, showering bouquets on Kuzmin, who stood beaming at the podium. It was, Orlov recalled, the "last demonstration of Leningrad's homosexuals" and Kuzmin's last public reading.

Once again he had attracted unnecessary attention, and in the years that followed, the GPU interrogated numerous friends about him. On the night of September 13, 1931, agents came to search the apartment. They seized the three most recent notebooks of the Diary, and papers and artworks by Yurkun. For well over a decade Yurkun had been doing sketches, small pictures, and collages that he sometimes sold (Hirschfeld had selected several) or gave to friends, and in February 1929 he had shown his works in Moscow with other members of the group that called itself the "Thirteen."[34] None of the material was returned. Both men had to sign a statement promising to say nothing about the search, but the next day Kuzmin courageously started a new Diary notebook: "Come what may, let anyone who wants read this, but I cannot do without writing about it, not any more than I could do without drinking or without sleeping. All right, I will refrain from describing the significant visit, which confirmed forever my love for Yur., for the persecuted art, for the only culture possible and homosexuality."[35]

On September 31 Yurkun was summoned to GPU headquarters and

interrogated. Several other summonses followed and stopped only when he agreed to sign a document recruiting him as a police inform- ant. Kuzmin noticed his agitation and depression in the weeks that followed, but, having been sworn to secrecy, Yurkun said nothing about it until November 6. It took Kuzmin until the twentieth to raise enough money to make a trip to Moscow, where he stayed for two weeks plead- ing Yurkun's case with the Briks, who were well connected with the secret police, and with Menzhinsky, his old debut comrade in *The Green Collection* and now the head of that organization. He succeeded in get- ting Yurkun released from his obligation, but the Leningrad "organs" did not forget or forgive the defiance. The arrest and exile of Vveden- sky, Kharms, and Bakhterev further blackened the grim year as the boundaries of the permitted kept narrowing.

With Hitler's rise to power, the Soviet press stepped up an anti-fascist campaign and started connecting the rise of fascism with Western "dec- adence," homosexuality in particular. The propaganda war culminated in a resolution announced on December 17, 1933, which became law on March 7, 1934, that recriminalized same-sex relations between men and prescribed up to five years of deprivation of freedom for voluntary sexual acts and up to eight for using force or for sex with a consent- ing minor. Thousands of arrests and a wave of suicides in the Red Army and Navy followed, but on May 23 Gorky welcomed the new law in an article titled "Proletarian Humanism" ("Proletarskii gumanizm"), which was published simultaneously in both the party newspaper *Pravda* and *Izvestiya*, the official govenment newspaper. At a time when German homosexuals were being arrested by the Nazis as carriers of the "Bolshevik plague," it concluded with the ringing assertion, "De- stroy homosexuality and fascism will disappear from this world."

A blow of another kind awaited Kuzmin that year. He had been ailing for a long time, and attacks of shortness of breath and chest pains, sometimes so severe that he lost consciousness, had hospitalized him three times early in 1934. In May he suffered a seizure so serious that the doctors doubted that he would survive it. They now diagnosed incurable angina pectoris and gave him no more than two years to live. On May 16 Yurkun came to visit the rest home at Detskoe Selo (the former Tsarskoe Selo) where Kuzmin was recuperating. He brought a new notebook in which he urged him to resume the Diary, asking him to write down his thoughts, poems, and reminiscences as well as daily events. Kuzmin wondered if he had the energy to do it, but that evening he began: "Fate has loudly pronounced the word 'death' to me and I have been brought face to face with this notion from some almost nonexistent distance. Now I know how I will die if, like Mistress Dombey, 'I do not make an effort.' So far, to the surprise of all, I have made those efforts." Only his "joy in every one of life's trifles" gave him the strength to make them again and again in the months that followed as the seizures increased in frequency and severity and stays in the hospital interrupted the new Diary.

The late Diary is not quite the prose poem that some friends remembered (probably because Kuzmin, as always, read from it selectively), but it is unlike the earlier volumes.[36] He at first tried to do what Yurkun had requested, following each listing of daily events with a "digression" of some kind, each given a title. He fretted when at times it turned into nothing but a chronicle, but then the original pattern would suddenly resume. Kuzmin now became even more attentive to his immediate surroundings than before, and his comments about "The Little Girl in the Neighboring Courtyard," "Sleeping Birds," "The Landscape with an Airplane," and observations on the slightest change in nature seen through the prism of his window reveal an authentic sense of wonder at life's inexhaustible variety. As he began to think about writing his memoirs, he "decided to record the past without any order, as fragments that I can then combine" (July 6, 1934). He set down recollections about Radlova ("I like her as I do few others"), Znosko-Borovsky and *Apollo*, his ancestors and parents, and a long series of entries on his childhood in Saratov and his life in the "Tower." He also fixed his thoughts on music and composers, of whom few but Mozart, Rossini, and Debussy escaped some stricture,[37] and even whimsical ruminations on "Eyeglasses": "They are one of the reasons for rationalism and pessimism. Nearsightedness is the basis of idealism and painting in the narrow sense of the word" (May 22).

The terrible blow of Vaginov's death from tuberculosis at the age of thirty-five and the failure of his own health to show any sign of improvement prompted more serious considerations:

Very Dangerous. What I am about to say is very dangerous, but very necessary to me. . . . It has to do neither more nor less than with faith. . . . I have been a believer all my life, but when it came to old

age and death, then I lost that faith. . . . As though I took offense
that faith will not save me from physical death. . . . I have lost faith
in the personal immortality of the soul, and in the case in question—death—that is most important. Therefore my attitude to
death is the same as toward the black hole of a Japanese print.
Obtuse, black, and hopeless. . . . Right now I had a flash of doubt
about my lack of faith. And furthermore, I know that (don't laugh)
were I looking at the clouds before sunset with someone whom I
trusted very much and whom I loved and he were to tell me that
the soul is immortal, I would believe it immediately. . . . But where
. . . is there a garden with clouds at evening and, most important,
the person whom I would believe? (September 14, 1934)

Paradoxically enough, it was the rediscovery of Erwin Rohde's *Psyche*
(1893), a classic study of the cult of the soul and the belief in immortality among the ancient Greeks, that bolstered his spirits: "To read only
the table of contents—Lord, what layers of tenderness, airiness, and
faith, which for some reason I had forgotten for a time, arose in me.
One must without fail re-read this book from time to time" (October
6–7, 1934). Existence may be "pale and swampy," but it is existence, and
there is the soul, "joyous, tremulous, light, affectionate, unstable." "I
have to read Erwin Rohde instead of the Apostle Paul," he concluded.[38]
That did nothing, however, to still his "inner and constant polemic with
Christianity because of its internationalism": "In my opinion, religion is
such a national, domestic, native, and intimate matter that it cannot be
international. . . . If Christianity had preserved its natural character—of
a Jewish idealist heresy—there would be sense and something touching.
But as the first international it immediately became a Jewish, odious
piece of work" (October 10). He recognized the existence of "various
Christianities," but the Church (like the Communist Party) had turned
into repressive "officialdom." As for "saints like St. Francis and St.
Ignatius [Loyola], well that is Italy and Spain, but not Christianity."[39]

"Everyone talks of nothing but the Congress [of the new Writers'
Union that was meeting in Moscow]," he wrote in the Diary on August
30, 1934. "I am entirely irrelevant everywhere."[40] He was, however,
elected to the Union, apparently because of the efforts of Samuil Marshak, who proposed him as a translator. Thanks to that and to the small
pension that he had been receiving since 1929, the sale of part of his

archive at the end of 1933, royalties from performances of plays and operas in his translations, and commissions for the Shakespeare, he and his little family no longer experienced the extreme privation of years past. But they had to watch every kopeck, and Kuzmin could never let up on the workload. It took an obvious toll. One acquaintance noted: "He looked older than his age. . . . Were one to believe the amateur photographs that have survived, one might form the impression that Kuzmin was a skinny little old man. . . . But that impression is false. . . . Charm has no effect on the camera. . . . The words 'old man' or 'little old man' were so incompatible with the image of Kuzmin that they would never have occurred to anyone."[41]

Nevertheless, he was obviously becoming the housebound invalid he had dreaded. Even short walks fatigued him, and his rare outings to the theater or the movies, where he enjoyed seeing once again favorite Germans and the "carefree Americans," among whom he included Chaplin, Buster Keaton, and Harold Lloyd, had to be carefully planned so as not to sap the energy he needed for the translating work. Yet nothing could diminish his appetite for beauty and his abiding curiosity. Visitors to the apartment now became his major contact with the world, and he rejected his doctor's advice to limit them severely, continuing to live as though life were indeed what happens when you're making other plans. (At the end of 1934 he thought a trip to Italy "not impossible," a complete fantasy given his health and Soviet travel restrictions.)

Visitors to apartment 9 at what was now Decembrist Ryleev Street, no. 17, climbed to the fifth floor (there was no elevator) and pressed the button of a communal doorbell three times. The door opened into a typical cluttered communal apartment that Kuzmin shared with a Jewish family with many noisy children, a fat man named Pipkin, and a Georgian family who used the telephone and kitchen. Kuzmin assured people that a communal apartment meant that life was never boring, but the Diary confirms one memoirist's opinion that "for all the sociability of his character . . . he must all the same have suffered . . . from the cramped quarters and the lack of peace and quiet in this not exactly boring apartment."[42] In fact, he hated it. He and Yurkun had two rooms with windows facing the courtyard. (A third, with a small balcony, had been taken away in 1931.) Yurkun's mother lived in one, and his life with Yurkun went on in the other, which also served as a passageway through which everyone living in the apartment had to pass on the way to the kitchen. He once again had a piano, and the large white instrument, kept slightly out of tune so as to sound like a harpsichord, dominated the room, whose walls were covered with pictures, icons, and bookshelves. Crowded into it were Kuzmin's small glass-topped desk (a present from Yurkun after his May 1934 illness), the couch where he slept, a few chairs, Yurkun's cot, and an enormous armoire chaotically stuffed with books and files where Yurkun kept his collections. In the center stood a round table with a samovar from which the host would pour tea into a mismatched array of old porcelain cups for his guests. Owning a tea service, he thought, was the height of bourgeois taste. "Strong tea substituted for spirits," one visitor recalled. "On two large platters there was a lot of bread and about two kilos of butter. That was it. As a result, wits (they had not become extinct on the banks of the Neva) usually said when they met on the street: 'Will you be at Kuzmin's butter next Thursday?'"[43]

Vsevolod Petrov, a young art critic who first came to the apartment in the spring of 1933, traced the source of Kuzmin's attraction to his "benevolent attentiveness to people, his lively interest in every person with whom he came into contact . . . and his aristocratic simplicity."[44] He never selfishly commanded the center of attention but drew everyone into the conversation and made them feel that they were unusually clever themselves. Even when he sat down at the piano and played, he minded not at all if the guests kept right on talking. Nikolay Khardzhiev, chronicler of Russia's "left art," remembered something else: "As a *causeur* Kuzmin had only one rival—Osip Mandelshtam. But unlike Mandelshtam, a convulsively fierce debater, Kuzmin uttered his 'verdicts' in an impassive 'white' voice."[45] Nadezhda Mandelshtam, who saw Kuzmin on occasion in the mid-twenties, believed that "he despised us all and did not even try to hide it."[46] He did loathe the Soviet reality around him, but Khardzhiev, who knew him in the thirties and noted the "caustic humor that showed through Kuzmin's mask of utter indifference," saw something more: "The poet could not hide his somehow childlike curiosity about people, about their passions and escapades." Akhmatova felt that Kuzmin never had a kind word to say about anyone. Every recollection of his friends disputes that. Ivan Likhachev, who was close to him in the thirties, recalled that he was "opinionated, even at times cruel," but added that he was "almost childishly unaware that anyone might find what he said objectionable and would have been mortified to learn that he had given offense."[47]

Whatever the reason for the attraction, the guests appeared every day without invitation between five and seven to visit what was one of the last centers of the once free-spirited intellectual atmosphere of Leningrad. Special friends were sometimes summoned to supper for later in the evening, and, knowing the host's constrained budget, brought the sweets and the German white wine that he now especially savored since he had had to give up smoking. (Even the wine went in 1935.) There were friends old and constantly new, fellow writers, critics, and translators, people from the city's theater and musical worlds, and always artists: the courteous and decorous Mitrokhin, Vladimir Lebedev ("an incomparable master, but slightly cold and too calculating," Kuzmin thought), Aleksandr Osmerkin, Aleksandr Tyshler, Pavel Basmanov, and participants in the "Thirteen."[48] And there were always the young men (most of whom, incidentally, were not gay): Rakov; the polyglot Ivan Likhachev, a gay poet and translator; Petrov; the poet and translator Aleksey Shadrin, a particularly loyal friend during Kuzmin's last illness; Aleksey Stepanov, a handsome young art specialist with a professional's knowledge of the theater and ballet, who brought a touch of "fashion" to the apartment; and the artist Konstantin Kozmin. The eccentric Viktor Panfilov, Kuzmin's last "crush," some thought, and the dedicatee of "A Stove in a Bathhouse," had been an almost daily guest after 1928, but he disappeared in the early thirties. Similarly, Andrey Egunov, a brilliant classicist and writer whose works Kuzmin especially prized, came only when he made a rare illegal visit to the city after his arrest and exile from Leningrad in 1933.[49]

Friends enjoyed Kuzmin's anecdotes and stories about the past, but to appreciate them they had quickly to learn the host's "code," as he had a comic name for everyone. Blok was the "notarized poet from a German family," Vyacheslav Ivanov the "reverend father," Sologub the "moneychanger," Remizov the "petty tyrant," Akhmatova the "poor relation," and after Georgy Ivanov began to publish his "reminiscences," he was dubbed the "milliner with the hatbox who carries gossip from house to house."[50] His irony did not even spare Yurkun (the "stableboy") and Radlova, whom he called the "Mother Superior with a past." He refused, however, to live in the past, and relied on his visitors to bring him news about contemporary cultural life abroad and the books that managed to make their way into the increasingly censorious Soviet state. By 1934 he had given up on Soviet literature, recognizing only the works of his friends (almost all of whom could not be published) or a few émigrés such as Remizov. But he remained curious and open-minded about foreign writers, and eagerly responded to anything that friends lent him.

He especially tried to keep track of developments in German-language literature, but was now inquisitive about new English and American writing as well. In April 1923 an acquaintance had "spoken interestingly about an Irishman named Joyce" (Diary), and Kuzmin found him remarkable when Valentin Stenich, who was doing translations, brought him *Dubliners* and *A Portrait of the Artist as a Young Man* in the original. (He seems not to have known *Ulysses*.) He also spoke with respect of Aldous Huxley and thought Hemingway worth keeping an eye on after reading the first Russian translation of his early stories. He first encountered Proust in Russian translation and found the prose of *À la recherche du temps perdu* too perfect and insufficiently alive, comparing it to a beautiful stillborn infant pickled in a jar. His opinion changed, however, when he finally got a chance to read the French original, and he remarked in the Diary: "Proust is right—to describe an object and everything that connects us with it means to wrest it from oblivion, to save ourselves from death. For the present is death. In a metaphysical sense, of course."

Livshits was working on an anthology of French poetry "from the Romantics to the Surrealists," and brought his friend some of the newest poets in the original. Kuzmin found the Surrealists "curious," but neither they nor others could displace Verlaine and Rimbaud in his affections. He had always taken a "highly sarcastic attitude toward the snobs of his homeland who were bewitched by the magic of the very sound of foreign names," and some reputations impressed him not at all: "Paul Valéry is boring, an inferior version of Leconte de Lisle. Paul Fort is a French Apollon Korinfsky [a once popular Russian poetaster]."[51] "I would have nothing against Régnier in the end," he remarked to Petrov, "but I am sick to death of his admirers."[52] He did not give a whit that one was no longer supposed to care for France or D'Annunzio. Their works still filled his shelves, but he made room for Gide ("such interesting portraits of young men," he remarked in 1928) and for Giraudoux, whose novels *Siegfried et le Limousin* and *Juliette au pays des hommes* he admired. But it was Goethe, Pushkin, Hoffmann, Dickens, Dostoevsky, the Elizabethans, classical authors, and the "ardent, carnal" writers of the Italian Renaissance to whom he returned over and over, and always Leskov: "I'll read through everything, and then I start all over again, and so it goes year in and year out."[53]

He was hospitalized again in March 1935. That summer he stayed at a sanatorium for writers in Detskoe Selo, but his health kept deteriorating. By the end of the year he reluctantly had to limit guests to a handful of his closest friends. He hated old age and dreaded the seizures that came with ever more menacing regularity. He knew that he was dying, but he worried more about what would become of Yurkun than he did about himself and, stoic to the end, complained little about his own condition. At the end of January 1936 he entered the Kuibyshev Hospital, which was overcrowded by one of Leningrad's usual winter flu epidemics. This time doctors held out no hope to the few friends who were allowed to visit. In February his bed was placed in a drafty corridor where, in his weakened condition, he caught the flu. At midnight on March 1, he died. Two months later Yurkun wrote to Vladimir Milashevsky and his wife in Moscow:

> Mikhail Alekseevich died in exceptional harmony: easily, elegantly, merrily, almost festively... On March first he talked for four hours with me about the most relaxed and easy things, about ballet most of all.
>
> There was no suffering, even in the death throes, which lasted about twenty minutes.
>
> About four days before his death he improved and escorted me through the corridors of the hospital as he planned a trip along the Volga in the summer and invited Olga Nikolaevna [Arbenina] and me...
>
> Then all of a sudden an attack of the flu, which turned into pneumonia, settled everything at once.[54]

He remembered the moment slightly differently in conversation with Lidiya Ginzburg, who wrote: "Yurkun was sitting with him in the hospital. They were chatting about various things. Suddenly Kuzmin said: 'Go home.' 'Why? I still want to stay with you.' 'No,' he said insistently, and added: 'Life on the whole is over, only details remain...' Yurkun left, and he died about an hour later."[55]

On Tuesday, March 3, the newspaper *Literary Leningrad* (Literaturnyi Leningrad) published on its last page the briefest announcement possible from the Leningrad section of the Writers' Union and the Literary Fund about Kuzmin's death and the date of the funeral. It spelled his last name wrong. *Izvestiya* got the name right in the seven-line bulletin that it published the next day, but it mentioned only his work as a translator. Ginzburg recalled that the Literary Fund "sent out typed notices with an invitation to the funeral of a member of the Writers' Union, 'Kuz'min M. A.' . . . The rudeness and the ignorance—the soft sign in the last name of the deceased and putting the initials after his name . . . Most of the invitations arrived the day after the funeral."[56]

On the early afternoon of March 5 about forty mourners waited on Liteinyi Prospect outside the gates of the hospital—all his friends and "fewer literary people than there were 'supposed to be,' but more, perhaps, than one would have liked to see... Remember that seven people walked behind Wilde's coffin, and then not all of them walked to the end."[57] Likhachev, Petrov, Shadrin, and Stepanov carried out the open casket. Gollerbakh, who was reminded of Baudelaire's death mask when he looked at the "severe, waxen face," assisted them, even though the coffin seemed to weigh almost nothing at all. "The silver strands of his hair, which he usually used to cover his bald pate, lay on his brow like a laurel wreath."[58] Arbenina placed a small icon in his hands, and others surrounded the casket in the modest open hearse with bunches of his favorite flowers. The literary organizations had not sent so much as a wreath.

Large flakes of heavy wet snow fell on the melancholy procession as it made its way along thoroughfares crowded with traffic, accompanied, just as Kuzmin had predicted, by the discordant strains of music from a "wretched" little band of three "despondent musicians" hastily thrown together by the Writers' Union. Akhmatova, who was too unwell to be present, sent her husband, Nikolay Punin, who remarked to Petrov, "We are burying Kuzmin, like Mozart, during a snowstorm."[59] The mourners made their way with difficulty from the Obvodnyi Canal through dirty narrow side streets to the Volkovo Cemetery:

For some reason the main street to it was closed—perhaps owing to repairs or construction. To the left ran fences and wooden houses, to the right a wintry canal covered with snow. A large clumsy cart was coming toward us on the narrow road. The driver, wearing a short yellow leather coat, was walking next to the horse and at the top of his voice shouted Russian words, terrible and insulting, at the funeral procession. The hearse tilted to one side as it passed the cart. The writers whispered among themselves in indignation. But of what concern to people passing by were these people who were walking behind a coffin—men in glasses, wet hats, caps, women wearing soaked fur coats, thin old coats, knitted caps. We walked around the cart with caution.[60]

Kuzmin was buried in the Literatorskie Mostki section of the cemetery in an "airy little bower-like chapel, transparent, resembling an aviary," not too far from the grave of Leskov.[61] The resting place was, however, at some distance from the plots of the most famous. Rozhdestvensky mumbled a few words on behalf of the Writers' Union to begin the civil funeral service. They struck all those present as inadequate. Sergey Spassky spoke not much better, but Vissarion Sayanov, another writer who had frequented Kuzmin's teas, made a fine speech that somewhat rectified the painful impression left by the previous remarks. "But Yurkun spoke even better. Very much from the heart and simply, as though on behalf of the living Mikhail Alekseevich, he thanked all who had come to see him off."[62]

The next day a few of his closest friends visited the grave, still mounded high with flowers, and attended a mass at the Cathedral of the Transfiguration. "Churches were rather empty in those years, and the nice aged priest took a visible interest in this unusual group of young people who had come to hear the memorial mass. . . . As he said goodbye to us, the priest said: 'Live long and live merrily!' 'A rather surprising wish after a funeral mass,' O. N. Gildebrandt whispered in my ear. I answered that in my opinion it was an entirely Christian wish and it seemed to me that Mikhail Alekseevich would have been pleased by it."[63]

Epilogue

"SO FAR (from my point of view), everyone is taking an almost ideal attitude to the memory of M[ikhail] A[lekseevich]," Yurkun wrote to Radlova on March 28, 1936. "Not once has anyone expressed to me sympathy either pompously excessive or affected. And for that I am deeply grateful to all."[1] A state agency that could claim the property of those who died without close family embroiled him, the executor, and his mother, the heir of Kuzmin's estate, in a nasty lawsuit for two months, but they won their rights and stayed on in the apartment. They also received the money from an insurance policy that Kuzmin had taken out shortly before his death. For the rest of their lives they lived on that, on the sale of books from Kuzmin's library, and on the modest royalties that continued to come into the estate from theaters and publishers. Yurkun spent his time as before, sketching, painting, and, still a passionate collector, buying old magazines from which he clipped illustrations for collages or for careful sorting and filing in the large portfolios that filled his room.

By 1936 the money from Kuzmin's sale of his Diary and other papers was long gone. As early as April 1918, Kuzmin, desperately in need of money, had hoped to sell the Diary to Pronin's wife, but that and several subsequent attempts to sell all or part of it to collectors or publishers fell through, even though he actually signed a contract for its sale to "Petropolis" in February 1921. In November 1933 Vladimir Bonch-

Bruevich, Lenin's former executive secretary and the founder and director of Moscow's State Literary Museum, persuaded him to part with it.[2] A special commission of the cultural-educational section of the Party's Central Committee criticized the purchase of the Diary, which it considered "notes, for the most part, on homosexual themes, something that has no museum or literary value." Bonch-Bruevich disagreed, finding much in the Diary "that is valuable and important for the study and understanding of that trend in left Symbolism to which Kuzmin belonged and which is such a graphic expression of our decaying bourgeois society at the end of the nineteenth and especially at the beginning of the twentieth century."

Kuzmin had long wondered about the propriety of selling such a personal document, but he knew that unless he were to destroy it, the Diary would remain among his papers after his death, and he decided to take advantage of the museum's generous offer while he needed the money. The director assured him that the Diary would be kept in strict confidence, and Kuzmin stipulated that it could be shown or published only after his death and "if in part during my lifetime, only and every time with my permission." What he never knew was that in February 1934, three months after his papers had arrived in Moscow, Mikhail Gorb, a ranking official of the NKVD, as the secret police was then called, "requested" that the museum turn over the Diary and other parts of Kuzmin's archive for examination "in connection with some case." The NKVD, despite several appeals and a direct letter to Lavrenty Beria, head of the organization, did not return the papers (and then not all of them) to the museum until March 1940.

Kuzmin had never kept his opinion of the regime and his sympathy for its victims a secret from the pages of the Diary. He was "horrified" when he saw in the newspapers the faces of those condemned to death by firing squad in the 1928 "Shakhty" show trial, and wrote, "A senseless phenomenon demands senseless bloodshed" (July 28, 1928). He had no illusions, but he was no active "oppositionist" for the simple fact that he was utterly indifferent to politics. "Kuzmin," Gollerbakh once remarked in his diary, "used to say that it made absolutely no difference to him who was 'there, at the top'—'let even a horse rule us, it is all the same to me.' He would not have tried to play up to the horse, not even the most thoroughbred, and would not have neighed to it for his own advantage."[3] To be sure, on December 1, 1934, Kuzmin noted in the

Diary: "This evening the murder of Kirov was announced. This may be fraught with consequences." The next day, however, he very typically wrote that the "death of Kirov has all the same introduced a kind of confusion in circles that are evidently completely uninterested," by which he apparently meant some friends who discussed the event with him. The remark confirms the statement of Gollerbakh and that of Petrov, who wrote: "It seems to me that Kuzmin *was bored to death* in this new era. The present was not the present for him, that is, it was not *authentic and indubitably real.* He perceived it as something accidental and erroneous. . . . Politics was organically alien to him, while the contemporary life around him was profoundly uninteresting."[4]

Kuzmin, like his friends, had no sense of the whirlwind to come in 1937–38. To suggest that the sale of his Diary, which certainly was examined by the secret police, was responsible for the subsequent fate of many friends because of some kind of naive thoughtlessness on his part would be cruelly unthinking, even reckless. True, at the end of the 1920s, he had written in it, "If the Diary is ever seized and read, then all of us will be shot." But three volumes had been seized in 1931 (and never returned) with no dire consequences, and he had tried to ensure—and had been assured of—confidentiality. Like others of the old intelligentsia who sold their papers to the Literary Museum and other repositories, only to have them "borrowed" by the police, he had been naive only in believing in promises made, in trusting in contracts signed by the director of a government agency, and in assuming that age-old standards of archival etiquette prevailed in a lawless state. And, most important, the security agencies never required "documentary evidence" for anything in an atmosphere for which "Kafkaesque" is a totally inadequate adjective. Something as simple as Kuzmin's apolitical but decidedly un-Soviet daily teas must have seemed extremely suspicious to the authorities and, when the times demanded, "proof" of sedition.

On the night of October 26–27, 1937, agents of the NKVD came to take Livshits to the remand prison attached to the "big house" *(bol'shoi dom)*, as its Leningrad headquarters on Liteinyi Prospect were known. Arrests of Valentin Stenich, the poet and translator Vilgelm Zorgenfrey, the young poet Sergey Dagaev, the writer Elena Tager, Nikolay Zabolotsky, and others followed. Yurkun's turn came on the night of February 3–4, 1938. All were accused of belonging to a counterrevolutionary organization of Leningrad writers that had been plotting the death of Stalin and the overthrow of the Soviet state. It was allegedly headed by Victor Serge, a prominent Trotskyite who had been released from a Soviet prison and exiled to his native Belgium in 1936 after appeals to Stalin by Rolland and other Western sympathizers of the Soviet Union.[5] Yurkun, like all the others who had been arrested, was subjected to the infamous "conveyer," a sadistic system of sleep deprivation, uninterrupted mental and verbal abuse, blackmail, threats against family, and physical torture that was designed to break the will and wring out false incriminations of "fellow conspirators" and "enemies of the people" and admissions of guilt for nonexistent crimes. In this case, as in many others, the victims were forced to sign statements that look to have been composed by their interrogators, who also sometimes faked their signatures.

At a "trial" that began shortly after eleven o'clock on the evening of September 20, 1938, and lasted fifteen minutes, Livshits, who was accused of being the conspiracy's ringleader, was condemned to immediate execution and confiscation of all personal property for taking part in an "anti-Soviet Right-Trotskyite terrorist and saboteur-wrecker organization." Dagaev, Stenich, Zorgenfrey, and Yurkun were given the same sentence after deliberations of similar brevity. All were shot sometime after midnight. Fate had indeed been benevolent to Kuzmin, as Akhmatova and others believed, by sending him death in 1936. Had he been alive, he would certainly have been arrested and, had he survived the brutal interrogations, shot with the others. His name (although never a reference to the Diary) figures prominently in the records of the interrogations and was included, with that of Vaginov, in a long list of those "uncovered" for involvement in the "writers' affair." Someone wrote in "already dead" after their names. Rakov, Likhachev, Shadrin, Spassky, and other friends were also taken, but they survived decades in the camps. The Radlovs were spared until 1945, when they were lured back to the Soviet Union from France, to which they had made their way after their theater troupe was caught behind German lines during the war. They were sentenced to the Gulag for nine years for "treason." She died there; he lived to be "rehabilitated" after Stalin's death.

Yurkun's mother died of heart failure a few weeks after her son's arrest. Arbenina had no inkling of his fate. Like the relatives of the other victims, she did know that the official sentence "ten years of confinement in remote camps without the right of correspondence" meant death. She had been able to gather up a few parts of Kuzmin and

Yurkun's archive from the apartment before the NKVD confiscated all the manuscripts, books, pictures, and other possessions on October 8. Two days later she appealed to Bonch-Bruevich for help in regaining the material. His letter to the Leningrad security organs was not answered. All the documents probably perished in the fires that burned for days when the NKVD destroyed countless "nonessential" papers in its holdings as the Germans approached Leningrad in 1941. Most of the portions of the archive that Arbenina left with a friend in Leningrad in May 1941 when she and her mother went to visit her sister in the Urals, where the outbreak of the war kept them, vanished during the siege.

"My Yurochka, I am writing you because I think that I will not live long," Arbenina began a letter to Yurkun on February 13, 1946, a bottle cast into the sea of the Gulag to a dead man and one of the most heartrending documents of the times. "I love you, believed in you, and waited for you for many years. . . . Most of all I want to learn that you are alive—and then die. Be happy. Try to achieve fame. Remember me. Don't scold me. I did everything that I could," she continued before telling him of the fate of his mother, their friends, and herself in the terrible years that followed his disappearance.[6] She did not learn about what had really happened to him for more than a decade.

When Arbenina returned to Leningrad in 1948 and visited the cemetery, Kuzmin's grave was still there, but she had to replace the wooden cross, which had probably been burned for firewood during the siege. All the little chapels were torn down sometime later, and a "reordering" of the graves took place. For a long time neither she nor friends could find the grave, but then it turned up in another spot, not far from the place of reburial of Blok and on a direct line from the graves of the mother and relatives of Lenin with their elaborate funerary monuments.[7] She and a few of the poet's old friends raised the money for the small white weathered marble stone that now lies over it. In 1907 Kuzmin had jokingly composed his own epitaph: "He lived for thirty years, drank, observed, loved, and smiled."[8] The inscription states simply:

MIKHAIL

ALEKSEEVICH

KUZMIN

1875–1936

POET

Abbreviations and Bibliographical Note
Notes
Index of Works by Kuzmin
General Index

Abbreviations and Bibliographical Note

HE	Mikhail Kuzmin, "Histoire édifiante de mes commencements," in *Mikhail Kuzmin i russkaya kul'tura XX veka*, ed. G. A. Morev (Leningrad, 1990)
IMLI	Gorky Institute of World Literature, Moscow
IRLI	Institute of Russian Literature (Pushkin House), St. Petersburg
JEM	John E. Malmstad
MK	N. A. Bogomolov and John E. Malmstad, *Mikhail Kuzmin: Iskusstvo, zhizn', epokha* (Moscow: Novoe literaturnoe obozrenie, 1996)
MKiRK	*Mikhail Kuzmin i russkaya kul'tura XX veka*, ed. G. A. Morev (Leningrad, 1990)
NAB	Nikolay Alekseevich Bogomolov
RGALI	Russian State Archive of Literature and Art, Moscow
RGB	Russian State Library, Moscow
RLM	Russian Literary Museum, Moscow
RNB	Russian National Library, St. Petersburg
S	Mikhail Kuzmin, *Stikhotvoreniya*, ed. N. A. Bogomolov, "Novaya Biblioteka poeta" (St. Petersburg: Gumanitarnoe agenstvo, "Akademicheskii proekt," 1996)
SS	Mikhail Kuzmin, *Sobranie stikhov*, ed. John E. Malmstad and Vladimir Markov, 3 vols. (Munich: Wilhelm Fink Verlag, 1977)
Studies	*Studies in the Life and Works of Mixail Kuzmin*, ed. John E. Malmstad, Wiener Slawistischer Almanach, *Sonderband* 24 (Vienna, 1989)
Zi	*Zhizn' iskusstva* (Petrograd-Leningrad)

In archival references the abbreviation "coll." (for "collection") renders the Russian *fond* and "inven." (for "inventory") *opis'*, while "item" corresponds to the Russian *edinitsa khraneniya*.

A good bibliography of Kuzmin's works and works about him can be found in Klaus Harer, *Michail Kuzmin: Studien zur Poetik der frühen und mittleren Schaffensperiode* (Munich: Verlag Otto Sagner, 1993), 253–306. P. V. Dmitriev and A. G. Timofeev published an almost complete bibliography of Kuzmin's critical writings in *De Visu*, 5/6 (16) (1994), 94–112.

Notes

Introduction

1. Evgeny Znosko-Borovsky expanded the talk and published it in the magazine *Apollon*, 4–5 (1917), under the title "O tvorchestve M. Kuzmina." B. P. Koz'min quoted almost verbatim from it, without attribution, in the entry on Kuzmin in his *Pisateli sovremennoi epokhi: Bio-bibliograficheskii slovar' pisatelei XX veka*, vol. 1 (Moscow, 1928), 158–160. He gives no sources at all for some of his other information about the writer.

2. Vladimir Markov, "Poeziya Mikhaila Kuzmina," in vol. 3 of Kuzmin's *Sobranie stikhov*, ed. John E. Malmstad (hereafter JEM) and Vladimir Markov (Munich: Wilhelm Fink Verlag, 1977), 323–325 (hereafter *SS* with volume number).

3. Leonid Dobychin's long story "Shurkina rodnya," discovered in the archives of Pushkinskii Dom and published for the first time in the *Ezhegodnik rukopisnogo otdela Pushkinskogo Doma na 1990 god* (St. Petersburg: Gumanitarnoe agentstvo "Akademicheskii proekt," 1993), caused a sensation. Some believe that he committed suicide in 1936 by throwing himself into the river Neva, although others dispute that.

4. A note to Kuzmin from Sergey Gorodetsky of September 14, 1910, allows us to fix with certainty the time of their meeting: "Dear Mikhail Alekseevich. Allow me to recommend to the attention of the Poetic Academy a young poet (fifteen years old), Georgy Vladimirovich Ivanov. I shake your hand." Manuscript Division, Russian National Library (Rossiiskaya natsional'naya biblioteka), St. Petersburg (hereafter RNB), coll. 124, item 1291.

5. Georgy Ivanov, *Stikhotvoreniya. Tretii Rim. Peterburgskie zimy. Kitaiskie teni* (Moscow: Kniga, 1989), 366.

6. Irina Odoevtseva, *Na beregakh Nevy* (Moscow: Khudozhestvennaya literatura, 1988), 97. She writes that Kuzmin had a Jewish grandmother; none of his relatives were Jews. Odoevtseva does, at least, call all this "stories" she heard about

Kuzmin from others, but then her supposedly eyewitness descriptions are equally fantastic.

7. Marina Tsvetaeva, "Nezdeshnii vecher," in *Izbrannaya proza v dvukh tomakh, 1917–1937*, vol. 2 (New York: Russica, 1979), 132.

8. Yury Tynyanov, statement in the collection *Kak my pishem* (Leningrad: Izdatel'stvo pisatelei v Leningrade, 1930), 161.

9. Margarita Woloschin, *Die grüne Schlange: Lebenserinnerungen* (Stuttgart: Deutsche Verlags-Anstalt, 1954), 178.

10. Znosko-Borovsky, "O tvorchestve M. Kuzmina," 29.

11. "A ustav, sredi zelenykh syadem trav, / V knige staroi prochitav ostatok glav: / Ty—chitatel' svoei zhizni, ne pisets, / Neizvesten tebe povesti konets," the final two couplets of the poem "Snova chist peredo mnoyu pervyi list," from the collection *Seti*. This, like all further citations from Kuzmin's poetry, is quoted from the 1996 edition of his collected verse, *Stikhotvoreniya*, "Novaya Biblioteka poeta," ed. N. A. Bogomolov (hereafter NAB) (St. Petersburg: Gumanitarnoe agenstvo, "Akademicheskii proekt," 1996), 91 (hereafter *S* with page number).

1. *"The Edifying Story of My Beginnings"*

1. NAB and JEM, *Mikhail Kuzmin: Iskusstvo, zhizn', epokha* (Moscow: Novoe literaturnoe obozrenie, 1996), 9 (hereafter *MK*). S. V. Shumikhin published and annotated the "Histoire édifiante de mes commencements" in *Mikhail Kuzmin i russkaya kul'tura XX veka*, ed. G. A. Morev (Leningrad, 1990), 146–155 (hereafter *MKiRK*). We shall refer to it simply as "Histoire édifiante" in the text and as HE in the notes. We have silently corrected his few misreadings of the text.

2. This "introduction" appears between entries for November 20 and 21, 1906. Kuzmin's Diary is held in the Russian State Archive of Literature and Art (Rossiiskii gosudarstvennyi arkhiv literatury i iskusstva), Moscow (hereafter RGALI), coll. 232, inven. 1, items 50–67a. All our citations in the text and notes will give only the date of the Diary entry without additional reference to item number. All entries are cited from the text prepared for publication by NAB and S. V. Shumikhin. For more information on the Diary, see S. V. Shumikhin, "Dnevnik Mikhaila Kuzmina: arkhivnaya predystoriya," *MKiRK*, 139–145.

3. In several documents, both private and public, Kuzmin varied the date of his birth, staying only within the range 1872–1877. A. G. Timofeev surveys Kuzmin's statements about the matter in "Materialy M. A. Kuzmina v rukopisnom otdele Pushkinskogo doma," in *Ezhegodnik rukopisnogo otdela Pushkinskogo Doma na 1990 god* (St. Petersburg: Gumanitarnoe agenstvo "Akademicheskii proekt," 1993), 18 (note 3).

4. "Za to, chto *vyros* v Yaroslavle, / Svoyu sud'bu blagoslovlyu!" from "Ya znayu vas ne ponaslyshke, / O verkhnei Volgi goroda!" *Vozhatyi* (*S*, 325); emphasis added.

5. Vsevolod Petrov recalled that "he loved the outline and sound of his ancient surname, and would get annoyed if it were written incorrectly, with a soft sign—'Kuz'min.' 'That isn't my name,' Mikhail Alekseevich would say." V. Petrov, "Kaliostro: Vospominaniya i razmyshleniya o M. A. Kuzmine," ed. Gennady Shmakov, *Novyi zhurnal*, 163 (1986), 105. Vladimir Milashevsky wrote in his memoirs: "Incidentally, Mikhail Alekseevich will also never ever forgive you if you insert

a soft sign into his last name. He values his gentry name very highly, that of seamen in the Russian fleet of tall ships, while 'Kuz'mins' with the soft sign... well, there are so many of that variety." See his "Pobegi topolya" in the magazine *Volga*, 11 (1970), 186. Volume sixteen of the Brockhaus and Efron *Entsiklopedicheskii slovar'* (St. Petersburg: Tipo-litografiya I. A. Efrona, 1895), under the entry "Kuzmin," identifies the family as of gentry (noble) descent (p. 932).

6. HE, 147.

7. "Moryaki starinnykh familii, / vlyublennye v dalekie gorizonty, / p'yushchie vino v temnykh portakh, / obnimaya veselykh inostranok . . . vazhnye, so zvezdami, generaly." "Moi predki" (*S*, 57).

8. See the memoirs of his brother Pavel Alekseevich (1819–1885), published in three issues (February, March, April) of *Russkaya starina* in 1895.

9. Voltaire mentions him often in his letters; see volume 103, General Index A–C, of *Voltaire's Correspondence*, ed. Theodore Besterman (Geneva: Institut et Musée Voltaire, Les Délices, 1965), 194. Kuzmin rather denigrated (and thus could take unboastful pride in) his distinguished ancestor in these lines from "Moi predki": "Dear actors of no great talent, / importing the school of a foreign land, / playing *Mahomet* in Russia / and dying with an innocent Voltaireanism" ("Milye aktery bez bol'shogo talanta, / prinesshie shkolu chuzhoi zemli, / igrayushchie v Rossii 'Magometa' / i umirayushchie s nevinnym vol'ter'yanstvom" [*S*, 57]).

10. Kuzmin found space to mention his French roots even in the very brief autobiographical statement he set down for M. L. Gofman's *Kniga o russkikh poetakh poslednego desyatiletiya* (Petersburg: M. O. Vol'f, 1907): "My native city is Yaroslavl, my family is of the gentry, my ancestors were French" (p. 383). He was also, he heard from his mother, distantly related to Théophile Gautier.

11. See Aleksey Remizov's reminiscence-necrology "Poslushnyi samokei," in *Plyashushchii demon: Tanets i slovo* (Paris, 1949), 44.

12. Tsvetaeva, "Nezdeshnii vecher," 131.

13. Marina Tsvetaeva, "Dva zareva!—net, zerkala!" in *Stikhotvoreniya i poemy*, "Biblioteka poeta," bol'shaya seriya (Leningrad: Sovetskii pisatel', 1990), 213–214.

14. Znosko-Borovsky, "O tvorchestve M. Kuzmina," 30.

15. HE, 148.

16. Ibid., 147.

17. See Simon Karlinsky, "Russia's Gay Literature and Culture: The Impact of the October Revolution," in *Hidden from History: Reclaiming the Gay and Lesbian Past*, ed. Martin Duberman, Martha Vicinus, and George Chauncey, Jr. (New York: Meridian, 1990), 347–363. The Legal Code, he writes, included "Article 995, which prohibited *muzhelozhstvo*, a term that the courts interpreted as anal intercourse between men. . . . The penalty prescribed for violating Article 995 was deprivation of all rights and resettlement in Siberia for four to five years" (p. 349). For the 1903 revision of the Legal Code, officially approved but never enacted, see Igor Kon, "Sexual Minorities," in *Sex and Russian Society*, ed. Igor Kon and James Riordan (Bloomington: Indiana University Press, 1993), 90. Kuzmin's Diary makes clear that a gay subculture existed quite openly in Petersburg at the time, with well-known cruising areas and many places where gay men could socialize publicly. It also records the anxiety, even panic, experienced by several of his friends who were employed by the government when they thought their inclinations might be exposed.

18. In a 1911 interview with a correspondent for a Moscow newspaper who had asked him did he not believe that "all the perversions" of modern Russian society were "the result of your preaching of free love? To a certain degree has not pornographic literature had an influence on the loosening of morals?" Kuzmin replied: "But pornography is one thing, while my works are another. I do not ascribe them to the category of the pornographic. [What are] pornographic are those works in which the relationship of the sexes is described in such a way as to arouse the reader in a sensual manner. . . . There is very little of the immoral [in my works]; I will say even more—the heroines whom I portray are in the majority chaste, because I take a simple and natural approach to the description, with no lip-smacking." *Moskovskaya gazeta*, no. 123, October 4, 1911.

19. Kuzmin's letters of 1890–1903 to G. V. Chicherin are in the Manuscript Division of the RNB, coll. 1030, items 17–22, 52–54; Chicherin's to Kuzmin of 1889–1926 are in RGALI, coll. 232, inven. 1, items 430–433, and in the Russian Literary Museum (Russkii literaturnyi muzei), Moscow (hereafter RLM), coll. 111, item 22. We will identify all further citations from this correspondence by date only in the text, without reference to item number or previous publications of fragments from it. Almost all citations given here appear at greater length in *MK*.

20. HE, 148; Znosko-Borovsky, "O tvorchestve M. Kuzmina," 30.

21. HE, 148.

22. Milashevsky, "Pobegi topolya," 187. In 1934, when a friend urged him to write his memoirs, Kuzmin set down some reminiscences about his life in Saratov in passages of the Diary entitled "Saratov Apartments" and "Saratov Dachas."

23. Autobiographical statement, Gofman, *Kniga o russkikh poetakh poslednego desyatiletiya*, 383.

24. HE, 148–149.

25. Ibid., 149.

26. Ibid., 147.

27. Kuzmin also described the suicide attempt, ibid.

28. Ibid., 149.

29. Ibid.

30. The Russian titles of the pieces are "Blednoe solntse osennego vechera," "Morskaya tsarevna" (probably a setting of Lermontov's poem of that title), "Zimnii les," and "Polden'." They are mentioned in a list (incomplete) of his musical compositions which Kuzmin set down (RGALI, coll. 232, inven. 1, item 14).

31. They saw each other only once again, in November 1926 (see Chapter 12). Chicherin was dismissed from his post in July 1930, ostensibly because of failing health. He had never got on with Stalin, and had found it difficult to conceal his contempt for Stalin's crudity and lack of culture. After his ouster from the foreign service, he experienced the full measure of the dictator's petty vengefulness: "Chicherin lived an isolated, solitary existence, as he ceased to play a role in government affairs and virtually dropped out of sight. In 1931 rumors circulated that he had become an alcoholic and was so impoverished that he was reduced to begging on the streets of Moscow. The Soviet government denied these reports, but they persisted, for he had been evicted from his room at Narkomindel on Kuznetskii Most. By the following year the Central Committee took action to provide for his care." See Timothy Edward O'Connor, *Diplomacy and Revolution: G. V. Chicherin and Soviet Foreign Affairs, 1918–1930* (Ames: Iowa State University Press, 1988), 167–168. In 1934 Stalin personally blocked the publication of an edition in 250

copies of Chicherin's book on Mozart. He died of a brain hemorrhage on July 7, 1936. He was not "rehabilitated" until 1962 (ibid., p. 168). O'Connor never mentions Chicherin's homosexuality or his friendship with Kuzmin.

32. HE, 150.

33. Ibid.

34. Ibid., 148.

35. Ibid. Kuzmin writes that his older, middle brother was "about 16–17" at the time, and that these sexual games took place when they were living in the country, about two years before they left for Petersburg, which would mean that he was about ten or eleven. It sounds as if these games consisted of mutual masturbation. The older brother clearly initiated the game, and from all that Kuzmin writes, he may also have been gay: "My brother, fearing that I would tell people at home, got mad at me, but started playing his games with Sasha Toplyakovsky, who was about five years older than me. My brother had a friend with whom he was in love and whom he drove away since he started paying too much attention to me. I didn't understand anything at the time." Kuzmin later had nothing whatsoever to do with him, but then he had little to do with most members of his immediate family, except for one sister.

36. Ibid., 149–150.

37. Aleksandr Timofeev, "Sovsem drugoe, proshloe solntse: Mikhail Kuzmin v Revele," *Zvezda*, 2 (1997), 153.

38. Mikhail Kuzmin, *Pervaya kniga rasskazov* (Moscow: Skorpion, 1910), 201; emphasis added. All quotations from *Kryl'ya* will be taken from that collection, which has been republished as volume one of Kuzmin's collected *Proza*, ed. Vladimir Markov (Berkeley: Berkeley Slavic Specialties, 1984). A very free rendering of the work can be found in Mikhail Kuzmin, *Selected Prose and Poetry* (Ann Arbor: Ardis, 1980). All translations are our own.

39. See letter of June 22, 1891, to Sergey Matveevsky, "Pis'ma M. A. Kuzmina S. K. Matveevskomu," published by NAB in *Minuvshee*, 22 (1997), 180.

40. HE, 150.

41. "At the Conservatory I was in Lyadov's class in solfeggio, [Nikolay] Solov'ev's in harmony, and Rimsky-Korsakov's in counterpoint and the fugue" (ibid).

42. Znosko-Borovsky, "O tvorchestve M. Kuzmina," 31.

43. HE, 150.

44. In a 1923 obituary of Loti, Kuzmin wrote of his "sentimental lyricism," adding, "Salon pessimism and enervated eroticism are among the most characteristic and now least acceptable features of Pierre Loti's talent." Kuzmin praised the "humanism" that on occasion shone through in his art, but found his "European disenchantment" with life "essentially empty and unnecessary and, therefore, harmful." *Vechernyaya Krasnaya gazeta*, no. 138, June 17, 1923, 2.

45. HE, 148. Kuzmin's answers of "None at all" to points five ("What was your attitude to Nekrasov in childhood?") and six ("What was your attitude to Nekrasov in your youth?") of Korney Chukovsky's 1921 questionnaire "Nekrasov and I" well show his early indifference to Russian literature and his lack of knowledge about many of its classic figures when he was young. See "Nekrasov i my," *Letopis' Doma literatorov*, 3 (December 1, 1921), 3. Kuzmin said that when he finally read Nekrasov, he did not particularly like him.

46. A comment about Offenbach in "Cheshuya v nevode," a selection "from

notes taken over the six years 1916–1921," makes clear how much censure Kuzmin intended: "Say what you will, Offenbach's *Le pont des soupirs* is boring nonsense. Lecocq never sank as low as Offenbach used to do. It is as if the composer were asleep and keeps purring commonplaces, the more banal the better, from memory. The posthumous appraisals are, in the long run, just, and attempts at galvanization succeed rarely, and then only briefly. *Avis aux snobs.*" Published in the collection *Strelets: Sbornik tretii i poslednii* (Petersburg, 1922), 99. In an article written not long after Lecocq's death, Kuzmin again made clear his preference for his "ingenuous, merry art" over the "brilliant, often vulgar buffooneries" of Offenbach: "Sharl' Lekok [Charles Lecocq] (1832–1918)," *Zhizn' iskusstva*, no. 5, November 2, 1918 (hereafter *Zi*), 5. The piece was republished in Kuzmin's only volume of collected critical essays and reviews, *Uslovnosti: Stat'i ob iskusstve* (Petrograd: Polyarnaya zvezda, 1923), 128–129.

47. "Dukh melochei, prelestnykh i vozdushnykh, / Lyubvi nochei, to nezhashchikh, to dushnykh, / Veseloi legkosti bezdumnogo zhit'ya! / Akh, veren ya, dalek chudes poslushnykh, / Tvoim tsvetam, veselaya zemlya!" From "Gde slog naidu, chtob opisat' progulku" (*S*, 59). There is an almost eighteenth-century quality in the fourth line's "dalek chudes [instead of "dalek ot chudes"] poslushnykh," and the compactness of the conceit makes for real questions about meaning. By "miracles at one's command" (or "obedient miracles") Kuzmin seems to mean the wonders that the imagination can summon up as opposed to those that exist in creation (earth's "flowers").

48. See, for example, a short piece by Akim Volynsky, an early champion of western European and Russian modernism, in the magazine *Severnyi vestnik*, 9 (1896), 57–58 (second pagination).

49. See T. V. Pavlova's excellent article on Wilde's reception in Russia, "Oskar Uail'd v russkoi literature (konets XIX—nachalo XX v.)," in *Na rubezhe XIX i XX vekov: Iz istorii mezhdunarodnykh svyazei russkoi literatury*, ed. Yu. D. Levin (Leningrad: Nauka, 1991), 77–128.

50. See the article "Gnilaya dusha" ("A Rotten Soul") by V. Artaban (pseudonym of the well-known religious publicist G. S. Petrov) in the newspaper *Russkoe slovo*, no. 43, February 12, 1904. N. Ya. Starodum (Stechkin), reviewing the first two issues of the magazine *Vesy*, did not deny Wilde's talent, but advised keeping silent about him in light of the scandal surrounding his name. He added that attempts to give Wilde a "special place" in literature "served only old degenerates and young neurasthenics." See his "Zhurnal'noe obozrenie ('Vesy'—yanvar', fevral' 1904 g.)," *Russkii vestnik*, 3 (1904), 342–343, 349.

51. HE, 150.

52. All our attempts to learn the identity of "Prince Georges"—Kuzmin always uses the French—have come to nothing, but there is no question that he existed; he is referred to on many later occasions in Kuzmin's Diary. Most likely this was nothing more than Kuzmin's nickname for the young officer.

53. HE, 150–151.

54. Ibid., 151.

55. Twelve years later the trip had lost none of its special aura. When he learned that an acquaintance was planning a trip to Istanbul, he wrote, "Constantinople, the memory of that unforgettable, enchanting city fills me almost with some kind of melancholy" (Diary, July 21, 1907).

56. "Chto zh delat', . . . / Chto moi stikhi, / dorogie mne, / tak zhe, kak Kalli-makhu / i vsyakomu drugomu velikomu, / kuda ya vlagayu lyubov' i vsyu nezhnost', / i legkie ot bogov mysli, / otrada utr moikh, / kogda nebo yasno / i v okna pakhnet zhasminom, / zavtra / zabudutsya kak i vsë? / Chto perestanu ya videt' / tvoe litso, / slyshat' tvoi golos? / chto vyp'etsya vino, / uletuchatsya aromaty / i sami dorogie tkani / istleyut / cherez stolet'ya? / Razve men'she ya stanu lyubit' / eti milye khrupkie veshchi / za ikh tlennost'?" "Mudrost'" (*S*, 121–122).

57. The opening line of the final stanza of Solov'ev's 1887 poem "Bednyi drug, istomil tebya put'."

58. Cavafy, whom Kuzmin might have met but did not, has a very different attitude to death in a cluster of epigraphs for young men struck down by an early death: they become ideal, since they have been spared time's corruption, which brings disillusion and infidelity.

59. HE, 151.

60. Ibid., 152.

61. Ibid. Klimenko was a well-known Petersburg specialist in nervous disorders.

62. "Spiritual rimes" renders *dukhovnye stikhi* (sometimes translated as "spiritual verses"), a special genre of Russian folk poetry with subject matter drawn from the Scriptures, lives of saints, and the Apocrypha. The *byliny* are a kind of epic folk song.

2. "I Am Searching . . . the Long, Long Path"

1. HE, 152.

2. A. G. Timofeev has published all of Kuzmin's letters to Chicherin from Italy as "'Ital'yanskoe puteshestvie' Mikhaila Kuzmina," in *Pamyatniki kul'tury: Novye otkrytiya, Ezhegodnik 1992* (Moscow: Nauka, 1993), 40–55. Kuzmin used the New Style, that is, the European calendar, in all his letters from abroad.

3. "Mladencheski teni zaslushalis' pen'ya Orfeya. / Iona pod ivoi vsë pomnit kitovye nedra. / No na plechi Pastyr' ovtsu vozlagaet, zhaleya, / I blagosten kruglyi zakat za verkhushkoyu kedra." "Katakomby" (*S*, 491).

4. He had written about the works of Bortnyansky and other Orthodox liturgical music in 1896, and he later made a special study of Russian liturgical singing.

5. G. I. Chulkov, *Gody stranstvii* (Moscow: Federatsiya, 1930), 164.

6. See, for example, Kuzmin's description of Mori's library, which he made good use of, reading up on Gnosticism and early Church history (*Pervaya kniga rasskazov*, 292–293), or the description of the young hero's walks through Florence with the fictional Mori (294–295).

7. Ibid., 293–294.

8. The "Fioretti" had particularly attracted him when he first encountered them in 1892, and he continued his study of the life and works of the saint while in Italy. Scholars have only begun to examine the saint's impact on Kuzmin's views of art and life. See the very brief article by I. G. Vishnevetsky, "Mikhail Kuzmin i Sv. Frantsisk: zametki k teme," *MKiRK*, 25–27.

9. These imaginary voyages explain why some sources, among them the *Enciplopedia italiana*, write of numerous trips to Italy when there was but one. After his return to Russia in 1897, Kuzmin never traveled abroad. In an autobiography writ-

ten for S. A. Vengerov in 1913, Kuzmin himself greatly exaggerated the length of his stay: "Of foreign countries I know Italy, where I lived more than a year, best of all." Manuscript Division, Institute of Russian Literature (Pushkinskii Dom), St. Petersburg (hereafter IRLI), coll. 377, inven. 6, no. 1982.

10. "Vo Florentsii my ne vstrechalis': / Ty tam ne byl, tebe bylo togda tri goda, / No vetki zhasmina kachalis' / I v serdtse byla lyubov' i trevoga." From "Kak lyublyu ya zapakh kozhi" (*S*, 163). The reference to the smell of leather and jasmine echoes a passage in *Kryl'ya* where the young hero, Vanya, and Mori visit a Florentine cobbler whose shop "smells of leather and jasmine, several sprigs of which stood in a bottle." Kuzmin, *Pervaya kniga rasskazov*, 311.

11. Contemporaries in Petersburg such as Vyacheslav Ivanov (who completed everything but the defense of his doctoral dissertation in Roman history from the University of Berlin) readily testified to Kuzmin's erudition. Pavel Muratov, one of Russia's most distinguished authorities on Italian culture and the author of the language's most perfect book on the subject (the two-volume *Obrazy Italii*) for his part called the play *O Aleksee cheloveke Bozh'em* "an astonishingly penetrating depiction of [early] Christian Rome." See P. P. Muratov, *Obrazy Italii*, vol. 1 (Moscow: Nauchnoe slovo, 1911), 13.

12. In several letters to Chicherin written immediately after his return to Petersburg in 1897, Kuzmin sounds almost conspiratorial when he talks about Catholicism, using "the house," for example, to refer to the Jesuits. Mori may indeed have given him the names of Jesuits secretly living in the capital who might be assigned to guide the process of his conversion or charged him with special plans connected with the activities of the Jesuits, banned in Russia since 1820. See a letter of June 29, 1897, *MK*, 45.

13. HE, 152. Aleksandra Ivanovna Peiker was the daughter of Mariya Grigor'evna Peiker, well known in religious circles as a supporter of the "Pashkov sect" (*pashkovtsy*) and the publisher of the religious magazine *Russkii rabochii*. After her mother's death in 1881, the daughter continued putting out the magazine. Both of Chicherin's parents were adherents of the Pashkovite movement, the Russian offshoot of a pietist sect founded by the third Baron Radstock, an English evangelical who enjoyed wide popularity in Russia. For a discussion of Radstock's work in Russia, see Hugh McLean, *Nikolai Leskov: The Man and His Art* (Cambridge, Mass.: Harvard University Press, 1977), 331–334. Aleksey Petrovich Kolokolov was the senior priest in the Church of St. George Martyr in Petersburg and a popular preacher in high society circles in the 1880s and 1890s.

14. The complete text of "V pustyne" can be found in *MK*, 47–48. The text was published with numerous errors in volume eight (1990) of Kuzmin's collected *Proza*, 239–240.

15. In the early part of 1898 Kuzmin sent a "mystery" with music on the theme of the death and resurrection of Attis, as well as a hymn to Adonis and a hymn to Antinous (written in September 1897), to several friends for comment and criticism (the works are apparently lost). In a letter to Chicherin that accompanied the work on Attis he wrote, "Amélineau [Emile, 1850–1915], the French Egyptologist and specialist in Egyptian Christianity, has translated and published two Gnostic manuscripts no shorter than *Pistis Sophia*," concrete evidence of his continuing serious interest in the subject.

16. In the poem that begins "Kak devushki o zhenikhakh mechtayut," he wrote of "Catherine, betrothed to Christ" ("Obruchena Khristu Ekaterina," *S*, 465).

17. The song "Dans ce nid furtif" bears a dedication to the famous baritone Leonid Georgievich Yakovlev (1858–1919), a soloist at the Mariinskii Theater and later its director, who may have performed it at one of his recitals. This information is drawn from Pavel Dmitriev's "K voprosu o pervoi publikatsii M. Kuzmina," *Novoe literaturnoe obozrenie*, 3 (1993), 154–158. Dmitriev rediscovered the scores, long forgotten, and gives the text of the third song. As he notes, basing his remark on Kuzmin's own list of his musical compositions written between April 1890 and December 1905 (RGALI, coll. 232, inven. 1, item 43), by the autumn of 1898 Kuzmin had composed more than 130 musical works.

18. The text of "Pines and Firs" ("Sosny i eli") and the letters of January 18 and 24, 1897, in which Kuzmin and Chicherin discussed the poem can be found in *MK*, 33–35. Kuzmin remarked that the poem had "no relation to music." That and references to several other poems refute the assertion of Znosko-Borovsky and many others that Kuzmin began to write poems, as distinct from texts for his own songs, only after 1905.

19. "Chto serdtse? ogorod nepolotyi, / Pomyat, chto dikim tabunom. / I kak mne zhizn'yu zhit' raskolotoi, / Kogda vse mysli ob odnom?" and "K kakim ya vozzovu ugodnikam, / Kto b mne pomog, kto b uslykhal? / Ved' tot, kto byl zdes' ogorodnikom, / Sam ogorod svoi rastoptal!" (*S*, 144).

20. The insistence on "fullness" *(polnota)* here, as in other letters, usually accompanied by talk of his "void" or "emptiness" *(pustota)*, reminds us how much he was translating his experience into terms he kept encountering in his reading: the two central concepts of the dualistic Gnostic view of the world, *pleroma*, a fullness of being, compared with which the promise of heaven looks meager, and *kenoma*, the pain, illusion, and emptiness of the lives we live. To draw the parallel does not, of course, deny the pain caused by the absence of one and the domination of the other in Kuzmin's life at the time.

21. HE, 152–153.

22. Manuscript Division, Gorky Institute of World Literature (Institut mirovoi literatury imeni Gor'kogo), Moscow (hereafter IMLI), coll. 192, inven. 1, item 18.

23. July 20, 1934, entry in the Diary, where the passage occurs in a reminiscence about Vyacheslav Ivanov's "Tower." Kuzmin seems to imply that inner conflicts about his homosexuality in part impelled him to find a resolution for them in the Old Belief.

24. HE, 153. One of the most often repeated legends about Kuzmin was that he came from a family with Old Believer roots. He did not. People probably concluded this from the fact that he was so closely tied to the regions around Saratov and Nizhnii Novgorod, which were strongholds of the Old Belief.

G. M. Kazakov owned a store in Petersburg which dealt in icons and religious artifacts. In 1888 the well-known musicologist Stepan Vasil'evich Smolensky (1848–1909), a specialist in Orthodox liturgical music, devised a system for transcribing the nonlinear neumes system of musical notation (called *kryuki* [literally "hooks"] in Russian) used in Byzantine and ancient Slavic Orthodox Church manuscripts, as well as in all Old Believer liturgical music, into the Western linear system. Kuzmin met with him at least twice: on December 7, 1901, and on January 24, 1902 (see letters to Chicherin of those dates).

A *nachetchik* among the Old Believers is a man (or woman, *nachetchitsa*) who performs the role of a theologian because of wide learning and knowledge of pre-

Nikonian ecclesiastical books. Among the "priestless" sects the word was used for the spiritual leader of a community of believers.

25. "Hermitage" renders *skit* (plural *skity*), a small monastic community in which the monks lived alone or in small groups, with a common church where they could celebrate religious services. They were very different in nature from the large monasteries, and were often located in extremely remote areas.

26. One of Kuzmin's contemporaries, Dmitry Filosofov, well summed up the "tragic situation of believers of learning and culture" *(kul'turnye veruyushchie)* at the turn of the century who, like Kuzmin, rejected an identification of the *divinum* with the religious establishment: "Those who do not want to join the sectarians and who, because of their convictions, cannot side with the numerous group of unbelieving intellectuals frankly do not know where to find a home. The Church for them is not a mother but a stepmother." D. V. Filosofov, *Neugasimaya lampada: Stat'i po tserkovnym i religioznym voprosam* (Moscow: Tipografiya T-va I. D. Sytina, 1912), 60.

27. The letters that the two friends exchanged on the topic are cited at length in *MK*, 52–67.

28. For a discussion of Strakhov, see Linda Gerstein, *Nikolai Strakhov* (Cambridge, Mass.: Harvard University Press, 1971).

29. In "Cheshuya v nevode," in a passage ridiculing the Russian penchant for "theorizing" and "arguing for the sake of arguing," he wrote, "I almost forgot the Merezhkovsky [-Gippius-Filosofov] trinity, but just what kind of theoreticians are they anyway? Querulous palace doormen out of work." *Strelets: Sbornik tretii i poslednii*, 101.

30. See *The Correspondence between Prince A. M. Kurbsky and Tsar Ivan IV of Russia, 1564–1579*, ed. with a translation and notes by J. L. I. Fennell (Cambridge: Cambridge University Press, 1955), 180–181.

31. A *lestovka* is a kind of rosary, usually made of leather, used during prayers by the Old Believers, but instead of being a string of beads, it is shaped like the rungs of a ladder.

32. There were several famous Orthodox monasteries located on the banks of the White Sea, as well as Old Believer settlements and hermitages in this remote area of the province of Olonets northeast of Petersburg. Belaya Krinitsa was a town with a monastery in Bukovina, in the Austro-Hungarian Empire, where a group of schismatics had settled to flee persecution by the Russian authorities. It became the focus of successful attempts in the late eighteenth and early nineteenth centuries to set up a hierarchy of metropolitan, bishops, and so on of one faction of the priested Old Believers. The so-called Belokrinitsian compact *(Belokrinitskoe soglasie)* enjoyed great influence and prestige among Old Believers throughout the Russian Empire because of this Belokrinitsian (or Austrian) Hierarchy.

33. HE, 153. The Brockhaus and Efron encyclopedia calls Chernoe a "lively summer retreat" *(dachnoe mesto)* much favored by people from Nizhnii and Moscow.

34. Kuzmin, *Pervaya kniga rasskazov*, 223.

35. Blok was writing about *Komediya o Evdokii iz Geliopolya*, a work in the vein of Byzantine "religious comedies," in his critical essay "O drame." A. A. Blok, *Sobranie sochinenii v 8 tomakh*, vol. 5 (Moscow: Khudozhestvennaya literatura, 1962), 182–183. See also A. Remizov, "Poslushnyi samokei," 48–49.

36. Kitezh is a legendary Old Russian city that sank to the bottom of Lake Svetloyar to save itself from the Tatars. (In another version the city turned into the

hills and banks that surround the lake.) The legend, particularly popular among the Old Believers, is the subject of several works of Russian "high culture," most notably an opera by Rimsky-Korsakov. Popular lore cited the city beneath a lake near the village of Vladimirskoe, about forty versts from the city of Semenov in the Nizhnii Novgorod province. It was a favorite goal of schismatic and sectarian pilgrims, who gathered around the lake every year on June 21, when, it was believed, the city's reflection could be seen in the lake at night and the chimes of its churches could be heard.

37. Solovki is the revered fortress-like Solovetskii Monastery, founded in 1429 on an island of the same name in the White Sea. It went to the side of the Old Belief, and was the first case of armed resistance to the Nikonian reforms. Its challenge to the authority of the patriarch and tsar lasted from 1667 to 1676, when it was recaptured by Muscovite troops. The Bolsheviks abolished the monastery in 1920 and turned it into one of their first concentration camps. Konovets is an island on Lake Ladoga (in the Olonets Province; thus "Korel'skii," i.e., "Karelian") with a revered monastery founded in 1393 (now a ruin being restored by the Orthodox Church). Sarov, in the province of Tambov, was the site of a monastery associated with the life and "spiritual victory" *(podvig)* of Saint Serafim (1759–1833), whose much-venerated relics were kept there. The Bolsheviks dissolved it and the neighboring convent of Diveevo in the 1920s; both are now being reconstructed. The saint's relics were returned to the Church in 1991.

38. As the adherents of the Old Belief rejected the authority of the official Church, it forbade them the practice of all religious rites, including having a clerical hierarchy, priests, and processions of the cross, using bells, and so on.

39. Robert O. Crummey has written a study of the Old Believer community on the Vyg River (in the province of Olonets), one of the focal points of their belief, *The Vyg Community and the Russian State, 1694–1855* (Madison: University of Wisconsin Press, 1970). The community was disbanded by the authorities in 1855. The sect of the so-called flagellants *(khlysty;* the name, which they never used for themselves, is probably a corruption of *khristy* or *khristovtsy,* as they believed their leaders to be "Christs"; they called themselves "people of God" [*lyudi Bozhii*]), like that of the even more violent castrators *(skoptsy),* intrigued many of the Russian modernists, Bal'mont and Bely among them, especially their "orgiastic" songs (in which Vyacheslav Ivanov saw echoes of the ancient Dionysian rites). Kuzmin imitated them in one poem entitled "Khlstovskaya" (1916) in the "Russian Paradise" cycle of *Vozhatyi (S,* 327–328). Government persecution of both the Old Believers and their sectarian offshoots made them go underground or seek refuge from the authorities in the most remote and inaccessible parts of Russia. Thus Kuzmin's mention of "tundras without roads." "Fugitives" renders the Russian *beguny,* but cannot at all convey what Kuzmin has in mind. The term denotes an especially extreme sect which appeared in the late eighteenth century. They recognized no authority, secular or ecclesiastical, as they believed that the Antichrist already reigned on earth. They spent their lives in wandering, refused to carry money or identity papers (as both bore the seal of the Antichrist, that is, tsarist emblems), and were required to leave no trace of their existence at death: they were to be buried secretly so that their names could never fall into any registry. "Graves while alive" *(zazhivo mogily)* on distant river islands possibly alludes to a series of collective suicides in 1896–97 by Old Believers living on such islands in the Dnestr River.

40. "Vtoroi volnoyu / Perechislit' / Khotelos' mne ugodnikov / I mestnye

svyatyni, / Kakikh izobrazhayut / Na starykh obrazakh, / Dvumya, tremya i che-tyr'mya ryadami. // Molebnye ruki, / Ochi goré,—/ Kitezha zvuki / V zimnei zare. // Pechora, Kreml', lesa i Solovki, / I Konevets Korel'skii, sinii Sarov, / Drozdy, lisitsy, otroki, knyaz'ya, / I tol'ko russkaya yurodivykh sem'ya, / I derevenskii krug bogomolenii. // Kogda zhe oslabnet / Etot priliv, / Plyvet neistoshchimo / Drugoi, zapretnyi, / Bez krestnykh khodov, / Bez kolokolov, / Bez patriarkhov... / Dymyat-sya sruby, tundry bez dorog, / Do Vyga ne dobrat'sya politseiskim. / Podpol'niki, khlysty i beguny / I v dal'nikh plavnyakh zazhivo mogily. / Otverzhennaya, pres-vyataya rat' / Svobodnogo i Bozheskogo Dukha!" From "'A eto—khuliganskaya,'—skazala" (*S,* 471).

41. The letter provides, once again, an example of how directly Kuzmin would later borrow from his experience for *Kryl'ya.* Kuzmin lived with an Old Believer family named Sorokin in the summer, and they provided the models for and the actual name of the family with whom Vanya lives in the second part of the novel.

42. Vasily Kandinsky, *Complete Writings on Art,* ed. Kenneth C. Lindsay and Peter Vergo, vol. 1 (1901–1921; Boston: G. K. Hall, 1982), 369. Kuzmin owned several of Kandinsky's early works on Russian themes. He had received them as payment for his contribution to the famous *Der Blaue Reiter* almanac.

43. The "Dukhovnye stikhi" were written 1901–1903, but published only in 1912, first as song texts and music (where the dedication to his lover at the time, Vsevolod Knyazev, obscures the actual period of composition), and then as a cycle in *Osennie ozera* (*S,* 214–221).

44. The text of "Petya, vstavai, grachi prileteli!" can be found in *MK,* 70.

45. "Mir sostoit iz chetyrekh veshchei: / Iz vozdukha, ognya, vody, zemli ... / I chelovek, kak budto malyi mir, / Iz chetyrekh zhe sostoit stikhii: / Iz krovi, flegmy, krasnoi, chernoi zhelchi. / Krov'—vozdukh, krasna zhelch'—ogon', / Zhelch' cher-naya—zemlya, voda—to flegma. / I kazhdyi vozrast, kak i vremya goda, / Svoei stikhiei upravlyaet. . . . / Tak v cheloveke, budto v malom mire, / Krugovorot vse-lennoi mozhesh' videt'" (*MK,* 70–71). The texts and music of "Vremena zhizni" were partially published around 1914 under the title "S Volgi."

46. Kuzmin, *Pervaya kniga rasskazov,* 248.

47. Ibid., 240.

3. *"Will a New Russia Arise?"*

1. HE, 153.

2. The *Domostroi* (a loan translation of the Greek *oikonomikos*) was a didactic work of the sixteenth century on the "management of the household." By Kuzmin's time, it had become emblematic of the "reactionary" nature of pre-Petrine Russia.

3. Kuzmin, *Pervaya kniga rasskazov,* 263.

4. Kuzmin acknowledged the importance of the whole family for his develop-ment in an autobiographical statement: "G. V. Chicherin . . . and the Verkhovsky family, who were interested in the new Russian art, exerted an enormous influence on me." Yury Medvedev published the statement in "Blok i Kuzmin v arkhive P. N. Medvedeva," in *Vestnik russkogo khristianskogo dvizheniya,* 167 (I-1993), 178.

5. HE, 153. On August 25, 1905, Kuzmin's nephew showed him his parting letter to Bekhli: "How long ago that was! Do I still love him? Would I be glad were I to encounter him? Perhaps. But all that is like a dream" (Diary).

6. The list of Kuzmin's early musical compositions mentions another work dedicated to Bekhli: a setting of Lermontov's famous "Pesnya pro kuptsa Kalashnikova," written in May–July 1903.

7. See L. Ya. Dvornikova, "Avtor odnogo romana," in *Vstrechi s proshlym*, fasc. 4 (Moscow: Sovetskaya Rossiya, 1982), 107–111. She is incorrect in her assertion that with this Menzhinsky dropped fiction. He published at least two other prose pieces in the miscellany *Protalina*, vol. 1 (Petersburg, 1907), 86–103.

8. *Obrazovanie*, 1 (1905), 147 (second pagination).

9. *Voprosy zhizni*, 7 (1905), 215–16; reprinted in volume five (1962) of Blok, *Sobranie sochinenii v 8 tomakh*, 587. On August 29, 1903, Kuzmin wrote to Chicherin: "Just imagine, I have started to work on the text of an opera conceived in scenes. It is, perhaps, too fantastical, it is a kind of mix of D[on] Juan, Faust, the Magic Flute, Oberon, and even D[on] Quixote, but it has something of its own."

10. *Vesy*, 1 (1905), 67; reprinted in Valery Bryusov, *Sredi stikhov, 1894–1924: Manifesty, stat'i, retsenzii* (Moscow: Sovetskii pisatel', 1990), 134.

11. This does not mean that the sonnets, which are in *S*, 594–600, went completely unnoticed or unappreciated by contemporary readers. One of them, Count Boris Berg, by all accounts a connoisseur of Russian poetry, remembered them at the end of the 1920s: "What a pity that there is no complete edition of his poetry, and that his charming sonnets, which appeared in *The Green Collection*, are nowhere reprinted" ("'Ne zabyta i Pallada...': Iz vospominanii grafa B. O. Berga," publication of R. D. Timenchik in the "Literaturnoe prilozhenie," no. 11, xi, of the Paris Russian newspaper *Russkaya mysl'*, November 2, 1990, no. 3852). Curiously enough, the sonnets contain motifs, such as the beloved's "greenish eyes" *(zelenovatye glaza)* and the references to the Arthurian legends, that would resurface in Kuzmin's verse much later, in the 1920s. Bekhli really did have greenish eyes: "The dear eyes in my past . . . the greenish eyes of Alesha" (Diary, August 30, 1905).

12. HE, 154. In a 1913 autobiography he wrote, "Through the Verkhovsky and Chicherin families I got acquainted with the 'Evenings of Contemporary Music' and the people who were close to them" (Manuscript Division, IRLI, coll. 377, inven. 6, no. 1982).

13. See Boris Gornung, "Iz vospominanii o Mikh. Al. Kuzmine," in "Moskovskaya literaturnaya i filologicheskaya zhizn' 1920-kh godov: mashinopisnyi zhurnal 'Germes,'" published by M. O. Chudakova and A. B. Ustinov in *Pyatye tynyanovskie chteniya* (Riga: Zinatne, 1990), 181.

14. When, a decade later, Nikolay Klyuev and Sergey Esenin appeared in the capital's literary circles wearing garish folk costumes, they were very consciously exploiting their peasant origins and skillfully playing the fashionable role of "peasant-poets." This, of course, Kuzmin never did. In 1934, reminiscing about the early years of the century, he did remark that there had been "no little masquerade" involved in his wearing Russian dress, "especially if one takes into account my completely Western complex of predilections and tastes." He concluded, "Long before Klyuev, I had been an aesthetic Rasputin of sorts" (Diary, July 20, 1934). He also complimented the discernment of his friends in the World of Art who had been able both to accept him in that Russian guise and to see through the "masquerade."

15. In HE, 153, he drew conclusions about his artistic tastes in 1904: "A series of works, which I value always and in every form, finally defined itself. This is almost always the epic of the *Prolog* [a Synaxary, a book of saints' Lives arranged

according to the calendar of the Church year], folktales, novellas, *fabliaux*; Shakespeare, *Don Quixote*, Molière and French comedies, Pushkin, Leskov. In music I kept returning without fail to the old French and Italian composers and to Mozart." He mentions not a single contemporary either here or in the whole HE.

16. Znosko-Borovsky's assertion that Kuzmin meant to publish *Kryl'ya* in *Zelenyi sbornik*, but was prevented from doing so by the "cowardice" of the editors ("O tvorchestve M. Kuzmina," p. 31) requires correction. Kuzmin did, apparently, start work on the novel in 1904, and he may indeed have discussed it with the Verkhovsky family, only to have them reject it as unsuitable, although there is no evidence for that. He had by no means finished it by the end of the year. He always gave 1905 as the date of the composition of *Kryl'ya*. The pointedly homoerotic "moral" of the "Istoriya rytsarya d'Alessio," after all, had not shocked the Verkhovsky family. When, in the work's final scene, the hero, Astorre, appears in a temple reminiscent of Sarastro's in *Die Zauberflöte*, a voice asks who has made his soul "ardent and winged," so that he "thirsted after light?" The chorus replies: "A spirit youth [*dukh otrok*], a spirit pure, a spirit invisible, a spirit eternal touched his lips with a kiss, and his soul became ardent and winged, and the kisses of women became cloying" (p. 126).

Kuzmin assigned the date 1905–1908 to the "Aleksandriiskie pesni" when he published them in *Seti*, but one of them ("V Kanope zhizn' privol'naya"), in the section "Kanopskie pesenki" (*S*, 130), can be found in the second scene of the second act of the 1904 *Komediya iz aleksandriiskoi zhizni*. The play was first published in Kuzmin's collected *Teatr*, bk. 2, vol. 4 (Berkeley: Berkeley Slavic Specialties, 1995).

17. In a lecture delivered in Moscow on December 4, 1925, Nina Vol'kenau, who based her remarks on interviews with Kuzmin, talked about his "captivation by the 'Sturm und Drang,' Hoffmann, the first centuries of Christianity." She added: "The turbulent, romantic era of Elizabethan England is close to Kuzmin. As for French poetry, according to him, he finds it extremely alien in the period between Villon and Verlaine, except for Ronsard. In the French eighteenth century only Laclos and Cazotte managed to captivate him." G. A. Morev published the lecture in "K istorii yubileya M. A. Kuzmina 1925 goda," *Minuvshee*, 21 (1997), 363.

18. This interest, evident in Kuzmin's earliest letters to Chicherin, never flagged. As Kuzmin grew older, his focus shifted to later periods in Goethe's life. On March 24, 1920, he noted in the Diary: "Examining the chronology of Goethe's life, what he wrote at my age."

19. Kuzmin, *Uslovnosti*, 165, where Kuzmin, tellingly, compares Hamann with the Russian poet-eccentric of genius, Velimir Khlebnikov. See, too, Isaiah Berlin, *The Magus of the North: J. G. Hamann and the Origins of Modern Irrationalism* (London: John Murray, 1993), 69 (footnote 2).

20. H. A. Salmony, *Johann Georg Hamanns metakritische Philosophie, Band* 1 (Zollikon: Evangelischer Verlag, 1958), 15–16. We have relied heavily on this study and that of Berlin, who calls the prolixities of Hamann's style "appalling" (*Magus of the North*, 19).

21. One of the most famous lyrics in *Vozhatyi*, "Gospod', ya vizhu, ya nedostoin" (*S*, 308–309), could be compared to all these aspects of Hamann's writings.

22. See W. M. Alexander, *Johann Georg Hamann: Philosophy and Faith* (The Hague: Martinus Nijhoff, 1966), 181.

23. Our translation of the German cited in Arthur Wald, *The Aesthetic Theories of the German Storm and Stress Movement* (Chicago: University of Chicago Libraries, 1924), 19.

24. Kuzmin, *Pervaya kniga rasskazov*, 256.

25. Ibid., 317. Mori's remark and a similar one by the composer Ugo Orsini (p. 307) echo the opinions of Pausanius in Plato's *Symposium;* see *The Collected Dialogues of Plato*, ed. Edith Hamilton and Huntington Cairns, Bollingen Series 71 (Princeton: Princeton University Press, 1980), 535.

26. Berlin, *Magus of the North*, 100.

27. Kuzmin, *Pervaya kniga rasskazov*, 218–220.

28. See Walther Brecht, *Heinse und der ästhetische Immoralismus* (Berlin: Weidmannsche Buchhandlung, 1911).

29. Nietzsche, who saw Heinse as a predecessor, aroused not the slightest interest in Kuzmin, not even when he found himself in the milieu of the World of Art, which admired Nietzsche's cult of the superior individual and held up the creative being as the perfect examplar of the strong personality. Kuzmin's view on the subject never wavered. In a 1934 Diary entry he wrote: "In *Lohengrin*, not to speak of *Tristan*, there is more philosophy of love and philosophy in general than in any of Nietzsche's books. The latter thought that he was writing philosophy, but in fact he was simply indulging in stylistics."

30. See the preface to Henry Hatfield, *Aesthetic Paganism in German Literature, from Winckelmann to the Death of Goethe* (Cambridge, Mass.: Harvard University Press, 1964).

31. Kuzmin, *Pervaya kniga rasskazov*, 204. Kuzmin echoed the thought in 1906 when he ordered a new bookplate with a representation of a male figure plucking fruit from a tree and with the inscription "Eritis sicut dei" ("Ye shall be as gods," Genesis 3:5). His previous *ex libris* had born a bouquet of flowers and the very Hamannian sentiment "Mieux être que paraître" ("Better to be than to seem"). See U. G. Ivask, *Opisanie russkikh knizhnikh znakov (Ex-Libris)*, fasc. 2 (Moscow: M. Ya. Paradelov, 1910), 67.

32. Kuzmin, *Pervaya kniga rasskazov*, 286–287. The remark paraphrases something Chicherin had written to Kuzmin on January 25, 1903: "Worlds will collapse, and an end will come to Phidias and Mozart, but what will have no end, what will not yield to time—that is true beauty, the ambrosial nature of Phidias, Mozart, and—you."

33. A. P. Ostroumova-Lebedeva, *Avtobiograficheskie zapiski*, vol. 1 (Moscow: Izobrazitel'noe iskusstvo, 1974), 169; Vladimir Pyast, *Vstrechi* (Moscow: Federatsiya, 1929), 100.

34. HE, 154. By 1912 Kuzmin had had enough of Nouvel's meddling in his private affairs and kept him at a distance. He never, however, lost his old affection for him: "I ran into Valechka, who exclaimed 'Misha'! And he really gladdened my heart, as he reminded me of so much, so much" (Diary, May 29, 1915).

35. See the article by Kuzmin, "Chekhov i Chaikovsky," first published in *Zi*, no. 1, October 29, 1918, 4, and republished in *Uslovnosti*, 144–147.

36. Stravinsky met Kuzmin at Nouvel's apartment, where, he recalled, the two friends often performed piano duets. See Igor Stravinsky and Robert Craft, *Dialogues and a Diary* (Garden City, N.Y.: Doubleday and Company, 1963), 72.

37. Kuzmin, *Uslovnosti*, 87. Kuzmin singled out the "comedies of Goldoni and

the theater of Gozzi, the writings of Restif de la Bretonne and English novels, the paintings of Longhi and the illustrations of Chodowiecki" as exemplary for the time.

38. Igor Stravinsky, *Poetics of Music in the Form of Six Lessons* (Cambridge, Mass.: Harvard University Press, 1970), 157.

39. Typical of the time were the remarks Diaghilev made at a dinner given in his honor on March 24, 1905, in Moscow: "We are living in a terrible time of crisis, we are fated to die. . . . We are the witnesses of the greatest historical moment of summing up and terminations in the name of a new, unknown culture which will arise because of us, but which will then surely sweep us away." Sergey Dyagilev, "V chas itogov," *Vesy,* 4 (1905), 46; reprinted in *Sergey Dyagilev i russkoe iskusstvo,* vol. 1 (Moscow: Izobrazitel'noe iskusstvo, 1982), 193–194.

40. On September 6, 1905, he noted only, "Can it be that not a year has passed since January 9," but in a context which suggests that the event had profoundly shaken the stability of his world.

41. HE, 154.

42. The initials A. B. figure in sonnets five and seven of the "Sonety" (*S,* 607–614). The homoerotic element is much more explicit in them than in the thirteen earlier sonnets.

43. The composer and music critic Boris Asaf'ev, writing under his usual pseudonym, Igor' Glebov, praised Kuzmin for the "integrity" of the opera's conception and for its "mastery" of dialogue and style. See his "Muzyka v tvorchestve M. A. Kuzmina," *Zi,* no. 580, October 12, 1920, 1.

44. Even though Kuzmin's work is set in ancient Rome, not Greece, he may have borrowed the hero's name from Wilhelm Adolf Becker's very popular *Charikles: Bilder altgriechischer Sitte: Zur genaueren Kenntniss des griechischen Privatsleben* (Leipzig: F. Fleischer, 1840). It was republished many times, and was widely translated. The "zweiter Excurs zur fünften Scene" deals with "Die Knabenliebe." English translations of Becker's work left out the section. Kuzmin could also have taken the name from the second-century A.D. Alexandrian Greek novel *The Adventures of Leucippe and Cleitophon* by Achilles Tatius. In one section Cleitophon meets a young man, Clinias, who has inadvertently killed his lover, Charicles. A discussion of same-sex love follows. Kuzmin knew both works, and later returned to the theme of "Charicles"—a conspiracy against an emperor interwoven with the love story of the gay hero, all of it redolent of magic and sorcery—in *Rimskie chudesa.*

45. HE, 149.

46. Kuzmin never intimated to anyone that their friendship had ever amounted to anything other than a close familial tie. The Diary, too, supports this. On September 14, 1905, for example, he wrote: "Varya [his sister] heatedly attacked the ideological tendency of my story [*Wings*] . . . as though she fears my influence on Serezha. In that regard she has no grounds at all for worry."

47. Letter of November 22, 1852, in Gustave Flaubert, *Correspondance,* 3rd series (1852–1854) (Paris: Conard, 1927), 53–54. On August 27, 1905, Kuzmin wrote in the Diary: "I can hardly wait . . . to live as much as possible in an ivory tower in elegant solitude."

48. See Joan Neuberger, *Hooliganism: Crime, Culture, and Power in St. Petersburg, 1900–1914* (Berkeley: University of California Press, 1993). Kuzmin's attraction to the iconoclastic energies of "hooligans" continued into 1906. He met a few

at the shop of Kazakov and at the Tavricheskii Garden, and his occasional carousing with some of them got him into a street brawl in June 1906, when he was beaten up. On June 5, 1906, he looked at his bruised face and exclaimed, "Poor Antinous, how dearly you've paid for your acquaintance with rowdies!" (Diary).

49. The Russian Assembly, founded in 1901, was one of the earliest organizations of the extreme Right. Originally an upper-class society for the dissemination of information about Russian achievements in the arts and sciences, it was by 1905 engaged in nationalistic and monarchist propaganda to oppose revolutionary agitation. It enjoyed some popularity among ultraconservative groups in the universities. Boris Nikol'sky, who had been an advocate of individual anarchism and of Nietzschean contempt for the herd in the 1890s (when he for a time exerted some influence on Chicherin), taught literature at Petersburg University, and himself wrote verse and translated. (Blok made his poetic debut in 1903 in a collection of student poems that Nikol'sky edited and published.) An outspoken anti-Semite, he joined the Russian Assembly in 1903, becoming one of its leaders and, in the years after 1905, a prominent spokesman for the extreme Right. Nikol'sky was executed by the Petrograd Cheka for counterrevolutionary activities in 1919.

50. Somov participated in the founding of one of the leading anti-tsarist satirical magazines that sprang up in those months and gave it its name, *Zhupel* (Bugbear). Nurok, Lancéray, and other World of Art members also took part in it and other similar magazines. In December 1905 Somov wrote to Benois: "I cannot give myself up heart and soul and, most important, with some kind of deed, to the revolutionary movement that has gripped Russia, because I am madly in love with beauty first and foremost and want to serve it; . . . I am an individualist, the whole world revolves around my 'I,' and in essence I don't give a damn about anything that goes beyond its limits and its narrow confines." K. A. Somov, *Pis'ma: Dnevniki: Suzhdeniya sovremennikov* (Moscow: Iskusstvo, 1979), 89.

51. The *oprichniki* were an administrative elite established by Ivan IV in 1565 as a private bodyguard and a force to assert his control over an old noble class of boyars which was resisting his increasingly authoritarian rule. They became symbols in Russian history of lawless cruelty. The young worker was doing much the same thing as someone shouting "Cossacks!" at mounted police patrolling a protest rally in the West, but he could, of course, hardly shout that at the real thing.

52. Kuzmin's views here, like the attraction he expressed on October 18 to the monarchist cause because it had been lost, recall *avant la lettre* Marina Tsvetaeva's attitude toward the Whites in her poetic cycle "Lebedinyi stan" (1917–1920).

53. G. S. Khrustalev-Nosar', a prominent lawyer and Menshevik, president of the Petersburg Soviet of Workers' Deputies. He had been arrested by order of Witte on November 26, an action marking the beginning of the end of the 1905 Revolution. He was the son of a peasant and was not Jewish.

54. Leonid Seleznev published a portion of this passage in a brief note entitled "Vstupal li Mikhail Kuzmin v 'Soyuz russkogo naroda'?" *Literaturnoe obozrenie*, 3–4 (1992), 110–111. Lev Erman was the first to assert that Kuzmin had joined the organization (see his *Intelligentsiya v pervoi russkoi revolyutsii* [Moscow: Nauka, 1966], 164), but he offered no evidence for the assertion. There the matter rested until *glasnost'* allowed Kuzmin to be published again in Russia. When Sergey Kunyaev, an odious ultranationalist ideologue, again made the assertion in the introduction to his highly tendentious selection of Kuzmin's lyrics published in Yaroslavl' in

1989 (with its notes based, without acknowledgment, on the Munich edition of Kuzmin's collected verse), it provoked a lively controversy both because Kunyaev offered no proof and because he was clearly trying, as it were, to enlist Kuzmin in his own ideological cause. Seleznev outlines the whole matter in his article.

55. The only subsequent mention occurs on May 23, 1906: "[Vyacheslav Ivanov] advised me to go to Moscow to meet Polyakov [who financed *Libra*], that he, a reader of *Moscow Gazette* [Moskovskie vedomosti], and I, a member of the 'Union of the Russian People,' decadents and exquisites, might hit it off. He said that I am *inaccessible* [he uses the French], *supérieur*, calm, disdainful—I didn't believe my ears." Kuzmin obviously had not hidden his action from Ivanov and his wife, even though they had taken a very leftist position during the events of 1905, and Ivanov himself had worked for the radical satirical magazine *Adskaya pochta*.

56. On October 31, while dining with the Chicherins, he had been told that somewhere there was a "merchant, a butcher, something like Minin" (Diary). That, of course, was entirely a fiction, but throughout November he kept hoping to find his address. Kuz'ma Minin, a butcher from Nizhnii-Novgorod, had helped organize the Russian army that drove the Poles from Muscovy in the early seventeenth century during the so-called Time of Troubles.

57. Early in March 1906 he accompanied his brother-in-law on a short business trip to the provinces. On the eighth, one of Moshkov's Jewish customers, a man named Gel'man, invited them to lunch with him and his family: "I don't remember a more vile (precisely vile) impression in my whole life. I did not imagine that the thought that I was a guest of Jews and was eating, eating with them, could so disturb and depress me. And eating is such an intimate matter, that I can understand the old rule about not dining with people of a different faith. . . . Everything seemed alien to me" (Diary). Fourteen years later he would be only too happy to dine with his Jewish publisher, with whose family he loved to spend long evenings. Even then he would on occasion remark "peculiar" Jewish ways of some of his Jewish friends, of whom he had many.

4. Buoyant Days

1. A remark by one of his friends may have prompted the reference to Casanova. On September 22, 1905, six days after he had shaved off his beard and moustache, much to the dismay of his Old Believer friends (Kazakov "flipped his lid" [*ochumel*]), he wrote, "When, in the evening, Mme. Kostrits found that I resemble Casanova or Cagliostro, that was the highest possible praise for me" (Diary). Kuzmin's nickname in the circle of Vyacheslav Ivanov was "the abbé"; it probably derived from this self-description, as Kuzmin may have read this part of the Diary to them.

2. In a Diary entry for September 7, 1905, Kuzmin wrote that he was "repelled" by "Dostoevskyism [*Dostoevshchina*], psychosis, lacerating emotion . . . darkness, insanity, suicide . . . everything that is coarse, dark, filthy, and tragic in its absurdity." Boris Asaf'ev observed, "Music exerts a pull on Kuzmin when it is modest, crystally clear, sunny (in a Mozartian way), when it does not lay bare, impudently and brazenly, the shame of the lusts of the human heart, does not seethe with passion" ("Muzyka v tvorchestve M. A. Kuzmina," 1).

3. There were no further readings because of the rapid deterioration of the political situation.

4. JEM examines at length the critical and popular reaction to the novel in "Bathhouses, Hustlers, and Sex Clubs: The Reception of Mikhail Kuzmin's *Wings*," *Journal of the History of Sexuality*, in press.

5. *Pereval*, 6 (1907), 51. Bely wrote that the "vulgarian Shtrup tempts the unhappy young hero with *muzhelozhstvo* [anal intercourse]," and that until he succeeds in his corruption has "to satisfy his sexual needs with a bathhouse attendant." Bely had kinder things to say about the "Alexandrian Songs," and did admit that Kuzmin had talent.

6. Blok, "O drame," 185.

7. André Gide, *Corydon* (New York: Farrar, Straus, 1950), 107.

8. Kuzmin, *Pervaya kniga rasskazov*, 321.

9. The poem "Kochevniki krasoty" first appeared in Ivanov's second collection of verse, *Prozrachnost'* (Moscow: Skorpion, 1904). He took the title from Gide's *Le Traité du Narcisse* (1891).

10. Donald C. Gillis has discussed the Platonic aspect of the novel in "The Platonic Theme in Kuzmin's *Wings*," *Slavic and East European Journal*, 22, no. 3 (1978), 336–47. Gide, too, pointed in the direction of Plato by casting *Corydon* in the form of a dialogue, but Kuzmin's utopian view of same-sex love has nothing in common with Gide's Darwinian defense of it.

11. Chicherin invents his "isms" from two common expressions, one French ("Revenons à nos moutons"—literally, "Let's get back to our sheep," that is, "Let's get back to our subject") and one Russian ("Vot gde sobaka zaryta"—literally, "That's where the dog is buried," that is, "That's the heart of the matter!").

12. Introduction to *Pesn' pesnei: V stikhotvornom perelozhenii s bibleiskogo teksta perevel Lev Yaroshevsky: Pod red. M. Kuzmina* (Petrograd: Sirius, 1917), 5. After reading the "Chansons" in February 1897, Kuzmin told Chicherin that he found "not a drop of the spirit of antiquity" in them, and he dismissed the work as a whole with "[the] piquancies are disgraceful." The question of Louÿs's impact and that of other French writers on the "Aleksandriiskie pesni" remains a matter for future study. Kuzmin admired Debussy's setting of several of the "Chansons," and in 1907 wrote, "The forerunner [*predtecha*, the Russian used for John the Baptist] of new music has already appeared, and his name is Claude Debussy." "Moskva i Peterburg," *Luch*, 4 (1907), 21.

13. Ya. Platek's article about Kuzmin as a musician and composer does not address the issue at all. "Radost' prostoty," *Muzykal'naya zhizn'*, nos. 20–23 (1989). Several of the poems were later set to music by composers other than Kuzmin.

14. See Bryusov's review of Kuzmin's *Priklyucheniya Eme Lebefa* and *Tri p'esy* in *Vesy*, 7 (1907), 80–81. He belittled Louÿs's "Chansons," and wrote that "no one among contemporary Russian writers has such a control of style" as Kuzmin (p. 81).

15. Probably A. H. Sayce, ed., *Records of the Past: Being English Translations of the Ancient Monuments of Egypt and Western Asia*, new series, vols. 1–6 (London: S. Bagster and Sons, 1888–1892). Kuzmin might also have known the earlier Samuel Birch, ed., *Records of the Past: Being English Translations of the Assyrian and Egyptian Monuments*, vols. 1–12 (London: S. Bagster and Sons, 1874–1881). Both were issued "under the sanction of the Society of Biblical Archaeology."

16. Morev, "K istorii yubileya M. A. Kuzmina 1925 goda," 364–365. Vol'kenau explored the connections between several of the "Pesni" and passages in *Records of the Past*.

17. On June 1, 1925, Kuzmin recalled that at the time he was writing the "Aleksandriiskie pesni" he had been "full of a European and modernist spirit, which somehow was associated for me with D'Annunzio" (Diary).

18. Letter of September 5, 1905. In 1929 Chicherin acquired a German edition of the "Aleksandriiskie pesni," and wrote to his brother that "they have made an even deeper impression on me than 30 years ago. The style is miniature, but how dense, rich, sharp, subtle, and elegant. . . . They are completely contemporary." Published in the appendix to Chicherin's *Motsart: Issledovatel'skii etyud*, 2nd ed. (Leningrad: Muzyka, 1971), 264.

19. Karatygin's article about the "Evenings" in *Vesy*, 3–4 (1906), 70–74, noted a generally hostile public reaction to the "Pesni" at the concert, but he gave an admiring, if not uncritical, appraisal of Kuzmin's music. "They sent me *Libra*, I am listed among the contributors; some more or less sharp, but, in my opinion, flattering lines are devoted to me in Karatygin's article about the 'E[venings] of C[ontemporary] M[usic]'" (Diary, March 31, 1906).

20. See the memoirs of Ivanov's daughter: Lidiya Ivanova, *Vospominaniya: Kniga ob ottse*, ed. JEM (Paris: Atheneum, 1990; Moscow: RIK, "Kul'tura," 1992), and a "biography" of the building in which the apartment was located, Aleksandr Kobak and Dmitry Severyukhin, "'Bashnya' na Tavricheskoi (biografiya doma)," *Dekorativnoe iskusstvo*, 1 (1987), 35–39, with excellent photographs of its exterior and its eclectic interior design.

21. See a fragment of her letter to M. M. Zamyatnina of April 3, 1906, quoted in *Literaturnoe nasledstvo*, vol. 92, *Aleksandr Blok: Novye materialy i issledovaniya*, bk. 3 (Moscow: Nauka: 1982), 243.

22. *Literaturnoe nasledstvo*, vol. 98, *Valery Bryusov i ego korrespondenty*, bk. 2 (Moscow: Nauka, 1994), 109.

23. Kuzmin well appreciated the magazine's meaning for his own career and Russian culture: "As I looked through *Libra* at the same time as *Mercure de France*, I noticed the whole importance and the cultural significance for Russian literature of the first magazine" (Diary, July 23, 1907).

24. To Bryusov belongs the dubious honor of having applied to Kuzmin's verse the phrase of Musset that became a French saying: "Mon verre n'est pas grand, mais je bois dans mon verre." The phrase appears in the verse dedication that precedes Musset's dramatic poem "La coupe et les lèvres" (1832). Bryusov used it in a brief notice about *Seti* that he included in his book of critical essays, *Dalekie i blizkie* (Moscow: Skorpion, 1912).

25. In 1923, on the occasion of the commemoration of Bryusov's fiftieth birthday, Kuzmin paid him a graceful tribute: "I think that the pose of magus that he assumed at one time was only a pose, but Bryusov is an enchanter, as only a few of the talented are, and I personally will always remember with tender gratitude the reception my first steps met from this poet." *Teatr*, 12 (December 18, 1923), 1. The obituary-article that Kuzmin published in *Zi*, 43 (1924), 2–3, was no less generous.

26. On April 18, 1906, Kuzmin wrote in the Diary: "Rarely does a person make such a charming impression as does Somov; all his gestures, words, works are so harmonious, so subtle, so dear, that the very sound 'Somov' is somehow telling."

27. In April 1906 Zinov'eva-Annibal wrote to M. M. Zamyatnina about the "striking Alexandrian, poet, and novelist Kuzmin—an altogether unusual phenomenon, with the quiet poison of elegant things half said, who is preparing a new future for life, art, and the whole erotic psyche of humanity" (Manuscript Division, Russian State Library [Rossiiskaya gosudarstvennaya biblioteka], Moscow; hereafter RGB, coll. 109, box 23, item 18).

28. In mid-May 1906 Zinov'eva-Annibal wrote to Zamyatnina: "For inspiration we have the Persian Hafiz, where wisdom, poetry, love, and sex were all mixed together, and the Cupbearer is a handsome young man, like a woman, who inspired the poet and inflamed his heart" (Manuscript Division, RGB, coll. 109, box 23, item 19). "Cupbearer" renders *kravchii*, a special rank at the medieval Russian court held by a boyar who supervised the ruler's table, including bearing his cup. The "Hafiz-ites" used it exclusively for the young man who was meant to pour wine at the gatherings.

29. For more detailed information about the circle, see NAB, "Peterburgskie Gafizity," in *Mikhail Kuzmin: Stat'i i materialy* (Moscow: Novoe literaturnoe obozrenie, 1995), 67–98.

30. Ivanov's diary, as published in his *Sobranie sochinenii*, vol. 2 (Brussels: Foyer Oriental Chrétien, 1974), 748. In a letter of February 17, 1907, to Zamyatnina, Zinov'eva-Annibal summarized Ivanov's remarks at one of the "Wednesdays" when the topic of discussion had been "The New Path of Eros": "There is no longer either ethics or aesthetics—both come down to eroticism, and every audacity born of Eros is sacred" (Manuscript Division, RGB, coll. 109, box 23, item 20).

31. Ivanov was himself infatuated with Gorodetsky at the time, and wanted to create with him a relationship in life, not theory, that would work out the Platonic model of Eros. See Pamela Davidson, *The Poetic Imagination of Vyacheslav Ivanov* (Cambridge: Cambridge University Press, 1989), 112–119.

32. Ivanov's diary, as published in the Brussels *Sobranie sochinenii*, 2:749–750. Ivanov made a marginal note about what sections Kuzmin read, so we know that he had pulled no punches, even reading parts describing his visits to the baths and his sexual encounters there. Of the June 13 reading Kuzmin wrote: "I read the Diary. . . . Vyach. Iv. not only spoke about the artistic side, but was not put off by the contents either and even agreed that it is chaste" (Diary).

33. Kuzmin wrote *Kuranty lyubvi* between October and December 8, 1906. It came out in a luxurious book, with the score and illustrations by Sergey Sudeikin and Nikolay Feofilaktov, in Moscow in November 1910 ("Skorpion"). Kuzmin performed the vocal-instrumental cycle many times, and it was at least twice mounted as a play.

34. When Kuzmin saw the frontispiece for the first time on January 15, 1907, he called it "boring," adding that it "for some reason or other unpleasantly recalls a figure in an anatomical textbook" (Diary). He said nothing to Somov about his misgivings, and when he received the first copy on May 22, he wrote, "It has come out very elegantly" (Diary).

35. It received its first performance in 1910 at a program given by Mariya Vedrinskaya, an actress at the Aleksandrinskii Theater. Auslender reviewed it in *Apollon*, 7 (1910), 52 (second pagination).

36. In the beginning of May 1908, Kuzmin was fined two hundred rubles or a month in prison for the *Tri p'esy*, a huge sum considering that, as usual, he was

penniless. Vyacheslav Ivanov gave moral support. Kuzmin would have preferred money. *Opasnaya predostorozhnost'* was apparently never staged, but *Dva pastukha* was performed in 1910 and 1916.

37. "Gde slog naidu, chtob opisat' progulku, / Shabli vo l'du, podzharennuyu bulku / I vishen spelykh sladostnyi agat?" (*S*, 59).

38. "Tvoi nezhnyi vzor, lukavyi i manyashchii,—/ Kak milyi vzdor komedii zven-yashchei / Il' Marivo kapriznoe pero. / Tvoi nos P'ero i gub razrez p'yanyashchii / Mne kruzhit um, kak 'Svad'ba Figaro'" (ibid.).

39. "Nashi maski ulybalis', / Nashi vzory ne vstrechalis', / I usta nashi nemy." From "Umyvalis', odevalis'" (*S*, 61).

40. "Zachem luna, podnyavshis', rozoveet, / I veter veet, teploi negi poln, / I cheln ne chuet zmeinoi zybi voln, / Kogda moi dukh vsë o tebe goveet?" (*S*, 62).

41. Vladimir Markov suggested a similar "tripartite" reading of *Seti* in his "Poeziya Mikhaila Kuzmina" (*SS*, 3:329–331). M. L. Gasparov analyzes the third part of the book in the article "Khudozhestvennyi mir pisatelya: tesaurus formal'nyi i tesaurus funktsional'nyi (M. Kuzmin, 'Seti,' ch. III)," in *Problemy strukturnoi lingvistiki, 1984* (Moscow: Nauka, 1988), 125–137.

42. Letter of May 30, 1907, Manuscript Division, RGB, coll. 386, box 91, item 12.

43. Blok, "O drame," 184. Blok had not at first liked the play when Kuzmin read an excerpt to him, but on April 3, 1907, when he read it aloud to Somov and Blok while the painter worked on his famous portrait of the latter, he reported: "I read *Eudoxia*, Somov liked it a lot, and so now does Blok" (Diary).

44. This tiresome polemic that for a time divided the Symbolist camp can be followed in the notes to the Bryusov-Ivanov correspondence in *Literaturnoe nasled-stvo*, vol. 85, *Valery Bryusov* (Moscow: Nauka, 1976). It is fairly summarized by William Richardson in *Zolotoe runo and Russian Modernism: 1905–1910* (Ann Arbor: Ardis, 1986), 117–129, and by Avril Pyman in *A History of Russian Symbolism* (Cambridge: Cambridge University Press, 1994), 278–281.

45. The three "religious comedies," written between March 1907 and June 1908, were published by "Oraea" at the end of 1908 as *Komedii*. The printers introduced an error into the subtitle of *O Aleksee:* "obrashchennyi" (converted) instead of the correct "obretennyi" (found).

46. Remizov, *Plyashushchii demon*, 42.

47. Pyast probably met Kuzmin on Sunday September 3, 1906, Kuzmin's first visit to Sologub's. Kuzmin wrote only this in the Diary: "At Sologub's Bely, Pyast, and Sologub himself read poems. . . . Upstairs I read my new poems. I don't know if anyone liked them. Vyach[eslav] Iv[anovich] assures me that Sologub liked them."

48. "Esli zavtra budet solntse, / My vo F'ezole poedem; / Esli zavtra budet dozhd', / To karetu my voz'mem. // Esli ty menya polyubish', / Ya tebe s vostorgom veryu; / Esli ne zakhoches' ty, / To druguyu my naidem." We cite the text not from Pyast's memoir (*Vstrechi*, 112–113), but from the sheet music (no date, but after 1911) issued by the Petersburg firm of Nikolay Davingof, which published most of Kuzmin's music. The gender of "somebody else" is marked in Russian. The text of the sheet music (and Pyast) gives the feminine accusative form (*druguyu*), whereas autographs have the masculine accusative form (*drugogo*).

49. On February 23, 1906, he learned from Nouvel that the "young Moscow artists Feofilaktov, Kuznetsov, Milioti, Sapunov [all to be associated with the "Blue

Rose" group] have become wildly enthusiastic about my music, and Feofilaktov thinks it possible to persuade Polyakov to publish the scores with his, Feofilaktov's, vignettes" (Diary).

50. Kuzmin's reminiscences of Sapunov, as published in *N. Sapunov: Stikhi, vospominaniya, kharakteristika* (Moscow: N. N. Karyshev, 1916), 47.

51. During the affair, Sudeikin began work on Kuzmin's portrait, which was apparently never completed. Kuzmin described it in the poem "Moi portret" as "Lyubov' vodila Vasheyu rukoyu, / Kogda pisali etot Vy portret" ("Love guided your hand when you painted this portrait" [*S*, 67]). "Sudeikin made the sketch, he will paint the portrait without me; very dark, *en face*, a wreath behind my head, two silver angels in the depths" (Diary, October 30, 1906). The first two lines of the poem's third stanza read: "Venok za golovoi, otkryty guby, / Dva angela naprasnykh za spinoi" ("A wreath behind [my] head, lips open, / two idle angels behind my back"). On February 7, 1915, Sudeikin did another portrait, in pencil, of Kuzmin in profile; see Irina Kravtsova, "Zabytyi portret M. Kuzmina," *Novoe literaturnoe obozrenie*, 3 (1993), 130–133.

52. The complete text of the story was published for the first time (not altogether accurately) in volume eight of Kuzmin's collected *Proza* (1990). The English translation of the first eleven chapters in the *Selected Prose and Poetry* mistakenly renders the title as "The House of Cards." *Kartonnyi domik* can mean that, but in the story and the poem cycle the man with whom the hero is in love gives him a "little cardboard house" before leaving him. On December 1, 1906, Sudeikin, whose mysterious comings and goings had kept Kuzmin in a state of constant anxiety in late November, left Kuzmin just such a present.

53. Manuscript Division, RGB, coll. 371, box 4, item 6.

54. One reviewer, signing himself "K. L.," assumed that the story was autobiographical ("Kuzmin . . . writes a little chronicle of several days in his private life"), and wrote that Kuzmin described the events with the kind of "simplicity and sincerity" that others might find difficult to muster even in the most private diary. See *Pereval*, 10 (1907), 53. A notice in *Zolotoe runo*, 5 (1907), 78, also pointed out the autobiographical dimension. The tabloid press savaged both works for their "pornography," as Kuzmin repeatedly reports in the Diary. The titles of two pieces on *Kryl'ya* and "Kartonnyi domik" by Vladimir Botsyanovsky, literary editor of the newspaper *Rus'*, make their contents clear: "V al'kove g. Kuzmina" ("In Mr. Kuzmin's Alcove," where "alcove" intimates a whorehouse and the baths), *Rus'*, no. 160, June 22, 1907, and "O 'grecheskoi' lyubvi" ("On 'Greek' Love"), *Rus'*, no. 170, July 2, 1907, 2. In both, Botsyanovsky blamed the appearance of "pornography" in Russian literature on translations from western European literature and native "ricochets" of their influence. Parodies of both works immediately followed their publication.

55. All the names of the principal characters are deciphered in *MK*, 116. There is a linguistic link between the name Myatlev and Sudeikin, as Marina Kostalevskaya pointed out to JEM after his lecture at Yale in the autumn of 1994: "Myatlev" is clearly related to the Old Russian *myatel'nik*, a judicial rank, while "Sudeikin" obviously points to the modern Russian word for judge (*sud'ya*). Only someone with Kuzmin's excellent knowledge of Slavonic and Old Russian would have been likely, however, to make the connection at the time. The "camouflage" of Sudeikin's identity was quite safe.

56. For the letter and several other instances of Kuzmin's appropriation of the Diary's life in the story, see *MK*, 117–118, and JEM, "Mikhail Kuzmin and the Autobiographical Imperative," *Slavonica*, 4/2 (1998), 7–27.

57. Someone (either Glebova-Sudeikina herself or possibly Akhmatova) told Eliane Moch-Bickert that Glebova only learned about the affair later, when she read Kuzmin's Diary, and that this led to the breakup of her marriage. See Eliane Moch-Bickert, "Olga Glebova-Soudeikina, amie et inspiratrice des poètes" (diss., Paris, 1972), 49 (an expanded Russian translation appeared in Petersburg in 1993). It is a nice self-serving story totally unsupported by the facts of letters and the Diary (and Kuzmin never gave his Diary to friends to read; he read to them from it). Sudeikin left his wife, not the other way around, as M. V. Tolmachev showed in a meticulously documented paper (read in May 1990 at a conference in what was still Leningrad devoted to "Kuzmin and Russian Culture of the Twentieth Century"), when he finally lost all patience with her behavior, which he found licentious even by the standards of their circle. Unfortunately, both Robert Craft, in the preface to his *Stravinsky: Glimpses of a Life* (New York: St. Martin's Press, 1992), and John Bowlt, in the notes to *The Salon Album of Vera Sudeikin-Stravinsky* (Princeton: Princeton University Press, 1995), have repeated Glebova's fabrication and further elaborations on it. Kuzmin did share an apartment with the couple for five months, from July 31, 1912, to January 1913, but he had no physical relationship with Sudeikin then (or ever after they broke up in 1906), and he left their apartment of his own volition; see Chapter 8.

58. Woloschin, *Die grüne Schlange*, 178.

59. "Vy i ya, i tolstaya dama, / Tikhon'ko zatvorivshi dveri, / Udalilis' ot obshchego gama. // Ya igral Vam svoi 'Kuranty', / Pominutno skripeli dveri, / Prikhodili modnitsy i franty. // Ya ponyal Vashikh glaz nameki, / I my vmeste vyshli za dveri, / I vse nam vdrug stali daleki. // U royalya tolstaya dama ostalas', / Franty stadom tolpilis' u dveri, / Tonkaya modnitsa gromko smeyalas'. // My vzoshli po lestnitse temnoi, / Otvorili znakomye dveri, / Vasha ulybka stala bolee tomnoi. // Zanavesilis' lyubov'yu ochi, / Uzhe drugie my zaperli dveri ... / Esli b chashche byvali takie nochi!" "Na vechere" (*S*, 68–69).

60. "Kak lyublyu ya steny posyrevshie / Belogo zritel'nogo zala." "V teatre" (*S*, 68). The contemporary was Evgeny Znosko-Borovsky, *Russkii teatr nachala XX veka* (Prague: Plamya, 1925), 271.

61. The actress Valentina Verigina describes the reading and the whole first season in her "Vospominaniya ob Aleksandre Bloke," in *Aleksandr Blok v vospominaniyakh sovremennikov*, vol. 1 (Moscow: Khudozhestvennaya literatura, 1980), 412–413.

62. See Kuzmin's letter to Meyerhold of December 3, 1906, in "Perepiska M. A. Kuzmina i V. E. Meierkhol'da 1906–1933," published by P. V. Dmitriev in *Minuvshee*, 20 (1996), 341. Kuzmin seems to have received no commission (or a very minimal one) for the music; see letter of December 22 (pp. 345–346). According to the Diary, Kuzmin at first regretted his acceptance when he had a lot of trouble with the score, and he would have preferred that Sudeikin be asked to do the designs. When he heard it performed in orchestration at a rehearsal, however, he was pleased with his result. Some of the music was included as an appendix to Blok's *Liricheskie dramy* (Petersburg: Shipovnik, 1908), 163–170.

63. Chulkov, *Gody stranstvii*, 221.

64. For contemporary reactions to the play and first performance, see the notes in volume four (1961) of Blok, *Sobranie sochinenii v 8 tomakh*, 567–571; Verigina, "Ob Aleksandre Bloke," 424–427; *Literaturnoe nasledstvo*, vol. 92, bk. 3, 264–266.

65. The first performance of the play, called *Pramater'* in Blok's translation, took place at the end of January 1909.

66. Verigina, "Ob Aleksandre Bloke," 430. She alludes to imagery from the poems in Blok's *Snezhnaya maska*.

67. A. M. Remizov, *Kukha: Rozanovy pis'ma* (Berlin: Izdatel'stvo Z. I. Grzhebina, 1923), 106. Stravinsky, in a communication to JEM, recalled his astonishment at first seeing Kuzmin at a concert of the "Evenings" wearing stylized Russian clothes, with his cheeks slightly rouged and his eyes carefully made up.

68. Cited by Yu. B. Demidenko in the article "Kostyum i stil' znizni: Obraz russkogo khudozhnika nachala XX veka," in *Panorama iskusstv 13* (Moscow: Sovetskii khudozhnik, 1990), 72.

69. Oscar Wilde, *The Picture of Dorian Gray* (London: Penguin, 1985), 53.

70. Tsvetaeva, "Nezdeshnii vecher," 132.

71. Documents of the time, including the Diary, give no clue as to whether a red necktie was in Russia, as in the United States in the early decades of the century, a popular article of clothing used to signal the wearer's homosexuality. See Jonathan Weinberg, *Speaking for Vice: Homosexuality in the Art of Charles Demuth, Marsden Hartley, and the First American Avant-Garde* (New Haven: Yale University Press, 1993), 33. Weinberg writes, "Havelock Ellis, writing about the late 1890s, suggests the red tie was an exclusive sign of homosexuality: 'It is notable that of recent years there has been a fashion for a red tie to be adopted by inverts as their badge.'"

72. Preface to Barbe d'Orevil'i, *Dendizm i Dzhordzh Bremmel'* (Moscow: Al'tsiona, 1912), III. Kuzmin noted that he was reading d'Aurevilly on June 1, 1907 (Diary).

73. Kuzmin wrote his introduction to the album *K. A. Somov* (Petrograd: Kamena, 1916 [1921]) on March 12, 1921. Despite the "1916" on the title page, the book came out in the early summer of 1921. The essay was reprinted in *Uslovnosti*, 180–185. Kuzmin wrote the following in "Cheshuya v nevode": "Somov. After his realistic strivings à la Serov and the light patina of the German decadents, how quickly he attained his own and tremendous thing. . . . Our time was very cultured and well read. The merit of aestheticism is a new humanism" (*Strelets: Sbornik tretii i poslednii*, 101).

74. "Pust' minutny kraski radug, / Milyi, khrupkii mir zagadok, / Mne gorit tvoya duga!" "Maskarad" (*S*, 80). In the 1921 essay on Somov, Kuzmin wrote: "Unease, irony, the puppet-like theatricality of the world, the comedy of eroticism, . . . the deceptive light of candles, fireworks, and rainbows—and suddenly a macabre tumbling down into death, sorcery . . . there you have the pathos of a whole series of Somov's works" (*Uslovnosti*, 181).

5. "Burning with a Double Love"

1. See Nikolay Berdyaev, "Ivanovskie sredy," in *Russkaya literatura XX veka*, vol. 3 (Moscow: Mir, 1916), 97–100; the biographical introduction by Olga Deschartes to volume one of Ivanov's *Sobranie sochinenii* (1971), 92; and Sergey Trotsky's "Vospominaniya," *Novoe literaturnoe obozrenie*, 10 (1994), 60.

2. "At the Ivanovs' they are now, it seems, cooking up the same thing with Sabashnikova that did not succeed last year with Gorodetsky, but I think that any kind of tercet with Diotima [Zinov'eva-Annibal] is unthinkable" (Diary, March 28, 1907).

3. S. I. Subbotin, "'...Moi vstrechi s vami netlenny...': Vyacheslav Ivanov v dnevnikakh, zapisnykh knizhkakh i pis'makh P. A. Zhurova," *Novoe literaturnoe obozrenie*, 10 (1994), 228–229.

4. Introduction to V. Ivanov, *Sobranie sochinenii*, 1:128.

5. On July 17, 1934, reminiscing about his life in the "Tower," Kuzmin summed up his opinion of Ivanov: "A most original poet in the style of the Munich School (Stefan George, Klinger, Nietzsche), a German paroxysm of the Wagnerian manner with German tastelessness, ponderousness, and depth" (Diary).

6. Feofilaktov had been a partisan of Kuzmin's works, which Bryusov showed him in manuscript, well before meeting their author. His plan to issue a luxurious edition of the "Aleksandriiskie pesni" with his illustrations never materialized, possibly because the publisher found the drawings too risqué. Kuzmin did dedicate them to Feofilaktov, and the artist later designed the covers for both *Seti* and *Kryl'ya*. Feofilaktov's cover for *Kryl'ya* depicts the upper torso of a winged figure wearing long gloves reaching to the elbow. More androgynous than female, it is a kind of fin-de-siècle Nike of Decadence.

7. *MK*, 129. Kuzmin noted receipt of the "rather incoherent" letter in his Diary on October 12, 1906.

8. The notebook Kuzmin kept in 1906–1910 contains an "approximate calculation of royalties" for those years (Manuscript Division, IRLI, coll. 172, inven. 1, no. 321, pp. 236 verso–237). He received 310 rubles in 1906, 1,080 in 1907, and 690 in 1908. The amounts were so small in 1909 that he gave only partial figures, which he did not bother to add up.

9. "Pis'ma M. F. Likiardopulo k M. A. Kuzminu," in NAB, *Mikhail Kuzmin: Stat'i i materialy*, 194. The letters (of 1907) record Likiardopulo's attempt to keep Kuzmin squarely in the camp of *Vesy*.

10. See *MK*, 129–130, for a detailed account of these literary skirmishes.

11. The letter appeared in the August issue of *Vesy* (1907). The signatories included Merezhkovsky, Gippius, Bryusov, Bely, Baltrushaitis, Likiardopulo, and Kuzmin. On August 21 and 22 the same signatories published letters in the newspaper *Stolichnoe utro* announcing their "departure" from *Zolotoe runo*.

12. *MK*, 129–130.

13. Nouvel's letter cites Bely's favorable review of *Priklyucheniya Eme Lebefa* in the August 1907 issue of *Pereval* (no. 10): "I must confess that in recent days one invariably finds repose in reading Kuzmin" (p. 52).

14. "Perepiska [M. A. Kuzmina] s V. F. Nuvelem," in NAB, *Mikhail Kuzmin: Stat'i i materialy*, 281.

15. "I wrote 'Phyllis'; Alexandria has again enveloped me" (Diary, June 24, 1907). After the publication of that story, however, mindful of his close financial ties to *Vesy* and "Skorpion," he still did not feel entirely comfortable about responding to the entreaties of Ryabushinksy for contributions and put him off until the summer of 1908.

16. See "Letters of N. N. Sapunov to M. A. Kuzmin," published in JEM, ed., *Studies in the Life and Works of Mixail Kuzmin*, Wiener Slawistischer Almanach,

Sonderband 24 (Vienna, 1989), 155–157 (hereafter *Studies*). Sapunov had hoped to design the production.

17. Letter of June 17, 1907, Dmitriev, "Perepiska Kuzmina i Meierkhol'da," 350. On July 17, 1907, he warmly recommended the play to Fedor Komissarzhevsky (ibid., note 3).

18. Vera Fedorovna Komissarzhevskaya, *Pis'ma aktrisy: Vospominaniya o nei: Materialy* (Leningrad: Iskusstvo, 1964), 165. Her theater never performed any of Kuzmin's plays.

19. In November 1907 Kuzmin wrote music for Remizov's *Besovskoe deistvo*. On the thirteenth he noted, "I went to the theater: even without costumes the 'ritual action' is ghastly" (Diary). He was not much more impressed by the first peformance on December 4, nor were the public and critics, who most admired the sets and costumes by Dobuzhinsky. See also Kuzmin's severe comments about the autumn season of Komissarzhevskaya's theater in the article "Otkrytie sezona" in the magazine *Luch*, 1 (1907), 20–22. He called the theater's "much-awaited" production of Wedekind's *Frühlings Erwachen* a "bore, alas."

20. The play's first act was published in *Tsvetnik Or* (1907). NAB published the manuscript of the remaining three acts in *Teatr*, 5 (1993), 159–191. Pamela Davidson discusses the play in "Lidiia Zinov'eva-Annibal's *The Singing Ass*: A Woman's View of Man and Eros," in *Gender and Russian Literature: New Perspectives*, ed. Rosalind Marsh (Cambridge: Cambridge University Press, 1996), 155–183.

21. Berdyaev wrote that she simply "disappeared forever. . . . Young people, disposed to see manifestations of an occult nature in everything, said either that she had gone into hiding in the West in a Catholic convent connected with the Rosicrucians, or that she had committed suicide because [Rudolf] Steiner had condemned her for the bad execution of his instructions." N. A. Berdyaev, *Samopoznanie*, 2nd corrected ed. (Paris: YMCA Press, 1983), 222. On June 6, 1910, Kuzmin wrote in the Diary: "An[na] Rud[ol'fovna], upset, in a swoon, has left for the North somewhere. Why, where? She's pathetic." On September 23–24, 1934, in one of his reminiscences about the "Tower," he fixed a version of her disappearance that is unique in its specificity: "One fine day Mintslova disappeared. Vyach[eslav Ivanov] told me that she had 'departed' [*ushla*] and that we would not see her again. It seems that she had exceeded her authority, had blurted out something she shouldn't have, was 'let go,' and drowned herself in Imatra [Falls]" (Diary).

22. Andrey Bely, *Mezhdu dvukh revolyutsii* (Moscow: Khudozhestvennaya literatura, 1990), 316–317.

23. Berdyaev, *Samopoznanie*, 221.

24. Kuzmin kept a list of letters written and received between March 1907 and January 1910 in his 1906–1910 notebook (Manuscript Division, IRLI, coll. 172, inven. 1, no. 321).

25. Kuzmin's sense of the playful extended only so far. On December 6, 1907, Blok's wife and the actress Nataliya Volokhova stopped by to invite him to perform, while wearing a Greek costume, *Kuranty lyubvi* for Isadora Duncan, who was making a triumphant visit to Petersburg. He declined, commenting in the Diary, "What nonsense, for God's sake!"

26. Let us recall again that Kuzmin's patron saint was the Archangel Michael, who is pictured on icons wearing armor, sword held aloft, while the mirror which

reflects the self and the self as "other" represents Kuzmin's variation, and an invariant motif in his art, of the Platonic myth of love as finding one's other half or double.

27. "Ya verno khozhu k vecherne / Opyat' i vnov', / Chtob byt' nedostupnei skverne" (*S*, 98).

28. "Istekai, o serdtse, istekai! / Rastsvetai, o roza, rastsvetai! / Serdtse, rozoi p'yanoe, trepeshchet. // Ot lyubvi sgorayu, ot lyubvi; / Ne zovi, o milyi, ne zovi: / Iz-za rozy mech grozyashchii bleshchet" (*S*, 105). See Davidson, *Poetic Imagination of Vyacheslav Ivanov*, 206–228, for a discussion of the sources of Ivanov's "Rosarium."

29. "Ogradi, o serdtse, ogradi. / Ne vredi, mech ostryi, ne vredi: / Opustis' na golubuyu vlagu. // Ya bedu lyubov'yu otvedu, / Ya pridu, o milyi, ya pridu / I pod mech s toboyu vmeste lyagu" (*S*, 105–106).

30. Mirsky's sage point about Kuzmin needs to be kept in mind before we assign him to Symbolism because of cycles like these: "There is a distinct religious strain in his [Kuzmin's] work, but it is not like that of the symbolists—it is not metaphysical, but devotional and ritual." D. S. Mirsky, *A History of Russian Literature*, ed. and abridged Francis J. Whitfield (New York: Alfred A. Knopf, 1966), 474.

31. See Kuzmin's letter to V. V. Ruslov of February 6, 1908, as published in "Vkhozhdenie v literaturnyi mir," in NAB, *Mikhail Kuzmin: Stat'i materialy*, 214–215. Kuzmin set the cycle to music in January 1908. On February 19, 1908, he and Ivanov "decided to publish 'The Wise Encounter,' 'The Guide,' 'Streams,' and the Spiritual Rimes in the spring, in a separate edition, in 'Oraea'" (Diary). Nothing came of the plan.

32. See "Mikhail Kuzmin osen'yu 1907 goda," in NAB, *Mikhail Kuzmin: Stat'i i materialy*, 99–116.

33. Aside from his writing, Kuzmin was closely involved in helping a group of gymnasium students mount a private production of *Kuranty lyubvi*. Among them was the future critic Prince Dmitry Svyatopolk-Mirsky, dubbed "il principino" in the Diary. Kuzmin had met him early in 1907, when some students from the First Petersburg Gymnasium, where Mirsky was studying, approached him for permission to use his music for a production of Blok's *Balaganchik* (nothing came of the idea). Kuzmin saw a lot of them in the autumn, when he clearly hoped they might be drawn into the "society" he was daydreaming about. The performance of *Kuranty lyubvi* on November 30, at an "Evening of the New Art" ("Vecher novogo iskusstva"), at which Blok, Gorodetsky, and Remizov read from their works, "flopped to laughter and boos" (Diary), but the author, at least, was pleased. He kept in touch with the young Mirsky and some of the others for several more months.

34. NAB, *Mikhail Kuzmin: Stat'i i materialy*, 203, 209–210. We have compressed the relevant passages of the two letters into one text. Comments in the Diary confirm many of the statements, while those in "Cheshuya v nevode," which was set down over ten years later, repeat many of them.

35. Johannes von Guenther, *Ein Leben im Ostwind: Zwischen Petersburg und München* (Munich: Biederstein Verlag, 1969), 225. Beethoven was the special favorite of Vyacheslav Ivanov, and he often asked Kuzmin to play piano transcriptions of the symphonies.

36. G. Ivanov, *Stikhotvoreniya*, 360.

37. Manuscript Division, IRLI, coll. 172, inven. 1, no. 319, pp. 246 verso–248 of a notebook Kuzmin used throughout the 1920s. Other Russians mentioned are Karamzin *(Pis'ma russkogo puteshestvennika)*, Khlebnikov, Mayakovsky, Remizov, Yurkun, the graphomaniacal Andrey Bolotov, and Kuzmin himself (the first volume of the "New Plutarch").

38. See K. L. Rudnitsky, *Russkoe rezhisserskoe iskusstvo, 1908–1917* (Moscow: Nauka, 1990), 19–24, and N. V. Drizen's "Starinnyi teatr (Vospominaniya)," *Stolitsa i usad'ba*, 71 (1916), 8–12.

39. Nothing came of Ivanov's plans beyond a program entitled "The Revival of Myth in Contemporary Poetry," which was held at the Tenishev School in January 1908, with Kuzmin, Meyerhold, Remizov, Gorodetsky, and Ivanov doing readings.

40. Andrey Bely, "Khudozhnik oskorbitelyam," *Vesy*, 1 (1907), 54. He excised the passage when he republished the piece in *Arabeski* (Moscow: Musaget, 1911) under the title "Khudozhniki oskorbitelyam," 326–330

41. At the end of January 1908, Bely wrote Blok that "I fell terribly in love with Kuzmin on this visit"; see Aleksandr Blok–Andrey Bely, *Perepiska* (Moscow: Izdanie Gosudarstvennogo Literaturnogo muzeya, 1940), 226. Bely wrote almost as effusively to Kuzmin himself; see Bely's letter to Kuzmin of January 30, 1908, Manuscript Division, RNB, coll. 124, no. 387.

42. Kuzmin did express guarded admiration for *Peterburg*, but Vsevolod Petrov recalled that he "actively disliked" all the prose Bely wrote thereafter (conversation with JEM, 1967). In the 1922 essay "Pis'mo v Pekin," Kuzmin wrote that after *Peterburg*, Bely "had come to a panicky dead end" in his prose and poetry (*Uslovnosti*, 164).

43. A remark in the Diary on September 19, 1906, helps explain the title: "And Pavlik [Maslov] keeps weaving his nets more and more." He also used the image to describe the relationship with Naumov: "Tomorrow I will see him again, these are sweet reciprocal nets" (December 15, 1907). Compare the opening stanza of the Faun's third song in the "Spring" section of *Kuranty lyubvi*: "Lyubov' rasstavlyaet seti / Iz krepkikh shelkov; / Lyubovniki, kak deti, / Ishchut okov" ("Love sets out nets / [made] of strong silk. / Lovers, like children, / search for fetters").

44. *Vesy*, 6 (1908), 64. A. V. Lavrov and R. D. Timenchik survey the critical reaction in the notes to Mikhail Kuzmin, *Izbrannye proizvedeniya* (Leningrad: Khudozhestvennaya literatura, 1990), 500–502.

45. Review of *Seti* in *Dalekie i blizkie*. See Valery Bryusov, *Sobranie sochinenii*, vol. 6 (Moscow: Khudozhestvennaya literatura, 1975), 340.

46. A. A. Blok, *Zapisnye knizhki, 1901–1920* (Moscow: Khudozhestvennaya literatura, 1965), 85.

47. A. A. Blok, "Pis'ma o russkoi poezii," *Zolotoe runo*, 10 (1908), 46–48; reprinted in volume five of the *Sobranie sochinenii v 8 tomakh*, 291, 294–295. On November 14, 1908, Kuzmin thanked Blok for sending him the article, adding: "I thank you also for the reproaches, because I more than anyone know their fairness and because, perhaps, I am trying a bit to make them less deserved" (*Literaturnoe nasledstvo*, vol. 92, bk. 2, 150). In a letter of May 13, 1908, Blok told Kuzmin that he was "in love with all of *Nets*," exclaiming, "Good Lord, what a poet you are and what a book you have written!"

48. "[I was] at Anichkov's, where were Shchegolev, Andrey Bely, Kuprin, everyone debating the question of homosexuality. 'It's in the air,' Diotima, who was at Somov's today, remarked" (Diary, September 2, 1906).

49. Maksimilian Voloshin, "Istoriya moei dushi," in Cherubina de Gabriak, *Ispoved'* (Moscow: Agraf, 1998), 278.

50. Guenther, *Ein Leben im Ostwind*, 205–206. Klaus Harer published Guenther's letters to Kuzmin in "Kuzmin i Gyunter," *Novoe literaturnoe obozrenie*, 24 (1997), 267–275.

51. Guenther gives an account of Kuzmin's and Ivanov's unsuccessful efforts to get the play produced by Komissarzhevskaya's troupe in his memoirs (*Ein Leben im Ostwind*, 219–226). His translation of *Kuranty lyubvi, Spieluhr der Liebe: Pastoral*, was published only twelve years later in Munich by the Musarion Verlag (1920). The Dreiländer Verlag of Munich issued his translation of the "Aleksandriiskie pesni," *Alexandrinische Gesänge*, the same year.

52. Guenther, *Ein Leben im Ostwind*, 207.

53. Kuzmin wrote of *The Thousand and One Nights*: "After it not only Defoe, but even Dickens and Balzac are insipid. Perhaps Shakespeare, Goethe, Dostoevsky can stand up to the comparison." See his "Cheshuya v nevode," in *Strelets: Sbornik tretii i poslednii*, 104.

54. The twelve *ghazals* that *Zolotoe runo* published in a summer issue (no. 7–9) in 1908 bore a dedication to Poznyakov. Kuzmin removed it when the entire cycle appeared in *Osennie ozera*.

55. "Kusmin nahm sich mit leichter Ironie und freundlicher Hingabe dieser Erzählung an." Letter to Vladimir Markov of October 5, 1971, cited in the notes to volume three of *SS*, 638–639.

56. The penetration of the "tight circle" ("uzkii krug") in the final stanza obviously suggests anal intercourse, and the "rose" of the last line ("O marvel of the rose of paradise!" ["O raiskoi rozy divo!"]), while obviously tinged with the mysticism of the "holy warrior" cycles, points more directly in the context to gay slang of the time, in which "rose" meant the anus. See, for example, the Diary: "We [Kuzmin and Poznyakov] went to the Remizovs'. He was alone, we discussed homosexuality [*gomoseksualizm*]. . . . I gave him information about fairies [*tapetki*], aunties [*tetki*], the bathhouses, *fendiller* [?] *de roses*, etc." (December 1, 1908).

57. Shortly before he began work on "Vsadnik," Kuzmin indulged in some mystical mummery with Guenther, an occult prank he seems to have enjoyed the more the German, and to an extent himself, was taken in by it. See the commentary to the poem in *S*, 719–720.

58. The first story appeared in *Vesy*, 9 (1908), 13–19, and the second in *Zolotoe runo*, 10 (1908) 27–37. Both magazines were, as usual, carelessly tardy in paying the author. Kuzmin, mindful of Ivanov's disapproval, never republished the second story.

59. Over the next seven years, Kuzmin now and again received letters from Naumov. His last contact with him seems to have been on August 28, 1915, when Naumov, on leave from the front and "in a panic" (Diary), spent much of the day with him strolling about Petersburg. We know nothing about his subsequent fate.

60. See *Zolotoe runo*, 10 (1908), 75. Remizov "elected" Kuzmin to his mythical "Great and Free Monkey Chamber," whose members received elaborate charters copied out in Remizov's stylized Old Russian calligraphy.

61. "Bez tebya tomlyusya v skuke, / Pri tebe tomlyus', revnuya; / Vse zhe tomnosti razluki / potselui predpochtu ya." A. G. Timofeev, "Neizdannye stikhotvoreniya M. Kuzmina vtoroi poloviny 1900-kh godov," *Novoe literaturnoe obozrenie*, 3 (1993), 127.

62. Other friends, under none of the obligation Bryusov felt, as he certainly did not want to risk alienating Kuzmin from his magazine, were brutally frank about Poznyakov's decidedly dilettantish efforts. Gorodetsky minced no words when he wrote Kuzmin on December 6, 1908: "You are creating a school, but all the same, Poznyakov's story won't do at all. . . . Either I am blind or Cupid's blindfold is putting you in an awkward position. . . . Aside from indecencies and parodying of you, there is nothing in the story. It is not up to your sweet voice to defend it" (Manuscript Division, RNB, coll. 124, item 1291).

63. See L. I. Tikhvinskaya, *Kabare i teatry miniatyur v Rossii: 1908–1917* (Moscow: RIK, "Kul'tura," 1995), 37–42.

64. Both Kuzmin's earlier picaresque heroes, Aimé and Eleusippus, had same-sex affairs in the course of their wanderings; the Englishman Fairfax has none—the author's mordant comment, perhaps, on the "truth" of the "English vice" cliché.

65. Review of the poet Viktor Gofman's collection of stories *Lyubov' k dalekoi* (Petersburg, 1912), in Kuzmin's column "Zametki o russkoi belletristike," *Apollon*, 1 (1912), 68. He went on to add, very shrewdly, "Of contemporary writers, we would name Gippius, Sologub, and Bely, whose prose somehow preserves the qualities of the prose of those who are not poets, although they are unquestionably poets." He found Gofman's weak efforts to be in the same category.

66. When he read through parts of the Diary on March 6, 1923, Kuzmin recalled the affair with Poznyakov as having been "not at all brilliant." It was his final word on the matter.

67. Kuzmin's close friendship with this Okulovka neighbor, a man named Godunov, provided the biographical subtext for the poem cycle "Troe," written in July–August 1909. The "three" were Kuzmin, his niece Varya, and Godunov. See JEM's article "'Real' and 'Ideal' in Kuzmin's 'The Three,'" in *For SK: In Celebration of the Life and Career of Simon Karlinsky* (Oakland: Berkeley Slavic Specialties, 1994), 173–183.

68. "Krov nashel bezdomnyi strannik / Posle zhizni kochevoi; / Uzh ne strannik, ne izgnannik, / Ya ot schast'ya sam ne svoi" (*S*, 190). "I wrote a poem to Vera, she kissed me for it. . . . I played the Seventh Symphony, we read [Bely's] *The Silver Dove* aloud. I saw an inexpensive copy of Wieland at a used-book shop. Peaceful, calm, holy. Lord, grant Thy blessing" (Diary, July 18, 1909).

6. Disciple to Master

1. V. Ivanov, *Sobranie sochinenii*, 2:780. Compare Kuzmin's Diary for the same day: "I worked hard on *Joseph*. In the evening I played *Don Giovanni* and read the Diary. . . . I would have to be an Eckermann to take down Vyacheslav's conversations, so interesting, brilliant, and instructive are they."

2. For a description of Kuzmin's rooms, see G. Ivanov, *Stikhotvoreniya*, 360. The reception room was dominated by Kuzmin's icon collection and a photograph of Botticelli's *Primavera*, which he had received from Chicherin on September 26, 1905. It was with him until the day he died.

3. V. Ivanov, *Sobranie sochinenii,* 2:784. Kuzmin notes, "Vyacheslav read the end of *Joseph,* expressed his wishes as regards the fourth part" (Diary, July 29). Of his reading to Ivanov on August 6 and the novel's conclusion, Kuzmin wrote with welcome irony, "Then we read *Joseph,* not bad, it seems, although in the end I developed an oratorio of sorts. Vyach[eslav] Iv[anovich] liked it."

4. In a 1913 autobiographical statement, Kuzmin singled out Blok's "Pis'ma o poezii" and Ivanov's article on his prose as genuine contributions to an understanding of his art, Ivanov's in particular because "the exact meaning of my short novels *Gentle Joseph* and *The Exploits of Alexander the Great* is disclosed in it" (IRLI, coll. 377, inven. 6, no. 1982).

5. Kuzmin received his copy on May 14, 1909 (Diary). Gumilev and Kuzmin both reviewed the second issue of *Ostrov* in the "Pis'ma o russkoi poezii" column of *Apollon,* 3 (December 1909), even though the second issue, which came out in August, received hardly any distribution at all. It contained no poems by Kuzmin.

6. See "I. F. Annensky: Pis'ma k S. K. Makovskomu," published by A. V. Lavrov and R. D. Timenchik, *Ezhegodnik rukopisnogo otdela Pushkinskogo Doma na 1976 god* (Leningrad: Nauka, 1978), 223.

7. See the chapter on Gumilev in Sergey Makovsky's often unreliable *Na Parnase serebryanogo veka* (Munich: Izdatel'stvo tsentral'nogo ob"edineniya politicheskikh emigrantov SSSR, 1962) and the chapter on *Apollon* by I. V. Koretskaya in *Russkaya literatura i zhurnalistika nachala XX veka, 1905–1917: Burzhuazno-liberal'nye i modernistskie izdaniya* (Moscow: Nauka, 1984).

8. I. F. Annensky, "O sovremennom lirizme," in *Kniga otrazhenii* (Moscow: Nauka, 1979), 364.

9. Ibid., 332–333.

10. Makovsky, *Na Parnase serebryanogo veka,* 199. Guenther himself wrote reviews of the theater season in Riga and reviews of German literature for *Apollon.* On September 29, 1909, Kuzmin noted, "Filosofov is saying: 'Just what kind of editorial board is this, with Gumilev, Kuzmin, cadets, young ladies, and a secretary who's all of fifteen years old?'" (Diary).

11. Makovsky, *Na Parnase serebryanogo veka,* 150. After Annensky's death, Faddey Zelinsky, a good friend of Ivanov's and a classical scholar teaching at the university, replaced him. Part of Kuzmin's duties involved approving candidates for membership in the society.

12. Vadim Kreid's attempt to assign authorship of the statement to Gumilev ("Neizvestnaya stat'ya N. S. Gumileva?" *Novyi zhurnal,* 166 [1987], 189–208), disregards all archival evidence. See Lavrov and Timenchik's publication of Annensky's letters to Makovsky (227–228), and K. F. Taranovsky's "Zametka o dialoge 'Skuchnyi razgovor' v pervom nomere *Apollona* (oktyabr' 1909 g.)," in *Russian Literature,* vol. 26 (1989), 417–424.

13. Review of *Osennie ozera,* first published in *Apollon,* 8 (1912), 62; republished in N. S. Gumilev, *Pis'ma o russkoi poezii* (Moscow: Sovremennik, 1990), 155.

14. None of Kuzmin's letters to Gumilev seems to have survived. Gumilev's to Kuzmin are in "Neizvestnye pis'ma N. S. Gumileva," published by R. D. Timenchik, *Izvestiya Akademii nauk SSSR,* Seriya literatury i yazyka, 46, no. 1, (1987), 50–78, and in N. S. Gumilev, *Neizdannye stikhi i pis'ma* (Paris: YMCA Press, 1980), 120–123. Kuzmin dedicated "Nadpis' na knige" (August 1909) to Gumilev, the poem whose final lines inflamed the romantic imagination of the fifteen-year-old

Marina Tsvetaeva and began her "cult" of Kuzmin's verse. Gumilev wrote a rather pretentious acrostic to the older poet (see *MK*, 149).

15. See Lavrov and Timenchik's commentary to Annensky's letters to Makovsky (241). After stopping by to visit Annensky at Tsarskoe Selo on October 4, Kuzmin noted that he looked very unwell (Diary).

16. For the best of the accounts, see Z. D. Davydov and V. P. Kupchenko, "Maksimilian Voloshin: Rasskaz o Cherubine de Gabriak," in *Pamyatniki kul'tury: Novye otkrytiya: Ezhegodnik 1988* (Moscow: Nauka, 1989), which contains Voloshin's "Istoriya Cherubiny" and Dmitrieva's "Ispoved'," and "Istoriya Cherubiny (Rasskaz M. Voloshina v zapisi T. Shan'ko)," in *Vospominaniya o Maksimiliane Voloshine* (Moscow: Sovetskii pisatel', 1990), 179–194. See too documents in her collected works, Cherubina de Gabriak *Ispoved'*, 267–288.

17. Nadezhda Voitinskaya was also doing a fine series of lithograph portraits of the leading figures around *Apollon*, Kuzmin included.

18. Mikhail Kuzmin, *Tret'ya kniga rasskazov* (Moscow: Skorpion, 1913), 130. The collection contains all the works mentioned, except "Okhotnichii zavtrak," which Kuzmin never republished after its first appearance in the second issue of the miscellany *Zhenshchina* (1910). NAB examines the polemical context of "Vysokoe iskusstvo," an artfully camouflaged comment on the "Symbolist debate" of 1910, in "Avtobiograficheskoe nachalo v rannem tvorchestve Kuzmina," in *Mikhail Kuzmin: Stat'i i materialy*, 140–144.

19. The translation, which remains the Russian standard, appeared in book form in 1913 (Petersburg, M. G. Kornfel'd). It was republished in 1968 in the prestigious series "Literaturnye pamyatniki." Two stories by Rachilde, the "Queen of the Decadents," as she was often called, that appeared in the second issue of *Apollon* in 1909 were apparently Kuzmin's first published prose translations.

20. In this, literary historians follow the dubious lead of Viktor Zhirmunsky's influential article "Preodolevshie simvolizm" ("Those Who Have Overcome Symbolism"), which was first published in *Russkaya mysl'*, 12 (1916), 30–32, 49–52 (second pagination).

21. V. Ivanov, *Sobranie sochinenii*, 2:785. Kuzmin's Diary mentions only that "Valechka [Nouvel] and Potemkin came in the evening. Chatted for such a long time. Went to bed very late."

22. Mikhail Kuzmin, "O prekrasnoi yasnosti," *Apollon*, 4 (1910), 7.

23. Heinrich Heine, *Sämtliche Werke*, vol. 6 (Munich: Georg Müller, 1935), 141; our translation and emphasis.

24. Kuzmin's Diary offers no help at all: 1910 is, as he put it in a footnote to the year, "very incomplete." There are no entries for January 19–31, all of February and March, April 1–18 and 20–26, October 1–27, November 5–13 and 20–30, and December 1–3, 5–12, and 15–31.

25. "Perepiska V. I. Ivanova s S. K. Makovskim," published by NAB, S. S. Grechiskin, and O. A. Kuznetsova in *Novoe literaturnoe obozrenie*, 10 (1994), 141–144.

26. Ibid., 155.

27. In an article summarizing the achivements of *Vesy*, which had ceased publication at the end of 1909, Kuzmin praised the magazine for never having been a "sectarian organ, narrow and intolerant," but rather one open to all that was "alive and new" in Russian and Western literature, and thus a defender of all "cultural values." "Khudozhestvennaya proza 'Vesov,'" *Apollon*, 9 (July–August 1910), 36.

402   *Notes to Pages 168–173*

28. See Ivanov's diary for September 5, 1909, in *Sobranie sochinenii*, 2:801.

29. Kuzmin, "O prekrasnoi yasnosti," 9. Makovsky's letter to Ivanov shows that the remarks about Remizov had particularly annoyed Ivanov.

30. Ibid., 6.

31. Ivanov, who continued to publish in *Apollon*, would certainly have found statements in Kuzmin's article to which he could take sharp exception, and he alluded to some of them in his 1910 article "Zavety simvolizma." John A. Barnstead examines some of the differences between the two men in "Mikhail Kuzmin's 'On Beautiful Clarity' and Viacheslav Ivanov: A Reconsideration," *Canadian Slavonic Papers*, 24, no. 1 (1982), 1–10. Ivanov removed a few sentences critical of Kuzmin's article from the draft of his own article; see O. A. Kuznetsova, "Diskussiya o sostoyanii russkogo simvolizma v 'Obshchestve revnitelei khudozhestvennogo slova' (Obsuzhdenie doklada Vyach. Ivanova)," *Russkaya literatura*, 1 (1990), 207.

32. Valery Bryusov, *Dnevniki, 1891–1910* (Moscow: Izdanie M. i S. Sabashnikovykh, 1927), 142.

33. *Pechat' i revolyutsiya*, 7 (1926), 46 (corrected from the autograph in IMLI, coll. 13, inven. 3, item 27).

34. Ivanov's lecture-article "Zavety simvolizma" and Blok's reply, "O sovremennom sostoyanii russkogo simvolizma," appeared one after the other in the eighth issue (May–June) of *Apollon* in 1910. Bryusov replied to both in the next issue with "O 'rechi rabskoi,' v zashchitu poezii," while Bely in turn disputed his views in the eleventh issue with the rather lame "Venok ili venets."

35. *Literaturnoe nasledstvo*, vol. 92, bk. 3, 370. We see evidence of those "tongue-lashings" in the Diary in the summer of 1910: "At dinner Vyach[eslav] carried on about the parasitism of the modernists, etc. I took offense and was rude. Now we hardly speak. He is stubborn and tactless, persistent and provocative" (July 7); "At dinner Vyach. attacked me terribly for *Apollo*, but then said that Zhenya [Znosko-Borovsky] and I are the best movement" (July 28); "Vyach. has calmed down a bit, but he still often grumbles at *Apollo*" (July 30). By the late summer Kuzmin began to think about moving out of the Ivanov apartment, but he stayed on because of his affection for the whole family and because he had no place to go, being plagued as usual by a lack of money.

36. Mikhail Kuzmin, "'Orfei i Evridika' kavalera Gluka," in *Uslovnosti*, 49. The article first appeared in *Apollon*, 10 (1911), 15–19.

37. Vas. Galakhov [Gippius's usual pseudonym], "Tsekh poetov," *Zhizn'* [an Odessa weekly], 5 (1918), 12. Cited by Roman Timenchik in his "Zametki ob akmeizme," *Russian Literature*, 7–8 (1974), 32.

38. *Literaturnoe nasledstvo*, vol. 98, bk. 2, 512.

39. Timenchik, "Zametki ob akmeizme," 32. Nadezhda Mandel'shtam wrote in her memoirs that "Mandel'shtam and Akhmatova always became enraged when literary historians attached to the Acmeists anyone they took it into their heads to: Kuzmin because of his 'clarism,' Lozinsky because of his friendship with the Acmeists, the young people who reckoned themselves Gumilev's pupils. . . . There were only six Acmeists." Nadezhda Mandel'shtam, *Vtoraya kniga* (Paris: YMCA Press, 1972), 38.

40. See her remarks in "K istorii akmeizma," in Anna Akhmatova, "Avtobiograficheskaya proza," *Literaturnoe obozrenie*, 5 (1989), 7, 9–10 (note 34). A number of Akhmatova's views on the rise of Acmeism need factual correction, but not this one.

41. Autobiographical statement, published in Medvedev, "Blok i Kuzmin v arkhive P. N. Medvedeva," 179.

42. [Mikhail Kuzmin], "Razdum'ya i nedoumen'ya Petra Otshel'nika," in *Petrogradskie vechera*, bk. 3 (Petrograd, 1914), 214. Kuzmin refers to himself in the third person in the article, which he did not sign with his own name, further evidence of the fact that though he certainly had views on art, he did not want at the time to take too public a position in the literary quarrels of the day.

43. Mikhail Kuzmin, "Mechtateli," *Zi*, nos. 764–766, June 29–July 1, 1921, 1. Kuzmin removed the remark when he republished the article in *Uslovnosti* in 1923, two years after Gumilev's execution, but he let stand a comment about the "stubborn dignity of Acmeism, which arbitrarily and quite obtusely restricts itself on all sides" (*Uslovnosti*, 154). See also his remark that "Acmeism is so obtuse and absurd that this mirage will soon pass" ("Cheshuya v nevode," in *Strelets: Sbornik tretii i poslednii*, 100). Akhmatova never forgave Kuzmin for this and other statements critical of Acmeism.

44. See Georgy Adamovich, "Moi vstrechi s Annoi Akhmatovoi," in *Vozdushnye puti*, vol. 5 (New York, 1967), 101.

45. In another comment on Acmeism, Kuzmin stressed the incompatibility of its major figures: "Such a non-organic but fabricated school as Acmeism, created by force alone, came apart at the seams from the very beginning as it tried to combine the uncombinable Gumilev, Akhmatova, Mandel'shtam, and Zenkevich." Mikhail Kuzmin, "Parnasskie zarosli," in the collection *Zavtra* (Berlin: Petropolis, 1923), 116. Interestingly enough, Mandel'shtam downplayed stylistic affinities as a defining quality for Acmeism, insisting, rather, on a moral dimension. In a letter to Lev Gornung of July–August 1923 he wrote, "It [Acmeism] wanted to be only the 'conscience' of poetry." *Literaturnoe obozrenie*, 9 (1986), 110.

46. *Apollon*, 5 (1912), 56.

47. Ibid.

48. On October 16, 1909, Khlebnikov wrote his parents, "I am an apprentice, and my teacher is Kuzmin," and on October 23 he reported to his brother, "I am an apprentice of the renowned Kuzmin. He is my *magister*." V. V. Khlebnikov, *Sobranie proizvedenii*, vol. 5 (Leningrad: Izdatel'stvo pisatelei v Leningrade, 1933), 287. See too Khlebnikov's poem "Vam," which is addressed to Kuzmin, in his *Tvoreniya* (Moscow: Sovetskii pisatel', 1986), 58. The poem was first published in 1922 in the miscellany *Chasy*, which Kuzmin edited.

49. A. E. Parnis, drawing exclusively on the Diary, describes what little we know of the relationship between the two writers in his essay "Khlebnikov v dnevnike M. A. Kuzmina," *MKiRK*, 156–165.

50. Kuzmin, *Uslovnosti*, 173. Not long after Khlebnikov's death in 1922, Kuzmin called him a "genius and a person of great visionary insights" who was probably fated to be little understood (ibid., 164).

51. Andrey Bely, "Rakkurs k 'Dnevniku': Materialy k biografii, 1899–1930," RGALI, coll. 53, inven. 1, item 100, sheets 51–52.

52. Andrey Bely, *Nachalo veka* (Moscow: Khudozhestvennaya literatura, 1990), 355. Bely freely blends descriptions of the "Tower" during two visits, one in January–February 1910 and another in January–February 1912. His account of the friction between Ivanov and Kuzmin belongs to the second, not the first, visit, as a comparison of the memoir with unpublished memoir documents such as the "Rakkurs k 'Dnevniku'" makes clear. See also Bely's "Vospominaniya o A. A. Bloke" in

the Berlin miscellany *Epopeya*, 4 (June 1923), 158. The merging of the two visits led Akhmatova to ridicule Bely's account of the rise of Acmeism, for it seems in the memoir to occur, preposterously, in 1910, not in the opening months of 1912 (see her "K istorii akmeizma" in "Avtobiograficheskaya proza," 7). In fact, most of what Bely writes about January–February 1912, including his discussions with Gumilev, can be confirmed from other sources, and it should not be dismissed as a fiction.

53. See Bely, *Nachalo veka*, 356, and *Epopeya*, 4, 159. Kuzmin's ability to work anywhere and at any time was legendary.

54. *Apollon*, 9 (1910), 41. Kuzmin and members of the Ivanov family read the novel aloud during the final months of 1909 (Diary).

55. When first published in Andrey Bely, *Stikhotvoreniya i poemy*, "Biblioteka poeta" (Moscow: Sovetskii pisatel', 1966), 466–467, the "improvisation" was misdated "between 1905 and 1907"; internal evidence contradicts that. Bely wrote the poem in the album of Vera Shvarsalon.

56. Kuzmin first mentions reading the play with the other members of the "Tower" and distributing the roles on November 3, 1909 (Diary). By the fourteenth, rehearsals were already under way. For a description of the planning, the rehearsals, and the production itself, see Pyast, *Vstrechi*, 166–180. Lidiya Ivanova acted the part of Menga in the play and describes the production in her memoirs, *Vospominaniya: Kniga ob ottse* (40–42).

57. See Znosko-Borovsky's detailed article about the production in *Apollon*, 8 (1910), 31–36.

58. In a photograph of the assembled players published opposite page 177 of V. E. Meierkhol'd, *Stat'i, pis'ma, rechi, besedy*, vol. 1 (1891–1917) (Moscow: Iskusstvo, 1968), Kuzmin is seated in the middle, costumed as an old man wearing a kind of turban. Another photograph of him and Vera Shvarsalon in their costumes is reproduced in this volume.

59. See his comments on the play, ibid., 254–255.

60. The Gluck opera, conducted by Napravnik, directed by Meyerhold, with choreography by Fokine and set and costume designs by Golovin, opened at the Mariinskii on December 21, 1911. In a March 16, 1926, review of the fourth revival of the production, Kuzmin called it "one of the highest points" of prerevolutionary Russian theater history (*Krasnaya gazeta*, no. 61, 6). He regretted that each revival got further and further away from the "brilliant" original, but still welcomed Golovin's "magnificent creation," which was "always magical in a new way," and "virtually determines the whole movement" of the production.

61. Aleksandr Golovin, *Vstrechi i vpechatleniya: Pis'ma: Vospominaniya o Golovine* (Leningrad: Iskusstvo, 1960), 100.

62. Ibid., 106. The volume contains a black-and-white reproduction of the portrait on page 103. There is a decent color reproduction in *Teatral'nyi portret kontsa XIX-nachala XX veka* (Leningrad: Avrora, 1973), which also has a reproduction of one of Somov's better-known portraits, painted in January 1909.

63. Golovin, *Vstrechi i vpechatleniya*, 102.

64. Kuzmin was so distressed by the changes someone at the theater had made to his translation that he wrote to Vladimir Telyakovsky, director of the Imperial Theaters, on January 24, 1913, asking that his name be removed as translator from the program and all advertising. See P. V. Dmitriev, "'Akademicheskii' Kuzmin," *Russian Studies*, 3 (I—1995), 146.

65. *Apollon*, 4 (1910), 79 (second pagination). He also reviewed a production of Shaw's *Caesar and Cleopatra*, designed by Sapunov and Sudeikin, in the same issue. On January 2, 1910, he notes, "[Sudeikin] dragged me to see 'Putanitsa.' . . . It is a very pleasant and nice piece, lively acting, we sat in the director's box. I met Belyaev, he resembles Apukhtin, spoke graciously and pompously" (Diary).

66. See section five ("Uslovnyi teatr") of Meierkhol'd's 1908 article "Teatr (K istorii i tekhnike)," republished in 1912 and in *Stat'i, pis'ma, rechi, besedy*, 1:141–142.

67. V. E. Meierkhol'd, "Russkie dramaturgi," ibid., 1:188.

68. See *Apollon*, 10 (1910), 32 (second pagination), and Tikhvinskaya, *Kabare i teatry miniatyur*, 69–86.

69. In a 1923 autobiography Kuzmin wrote: "The founding of the 'House of Interludes' with Meyerhold and Sapunov and participation in the editorial work of *Apollo* were to a certain extent my civic activities. Incidentally, the 'House of Interludes' did not last for very long." See Medvedev, "Blok i Kuzmin v arkhive P. N. Medvedeva," 179.

70. See Auslender's review of the opening in *Apollon*, 12 (December 1910), 26–27 (second pagination). Unfortunately, we have no description of it in Kuzmin's Diary. He was so busy with the preparations for the opening and throughout the days that followed that he made no entries for October 1–27, 1910.

71. Ibid., 27.

72. The text of *Gollandka Liza*, dated September 1910, appeared in the miscellany *Severnye tsvety na 1911 god*, fasc. 5 (Moscow: Skorpion, 1911). (Kuzmin received the page proofs on March 4, 1911.) Another of Kuzmin's comedies written in 1910, in expectation of a production at the "House of Interludes," *Prints s myzy*, was never performed; he published it in the miscellany *Al'tsiona*, bk. 1 (Moscow, 1914).

73. Nikolay Volkov, *Meierkhol'd*, vol. 2 (Moscow-Leningrad: Academia, 1929), 155. Kuzmin's 1929 reminiscences about Kazaroza appeared in *Kazaroza* (Moscow, 1930), 23–27.

74. "Ditya, ne tyanisya vesnoyu za rozoi, / Rozu i letom sorvesh', / Rannei vesnoyu sbirayut fialki, / Pomni, chto letom fialok uzh net." "Ditya i roza," quoted from the sheet music issued in 1913 by the firm of Nikolay Davingof; the complete text is in *SS*, 3:522. The song enjoyed widespread popularity well into the postrevolutionary period; see the memoirs of T. A. Aksakova-Sivers, *Semeinaya khronika* (Paris: Atheneum, 1988), 216.

75. There had also been a conflict among the theater's board members since December 1910. See Kuzmin and Sapunov's letters to Meierkhol'd in Dmitriev, "Perepiska Kuzmina i Meierkhol'da," 361–366.

76. "Dragunskii kornet so stikhami / I s bessmyslennoi smert'yu v grudi." Anna Akhmatova, *Stikhotvoreniya i poemy*, "Biblioteka poeta" (Leningrad: Sovetskii pisatel', 1976), 368, ll. 468–469.

77. Guenther, *Ein Leben im Ostwind*, 399. Knyazev's father, a high school teacher of Russian literature, included a photograph of his son in the edition of his verse that he published at his own expense after his son's death; see Vsevolod Knyazev, *Stikhi: Posmertnoe izdanie* (Petersburg: Tipografiya imperatorskikh SPb teatrov, 1914). See also R. D. Timenchik, "Rizhskii epizod v 'Poeme bez geroya' Anny Akhmatovoi," *Daugava*, 2 (1984), 113–121.

78. See R. D. Timenchik's bio-bibliographical entry about her under that name in volume one of *Russkie pisateli 1800–1917: Biograficheskii slovar'* (Moscow:

Sovetskaya entsiklopediya, 1989), 299. It contains a photograph of her. See, too, R. D. Timenchik, "'Ne zabyta i Pallada...': Iz vospominanii grafa B. O. Berga." Two of Pallada's admirers committed suicide: one shot himself under her picture, while another shot himself before her very eyes. These well-known incidents certainly shaped Akhmatova's portrayal of the death of the Knyazev-like character in *Poema bez geroya*.

79. "Yanvarskii den'. Na beregu Nevy / Nesetsya veter, razrushen'em veya," 1923. G. Ivanov, *Stikhotvoreniya*, 74.

80. Lidiya Chukovskaya, *Zapiski ob Anne Akhmatovoi: 1938–1941*, vol. 1 (Moscow: Soglasie, 1997), 33–34. Pallada did, in fact, wear an ankle bracelet (as several note in their memoirs), but Akhmatova's reference to "ankle bracelets" ("braslety na nogakh") functions in the same way as do her constant allusions in the *Poema bez geroya*: she counts on the fact that readers in the know will recall Pallada's description of a Petersburg courtesan in the opening poem of her 1915 collection *Amulety*—"Amulets entwined around her ankles" ("Na nogakh spleteny amulety")—and that they will then draw their own conclusions about the character and real "profession" of the author herself, about which Akhmatova otherwise keeps silent.

81. See Diary entry for May 30, 1910, for example (*MK*, 166).

82. Kuzmin was able to persuade the editors of the mass-circulation *Novyi zhurnal dlya vsekh* to publish the poem "Mne mnitsya inogda pri bleske lunnom nochi" in 1910 (no. 21 [July], 10). Only one other of his poems, "Kogda ona govorit,—istselyayutsya rany," appeared in print in his lifetime, in the equally popular magazine *Novaya zhizn'*, 4 (March 1911), 4.

83. "S chego nachat'? tolpoyu toroplivoi / K moei dushe, tak dolgo molchalivoi, / Begut stikhi, kak stado rezvykh koz. . . . / Yavilis' Vy . . . / Teper' ya znayu, gordyi i schastlivyi, / S chego nachat'" (*S*, 145–146).

84. "Bledny vse imena, i stary vse nazvan'ya— / Lyubov' zhe kazhdyi raz nova," and "Stareyutsya slova, no serdtse ne stareet" (*S*, 149).

85. "'Dlya nas i v avguste nastupit mai!',," the final poem of "Osennii mai" (*S*, 152).

86. *The Poetry of Michelangelo*, an annotated translation by James M. Saslow (New Haven: Yale University Press, 1991), 133 (poem no. 49). In 1919 Kuzmin translated a selection of the sonnets for an edition that a small private publisher, "Stranstvuyushchii entuziast," planned to issue. It never came out (see Diary, April 19, 1919).

87. "Zelenyi doloman," in "Chto za Paskha! sneg, tuman," the eighth poem of the cycle "Kholm vdali," written in May–October 1912 and addressed to Knyazev (*S*, 242).

88. "Po-prezhnemu dlya nas Amur krylatyi reet / I ostroyu streloi grozit" (*S*, 149).

89. "Trizhdy v temnyi sklep strastei tomyashchikh / Ty yavlyalsya, vestnik mechenosnyi, / I manil menya v stranu inuyu. / Kak zhe nynche tvoi prizyv minuyu? / Zhgu, zhenikh moi, zheltyi ladan rosnyi, / Chuya blizost' belykh kryl blestyashchikh" (*S*, 146).

90. In a list of Kuzmin's works appended to the 1913 *Tret'ya kniga rasskazov*, for example, the book is described as "In preparation" (*gotovitsya*).

91. "Krepko vyazhet serdtsa v chas rasstavan'ya lyubov'" (*S*, 150).

92. "No vdrug sluchitsya vetrenoi Fortune / Osennii mai nam sdelat' okty-abrem?" (*S*, 152).

93. It is poem no. 50 in Knyazev's *Stikhi*, 50.

7. *"Where Is Life's Enchantment?"*

1. See *Rech'*, no. 55, February 26, 1911.

2. "The apotheosis of Komissarzhevskaya has been planned by the kikes" was one of the speech's milder remarks. The full text can be found in the stenographic record of the proceedings of the Third Duma, *Gosudarstvennaya Duma, sozyv tretii: Stenograficheskie otchety, sessiya chetvertaya, chast' II, zasedaniya 39–73* (St. Petersburg, 1911), 2814–2840. Kuzmin included a graceful note about Komissarzhevskaya's passing in the "Chronicle" section of *Apollon*, 5 (1910), 36 (second pagination).

3. For a description of the performance and a photograph of one scene, see *Ogonek*, 19 (1911). The text of the "comic opera" (its subtitle) was first published in Kuzmin's *Teatr*, bk. 2, vol. 4 (1995), 84–139; the reviews are summarized on pages 388–390. One critic wrote that "considering that the author is Kuzmin, there is comparatively little pornography," while another saw the "seed of the rebirth of the Russian operetta" in it. The theater advertised the new production in August 1911 in a tiny magazine called *Veer*, which was printed in the shape of a fan; see Pavel Dmitriev, "Zhurnal 'Veer' (1911: no. 1)," *Novoe literaturnoe obozrenie*, 3 (1993), 336–340.

4. Dora Kogan discusses Sudeikin's work on the operetta in her *Sergey Yur'evich Sudeikin* (Moscow: Iskusstvo, 1974), 57–64; the book provides several re-productions of the set and costume designs.

5. The text of the duet, "Poletim daleko za more," is on pp. 117–120 of Kuzmin's *Teatr*, bk. 2, vol. 4.

6. See Kuzmin's essay "Uslovnosti" which opens the collection of that name (11–22).

7. Mikhail Kuzmin, "Doch' ploshchadei, sputnitsa revolyutsii," in *Uslovnosti*, 125–127.

8. E. A. Znosko-Borovsky, "Malyi teatr," *Russkaya khudozhestvennaya letopis'* [an irregular supplement to *Apollon*], 13 (September 1911), 200–202.

9. "Bednyi, bednyi Telemakh, / On boitsya cherepakh!"—literally, "he fears tortoises." Dmitry Bouchêne recalled the couplet in conversation with JEM in Paris in 1970. The text of the operetta was first published in Kuzmin's *Teatr*, bk. 2, vol. 4, 140–181. The critical reaction is summarized in the notes (393–396). The song text as published has only "A Telemakh boitsya cherepakh" (149).

10. The copy is in a private collection in the West.

11. "Mozhet byt', ya bezrassuden, / Ne strashas' nezhdannykh kov, / No ot"ezd Vash khot' i truden, / Mne ne strashen dal'nii Pskov. // Schast'e mne som-nen'ya tupit / Vest'yu vernoi i pryamoi: / 'Sorok muchenik' nastupit—/ I vernetes' Vy domoi" (*S*, 152–153).

12. See "Kogda k chernym i belym klavisham" in Knyazev, *Stikhi*, 53.

13. "Mne kazhetsya, skoro pridet ko mne nezhnyi, / Moi milyi, zhelannyi, nevedomyi drug" (ibid., 56).

14. "Kak radostna vesna v aprele, / Kak nam plenitel'na ona! / V nachale budushchei nedeli / Poidem snimat'sya k Buasona. // Lyubvi pokorstvuya

obryadam, / Ne razmyshlyaya ni o chem, / My pomestimsya nezhno ryadom, / Ruka s rukoi, plecho s plechom. // Somnenii slezy ne vo sne li? / (Obmanchivy byvayut sny!) / I razve stranny nam v aprele / Kaprizy milye vesny?" (*S*, 153).

15. G. Ivanov, *Stikhotvoreniya*, 365. The shop of Boissonnas et Egler, Photographes de la Cour Impériale de Russie, was located at Nevsky Prospect, no. 24 (see the *Almanach de St. Pétersbourg* for 1910).

16. For a discussion of Kuzmin's use of "April," see JEM, "'You Must Remember This': Memory's Shorthand in a Late Poem of Kuzmin," in *Studies*, 130–131.

17. "Scorpio" included the translations of "The Three Musicians" and "The Ballad of a Barber" in its 1912 collection of Beardsley's *Izbrannye risunki* (Selected Drawings).

18. Kuzmin saw a lot of Yur'ev in 1911 and 1912, when, on the occasion of the twentieth anniversary of his debut, he saluted him in a poem published in *Glinyanye golubki* (*S*, 262).

19. Kuzmin dedicated three lyrics of 1912 to Rakitin himself, as well as the only short story he wrote in 1911, "Vanina rodinka," finished in September.

20. Kuzmin completed the score on time but was not paid. The project, rescheduled for celebrations to mark the one hundredth anniversary of Lermontov's birth in October 1914, finally opened on February 25, 1917, with a score by Glazunov and with sets and costumes by Golovin so lavish that their likes would never again be seen in Petersburg.

21. The Moscow publishing house "Alcyone" ("Al'tsiona") put out the d'Aurevilly in 1912. The Gourmont, done in collaboration with V. M. Blinova and edited by Akim Volynsky, appeared in 1913 from the Petersburg firm "The Day to Come" ("Gryadushchii Den'"). See the review by "Alex. St." in *Apollon*, 6 (1913), 84–85.

22. Many of the reviews are quoted and summarized on pages 512–514 of Kuzmin, *Izbrannye proizvedeniya*.

23. First published in *Apollon*, 8 (1912), the review is reprinted in Gumilev, *Pis'ma o russkoi poezii*, 155. Gumilev's two other reviews are on pages 156–158 of the same volume.

24. *Novyi entsiklopedicheskii slovar'*, vol. 23 (Petrograd: Brockhaus-Efron, n.d.), column 587, signed "M. Lopatin."

25. In a September 23–24, 1934, Diary reminiscence about his life in the "Tower," Kuzmin wrote that he had been curious enough about Masonry to ask Evgeny Anichkov, whom he suspected of being a Mason, how one could join. Anichkov, one of Vyacheslav Ivanov's closest friends, told him that he would have to go to Prague or Paris, as there were no lodges in Russia, and he suggested that he turn to Ivanov, who was a Mason, for further advice. (Compare the February 12, 1912, entry in the Diary: "Anichkov was nice. . . . There are no lodges in Russia. Vyacheslav is also a Mason.") Kuzmin noted only that he believed Ivanov had been more involved with the Rosicrucians and with anthroposophy than Masonry, adding: "Rosicrucianism always seemed a pathetic masquerade to me, but Steinerism was a reality." Kuzmin never did join the Masons, but notes that they "always interested me because of Mozart and as a secret society and, perhaps this is the most important, as an organization drawn up without any orientation to women, just like the army, closed learned establishments, and monasteries." Allow women into them, English clubs, officers' associations, and the like, and, he believed, they lose all their meaning and "poetry." "Of all sports," he concluded, "I perhaps like soccer the most as the one least accessible to women."

26. Kuzmin finished the translation in April, and it was announced for publication by "Gryadushchii Den'," but, like so many of his translations, it never came out.

27. The complete text of this letter, as well as the full text of the review, are published in NAB, "Istoriya odnoi retsenzii (*Cor ardens* Vyach. Ivanova v otsenke M. Kuzmina)," *Philologica*, 1, no. 1–2 (1994), 135–148.

28. Blok, *Sobranie sochinenii*, vol. 8 (1963), 386–387, letter of April 16, 1912. The penultimate paragraph of the review as published read, "Vyacheslav Ivanov's poetry is the sound of trumpets and flutes, the rustling of wings, the coursing of white horses who moan with a tender neighing only in the hour of sacrificial quiet...."

29. *Apollon*, 5 (1912), 57. See also Chapter 6.

30. Letter of September 12, 1912, cited in NAB, "Istoriya odnoi retsenzii," 144.

31. "Moi brat v del'fiiskom Apollone, / A v tom—na Moike—chut' ne vrag!" V. Ivanov, *Sobranie sochinenii*, 3 (1979), 48. The poem was written on January 21, 1911.

32. Shvarsalon's diary for 1908–1910 recounts the story of her relationship with Kuzmin. NAB published those parts of it touching on him in *Mikhail Kuzmin: Stat'i i materialy*, 310–337.

33. Aleksey Skaldin made the comparison in a poem addressed to her; see Sergey Trotsky's "Vospominaniya," 66.

34. See the entry for November 14, 1909, in her diary, published in NAB, *Mikhail Kuzmin: Stat'i i materialy*, 332.

35. "Detskii spisok docheri-bogini, / Prestupivshei zapovednyi prag," from the 1912 poem "Ee docheri" ("To Her Daughter") that mythologized the events of the previous summer. V. Ivanov, *Sobranie sochinenii*, 3:53. Ivanov later exclaimed to Sergey Trotsky, one of many friends who found it difficult to accept the relationship, "But understand, understand that I love Vera precisely because she is *her* daughter." Trotsky, "Vospominaniya," 66.

36. Guenther was the first to do more than hint at this story in his memoirs, *Ein Leben im Ostwind*, 399–400. Ivanov's biographer Olga Deschartes wrote only of "pernicious slander" in Petersburg about the couple; see her introduction to volume one of Ivanov's *Sobranie sochinenii*, 138.

37. M. V. Alpatov and E. A. Gunst, *Nikolay Nikolaevich Sapunov* (Moscow: Iskusstvo, 1965), 37–38. They write that Kuzmin is holding a book in the portrait, but none is visible in the photograph of it that JEM received from the Minsk museum that owns it.

38. For a description of the venture, see A. A. Mgebrov, *Zhizn' v teatre*, vol. 2 (Moscow: Academia, 1932), 189–222.

39. Ibid., 206.

40. Blok, *Sobranie sochinenii*, 8:393, letter of June 24, 1912. Kuzmin, who attended the funeral with Miller, who had dropped by unexpectedly that morning, wrote only, "It was utterly gloomy, they did not even give us any candles to hold" (Diary).

41. "O zhutkom i misticheskom," *Sinii zhurnal*, 51 (1913), 5.

42. Mikhail Kuzmin, "Vospominaniya o N. N. Sapunove," in *N. Sapunov: Stikhi, vospominaniya, kharakteristiki* (Moscow: N. N. Karyshev, 1916), 51.

43. "Skazal: 'Ya ne umeyu plavat','—/ I vot otplyl, plokhoi plovets, / Tuda, gde uzh spletala slava / Tebe lazorevyi venets" ("Sapunovu," *S*, 427).

44. "Khudozhnik utonuvshii / Topochet kabluchkom"; "Za nim gusarskii mal'chik" (*S*, 532).

45. "Devyat' rodinok prelestnykh / Potseluyami schitayu, / I, schitaya, ya chitayu / Tainu, slashche tain nebesnykh. / Na shchekakh, na miloi shee, / U grudi, gde serdtse b'etsya… / Ot lobzanii ne sotretsya / To, chto muskusa temnee. / Tak, po lestnitse nebesnoi, / Chetki neg perebiraya, / Ya dverei dostignu raya / Krasoty tvoei chudesnoi. / Ta li rodinka vos'maya / Mne milei vsego na svete, / Slashche teni v teplom lete / I milei, chem veter maya. / A doidu ya do devyatoi— / Tut uzh bol'she ne schitayu… / Tol'ko tayu, tayu, tayu, / Nezhnym plamenem ob"yatyi" (*S*, 246). This is the second poem of the "Ostanovka" cycle, which was written in 1912–13.

46. "Ya tikho ot tebya idu, / A ty ostalsya na balkone. / 'Kol' slaven nash Gospod' v Sione' / Trubyat v Tavricheskom sadu. / Ya vizhu blednuyu zvezdu / Na teplom, svetlom nebosklone, / I luchshikh slov ya ne naidu, / Kogda ya ot tebya idu, / Kak 'slaven nash Gospod' v Sione'" (*S*, 241). The poem is the sixth of the cycle "Kholm vdali," which was written between May and October 1912 and addressed to Knyazev.

47. "Ne mozhet iz"yasnit' yazyk." The hymn, with music by Dmitry Bortnyansky, used the text of a Psalm written by the eighteenth-century poet Mikhail Kheraskov. The full text, which was long banned in the Soviet period, can be found in *Russkaya literatura—vek XVIII: Lirika*, vol. 1 (Moscow: Khudozhestvennaya literatura, 1990), 228–229.

48. "Tselovannye mnoyu ruki / Ty ne szhigai, no beregi," the second poem of the cycle "Kholm vdali" (*S*, 239).

49. "Plenennyi prelest'yu pevuchei," in Knyazev, *Stikhi*, 79. The masculine adjective *blizok* ("close") in the second line of the poem's second stanza makes it obvious that the poem is addressed to a man.

50. See the eleventh poem, "Smutish'sya l' serdtsem orobelym?" of the cycle "Kholm vdali" (*S*, 244). Kuzmin's part of the proposed volume was entitled "Zelenyi doloman" (*S*, 621–625, 781–782).

51. Cited by NAB, "Peterburgskie gafizity," in *Mikhail Kuzmin: Stat'i i materialy*, 88.

52. "Dorozhe syna, rodnee brata," "Moi neizmennyi, zhelannyi drug" (*S*, 241).

53. Kuzmin captured the atmosphere of Riga's Old Town—"Tall old buildings, tiled roofs, narrow streets or boulevards, street signs in German. Everything was unaccustomed" (Diary)—in *Plavayushchie puteshestvuyushchie* and in the opening poem of the "Kholm vdali" cycle, "Schastlivyi son li sladko snitsya" (*S*, 239).

54. Kuzmin recalled the time in Mitau in the seventh poem of "Kholm vdali," "Pokoisya, mirnaya Mitava" (*S*, 242). Knyazev wrote at least two poems during their stay there (*Stikhi*, 94–95).

55. The first of them, entitled simply "O. A. S." and dated July 1912, has the poet standing on his balcony thinking only of her, his "distant, white star." Knyazev, *Stikhi*, 81.

56. "Bisernye koshel'ki" (*S*, 271–274). Sudeikina had asked Kuzmin for something she could use at her verse recitals; the cycle became one her "signature pieces."

57. "Odna nizhu ya biser na svobode: / Malinovyi, zelenyi, zheltyi tsvet— / Tvoi tsveta" (*S*, 271).

58. The drawing had appeared in the beginning of September in *Satirikon*, 36 (1912), 9. Knyazev immediately wrote a poem about it, "Na risunok S. Yu. Sudeikina," in which he pictured himself as the officer receiving the rose. When it was published in his *Stikhi*, 93, the reader was referred to the drawing. In the cycle, Kuzmin transferred his own doubts about Knyazev to the young woman of "Bisernye koshel'ki," from whose point of view the first two poems are told: she realizes her lover's betrayal when he stands with another woman "on a balcony."

59. J. Douglas Clayton gives a reliable survey of one aspect of the age's obsession in his *Pierrot in Petrograd: The Commedia dell'Arte/Balagan in Twentieth-Century Russian Theatre and Drama* (Montreal: McGill–Queen's University Press, 1993).

60. "Vy—milaya, nezhnaya Kolombina," in Knyazev, *Stikhi*, 82.

61. "V grustnom i blednom grime" (*S*, 247–248)).

62. "Moi milyi, molyu, na mgnoven'e / Predstav', budto ya—ona" ("Ya znayu, ty lyubish' druguyu," *S*, 249).

63. The play may in part have been inspired by Kuzmin's work over the summer on a translation of *Il re corvo* by Carlo Gozzi for the publishing house of Konstantin Nekrasov in Yaroslavl', which went out of business before it could be issued. Translations of four poems by Oscar Wilde did appear in the 1912 Marks edition of his collected works.

64. *Russkaya mysl'*, 7 and 8 (1913). Kuzmin republished it in his fourth book of stories, *Pokoinitsa v dome: Skazki* (St. Petersburg: M. I. Semenov, 1914).

65. The text of the play can be found in *Russkaya teatral'naya parodiya XIX— nachala XX veka* (Moscow: Iskusstvo, 1976), 588–597.

66. Full details about the whole sorry tale, related in letters, can be found in NAB, "K odnomu temnomu epizodu v biografii Kuzmina," *MKiRK*, 166–169, and Konstantin Azadovsky, "Epizody," *Novoe literaturnoe obozrenie*, 10 (1994), 123–129.

67. On November 13, 1909, Kuzmin wrote in the Diary: "The Tolstoys were not there. They had probably gone to the meeting about the cabaret which Komissarzh[evsky], Sudeikin, etc. are organizing." Pronin had invited Kuzmin to take part, but he had to be at Golovin's studio to pose for the *Apollon* group portrait.

68. A. E. Parnis and R. D. Timenchik survey its history and give all the programs performed there in "Programmy 'Brodyachei sobaki,'" in *Pamyatniki kul'tury: Novye otkrytiya, Ezhegodnik 1983* (Leningrad: Nauka, 1985), 160–257.

69. "A!.. / Ne zabyta i Pallada / V titulovannom krugu, / Slovno drevnyaya driada, / Chto rezvitsya na lugu, / Ei lyubov' odna otrada, / I gde nado, i ne nado / Ne otvetit (3 raza) 'ne mogu.'" Benedikt Livshits first gave the "Hymn" wide circulation when he included its complete text in his memoirs in 1933. A paraphrase of it can be found in John Bowlt's translation of the memoirs, *The One-and-a-Half-Eyed Archer* (Newtonville, Mass.: Oriental Research Partners, 1977), 215–216. For the Russian text, see Parnis and Timenchik, "Programmy 'Brodyachei sobaki,'" 202–203.

8. *"Everything Will Be as It Is Destined"*

1. Sergey Auslender reviewed the "touchingly childlike play" in *Apollon*, 2 (1913), 66–67. The text can be found in Kuzmin, *Teatr*, bk. 1, vol. 1, 61–67.

2. Vsevolod Knyazev, "I net napevov, net sozvuchii," *Stikhi*, 103, dated December 1912.

3. "Ya tseloval 'vrata Damaska,' / Vrata s shchitom, uvitom v mekh" (ibid., 105). They are the first two lines of the last stanza of "Ya byl v strane."

4. Timenchik, "Rizhskii epizod v 'Poeme bez geroya' Anny Akhmatovoi," 120. On Sunday April 7, 1913, the Petersburg newspaper *Rech'* contained a notice of his death.

5. Elaine Moch-Bickert reports the first version in her *"Kolombina desyatykh godov...": Kniga ob Ol'ge Glebovoi-Sudeikinoi* (Paris: Izdatel'stvo Grzhebina, AO "Arsis," 1993), 101, while JEM heard the other as recently as 1995 in Petersburg.

6. Ibid.

7. "Kto nad mertvym so mnoi ne plachet, / Kto ne znaet, chto sovest' znachit / I zachem sushchestvuet ona." Akhmatova, *Stikhotvoreniya i poemy*, 372.

8. R. D. Timenchik, "Neopublikovannye prozaicheskie zametki Anny Akhmatovoi," *Izvestiya Akademii Nauk SSSR: seriya literatury i yazyka*, 43, no. 1 (1984), 71.

9. Chukovskaya, *Zapiski ob Anne Akhmatovoi*, 1:192.

10. See her conversation with Chukovskaya on August 8, 1940, ibid., 173.

11. "Zaletnoyu golubkoi k nam sletela" (*S*, 261). *Vecher* came out in March 1912 (St. Petersburg: Tsekh poetov).

12. Dmitry Maksimov told JEM in 1969 that he had once been "tactless" enough to ask Akhmatova about Kuzmin's preface to *Vecher* and, as a literary historian curious about matters of genealogy, about her view of the relationship of her verse to that of Kuzmin, only to be met with icy silence and "banishment" from her apartment for several months (they were neighbors living in the same building). The usually indomitable Lidiya Ginzburg told JEM during their last long conversation in 1990 that she had never "dared" to raise the matter with Akhmatova, an old friend, knowing all too well what the reaction would be.

13. P. N. Luknitsky, *Acumiana: Vstrechi s Annoi Akhmatovoi*, vol. 1, *1924–1925* (Paris: YMCA Press, 1991), 124, entry for April 12, 1925.

14. Chukovskaya, *Zapiski ob Anne Akhmatovoi*, 1:173–174. Vsevolod Petrov also writes, "I heard from A. A. Akhmatova that she was convinced that Gumilev's review had forever alienated Kuzmin from the whole group of Acmeists" ("Kaliostro," 90).

15. *Apollon*, 8 (1912), 61. The review is republished in Gumilev, *Pis'ma o russkoi poezii*, 153–154.

16. *Apollon*, 2 (1912), 73–74.

17. *Niva: Prilozheniya na 1913*, vol. 1, columns 161–162.

18. See, for example, the Diary entry for December 14, 1913: "Gumilev wanted to come by at 5 o'clock. . . . Gumilev was with Anna Andr[eevna], who reminded me of Tsarskoe, my living there, *Apollo*, Knyazev, for some reason."

19. Fedor Ivanov, "Staromu Peterburgu (Chto vspomnilos')," in the Berlin Russian journal *Zhizn'*, 9 (1920).

20. In an answer to a newspaper questionnaire about suicide that he wrote a few weeks after Knyazev's death, Kuzmin stated simply, "About the voluntary or unintentional suicides themselves, we have no right to judge: they perform a mysterious sacrifice whose meaning is secret from us." See "Samoubiistvo," *Birzhevye vedomosti* (evening edition), no. 12944, May 19, 1912, 4; reprinted in *Novoe slovo*, 6 (1912), 8.

21. "Puskai nas svyazyval izdávna / Veselyi i pechal'nyi rok" (*S*, 635).

22. "Pustit'sya by po belu svetu," the first poem of the cycle "Raznye stikhotvoreniya" in *Glinyanye golubki* (*S*, 260).

23. See "Vsegda stremyas' k lyubvi neulovimoi" (*S*, 244–245), the twelfth and final poem of the cycle "Kholm vdali."

24. "Zemlya, ty mne dala tsvetok" (*SS*, 3:457). Kuzmin never included the poem in any of his verse collections.

25. "Nakhodit strannoe molchanie / Po vremenam na nas, / No v nem taitsya uvenchanie, / Spokoinyi schast'ya chas. / Zadumavshiisya nad stupenyami, / Nash angel smotrit vniz, / Gde mezh derev'yami osennimi / Zlatistyi dym povis. / Zatem opyat' nash kon' prishporennyi / Privetlivo zarzhet / I po doroge neprotorennoi / Nas poneset vpered. / No ne smushchaisya ostanovkami, / Moi nezhnyi, nezhnyi drug, / I ob"yasnen'yami nelovkimi / Ne narushai nash krug. / Sluchitsya vsë, chto prednaznacheno, / Vozhatyi nas vedet. / Za te chasy, chto zdes' utracheny, / Nebesnyi vkusim med," in the collection *Vozhatyi* (*S*, 310–311).

26. The two poems and another, "Vnizu nedvizhen kruglyi prud," appeared in the magazine *Severnye zapiski*, 3 (1914), 83–84. The autograph of "Nakhodit strannoe molchanie" is inscribed "To My Vsevolod."

27. "Iz gliny golubykh golubok" (*S*, 231).

28. Yurkun was born in Vilnius. "It's a pity for Yurkun personally that he's a Pole. Incidentally, he is a Lithuanian, although I do not know what that means. Like Montenegrins. Not a distinctive *universal* nation," Kuzmin wrote in "Cheshuya v nevode," in *Strelets: Sbornik tretii i poslednii*, 101.

29. "Lyubov'—vsegdashnyaya moya vera," the fourth line of the first stanza of the first poem of the cycle "Radostnyi putnik," in *Seti* (*S*, 90).

30. On February 5, 1925, Kuzmin wrote in the Diary: "And how sad, catastrophic is the Diary for the years 1911–12–13. Yur.'s appearance on the scene was necessary for everything to take proper shape."

31. On August 15, 1915, "Serg[ey] Yur['evich] drew Yurochka's portrait, successfully" (Diary). This is apparently the portrait that is now in the collection of the Russian Museum in Petersburg and that can be found in a black and white reproduction on page 136 of the article "Artisticheskoe kabare 'Prival komediantov'" by A. M. Konechnyi, V. Ya. Morderer, A. E. Parnis, and R. D. Timenchik, in *Pamyatniki kul'tury: Novye otkrytiya, Ezhegodnik 1988* (Moscow: Nauka, 1989). When one compares the portrait with photographs of Yurkun from the 1930s, one can understand why Kuzmin nicknamed him Dorian: he not only reminded him of Wilde's description of his hero, but seemed to age rather little.

32. "Net, zhizni mel'nitsa ne sterla / Lyubovnoi smelosti v krovi,— / Khochu zapet' vo vsë ya gorlo / Mal'chisheskuyu pesn' lyubvi!" (*S*, 232), the first poem of the cycle "V doroge."

33. "Nezhnost' brata, / vernost' druga / i strastnost' lyubovnika" in "Pokhozha li moya lyubov'," the second poem of the free verse cycle "Nochnye razgovory," which is dedicated to Yurkun (*S*, 256). On April 13, 1913, Kuzmin wrote in the Diary, "Yurochka is sweet, like a young god, jolly and young, like spring." He wrote only "To Yurochka" under the heading "Poems" in a list of his works for 1913.

34. "Chto eto—ne lyubov' yunoshi, / no rebenka—muzha / (mozhet byt', startsa)" (*S*, 256).

35. "Bez tebya moya zhizn' pusta. / S toboi proidu do mogily" (*S*, 238), from "My dumali, konchilos' vsë," the final poem of the cycle "V doroge."

36. See Margaret Dalton, "A Russian Best-Seller of the Early Twentieth Century: Evdokiya Apollonovna Nagrodskaya's *The Wrath of Dionysus*," in *Studies in Russian Literature in Honor of Vsevolod Setchkarev*, ed. Julian W. Connolly and Sonia I. Ketchian (Columbus, Ohio: Slavica, 1986), 102–112, and S. Savitsky's introduction to the 1994 reprint of the novel published in St. Petersburg by "Severo-Zapad" (5–10).

37. *Apollon*, 9 (July–August 1910), 34 (second pagination).

38. Ryurik Ivnev, "Vstrechi s M. A. Kuzminym," *Zvezda*, 5 (1982), 161.

39. G. Ivanov, *Stikhotvoreniya*, 364.

40. Vsevolod Petrov in conversation with JEM in 1969. Was Kuzmin recalling Lord Henry's remark in *The Picture of Dorian Gray*, "My dear fellow, she tried to found a *salon*, and only succeeded in opening a restaurant"? Wilde, *Picture of Dorian Gray*, 30.

41. From 1914 to 1918, when Semenov's enterprise collapsed in the economic chaos that enused after the events of 1917, he published nine volumes, all but one of which (the 1915 second edition of *Seti* that was mutilated by the war censorship) were actually new works, not the simple reprints one would expect from something called a "collected edition" *(sobranie sochinenii)*. The ninth volume, to be sure, included four stories first published by "Scorpio."

42. See Kuzmin's letter to her of May 1913 in A. G. Timofeev, "M. Kuzmin. Stikhotvoreniya: P'esa: Perepiska," in *Ezhegodnik rukopisnogo otdela Pushkinskogo Doma na 1990 god* (St. Petersburg: Gumanitarnoe agenstvo "Akademicheskii proekt," 1993), 62–63. Other letters are quoted in notes to individual stories in *Durnaya kompaniya* (St. Petersburg: Izdatel'skii tsentr "Terra," izdatel'stvo "Azbuka," 1995), a volume of Yurkun's collected prose.

43. See Mikhail Kuzmin, "Kak ya chital doklad v 'Brodyachei sobake'," *Sinii zhurnal*, 18 (1914), 6; and Parnis and Timenchik, "Programmy 'Brodyachei sobaky,'" 233–234.

44. Nagrodskaya brought *Glinyanye golubki* to Kuzmin, who was staying at her dacha at Pavlovsk, on May 20, 1914. Yurkun brought him a copy of the novel on June 8. Kuzmin inscribed Yurkun's copy of the collection with "To the one and only Yurochka, whom I love, the first copy of this book, rejoicing that it will come out at the same time as his *Swedish Gloves*."

45. The reviews are summarized in the notes to Yurkun, *Durnaya kompaniya*, 473–475. See also T. L. Nikol'skaya, "O tvorchestve Yu. I. Yurkuna," in *Sed'mye Tynyanovskie chteniya*, fasc. 9 (Riga, 1995–96), 173–178.

46. Somov, *Pis'ma: Dnevniki: Suzhdeniya sovremennikov*, 143.

47. See Lev Rubanov, "Klub 'Mednyi vsadnik'," *Mosty*, 12 (1966), 376–384.

48. "Kosnoyazychnymi namekami / To naklikaetsya, / To otvrashchaetsya / Gryadushchaya beda," from "Byvayut strannymi prorokami / Poety inogda" ("Poets are sometimes strange prophets") (*S*, 249).

49. The volumes were *Pokoinitsa v dome: Skazki: Chetvertaya kniga rasskazov*, ten stories of 1912–13 (vol. 4 of the collected works, 1914); *Zelenyi solovei: Pyataya kniga rasskazov*, eleven stories of 1914–15 (vol. 5, 1915); *Antrakt v ovrage*, seventeen stories of 1914–15 (vol. 8, 1916); *Babushkina shkatulka*, eleven stories of 1916 (vol. 2, 1918); and *Devstvennyi Viktor*, thirteen stories of 1916–17 and reprints of some earlier works (vol. 9, 1918).

50. His last prose contribution, an article entitled "Analogiya ili providenie? (O

A. S. Khomyakove kak o poete)" in issue 6–7 of 1914, used citations from the poetry of the influential nineteenth-century Slavophile Aleksey Khomyakov to make an anti-German statement and predict Russia's victory in the war.

51. Kuzmin notes, "I was at the offices of *Satyricon* and at *Northern Annals*—an editorial office of rare politeness and kindness" (Diary, December 13, 1913). He was unhappy that the latter would not accept Yurkun's stories, but he published some of his finest poems of the period in the magazine.

52. Mikhail Kuzmin, "Prival komediantov," *Obozrenie teatrov*, no. 3076, April 20, 1916, 12.

53. Benedikt Livshits wrote in his memoirs that by the time he began to visit the cabaret, Kuzmin was "already a rather rare guest." Benedikt Livshits, *Polutor-aglazyi strelets* (Leningrad: Sovetskii pisatel', 1989), 512. The Diary confirms his account. Not even a special evening of eighteenth-century dances on March 28, 1914, honoring Tamara Karsavina, whom he "worshiped," could entice Kuzmin to the cabaret. He wrote a poem for the "bouquet" of poems, portraits, and essays that she received on the special night, but he preferred to spend a quiet evening with her the day before her performance rather than go to the cabaret itself.

54. See the chapter "Peterburgskie teatry miniatyur i 'Krivoe zerkalo'" in Tikhvinskaya, *Kabare i teatry miniatyur*, 137–204.

55. The texts of the majority of the plays to have survived are published in Kuzmin's two-volume *Teatr*, where notes give what information we have about their performance history.

56. A translation can be found in Michael Green, ed. and trans., *The Russian Symbolist Theatre: An Anthology of Plays and Critical Texts* (Ann Arbor: Ardis, 1986).

57. Anatoly Shaikevich, "Peterburgskaya Bogema (M. A. Kuzmin)," *Orion* (Paris, 1947), 139; the memoirs were republished in *Russkaya literatura*, 2 (1991), 104–112.

58. Artur Lur'e, "O. A. Glebova-Sudeikina," *Opyty*, 5 (1967), 142.

59. Hubertus F. Jahn excludes literature and the fine arts from his *Patriotic Culture in Russia during World War I* (Ithaca, N.Y.: Cornell University Press, 1995) and focuses instead on mass culture and popular entertainment in his survey of popular attitudes to the war.

60. Ern gave his speech on October 6, 1914, at Moscow's Religious-Philo-sophical Society. He published it in *Russkaya mysl'*, 12 (1914), and in his *Mech i Krest: Stat'i o sovremennykh sobytiyakh* (Moscow: Tipografiya t-va I. D. Sytina, 1915).

61. "Vse o nemtsakh," *Sinii zhurnal*, 31 (1914), 12–13.

62. "Odumaetsya li Germaniya / Ostavit' pagubnyi marshrut, / Kuda vedet smeshnaya maniya / I v kaske Vagnerovskii shut?!" from the poem "Tyazhelovesnym groznym shorokhom," *Petrogradskie vechera*, 3 (1914), 7; republished in *SS*, 3:460–461.

63. Mikhail Kuzmin, "Razdum'ya i nedoumen'ya Petra Otshel'nika," *Petrogradskie vechera*, 3 (1914), 216.

64. Kuzmin, "Cheshuya v nevode," 98.

65. Georgy Adamovich, "Kuzmin," *Poslednie novosti*, no. 5538, May 22, 1936, 3.

66. Mikhail Kuzmin, "Elegiya Tristana," in *Paraboly* (*S*, 482–483).

67. Unlike that of England, France, or Germany, Russian literature produced not a single memorable, much less classic, work on the World War. Gumilev's death-haunted war poetry is incomparably better than the run-of-the-mill stuff

written by other poets, perhaps because, unlike most, he served at the front, but it is hardly his best work; in a few years, of course, revolutions and civil war would move to the center of the literary imagination.

68. See, for example, his article "Prichiny i sledstviya," *Birzhevye vedomosti*, no. 15832, evening edition, September 29, 1916, 4, where he wrote: "In general, various consequences are ascribed to the movies: the decline of theaters, the influx of refugees, the lack of heat in the capital, and, of course, juvenile crime. Viewers, they say, who have seen a lot of the exploits of cunning thieves, themselves put into practice all that they have seen. One could as well say that a child who has learned how to use a knife from his grandmother will use it to stab her."

69. "O pantomime, kinematografe i razgovornykh p'esakh," in *Dnevniki pisatelei*, 3–4 (May–June, 1914), 12–16. Fedor Sologub edited the short-lived magazine.

70. Meyerhold again used Kuzmin's music for a revival of Blok's play *Balaganchik*, which his "Studio" pupils performed on April 7, 1914. Kuzmin now dismissed the piece as "unbelievable nonsense" ("neveroyatnyi vzdor" [Diary]) and wondered what he had ever seen in it.

71. Cited by A. G. Timofeev in the introduction to his publication of Kuzmin's "Arabian fairy tale" *Zerkalo dev*, in "Kabaretnaya efemerida," *Novoe literaturnoe obozrenie*, 3 (1993), 144. It opened the cabaret's second season on October 25, 1916. The whole history of the new cabaret can be found in Konechnyi, Morderer, Parnis, and Timenchik, "Artisticheskoe kabare 'Prival komediantov.'"

72. Mikhail Kuzmin, "Prival komediantov," *Obozrenie teatrov*, no. 3076, April 20, 1916, 12.

73. Kuzmin had made his real debut, of course, in the 1905 *Zelenyi sbornik*, of which the organizers were probably unaware. Kuzmin was probably just as happy to ignore their imprecision, considering as he did the 1906 publication of the "Aleksandriiskie pesni" and *Kryl'ya* in *Vesy* his real entrance into Russian literature.

74. "Slav'sya likho, / Slav'sya Mikha- / Il Alekseevich Kuzmin!" The full text can be found in Konechnyi, Morderer, Parnis, and Timenchik, "Artisticheskoe kabare 'Prival komediantov,'" 130.

75. "Ognisto-l'distyi, / Morozno-zharkii, russkii rai," "zhelannyi, neiskorenimyi, / Dushi moei davnishnii son!" The lines are from the 1915 poem "Vsë tot zhe son, zhivoi i davnii," which opens the "Russkii rai" cycle in *Vozhatyi* (*S*, 323–324).

76. "Menya trevozhit vzdokh myatezhnyi / (Ot etikh vzdokhov, Gospod', spasi!), / Kogda prizyv ya slyshu nezhnyi / To Motsarta, to Debyussi. / Eshche khochu zabyt' ya o gore, / I zagoraetsya nadezhdoyu vzor, / Kogda ya chuvstvuyu veter s morya / I grezhu o tebe, Bosfor!" From "Gospod', ya vizhu, ya nedostoin," the third poem of the cycle "Plod zreet" in *Vozhatyi* (*S*, 309).

77. Igor Stravinsky, "The Avatars of Russian Music," in *Poetics of Music in the Form of Six Lessons* (Cambridge, Mass.: Harvard University Press, 1970), 97.

78. See Robert Craft's article "Where's Vera? She's Painting," *Saturday Review*, February 26, 1972, 46. Kuzmin alluded to her ancestry in the penultimate stanza of his poem: "In my land, you are all the same foreign [or 'someone else's'], / and yet you could not be more native to Russia" ("V moem krayu vy vse-taki chuzhaya, / I vsë zh nel'zya Rossii byt' rodnei") (*S*, 398).

79. "Ya—Figaro, a vy... vy—donna Anna. / Net, don Zhuana net, i ne pridet

Suzanna!" (*S*, 396). The autograph of "Chuzhaya poema" is item number 17a in the album that Vera Arturovna kept during her peregrinations with Sudeikin throughout Russia, the Crimea, and the Caucasus in 1917–1920 before they fled for France. See Bowlt, *The Salon Album of Vera Sudeikin-Stravinsky*, 16–17.

80. "Besformennoi prizrak svobody, / bolotno lzhivyi, kak beloglazye lyudi, / ty razdelyaesh' narody, / bormocha o nebyvshem chude. / I vot, / kak ristalishchnyi kon', / rinesh'sya vzryvom vod, / vz"yarish'sya, khrapish', mechesh' / mokryi ogon'/ na beloe nebo, rushas' i rusha, / sverlivoi voronkoi, buravya / svoi zhe nedra!" "Vrazhdebnoe more" (*S*, 332–333).

81. Yury Tynyanov, *Arkhaisty i novatory* (Leningrad: Priboi, 1929), 553.

82. See Kuzmin's "Futuristy" in "Pis'ma iz Italii" ("Letters from Italy"), *Apollon*, 9 (1910), 20, of the "Khronika" section. There he said of it what he would later say of Acmeism: "If this movement has been provoked by life, it will, of course, change its form and will be effective, but if it has been fabricated by two or three disgruntled people, it will, of course, disappear" (21).

83. Kuzmin, "Kak ya chital doklad v 'Brodyachei sobake.'" See also Parnis and Timenchik, "Programmy 'Brodyachei sobaki,'" 233–234. Two years later Kuzmin wrote incidental music for a private performance on December 3, 1916, of Zdanevich's "dra" *Yanko krul' albanskai*, the last two words deformations of the Russian for "Albanian king"—the play was ostensibly written in Albanian!

84. Kuzmin made the remarks about Khlebnikov and Futurism in the 1922 "Pis'mo v Pekin," in *Uslovnosti*, 165.

85. The recollections of Boris Pronin as quoted in Parnis and Timenchik, "Programmy 'Brodyachei sobaki,'" 166.

86. "Priyatno marsovym vécherom / Pit' kuzminskoi réchi rom." Quoted in Leonid Seleznev, "Mikhail Kuzmin i Vladimir Mayakovsky (K istorii odnogo posvyashcheniya)," *Voprosy literatury*, 11 (1989), 68.

87. We have in mind lines such as "I tyazhelaya ot myasa fantaziya / medlenno, kak pishchevarenie, grezit o vechnoi narodov bitve, / ryzhaya zhena Menelaya, toboi, tsarevich troyanskii, toboi / uyazvlennaya!" ("And fantasy, heavy from meat, slowly, like digestion, dreams of the eternal battle of peoples, the russet[-haired] wife of Menelaus, by you, Trojan tsarevich, by you—stung!") (*S*, 334).

88. Mikhail Kuzmin, "Parnasskie zarosli," in *Zavtra: Literaturno-kriticheskii sbornik*, 1 (Berlin, 1923), 117. The article was written in March 1922 and slightly revised in September.

89. Seleznev, "Mikhail Kuzmin i Vladimir Mayakovsky," 76.

90. When Kuzmin re-read the novel in March 1922, he detected Nagrodskaya's pernicious influence and dismissed it as an "unpleasant and slack work" (Diary, March 21).

91. A notebook dating from the beginning of the 1920s held in the archives of IRLI, coll. 172, inven. 1, no. 319, 245 verso. "Then we [he and Yurkun] chatted about 'Plutarch,' drew up lists" (Diary, August 12, 1915).

92. The short novel, which he dedicated to Meyerhold, first appeared on the pages of the miscellany *Strelets: Sbornik vtoroi* (1916), 1–103. The 1919 book edition is reproduced in volume eight of the collected *Proza*.

93. Charles Dickens, *Our Mutual Friend*, Book the Third (London: Oxford University Press, 1970), 476 (chap. 6).

94. Kuzmin, *Proza*, 8:8.

95. Kuzmin turned to all available accounts of Cagliostro's life and a variety of secondary sources on alchemy, Masonry, and the occult when writing the novel. His dissatisfaction with them made him turn to Anatoly Shaikevich for help in setting up a meeting with a primary source, the occult thinker and "hyperspace philosopher" Petr Uspensky. See Shaikevich, "Peterburgskaya Bogema," 141–142.

96. Mikhail Kuzmin, Introduction to *Cagliostro*, in *Proza*, 8:8–9.

97. Georgy Adamovich, "Russkaya poeziya," *Zi*, 2 (1923), 4.

98. Letter to Pasternak of February 14, 1923, in Marina Tsvetaeva, *Neizdannye pis'ma* (Paris: YMCA Press, 1972), 280.

99. The poem "O visokosnye goda" (*SS*, 3:467).

9. "The End of Everything"

1. Georgy Adamovich, "Kuzmin," *Poslednie novosti*, no. 5538, May 22, 1936, 3.

2. "Slovno sto let proshlo, a slovno nedelya! / Kakoe nedelya ... dvadtsat' chetyre chasa!" from "Russkaya revolyutsiya," *Niva*, 15 (1917), 215. He never republished it or the other poems he wrote in the months immediately following February 1917. Some of them can be found in *S*, 630–633.

3. "Krovavuyu razveya ten', / Protrubit krasnyi maiskii den', / Chto vse narody mira—brat'ya!" "Maiskii den'," *Russkaya volya*, no. 69, April 18, 1917, 3; republished in *SS*, 3:469–470.

4. E. A. Dinershtein, "Mayakovsky v fevrale–oktyabre 1917 g.," *Literaturnoe nasledstvo*, vol. 65, *Novoe o Mayakovskom* (Moscow: Izdatel'stvo Akademii Nauk SSSR, 1958), 543–544; and Seleznev, "Mikhail Kuzmin i Vladimir Mayakovsky," 72–74.

5. Somov, *Pis'ma*, 169 and 176.

6. Moisey Bamdas, *Predrassvetnyi vecher* (Petrograd: Izdatel'stvo "Marsel'skikh matrosov," [1917]), 3–5. Kuzmin dedicated a story to him ("Slava v plyushevoi ramke," 1915; in volume eight of the collected works), and the fine poem "Ved' eto iz Geine chto-to..." ("But this is something from Heine..." *S*, 411–12). In the preface to Bamdas's poems, Kuzmin wrote that they were the "voice of a Jewish boy" and called him a "relative" of Heine, "only without his grimaces and, alas, without his humor" (p. 5).

7. See T. L. Nikol'skaya, "Yury Degen," *Russian Literature*, XXIII–II (February 15, 1988), 101–112, and the entry on Degen by Nikol'skaya and NAB in *Russkie pisateli 1800–1917: Biograficheskii slovar'*, vol. 2 (Moscow: Bol'shaya rossiiskaya entsiklopediya, 1992), 92–93. Degen was shot by the Cheka in 1923.

8. NAB, "Dokumental'noe pribavlenie," *Novoe literaturnoe obozrenie*, 11 (1995), 333–334.

9. "The more I read Casanova, the less I like him. A paltry and insolent wretch. The adventures are monotonous and boorishly narrated." Kuzmin, "Cheshuya v nevode," in *Strelets*, 103.

10. Daily entries for amounts of money received began to appear in the Diary in 1917 and continued for years after.

11. "Dusha, ya gorem ne terzaem, / No plachu, vetrenaya strannitsa. / Vsë prodaem my, vsem dolzhaem, / Skoro u nas nichego ne ostanetsya. // Konechno, est' i Bog, i nebo, / I voobrazhenie, kotoroe ne lenitsya, / No kogda sidish' pochti bez khleba, / Stanovish'sya kak smeshnaya plennitsa. // Muza vskochit, pro lyubov'

rasskazhet / (Ona ved' glupen'kaya, durochka), / No vzglyanesh', kak verevkoi vyazhet / Poslednii tyuk nash milyi Yurochka,— // I ostanovish'sya. Otrada / Minutnaya, stradan'e melkoe, / No, Bozhe moi, komu eto nado, / Chtoby vertelsya, kak belka, ya?" (*S*, 321–322).

12. Klaus Harer explores the complex sources of the cantata in *Michail Kuzmin: Studien zur Poetik der frühen und mittleren Schaffensperiode* (Munich: Verlag Otto Sagner, 1993), 90–168.

13. See Konechnyi, Morderer, Parnis, and Timenchik, "Artisticheskoe kabare 'Prival komediantov,'" 139–142, for the whole program and contemporary descriptions of it.

14. Georgy Chulkov had been astonished when Kuzmin told him in August or September that "it goes without saying that I am a Bolshevik," adding: "I confess I like Lenin more than all these liberals of ours who shout about the defense of the fatherland. It is both strange and offensive to fight in the twentieth century." Chulkov set down a lengthy account of the conversation in "Vchera i segodnya," *Narodopravstvo*, 12 (October 16, 1917), 9. Blok shared Kuzmin's views.

15. "Na prestole semistolbnom / Ya, kak yakhont, plamenela / I khoten'em beskhotennym / O Tebe, Khristos, khotela! / Govorila: 'Bezzakonno / Zakovat' zakonom dushu, / Samovol'no li, nevol'no l', / A zapret lyubvi narushu!'" "Sofiya" (*S*, 436–437).

16. Kuzmin, "Cheshuya v nevode," 106–108.

17. Mikhail Kuzmin, "Emotsional'nost' i faktura," in *Uslovnosti*, 177.

18. Kuzmin, "Cheshuya v nevode," 99–100.

19. The bibliophile Sergey Mukhin described the volume in the 1925 booklet he prepared to mark the twentieth anniversary of Kuzmin's literary debut. A. A. Sidorov included one of Kuznetsov's illustrations in *Russkaya grafika nachala XX veka* (Moscow: Iskusstvo, 1969), 216.

20. Mikhail Kuzmin, "Pyat' razgovorov i odin sluchai," in *Proza*, 9:380. Written in November 1925, it was unprintable in Soviet Russia.

21. Blok, *Sobranie sochinenii*, 6:314–315.

22. See G. A. Morev's detailed introduction and notes to his publication of O. N. Gil'debrandt-Arbenina's reminiscences about the Kannegiser family, "Iz istorii russkoi literatury 1910-kh godov: k biografii Leonida Kannegisera," *Minuvshee*, 16 (1994) 115–149. Adamovich, Georgy Ivanov, and the novelist Mark Aldanov thought highly enough of his verse to issue a slim volume of it, *Leonid Kannegiser: 1918–1928*, with their articles and four photographs of him, in Paris in 1928.

23. *Petrogradskaya pravda*, no. 191, September 4, 1918. Cited in G. A. Morev's "Iz kommentariev k tekstam Kuzmina ('Barzhi zatopili v Kronshtadte...')," *Shestye Tynyanovskie chteniya* (Riga, 1992), 27.

24. "Barzhi zatopili v Kronshtadte, / Rasstrelyan kazhdyi desyatyi,— / Yurochka, Yurochka moi, / Dai Bog, chtob Vy byli vos'moi. // Kazarmy na zatonnom vzmor'e, / Prezhnii, ya kriknul by: 'Lyudi!' / Teper' molyus' v podpol'e, / Dumaya o belom chude" (*S*, 555).

25. The firm's beautifully printed catalogues give a good idea of the scope of the plans. See *Katalog izd. "Vsemirnaya literatura"* (Petrograd, 1919), with an introduction by Gorky, and *Katalog izd. "Vsemirnaya literatura": Literatura vostoka* (Petrograd, 1919). In April 1919 a series for twentieth-century Russian literature was added to the translation plan.

26. See A. D. Zaidman, "Literaturnye studii 'Vsemirnoi literatury' i 'Doma Iskusstv' (1919–1921)," *Russkaya literatura*, 1 (1973), 141–147.

27. *L'Île des pingouins* (vol. 6, 1919) and *La Révolte des anges* and *Les Sept femmes de la Barbe-Bleue et autres contes merveilleux* (vol. 9, 1919). Kuzmin not only edited previous translations but also did several new ones himself over the next few years; only one, *Crainquebille, Putois, Riquet, et plusieurs autres récits profitables*, came out in 1922 (vol. 8). Another publisher issued his translation of France's *Petit Pierre* the same year.

28. Kuzmin, "Cheshuya v nevode," 108.

29. *Zi*, no. 178, July 2, 1919, 1; the essay was republished in Kuzmin, *Uslovnosti*, 35–37.

30. See *Zi*, no. 13, November 14, 1918, 4. The ballet was performed at the Malyi Theater in February 1919 at a special Mardi Gras evening, and at a fundraising evening for Petersburg actors at the Mikhailovskii Theater on May 14.

31. See the review by Konstantin Petrov in *Zi*, no. 54, January 8, 1919, 1, and notes to the play in Kuzmin, *Teatr*, bk. 2, vol. 4, 323–328. Bryantsev became one of the most celebrated directors in the history of Soviet children's theater. Kuzmin praised the "enlightening," even "pedagogical" role that Gaideburov's theater (the adjective "peredvizhnoi" in its name may also be translated as "traveling," "mobile") had played since its founding in 1903, but he found its productions a bit too ascetic and "Salvation Army–like," too lacking in the "joy" that he considered essential for any theater. See "Mudroe delanie (Peredvizhnoi teatr)," *Zi*, no. 3, October 31, 1918, 6. Kuzmin met Gaideburov in 1907.

32. See "Teatr-Studiya" (unsigned), in *Zi*, no. 24, November 27, 1918, 4. It lists the suggestions that Kuzmin had made to fellow members of its artistic board on November 22 for a repertory of Russian and foreign works, many of them children's classics that he considered suitable for adaptation.

33. *Zi*, no. 80, February 18, 1919, 1–2; republished in Kuzmin, *Uslovnosti*, 76–79. Until 1920 the theater gave its performances in the great hall of the Conservatory.

34. In his review, Kuzmin objected to the fact that Benelli's was the only new play by a contemporary foreign writer in the theater's second season; see "Rvanyi plashch," *Zi*, no. 249, September 23, 1919, 1.

35. Mikhail Kuzmin, "Pafos yunosheskikh dram Shillera," *Dela i dni Bol'shogo Dramaticheskogo teatra*, 1 (1919), 18–25. The issue also contained articles by Blok and Gorky.

36. Mikhail Kuzmin "Vecher poetov," *Zi*, no. 91, March 5, 1919, 1–2. That night Lunacharsky also read his play, *Magi*, at the Pronins' apartment, which was located above the cabaret. Kuzmin called it "nonsense, of course. Senile sensuality and mysticism" (Diary). The cabaret closed at the end of April 1919.

37. "Bats! / Po morde smazali gryaznoi tryapkoi, / Otnyali khleb, svet, teplo, myaso, / Moloko, mylo, bumagu, knigi, / Odezhdu, sapogi, odeyalo, maslo, / Kerosin, svechi, sol', sakhar, / Tabak, spichki, kashu,—/ Vsë / I skazali: / 'Zhivi i bud' svoboden!' / Bats! / Zaperli v kletku, v kazarmy, / V bogadel'nyu, v sumasshedshii dom, / Tosku i nenavist' poseyav... / Ne tvoi li ideal osushchestvlyaetsya, Arakcheev? / 'Zhivi i bud' svoboden!' / Bats! . . . / Zatoptannye / Dazhe ne sapogami, / Ne laptyami, / A kradennymi s chuzhoi nogi botinkami, / Zhivem svobodnye, / Drozhim u netoplennoi pechi / (Vdokhnoven'e). / Khodim vpot'makh k takim zhe drozhashchim druz'yam. / Ikh tak malo,—/ Edim otbrosy,

zhadno kosyas' na chuzhoi kusok. / Tup um, . . . / Podlye vystrely, / Seraya nenavist', / Tyazhkaya zhizn' podpol'naya / Chervei nerozhdennykh. / Razve i vpravdu /
Navoz my, / Kak govorit navoznaya kucha . . . / Nas zavalivshaya? / Net. /
Zadavlennye, ispugannye, / Rasteryannye, mozhet byt', podlye,—/ No my—lyudi,
/ I potomu eto—tol'ko son / (Bozhe, dvukhletnii son). / Potomu ne navek / Otletel
ot menya / Angel blagovestvuyushchii. / Zhdu ego, / Dumaya o chude." "Angel
blagovestvuyushchii" (*S*, 637–639). Kuzmin refers to the hated minister of Alexander I, Count Aleksey Arakcheev, who a century earlier had instituted a series of
"military colonies" and dreamed of regimenting Russian life along military lines.

38. "Togda svobodno, bezo vsyakogo gruza, / Sladko svyazhem uzel / I
svobodno (ponimaete: svobodno) poidem / V goryachie, soderzhimye chastnym
litsom, / Svobodnym, / Nazhivayushchim dvesti tysyach v god / (Togda eto budut
ogromnye den'gi), / Bani. / Slovom dovol'no gadkim / Stikhi konchayu ya, / Pod-
vergalsya stol'kim napadkam / Za eto slovo ya. . . . / No eto bylo davno ved', / S
tekh por izmenilsya ya. / V etom ubeditsya vsyakii bespristrastnyi chitatel'. / Pri-
tom est' angliiskoe (na frantsuzskom yazyke) motto, / Kotoroe mozhno videt' / Na
lyubom portsigare, podvyazkakh i myle: / 'Honny [rather than the usual 'Honi']
soit qui mal y pense'" (*S*, 641).

39. The poems were first "published" in 1920 in a manuscript booklet, with a
cover by Yurkun, which Kuzmin wrote out by hand in five copies. They first appeared in print in the collection *Nezdeshnie vechera*.

40. See Barry Scherr, "Notes on Literary Life in Petrograd, 1918–1922: A Tale
of Three Houses," *Slavic Review*, 36, no. 2 (June 1977), 256–267; note 19 lists the
major memoirs and fictional accounts about life in the famous House of Arts. See
also the chronicle section of the first issue of the miscellany *Dom Iskusstv* (1921;
1920 on the cover), 68–71, for information on the aims and board members of both
it and the Writers' House.

41. Kuzmin had been assigned to "category number 2" for the academic ration,
a gratuitous slap in the face as it was meant for those "practitioners of the arts" who
were "young, but already formed and have an unquestionable and clear-cut gift."
The third, given to Akhmatova, Dobuzhinsky, Sologub, and Mayakovsky, was for
those who possessed an "entirely mature gift and a record of major artistic accom-
plishment." There were two even higher categories. See Aleksandr Galushkin,
"'Tak zhili poety...' Neakademicheskie zametki ob 'akademicheskikh paikakh,'"
Russkaya mysl' (Paris), no. 4152, December 5–11, 1996.

42. Nina Kannegiser, "O M. A. Kuzmine," published by N. G. Knyazeva and
G. A. Morev in *Iskusstvo Leningrada*, 9 (1990), 65–66.

43. Ibid., 66.

44. Book production in Russia dropped from 26,000 titles in 1913 to 4,500
between 1920 and 1921, and the country experienced an 85 percent reduction in
the publication of periodicals from 1918 to 1921. See Robert A. Maguire, *Red
Virgin Soil* (Princeton: Princeton University Press, 1968), 6–7.

45. See Mikhail Slonimsky's account of the evening in *Zi*, no. 334–336, January
3–5, 1920, 1; Blok, Gumilev, Pyast, and Rozhdestvensky read on the same program.

46. Mikhail Kuzmin, "Iz zapisok Tivurtiya Pentslya," *Dom Iskusstv*, 1 (1921),
14–20.

47. See the account of the evening, signed "Dzhikill'," in *Zi*, no. 462, May 27,
1920.

48. F. Groshikov, "Na zadvorkakh deistvitel'nosti: Vecher M. Kuzmina v dome

literatorov," *Krasnaya gazeta* no. 116, morning edition, May 29, 1920. Groshikov noted that the public had warmly received Kuzmin, but added that he had not seen a single worker or member of the Red Army.

49. "Skorokhody istorii," *Zi*, no. 488–489, June 27, 1920, 1. Kuzmin wrote the article on June 24. The censorship forced major cuts when it was republished three years later in *Uslovnosti*, 23–24.

50. See chap. 9, "Simon Magus and the Origins of Gnosticism," in Giovanni Filoramo, *A History of Gnosticism*, trans. Anthony Alcock (Oxford: Basil Blackwell, 1990), 142–152.

51. Kuzmin, "Cheshuya v nevode," 102–103; emphasis added. Khlebnikov had worked out elaborate mathematical formulas that he believed allowed him to predict historical patterns. They intrigued Kuzmin, who on May 30, 1920, wrote in the Diary, "We got really excited by the calculations of Khlebnikov."

52. All traces of another novel that he worked on in 1920, *Propavshaya Veronika*, and that he hoped to return to as late as 1934 have also disappeared.

53. Mikhail Kuzmin, "Zlatoe nebo," *Abraksas*, 3 (1923), 4–10.

54. Grzhebin oversaw the practical affairs both of "World Literature" and Persits's "Wandering Enthusiast," and had his own publishing house. In 1919 he negotiated with Kuzmin to issue an edition of his collected works, and the "Chronicle" section of *Zi* for July 13, 1920 (no. 502), noted that Kuzmin "is completing" monographs on Grétry, Rossini, and Delibes for Grzhebin. Nothing came of any of the projects.

55. See A. G. Timofeev, "Mikhail Kuzmin i izdatel'stvo 'Petropolis' (Novye materialy po istorii 'russkogo Berlina')," *Russkaya literatura*, 1 (1991), 189–204.

56. Yu. Ofrosimov, "O Gumileve, Kuzmine, Mandel'shtame... Vstrecha s izdatelem," *Novoe russkoe slovo* (New York), December 13, 1953.

57. English publishers used the same ruse in the nineteenth century; the pornographic classic *My Secret Life* also bore "Amsterdam" as the place of publication.

58. Nikolay Berezhansky, the political editor of the Riga Russian newspaper *Segodnya*, for example, noted "with surprise" in a 1921 article that pornography was now being legally sold in Soviet Russia. He singled out Kuzmin's book, with its "indecent" drawings, the Régnier, and Remizov's *Zavetnye skazy* (Petersburg: Alkonost, 1920) and *Tsar' Dodon* (Petersburg: Alkonost, 1921), with drawings by Bakst, as his examples. His article, "Nenuzhnye lyudi nenuzhnogo dela," appeared in the Berlin Russian magazine *Russkaya kniga*, 7–8 (1921), 7, whose editors added a note professing their doubts that the books could be categorized as "pornographic."

59. Gorky sent the copy to Salomé Andronikova-Halpern in England through his adopted son. She tried without success to sell the manuscript, and then returned it to Gorky, but not before making a copy, which she sent to JEM in 1970. The copy carries the inscription "Poems not intended for print, 1919."

60. Blokh had submitted only titles and authors, not texts, listing the Régnier simply as "Seven Portraits." One wag surmised that the censor, unfamiliar with that name, had assumed that the book must be portraits of revolutionary heroes, and so had approved it. Given the level of literacy in the early Soviet censorship, the surmise is entirely plausible. See Grigory Lozinsky, "Petropolis," in *Vremennik Obshchestva druzei russkoi knigi*, vol. 2 (Paris, 1928), 36. Some early censors, appointed for their "political reliability," were virtually illiterate; see A. V. Blyum, *Za*

kulisami "Ministerstva Pravdy": Tainaya istoriya sovetskoi tsenzury, 1917–1929 (St. Petersburg: Gumanitarnoe agenstvo "Akademicheskii proekt," 1994), 91–92.

61. Some of the evaluations done by the committee, made up of Blok, Gumilev, Mikhail Lozinsky, and Kuzmin, can be found in "Blok i Soyuz poetov," in *Literaturnoe nasledstvo*, vol. 92, bk. 4 (Moscow: Nauka, 1987), 684–695. Several more are published in Yury Medvedev's "Blok i Kuzmin v arkhive P. N. Medvedeva," 172–174.

62. The text of Blok's speech can be found in volume six of his *Sobranie sochinenii* (1962), 439–440. Kuzmin noted in the Diary: "Blok, Rozhdestvensky, Otsup, Grushko took good care of me. It all turned out fine, affable and proper. Blok made a very touching speech."

63. Erikh Gollerbakh gave a full account of the evening in *Zi*, no. 574, October 5, 1920, 2. The chronicle of the first issue of the miscellany *Dom Iskusstv* (1921), 74, called the evening the most successful of all the projects organized by the Poets' Union, adding that it had been carried off with "exceptional enterprise and success."

64. *Zi*, no. 569, September 29, 1920, contains Eikhenbaum's long article "O proze M. Kuzmina" and an essay, "Neobkhodimyi paradoks (M. A. Kuzmin i 'Zhizn' iskusstva')" by Yakov Pushchin (the pseudonym of the composer Nikolay Strel'nikov). The issue of October 7 (no. 576) had an article by Zhirmunsky, "Poeziya Kuzmina," while that of October 12 (no. 580) had Igor' Glebov's "Muzyka v tvorchestve M. A. Kuzmina."

65. When the Goldoni opened at the end of March 1921, the theater used a pastiche of music by Scarlatti and Rameau arranged by Asaf'ev. In his review in *Zi*, no. 706–708, March 30/31–April 1, 1921, 1, Kuzmin objected that the music, "charming in itself," was stylistically anachronistic and slowed the play's tempo.

66. "Dekabr' morozit v nebe rozovom, / Netoplennyi mrachneet dom. / A my, kak Menshikov v Berezove, / Chitaem Bibliyu i zhdem. // I zhdem chego? samim izvestno li? / Kakoi spasitel'noi ruki? / Uzh vzbukhnuvshie pal'tsy tresnuli / I razvalilis' bashmaki. // Nikto ne govorit o Vrangele, / Tupye protekayut dni. / Na zlatokovannom Arkhangele / Lish' mleyut sladostno ogni. // Poshli nam krepkoe terpenie, / I krotkii dukh, i legkii son, / I milykh knig svyatoe chtenie, / I neizmennyi nebosklon! // No esli angel skorbno sklonitsya, / Zaplakav: 'Eto navsegda!'— / Pust' upadet, kak bezzakonnitsa, / Menya vodivshaya zvezda. // Net, tol'ko v ssylke, tol'ko v ssylke my. . . ." (*S*, 644–645). The poem's opening stanza alludes to a famous picture *Menshikov in Berezov* (1883) by the Itinerant master, Vasily Surikov, whom Kuzmin admired. It depicts the Siberian exile of the once all-powerful friend of Peter I, who sits in winter, surrounded by his daughters, in a mean hut with a Bible open on the table in front of them. Light gleams on icons in one corner. General Petr Vrangel' commanded the White Army, the remnants of whose troops were evacuated from Sevastopol in 1920.

67. Vladimir Milashevsky, "V dome na Moike: Iz zapisok khudozhnika," *Zvezda*, 12 (1970), 193. Milashevsky quoted only four lines from the poem, whose complete text was not printed in the Soviet Union until 1988. See G. A. Morev, "Iz kommentariev k tekstam Kuzmina: II ('Dekabr' morozit v nebe rozovom...')," *Novoe literaturnoe obozrenie*, 5 (1993), 165–167, and Leonid Seleznev, "K voprosu o prizhiznennykh publikatsiyakh stikhotvoreniya M. Kuzmina 'Dekabr' morozit v nebe rozovom...' ('Men'shikov v Berezove')," *Novoe literaturnoe obozrenie*, 24 (1997), 281–282.

10. "Will I Have Time to Show the Magic in Me?"

1. None of Kuzmin's friends shared his high evaluation of Yurkun's talents, and some did little to hide their condescension. After the tepid response accorded his 1915 volume of stories, Yurkun had to wait until the beginning of 1918 for "Felana," a small firm organized by Konstantin Lyandau, to publish his novel *Durnaya kompaniya* and a story entitled "Klub blagotvoritel'nykh skeletov" under one cover with illustrations by another friend, Yury Annenkov. His novel *Tumannyi gorod*, on which he worked throughout the 1920s and which Kuzmin believed to be his finest work, was never published. Two chapters from it appeared in *Abraksas*, 2 (1922).

2. Both Gumilev and Mandel'shtam had also pursued Arbenina, but it was Yurkun who captured her affection, prompting a witty "fable" from Georgy Ivanov; see *MK*, 228–229.

3. "Lyubov' chuzhaya zatsvela / Pod novogodneyu zvezdoyu" (*S*, 496).

4. See her "O Yurochke" in Yurkun, *Durnaya kompaniya*, 455–469.

5. *Pushkin—Dostoevsky* (Petersburg: Izdanie Doma literatorov, 1921), 3. The book contains the contributions of the main participants in the festivities as well as those given at the Writers' House that month to mark the fortieth anniversary of Dostoevsky's death.

6. "Svidetel'stvo ochevidtsa. Dnevnikovye zapisi E. P. Kazanovich," *Literaturnoe obozrenie*, 10 (1980), 108–109. When Tsvetaeva, dispirited and lonely in Moscow, encountered the poem "Pushkin" later that year in the collection *Nezdeshnie vechera* (*S*, 424–425), she wrote to thank Kuzmin in her first and only letter to him: "If there are still such poems...." Tsvetaeva cited the letter in her memoir "Nezdeshnii vecher," 139–140.

7. *Zi*, no. 16, November 18, 1918, 4.

8. Mikhail Kuzmin, "Golos poeta (Anna Radlova: 'Korabli')," *Zi*, no. 702–705, March 26–29, 1921, 1; reprinted with major cuts in *Uslovnosti*, 169–171.

9. Kuzmin met Odoevtseva on January 19, 1921, when she "read her complete collected works" at the house of friends. "She's sweet," he wrote, but in "Parnasskie zarosli" he dismissed her work and that of other of Gumilev's pupils: "I do not think that forced fantasy and the utter irresponsibility of a mechanical imagination can be considered some kind of theme or originality. Incidentally, aside from those qualities and a facile manner, Irina Odoevtseva has nothing else. . . . The books of Otsup and Nel'dikhen seem to me pure and simple exercises in fashionable devices." *Zavtra: Literaturno-kriticheskii sbornik*, 1 (Berlin, 1923), 121.

10. Kuzmin reviewed the Goldoni in *Zi*, no. 706–708, March 30/31–April 1, 1921, 1; a revised version appeared in *Uslovnosti*, 87–89.

11. Nothing is known about the "Vol'noe sodruzhestvo poetov" in which Konstantin Erberg invited Akhmatova, Sologub, Khodasevich, Radlova, Kuzmin, and a few others to take part. The "Kol'tso poetov" tried to start a genuine literary movement based on a revival of Ego-Futurism. Kuzmin accepted their invitation to become a member "with gratitude" (see his letter of June 14, 1921, IRLI, coll. 355, no. 29), but was hardly active in it, as its organizers claimed. It was banned by the Cheka in September 1922. See Anthony Anemone and Ivan Martynov, "Towards the History of the Leningrad Avant-Garde: The 'Ring of Poets,'" *Wiener Slawistischer Almanach, Band* 17 (1986), 131–148.

12. Announcements for the Fielding volume, edited by Blokh, Mikhail Lozinsky, and Kuzmin for the series "Monuments of the World Repertory" and with music by Kuzmin, appeared over that summer, but it seems not to have been published, as no copy of the book has ever surfaced in a Russian library. Kuzmin was listed as having translated "Tumble-Down Dick or Phaeton in the Suds" and "The Old Man Taught Wisdom; or the Virgin Unmasked."

13. A second edition for "Petropolis," with illustrations by Dobuzhinsky and the full score, on which Kuzmin worked until August 1923, never materialized. Joachim T. Baer describes the work's contents well enough, if rather trivializing it in his "Mixail Kuzmin's *Lesok*: A Rococo Work in the Twentieth Century," in *American Contributions to the Eighth International Congress of Slavists*, vol. 2, *Literature*, ed. Victor Terras (Columbus, Ohio: Slavica, 1978), 7–23.

14. See V. A. Reshchikova, "Vysylka iz RSFSR," *Minuvshee*, 11 (1991), 199–208, and L. A. Kogan, "'Vyslat' za granitsu bezzhalostno' (Novoe ob izgnanii dukhovnoi elity)," *Voprosy filosofii*, 9 (1993), 61–84.

15. Mikhail Kuzmin, "Kapusta na yablonyakh," *Zi*, no. 786–791, July 26–31, 1921, 2. A note from the editors explained that the article was being published "for purposes of discussion," a formula already typical in Soviet periodicals whenever the editors wished to avert responsibility should the views expressed prove too controversial, even subversive, to the authorities. No discussion, of course, followed.

16. "Leti, leti! . . . / Ved' ad voochiyu my videli, / I nam geenna ne strashna" from "Rodina Virgiliya" (*S*, 489). At the end of the "Hoffmann grove" in *Lesok*, Faust and Mephistopheles, to allay human suffering, create a "paradise" which is a nightmare vision of a faceless, totally regimented totalitarian state. The narrative voice comments, "We are already in hell, my children!" (*Lesok*, 25).

17. We have concluded that Milashevsky's reminiscences (see *MK*, 237) about an evening in May 1921 when Kuzmin gave a small dinner party for a few close friends, Blok among them, at the House of Arts must be a fiction or that his memory "misdated" it and that he refers to an earlier occasion, the fifteenth "jubilee" evening of September 29, 1920, when Blok spoke. After it, Kuzmin wrote in the Diary, "Our crowd stayed for tea afterwards." Certainly either Kuzmin or Blok would have mentioned such an event in their respective diaries in 1921, but there are no references to it.

18. Mikhail Kuzmin, "A. Blok," *Zi*, no. 804, August 16–21, 1921, 5.

19. "Zhivetsya nam ne plokho: / Voditsa da pesok..." "Ne bolen, ne utoplen, / Ne spyatal, ne ubit! / Ne znaet vovse voplei / Nash krolikovyi skit" (*S*, 646).

20. "Kogo on raz privetil, / Tot sirym ne umret" (*S*, 647).

21. Kuzmin stated that *Chasy* for the first time united the people he would call "Emotionalists." See his autobiography in Medvedev, "Blok i Kuzmin v arkhive P. N. Medvedeva," 179. That is not altogether accurate. Among the contributors to the miscellany, he, Anna Radlova, Boris Paparigopulo, and Yurkun were asssociated with the "Emotionalists," but the others—I. Evert, Viktor Shklovsky, and, of course, the late Khlebnikov—had nothing to do with it.

22. Kuzmin reviewed three of their productions in *Zi*: Gumilev's *Gondla*, the fifteenth-century *Farce de maistre Pierre Pathelin*, and Remizov's *Tragediya o Iude, printse Iskariotskom*. The reviews were reprinted in *Uslovnosti*, 107–113.

23. See Ida Nappel'baum, *Ugol otrazheniya: Kratkie vstrechi dolgoi zhizni* (St.

Petersburg: Logos, 1995), 20–24, 32–34, and Ol'ga Grudtsova, "Dovol'no, ya bol'she ne igrayu... Povest' o moei zhizni," *Minuvshee*, 19 (1996), 7–28, 114–116. On July 2, 1922, Nappel'baum made a fine studio portrait of Kuzmin in his Old Master style of heavily retouching the background in a "painterly" manner. It is reproduced in his daughter's book, with photographs of Yurkun, Arbenina, Radlova, and many others.

24. Sergey Bobrov, "Ekho," *Pechat' i revolyutsiya*, 3 (1921), 272–274.

25. Nikolay Chukovsky recalled that "every Monday about thirty people recited their verse at the Nappel'baums'. But only five truly moved the listeners: [Nikolay] Tikhonov, Vaginov, Rozhdestvensky, Kuzmin, and Khodasevich." N. K. Chukovsky, *Literaturnye vospominaniya* (Moscow: Sovetskii pisatel', 1989), 104.

26. Mikhail Kuzmin, "Parnasskie zarosli," *Zavtra*, 1 (1923), 122.

27. On December 15, 1923, Kuzmin noted "to Ionov [the head of the Petrograd branch of Gozisdat, the State Publishing House]. *Parables* is permitted [for import] and is available (where?)." In March 1924 he wrote to Blokh about the matter: "Ionov assured me again and again that it [*Parables*] is not banned (which, to tell the truth, I don't much believe), but in the meantime it is and never was available anywhere. . . . What is going on? Everyone is longing for *Parables*." See JEM, "Letter of M. A. Kuzmin to Ja. N. Blox," in *Studies*, 175.

28. "Esli budesh', strannik, v Berline, / u dorogikh moemu serdtsu nemtsev, / gde byli Gofman, Motsart i Khodovetskii / (i Gete, Gete, konechno),— / klanyaisya domam i prokhozhim, / i starym, chopornym lipkam, / i okrestnym ploskim ravninam. / Tam, naverno, vsë po-drugomu,— / ne uznal by, esli b poekhal, / no ya znayu, chto v Sharlottenburge, / na kakoi-to, kakoi-to shtrasse, / zhivet belokuraya Tamara / s mamoi, sestroi i bratom. . . . / Rasskazhi ei, chto my zhivy, zdorovy, / chasto ee vspominaem, / ne umerli, a dazhe zakalilis', / skoro sovsem popadem v svyatye, / chto ne pili, ne eli, ne obuvalis', / dukhovnymi slovesami pitalis', / chto bedny my (no eto ne novost': / kakoe zhe u vorob'ev imen'e?), / zanyalis' zamechatel'noi torgovlei: / vsë prodaem i nichego ne pokupaem, / smotrim na vesennee nebo / i dumaem o druz'yakh dalekikh. / Ustalo li nashe serdtse, / oslabeli li nashi ruki, / pust' sudyat po novym knigam, / kotorye kogda-nibud' vyidut. . . . / No esli ty poedesh' dal'she / i vstretish' druguyu Tamaru—/ vzdrogni, vzdrogni, strannik . . . / sledya za dvizhen'yami veshchei Zhar-Ptitsy, / smotrya na temnoe, letuchee solntse." "Poruchenie" (*S*, 497–498). In 1922–23 Persits sent him several packages with delicacies such as chocolates and soap. She took up with Lourié when he emigrated to Berlin. Tamara Karsavina had been the first to dance the Firebird in the Stravinsky-Fokine ballet.

29. Mikhail Kuzmin, "Podzemnye ruch'i," first published in the miscellany *Novaya Rossiya* (Moscow-Petrograd, 1922), 28; republished in *Proza*, 9:308. When he received a letter from Persits on November 9, 1921, he wrote, "She is very homesick there, in Berlin" (Diary).

30. Marietta Shaginyan, "Literaturnyi dnevnik: Novye poety," *Literaturnaya nedelya*, no. 7, July 9, 1922, the literary supplement to the newspaper *Petrogradskaya pravda*, no. 151.

31. Mikhail Kuzmin, "Krylatyi gost', gerbarii i ekzameny," *Zi*, no. 28 (851), July 18, 1922, 2; republished in *Uslovnosti*, 172–176.

32. Adamovich in conversation with JEM in Paris in 1970. In 1923 Adamovich wrote that ever since "Vrazhdebnoe more," Kuzmin's verse had suffered from the

"childish illness of leftism" and that his new works showed his "profound artistic confusion." G. V. Adamovich, "Russkaya poeziya," *Zi*, no. 2 (876), January 16, 1923, 4. When Radlova returned from a visit to Paris, she told Kuzmin about the "despicable" attacks that Adamovich was making on his recent verse in the émigré press (Diary, October 10, 1925).

33. L. D. Trotsky, *Literatura i revolyutsiya* (Moscow: Izdatel'stvo politicheskoi literatury, 1991), 37. This collection of Trotsky's newspaper articles on literature first came out in 1923. His attack on the contributors to *Strelets* and on Futurism, Blok, Bely, Rozanov, Akhmatova, Radlova, Gippius, and others is dated September 8, 1922. Kuzmin's concern about the possibility of being exiled was entirely justified. Among the contributors to *Strelets*, where Kuzmin had published fragments from *Rimskie chudesa* and "Cheshuya v nevode," was Lev Karsavin, the brother of the ballerina and a brilliant religious philosopher. He had been arrested in August and was exiled from Russia in November.

34. Kuzmin, *Uslovnosti*, 172. Kuzmin was one of several major poets who had nothing good to say about Formalism. Bely, Vyacheslav Ivanov, Pasternak, and Khodasevich all excoriated it; see JEM, "Khodasevich and Formalism: A Poet's Dissent," in *Russian Formalism: A Retrospective Glance: A Festschrift in Honor of Victor Erlich*, ed. R. L. Jackson and Stephen Rudy (New Haven: Yale Center for International and Area Studies, 1985), 68–81.

35. "Its [the word *abraxas's*] numerical meaning according to the Pythagorean or Cabalistic system is 365, the fullness of the world's creative forces," Kuzmin explained in 1923. Cited in Kuzmin, *Izbrannye proizvedeniya*, 535.

36. NAB, "Pis'mo B. Pasternaka Yu. Yurkunu," *Voprosy literatury*, 7 (1981), 225–232.

37. Mikhail Kuzmin, "Govoryashchie," *Zi*, no. 31 (854), August 8–15, 1922, 1; reprinted in *Uslovnosti*, 158–161.

38. See Lazar Fleishman, *Boris Pasternak: The Poet and His Politics* (Cambridge, Mass.: Harvard University Press, 1990), 117–118.

39. At the beginning of November 1925, the young critic Lev Gornung was given the task of obtaining Pasternak's signature for a "congratulatory address to Mikhail Kuzmin in connection with the twentieth anniversary of his literary debut. . . . Boris Leonidovich told me that he was ready to sign with great pleasure since he liked Kuzmin's poems very much, although the latter probably did not know that." Lev Gornung, "Vstrecha za vstrechei: Po dnevnikovym zapisyam," *Literaturnoe obozrenie*, 5 (1990), 103. Pasternak equally admired Kuzmin's prose.

40. Nadezhda Mandel'shtam wrote that when she and her husband, whose brother was married to Radlova's sister, visited Petersburg in the late summer of 1922, he was invited to join the circle that the Radlovs and Kuzmin were assembling during a visit to the Radlovs' apartment, where Kuzmin and Yurkun were present; see N. Mandel'shtam, *Vtoraya kniga*, 139–140. One questions the reliability of her memory, as Kuzmin makes no mention of any meeting with the Mandel'shtams at that time. Mandel'shtam had no affiliation with them, but two of his poems did appear in the second issue of *Abraksas*.

41. When Kuzmin received the book on June 10, 1926, he remarked in the Diary, "Pasternak wrote me a whole piece of literature in the book." George Cheron reproduced the text in "B. Pasternak and M. Kuzmin (An Inscription)," *Wiener Slawistischer Almanach*, Band 5 (1980), 67–69.

42. *Abraksas*, 3 (February 1923), 3. The entire "Declaration" is reprinted in T. L. Nikol'skaya, "Emotsionalisty," *Russian Literature*, XX-1 (1986), 62–63.

43. Vladimir Veidle's "Po povodu dvukh statei o Bloke," *Zavtra*, 1 (1923), 107–113, dated "Petersburg. 1 January 1922," is a polemical response to two articles by Boris Eikhenbaum and Yury Tynyanov in *Ob Aleksandre Bloke* (Petersburg: Kartonnyi domik, 1921). The phrase "emotional art" is on p. 112.

44. Kuzmin, *Uslovnosti*, 173 and 163.

45. Mikhail Kuzmin, "Emotsional'nost' i faktura," *Zi*, no. 51 (874), December 26, 1922, 1; reprinted in *Uslovnosti*, 177–179.

46. Kuzmin's "Emotsional'nost' kak osnovnoi element iskusstva" was published in December 1923 in *Arena: Teatral'nyi al'manakh* (Petersburg, 1924), 8–12.

47. Mikhail Kuzmin, "Skachushchaya sovremennost'," *Birzhevye vedomosti*, no. 15792, evening edition, September 9, 1916, 5; reprinted in *Uslovnosti*, 151–153.

48. See JEM, "You Must Remember This," 115–140.

49. "Emotsionalizm," *Poslednie novosti* (Petrograd), no. 18 (40), April 30, 1923, signed "Aristarkh."

50. "Privetstvie khudozhnikam molodoi Germanii ot gruppy emotsionalistov," *Zi*, no. 10, March 13, 1923, 8, signed by Kuzmin, Vaginov, Dmitriev, Piotrovsky, Radlova, Radlov, and Yurkun (in that order). The text is reprinted in Nikol'skaya, "Emotsionalisty," 64–65. "We read, spoke about the Germans, we want to send them a greeting" (Diary, January 20, 1923).

51. Although not unqualified, to be sure, Kuzmin's admiration for German culture even shaped his response to the painters of the World of Art. In a July 14, 1934, entry in the Diary entitled "The German Element," he wrote: "What do Somov, Golovin, Benois, Lancéray, Dobuzhinsky, even Bakst have in common with the French? Nothing. Utter and complete *Sezession* and a German perception of world literature. A German or in the last resort an English (the Pre-Raphaelites as a complex of modernism) movement, of course."

52. Kuzmin wrote in one of his autobiographies: "I am exclusively interested in the Expressionists among contemporaries. I highly value Khlebnikov, Anna Radlova, Vaginov, Remizov, Yurkun, and Pasternak among the Russians. Of course, I am not impartial." See Medvedev, "Blok i Kuzmin v arkhive P. N. Medvedeva," 180.

53. Kuzmin, "Emotsional'nost' kak osnovnoi element iskusstva," 12.

54. "Radlov wants me to write the music for Toller. He wants to show homosexual and lesbian Berlin for the first time" (Diary, August 8, 1923). Kuzmin began work on the score in August, but did not finish orchestrating it until early December.

55. Mikhail Kuzmin, "Pafos ekspressionizma," *Teatr*, 11 (1923), 1–2.

56. Mikhail Kuzmin, "Teatr aktera–5 ili 25," *Teatr*, 7 (1924), 1. The article celebrated the first five years of the Bol'shoi Drama Theater. The Expressionist plays, Kuzmin wrote, were entirely appropriate to the "Schillerian revolutionary lyricism" of so many of the plays it had mounted.

57. "Germaniya" (*S*, 653–654) was first published in *Zi*, 18 (893) (1923), 6.

58. Kuzmin compared Dr. Caligari to Hoffmann's Dr. Coppelius in "Benefisy," *Zi*, 21 (896) (1923), 17–18, an article about recent benefit evenings for operetta performers. He saw the "convulsive exaltation" of Expressionism in some of the new German and Austrian operettas that he reviewed. A necrology of Bryusov did

appear on October 21, 1924, in *Zi*, 43 (1016), 2–3, but it was his last contribution to it (and his first since August 1923).

59. Letter of July 5, 1924, to V. V. Ruslov, *MKiRK*, 191.

60. See his survey of the 1922–23 season, "Petrogradskii teatral'nyi sezon (Pis'mo iz Petrograda)," *Izvestiya*, no. 118, May 31, 1923, 6. He wrote music for Sophocles' *Oedipus* and finished an adaptation for the stage of *Don Quixote* which the Academic Drama Theater commissioned as a vehicle for his old friend Yury Yur'ev. He would do other projects for it over the next few years, but never as many as he would have liked.

61. Somov emigrated at the end of 1923, Dobuzhinsky in 1924.

62. On November 19, 1921, Kuzmin read the article "Kolebanie zhiznennykh tokov" to Annenkov. It was published in Yury Annenkov, *Portrety* (Petersburg: Petropolis, 1922), 43–56, with another article by Zamyatin. The album of portraits, which came out in November 1922, contained the one of Kuzmin that Annenkov had begun in March 1918 and finished a year later. Kuzmin did not much care for it. Kuzmin's article "G. Narbut (Po povodu posmertnoi vystavki)," written at the end of August 1922, appeared in *Russkoe iskusstvo*, 1 (1923), 36. The article on Mitrokhin that he wrote in March 1922 came out at the end of the year in *Tvorchestvo D. I. Mitrokhina* (Moscow: Gosizdat, 1922), 7–18, where it was accompanied by an article by Vsevolod Voinov, who had done Kuzmin's portrait in May 1921. The book was also issued in German and French translations.

63. Mikhail Kuzmin, *Rerikh* (Moscow: Izdatel'stvo Vserossiiskogo Komiteta pomoshchi invalidam voiny pri VTsIK Sovetov, [1923]), 1–15. Kuzmin received a piano score of the *Rite* and of Stravinsky's ballet *Pulcinella* in 1923 and played them over and over to friends. He called the *Rite* an "event in the history of the Russian theater." In 1924 the Petrograd section of Gosizdat asked Kuzmin, Benois, Dobuzhinsky, Gollerbakh, Golovin, and Voinov to contribute to a special volume being prepared to mark the twenty-fifth anniversary of the World of Art. It was never published.

64. Kuzmin, "Cheshuya v nevode," 104.

65. In 1923 Kuzmin edited translations of *La Double Maîtresse* and *Les Vacances d'un jeune homme sage* and translated *Les Recontres de M. de Bréot*, for which he also wrote the introduction. Details on the publishing of these and other Kuzmin translations of Régnier can be found in the catalogue that was prepared for an exhibition in 1980, *Izdatel'stvo "Academia," 1922–1937: Vystavka izdanii i knizhnoi grafiki* (Moscow: Kniga, 1980), 50–51 (item 175).

66. On October 5, 1923, Kuzmin saw a German catalogue of translations from the Russian: "A lot of mine. Gyugus [Guenther] is working to his utmost there. That cheers me up, but what will become of us here?" (Diary).

67. "Zerkal'nym zolotom vrashchayas'" (*S*, 654–655). The poem, written in April 1923, appeared in the fourth issue of the journal.

11. *"Like a Ragged Squirrel on a Treadmill . . ."*

1. Mikhail Kuzmin "Pis'mo v Pekin," in *Uslovnosti*, 163.

2. Vaginov's story first appeared in the second number of *Abraksas*. The text of *Smert' Nerona*, which Vladimir Markov and JEM first published in *SS*, 3:569–613, can be found in *Teatr*, bk. 2, vol. 3, 322–380. Kuzmin finished it on July 8,

1929, and dedicated it to Sergey Radlov. Vaginov developed the historical parallel between the falls of the Roman and Russian empires in another story as well, "Monastyr' Gospoda nashego Apollona," published in the first issue of *Abraksas*.

3. Marie-Luise Bott traces some of the play's many allusions to early Soviet history in "O postroenii p'esy Mikhaila Kuzmina 'Smert' Nerona' (1928–1929 g.): Tema s variatsiyami ot Mandel'shtama do Bulgakova," in *Studies*, 141–151. She suggests that the play's temporal shifts influenced Bulgakov's *Master i Margarita*.

4. "S. E." [Akim Volynsky], "Amsterdamskaya pornografiya," *Zi*, no. 5 (929), January 29, 1924, 14–15.

5. Manuscript Division, RLM, coll. 9, item 37.

6. "Kinematograf v Germanii," *Vechernyaya Krasnaya gazeta*, no. 135, June 14, 1923, 3.

7. "Letter of M. A. Kuzmin to Ja. N. Blox," in *Studies*, 174.

8. In the early 1930s, Rakov published a brochure on ancient Rome which almost got him into serious trouble. Developing the thesis of his graduate adviser, Sergey Kovalev, he argued that slave revolts had not turned and could not turn into genuine revolution. Typesetting and binding had been almost finished when Stalin, at a congress of collective farm shock workers, declared on February 19, 1933, that the "revolution of the slaves liquidated slaveholders and replaced the slaveholding form of the exploitation of the workers." I. V. Stalin, *Voprosy leninizma* [Moscow: Politizdat, 1935], 527. Rakov, famous for his quick wit, later called the days that followed, when the last page of his brochure had to be torn out and replaced with a new one, "The Ten Days that Shook the Slaveholding World." See B. Ya. Koprzhiva-Lur'e [Ya. S. Lur'e], *Istoriya odnoi zhizni* (Paris: Atheneum, 1987), 143–144. In December 1938, Kovalev, himself under arrest, denounced Rakov as a homosexual and counterrevolutionary before even being questioned. His former pupil received a sentence of twenty-five years in the Gulag, from which he was released only after Stalin's death.

9. Kuzmin gave a droll example of Yurkun's "boosterism": Yurkun "asks everyone who our foremost poet is, thinking that they will name me, but no one does." Kuzmin, "Cheshuya v nevode," 99.

10. See M. G. Ratgaus, "Kuzmin—kinozritel'," *Kinovedcheskie zapiski*, 13 (1992), 52–86.

11. "Amerikanets yunyi Gul' / Ubit byl doktorom Mabuzo: / On tak pokhozh... Ne potomu l' / O nem zagovorila muza? / Ved' ya sovsem i pozabyl, / Kakim on na ekrane byl!" (*S*, 519). Kuzmin explained the reference to the movie in a brief footnote to the poem. He had purchased several of Gilbert's operettas in May 1923, and Rakov often asked him to play them. He reviewed Viktor Rappaport's May 1924 staging of *Dorine und der Zufall* at the Musical Comedy Theater in "Novaya kladka," *Vechernyaya Krasnaya gazeta*, no. 124, June 3, 1924, 5.

12. "Vot on sidit / (Il' eto Vy sidite?) v lozhe" (*S*, 519).

13. In both letters Kuzmin referred to it as *Hull's Stroll*, not "Strolls," and both titles appear in the Diary and elsewhere. Manuscript copies have the plural. The text was first published in *SS*, 3:559–567, and then in *Teatr*, bk. 1, vol. 3, 311–321, and in Dmitriev, "'Akademicheskii' Kuzmin," 154–164.

14. Kuzmin's cinematic borrowings continued in *Progulki Gulya*. He took the names "Sammy" and "Tommy," the two London dandies who sometimes visit Hull, from another German movie, Joe May's *Indische Grabmal* (1921), where they are the servants of the English officer MacAllan, a role played by Paul Richter. Kuzmin

thought Conrad Veidt was "incomparable" in the role of Ayan, Maharadscha von Eschnapur, and saw the movie seven or eight times.

15. *SS*, 3:735; *Teatr*, bk. 2, vol. 4, 372. In the 1929 scenario, Kuzmin called the work a "theatrical-musical suite in fifteen episodes."

16. Letter of October 15, 1924, in Klaus Harer, "'Verchus' kak obodrannaya belka v kolese': Pis'ma Mikhaila Kuzmina k Ya. N. Blokhu (1924–1928)," in *Shestye Tynyanovskie chteniya: Tezisy dokladov i materialy dlya obsuzhdeniya* (Riga, 1992), 225. Kuzmin proposed that Blokh contract Hans Meid, Karl Walser, and Richard J. M. Seewald to illustrate *Progulki Gulya*. Meid had done twenty-four illustrations for a luxurious German translation of *Die Abenteuer des Aimé Lebeuf* (Berlin: Gurlitt, 1922).

17. A. G. Timofeev, "Progulka bez Gulya? (K istorii organizatsii avtorskogo vechera M. A. Kuzmina v mae 1924 g.)," *MKiRK*, 181–182. All further citations from the eleven letters and telegrams that Kuzmin, Ruslov, and Auslender exchanged between March and early June 1924 are from this publication. Timofeev corrected some of his mistakes in "Eshche raz o vechere M. Kuzmina v studii 'Sinyaya ptitsa' (1924)," *Novoe literaturnoe obozrenie*, 3 (1993), 158–160.

18. Kuzmin saw many at an evening that Boris Gornung and his associates at the magazine *Germes* put together on the eleventh. Gornung misdated Kuzmin's arrival and greatly exaggerated the length of his stay in his "Iz vospominanii o Mikh. Al. Kuzmine," 179–180.

19. Mikhail Kuzmin, "Struzhki," *Rossiya*, 5 (1925), 164.

20. Ibid., 165.

21. Ibid., 166–167.

22. Mikhail Kuzmin, "Anatol' Frans," *Rossiya*, 4 (1925), 281–286.

23. Harer, "'Verchus' kak obodrannaya belka v kolese,'" 225–226. More than fifteen articles, as well as translations of Eduard Künneke's operetta *Der Vetter aus Dingsda* (1921) and Régnier's *Le Bon plaisir* kept the treadmill going in the final months of 1924.

24. He reviewed its production of the Minkus-Petipa *Don Quixote* on October 14, 1924, in *Vechernyaya Krasnaya gazeta*, no. 234. It so dispirited him that he did not write the other ballet reviews Kuznetsov had assigned him.

25. "Ne gubernatorsha sidela s ofitserom, / Ne gosudarynya vnimala ordinartsu, / Na zolochenom, zakruchennom stule, / Sidela Bogoroditsa i shila. / A pered nei stoyal Mikhal-Arkhangel" (*S*, 666). The poem was first published in Russia in 1989.

26. "Arkhangelu Vladychitsa skazala: / 'Uz, pravo, ya, Mikhailushka, ne znayu, / Chto i podumat'. . . . / Prozhit' nel'zya bez very i nadezhdy / I bez tsarya, nisposlannogo Bogom. / Ya zhenshchina. Zhaleyu i zlodeya. / No etikh za lyudei ya ne schitayu. / Ved' sami ot sebya oni otverglis' / I ot dushi bessmertnoi otkazalis'. / Tebe predam ikh. Deistvui spravedlivo.' / Umolkla, ot shit'ya ne otryvayas'. / No slezy ne blesnuli na resnitsakh. . . . / 'Nu, s Bogom!'—Bogoroditsa skazala, / Potom v okoshko tikho posmotrela / I molvila: 'Proidet eshche nedelya, / I stanet polotno belee snega.'" (*S*, 667).

27. Harer, "'Verchus' kak obodrannaya belka v kolese,'" 230.

28. Kuzmin finished the fourth chapter of *Rimskie chudesa* in December 1925 and never returned to it, although he talked about doing so as late as 1934 in the Diary.

29. Harer, "'Verchus' kak obodrannaya belka v kolese,'" 231–232.

30. *Le bon plaisir* came out under the title *Po prikhoti korolya* in 1925 as volume four of the "Academia" Régnier edition and *L'Amphisbène* in 1926 as volume twelve, with the introduction Kuzmin had written in December 1925.

31. "Na ulitse motornyi fonar' / Dnem. Svet bez luchei / Kazalsya nezdeshnim rassvetom. / Budto i teper', kak vstar', / Zabludilsya Orfei / Mezhdu zimoi i letom. / Nadezhdinskaya stala luzhaikoi / S zagrobnymi anemonami v ruke, / A Vy, malen'kii, idete s Faikoi, / Zapletaya nogami, vdaleke, vdaleke. / Sobaka v sumerechnom zale / Laet, chtoby Vas ne zhdali" (*S*, 555).

32. Aleksandr Shatalov discusses the cycle in his article "Predmet vlyublennykh mezhdometii: Yu. Yurkun i M. Kuzmin—k istorii literaturnykh otnoshenii," *Voprosy literatury* (November–December 1996), 80–89.

33. The text of the letter is given in a note to the memoirs of Ida's younger sister, Ol'ga Grudtsova, "Dovol'no, ya bol'she ne igrayu," 116.

34. The photo is reproduced in the "Novaya Biblioteka poeta" edition of Kuzmin's verse. The second photograph, in which Akhmatova stands behind Kuzmin, can be found in this volume.

35. One wonders whether Kuzmin had ever actually read any of Klyuev's highly original verse or whether he was so put off by the persona that he never bothered. The "Khlysty songs" had been published as "Radel'nye pesni" in Klyuev's 1912 collection *Bratskie pesni*. The two arrests had also taken place before Kuzmin met him in 1915. He would be arrested again in 1934 and exiled from Moscow. He was summarily tried and executed in October 1937.

36. See T. L. Nikol'skaya, "Poeticheskaya sud'ba Ol'gi Cheremshanovoi," *Litsa: Biograficheskii al'manakh*, 3 (1993), 40–48, and her "Tema misticheskogo sektanstva v russkoi poezii 20-kh godov XX veka," in *Puti razvitiya russkoi literatury. Literaturovedenie. Trudy po russkoi i slavyanskoi filologii*, Uchenye zapiski Tartuskogo universiteta, no. 883 (Tartu, 1990), 157–169. Kuzmin met Cheremshanova at the end of 1924.

37. Ol'ga Cheremshanova, *Sklep: Stikhi* (Leningrad: Tipografiya Torgovoi palaty, 1925), 4, 7. A year before, in March 1924, he had written a brief introduction for a book of poems called *Elegii i stansy* (Leningrad: Academia, 1924) by the now totally forgotten Anatoly Nal', a Moscow actor. Kuzmin did not actually meet him until July 2, 1926.

38. See, for example, the review signed "Apakhito" in *Vechernyaya Krasnaya gazeta*, no. 188 (876), July 31, 1925.

39. Two years later he drew Cheremshanova's portrait in verse in "Byl by ya khudozhnik, napisal by" (*S*, 676–677).

40. *K XX-letiyu literaturnoi deyatel'nosti Mikhaila Alekseevicha Kuzmina* (Leningrad, 1925). Only two hundred copies were printed. It contains a description of the exhibit, two poems addressed to Kuzmin by Erikh Gollerbakh, the guiding spirit of the Society, and Rozhdestvensky, and his lithograph portrait by Vsevolod Voinov. The Society included a detailed description of the evening in the chronicle of its activities from 1925 to January 1928 that appeared in its *Al'manakh bibliofila* (Leningrad: Leningradskoe obshchestvo bibliofilov, 1929), 361–363, of which three hundred copies were issued. The Russian Literature section of GAKhN marked Kuzmin's anniversary in Moscow on December 4, 1925; see Morev, "K istorii yubileya M. A. Kuzmina 1925 goda."

41. Viktor Pertsov, "Po literaturnym vodorazdelam: 1: Zatish'e," *Zi*, no. 43 (1070), October 27, 1925, 5–6.

42. Mikhail Kuzmin, "Pyat' razgovorov i sluchai," in *Proza*, 9:391. On May 2, 1928, Kuzmin wrote in the Diary, "There is no longer any self-delusion, but simply delusion so that one can live."

43. Mikhail Kuzmin, Preface to Evgeny Gerken, *Bashnya: Stikhi* (Leningrad: Tipografiya Sev.-zap. obl. Upravleniya svyazi, 1926), 3–4. Gerken was arrested in 1932 during an antihomosexual witch-hunt and was not released from prison camp until 1954.

44. Mikhail Kuzmin, "Monakhov v operette," "Monakhov—'Filipp,'" and "Monakhov—'Sheilok,'" in *Nikolay Fedorovich Monakhov: K 30-letiyu artisticheskoi deyatel'nosti, 1896–1926* (Leningrad: Academia, 1926), 21–22; 23, 25; 26. The booklet was the second miscellany of *Dela i dni Bol'shogo Dramaticheskogo teatra*. Kuzmin was also asked to be a member of the commission arranging the anniversary.

45. "Chuzhoe solntse za chuzhim bolotom / Neistovo saditsya na nasest, / A zavtra vnov' samoderzhavno vstanet, / Ne nakazuya, ne blagovolya. . . . / O Bozhe, Bozhe, Bozhe, Bozhe, Bozhe! / Zachem nam prosypat'sya, esli zavtra / Uvidim te zhe kochki i dorogu, / Gde palka s nadpis'yu 'Prospekt pobed,' . . . / A deti vyrastut, kak svinopasy: / Razuchatsya chitat', pisat', molit'sya, / Skupuyu zemlyu stanut kovyryat' / Da prigovarivat', chto vremya—den'gi, . . . / Plodit' detei i tupo umirat', / Pochti ne soznavaya skuchnoi slavy / Obmanchivogo slova 'pionery'!.. / Prospite luchshe, Molli, do poludnya. / Byt' mozhet, vam prisnitsya bereg Temzy / I khmelem uvitoi rodimyi dom..." (*S*, 672–673). On April 12, 1926, Kuzmin wrote in the Diary, "I am thrilled by *Martin Chuzzlewit*."

46. Petrov, "Kaliostro," 110.

47. Harer, "'Verchus' kak obodrannaya belka v kolese,'" 235.

48. Mikhail Kuzmin, "Pechka v bane (Kafel'nye peizazhi)," in *Proza*, 9:373, 375, 376. JEM and Gennady Shmakov first published the work in the miscellany *Apollon—77* (Paris, 1977), 191–193.

49. According to the testimony of Igor' Bakhterev, Kuzmin came to believe that Vvedensky was one of the "most outstanding poets of the twentieth century, a poet of the same importance and scale as Khlebnikov." Cited by Mikhail Meilakh in his commentary to Aleksandr Vvedensky, *Polnoe sobranie sochinenii*, vol. 2 (Ann Arbor: Ardis, 1984). 346. To judge by the Diary, Kuzmin quickly tired of the works of Vvedensky's fellow avant-gardist Daniil Kharms.

50. Vvedensky first brought Zabolotsky to Kuzmin's apartment on October 9, 1926. Petrov wrote that the "representatives of the poetic avant-garde of those years, especially its most extreme left flank, emphatically singled out Kuzmin from all the poets of the older generation, and, it seems, took him alone into account" ("Kaliostro," 96).

51. George Cheron's "Mixail Kuzmin and the Oberiuty: An Overview," *Wiener Slawistischer Almanach, Band* 12 (1983), 87–101, is so general as to be of little help in the study of a topic that remains open.

52. Mikhail Padvo, "Neskol'ko slov retsenzentam i o retsenzentakh; poputno o Sade Otdykha i o prem'ere v Muzykal'noi Komedii," *Zi*, no. 23, June 8, 1926, 16.

53. Ibid.

54. "V zashchitu dostoinstva sovetskoi kritiki," *Vechernyaya Krasnaya gazeta*, no. 137, June 14, 1926. Among the signatories were Sergey Radlov, Adrian Piotrovsky, Konstantin Fedin, Nikolay Tikhonov, Nikolay Nikitin, Boris Lavrenev, Mikhail Slonimsky, Igor' Glebov, Monakhov, and Andrey Bely, who was in Leningrad on a two-month visit, during which Kuzmin saw him on several occasions.

55. The text of the entire letter may be found in *MK*, 257–258.

56. Mikhail Kuzmin, "'Sonya' (Sad Otdykha)," *Vechernyaya Krasnaya gazeta*, no. 153, July 3, 1926, 4.

57. Mikhail Kuzmin, "V. M. Khodasevich," in *Valentina Khodasevich: Stat'i M. Kuzmina, Sergeya Radlova, S. Mokul'skogo, A. Movshensona* (Leningrad: Academia, 1927), 5–18; idem, "Eduard Bagritsky," *Literaturnaya gazeta*, no. 23, May 17, 1933, 3.

12. Dissenting to the End

1. For an account of Kuzmin's work for the Russian Jubilee Goethe edition, see "Perepiska A. G. Gabrichevskogo i M. A. Kuzmina," *Literaturnoe obozrenie*, 11–12 (1993), 58–75. On January 15, 1930, Kuzmin sent Gabrichevsky not so much a letter as an article outlining his views of "methods of translation" (63–64).

2. Klaus Harer gives a relatively complete list of the translations in his *Michail Kuzmin*, 276–282. He does not mention the work on Hoffmann in 1927–28 (it may not have been published) or the songs from the Brecht-Weill *Die Dreigroschenoper* in the late twenties.

3. "Proshchanie Gektora" appeared in *Zvezda*, 6 (1933), 69–73, with Kuzmin's brief "A Few Words about the Translation."

4. See *Krasnaya nov'*, 1 (1935), 182–196. Kuzmin was so upset by the "devastating" review that he fell ill and had to be hospitalized for several weeks.

5. The other translations were *The Tempest, The Two Gentlemen of Verona, The Merry Wives of Windsor, Much Ado about Nothing, Love's Labour's Lost, The Taming of the Shrew*, and *King Henry IV*, Parts One and Two. *The Tempest* was not published until 1990. Anna Radlova, who also participated in the Shakespeare translation project, describes its genesis in her article "Kak ya rabotayu nad perevodom Shekspira," *Literaturnyi sovremennik*, 3 (1934). Chukovsky was especially critical of her translations.

6. See M. L. Gasparov, "Neizvestnye russkie perevody baironovskogo 'Don-Zhuana,'" *Izvestiya Akademii Nauk SSSR*, seriya literatury i yazyka, 47, no. 4 (1988), 359–367. He writes that "Kuzmin's translation is more precise [than Adamovich's], but heavy-handed and clumsy, with unnaturally constructed phrases" (364).

7. Petrov, "Kaliostro," 101.

8. In *Lesok*, Kuzmin referred to Wilde's fictional hypothesis, in "The Portrait of Mr. W. H.," that he was a "wonderful boy actor of great beauty" named Willie Hughes and also the "rose-cheeked Adonis" of *Venus and Adonis*.

9. Ivan Likhachev in a 1969 conversation with JEM.

10. "M. A. Kuzmin v dnevnikakh E. F. Gollerbakha," published by E. A. Gollerbakh, *MKiRK*, 234.

11. "Novoe slovo v opere," *Vechernyaya Krasnaya gazeta*, no. 132, June 7, 1926, 4.

12. See Berg's letter to Kuzmin in S. Volkov and L. Fleishman, "Al'ban Berg i Mikhail Kuzmin," *Russian Literature Triquarterly*, 14 (Winter 1976), 451–456.

13. A. Dorokhov, "'Tsyganskii baron' v Muzkomedii Gosnardoma," *Rabochii i teatr*, 8 (1932), 18.

14. Kuzmin translated Schoenberg's *Gurrelieder* and his opus 8, *Sechs Orchester-Lieder*, for the 1927–28 season, and the following for the 1928–29 season: the Goethe texts in Beethoven's *Egmont*; Berg's 7 *Frühe Lieder*; Mahler's *Lied von der*

Erde (Otto Klemperer, who had the effect of a "magician" on Kuzmin when he conducted, led the performance); the Speaker's part in Stravinsky's *Oedipus Rex*, which Ansermet conducted on May 18, 1929; and Monteverdi's *Orfeo*, which was given a concert performance on December 5, 1928, the first ever in Russia. The texts of the translations and information about the performances can be found in Dmitriev, "'Akademicheskii' Kuzmin," 164–227.

15. See Kuzmin's letter to the director of September 7, 1927, in Dmitriev, "Perepiska," 381.

16. See Dmitriev, "'Akademicheskii' Kuzmin," 146–151.

17. See Meierkhol'd's letter to V. Ya. Shebalin of June 24, 1933, in Meierkhol'd, *Stat'i*, 2:289, and the Meierkhol'd-Kuzmin letters of July–November 1933 (Dmitriev, "Perepiska," 383–386). In June 1915 the director had asked Kuzmin to translate the play itself, but nothing came of the project.

18. Mikhail Kuzmin, "Temnye ulitsy rozhdayut temnye chuvstva" (*S*, 550–551).

19. Mikhail Kuzmin, "Lidiya Ivanova," *Vechernyaya Krasnaya gazeta*, no. 135, June 18, 1924. *Zi* published articles on her by Volynsky and others throughout June and July.

20. See JEM, "The Mystery of Iniquity: Kuzmin's 'Temnye ulitsy rozhdaiut temnye mysli," *Slavic Review*, 34, no. 1 (1975), 44–64; Gennady Shmakov, "Zagadka Lidochki Ivanovoi," *Russkaya mysl'*, no. 3625, June 13, 1986, 10–11; and *MK*, 265–272. Kuzmin's article "Dve stikhii" appeared in the brochure *Lidiya Ivanova: 1903–1924* (Leningrad, 1927) along with articles by Volynsky, Mikhail Chekhov, and Erikh Gollerbakh.

21. Kuzmin "Dve stikhii," 16–17.

22. The text of Kuzmin's letter may be found in George Cheron, "Kuzmin's 'Forel razbivaet led': The Austrian Connection," *Wiener Slawistischer Almanach*, *Band* 12 (1983), 107–111. To judge by Diary entries for September 1927, Arbenina was not so naive as to believe him.

23. Letter to Evgeny Arkhippov of October 5, 1927, cited in M. V. Rozhdestvenskaya, "Mikhail Kuzmin v arkhive Vs. Rozhdestvenskogo," *MKiRK*, 217.

24. "Tolpoi nakhlynuli vospominan'ya, / Otryvki iz prochitannykh romanov, / Pokoiniki smeshalisya s zhivymi" (*S*, 546). JEM and Gennady Shmakov first explored the work and its many sources in "Kuzmin's 'The Trout Breaking through the Ice'," in *Russian Modernism: Culture and the Avant-Garde*, ed. George Gibian and H. W. Tjalsma (Ithaca, N.Y.: Cornell University Press, 1976), 132–164. See, too, NAB, "'Otryvki iz prochitannykh romanov,'" in *Mikhail Kuzmin: Stat'i i materialy*, 163–173, and articles by Boris Gasparov and Irina Paperno, in *Studies*, 57–114.

25. *Zvezda*, 5 (1929), 171–172.

26. Boris Ol'khovy, "O poputnichestve i poputchikakh," *Pechat' i revolyutsiya*, 6 (1929), 5.

27. *Chisla* (Paris), 4 (1931), 263, signed "Yu. Sushchev." "Gulliver," the pseudonym used by Nina Berberova and Khodasevich for their weekly column in the Paris newspaper *Vozrozhdenie*, called the poems "senile, alas," adding that "Kuzmin is of little interest to a contemporary reader—in this, Soviet criticism is for once right" (no. 1493, July 4, 1929). Nikolay Otsup in "O poezii i poetakh v SSSR" saw only "decrepitude" and proof that "leftishness" had destroyed Kuzmin's "charming, light" poetry; see *Chisla*, 7–8 (1933), 238.

28. July 20, 1934, in the Diary. The brook in question was a favorite destina-

tion of Kuzmin and Yurkun on the walks that they took during visits to Detskoe Selo. The poem to Arbenina is in *S*, 677–678.

29. Cited by Shmakov in "Mikhail Kuzmin i Rikhard Vagner," *Studies*, 34.

30. Ibid., 41–42.

31. *MKiRK*, 170.

32. Petrov, "Kaliostro," 101, 97.

33. Orlov, who became a well-known editor of Blok and the head of the editorial board of the "Poet's Library" before being dismissed for opening it to long-suppressed modernist poets, told the story to JEM in 1969.

34. See M. A. Nemirovskaya, *Khudozhniki gruppy "Trinadtsat"*: *Iz istorii khudozhestvennoi zhizni 1920–1930-kh godov* (Moscow: Sovetskii khudozhnik, 1986). Arbenina, who had also been painting for several years, exhibited with the group under her real name, Gil'debrandt.

35. All this information is drawn from S. V. Shumikhin's publication of the 1931 Diary, "M. Kuzmin: Dnevnik 1931 goda," *Novoe literaturnoe obozrenie*, 7 (1994), 163–204.

36. See, for example, the diary of Erik Gollerbakh for June 9, 1935: "M. A. read his current diary, exceptionally interesting. Every section of the diary consists of recollections about the past or reflections on art and literature, and a few lines about the past day. . . . This is real art . . . these interlacings of the commonplace and the amusing with the elevated and significant" (*MKiRK*, 225). Sometime after Kuzmin's death a typescript was made of the 1934 Diary (and possibly more); it was long in the possession of Arbenina. JEM thanks the director and staff of the Akhmatova Museum in Petersburg for the opportunity to examine it in June 1997. G. A. Morev has prepared it for publication. Gollerbakh described portions from 1935, but neither it nor any other parts after 1932 seem to have survived, except for 1934.

37. In her memoirs of Kuzmin, Arbenina wrote: "He loved Mozart most of all in art—simply prayerfully. . . . M. A. considered Beethoven a 'protestant' (on his lips almost a censure). . . . I did not notice any special tenderness for Chopin. He loved Bizet, Delibes (I entirely understood), and Debussy. Ravel not so ardently. Of the Russians—Musorgsky (I don't understand that!), even more than Borodin. Had a slightly sarcastic attitude to Tchaikovsky. . . . He liked Stravinsky—Shostakovich was as if in second place, before Prokofiev. He had an extraordinary love for Webern. Was interested in Alban Berg." O. N. Gil'debrandt, "M. A. Kuzmin," introduction and commentary by G. A. Morev, in *Litsa*, 1 (1992), 267.

38. Petrov reports that Kuzmin told him that he read Rohde's book "constantly," "more often than Holy Writ" ("Kaliostro," 98).

39. Kuzmin drew even darker parallels between communism and early Christianity, and "settled his score with Christianity" even more severely in Diary entries for April 8, 12, and 13 and May 27, 1928.

40. In 1933, following the April 1932 disbanding of the intolerant Russian Association of Proletarian Writers (RAPP) and as plans were under way for a new Writers' Union, some saw a "thaw" in Soviet cultural life. Kuzmin tested the waters, unsuccessfully it turned out, with his piece on Bagritsky in *Literaturnaya gazeta*, no. 23, May 17, 1933. See G. A. Morev, "Sovetskie otnosheniya M. Kuzmina (K postroeniyu literaturnoi biografii)," *Novoe literaturnoe obozrenie*, 23 (1997), 78–86.

41. Petrov, "Kaliostro," 88.

42. Ibid., 82. Our description of the apartment paraphrases parts of Petrov's account of its appearance in the 1930s.

43. Ivnev, "Vstrechi s M. A. Kuzminym," 165.

44. Petrov, "Kaliostro," 105.

45. Nikolay Khardzhiev, "Mitrokhin v obratnoi perspektive," in *Kniga o Mitrokhine* (Leningrad: Khudozhnik RSFSR, 1986), 390.

46. N. Mandel'shtam, *Vtoraya kniga*, 234.

47. Ivan Likhachev in conversation with JEM in 1969.

48. Some of the artists asked to paint his portrait, but after the experience of Nikolay Radlov's "vile" 1926 effort, which Kuzmin regretted that Petrov had not tossed into the Neva when he carried it from Pushkin House to an exhibit, he declined. Why, Petrov, once asked, did Kuzmin so dislike Radlov's portrait, to which he replied: "'What an absurd idea to depict me with my own book! I never read my books. I only see their faults.' And after falling silent for a moment, he added: 'Incidentally, if someone else had written these poems, I might perhaps like them'" (Petrov, "Kaliostro," 93–94). Radlov's portrait is reproduced opposite page 161 in *MK*. A 1931 pencil portrait by Evgeny Krshizhanovsky, a frequent visitor in the late 1920s, appears in *Literaturnoe nasledstvo*, 27–28 (1937), 47.

49. Egunov published prose and poetry under the name Andrey Nikolev. See Andrey Nikolev (Andrey N. Egunov), *Sobranie proizvedenii*, ed. Gleb Morev and Valery Somsikov, *Wiener Slawistischer Almanach, Sonderband* 35 (Vienna, 1993).

50. Gil'debrandt, "M. A. Kuzmin," 265. She writes: "I never heard anything bad [about Akhmatova] from Kuzmin, but Yury [Yurkun]—yes—he was indignant about Akhmatova's 'ingratitude' for the introduction to *Evening* (a 'start in life' we would say now!)" (269). The reference is to the immensely popular 1931 *Putevka v zhizn'*, the first real Soviet sound movie. Arbenina dismissed Akhmatova's belief that Radlova was connected with the secret police as "utter nonsense" (270).

51. Khardzhiev, "Mitrokhin v obratnoi perspektive," 390.

52. Petrov, "Kaliostro," 100.

53. Innokenty Basalaev, "Zapiski dlya sebya," *Minuvshee*, 19 (1996), 466.

54. *MKiRK*, 242. Emphysema further complicated the pneumonia, and at the end Kuzmin was on oxygen. *Kratkaya literaturnaya entsiklopediya*, vol. 3 (1966), 875, incorrectly gives the date of Kuzmin's death as "3. III. 1936."

55. Lidiya Ginzburg, "Mysl', opisavshaya krug," in *Chelovek za pis'mennym stolom* (Leningrad: Sovetskii pisatel', 1989), 431. In a letter of March 15, 1936, to Evgeny Arkhippov, Gollerbakh wrote: "According to Yu. I. Yurkun, there were no death throes, death approached quietly, almost imperceptibly. Not long before the end, M. A. talked about how he felt absolutely fine, how inwardly he felt light and at ease. He was not conscious of the impending danger. He conversed about routine matters, about various humdrum trifles, planned on going to the ballet." "Iz dnevnika Mikhaila Kuzmina," published by S. V. Shumikhin in *Vstrechi s proshlym*, fasc. 7 (Moscow: Sovetskaya Rossiya, 1990), 246–247.

56. Ginzburg, "Mysl', opisavshaya krug," 430.

57. March 15, 1936, letter of Gollerbakh to Evgeny Arkhippov, p. 247.

58. Petrov, "Kaliostro," 112.

59. Ibid. Ginzburg, who visited Akhmatova and Punin the night of the funeral, recalled that Akhmatova was upset that she had not been able to attend the funeral

"because she could not stand the deceased (in the capacity of the leading light of Anna Radlova's salon), and she would have taken pleasure in demonstrating her impartiality." Ginzburg, "Mysl', opisavshaya krug," 431.

60. Basalaev, "Zapiski dlya sebya," 466.

61. Yurkun to Milashevsky, *MKiRK*, 242–243.

62. Petrov, "Kaliostro," 112–113. Gil'debrandt's estimation of the speakers coincides with Petrov's assessment ("M. A. Kuzmin," 272).

63. Petrov, "Kaliostro," 113.

Epilogue

1. "Pis'ma M. Kuzmina 30-kh godov," *Novyi zhurnal*, 183 (1991), 364. The night of the funeral, Gollerbakh wrote Yurkun a letter of such warmth and sensitivity that from then on Radlova, to whom Gil'debrandt showed it, made Gollerbakh sit to her immediate left whenever he was a guest. This was the seat Kuzmin had always occupied at her table. G. A. Morev published the text of its rough draft (the original perished) in *MKiRK*, 236–239.

2. See S. V. Shumikhin, "Dnevnik Mikhaila Kuzmina: arkhivnaya predystoriya," *MKiRK*, 139–145. All information on the Diary and its fate is drawn from that article.

3. Gollerbakh diary entry for December 1936, *MKiRK*, 227.

4. Petrov, "Kaliostro," 107–108.

5. All information for the account of the fate of Livshits, Yurkun, and the others is drawn from Eduard Shneiderman, "Benedikt Livshits: arest, sledstvie, rasstrel," *Zvezda*, 1 (1996), 82–126.

6. G. A. Morev published the complete text of her letter in *MKiRK*, 247–252.

7. Gil'debrandt, "M. A. Kuzmin," 272.

8. Gofman, *Kniga o russkikh poetakh poslednego desyatiletiya*, 383.

Index of Works by Kuzmin

General Index

Achilles Tatius, 384n44
Adamovich, Georgy Viktorovich
(1892–1972), 233, 239, 252, 255, 302,
347, 403n44, 415n65, 418nn97,1,
419n22, 426n32, 427n32, 434n6
Adonts, Gaik Georgievich (1892–1937),
308, 315–316
Aeschylus, 99
Akhmatova, Anna Andreevna (real name:
Gorenko, 1889–1966), 3, 36, 153, 162,
172, 173, 174, 179, 182, 183, 198–199,
201, 214, 221–225, 234, 252, 283, 285,
292, 295, 296, 304, 330, 332, 354, 355,
358, 363, 392n57, 402nn39,40, 403nn43,
45, 404n52, 405n76, 406nn78,80,
412nn7,12,14,18, 421n41, 424n11,
427n33, 432n34, 437nn50,59
Aksakova-Sivers, T. A., 405n74
Alcaeus, 236
Aldanov, Mark Aleksandrovich (real name:
Landau, 1886–1957), 419n22
Alexander, W. M., 382n22
Alexander of Macedonia, 149, 250
Aloysius Gonzaga, St., 36, 40–41
Alpatov, M. V., 409n37
Al'tman, Natan Isaevich (1889–1970), 244,
264, 267
Ambrozevich, Veronika Karlovna
(1870?-1938, mother of Yury Yurkun),
252, 260, 265, 266, 267, 279, 289, 328,
353, 360, 363

Amélineau, Emile, 376n15
Anacreon, 210
Andersen, Hans Christian, 265, 299
Andreev, Leonid Nikolaevich (1871–1919),
93, 129, 248, 255
Andreeva, Mariya Fedorovna (1868–1953),
272, 280
Andronikova, Salomeya Nikolaevna
(1889–1982), 183, 422n59
Anemone, Anthony, 424n11
Anichkov, A. I., 47
Anichkov, Evgeny Vasil'evich (1866–1937),
142, 398n48, 408n25
Annenkov, Yury Pavlovich (1889–1974),
247, 255, 264, 284, 296, 301, 310, 424n1,
429n62
Annensky, Innokenty Fedorovich
(1855–1909), 159–160, 161, 162, 167,
178, 400nn6,8,11, 401n15
Ansermet, Ernest, 435n14
Antinous, 74, 96, 98, 99, 100, 103, 104, 118,
194, 281, 376n15, 385n48
Antoninus, Marcus Aurelius, 281
Apollodorus of Athens, 201
Apukhtin, Aleksey Nikolaevich
(1840–1893), 405n65
Apuleius, 27, 34, 140, 169, 251, 256, 294, 341
Arakcheev, Aleksey Andreevich
(1769–1834), 274, 421n37
Arapov, Anatoly Afanas'evich (1876–1949),
181, 330

MAY 2 5 1988